S0-ANF-120

BASIC ACCOUNTING

SECOND
CANADIAN
EDITION
REVISED

Henry Dauderis
Concordia University
Albert Slavin
Northeastern University
Isaac N. Reynolds
University of North Carolina at Chapel Hill
Consulting Editor
Allen B. Sanders
Elon College

Holt, Rinehart and Winston of Canada, Limited

Canadian Cataloguing in Publication Data

Dauderis, Henry, 1941—
Basic Accounting

In the 1st Canadian ed. (1975), Albert Slavin's name appeared first on the t. p.

ISBN 0-03-928001-2

1. Accounting. I. Slavin, Albert. II. Reynolds, Isaac N. III. Title.

HF5635.S6318 1978 657 C77-001790-8

Library of Congress Catalog Card Number 77-095060

Printed in the United States of America
3 4 5 82 81 80 79

To our wives
Jurate
Beatrice
Dorothy
for their patience,
understanding,
and
inspiration

Preface

Basic Accounting is designed to provide a comprehensive first course in accounting at the university and college level. The objective is to provide students of business and administration with the basic concepts and uses of accounting, and accounting majors with a broad foundation for advanced study. This is accomplished by presenting the financial and managerial uses of accounting as an aid for decision making.

This second Canadian edition includes the important changes in accounting practice and corporation law that have occurred since the first edition was published. In particular, the effect of the provisions of the Canada Business Corporations Act (1975) on shareholders' equity transactions are highlighted. The subject matter has also been reorganized, emphasizing concepts and deemphasizing material that is less important. Every chapter has been reviewed in detail and numerous changes have been made. The number of chapters has been increased to include additional managerial accounting topics so as to provide a bridge for the further study of managerial accounting. The second Canadian edition also continues and accelerates the evolution of *Basic Accounting* into a distinctly Canadian text.

This edition meets several different needs. For the first introductory course every chapter can be used. For schools that have only one accounting course, Chapters 1-16, with some careful deletions, constitute a high-level course. Several chapters are divided into sections and some include the more complex concepts in appendices which can be omitted without interrupting the continuity of the book.

The book is divided into four parts:

1. Basic Concepts and Methodology: Service and Merchandising Businesses
2. Income Measurement and Valuation Problems Related to Sources and Uses of Invested Capital
3. Financial Reporting: Analysis and Interpretive Problems
4. Cost Accumulation, Cost Control, and Financial Planning

Part 1 consists of six chapters that cover the basic accounting cycle and the functioning of an accounting system. Accounting principles and the accounting equation are introduced in Chapter 1 because they are building blocks for the chapters that follow. Balance sheet and income statement preparation and the end-of-period process are covered in separate chapters. The accounting cycle is presented in Chapters 3 and 4. The accounting for merchandising operations and an introduction to accounting systems conclude Part 1. A mini practice case which can be completed in the space provided is included at the end of Chapter 6.

Part 2 covers the accounting for components of the balance sheet. Chapters 7 through 9 deal with individual asset items. Owners' equity accounting is discussed in Chapters 10 through 13. Creditors' equity, discussed in Chapter 14, is followed by the accounting for investments. This sequence helps students to understand that the accounting for debt financing instruments are practically the mirror image of accounting for investments. The retirement and refunding of bonds payable and short-term debt financing are covered in the Appendix to Chapter 13.

Part 3 covers the analysis and interpretation of financial statements and the preparation of the fourth major statement, the statement of changes in financial position. The importance of financial reporting is stressed in these chapters. A discussion of accounting policies and footnotes to financial statements is included as an Appendix to Chapter 15.

Part 4 covers the managerial uses of accounting data. Chapters 17 through 21 introduce cost accumulation and control for general manufacturing operations, job and process cost accounting systems, standard costs and direct costs, cost volume and income analysis, and capital budgeting decisions. The new managerial accounting chapters are intended to provide a bridge for students completing an introductory financial accounting course and beginning a second managerial accounting course.

Simple and compound interest is in Appendix I, following Chapter 21. This is so that instructors can have greater flexibility in choosing when to cover this topic.

Actual published financial statements of major corporations, together with notes and the auditor's report, are included in a second Appendix following Chapter 21. Although some concepts are not usually covered in an introductory course, all data applicable to the financial statements are included for discussion and illustration purposes. In particular, the treatment of inflation accounting by several corporations should be useful for classroom discussions.

The second Canadian edition has the following important characteristics:

1. *Easy teachability.* The examples are presented in a manner that proceeds from the simple to the complex. The end-of-chapter materials are well coordinated with the chapter material.
2. *Contemporary and modern coverage.* The theory sections are up to date and are integrated with text material.
3. *Flexibility.* Chapter appendices may or may not be used; many of the other chapters can be taught in a sequence other than that in which they appear in the book.

The end-of-chapter material is divided into three parts: (1) questions for class discussion; (2) class demonstration problems designed for the use of the instructor; and (3) problems. Some of the end-of-chapter material is identified as accounting policy decision problems, financial policy decision problems, and management policy decision problems. The demonstration problems exemplify highlights of each chapter. The questions are designed either for class discussion or for outside assignment; they test the student's understanding of the chapter contents. The problems stress both theory and practice and are graded by level of difficulty and approximate completion time.

The decision problems are also correlated to the chapter material but are set within a broader business background and furnish a specific business orientation for in-depth analysis and class discussion.

An optional self-study guide, prepared by Allen B. Sanders and Henry Dauderis, not only tests the student's comprehension of the text, but also reduces the amount of class time required to cover the individual chapters. Each chapter of the study guide has three basic components: (1) a concise explanation of the most important concepts in the corresponding textbook chapter; (2) interactive exercises with the text books that follow the sequence of, and are tied directly to, the textbook examples; and (3) a short set of questions and exercises to evaluate the student's comprehension of the chapter material. The interactive exercises are accompanied by answers. A short practice set, including narrative and working papers, is included in the self-study guide.

An optional set of working papers, which should be sufficient for most of the text, is also available for student use. The set of working papers is designed in such a way that it can be used for any part of the text.

The chapter glossaries, the wide margins, and a comprehensive index greatly enhance the usefulness of the book. The discussions and problems in the text and all the supplementary materials have been classroom-tested over a sustained period of time.

We are grateful to our colleagues and students for their help and encouragement, and are indebted to the users of the first edition for their support and their constructive criticisms and comments. We hope that they and others will continue in the future, as they have done in the past, to furnish us with their invaluable suggestions. Whatever deficiencies still persist, whatever errors of omission or commission still remain are, of course, entirely attributable to the authors. We are also indebted to many individuals and organizations for their permission to use certain material created by them.

Henry Dauderis
Montreal, Quebec
January, 1978

Albert Slavin
Isaac N. Reynolds

Contents

Part 1 *Basic Concepts and Methodology: Service and Merchandising Business* 1

1 **Introduction to Accounting and the Accounting Equation** 3

Present-Day External Users of Accounting **4**
Present-Day Internal Users of Accounting **5**
Relation of Accounting to other Disciplines **5**
Communication of Accounting Information **6**
Accounting Principles **6**
Authoritative Bodies **8**
The Basic Accounting Model **9**

The Accounting Equation **9**

The Entity Concept **9**
Assets **10**
Equities: Liability and Owner's Equity **10**
The Accounting Equation **10**
Balance Sheet **12**
Development of the Basic Model **18**
Expansion of the Accounting Equation **21**
Glossary **22**

2 **Balance Sheet Preparation** 31

The Creation of Accounts 31
Debits and Credits 32
Illustration of Debits and Credits 34
The Trial Balance 37
The Balance Sheet 39
The General Journal and Posting 39
Glossary 45

3 **Income Statement Preparation** 53

Basic Operating Concepts and Procedures 53

Revenues 53
Expenses 55
Dividends 57
Expanded Rules for Debits and Credits 57
The Accounting Sequence 64
Interrelationship of Financial Statements 74
Selecting a Chart of Accounts 75
Glossary 76

4 **The End-of-Period Process** 87

Two Accounting Methods 87

Cash Basis 87
Accrual Basis 88

Adjustments 89

Need for Adjusting Entries 89
Process of Recording Adjustments 90

The Work Sheet 100

Preparation of the Work Sheet 100

Updating of Accounts After Preparation of the Work Sheet **107**

Recording Adjustments in the General Journal and Posting to the General Ledger **107**
Closing Entries May Be Recorded Directly from the Work Sheet **109**
The Postclosing Trial Balance **109**

The Accounting Cycle **110**

Split Entries **111**

Purpose of Split Entries **111**
Glossary **112**

5 Accounting for Merchandising Operations **127**

Accounts for a Merchandising Business **127**
Functions of the Merchandise Accounts **132**
Cost of Goods Sold and Gross Margin on Sales **133**
The Operating Expense Accounts **134**
Other Revenue and Other Expenses **134**
Completion of the Work Sheet **136**
Completed Financial Statements **138**
Closing Entries **139**
Interim Financial Statements **140**
Cash Discounts—Implications to Management **140**
Management Control—The Exception Principle **141**
Trade Discounts **142**
Glossary **143**

6 Accounting Systems **155**

Design of a Record System **155**
The General Ledger and Subsidiary Ledgers **156**
Expansion of General Journal: Evolution of a Simple Manual System **159**
The General Journal **175**
Bookkeeping Machine Processing **177**
Other Accounting Systems **178**
Mini Practice Case **179**
Appendix: The Voucher System **182**
Glossary **185**

Part 2 ***Income Measurement and Valuation Problems Related to Sources and Uses of Invested Capital*** **197**

7 **Cash and Receivables** **199**

Control of Cash **199**

Internal Control **199**

Accounts Receivable Measurement **209**

Recognition of Losses on Uncollectible Accounts **210**
Correction of Errors in Allowance for Doubtful Accounts **218**
Internal Control—Accounts Receivable **219**
Appendix: Payroll Procedures **219**
Glossary **221**

8 **Inventory** **233**

Basis of Inventory Valuation **233**
Inventory Systems **234**
Physical Count Method **235**
Inventory Costing Methods Compared and Analyzed **238**
Continuous Record Method **239**
Balance Sheet Disclosure **243**
Lower of Cost and Market (LCM) **243**
Consistency in Application of Procedures **244**
Perpetual and Periodic Inventory Systems Compared **245**
Gross Margin Method **246**
Retail Method **248**
Importance of Inventory Valuation **248**
Inventory Control **249**
Glossary **250**

9 **Plant and Equipment** **261**

Cost of Plant and Equipment **262**
Capital and Revenue Expenditures **263**
Depreciation of Plant and Equipment **263**
Revision of Depreciation Charges **269**
Disposal of Plant and Equipment **270**

Disclosure Requirements **274**
Reporting the Effects of Inflation **274**
Depletion of Natural Resources **275**
Appendix: Intangible Assets **277**
Glossary **279**

10 **Shareholders' Equity** **287**

Characteristics of a Corporation **287**
Capital Stock Transactions **291**
Incorporation under the Canada Business Corporations Act (1975) **292**
Accounting for Companies Incorporated under Laws Other Than the Canada Business Corporations Act (1975) **294**
Sources of Shareholders' Equity **296**
Contributed Surplus **297**
Appraisal Increase **298**
Retained Earnings **299**
Balance Sheet Presentation **300**
Appendix: Stock Subscriptions **301**
Glossary **304**

11 **Dividends and Retained Earnings** **313**

Dividends **313**
Appendix: Treasury Stock **322**
Glossary **327**

12 **Proprietorship and Partnership Capital** **337**

Proprietorships **338**
Partnerships **342**
Glossary **351**

13 **Debt Financing** **361**

Review of Current Liabilities **361**

Bonds Payable **362**

Bonds Compared with Capital Stock **362**
Classification of Bonds **363**
Management Reasons for Issuing Bonds Instead of Capital Stock **364**
Authorizing the Bond Issue **366**
Accounting for Issuance of Bonds **367**

Other Long-Term Liabilities **376**

Appendix I: Retirement and Refunding of Bonds Payable **376**
Appendix II: Short-Term Financing Devices **380**
Appendix III: Compound-Interest Method of Premium and Discount Amortization **384**
Glossary **386**

14 Investments **399**

Temporary Investments in Marketable Securities **399**

Temporary Investments in Bonds **399**
Temporary Investments in Stocks **401**
Valuation of Temporary Investments **402**

Long-Term Investments **404**

Investment in Stocks **404**
Investment in Bonds **406**
Accounting for Investment in Subsidiary **407**
Long-Term Investment in Secured and Unsecured Notes **408**
Appendix: Investment in Bonds—Compound Interest Amortization **408**
Glossary **409**

Part 3 Financial Reporting: Analysis and Interpretive Problems **417**

15 Analysis and Interpretation of Financial Statements **419**

Analysis and Interpretation of Financial Statements **419**
Ratio Analysis **420**
Measurement of Short-Run Solvency **420**
Measurement of Long-Run Solvency **424**
Measurement of Earning Power **428**
Comparative Statements **431**
Financial Statement Analysis—Influences **438**
Appendix: Disclosure Issues **440**
Glossary **443**

16 **Statement of Changes in Financial Position** 455

Evolution of Content of Statement of Changes in Financial Position **455**
Statement of Changes in Financial Position—Working Capital Basis **456**
All-Financial Resources Concept of Funds **472**
Statement of Changes in Financial Position—Cash Basis **474**
Glossary **475**

Part 4 Cost Accumulation, Cost Control, and Financial Planning *491*

17 **Accounting for Manufacturing Operations** 493

Materials Used **493**
Direct Labor **495**
Manufacturing Overhead **495**
Work-in-Process Inventory **497**
Total Period Manufacturing Costs **498**
Finished Goods and Cost of Goods Sold **499**
Work Sheet for a Manufacturing Company **499**
Ending Inventories on the Work Sheet **499**
Financial Statements **502**
Accounting Entries **504**
Glossary **504**

18 **Cost Accounting Systems** 515

Cost Accumulation **515**
Job Order Cost System **518**
The Manufacturing Overhead Rate **520**
Evaluation of the Job Order Cost System **522**
Process Cost System **522**
Costs Used in Cost Accounting Systems **530**
Glossary **530**

19 **Standard Costs, Direct Costing, Responsibility Accounting** 543

Standard Costs **543**

Use of Standards for Budgets **543**
Flexible Manufacturing Overhead Budget **544**
Managerial Interpretation of Variances **553**

Responsibility Accounting **557**

Glossary **559**

20 Cost, Volume, and Income Analyses **569**

Views of Cost **569**
Break-Even Analysis, **570**
Marginal Income Statements **575**
Margin of Safety **576**
Marginal Income Planning **577**
Pricing of Special Orders **578**
Product Pricing **580**
Deciding to Make or Buy **582**
Department, Territory, or Product Abandonment **583**
Glossary **585**

21 Capital Budgeting Decisions **599**
Budgeting Capital Expenditures **599**
Comparing Capital Expenditures **602**
Limitations **610**
Glossary **611**

Appendix I: Simple Interest and Compound Interest **617**

Definitions of Interest **617**
Simple Interest **617**
Compound Interest **619**
Compound Interest Tables **628**

Appendix II: Annual Reports **632**

Index **665**

Part One

Basic Concepts and Methodology: Service and Merchandising Businesses

1

Introduction to Accounting and the Accounting Equation

Accounting arose out of the needs of its environment. In the earliest civilizations it became necessary to develop bookkeeping methods to maintain records of grain stored in the custody of the temple priests. Later came the need for expansion of bookkeeping to include such things as tax records, payroll systems, and records of production costs. As conditions changed, accounting methods also had to change to keep pace; thus, accounting has always been a creature of its environment.

Accounting has also done much to shape the environment. In 1494, when an Italian monk named Luca Pacioli wrote a chapter in a mathematics textbook, double-entry bookkeeping was promulgated. The mechanics of the double-entry system—still with us today—provided the means by which adequate determinations could be made of the profitability of cooperative business ventures. Ability to render reports that disclosed the results of operations, the financial status of the venture as a whole, and the status of each individual member's share provided the incentive for individuals to invest in voyages for trading and exploration. Also among the primary instances of accounting's influence on the environment is the enlargement in the first half of the twentieth century of the *attest function,* the certification by independent professional accountants of the fairness of financial statements. Such independent auditors are called chartered accountants (CAs) in Canada and certified public accountants (CPAs) in the United States. The rise of the attest function of accounting has been a major factor in the willingness of millions of absentee owners to invest money in share capital, thus enabling the growth of today's large business corporations.

Accounting, therefore, is not a new discipline; it is as old as civilization itself. It has developed as a product of its environment, but has also exerted an influence on the shape of that environment. In both roles, accounting continues to expand. The following two sections will describe the nature of accounting in terms of some of its users.

PRESENT-DAY EXTERNAL USERS OF ACCOUNTING

External users are those persons or groups outside the organization for which accounting is performed. Following are examples of such external users.

1. Investors, both individual and institutional, who seek information that will allow them to evaluate and compare the financial health and economic potential of business firms. Individuals and organizations, sometimes finding themselves with excess cash for a temporary period, desire to use it in an investment that is safe, at the same time yielding the highest possible rate of return for that type of investment. Individuals buy shares or bonds for long-term savings and for retirement plans; large institutions such as insurance companies or universities tend to accumulate cash in various funds. Both groups must keep their investments under constant review and revision. As a basis for their investment decisions, all these investors are dependent upon accounting information included in the annual reports of corporations.
2. Members of or contributors to *not-for-profit* organizations such as community funds, churches, colleges, fraternities and sororities, service clubs, and numerous other such entities need accounting reports to see how their funds are bieng used and to determine if the organization deserves continued support, the amount of such support, or if the support should be transferred to another group. Although cost effectiveness (that is, the extent of organizational goal attainment per dollar contributed) is only one of several factors considered by external users of information about not-for-profit agencies, it is an important criterion in the decision regarding continuation of participation and support.
3. Taxing authorities, regulatory agencies, and other governmental institutions use accounting information. Income tax returns are examples of financial reports to governmental agencies prepared with information taken directly from accounting records of individuals and businesses. The reports accompanying remittances of taxes to fund federal or provincial old age and medical-care programs and to fund unemployment insurance payments are determined from payroll accounts. Reports of collection of sales taxes as well as federal excise taxes must be based on accurate records of sales.

Important to consumers is the use of accounting reports by governmental regulatory commissions, especially those which have the authority to prescribe the rates that may be charged for services to the public. Rate setting for public utilities usually hinges on the concept of a "fair return on investment."

An inclusive list of other government users of accounting information is too long for our purpose. Note should be taken, however, of the national income accounting system used by Statistics Canada, which compiles accounting information from all segments of the economy to determine indicators of national economic growth such as gross national product and a host of other summarized data. Such data are used by the federal government to formulate fiscal and monetary policies in an effort to maintain a more stable economy.

PRESENT-DAY INTERNAL USERS OF ACCOUNTING

Planning and Controlling

Two of the most frequently listed functions of management are planning and controlling. *Planning* is the function that defines the goals and objectives of the organization; a major portion of planning is financial.

> Organizations of all types prepare budgets; a *budget* is simply a financial plan for a future period. Usually a budget covers a period of one year and is developed in organizational detail showing planned activity in terms of output of goods and services and in terms of man-hours and machine-hours, together with planned inflows and outflows of money and other resources.

Budget preparation is an important part of the planning function, and its starting point is the accounting records for the prior year.

Controlling is the function of monitoring budget execution (the day-to-day operations of the enterprise) and intervening when necessary to redirect operations toward accomplishment of plans. The primary element of the monitoring process is a group of special reports provided by the accounting system to each responsible manager. These periodic reports contain data that compare budgeted performance with actual performance, enabling the manager to exercise control.

Cost Determination

Many internal decisions require details of product cost information. The determination of prices in the environment in which today's business operates is rarely an automatic result of the interaction between supply and demand. A firm may have to bid competitively against other firms for a specific job; if its bid exceeds cost plus a reasonable rate of return, it probably will not be awarded the contract. On the other hand, if the firm bids less than its cost to perform the job, it will be awarded the contract but will also incur a loss.

Other Decisions

Managers are faced daily with capital budgeting decisions, those decisions involving a commitment of funds for replacement, overhaul, or repair of machinery, buildings, or equipment. Also, most businesses invest substantial sums in inventory, the merchandise items they intend to resell. For each inventory item carried, decisions must continually be made about the optimum quantity to be bought on the next order. Sometimes the question is one of "make or buy." In production operations, choices must be made between hiring of additional work force or use of overtime. In all these situations—as in numerous others—managers require cost data provided by the accounting system.

RELATION OF ACCOUNTING TO OTHER DISCIPLINES

From the foregoing, it can easily be seen that a close relation exists between the concepts of accounting and the other disciplines. Economics is basically a study of the processes of allocation of scarce resources. Using the monetary unit of the society as the yardstick of value measurements, accounting information is needed to evaluate alternative uses of economic resources, thereby forming the basis for ultimate allocation decisions.

Accounting has an impact on personal behavior—sometimes in a very direct way and at other times in a more subtle manner. Incentive pay systems, which depend upon accounting for measurement, are part of the reward structure of many firms with a direct effect on personal behavior. Recent behavioral science research has begun to question the impact on people of the use of accounting-based budgetary controls. Some findings suggest an adverse effect on employee motivation that leads to lower worker productivity. Attention is now being focused on environmental and social welfare aspects of our industrial and financial institutions. Questions are being raised about the true social costs of production which today's accounting systems do not measure. The current interest in research in *social accounting* serves to emphasize the relation between accounting and social welfare.

The structure of government in Canada is based on a legal framework; an example is the concept of property rights. It is a legal function to define those property rights (ownership, suretyship, and other rights), but it is an accounting function to measure their value, thus enabling comparisons on which to base exchanges of property. This same measurement function of accounting creates another set of close relationships—the interdependence of accounting and *quantitative decision models.* The use of quantitative analysis together with the development of high-capacity electronic computors constitutes a revolution in the business environment, and accounting must provide the underlying information.

COMMUNICATION OF ACCOUNTING INFORMATION

Accounting records constitute a history of economic events that take place in an organization. Purchases of merchandise, equipment, or services occur daily; sales of merchandise and other services occur almost continually. So that the events are recorded in an organized and acceptable manner, we have to review the basic principles that form the foundation for accounting entries. The term *generally accepted accounting principles* has been used to describe a set of broad rules having substantial authorative support.

Conceptually, accounting is the discipline that provides information on which external and internal users of the information may base decisions that result in the allocation of economic resources in society.

Generally accepted accounting principles help in the communication of this information by providing a basis for acceptance or rejection of proper accounting methods in reporting this information to users.

ACCOUNTING PRINCIPLES

The following is an outline of some of the more important generally accepted accounting principles.

Entity Concept. The accountant must maintain separate sets of records for each business enterprise of an owner, and must guard against intermingling of transactions of the enterprise and personal transactions of the owner.

Going Concern. It is assumed that the entity will continue in operation indefinitely unless there is evidence to the contrary. For example, the accountant in a going concern does not record assets at liquidation value; instead the basis chosen for valuation will be one consistent with the idea that the business will continue in existence over the expected useful life of any asset.

Consistency. In some instances there are acceptable alternative methods that can be used in accounting records. Once a choice has been made, the principle of *consistency* holds that the chosen procedure should be followed in all future entries in order to enhance comparability of statements covering different time periods.

Conservatism. Where acceptable alternatives exist, the one normally chosen would be that which produces the least favorable immediate result. The principle of conservatism aims to avoid favorable exaggeration in accounting reports.

Periodicity. Financial statements will be prepared at regular specified time periods before the end of the lifetime of the firm. This principle holds that items of expense and revenue can be allocated to such time periods. Such an assignment to periods is necessary for proper matching of expenses and revenue for income determination.

Objective Evidence Principle. To the greatest extent possible, the amounts used in recording events will be based upon objective evidence as compared to subjective judgment. It will follow that two separate accountants, given the same set of data, would be expected to arrive at the same result. (Without the objective evidence principle, the attest function of CAs and CPAs could not hold the high degree of confidence which it enjoys today.)

Materiality. An item small enough (in dollar amount or in proportion to other items) such that it would not influence a decision based upon the statement in which it is used is immaterial, and the accounting treatment thereof need not follow prescribed accounting principles. (For example, the inventory value of unused stationery in the typing pool or paper clips in the office would not be counted as part of the supplies inventory at the end of a period.)

Full Disclosure. Financial statements should report all significant financial and economic information relating to an entry. If the accounting system does not automatically capture some specific item of significance, it should be included in a footnote to the accounting statements.

Stable-Dollar Concept. This principle assumes that the dollar is sufficiently stable in value to be used as the basic unit of measure in accounting without adjustment for price-level fluctuations. Many accountants challenge the general use of this principle on the grounds that it simply is not true.

Historical Cost Concept. The cost principle holds that actual cost—arrived at through arm's-length bargaining—is the appropriate amount to be used to record the value of a newly acquired asset.

Accrual Basis. Items of expense and revenue should be recognized at the time of occurrence of the economic events that caused them without regard to the timing and amount of cash collections or payments.

Many other concepts and assumptions might be included in the list. As research and study continue, certain standards will be revised and new ones can be expected.

Accounting is a social system designed to meet users' needs. These needs continue to increase in scope and complexity as changes occur in the environment in which users make economic decisions.

AUTHORITATIVE BODIES

Accounting bodies are usually classified according to their primary areas of interest: external accounting and internal accounting. In external accounting, the independent public accountant—usually thought of as the chartered accountant—examines the financial statements prepared by a corporation or other form of organization, and relies on accounting principles to express an opinion on these financial statements. Internal accounting is usually thought of as the practice of accounting within an organization and is referred to as management accounting.

A number of authoritative accounting organizations are concerned with the formulation of generally accepted accounting principles. Each Canadian organization is incorporated under federal legislation and has associations in every province. Everyone who holds membership in a provincial association is automatically a member of the national group and membership is fully portable between provinces. The senior accounting body in North America was formed in Canada in 1880 and was called the Association of Accountants in Montreal (now the Order of Chartered Accountants of Québec).

The most important group of public accountants is the chartered accountants (CAs) who belong to the Canadian Institute of Chartered Accountants (CICA). CICA research pronouncements and accounting principles are published in the *CICA Handbook,* and represent standards to be adhered to in most cases by members of the Institute. The Accounting Research Committee (ARC) of the CICA is responsible for the issuance of pronouncements relating to accounting. Membership in ARC includes representatives from other organizations such as Financial Analysts Federation, the Financial Executives Institute of Canada, the General Accountants Association, and the Society of Management Accountants. In developing Canadian accounting standards and research, ARC uses exposure drafts to obtain views of members and the business community on proposed recommendations.

The next largest group of public accountants is the General Accountants Association (GAA). Its members use the designation Certified General Accountant (CGA). Although CGAs practise public accounting, most specialize in management and government accounting. The GAA serves to co-ordinate the work and opinions of the various provincial bodies in matters of national concern, such as the submission of briefs to the federal government and its agencies.

The dominant group of management acountants is the Society of Management Accountants (SMA)—formerly the Society of Industrial Accountants—whose members use the designation Registered Industrial Accountant (RIA). The SMA develops managerial accounting education materials and publishes special studies dealing with areas of management accounting. The overall objective of the society is to set standards and help develop professional skills for those engaged in professional management accountant occupations.

In addition to the above bodies, each province has a securities commission or other governmental body that exercises a considerable amount of control in the securities markets, particularly in the area of prospectuses. These provincial commissions have formally defined, generally accepted accounting principles for financial disclosure as those pronouncements which are set out in the *CICA Handbook.*

The American Institute of Certified Public Accountants (AICPA) is the most important accounting organization in the United States. Since its members—called Certified Public Accountants (CPAs)—are mostly the auditors of public corporations in the United States, it is easy to understand its power in developing and prescribing accounting principles.

The Financial Accounting Standards Board (FASB) is the leading independent nongovernmental body in the United States responsible for the development and issuance of financial accounting standards. CAs and other public accountants in Canada are strongly influenced by these and other American accounting pronouncements and research.

THE BASIC ACCOUNTING MODEL

The presentation of accounting information in a meaningful format and the submission of this information to those who use it as a guide to action make it necessary that the preparer of accounting data understand precisely how to use the basic accounting model that has been developed over the past seven hundred years. The following discussion illustrates the boundary line of the business unit, the entity; the components included in the model; the development of the accounting equation; and the preparation of the balance sheet.

THE ACCOUNTING EQUATION

THE ENTITY CONCEPT

In order to provide meaningful decision-making information about a business unit, the accountant must maintain a separate set of records for each business enterprise of an owner. The focal point of attention is not the owner but each independent unit, which has well-defined boundaries. For example, suppose that John Goodwin owns a grocery store, a hardware store, and a service station, and that he also has a car, a residence, some stocks and bonds, and other personal items of value. These are shown in graphic form below.

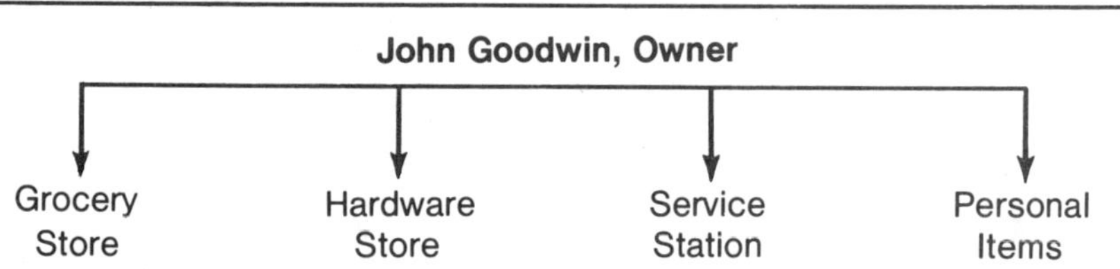

If the accountant's total attention is focused on John Goodwin, he may lose sight of the individual economic units. Thus, in this case, the accounting information for all Goodwin's activities lumped together is useless in making decisions for any single unit.

> **In order to accomplish the accounting objectives mentioned in the preceding paragraph, a set of records must be provided for each of the individual business units, and the focal point of attention must be the individual unit rather than the owner.**

This is referred to as the *entity* concept.

ASSETS

The *assets* of a business are everything of value found in the business. The word *value* is used here in the sense of future usefulness to a continuing business enterprise; it does not necessarily indicate the cost of replacing the asset nor how much it may bring in if offered for sale. Cash, notes and accounts receivable (amounts owed to the business through transactions on credit), land, buildings, and high-grade, readily marketable stocks or bonds of other companies *(marketable securities)* are examples of assets in a business. An asset is placed on the books of the acquiring entity at its full cost even though it has not been fully paid for in cash; the amount of any debt or claim against the asset is shown as a liability.

EQUITIES: LIABILITIES AND OWNER'S EQUITY

The *equities* represent claims against, or rights in, the assets of a business. The two major classifications of individuals who have equities in a business are the *creditors* (liability holders) and the *owners.*

The *liabilities* of a business are everything owed to creditors. Liabilities represent claims of the creditors against the assets of the business unit. *Accounts payable* and *notes payable,* which are amounts owed by the business through purchases on credit, are some liabilities that a business may have. Wages owed to employees is another example.

The *owner's equity (capital and proprietorship* are alternative terms) represents the proprietor's, the partners', or the shareholders' claims against the assets of a business, or the *excess* of all assets over all liabilities.

THE ACCOUNTING EQUATION

Because equities, by definition, represent the total claims against assets, then assets must equal equities. This relationship is shown here.

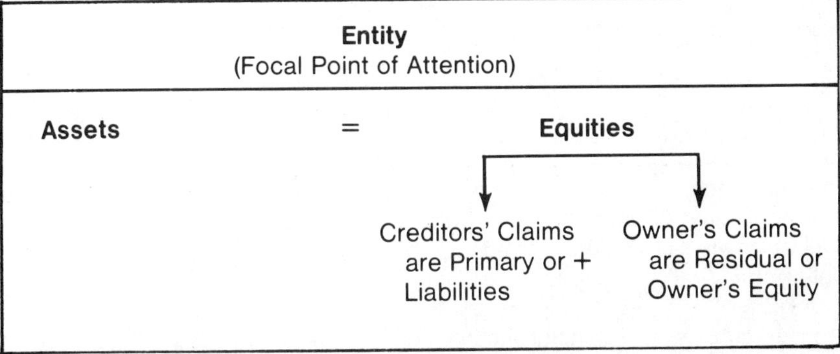

The equities of the unit are broken down into the *primary claims,* those of the creditors, and the *residual claims,* those of the owner(s). Since assets are derived primarily from these two sources, the truth of the equation is reinforced. Another source is a *gift* of assets, which increase the owner's equity.

The following equation, then, is the *basic accounting equation* of any business entity at all times.

Assets = Liabilities + Owner's equity

This equation means that the total of the balances of all asset accounts is equal to the total of the balances of liability and owner equity accounts. For example, if a business owns only one asset (land) which costs $25,000 to purchase, and $20,000 had been paid at the purchase date with a $5,000 balance (mortgage) remaining, the equation would be completed as follows:

Assets	=	**Liabilities**	+	**Owner's equity**
$25,000	=	$5,000	+	$20,000

This illustration indicates that this entity owns $25,000 assets (land), that creditors (those who sold the land) have primary claims of $5,000, and that the entity's owners have residual claims of $20,000. From this example it is clear that the total of the asset side of the equation ($25,000) equals the total of the equity side of the equation ($5,000 + $20, 000). In other words, since the assets must be derived from some source, the relationship can be expressed as follows:

Assets = Sources of Assets
or
Assets = Equities
$25,000 = $25,000

The accounting equation may be restated for analytical purposes in the following manner:

Assets	−	**Liabilities**	=	**Owner's equity**
$25,000	−	$5,000	=	$20,000

This relationship is important to the development of accounts and accounting records. In essence, bookkeeping is the recording of changes in the components of the equation resulting from business operations.

The term *net assets* is often used in business; it may be expressed as follows:

Assets	−	**Liabilities**	=	**Net Assets**
$25,000	−	$5,000	=	$20,000

Since total assets minus total liabilities also equal owner's equity, it is obvious that net assets is synonymous with the owner equity interest in total assets.

To add an element of preciseness, the equation is modified to indicate the particular kind of business organization: *proprietorship, partnership,* or *corporation.* For example, in a partnership the equation is

Assets = Liabilities + Partner's Equity

and in a corporation the equation is

Assets = Liabilities + Shareholders' Equity

The accounting equation for a corporation is then understood as follows:

Assets	=	Liabilities	+	Shareholders' Equity
(Property Owned by a Business)	=	(Creditor's Claims to Assets)	+	(Owner's Claims to Assets)

BALANCE SHEET

The balance sheet (Figure 1-1) is an expanded expression of the accounting equation. It summarizes the assets, liabilities, and shareholders' equity of a business entity at a specific time. This statement is also referred to as a statement of financial position. This term is used interchangeably with balance sheet.

The heading of a balance sheet usually contains three lines of information: (1) name of business, (2) name of the statement, and (3) date of the statement. The date given in the example shows that it presents the balance sheet of the firm as of the close of business on December 31.

Dollar signs are used on formal typed or printed statements at the top of each column of figures. A new column is created whenever a line is drawn for addition, subtraction, or other reasons. A double line is drawn under any amount that is the final result of a series of calculations.

Need for Classification in a Balance Sheet

> Note that the assets and liabilities in the balance sheet for Murrow Clothing Store Ltd. are ***classified.***

A balánce sheet should be classified so as to be of maximum value to an analyst, banker, creditor, employee, or other interested person; it can be made more easily understandable by the manner in which the items are arranged. The kind of classifications and the order of arrangements to be shown in the statement depend on tradition, the nature of the business activity, and the expected use of the statement.

Figure 1-1 Balance Sheet

ASSETS = LIABILITIES + SHAREHOLDERS' EQUITY

MURROW CLOTHING STORE LTD.
Balance sheet
December 31, 19XX

Assets		
Current Assets		
Cash	$ 325	
Marketable Securities	1,900	
Accounts Receivable	11,025	
Notes Receivable	2,520	
Merchandise Inventory	14,750	
Prepaid Insurance	275	
Office Supplies	26	
Store Supplies	89	
Total Current Assets		$30,910
Plant and Equipment		
Land	$ 3,000	
Building	10,000	
Store Equipment	2,500	
Delivery Equipment	3,250	
Total Plant and Equipment		18,750
Total Assets		$49,660

Liabilities and Shareholders' Equity		
Current Liabilities		
Accounts Payable	$12,060	
Notes Payable	2,060	
Accrued Wages Payable	970	
Total Current Liabilities		$15,090
Long-Term Liabilities		
Bank Loan Payable (due June 1991)	$ 4,000	
Mortgage Payable	10,000	
Total Long-Term Liabilities		14,000
Total Liabilities		$29,090
Shareholders' Equity		
Capital Stock	$20,000	
Retained Earnings	570	
Total Shareholders' Equity		20,570
Total Liability and Shareholders' Equity		$49,660

Classification of Assets—Current

Current assets consist of cash and other assets that are expected to be converted into cash or to be used in the operation of the business typically within one year or within the normal operating cycle, where that is longer than one year. Current assets are usually listed in the order of their probable *liquidity,* or their expected conversion into cash. The current assets, listed in order of liquidity, of Murrow Clothing Store Ltd. are the following.

Cash. Cash is any item that a bank will accept as a deposit and which is immediately available and acceptable as a means of payment. Cash includes coins, currency, checks, bank drafts, money orders, and demand deposits in financial institutions.

Marketable Securities. Businesses that have a temporary excess of cash on hand and want to earn interest on it may buy promises to pay issued by other companies (usually referred to as ***commercial paper)*** or by governmental agencies or institutions (called ***notes*** or ***bonds).*** Many finance companies, for example, sell short-term financial paper that will usually mature within sixty days to six months. The Canadian government also issues short-term bills that are often acquired by organizations as temporary investments of excess cash. Also, high-grade industrial bonds and stocks may be purchased as temporary investments.

Accounts Receivable. Accounts receivable represents the amounts due from customers for services rendered or for merchandise, or for any asset, sold on credit (***open account***). A business with a limited number of customers could list them individually in the statement of financial position. If the debtors are numerous, however, the individual names are eliminated and the statement shows the total amount of accounts receivable in one figure. Information about amounts due from each customer must be maintained on a separate supporting record.

Notes Receivable. A note receivable is an unconditional formal written promise by a customer to pay a fixed amount of money on demand or on a specific date. Since the note is usually transferable by endorsement to another party or to a bank, it represents an asset that can be converted readily into cash.

Merchandise Inventory. Businesses that offer products for sale must have them readily available. All the merchandise on hand at any given time is called ***merchandise inventory.*** Merchandise inventories are found on retail store shelves and in stockrooms or warehouses.

Prepaid Items. Prepaid items are current assets that have been acquired for purpose of consumption during the next twelve months. The items, however, that are placed on the balance sheet have not been used up at the statement date. A physical inventory (or other method of computing the inventory) is usually taken of these assets at the statement date so that the cost of the unconsumed portion may be shown. Some common prepaid items are described in the following paragraphs.

Prepaid Insurance. Every business must protect itself against hazards. Consequently, businesses take out insurance policies for protection. The cost of this type of protection is called an insurance premium and is paid in advance. Insurance policies commonly are issued against such hazards as fire, burglary, personal injury, business interruption, and injury to employees (workmen's compensation). The unexpired portion is listed on the statement.

Office Supplies. Supplies such as stamps, stationery, and business forms required in an office are grouped under the title Office Supplies and are current assets of the business.

Store Supplies. Store supplies include wrapping paper, twine, paper bags, and similar items used in a store. They are also classified as current assets.

Assets used in the general operation of the business should not be included in the merchandise inventory.

Classification of Assets—Plant and Equipment

Plant and Equipment comprises assets that will be used in the business over a period longer than a year, or a period longer than the normal operating cycle where that is longer than a year. These assets are customarily listed on the balance sheet according to the degree of permanency; the most permanent item is listed first. Some typical plant and equipment assets are the following.

Land is shown separately on the balance sheet, although land and the buildings on the land are usually sold together. Land and buildings are classified separately because the buildings will deteriorate through usage, whereas the land will not.

Buildings. In order for a building to appear on the balance sheet, it must be owned by the business or held under a long-term lease whose provisions, for all practical purposes, amounts to ownership.

Store Equipment. Showcases, counters, and shelves are typical permanent items of store equipment used in selling the merchandise inventory.

Delivery Equipment. Delivery equipment consists of trucks, cars, and other types of equipment owned that are used for the delivery of products to the customer.

Other Classification Groupings

Other groupings are used for such items as long-term investments in stocks and bonds (Long-Term Investment) and for intangible plant items such as goodwill and trademarks (Intangible Assets).

Classification of Liabilities—Current

The term *current liabilities* is used principally to designate obligations whose *liquidation* (payment or settlement) is reasonably expected to require the use of current assets or the creation (substitution) of other current liabilities.

All liabilities to be paid within a one-year period, or within the normal operating cycle where that is longer than a year, are classified as current. In general, current liabilities are listed on the balance sheet in their probable order of liquidation; those that, on the average, will be paid first are shown first, those to be paid next are next, and so on. Typical current liabilities are the following.

Accounts Payable. Accounts payable represent amounts owed to creditors resulting from purchases on credit (open charge account). If creditors are few, their names may be listed separately on the balance sheet. If creditors are numerous, the balance sheet shows only the total amount of accounts payable. Information about amounts owed to each creditor must be maintained in a separate supporting record.

Notes Payable. A note payable is an unconditional formal written promise to pay money to a creditor on demand at a specified time for value received. A *trade note payable* arises from the purchase of merchandise or services used in the course of business. A note payable to a bank arises when a company borrows money from a bank for business use. Generally these two items are *short term* and are classified as current liabilities, unless the note is for more than one year.

Accrued Liabilities. Accrued wages payable and accrued interest payable are typical *accrued liabilities,* which are debts that have accumulated because of the passage of time but that are not yet due for payment. These items are customarily placed last among the current liabilities.

Classification of Liabilities—Long Term

Debts that are not due for at least a year are called *long-term,* or *fixed,* liabilities. If part of a long-term liability is due within a year from the date of the balance sheet, the amount of that part should be shown as current. There is no particular sequence in which long-term liabilities appear in the balance sheet; however, size may be one criterion.

Mortgage Payable. A mortgage payable is a debt owed by the business that is secured by a specific asset or assets. The legal document by which the debt is secured is called a *mortgage.* A business may arrange a long-term loan with a bank, for example, and give to the bank as security a mortgage on its land and building. If the business fails to meet the terms of payment of the mortgage, the bank can take necessary legal action to take possession of the asset, or to sell it and satisfy the mortgage claim from the proceeds of the sale. Any balance remaining from the sale of the asset reverts to the business.

Bonds Payable. As a means of raising funds, corporations issue *bonds,* which are long-term promises to repay funds that are borrowed. These obligations may or may not be secured by assets of the borrowing company. Many corporations have excellent credit ratings and therefore do not need to offer specific security for loans.

Owner's Equity on the Balance Sheet

The form of a business organization determines the manner of reporting the owner's equity on the balance sheet. The three common forms of business organization are (1) the corporation, (2) the proprietorship, and (3) the partnership. The ownership interest in each of these organizational forms is disclosed in a slightly different manner on the balance sheet.

A corporation is a separate legal entity, created by a *charter* from the federal or a provincial government; it is owned by several shareholders. Each shareholder owns a certain portion of the corporation, expressed in *shares* of *stock. Share certificates* are issued to him as evidence of his ownership. *Capital stock* is a term describing investments by the shareholders. Shares are issued for a consideration determined from time to time by the directors of the corporation.

The primary advantage of the corporation to its owners is that the shareholders' personal assets cannot be taken by creditors to satisfy the debts of the business; only the assets of the business itself can be taken; this concept is referred to as *limited liability* of the shareholders. There are also other significant legal advantages, which will be studied in later chapters. In turn, corporations are subject to special government regulation and taxation. Because the corporate form is the most important form of business ownership today, it is stressed throughout this text. Moreover, the use of the simple form of corporate ownership accentuates the entity concept of accounting.

The income, or profits, of the corporation may be distributed to the shareholders in the form of *dividends* or may be retained in the corporation. The part that is kept is referred to as *retained earnings.* Retained earnings are not a part of the capital stock, but are a part of the total shareholders' equity. They represent the accumulated undistributed earnings of the corporation—that is, the total net income of the business from the date it was organized less the total dividends paid and the total losses sustained during the same period. Retained earnings must be accounted for separately from the capital stock because of the legal restrictions placed on the original capital paid in by investors.

Corporation. The owners' equity section of a balance sheet for a corporation is shown as

Shareholders' Equity		
Capital Stock	$20,000	
Retained Earnings	570	
Total Shareholders' Equity		$20,570

Proprietorship. Many businesses are owned by individuals; they are referred to as *proprietorships.* If a business is small and its operations are comparatively simple, the proprietorship form of ownership offers several advantages over the corporate form: the owner has a more direct control of the business; he does not have to report to several shareholders; and the business is not subject to the special regulations and taxes for corporations. But his personal assets can be taken as payment for the debts of the business. Careful management will, of course, minimize the chances of such an event.

If the Murrow Clothing Store is a proprietorship owned by Douglas Murrow, then his equity would be shown on the balance sheet as follows:

Owner's Equity	
Douglas Murrow, Capital	$20,570

The owner's equity for the proprietorship is listed with the name of the proprietor, followed by the word "Capital." The total owner's equity may be shown as one item, because there are no legal restrictions on withdrawals by a proprietor as there are for the shareholders of a corporation.

Partnership. Often several individuals find it advantageous to form a business by establishing a *partnership.* In this case, the owners are the *partners* of the business. The advantages of a partnership are similar to those of a proprietorship, with the added advantages of a greater amount of capital contributed by the several partners and the different abilities that the partners can bring to the management of the business. The primary disadvantage of the partnership is that each partner may be held personally responsible for all the debts of the business.

If Douglas Murrow and John Wells own the Murrow Clothing Store as partners, their equity would be shown on the balance sheet as follows:

Partners' Equity		
Douglas Murrow, Capital	$10,085	
John Wells, Capital	10,485	
Total Partners' Equity		$20,570

DEVELOPMENT OF THE BASIC MODEL

In this section of this chapter and in the following two chapters, *service businesses,* which sell services rather than merchandise, are used as illustrations. Service businesses are used first to illustrate the operation of an accounting system because they do not offer the added complications of the inventories required in *merchandising businesses.*

All businesses go through an initial cycle, during which the owners invest in shares of the corporation and the corporation then acquires plant and equipment prior to beginning regular operations. The transactions involved in the organization of the Whitside Realty Corporation Limited follow:[1]

Transaction 1:

July 3 The Whitside Realty Corporation Limited was organized by John Whitside, Ronald Raymond, and James Baker. The charter was received and capital stock in the amount of $50,000 was issued at par (sold for face amount) for cash; that is, the shareholders—Whitside, Raymond, and Baker—made an investment of $50,000 in the business. Whitside invested $40,000; Raymond, $6,000; and Baker, $4,000.

This transaction involves an increase of an asset, Cash, accompanied by an increase in a shareholders' equity item, Capital Stock. The plus and minus signs show the direction of change of each item in the transaction; they would not be part of the actual statement.

After issuance of Capital Stock

Balance Sheet

Assets		*Liabilities and Shareholders' Equity*	
Current Assets		Shareholders' Equity	
(+) Cash	$50,000	(+) Capital Stock	$50,000

Transaction 2:

July 5 Purchased land and building for $30,000 in cash. The land was appraised at $5,000, the building at $25,000.

This transaction involves increases of assets, Land and Building, accompanied by a decrease of an asset, Cash, with no change occurring in the shareholders' equity.

After purchase of Land and Building for Cash

Balance Sheet

Assets			*Liabilities and Shareholders' Equity*	
Current Assets			Shareholders' Equity	
(—) Cash $(50,000-30,000)		$20,000	Capital Stock	$50,000
Plant and Equipment				
(+) Land	$ 5,000			
(+) Building	25,000			
Total Plant and Equipment		30,000		
Total Assets		$50,000	Total Shareholders' Equity	$50,000

[1] The word *Limited, Incorporated, or Corporation* must be used as the last word of the name of a company incorporated in Canada, depending on the legislation of the jurisdiction where incorporation takes place.

Transaction 3:

July 10 Purchased furniture on account from the Jones company for $8,000. This transaction involves an increase of an asset, Furniture, accompanied by an increase of a liability, Accounts Payable, with no change occurring in the shareholders' equity and no change in any other assets.

Balance Sheet

After purchase of Furniture on Account

Assets			*Liabilities and Shareholders' Equity*	
Current Assets			Current Liabilities	
Cash		$20,000	(+) Accounts Payable	$ 8,000
Plant and Equipment			Shareholders' Equity	
Land	$ 5,000		Capital Stock	50,000
Building	25,000			
(+) Furniture	8,000			
Total Plant and Equipment		38,000		
Total Assets		$58,000	Total Liabilities and Shareholders' Equity	$58,000

Transaction 4:

July 20 Paid the Jones Company $5,000 on account.
The transaction reflected in this statement involves a decrease of a liability, Accounts Payable, accompanied by a decrease of an asset, Cash.

Balance Sheet

After payment of Accounts Payable

Assets			*Liabilities and Shareholders' Equity*	
Current Assets			Current Liabilities	
(−) Cash $(20,000 - 5,000)		$15,000	(−) Accounts Payable $(8,000 - 5,000)	$ 3,000
Plant and Equipment				
Land	$ 5,000			
Building	25,000		Shareholders' Equity	
Furniture	8,000		Capital Stock	50,000
Total Plant and Equipment		38,000		
Total Assets		$53,000	Total Liabilities and Shareholders' Equity	$53,000

Transaction 5:

July 25 The corporation found that some of the furniture was not what it wanted, so it sold the furniture, which had cost $1,800, to James Hill for $1,800 on account.

1. The amount of money yet to be received from James Hill is reflected as an asset, Accounts Receivable. It is a current asset because it is collectible within a year.

2. This transaction involves an increase of an asset, Accounts Receivable, accompanied by a decrease of an asset, Furniture. It is similar to the transaction of July 5 in that it consists of an exchange of one asset for another.
3. The furniture was sold at cost. If it had been sold at a price above its cost, a shareholders' equity item, Retained Earnings, would have been increased by the amount of the gain.

After sale of Furniture on Account

Balance Sheet

Assets			*Liabilities and Shareholders' Equity*	
Current Assets			Current Liabilities	
Cash	$15,000		Accounts Payable	$ 3,000
(+) Accounts Receivable	1,800		Shareholders' Equity	
			Capital Stock	50,000
Total Current Assets		$16,800		
Plant and Equipment				
Land	$ 5,000			
Building	25,000			
(–) Furniture (8,000 – 1,800)	6,200			
Total Plant and Equipment		36,200		
Total Assets		$53,000	Total Liabilities and Shareholders' Equity	$53,000

Transaction 6:

July 31 Collected $1,000 from James Hill on account.

After James Hill makes a payment of $1,000, the following balance sheet is prepared. As in the above balance sheet, this transaction involves an increase of an asset, Cash, accompanied by a decrease of an asset, Accounts Receivable.

After collection of Accounts Receivable

Balance Sheet

Assets			*Liabilities and Shareholders' Equity*	
Current Assets			Current Liabilities	
(+) Cash (15,000 + 1,000)	$16,000		Accounts Payable	$ 3,000
(–) Accounts Receivable (1,800 – 1,000)	800		Shareholders' Equity	
			Capital Stock	50,000
Total Current Assets		$16,800		
Plant and Equipment				
Land	$ 5,000			
Building	25,000			
Furniture	6,200			
Total Plant and Equipment		36,200		
Total Assets		$53,000	Total Liabilities and Shareholders' Equity	$53,000

The method of accumulating accounting data illustrated thus far gives the desired results of enabling a business to prepare a balance sheet but, in most instances, the time and expense involved would prohibit its use. Moreover, a balance sheet prepared after each transaction is not needed by those who use accounting information as a guide to action. A balance sheet prepared at the end of each month is usually sufficient.

Balance Sheet

The following is the formal balance sheet for the Whitside Realty Corporation Limited (Figure 1-2).

Figure 1-2 Formal Balance Sheet

WHITSIDE REALTY CORPORATION LIMITED
Balance Sheet
July 31, 19XX

Assets			*Liabilities and Shareholders' Equity*	
Current Assets			Current Liabilities	
Cash	$16,000		Accounts Payable	$ 3,000
Accounts Receivable	800		Shareholders' Equity	
Total Current Assets		$16,800	Capital Stock	50,000
Plant and Equipment				
Land	$ 5,000			
Building	25,000			
Furniture	6,200			
Total Plant and Equipment		36,200		
Total Assets		$53,000	Total Liabilities and Shareholders' Equity	$53,000

EXPANSION OF THE ACCOUNTING EQUATION

Since the procedure described in the foregoing section is cumbersome, a better methodology is called for. Using the basic accounting equation, it is possible to show how each transaction will effect the balance sheet and yet have all six transactions combined in one statement. In Figure 1-3 the balances are brought down after each transaction and form an equation from which a formal statement similar to Figure 1-2 could be prepared.

Figure 1-3 Expanded Accounting Equation

Date		Business Transaction	Cash	+	Accounts Receivable	+	Land	+	Building	+	Furniture	=	Accounts Payable	+	Capital Stock
			Assets									=	*Liabilities*	+	*Shareholders' Equity*
July	3	Issued capital stock for $50,000 in cash	+$50,000									=			+$50,000
	5	Purchased land and building for $30,000 in cash. Land is appraised at $5,000; building at $25,000.	−30,000				+ $5,000		+ $25,000						
		Balances	$20,000	+			$5,000	+	$25,000			=			$50,000
	10	Purchased furniture on account from the Jones Company for $8,000.									+$8,000	=	+$8,000		
		Balances	$20,000	+			$5,000	+	$25,000	+	$8,000	=	$8,000	+	$50,000
	20	Paid the Jones Company $5,000 on account.	−5,000										−5,000		
		Balances	$15,000	+			$5,000	+	$25,000	+	$8,000	=	$3,000	+	$50,000
	25	Sold furniture at cost to James Hill for $1,800 on account.			+$1,800						−1,800				
		Balances	$15,000	+	$1,800	+	$5,000	+	$25,000	+	$6,200	=	$3,000	+	$50,000
	31	Collected $1,000 from James Hill on account.	+1,000		−1,000										
		Balances	$16,000	+	$ 800	+	$5,000	+	$25,000	+	$6,200	=	$3,000	+	$50,000

After each transaction, the total of the Assets columns equals the total of the Liabilities and Shareholders' Equity columns. For example, after the July 25 transaction, the assets total $53,000 = ($15,000 + $1,800 + $5,000 + $25,000 + $6,200) equals the liabilities and shareholders' equity total of $53,000 =($3,000 + $50,000). A formal balance sheet could be prepared from Figure 1-3 after the July 31 transaction by simply arranging the various assets, liabilities, and shareholders' equity items in the form illustrated in Figure 1-2.

Although this method tends to shorten the accounting process, it is unsuitable for most companies because it cannot easily be expanded to provide for a large number of asset and liability items. For example, it would be virtually impossible to use this procedure in a company that has fifty assets and twenty-five liabilities.

GLOSSARY

Accounting The discipline that provides information that is useful for the making of economic decisions.

Accounting Objective A basic statement identifying a goal or purpose of accounting.

Accounting Practice A specific method for recording of an economic event.

Accounting Principle See *Accounting Standard.*

Accounting Standard A fundamental guideline that serves as a basis for acceptance or rejection of an accounting method. (Formerly called an "accounting principle.")

Annual Report A report containing basic accounting statements rendered by firms at the close of each business year. It is designed for external users of accounting data.

ARC Accounting Research Committee of the CICA.

Asset A thing of value held by an economic enterprise.

Balance Sheet The statement that summarizes the assets, liabilities, and owner's (or owners') equity of a business unit as of a specific time.

Budget A financial plan for a future period developed in organizational detail.

CA (Chartered Accountant) An accountant who has passed the Uniform Final Examination and has been admitted into membership of a provincial Institute. Everyone who holds membership in a provincial Institute is automatically a member of the Canadian Institute.

Contolling The management function which consists of monitoring actual versus planned activity, and taking corrective action where appropriate.

Current Assets Cash and other assets that are expected to be converted into cash or to be used in the operations of the business within one year or within the normal operating cycle, where that is longer than a year.

Current Liabilities Obligations whose payment or settlement is reasonably expected to require the use of current assets or the creation of other current liabilities within a one-year period or within the normal cycle, where that is longer than a year.

Entity Concept A term referring to the notion of placing emphasis on the business unit for purposes of accounting rather than on the owner(s) of the business.

Equities Claims against, or property rights in, the assets of a business.

External Users Individuals, groups, or institutions outside the enterprise.

Generally Accepted Accounting Principles The set of accounting standards that are generally accepted as valid.

Liability An obligation of a business, or a creditors' claim against the assets of a business.

Long-Term Liability An obligation that matures after one year.

Merchandising Business A business that sells products or merchandise.

Net Assets Assets minus liabilities.

Not-for-Profit Organizations Enterprises organized for purposes other than engaging in business operations for profit. Examples include charitable groups, service and civic clubs, churches, social clubs, and numerous other nonbusiness enterprises.

Owner's Equity The owner's or owners' claims against assets of a business. As used in this text, owner's equity implies that the business is a proprietorship and, therefore, represents the proprietor's claims against assets of the proprietorship.

Partners' Equity The partners' claims against the assets of a partnership business.

Planning The function that defines the goals and objectives of an organization.

Plant and Equipment The tangible long-lived assets of a firm that are used in the operations of the firm and are not held for resale.

Service Business A business that sells a service, for example, a public accounting firm.

Shareholders' Equity The shareholders' claims against the assets of a corporation.

Social Accounting A relatively new concept in which measurement of social-welfare aspects of events would be considered along with measurement of economic aspects of events.

QUESTIONS

Q1-1. What is the basic role of accounting in society?

Q1-2. Why can we claim that accounting is both a product of its environment and an influence on its environment?

Q1-3. What is a CA?

Q1-4. Cite three examples of users of accounting reports who are external to the organization for which accounting is being performed.

Q1-5. What role does accounting play in the planning function of management? in the controlling function?

Q1-6. What is the relationship between accounting and economics? accounting and social welfare? accounting and law? accounting and quantative decision models?

Q1-7. What is the entity concept? Identify the ways in which this concept aids the accounting function.

Q1-8. Define and give three examples of each of the following terms: (a) assets, (b) liabilities, (c) owner's equity.

Q1-9. What are current assets? Give five examples. In what order should these items be listed on the balance sheet?

Q1-10. What is the purpose of the balance sheet?

Q1-11. What is plant and equipment? Give five examples.

Q1-12. What are current liabilities? Give five examples.

Q1-13. What is a business transaction? Give eight examples.

Q1-14. Why are the assets and liabilities classified in the balance sheet?

Q1-15. Give an example of a transaction that would result (a) in an increase of an asset accompanied by an increase in the owner's equity; (b) in an increase of an asset accompanied by an increase of a liability; (c) in an increase of an asset accompanied by a decrease of an asset; (d) in a decrease of an asset accompanied by a decrease of a liability.

DEMONSTRATION PROBLEMS

DP1-1. *(Corporate balance sheet)* The following alphabetical list of accounts is taken from the records of Jensen Company Ltd. at December 31:

Accounts Payable	$125,000
Accounts Receivable	138,000
Building	400,000
Capital Stock	400,000
Cash	250,000
Delivery Equipment	140,000
Land	115,000
Merchandise Inventory	70,000

(Ch. 1)

Mortgage Payable (due July 1, 1993)	280,000
Notes Payable	110,000
Notes Receivable	18,000
Prepaid Insurance	12,000
Retained Earnings	214,000
Wages Payable	14,000

Required: Prepare a classified balance sheet.

DP1-2. *(Development of an accounting system: corporation)* The following transactions occurred at Westerlin Corporation during its first month of operations:

May 1 Received a corporate charter and issued all its authorized stock for $100,000 in cash.

2 Purchased land and building for $60,000. The company paid $20,000 in cash and issued a 20-year mortgage payable for the balance. The land was appraised at $15,000; the building, at $45,000.

3 Purchased furniture from the Goodwin Company for $10,500 on account.

15 Paid the Goodwin Company $6,500 on account.

20 Sold a portion of the land purchased on May 2 at its approximate cost of $5,000 to the Durham Realty Company on account.

31 Received $4,000 in cash and a 90-day note for $1,000 from the Durham Realty Company.

Required: Using these six transactions:

1. Prepare a balance sheet after each transaction.
2. Record the transactions in an expanded accounting equation.

DP1-3. The following lists show selected statement totals for four different firms: Able, Baker, Charles, and Dawson. In each case, the amount for one total is omitted.

	Able	Baker	Charles	Dawson
Current Assets	$200,000	$ 70,000	$?	$ 35,000
Plant and Equipment	400,000	120,000	100,000	180,000
Current Liabilities	100,000	20,000	10,000	15,000
Long-Term Liabilities	150,000	?	26,000	60,000
Capital Stock	350,000	60,000	100,000	?
Retained Earnings	?	10,000	14,000	25,000

Required: Compute the missing figure for each firm.

PROBLEMS

P1-1. Assume that Chapel Hill Corporation Ltd. has the following items at the end of the year.

Total Assets	$405,000
Total Long-Term Liabilities	50,000
Capital Stock	150,000
Retained Earnings	135,000
Current Assets	80,000

Compute the amount of current liabilities.

P1-2. The books of Travis Armour Company Ltd. contain the following items:

Retained Earnings	$ 75,000
Cash	45,000
Capital Stock	150,000
Accounts Receivable	9,000
Accounts Payable	6,400
Prepaid Insurance	1,600

Select the current assets and prepare in good form the Current Assets section of the balance sheet as of December 31.

P1-3. The books of Bunker Company Ltd. contain the following items:

Cash	$ 10,500
Land	20,000
Capital Stock	200,000
Building	320,000
Long-Term Notes Payable (due July 1, 1999)	100,000
Delivery Equipment	20,000
Office Supplies	2,000

Select the plant and equipment items, and prepare in good form the Plant and Equipment section of the balance sheet as of December 31.

P1-4. The books of Canyon Company Ltd. contain the following items:

Accounts Receivable	$ 3,500
Accounts Payable	12,000
Notes Receivable	2,000
Notes Payable	4,000
Accrued Wages Payable	1,500
Retained Earnings	45,000
Bonds Payable (due July 1, 1999)	35,000

Select the current liabilities, and prepare in good form the Current Liabilities section of the balance sheet as of December 31.

P1-5. Branson Corporation Ltd. engaged in the following transactions during the first week of operations:

June 1 Issued capital stock at par to the four incorporators for $50,000 in cash.

3 Purchased office equipment from Black and Sons for $6,000 on account.

5 Purchased land for a future building site at a cost of $30,000; paid $10,000 down and issued a mortgage note payable in 10 years for the balance.

Prepare a classified balance sheet after each transaction.

P1-6. Assume that a firm has current assets, $50,000; current liabilities, $20,000; long-term liabilities, $60,000; and shareholders' equity, $250,000 at the end of the year. Compute the amount of plant and equipment.

P1-7. The following financial information is available for Aprile Company Ltd. as of December 31:

Marketable Securities	$ 20,000
Accounts Receivable	80,000
Wages Payable	120,000
Buildings	100,000
Prepaid Insurance	2,000
Inventories	90,000
Capital Stock	100,000
Accounts Payable	65,000
Cash on Hand	4,500
Cash in Bank	210,000
Retained Earnings	?
Land	40,000
Bonds Payable	200,000

Prepare a balance sheet for Aprile Company Ltd. as of December 31.

P1-8. The following balance sheets were prepared immediately following each of three transactions engaged in by the Cimeron Corporation.

July 1

Assets			*Shareholders' Equity*	
Current Assets			Shareholders' Equity	
Cash		$ 50,000	Capital Stock	$ 50,000

July 3

Assets			*Liabilities and Shareholders' Equity*	
Current Assets			Long-Term Liabilities	
Cash		$ 35,000	Mortgage Payable	$ 55,000
Plant and Equipment			Shareholders' Equity	
Land	$10,000		Capital Stock	50,000
Building	60,000			
Total Plant and Equipment		70,000		
Total Assets		$105,000	Total Liabilities and Shareholders' Equity	$105,000

July 5

Assets			*Liabilities and Shareholders' Equity*	
Current Assets			Current Liabilities	
Cash	$35,000		Accounts Payable	$ 2,000
Office Supplies	2,000		Long-Term Liabilities	
Total Current Assets		$ 37,000	Mortgage Payable	55,000
Plant and Equipment			Total Liabilities	$ 57,000
Land	$10,000		Shareholders' Equity	
Building	60,000		Capital Stock	50,000
Total Plant and Equipment		70,000		
Total Assets		$107,000	Total Liabilities and Shareholders' Equity	$107,000

Date and describe each transaction.

P1-9. On December 31 the assets, liabilities, and shareholders' equity of Jackson Company Ltd. are as follows:

Assets (in alphabetical order)	
Accounts Receivable	$ 38,000
Building	100,000
Cash	40,000
Equipment	120,000
Land	20,000
Marketable Securities	90,000
Merchandise Inventory	40,000
Supplies	18,000
Liabilities (in alphabetical order)	
Accounts Payable	40,000
Bonds Payable (due July 1, 1995)	90,000
Dividends Payable	8,000
Interest Payable	12,000
Shareholders' Equity	
Capital Stock	300,000
Retained Earnings	?

Required: Prepare a properly classified balance sheet.

P1-10. The following is an alphabetical list of the assets, liabilities, and shareholders' equity of Michael Company Ltd. as of December 31:

Accounts Payable	$ 16,000
Accounts Receivable	17,000
Building	150,000
Cash	60,000
Delivery Equipment	30,000
Land	25,000
Long-Term Notes Payable (due August 1, 2005)	80,000
Marketable Securities	5,000
Merchandise Inventory	32,000
Mortgage Payable (due March 1, 1985)	50,000
Notes Payable	6,000
Capital Stock	?
Prepaid Insurance	2,000
Salaries Payable	1,000

Required: Prepare a properly classified balance sheet.

P1-11. The assets, liabilities, and shareholders' equity of Tombstone Company Ltd. as of December 31, are as follows:

Cash	$ 8,000
Accounts Receivable	25,000
Notes Receivable	4,000
Merchandise Inventory	8,500
Office Supplies	500
Prepaid Insurance	1,000
Store Equipment	6,000
Building	26,000
Land	7,500
Accounts Payable	15,000
Notes Payable	8,000
Mortgage Payable (due Feb. 1, 2012)	12,000
Capital Stock	51,500

Required: Prepare a balance sheet in good form.

P1-12. Successive balance sheets for the Hand Corporation are given below.

August 1

Assets			*Liabilities and Shareholders' Equity*	
Current Assets			Shareholders' Equity	
Cash		$130,000	Capital Stock	$130,000

August 2

Assets			*Liabilities and Shareholders' Equity*	
Current Assets			Long-Term Liabilities	
Cash		$116,000	Mortgage Payable	$ 86,000
Plant and Equipment			Shareholders' Equity	
Land	$15,000		Capital Stock	130,000
Building	85,000	100,000		
Total Assets		$216,000	Total Liabilities and Shareholders' Equity	$216,000

August 3

Assets			*Liabilities and Shareholders' Equity*	
Current Assets			Current Liabilities	
Cash	$116,000		Accounts Payable	$ 6,000
Medical Supplies	6,000	$122,000	Long-Term Liabilities	
Plant and Equipment			Mortgage Payable	86,000
Land	$ 15,000		Total Liabilities	$ 92,000
Building	85,000	100,000	Shareholders' Equity	
			Capital Stock	130,000
Total Assets		$222,000	Total Liabilities and Shareholders' Equity	$222,000

August 4

Assets			*Liabilities and Shareholders' Equity*	
Current Assets			Current Liabilities	
Cash	$116,000		Accounts Payable	$ 6,000
Notes Receivable	3,000		Long-Term Liabilities	
Medical Supplies	6,000	$125,000	Mortgage Payable	86,000
Plant and Equipment			Total Liabilities	$ 92,000
Land	$ 12,000		Shareholders' Equity	
Building	85,000	97,000	Capital Stock	130,000
Total Assets		$222,000	Total Liabilities and Shareholders' Equity	$222,000

August 5

Assets			*Liabilities and Shareholders' Equity*	
Current Assets			Current Liabilities	
Cash	$116,000		Accounts Payable	$ 2,000
Notes Receivable	3,000		Long-Term Liabilities	
Medical Supplies	6,000	$125,000	Mortgage Payable	86,000
Plant and Equipment			Total Liabilities	88,000
Land	$ 12,000		Shareholders' Equity	
Building	85,000	97,000	Capital Stock	134,000
Total Assets		$222,000	Total Liabilities and Shareholders' Equity	$222,000

August 7

Assets			*Liabilities and Shareholders' Equity*	
Current Assets			Current Liabilities	
Cash	$119,000		Accounts Payable.	$ 2,000
Medical Supplies	6,000	$125,000	Long-Term Liabilities	
Plant and Equipment			Mortgage Payable	86,000
Land	$ 12,000		Total Liabilities	$ 88,000
Building	85,000	97,000	Shareholders' Equity	
			Capital Stock	134,000
Total Assets		$222,000	Total Liabilities and Shareholders' Equity	$222,000

Required: Study the successive balance sheets to determine what transactions have occurred. Prepare a list of these transactions giving the date and description of each.

P1-13. The transactions of the newly organized Finetime Services, Inc., for the week of June 1 to 6, are given below.

June 1 Received a charter and issued all its authorized capital stock for $50,000 in cash.

2 Purchased land and building at a cost of $60,000. Paid $15,000 in cash and issued a 20-year mortgage payable for the balance. The land is appraised at $15,000; the building, at $45,000.

3 Purchased furniture for $3,000 from the Sanford Chair Company on account.

4 Purchased office supplies (stationery, stamps, and envelopes) for $400 in cash.

5 Some of the furniture was found to be defective and was returned to the Sanford Chair Company. The account was reduced by $1,000.

6 Paid the balance due the Sanford Chair Company.

Required: Prepare a classified balance sheet after each transaction.

2

Balance Sheet Preparation

In Chapter 1 a new balance sheet was prepared following each transaction to illustrate that every transaction affects another component of the accounting equation. The preparation of balance sheets after each exchange would be impractical in actual practice and a less cumbersome method must be devised to record increases and decreases in assets, liability, and shareholders' equity components of the equation.

This chapter deals with the methodology that has been developed to record increases and decreases. The discussion in this chapter centers on the creation of accounts, the development of debits and credits, the preparation and recording of journal entries, and the preparation of a trial balance and balance sheet following the recording of all transactions.

THE CREATION OF ACCOUNTS

One solution to the problem of accumulating data for each component of the accounting equation is to make use of the devise called an account. A simplified account often used for illustrative purposes is referred to as a T account, so called because it resembles the letter T as shown below:

T accounts are used for each asset, liability, and shareholders' equity item and a separate T account page contains the increases and decreases applicable to each item. For example, in Figure 1-3, there would be a separate T account for each of the following: Cash, Accounts Receivable, Land, Building, Furniture, Accounts Payable, and Capital Stock.

DEBITS AND CREDITS

Each account consists of a left side and a right side. The left side of an account is called the *debit* side, and the right side of an account is called the *credit* side. The name of each account is written across the top of the T as shown below:

Name of Account

Debit (always the left side)	*Credit* (always the right side)

The two sides of each account are used for the purpose of recording increases and decreases in the account.

The application of the above debit and credit methodology to the components of the accounting equation is now discussed. The accounting equation suggests the following:

Assets = **Liabilities + Shareholders' Equity**

Assets appear on the left side of the equation; therefore, the left side of an account is used to record increases of assets.

All Asset Accounts

A debit records an increase in assets.	

Since an account also has a credit side, therefore, the right side is used to record decreases in assets.

All Asset Accounts

	A credit records a decrease in assets.

Liabilities and shareholders' equity appear on the right side of the equation; therefore, the right side of the account is used to record increases in liability and shareholders' equity accounts.

All Liability and Shareholders' Equity Accounts

	A credit records an increase in liability and shareholders' equity accounts.

Since an account also has a debit side, therefore, the left side is used to record decreases in liabilities and shareholders' equity.

All Liability and Shareholders' Equity Accounts

A debit records a decrease in liability and shareholders' equity accounts.	

Each account page, then, contains the increases and decreases that occur in that individual item. For example, the Accounts Receivable and Accounts Payable transactions for the Whitside Realty Corporation Limited summarized in Figure 1-3 would appear in T accounts as follows:

Accounts Receivable

Increases *Debit*	*Decreases* *Credit*
July 25 1,800	July 31 1,000

Explanation

The July 25 sale of furniture on account for $1,800 increases Accounts Receivable. An increase in Accounts Receivable is recorded on the debit side.
The July 31 collection of $1,000 reduces Accounts Receivable. A decrease in Accounts Receivable is recorded on the credit side of the account.

Accounts Payable

Decreases *Debit*	*Increases* *Credit*
July 20 5,000	July 10 8,000

Explanation

The July 10 purchase of $8,000 furniture on account increases Accounts Payable. An increase in Accounts Payable is recorded on the credit side of the account.
The July 20 payment of $5,000 of the Accounts Payable reduces Accounts Payable. A decrease in Accounts Payable is recorded on the debit side of the account.

In the above illustrated T accounts for Accounts Receivable and Accounts Payable, the dates and related amounts are shown so that each entry is cross-referenced to the appropriate transaction recorded elsewhere. An alternate method used in Chapter 3 shows a transaction number in the T account rather than the date.

Rules for debit and credit

Using debits and credits for asset accounts:	Using debits and credits for liability and shareholders' equity accounts:
Debit for Increases *Credit for Decreases*	*Debit for Decreases* *Credit for Increases*

The following summaries can now be made. Firstly, the relationship of the rules of debit and credit to the balance sheet and to the accounting equation may be illustrated as follows:

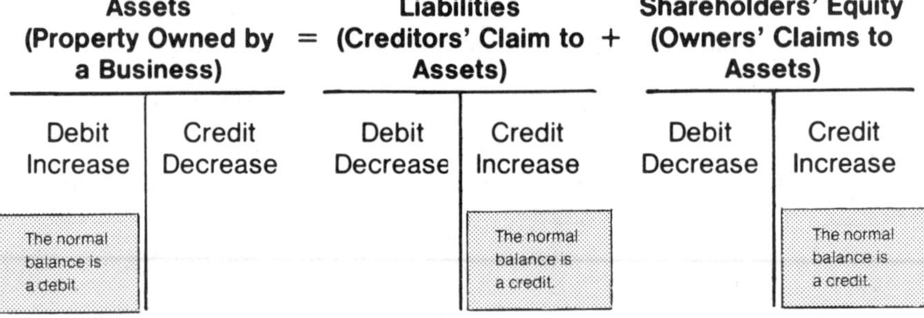

The abbreviation for credit is *Cr.;* for debit it is *Dr.*

Secondly, the following rules can be summarized for the applicability of the debit and credit terminology to T accounts.

Debit to record:
1. An increase of an asset
2. A decrease of a liability
3. A decrease in the shareholders' equity

Credit to record:
1. A decrease of an asset
2. An increase of a liability
3. An increase in the shareholders' equity

ILLUSTRATION OF DEBITS AND CREDITS

Again, using the six transactions of the Whitside Realty Corporation Limited, the mechanics of debits and credits are demonstrated. Each transaction is analyzed in the light of the foregoing suggestions for recording the information, the appropriate debits and credits are illustrated, and the amounts are entered directly into the accounts.

Transaction 1:

July 3 The Whitside Realty Corporation Limited was organized and capital stock was issued for cash in the amount of $50,000. Cash, an asset, is increased by $50,000, and Capital Stock, a shareholders' equity item, is likewise increased.

An increase in the asset, Cash, is recorded by a Debit.

Debit	Cash	$50,000

An increase in an equity account is recorded by a credit. The increase in Capital Stock is recorded by a Credit.

Credit	Capital Stock	$50,000

This transaction is recorded in the T accounts as follows:

Cash

Debit	*Credit*
50,000	

Capital Stock

Debit	*Credit*
	50,000

Transaction 2:

July 5 Purchased land and building for $30,000 in cash. The land was appraised at $5,000; the building, at $25,000. Both land and building are assets that have been increased.

An increase in assets is recorded by a Debit.

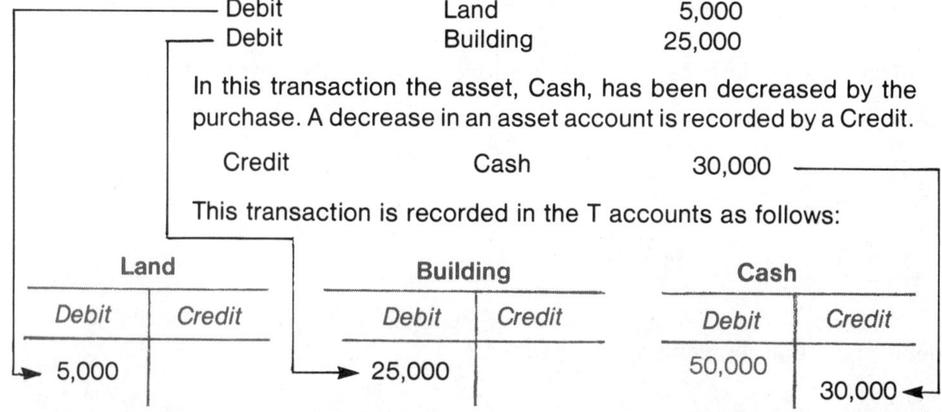

Debit	Land	5,000
Debit	Building	25,000

In this transaction the asset, Cash, has been decreased by the purchase. A decrease in an asset account is recorded by a Credit.

Credit	Cash	30,000

This transaction is recorded in the T accounts as follows:

Land

Debit	*Credit*
5,000	

Building

Debit	*Credit*
25,000	

Cash

Debit	*Credit*
50,000	
	30,000

Transaction 3:

July 10 Purchased furniture on account from the Jones Company for $8,000.

In this transaction the asset, Furniture, has been increased. Since the purchase was on credit, the liability of the company has also been increased.

An increase in the asset, Furniture, is recorded by a Debit.

Debit	Furniture	8,000

An increase in the Liability, Accounts Payable, is recorded by a Credit.

Credit	Accounts Payable	8,000

This transaction is recorded in the T accounts as follows:

Furniture

Debit	*Credit*
8,000	

Accounts Payable

Debit	*Credit*
	8,000

Transaction 4:

July 20 Paid the Jones Company $5,000 on account. The liability, Accounts Payable, is decreased and the asset, Cash, is also decreased.

A decrease in a liability is recorded by a Debit.

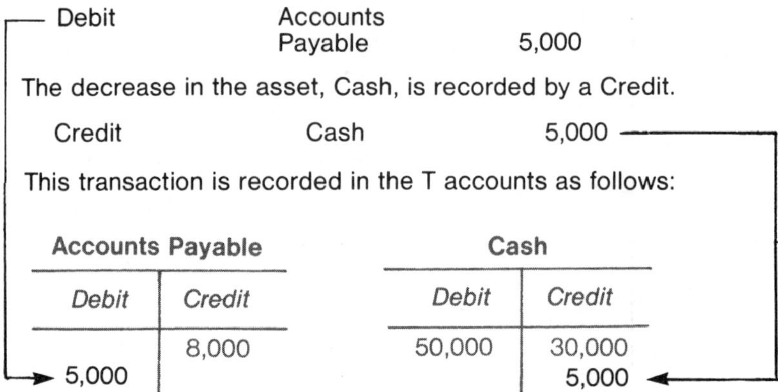

Debit	Accounts Payable	5,000

The decrease in the asset, Cash, is recorded by a Credit.

Credit	Cash	5,000

This transaction is recorded in the T accounts as follows:

Accounts Payable

Debit	*Credit*
	8,000
5,000	

Cash

Debit	*Credit*
50,000	30,000
	5,000

Transaction 5:

July 25 Sold furniture that cost $1,800 to James Hill for $1,800 on account. The asset, Accounts Receivable, is increased by $1,800 and the asset, Furniture, is decreased by $1,800.

The increase in the asset, Accounts Receivable, is recorded by a Debit.

Debit	Accounts Receivable	1,800

The decrease in the asset, Furniture, is recorded by a Credit.

Credit	Furniture	1,800

This transaction is recorded in the T accounts as follows:

Accounts Receivable

Debit	*Credit*
1,800	

Furniture

Debit	*Credit*
8,000	
	1,800

Transaction 6:

July 31 Collected $1,000 from James Hill on account. The asset, Cash, is increased by $1,000; the asset, Accounts Receivable, is decreased by $1,000. The increase in the asset, Cash, is recorded by a Debit.

Debit	Cash	1,000

The asset, Accounts Receivable, has been decreased by this transaction and is recorded by a Credit.

Credit	Accounts Receivable	1,000

This transaction is recorded in the T accounts as follows:

Cash

Debit	*Credit*
50,000	30,000
	5,000
1,000	

Accounts Receivable

Debit	*Credit*
1,800	
	1,000

THE TRIAL BALANCE

After all the transactions are recorded, the accounts are *footed;* that is, each amount column containing more than one entry is totaled under the last amount on each side (see the Cash account, for example). Then the balance of each account is determined by subtracting the smaller amount from the larger; the balance is placed in the side with the larger amount. This is illustrated in Figure 2-1.

Figure 2-1 Company T Accounts

Assets (Property Owned by a Business)	=	Liabilities (Creditors' Claims to Assets)	+	Shareholders' Equity (Owners' Claims to Assets)

Cash	**Acct. No. 101**
50,000	30,000
1,000	5,000
51,000	**35,000**
Bal. 16,000	

Accounts Receivable Acct. No. 111	
1,800	1,000
1,800	**1,000**
Bal. 800	

Land	**Acct. No. 151**
5,000	

Building	**Acct. No. 152**
25,000	

Furniture	**Acct. No. 157**
8,000	1,800
8,000	**1,800**
Bal. 6,200	

Accounts Payable	**Acct. No. 201**
5,000	8,000
5,000	**8,000**
	Bal. 3,000

Capital Stock	**Acct. No. 251**
	50,000

A comment about the page numbering system should be made. The pages could be numbered 1, 2, 3, 4, 5, 6, 7; but if the numbers are to have a specific meaning—for example, 100-199 for assets, 200-249 for liabilities, and 250-299 for shareholders' equity items—and if expansion is contemplated (the insertion of new pages for new items), then the numbering system should be something like the one shown in Figure 2-1.

As a check on the accuracy of the work in relation to the accounting equation, it is customary to compare the total of the debit balances to the total of the credit balances. If the totals agree, it is presumed that the accounting is correct up to this point. This listing of account balances is called a trial balance. The trial balance for Whitside Realty Corporation Limited is shown below.

WHITSIDE REALTY CORPORATION LIMITED
Trial Balance
July 31, 19XX

Acct. No.	*Account Title*	*Debits*	*Credits*
101	Cash	$16,000	
111	Accounts Receivable	800	
151	Land	5,000	
152	Building	25,000	
157	Furniture	6,200	
201	Accounts Payable		$ 3,000
251	Capital Stock		50,000
	Totals	$53,000	$53,000

The trial balance proves the equality of debits and credits, but this does not insure the accuracy of the accounts; for example, an entire transaction could be omitted, the debit and credit amounts of an entry could be identically incorrect, a wrong account could be debited or credited, or both the debit and credit amounts for a given transaction could be posted twice. If the trial balance is in balance, however, the accountant considers this strong presumptive evidence of accuracy and proceeds from that point.

The trial balance is useful to the accountant in preparing periodic financial statements. The accountant could prepare a balance sheet directly from the accounts; but the trial balance furnishes a convenient summary of the information for the preparation of the statement of financial position.

If a trial balance does not balance, the following steps should be followed in the indicated sequence to locate the error.

1. Find the difference between the trial balance totals.
2. Examine the trial balance for balances that may be in the wrong column.
3. Re-add the trial balance columns.
4. Check the trial balance figures against those appearing in the ledger to see whether the amounts correspond and whether they have been entered in the proper columns.
5. Check the additions on each side of each ledger account and recompute the balances.
6. Check postings from journal to ledger.

The trial balance may not balance because of a single error. Time and effort may be saved by applying the following special tests after step 1:

1. Errors in the amount of $0.01, $0.10, $1, $10, $100, and so on, may be due to errors in addition or subtraction.
2. If the trial balance difference is divisible by 2, the error may be due to a debit amount entered as a credit amount, or vice versa.
3. If the trial balance difference is divisible by 9 or 99, the error may be due to a transposition of figures ($83.41 posted as $38.41) or a slide ($1.05 posted as $105.00).

THE BALANCE SHEET

After the trial balance is completed, a balance sheet identical to Figure 1-2 can be prepared.

Figure 2-2 Formal Balance Sheet

WHITSIDE REALTY CORPORATION LIMITED
Balance Sheet
July 31, 19XX

Assets			*Liabilities and Shareholders' Equity*	
Current Assets			Current Liabilities	
Cash	$16,000		Accounts Payable	$ 3,000
Accounts Receivable	800		Shareholders' Equity	
Total Current Assets		$16,800	Capital Stock	50,000
Plant and Equipment				
Land	$ 5,000			
Building	25,000			
Furniture	6,200			
Total Plant and Equipment		36,200		
Total Assets		$53,000	Total Liabilities and Shareholders' Equity	$53,000

THE GENERAL JOURNAL AND POSTING

In the preceding sections of this chapter, the six transactions of the Whitside Realty Corporation Limited were analyzed in terms of their effect on assets, and shareholders' equity accounts, the appropriate use of debits and credits was illustrated for each transaction, and the information was entered directly into the accounts. Records can be kept in this manner; however, most businesses need more detailed information as well as a means of ensuring a properly functioning and systematic procedure for the recording of transactions. The desired additional information includes a chronological record of transactions and a complete history of each transaction recorded *in one place.* It is often necessary to view a transaction in its entirety, including reference to the underlying documents and supporting papers. Since every entry consists of at least one debit and one credit, the transaction is recorded on different ledger pages. If the ledger contains many accounts, it may be difficult to reconstruct the complete transaction.

The recording process is commonly divided into two parts:

1. *Journalizing,* or recording transactions in a book called a *journal.* The record of a transaction in the journal is called a *journal entry.*
2. *Posting,* or transferring amounts in the journal to the correct accounts in the ledger.

Entering Transactions in the Journal

The following entry, in the basic form of a journal, the *general journal,* shows the July 3 transaction of the Whitside Realty Corporation Limited.

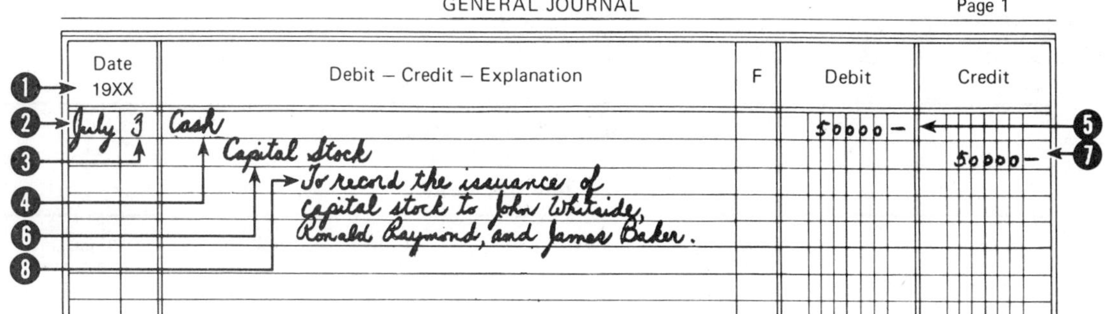

❶ The year is written in small figures at the top of the Date column. It should be written in that position on every page of the journal.

❷ The month of the first transaction recorded on this page is entered. It is not necessary to write the month again on this page unless it changes.

❸ The date of each transaction is entered.

❹ The title of the account debited is placed in the Explanation column against the date line. In order to eliminate confusion, it is important that the account title written in the journal entry should be the exact title of the account as it appears in the ledger.

❺ The amount of the debit is entered in the Debit money column.

❻ The title of the account credited is indented approximately one inch from the Date column.

❼ The amount of the credit is entered in the Credit money column.

❽ The explanation is entered on the next line, indented an additional one inch. The explanation should contain all the essential information as well as a reference to the relevant source document from which the information was obtained—inspection report, receiver's report, check number, and so on.

In journals, ledger accounts, and trial balances, the use of two zeros or a dash in the cents column is a matter of choice. Thus, an amount may be written 2,357.00 or 2,357.—. Many accountants feel that a dash is more easily written than two zeros, and that the use of dashes facilitates the addition of the cents column.

In a balance sheet and other statements it is preferable, for the sake of appearance, to use zeros. In the interest of space and time, the zero column will be omitted in most of the journals, ledgers, and statements that are illustrated in the remaining pages of this book.

The Three-Column Account Form

A variation of the T account method is used in actual practice by companies with a manual accounting system. This more formal account consists of three columns and shows separately debits, credits, and the balance resulting when debits and credits are added to or subtracted from the balance. The following illustration of the cash account for Whitside Realty Corporation Limited shows the workings of the three-column form.

Cash — Acct. No. 101

Date 19XX		Explanation	F	Debit	Credit	DR. or CR.	Balance
July	3	Issuance of Capital Stock		50000 —		DR	50000 —
	5	Purchased land and building			30000 —	DR	20000 —
	20	Payment to Jones Company Ltd.			5000 —	DR	15000 —
	31	Collection from Hill		1000 —		DR	16000 —

This method indicates whether the balance is a debit or credit. Sometimes accountants do not indicate whether the balance is a Dr. or Cr. since they know that the normal balance for assets is a debit, and the normal balance for liability and equity accounts is a credit. In some cases an account may have a balance other than its normal balance. For example, if the above cash account was overdrawn—more disbursements were made than there was cash available—then the resulting credit balance would have a Cr. notation entered in front of the balance. Similarly, if a debit balance resulted in a liability account from an error, for example, a Dr. would be placed in front of the balance.

Figure 2-3 Posting Flow Chart

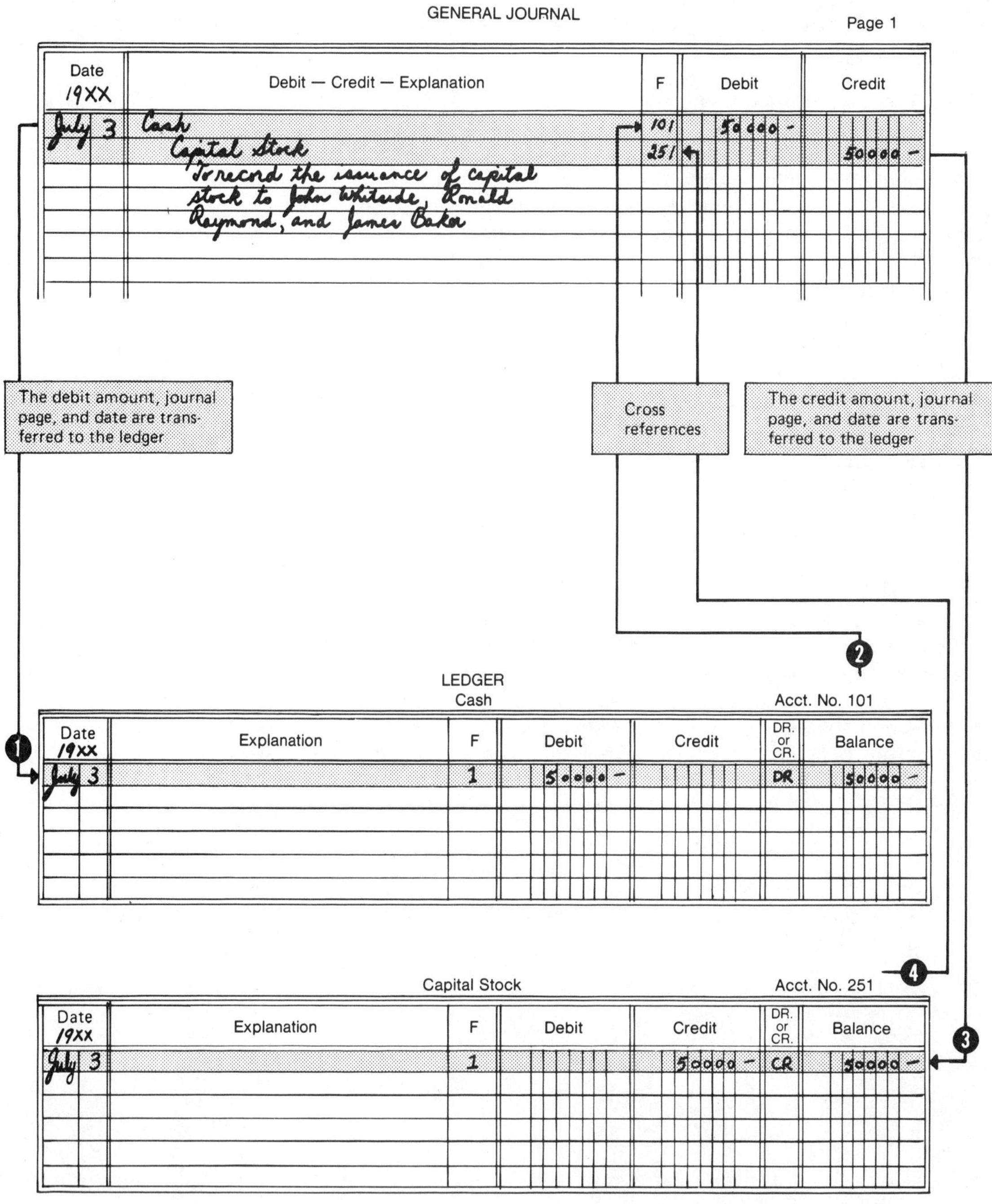

Dollar signs need not be written in journals and ledger accounts. They should be used in balance sheets and other formal statements.

Posting from the General Journal

It should be emphasized that the journal does not *replace* the ledger account. The journal is called a *book of original entry,* because it is necessary first to journalize the transaction and then to post to the proper accounts in the ledger(the *book of final entry*).

Figure 2-3 illustrates the posting of the July 3 entry from the general journal of the corporation to its ledger. Posting normally should be done daily. Explanations of the encircled numbers in Figure 2-3 follow:

❶ The debit amount, $50,000, the journal page, 1, and the date, July 3, are entered in the Cash account of the ledger. The year, 19XX, is written at the top of the Date column. Dollar signs are not used in journals or ledgers.

❷ The ledger account number for the debit entry, 101, is entered in the folio (F) column of the journal to cross-reference the journal and the ledger.

❸ The credit amount, $50,000, the journal page, 1, and the date, July 3, are entered in the Capital Stock account of the ledger. The year, 19XX, is written at the top of the Date column.

❹ The ledger account number for the credit entry, 251, is entered in the folio column of the journal to complete the cross referencing. It follows that the cross reference in the journal also indicates that the posting to the ledger has been completed.

It should be observed that explanations are not usually used in the Explanation columns of the ledger accounts. The cross reference to the journal page from which the information was recorded permits any interested person to quickly find a complete story of the transaction. Short explanations are used in the ledger accounts only when it is deemed that they will be especially useful in particular transactions.

The Accounting Sequence for the Whitside Realty Corporation Limited

The stage of accounting methodology used in actual practice is illustrated with the six transactions of the Whitside Realty Corporation Limited. The steps in the accounting sequence are:

1. Journalizing
2. Posting
3. Preparing a trial balance
4. Preparing a balance sheet

Journalizing. The six transactions of the Whitside Realty Corporation Limited appear in the general journal as follows:

GENERAL JOURNAL					Page 1
19XX					
July	3	Cash	101	50,000	
		Capital Stock	251		50,000
		To record the issuance of capital stock to John Whitside, Ronald Raymond, and James Baker.			
	5	Land	151	5,000	
		Building	152	25,000	
		Cash	101		30,000
		To record purchase of land and building for cash.			
	10	Furniture	157	8,000	
		Accounts Payable— Jones Company	201		8,000
		To record purchase of furniture on account.			
	20	Accounts Payable— Jones Company	201	5,000	
		Cash	101		5,000
		To record payment on account.			
	25	Accounts Receivable—James Hill	111	1,800	
		Furniture	157		1,800
		To record credit sale of furniture at cost.			
	31	Cash	101	1,000	
		Accounts Receivable— James Hill	111		1,000
		To record collection on account.			

Posting. The transactions are posted from page 1 of the general journal to the ledger accounts as illustrated previously.

The system under discussion is called *double-entry accounting,* because it requires that each record of a transaction has debits and credits of equal amount. Every transaction does not necessarily have a single debit and a single credit. For example, the July 5 entry of the corporation involves two debits totaling $30,000 and one credit of $30,000. This is called a *compound entry.* Regardless of the number of accounts debited in a single transaction, the total amount of all debits and the total amount of all credits in each transaction must be equal. It follows that the total of the debit and the credit balances in all the accounts must also be equal.

GLOSSARY

Account A statistical devise used for sorting accounting information into homogeneous groupings.

Asset A thing of value held by an economic enterprise.

Balance The difference between the total of the debit amount in an account and the total of the credit amount in an account.

Compound Entry A journal entry with more than one debit account or more than one credit account.

Credit The right side of an account, the amount shown on the right side of an account, or the process of placing an amount on the right side of an account.

Debit The left side of an account; the amount shown on the left side of an account; or the process of placing an amount on the left side of an account.

Folio The cross-reference column in a journal or a ledger.

Footing The totaling of a column of figures and showing of the total in small pencil figures under the last amount in the column (also used as a noun).

Journal The book(s) of original entry for all transactions.

Journalizing The process of recording a transaction, analyzed in terms of its debits and credits, in a record of original entry, referred to as a journal.

Ledger The book that contains all the ledger accounts; or any collection of ledger accounts.

Posting The process of transferring an amount recorded in the journal to the indicated account in the ledger.

T Account A simple form of ledger account in the shape of a T used for analyzing transactions and for teaching purposes.

Trial Balance A statement that shows the balances of all ledger accounts arranged according to whether they are debits or credits, the total of the debits must equal the total of the credits in this statement.

QUESTIONS

Q2-1. What is the difference between the terms *debit* and *credit?*

Q2-2. What is the function (a) of the general journal? (b) of the ledger?

Q2-3. A balanced trial balance is a correct trial balance. Discuss.

Q2-4. Robert Hanson purchased furniture on account from the Jones Company. Hanson debited the Furniture account for $800, and erroneously credited the Accounts Receivable account for $800. (a) What effect would the error have on the debit and credit totals of the trial balance taken at the end of the period? (b) What accounts in the trial balance would be incorrectly stated?

Q2-5. What does the term *ledger account* mean? Indicate two forms of the account. State the reasons and circumstances for using each form.

DEMONSTRATION PROBLEMS

DP2-1. *(Development of an accounting system: corporation)* Thurston Eaton Ltd. was incorporated in March and engaged in the following transactions:

March 1	Received a charter and issued all authorized capital stock for $40,000 cash.
2	Purchased land and building for $30,000. Paid $10,000 in cash and issued a 20-year mortgage payable for the balance. The land was appraised at $5,000; the building, at $25,000.
3	Purchased equipment and furniture from the Gummo Company for $8,000 on account.
12	Paid $3,000 in part payment of the Gummo Company account.
15	Some of the furniture purchased on March 3 was not satisfactory for office needs, so Eaton sold it on account to a lawyer, Thomas Schuester, at its cost of $800.
31	Received $700 from Schuester on account.

Required: Journalize the six transactions, post to formal ledger accounts, take a trial balance, and prepare a balance sheet.

DP2-2. The assets, liabilities, and equity of Tombstone Company Ltd. as of December 31, are as follows:

Cash	$ 8,000
Accounts Receivable	25,000
Notes Receivable	4,000
Merchandise Inventory	8,500
Office Supplies	500
Prepaid Insurance	1,000
Store Equipment	6,000
Building	26,000
Land	7,500
Accounts Payable	15,000
Notes Payable	8,000
Mortgage Payable (due Feb. 1, 2012)	12,000
Capital Stock	51,500

Required:
1. Prepare a trial balance from the above accounts.
2. Prepare a balance sheet.

PROBLEMS

P2-1. The following are among the transactions of Anderson Corporation Ltd.:

Dec. 1	Capital stock of $50,000 par value was issued for cash.
4	Purchased land for $10,000 in cash.
8	Purchased temporary investments for $5,000 in cash.
14	Purchased service supplies from Baltimore Company for $800 on account.
18	Sold the land at cost for $10,000 cash.
31	Paid $800 to Baltimore Company for balance of account.

Journalize the transactions, post to T accounts, and prepare a trial balance. (Assign appropriate numbers to accounts.)

P2-2. Branson Corporation Ltd. engaged in the following transactions during the first week of operations:

June 1 Issued capital stock at par to the four incorporators for $20,000 in cash.
3 Purchased office equipment from Black and Sons for $5,000 on account.
5 Purchased land for a future building site at a cost of $30,000; paid $10,000 down and issued a mortgage note payable in 10 years for the balance.

Journalize the transactions.

P2-3. The following transactions were engaged in by Calvin Corporation Ltd. during the month of March:

March 1 Received a charter and issued all authorized capital stock for $200,000 in cash.
2 Purchased land and buildings for $60,000 in cash and a 20-year mortgage payable for $40,000. The land was appraised at $30,000; the building, at $70,000.
3 Purchased service supplies from the Rand Company for $2,000 on account.
31 Sold a portion of the lot purchased on March 2 for its approximate cost of $5,000. The buyer, the White Sands Company, paid $3,000 in cash and issued a 90-day note for $2,000.

1. Journalize the transactions.
2. Post to formal ledger accounts.
3. Take a trial balance.
4. Prepare a classified balance sheet in good form.

P2-4. The following transactions occurred at Westerlin Company Ltd. during its first month of operations:

May 1 Received a corporate charter and issued all its authorized stock for $100,000 in cash.
2 Purchased land and building for $60,000. The company paid $20,000 in cash and issued a 20-year mortgage payable for the balance. The land was appraised at $15,000; the building, at $45,000.
3 Purchased furniture from the Godwin Company for $10,500 on account.
15 Paid the Godwin Company $6,500 on account.
20 Sold a portion of the land purchased on May 2 at its approximate cost of $5,000 to the Durham Realty Company on account.
31 Received $4,000 in cash and a 90-day note for $1,000 from the Durham Realty Company.

Journalize the transactions, post to formal ledger accounts, take a trial balance and prepare a classified balance sheet.

P2-5. The following T accounts were taken from the ledger of Raleigh Company Ltd.

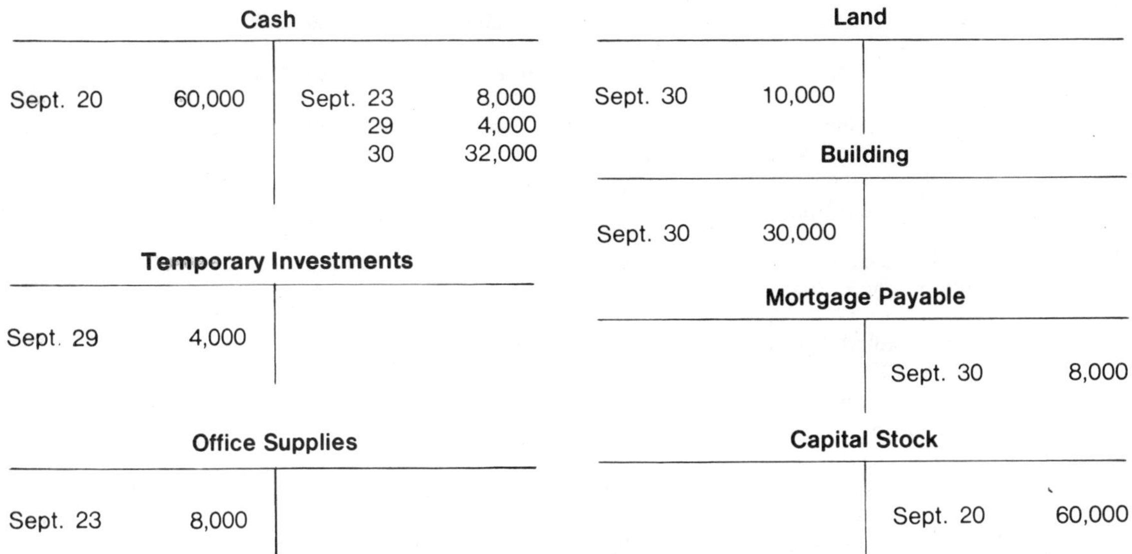

Cash

Sept. 20	60,000	Sept. 23	8,000
		29	4,000
		30	32,000

Temporary Investments

Sept. 29	4,000		

Office Supplies

Sept. 23	8,000		

Land

Sept. 30	10,000		

Building

Sept. 30	30,000		

Mortgage Payable

		Sept. 30	8,000

Capital Stock

		Sept. 20	60,000

Analyze these accounts and journalize each transaction.

P2-6. The following trial balance was prepared by Henry Donnan Company Ltd. The trial balance is not in balance and the accounts are not in the proper order, but the account balances are correct.

Account Title	*Debits*	*Credits*
Cash	$120,000	
Capital Stock		$170,000
Accounts Payable	20,000	
Notes Payable	10,000	
Land		8,000
Building		120,000
Accounts Receiveble		14,000
Notes Receivable		12,000
Service Supplies	6,000	
Mortgage Payable		80,000
Totals	$156,000	$404,000

1. Prepare a corrected trial balance showing the accounts in proper order.
2. Prepare a classified balance sheet.

P2-7. The Ernest Gray Company Ltd. had the following ledger accounts at June 30:

Cash	Acct. No. 101
110,000	6,000
800	2,000
	5,000

Notes Receivable	Acct. No. 112
3,000	800

Service Supplies	Acct. No. 131
8,000	3,000

Land	Acct. No. 151
20,000	

Accounts Payable	Acct. No. 201
5,000	14,000
	6,000

Capital Stock	Acct. No. 251
	110,000

1. Compute the account balances.
2. Prepare a trial balance.
3. Prepare a balance sheet.

P2-8. Nance Stenographic Service Inc., a newly incorporated company, plans to provide typing, duplicating, and stenographic services. The following ledger accounts as of August 31 are not in proper sequence.

Cash	
31,470	25,000
	1,000
	200
	700
	200
	100

Office Supplies	
50	
225	

Land	
5,000	

Accounts Payable	
100	350
[illegible]	60

Maintenance Supplies	
250	
220	
515	

Prepaid Insurance	
1,200	

Duplicating Equipment	
20,000	

Building	
70,000	

Mortgage Payable	
	25,000

Capital Stock	
	80,000

Delivery Equipment	
2,500	

Office Equipment	
1,000	

Required:

1. Determine the account balances and prepare a trial balance as of August 31, listing the accounts in proper sequence.
2. Prepare a balance sheet.

P2-9. During the first month of operation of the Herman Car Rental System Ltd., a corporation, the following transactions occurred:

Dec.	1	Received a charter and issued capital stock for $100,000.
	3	Purchased land for $10,000 and a building on the lot for $40,000. A cash payment of $20,000 was made, and a promissory note was issued for the balance.
	4	Purchased 15 new automobiles at $3,000 each from the Foreign Motor Company. A down payment of $30,000 in cash was made; the balance was promised to be paid in 30 days.
	5	Sold one automobile to Hilton Hertz, one of the company's employees, at cost. The employee paid $2,000 in cash and agreed to pay the balance within 30 days.
	6	One automobile proved to be defective and was returned to the Foreign Motor Company. The amount due was reduced by $3,000.
	11	Purchased a cash register and office desks for $2,500 for cash.
	31	Paid $10,000 in cash to the Foreign Motor Company on account.

Required:
1. Journalize the transactions.
2. Post to T accounts.

P2-10. The Barringer Garage Ltd. was incorporated on August 20. During the first several days of operations, its part-time bookkeeper (a high school student who had had a few months' instruction in bookkeeping) recorded the transactions and rendered the following unbalanced trial balance as of August 31.

Account Title	Debits	Credits
Accounts Payable	$ 37,100	
Accounts Receivable		$ 20,000
Building	100,000	
Capital Stock	150,000	
Cash	31,000	
Furniture	12,000	
Land		24,000
Marketable Securities		19,200
Mortgage Payable		40,000
Notes Payable	20,700	
Notes Receivable		36,000
Service Supplies	5,600	
Totals	$356,400	$139,200

Required:
1. Assuming that the amounts are correct but that the bookkeeper did not understand the proper debit-credit position of some accounts, prepare a trial balance showing the accounts in correct balance sheet order.
2. Prepare a balance sheet.

P2-11. *(Accounting policy decision problem)* Barton Corporation Ltd. has been operating for some years. In November 19XX the accountant of the company disappeared taking the records with him.

You are hired to reconstruct the accounting records, and with this in mind you make an inventory of all company assets. By checking with banks, counting the materials on hand, investigating the ownership of buildings and equipment, and so on, you develop the following information as of December 31:

Account Title	*Balance*	*Account Title*	*Balance*
Land	$30,000	Marketable Securities	$ 10,000
Equipment	50,000	Inventories	28,000
Buildings	60,000	Cash on Hand	6,000
Accounts Receivable	20,000	Cash in Banks	106,000

Statements from creditors and unpaid invoices found in the office indicate that $80,000 is owed to trade creditors. A $20,000 long-term mortgage (30 years) is outstanding.
Interviews with the board of directors and a check of the capital stock record bo[illegible] indicate that 2,000 shares of the capital stock are outstanding and that the [illegible]holders have contributed $60,000 to the corporation. No record is available regarding past retained earnings.

Required:

1. Prepare a trial balance and a balance sheet as at December 31.
2. Write a report to management indicating a simple accounting system that could be used and why you recommend such a system. *(Hint:* Include in the report the kinds of journals, ledgers, and overall system you recommend.)

P2-12. *(Financial policy decision problem)* Accounts included in the trial balance of the Karl Kutz Corporation as of November 30, were as follows:

Acct. No	*Account Title*	*Balance*
101	Cash	$ 25,200
111	Accounts Receivable	12,000
150	Office Supplies	1,500
200	Land	?
250	Building	?
300	Furniture and Fixtures	9,000
350	Machines	75,000
400	Delivery Equipment	3,500
600	Accounts Payable	4,000
650	Notes Payable	30,000
800	Capital Stock	?

Land and building were acquired at a cost of $36,000. It was determined that one-third of the total cost should be applied to the cost of land.

The following transactions were completed during the month of December:

Dec. 2 Paid in full an open-account liability of $200 to the Duncan Company.

3 Collected in full an account receivable of $700 from the Papermoon Corporation.

4 Purchased office equipment from Boozier Corporation Ltd. for $500 on account.

8 Additional shares were issued for $20,000 in cash.

10 Collected $1,500 from the Parker Company on account.

11 Purchased a machine from the Iber Business Machine Company for $25,000; paid $5,000 in cash, the balance to be paid within 30 days.

15 Paid in full an open-account liability of $600 to the Milton Company.

20 Paid $15,000 in cash to the Iber Business Machine Company in partial settlement of the liability of December 11. Issued a note payable for the balance.

31 Collected in full an account receivable of $400 from the Downy Company.

Required:

1. Journalize these transactions.
2. Enter the balances of November 30 in ledger accounts, post the December entries, and determine the new balances.
3. Prepare a trial balance as of December 31.
4. Prepare a balance sheet.

3

Income Statement Preparation

In the previous chapter, changes in the shareholders' equity caused by shareholder investments were discussed. Other changes may be caused by revenues, expenses, and dividends to shareholders. These changes, and the statements on which they are reflected, are explained in this chapter.

BASIC OPERATING CONCEPTS AND PROCEDURES

REVENUES

The term *revenue* describes the source of inflows of assets received in exchange for services rendered, sales of products or merchandise, gains from sales or exchanges of assets other than stock in trade, and earnings of interest and dividends on investments. It does *not include* increases arising from owners' contributions or from borrowed funds. For revenue to be earned, it does not have to be collected immediately in cash; it is sufficient that claims for cash on customers or clients exist.

Revenue accounts are created to accumulate the amounts earned during a *specified* period; the typical accounting period is one year. Often, however, progressive statements are prepared each month for the information of the management. The title of a revenue account should indicate the nature of the particular revenue; examples are Commissions Earned, Sales, Interest Earned, Dividends Earned, Accounting Fees Earned, and Garage Repair Revenue.

Revenue accounts are *credited when revenue increases;* the particular asset that is received is *debited.* To illustrate the journalizing of revenue transactions, several companies that earned different kinds of revenue are considered.

First, suppose that on August 2, 19XX, the Whitside Realty Corporation Limited sells a house and a lot and receives a commission of $500 in cash; this increase in the asset Cash is recorded by a debit, while the increase to the revenue account, Commissions Earned, is recorded by a credit. The journal entry follows:

Aug.	2	Cash		500	
		Commissions Earned			500
		To record receipt of commission on sale of house and lot.			

Next, assume that on July 30, 19XX, I.N. Malvin, C.A., bills the Anderson Company Ltd. for $1,000 for an annual audit that he had made. Accounts Receivable is the asset that is increased here and this increase is recorded by a debit. Since revenue was increased, and an increase to a revenue account is recorded by a credit, the account, Accounting Fees Earned, is credited.

July	30	Accounts Receivable		1,000	
		Accounting Fees Earned			1,000
		To record billing of following client for audit: Anderson Company Ltd. $1,000			

Suppose that on January 2, 19XX, the Georgetown Rental Agency Ltd. receives $750 in cash for January rent. Cash, an asset, is received; to record the increase of this asset, the Cash account must be debited. The source of this asset is a revenue. To record an increase in the revenue, Rent Earned, is credited.

Jan.	2	Cash		750	
		Rent Earned			750
		To record rental receipts for month of January.			

Rules for Recording Revenues

The above examples illustrate that an increase in revenue is recorded by a credit. This procedure can be related to the accounting equation discussed in Chapter 2, where increases in shareholders' equity are shown to be also recorded by a credit. A revenue can be considered as an increase in shareholders' equity; revenue accounts can be thought of as an extension of the shareholders' equity account, Retained Earnings (discussed later in this chapter). The relationship between revenue accounts and the Retained Earnings account is illustrated as follows:

Shareholders' Equity Accounts (Retained Earnings)

	An increase in retained earnings is recorded by a credit. An increase in revenue increases retained earnings.

All Revenue Accounts

	A credit records an increase in revenue.

EXPENSES

Expenses are expired costs of the materials consumed and services received during a specified period and used in the production of revenue during that same period. Examples of *expense accounts* are Salaries Expense, Rent Expense, and Office Supplies Expense. Expenses are recorded by a debit to the appropriate expense account and a credit to the Cash account, to a liability account, or possibly to some other type of account. The recording process for expenses is illustrated by the following transactions, which took place at the Mason Company.

Jan. 2 Paid $400 in rent for the month of January.
10 Purchased an advertisement in the local newspaper for $75 in cash.
15 Paid semimonthly salaries of $600.
20 Had some office machinery repaired at a cost of $45.

Each of the above transactions involves an increase in an expense account which is recorded by a debit to the appropriate account. The asset, Cash, is decreased in each of these transactions and is recorded by a credit to Cash.

These transactions are recorded in the general journal as follows:

GENERAL JOURNAL

Jan.	2	Rent Expense		400	
		Cash			400
		To record payment of rent for month of January.			
	10	Advertising Expense		75	
		Cash			75
		To record payment for advertising.			
	15	Salaries Expense		600	
		Cash			600
		To record payment of semimonthly salaries.			
	20	Repairs Expense—Office Equipment		45	
		Cash			45
		To record payment of repairs to office equipment.			

Rules for Recording Expenses

The preceding journal entries recording increases in expenses illustrate that an increase in expense is recorded by a debit. The logic of this debit procedure is clearer when the relationship between expense accounts and shareholders' equity is explained. An expense can be considered as a decrease in shareholders' equity and expense accounts can be thought of as an extension of the shareholders' account, Retained Earnings. The relationship between expense accounts and the Retained Earnings account is illustrated as follows:

Shareholders' Equity Accounts
(Retained Earnings)

A decrease in retained earnings is recorded by a debit. An expense decreases retained earnings.	

All Expense Accounts

A debit records an increase in expense.	

Distinction Between Costs and Expenses

It is necessary to distinguish between an *expense* and a *cost.* A cost is the amount paid or payable in either cash or the equivalent, for goods, services, or other assets purchased. When a cost no longer has asset status—that is, when its potential to produce future revenue is lost—it is said to be expired and thus to have become an *expense.*

From this statement the following conclusions are warranted:

Expenses = Expired costs (used up in producing this period's revenue)
Assets = Unexpired costs (to be used to produce future revenue)

For example, rent paid in advance for three months is an asset, Prepaid Rent. As time passes, this becomes Rent Expense. The required adjusting process is discussed in detail in the next chapter.

A *disbursement* is a payment in cash or by check. Hence, a machine may be acquired at a cost of $10,000; the transaction is completed by a disbursement in the form of a check for $10,000; and, as the machine is used in operations, it loses part of its service value, or *depreciates.* This is an element of expense, Depreciation Expense.

DIVIDENDS

Dividends are distributions of net income regardless of whether that income is earned in the current period or in past periods. Although dividends reduce the shareholders' equity, they are *not* expenses; they are not declared and paid for the purpose of producing revenue. A dividend may be recorded by a debit to a special Dividends account and a credit to Cash, or to a liability account if it is to be paid at a date subsequent to the date of declaration. For example, suppose that the Sandra Corporation declared and paid a regular quarterly cash dividend of $1,000 to its shareholders on November 10, 19XX. This transaction involves an increase in the account, Dividends; an increase in this account is recorded by a debit. The decrease of the asset, Cash, is recorded by a credit to Cash. The journal entry follows:

Nov.	10	Dividends		1,000	
		Cash			1,000
		To record declaration and payment of fourth quarterly dividend.			

EXPANDED RULES FOR DEBITS AND CREDITS

Since new types of accounts have been introduced, the rules for debiting and crediting accounts are expanded and summarized as follows:

Account Title

Debit to record:	*Credit to record:*
1. An increase of an asset	1. A decrease of an asset
2. An increase of an expense	2. A decrease of an expense
3. An increase of dividends	3. A decrease of dividends
4. A decrease of a liability	4. An increase of a liability
5. A decrease in the shareholders' equity	5. An increase in the shareholders' equity
6. A decrease in revenue	6. An increase in revenue

The relationship of the rules of debits and credits to the accounting equation may be diagramed as follows. The normal balance of each account is indicated by a *. For example, the normal balance of asset accounts is a debit.

EXPANDED ACCOUNTING EQUATION

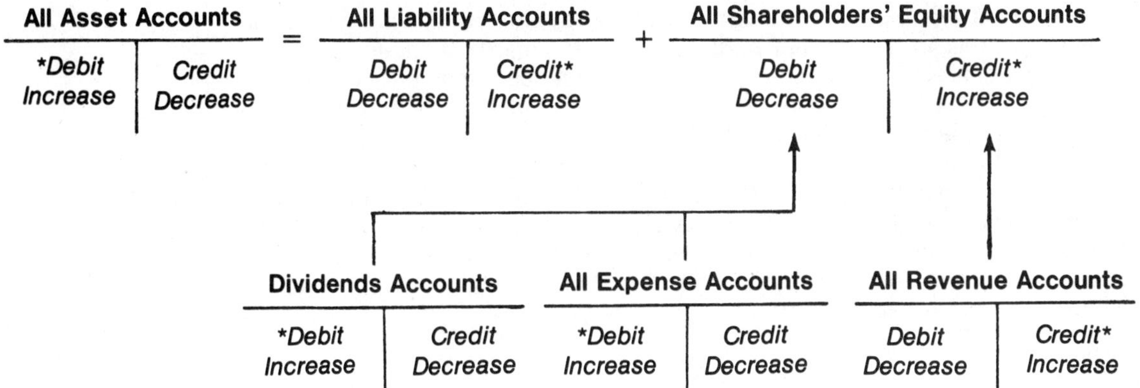

Analyzing Transactions and Journalizing

The transactions of Nelson Garage Ltd. that occurred during January 19XX are given. Before making entries in the journal, the accountant must analyze each transaction in terms of the basic system of debits and credits that has already been outlined. Following the transactions listed, a description of the analytical thinking that must precede the journalizing of these transactions is given as a guide to future action. Posting of these transactions to the apporpriate accounts is then illustrated.

Transaction 1:

The Corporate charter for the Nelson Garage Ltd. was received on this date, and the 3,000 shares of authorized capital stock were issued to three shareholders for $30,000 in cash. An asset, Cash, is received; to record an increase of an asset, it must be debited; therefore, the Cash account is debited for $30,000. The shareholders have a claim against the business; the increase in the shareholders' equity account, Capital Stock, is shown by a credit to that account.

Cash	30,000	
Capital Stock		30,000

The accounts would be posted as follows:

Cash

Debit	Credit
(1) 30,000	

Capital Stock

Debit	Credit
	(1) 30,000

Transaction 2:

Rented a temporary garage and paid $300 for the January rent; issued check No. 1. Since all the rent will have expired by the time the financial statements are prepared, it is considered an expense of the month of January. An increase of an expense account is recorded by a debit; therefore, the Rent Expense—Garage Building account is debited. The decrease of the asset Cash, is recorded by a credit to Cash. A single rent account may be sufficient for all rented buildings and equipment. In this case, the accountant felt that managerial analyses required a separate rent expense account for the garage building.

Rent Expense—Garage Building	300	
Cash		300

The accounts would be posted as follows:

Rent Expense—Garage Building

Debit		Credit	
(2)	300		

Cash

Debit		Credit	
(1)	30,000	(2)	300

Transaction 3:

Rented automotive tools and equipment pending purchase of the firm's own. Rent in the amount of $80 was paid for January; issued check No. 2. As in the preceding transaction, all this rent will have expired before the financial statements are prepared; therefore it is considered an expense of January. An increase of an expense account is recorded by a debit—in this case to Rent Expense—Automotive Tools and Equipment. The decrease of the asset, Cash, is recorded by a credit to Cash. Again, a single rent expense account may have been sufficient.

Rent Expense—Automotive Tools and Equipment	80	
Cash		80

The accounts would be posted as follows:

Rent Expense—Auto Tools and Equipment

Debit		Credit	
(3)	80		

Cash

Debit		Credit	
(1)	30,000	(2)	300
		(3)	80

Transaction 4:

Purchased garage parts and supplies described on invoice No. 306 from the Southern Supply Company for $650 on account. The Garage Parts and Supplies account is an asset and is increased by the transaction; the increase in the asset is shown by a debit to Garage Parts and Supplies. Since the purchase was on credit, a liability is created. To record the increase in the liability, the Accounts Payable account is credited.

Garage Parts and Supplies	650	
Accounts Payable		650

The accounts would be posted as follows:

Garage Parts and Supplies

Debit	Credit
(4) 650	

Accounts Payable

Debit	Credit
	(4) 650

Transaction 5:

Performed garage repairs for several cash customers; received $4,800 in cash. Cash, an asset, is received; to record the increase of the asset, the Cash account must be debited. The particular source of this asset is a revenue. To record an increase in the revenue, Garage Repairs Revenue is credited.

Cash	4,800	
Garage Repair Revenue		4,800

The accounts would be posted as follows:

Cash

Debit	Credit
(1) 30,000	(2) 300
(5) 4,800	(3) 80

Garage Repair Revenue

Debit	Credit
	(5) 4,800

Transaction 6:

Purchased land as a prospective building site for $10,000. Paid $4,000 in cash (check No. 3) and issued a one-year note for the balance. An increase in an asset account is recorded by a debit—in this case, to Land—and a decrease to the asset, Cash, is recorded by a credit. Since the land was not completely paid for, a liability is created. To record an increase in this liability, the Notes Payable account is credited.

Land	10,000	
Cash		4,000
Notes Payable		6,000

The accounts would be posted as follows:

Land

Debit	Credit
(6) 10,000	

Cash

Debit	Credit
(1) 30,000	(2) 300
(5) 4,800	(3) 80
	(6) 4,000

Notes Payable

Debit	Credit
	(6) 6,000

Transaction 7:

Paid $1,700 in salaries for first half of month (check No. 4 issued to obtain payroll cash). The increase in Salaries Expense is recorded by a debit. The decrease in the asset, Cash, is recorded by a credit.

	Debit	Credit
Salaries Expense	1,700	
Cash		1,700

The accounts would be posted as follows:

Salaries Expense

	Debit		Credit
(7)	1,700		

Cash

	Debit		Credit
(1)	30,000	(2)	300
(5)	4,800	(3)	80
		(6)	4,000
		(7)	1,700

Transaction 8:

Paid to the Southern Supply Company $300 on account (check No. 5). To record the decrease in the liability, the Accounts Payable account is debited. The decrease of the asset, Cash, is recorded by a credit to Cash.

	Debit	Credit
Accounts Payable	300	
Cash		300

The accounts would be posted as follows:

Accounts Payable

	Debit		Credit
(8)	300	(4)	650

Cash

	Debit		Credit
(1)	30,000	(2)	300
(5)	4,800	(3)	80
		(6)	4,000
		(7)	1,700
		(8)	300

Transaction 9:

Paid electricity and water bills for January, $80 (check No. 6). An increase in an expense account is recorded by a debit. The decrease in the asset, Cash, is recorded by a credit.

	Debit	Credit
Electricity and Water Expense	80	
Cash		80

The accounts would be posted as follows:

Electricity and Water Expense			
(9)	80		

Cash			
(1)	30,000	(2)	300
(5)	4,800	(3)	80
		(6)	4,000
		(7)	1,700
		(8)	300
		(9)	80

Transaction 10:

Paid a $300 cash dividend to the three shareholders (checks No. 7, 8, and 9). An increase in the dividend account is recorded by a debit. The decrease in the asset, Cash, is recorded by a credit.

Dividends	300	
Cash		300

The accounts would be posted as follows:

Dividends			
(10)	300		

Cash			
(1)	30,000	(2)	300
(5)	4,800	(3)	80
		(6)	4,000
		(7)	1,700
		(8)	300
		(9)	80
		(10)	300

Transaction 11:

Purchased automotive tools and equipment for cash, $4,000 (check No. 10). The list price was $5,000. The Automotive Tools and Equipment account is an asset and is increased by this transaction; the increase is recorded by a debit. The amount of the increase is $4,000 since assets are recorded at cost. The decrease in the asset, Cash, is recorded by a credit.

Automotive Tools and Equipment	4,000	
Cash		4,000

The accounts would be posted as follows:

Automotive Tools and Equipment			
(11)	4,000		

Cash			
(1)	30,000	(2)	300
(5)	4,800	(3)	80
		(6)	4,000
		(7)	1,700
		(8)	300
		(9)	80
		(10)	300
		(11)	4,000

Transaction 12:

Paid a premium of $600 (check No. 11) on a 12-month comprehensive insurance policy; the policy becomes effective on February 1, 19XX. Since none of the insurance will expire by the time the financial statements are prepared, it is considered as an asset and recorded by a debit to the Prepaid Insurance asset account. The decrease in the asset, Cash, is recorded by a credit.

Prepaid Insurance	600	
Cash		600

The accounts would be posted as follows:

Prepaid Insurance

(12)	600		

Cash

(1)	30,000	(2)	300
(5)	4,800	(3)	80
		(6)	4,000
		(7)	1,700
		(8)	300
		(9)	80
		(10)	300
		(11)	4,000
		(12)	600

Transaction 13:

Performed garage repairs for $210 on account, and for $10 cash. Since some repairs are made on credit, an asset account is created. To record an increase in the asset, the Accounts Receivable account is debited for $210. The increase in Cash is recorded by a debit. To record an increase in revenue, Garage Repairs Revenue is credited.

Cash	10	
Accounts Receivable	210	
Garage Repairs Revenue		220

The accounts would be posted as follows:

Cash

(1)	30,000	(2)	300
(5)	4,800	(3)	80
		(6)	4,000
(13)	10	(7)	1,700
		(8)	300
		(9)	80
		(10)	300
		(11)	4,000
		(12)	600

Accounts Receivable

(13)	210		

Garage Repairs Revenue

		(5)	4,800
		(13)	220

Transaction 14:

Took a physical inventory of garage parts and supplies; it showed that parts and supplies costing $375 were on hand, thus indicating that $275 (amount purchased $650, minus inventory, $375) worth of garage parts and supplies had been used, becoming an expense. Originally, as parts and supplies were purchased, they were debited to an asset account. Now, as the amount used becomes known, an entry is made debiting an expense account, Garage Parts and Supplies Used, to show that the expense account has been increased, and crediting an asset account, Garage Parts and Supplies, to show that the asset account has been decreased. (This type of transaction is normally recorded in an ***adjusting entry,*** explained in Chapter 4. It is presented here to broaden the scope of this illustration.)

Garage Parts and Supplies Used	275	
Garage Parts and Supplies		275

The accounts would be posted as follows:

Garage Parts and Supplies Used

(14)	275		

Garage Parts and Supplies

(4)	650	(14)	275

THE ACCOUNTING SEQUENCE

Six steps in the accounting sequence are illustrated through the example of a newly incorporated business called Nelson Garage Ltd. These steps are: (1) journalizing the transactions, (2) posting to the ledgers, (3) preparing a trial balance, (4) preparing the financial statements, (5) closing the temporary accounts, and (6) taking a postclosing trial balance. An explanation of each step in the sequence is presented along with the accounting procedure for the step.

Step 1

Journalizing the Transactions

The results of this analytical reasoning are presented in the following general journal. Note that space is left between entries to ensure that they are separate and distinct.

GENERAL JOURNAL — Page 1

			F	Debit	Credit
Jan.	2	Cash	101	30,000	
		Capital Stock	401		30,000
		To record issuance of Capital stock for cash.			
	3	Rent Expense—Garage Building	601	300	
		Cash	101		300
		To record payment of rent on garage building for month of January; issued check No. 1.			
	5	Rent Expense—Automotive Tools and Equipment	602	80	
		Cash	101		80
		To record payment of rent for automotive tools and equipment for month of January; issued check No. 2.			
	5	Garage Parts and Supplies	131	650	
		Accounts Payable	301		650
		To record purchase of parts and supplies on account.			
	6	Cash	101	4,800	
		Garage Repair Revenue	501		4,800
		To record collection from cash customers for services rendered.			
	10	Land	201	10,000	
		Cash	101		4,000
		Notes Payable	302		6,000
		To record purchase of land; issued check No. 3.			
	15	Salaries Expense	604	1,700	
		Cash	101		1,700
		To record payment of semimonthly salaries; issued check No. 4 to obtain payroll cash.			

GENERAL JOURNAL — Page 2

			F	Debit	Credit
Jan.	30	Accounts Payable	301	300	
		Cash	101		300
		To record payment; issued check No. 5 to Southern Supply Company.			
	31	Electricity and Water Expense	608	80	
		Cash	101		80
		To record payment of electricity and water bills for month of January; issued check No. 6.			
	31	Dividends	421	300	
		Cash	101		300
		To record payment of dividends to stockholders; issued checks No. 7, 8, and 9.			
	31	Automotive Tools and Equipment	221	4,000	
		Cash	101		4,000
		To record purchase of tools and equipment at a cost of $4,000 (list price, $5,000); issued check No. 10.			
	31	Prepaid Insurance	141	600	
		Cash	101		600
		To record payment of insurance premium for 12 months. Insurance is effective February 1, issued check No. 11.			
	31	Cash	101	10	
		Accounts Receivable	121	210	
		Garage Repair Revenue	501		220
		To record repair revenue.			
	31	Garage Parts and Supplies Used	609	275	
		Garage Parts and Supplies	131		275
		To record cost of parts and supplies used during month of January.			

Posting to the Ledgers

Step 2

As the transactions are posted to the ledger, the account numbers are entered in the general journal folio (F) column.

The timing of the posting process is a matter of personal preference and expediency. All postings, however, must be completed before financial statements can be prepared.

The posted ledger accounts are shown on the following page.

After all the transactions are posted, the accounts are footed; that is, each amount column containing more than one entry is totaled under the last amount on each side. Then the balance of each of these accounts is determined by subtracting the smaller amount from the larger; the balance is placed on the side with the larger amount.

ASSETS = LIABILITIES + [Capital Stock + Retained Earnings]

Cash Acct. No. 101

(1)	30,000	(2)	300
(5)	4,800	(3)	80
(13)	10	(6)	4,000
		(7)	1,700
		(8)	300
		(9)	80
		(10)	300
		(11)	4,000
		(12)	600
	34,810		11,360
Bal.	23,450		

Accounts Receivable Acct. No. 121

(13)	210		

Garage Parts and Supplies Acct. No. 131

(4)	650	(14)	275
	650		275
Bal.	375		

Prepaid Insurance Acct. No. 141

(12)	600		

Land Acct. No. 201

(6)	10,000		

Automotive Tools and Equipment Acct. No. 221

(11)	4,000		

Accounts Payable Acct. No. 301

(8)	300	(4)	650
	300		650
		Bal.	350

Notes Payable Acct. No. 302

		(6)	6,000

Capital Stock Acct. No. 401

		(1)	30,000

Retained Earnings Acct. No. 411

The use of the Retained Earnings account is explained in Step 5.

SHAREHOLDERS' EQUITY →

−[Dividends] + [Revenue] − [Expense]

Dividends Acct. No. 421

(10) 300	

Garage Repair Revenue Acct. No. 501

	(5) 4,800
	(13) 220
	Bal. 5,020

Rent Expense—Automotive Tools and Equipment Acct. No. 602

(3) 80	

Salaries Expense Acct. No. 604

(7) 1,700	

Electricity and Water Expense Acct. No. 608

(9) 80	

Garage Parts and Supplies Used Acct. No. 609

(14) 275	

Income Summary Acct. No. 901

The use of the Income Summary account is explained in Step 5.

Step 3

Preparing a Trial Balance

After the accounts in the general ledger are footed and the balances are obtained, the following trial balance is taken:

NELSON GARAGE LTD.
Trial Balance
January 31, 19XX

Acct. No.	*Account Title*	*Debits*	*Credits*
101	Cash	$23,450	
121	Accounts Receivable	210	
131	Garage Parts and Supplies	375	
141	Prepaid Insurance	600	
201	Land	10,000	
221	Automotive Tools and Equipment	4,000	
301	Accounts Payable		$ 350
302	Notes Payable		6,000
401	Capital Stock		30,000
421	Dividends	300	
501	Garage Repair Revenue		5,020
601	Rent Expense—Garage Building	300	
602	Rent Expense—Automotive Tools and Equipment	80	
604	Salaries Expense	1,700	
608	Electricity and Water Expense	80	
609	Garage Parts and Supplies Used	275	
	Totals	$41,370	$41,370

These accounts are used to prepare the Income Statement.

Step 4

Preparing the Financial Statements

The Income Statement

The total expenses for a period are deducted from the total revenues to measure the *net income* (profit) for the period, which in turn reflects the increase in the shareholders' equity resulting from business operations.

This may be expressed in equation form:

Total revenues − Total expenses = Net income

If the expenses for a period exceed the revenues for that period, a *net loss* results, and the shareholders' equity is decreased. The equation now becomes

Total expenses − Total revenues = Net loss

The basic objective of operating a business is to produce a net income, which results from receiving more from a customer for services rendered than the total expense to the business of producing the services; a loss is incurred when the expense of the services to the enterprise is more than the income received from customers for the services rendered.

At the end of the period, the period's expenses are matched against the period's revenue to determine the net income or net loss for that period. This information is contained in a financial statement called an *income statement,* discussed and illustrated below.

The income statement shown in Figure 3-1 was prepared from the trial balance of Nelson Garage Ltd.

The heading of the income statement shows the following:

1. Name of the business
2. Name of the statement
3. Period covered by the statement

It is important that the period covered be specified clearly. The date January 31, 19XX, is not sufficient; it, alone, does not indicate whether the net income of $2,585 was earned in one day, one month, or one year ended January 31, 19XX. The analyst must know how long a period it took for the firm to earn the $2,585.

Figure 3-1
Income Statement

NELSON GARAGE LTD.
Income Statement
For the Month Ended January 31, 19XX

Revenue		
Garage Repair Revenue		$5,020
Expenses		
Rent Expense—Garage Building	$ 300	
and Equipment	80	
Salaries Expense	1,700	
Electricity and Water Expense	80	
Garage Parts and Supplies Used	275	
Total Expenses		2,435
Net Income		$2,585

The determination of net income for Nelson Garage Ltd. at this level should not be interpreted as being definitive. For example, a corporation is subject to income taxes; the accounting for income taxes and certain other more complex problems are deferred to later chapters.

There is no standard order for listing accounts in the income statement. Size of each revenue and expense item may be one criterion; or the sequence of the accounts in the general ledger may be used as the basis for establishing the order used in listing the accounts in the income statement.

The Statement of Retained Earnings. Since the corporation is a creature of the law, there are certain legal restrictions on it, including a requirement that the net income retained in a business be recorded separately from the Capital Stock account. The typical title of the account used to accumulate this information is Retained Earnings. ***The statement of retained earnings*** shows the changes in that part of the shareholders' equity designated as "retained earnings"; it should cover the same period as the income statement. Since by definition retained earnings are the accumulation of all past net income less any dividends paid out, it follows that net income and dividends for a period must be reflected in the statement. The first end-of-period statement of retained earnings of Nelson Garage Ltd. is shown in Figure 3-2.

Figure 3-2
Statement of Retained Earnings

NELSON GARAGE LTD.
Statement of Retained Earnings
For the Month Ended January 31, 19XX

Net income for January	$2,585
Deduct Dividends	300
Retained Earnings, January 31	$2,285

The heading of the statement of retained earnings is similar to that of the income statement.

For a business that has been in existence prior to the current period, there would be an additional item in the statement of retained earnings, the beginning-of-period balance. For example, the statement of Elizabeth Calloway Company Ltd. is shown in Figure 3-3.

Figure 3-3
Statement of Retained Earnings

ELIZABETH CALLOWAY COMPANY LTD.
Statement of Retained Earnings
For the Month Ended January 31, 19XX

Retained Earnings, January 1	$5,000,000
Add Net Income for January	400,000
Total	$5,400,000
Deduct Dividends	300,000
Retained Earnings, January 31	$5,100,000

The Balance Sheet. Since the retained earnings of Nelson Garage Ltd., as of January 31, 19XX, have now been determined (Figure 3-2), it is possible to prepare the balance sheet, as shown in Figure 3-4.

Figure 3-4 Formal Balance Sheet

NELSON GARAGE LTD.
Balance Sheet
January 31, 19XX

Assets			*Liabilities and Shareholders' Equity*		
Current Assets			Current Liabilities		
Cash	$23,450		Accounts Payable	$ 350	
Accounts Receivable	210		Notes Payable	6,000	
Garage Parts and Supplies	375		Total Current Liabilities		$ 6,350
Prepaid Insurance	600				
			Shareholders' Equity		
Total Current Assets		$24,635	Capital Stock	$30,000	
Plant and Equipment			Retained Earnings	2,285	
Land	$10,000				
Automotive Tools and Equipment	4,000		Total Shareholders' Equity		32,285
Total Plant and Equipment		14,000			
Total Assets		$38,635	Total Liabilities and Shareholders' Equity		$38,635

Note that the heading of the balance sheet contains the single date *January 31, 19XX.* This statement reveals the financial position as of the close of business on January 31. It is analogous to a still photograph, whereas the income statement and statement of retained earnings are like moving pictures—they show the changes that have taken place during a specific period.

Closing the Temporary Accounts

Step 5

The revenue, expense, and dividends accounts are used to measure part of the changes that take place in retained earnings during a specified period. For this reason, these accounts are often called ***temporary owner's equity accounts*** or ***nominal accounts.***

At the end of an accounting period, these accounts must be emptied—or *closed*—so that they may be used to accumulate the changes in retained earnings for the next period. Therefore, *closing entries* are made to transfer the final effects of the temporaty shareholders' equity accounts to the Retained Earnings account, which is a *permanent,* or *real,* account.

The Closing Procedure. To simplify the transfer of revenue and expense account balances, an intermediate ***summary account,*** called Income Summary, is used. The balances of all revenue and expense accounts are transferred to this account. The Income Summary account, the balance of which reveals the net income or loss for the period, is then closed by transferring its balance to the Retained Earnings account, a part of the shareholders' equity. This action is justified because net income or net loss accrues to the owners. Since the Dividends account is not an expense account, it is not closed to Income Summary; rather, it is closed directly to Retained Earnings.

The closing procedure is illustrated in Figure 3-5. An explanation of encircled figures in this figure is as follows:

Entry ❶ —The revenue accounts are closed.
Entry ❷ —The expense accounts are closed.
Entry ❸ —The Income Summary account is closed.
Entry ❹ —The Dividends account is closed.

Figure 3-5 The Closing Procedure

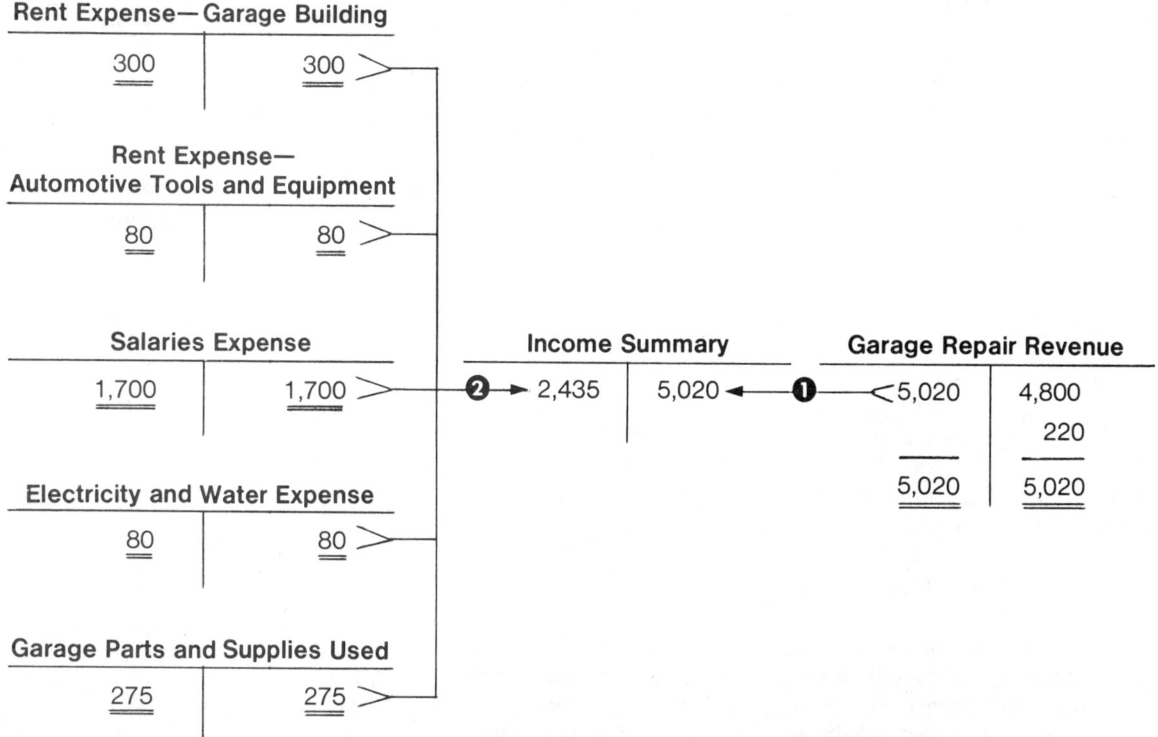

Following the closing of the revenue and expense accounts to Income Summary, the balance in Income Summary is equal to the net income of $2,585. The Income Summary and Dividend accounts are now closed to Retained Earnings.

Dividends	
300	300 ❹ →

Retained Earnings	
300	
	2,585 ← ❸
300	2,585
	Bal. 2,285

Income Summary	
2,435	5,020
2,585	
5,020	5,020

Ruling the Closed Temporary Accounts. After the closing entries have been posted, the temporary shareholders' equity accounts consist of equal debit and credit totals; that is, they have zero balances. These accounts (revenue, expense, and dividend) are ruled to separate the amounts entered during one accounting period from the amounts to be entered during the next. Each side is totaled; and the equal debit and credit totals are written on the first available full line. Double lines are then drawn below all the totals to signify that the accounts have a zero balance. If an account has only one debit and one credit, it is unnecessary to foot the account; double lines are drawn below the individual amounts. Figure 3-5 shows the posted closing entries and the ruling of the nominal accounts.

Unlike regular transaction entries, which require analysis and judgment, the closing process is purely mechanical and involves only the shifting and summarizing of previously determined amounts. The closing journal entries of Nelson Garage Ltd. on January 31, 19XX, are shown in Figure 3-6.

The presence of account numbers in the folio column of the journal indicates that the closing journal entries have been posted to the ledger accounts indicated in the journal. Closing may be indicated by the words *to close* in the columns of the temporary accounts.

Figure 3-6
Closing Entries

GENERAL JOURNAL

Page 3

		Closing Entries			
19XX					
Jan.	31	Garage Repair Revenue	501	5,020	
		Income Summary	901		5,020
		To close revenue to summary account.			
	31	Income Summary	901	2,435	
		Rent Expense—Garage Building	601		300
		Rent Expense—Automotive Tools and Equipment	602		80
		Salaries Expense	604		1,700
		Electricity and Water Expense	608		80
		Garage Parts and Supplies Used	609		275
		To close expenses to summary account.			
	31	Income Summary	901	2,585	
		Retained Earnings	411		2,585
		To transfer net income to retained earnings.			
	31	Retained Earnings	411	300	
		Dividends	421		300
		To close dividends to retained earnings.			

Entry 1.
All the revenue accounts are debited in a compound journal entry, and the total is credited to the Income Summary account.

Entry 2.
All the expense accounts are credited in a second compound entry, and the total is debited to the Income Summary account.

Entry 3.
After entries 1 and 2 are posted, a credit balance in the Income Summary account represents net income. The balance of the account is credited to Retained Earnings.

Entry 4.
The dividends account is closed directly to Retained Earnings.

Step 6

Taking a Postclosing Trial Balance

After the closing entries have been posted and the accounts are ruled and balanced, a ***postclosing trial balance*** is taken from the general ledger. Since the only accounts with open balances are the real accounts, the accounts and amounts in the postclosing trial balance are the same as those in the balance sheet. The postclosing trial balance tests the debit and credit equality of the general ledger before the accounts receive postings of the next accounting period. Its use, however, is optional, and a comparison of the general ledger account balances with the balance sheet will serve the same purpose. In any case, it is absolutely essential to start a new period with the accounts in proper balance; even though the trial balance at the end of the new period would indicate an error; errors made in previous accounting periods are very difficult to trace.

The postclosing trial balance of Nelson Garage Ltd. is shown:

NELSON GARAGE LTD.
Postclosing Trial Balance
January 31, 19XX

Acct. No.	*Account Title*	*Debits*	*Credits*
101	Cash	$23,450	
121	Accounts Receivable	210	
131	Garage Parts and Supplies	375	
141	Prepaid Insurance	600	
201	Land	10,000	
221	Automotive Tools and Equipment	4,000	
301	Accounts Payable		$ 350
302	Notes Payable		6,000
401	Capital Stock		30,000
411	Retained Earnings		2,285
	Totals	$38,635	$38,635

INTERRELATIONSHIP OF THE FINANCIAL STATEMENTS

There is a significant interrelationship between the balance sheet, the statement of retained earnings, and the income statement. The income statement shows the net amount remaining after revenues have been matched with expenses for a given period. This amount, the net income, is transferred to the statement of retained earnings, which shows the changes that have taken place in shareholders' equity as a result of the operations of a period. The statement of retained earnings shows additional changes that have taken place in shareholders' equity—in this particular case, dividend payments. The end-of-period balance of retained earnings is transferred to the end-of-period balance sheets, which presents information as of a moment of time—that is, at the end of the accounting period. The income statement and the statement of retained earnings help to account for the changes in the shareholders' equity during the interval between balance sheets. For this reason, it is helpful if the statements are prepared in this sequence: income statement, statement of retained earnings, and balance sheet.

SELECTING A CHART OF ACCOUNTS

An important step in establishing an efficient accounting system that will satisfy the needs of management, government agencies, and other interested groups is the construction of a *chart of accounts.*

> A separate account should be set up for each item that appears in the financial statements to make the statements easier to prepare. The *chart of accounts* is the complete listing of account titles to be used in the entity.

The classification and the order of the items in the chart of accounts corresponds to those of the statements.

Account titles should be carefully selected to suit the needs of the business, and should indicate clearly and precisely the nature of the accounts to ensure proper recording of transactions. However, titles are not standardized; for example, one business may use Unexpired Insurance and another Prepaid Insurance to describe the same asset.

The accountant of Nelson Garage Ltd., expecting the company to grow rapidly, sets up the following chart of accounts—the accounts that he expects to use during the first month of operations are listed with numbers skipped to provide for future expansion.

NELSON GARAGE LTD.
Chart of Accounts

Asset Accounts (100-299)

Current Assets (100-199)
- 101 Cash
- 121 Accounts Receivable
- 131 Garage Parts and Supplies
- 141 Prepaid Insurance

Plant and Equipment (200-299)
- 210 Land
- 221 Automotive Tools and Equipment

Liability and Shareholders' Equity Accounts (300-499)

Current Liabilities (300-350)
- 301 Accounts Payable
- 302 Notes Payable

Long-Term Liabilities (351-399)

Shareholders' Equity (400-499)
- 401 Capital Stock
- 411 Retained Earnings
- 421 Dividends

Income Statement Accounts (500-999)

Revenue (500-599)
- 501 Garage Repair Revenue

Expenses (600-699)
- 601 Rent Expense—Garage Building
- 602 Rent Expense—Automotive Tools and Equipment
- 604 Salaries Expense
- 608 Electricity and Water Expense
- 609 Garage Parts and Supplies Used

Clearing and Summary Accounts (900-999)
- 901 Income Summary

In this example, a three-digit system is used to number the accounts; a larger business with a number of departments or branches may use four or more digits. Notice that accounts 100-299 represent assets; that accounts 300-499 represent liabilities and shareholders' (owners') equity; and that accounts 500-999 represent income statement accounts. The more detailed breakdown for current assets, plant and equipment; and current liabilities, for example, can be seen in the chart. As stated previously, the gaps between the assigned account numbers allow for additional accounts as they are needed by the business.

GLOSSARY

Chart of Accounts A list of all accounts in the general ledger which are anticipated to be used. Their numbering system indicates the types of accounts by subgroups.

Closing the Books The process of clearing the temporary or the nominal accounts at the end of a period; this process requires preparation of closing journal entries, posting of these entries, and ruling of the nominal accounts that are closed.

Cost The amount paid or payable in either cash or its equivalent for goods, services, or other assets purchased.

Dividend A distribution of net income whether such income is earned during the current period or in a previous period.

Expense Expired costs; the materials used and services utilized in the production of revenue during a specific period.

Income Statement A statement showing all revenue and expense items for a given period arranged in such a manner that the total of the expenses are subtracted from the total of the revenues, thus revealing the net income earned during that period.

Matching Concept The identification of incurred expenses to a given time period, and matching them against earned revenue identified to the same time period, to determine net income for that period.

Net Income Excess of revenue over expenses for a given period.

Net Loss Excess of expenses over revenue for a given period.

Permanent Accounts The accounts that are not closed and which are incorporated in the balance sheet.

Postclosing Trial Balance A trial balance taken of the ledger accounts that have any balances in them—the real accounts—after closing entries have been recorded and posted.

Revenue A term describing the source of inflows of assets received in exchange for services rendered, sales of products or merchandise, gains from sales or exchange of assets other than stock in trade, and earnings from interest and dividends on investments.

Statement of Retained Earnings A statement showing the changes that occurred in retained earnings during a given period.

Temporary Accounts Temporary accounts that are set up to collect and to measure part of the change that takes place in retained earnings or other applicable owners' equity accounts. They are closed out at the end of each accounting period.

QUESTIONS

Q3-1. Define the term *revenue.* Does the receipt of cash by a business indicate that revenue has been earned? Explain. List ten small businesses and professions, and name the major source of revenue for each.

Q3-2. Define the term *expense.* Does the payment of cash by a business indicate that an expense has been incurred? Explain. Distinguish between a dividend and an expense.

Q3-3. Russell Carter purchased electrical supplies on account from the Dunlap Company for $350 and from Hanlon, Inc., for $100. Carter debited Electrical Supplies, $450, and erroneously credited Accounts Receivable for $450 in the general ledger. The credit postings to the accounts payable ledger were properly made. (a) What effect would the error have on the debit and credit totals of the trial balance taken at the end of the month? (b) What accounts in the trial balance would be incorrectly stated? (c) Would the error be discovered? How?

Q3-4. What is the purpose of closing the books? Using T accounts for Revenue, Expenses, Dividends, Income Summary, and Retained Earnings, diagram the closing process.

Q3-5. The balance of retained earnings of Hudson Company Ltd. on December 31, 19X2, was $2,000 less than on December 31, 19X1. Give two possible reasons for the decrease.

DEMONSTRATION PROBLEMS

DP3-1. *(Journalizing, posting, and trial balance)* The chart of accounts of the Wilson Corporation includes the following accounts and identifying numbers: Cash, 101; Accounts Receivable, 111; Cleaning Supplies, 131; Cleaning and Pressing Equipment, 161; Capital Stock, 251; Cleaning Revenue, 301; Miscellaneous General Expense, 412; Wages Expense, 414.

The company's transactions for December follow:

Dec.	1	Issued capital stock for $10,000 in cash to start a cleaning business.
	3	Purchased cleaning and pressing equipment for $900 in cash.
	10	Paid $100 in cash for cleaning supplies.
	15	Billed $370 for cleaning work for the first half of the month.
	15	Paid $300 in salaries.
	21	Paid $120 for miscellaneous general expenses.
	26	Received $225 cash from customers to apply on acount.
	31	Paid $300 in salaries.
	31	Billed $290 for cleaning work for the second half of the month.
	31	Received $600 from cash customers for the month.

Required:

1. Journalize the transactions.
2. Open accounts and post from the journal to the appropriate ledgers. (Use assigned account numbers for general ledger accounts.)
3. Take a trial balance.

DP3-2. *(Journalizing, posting, and statements)* Elizabeth Taylor opened an office for the general practice of dentistry. During the month of July the following transactions occurred:

July	2	Issued capital stock for $4,000 in cash.
	3	Purchased $700 dental supplies on account.
	3	Paid $400 for July rent.
	7	Paid $300 for miscellaneous general expenses.
	9	Received $2,000 in cash for services rendered.
	10	Purchased dental equipment for $6,000 on account.
	15	Paid $450 on account to suppliers.
	26	Billed patients $450. for services rendered. Dorothy Reynolds $ 350 Paul Williams 100
	31	Paid $2,000 in cash and issued a note payble for $4,000 for the amount due for dental equipment.
	31	Received on account in cash $225 from patients.
	31	Determined that $200 of dental supplies had been consumed.

Required:

1. Journalize the transactions.
2. Post to the general ledger. (Assign numbers to the general ledger accounts)
3. Take a trial balance.
4. Prepare an income statement, a statement of retained earnings, and a balance sheet.
5. Journalize the closing entries and post them.
6. Prepare a postclosing trial balance.

DP3-3. *(Closing entries and postclosing trial balance)* The trial balance of the Fuller Corporation on December 31 follows:

Acct. No.	*Account Title*	*Debits*	*Credits*
101	Cash	$100,000	
111	Accounts Receivable	8,000	
121	Supplies	3,600	
201	Equipment	40,000	
301	Accounts Payable		$ 8,000
401	Capital Stock		100,000
411	Retained Earnings, January 1		29,700

421	Dividends	4,000	
501	Commissions Earned		30,000
511	Rent Earned		10,000
601	Salaries Expense	13,400	
602	Advertising Expense	2,000	
603	Supplies Used	3,200	
604	Miscellaneous Expense	3,500	
	Totals	$177,700	$177,700

Required:

1. Set up T accounts for Retained Earnings, Dividends, and each revenue and expense account listed in the trial balances.Enter the account balances.
2. Journalize the closing entries and post to the T accounts.
3. Prepare a postclosing trial balance.

PROBLEMS

P3-1. A new accountant began work on January 2, 19XX. Unfortunately, he made several errors that were discovered by the auditor during the year-end review. For each error described below, indicate the effect of the error by completing the following solution form. Treat each error separately; do not attempt to relate the errors to one another.

Suggested Solution Form

Error	Would the December 31 Trial Balance Be Out of Balance		If Yes, by How Much	Which Would Be Larger?	
	YES	NO		Debit Total	Credit Total
a b etc.					

a. A typewriter was purchased for $450 and cash was paid and credited. The debit was entered twice in the asset account.
b. A debit to the Cash account of $1,192 was posted as $1,129.
c. Cash collections of $925 from customers in settlement of their accounts were not posted to the Accounts Receivable account, but were posted correctly to the Cash account.
d. A purchase of office supplies of $250 was recorded as a credit to Cash and also as a credit to Office Supplies.

P3-2. Some of the possible effects of a transaction are listed:

1. An asset increase accompanied by an asset decrease.
2. An asset increase accompanied by an owner's equity increase.
3. An asset increase accompanied by a liability increase.
4. An asset increase accompanied by a revenue increase.
5. An asset decrease accompanied by a liability decrease.
6. An asset decrease accompanied by owner's equity decrease.
7. An asset decrease accompanied by an expense increase.
8. An expense increase accompanied by a liability increase.

Using the identifying numbers to the left of the listed combinations, indicate the effect of each of the following transactions:

Example: Issued capital stock for cash. *Answer:* (2)

a. Collected a commission on a sale made today.
b. Borrowed money from a bank and issued a note.
c. Collected an account receivable.
d. Paid an account payable.
e. Paid for an ad in a magazine.

P3-3. The following cash receipt transactions occurred at the Amity Realty Corporation during the month of August:

Aug 1 Issued additional stock for $50,000 in cash.
7 Received a commission of $2,400 from the sale of a house and lot.
8 Received $4,500 in cash from the issuance of a note payable to a bank.
31 Received $250 in interest from federal government bonds.
31 Received $250 in cash for August rent of part of the corporation's building.

Journalize the revenue transactions only.

P3-4. The following were among the cash payment transactions at Sir Park Garage Ltd. during month of May:

May 3 Paid $4,500 for a truck.
7 Paid $900 in salaries for the month.
9 Paid $4,000 in settlement of an account.
12 Paid $300 for a typewriter.
16 Declared and paid a $1,500 cash dividend to shareholders .
22 Paid $200 for rent of the office for May.

Journalize the expense transactions only.

P3-5. The August transactions of the Farrell Travel Service Ltd. are given below:

Aug. 1 Paid $250 for an advertisement in the Travel section of the *Globe and Mail.*

2 Arranged a round-the-world trip for Mr. and Mrs. Clyde J. Davis. Collected a commission of $200 in cash from the steamship company.

3 Arranged fly-now, pay-later European trips for several clients. The Trans-Islandic Airway System agreed to a commission of $700 for services rendered, payment to be made at the end of the month.

4 Another advertisement was placed in the *Globe and Mail* for $300, payment to be made in 10 days.

16 The company paid $450 in dividends.

19 Collected $700 from the Trans-Islandic Airway System.

Following the example given for the August 1 transaction, analyze each transaction and prepare the necessary journal entry.

Example:

Aug. 1 **a.** Advertising is an operating expense. Increases in expenses are recorded by debits. Debit Advertising Expense for $250.

b. The asset, Cash, was decreased. Decreases of assets are recorded by credits. Credit Cash for $250.

c. Journal entry:

	Debit	Credit
Advertising Expense	250	
Cash		250

P3-6. As of December 31, 19XX, the ledger of Baggett Company Ltd. contained the following accounts and account balances, among others: Cash, $50,000; Accounts Receivable, $30,000; Retained Earnings $72,500; Commissions Earned, $70,000; Rent Earned, $5,000; Salaries Expense, $40,000; Office Expense, $6,000; Miscellaneous Expense, $15,000; Dividends, $7,000. Journalize the closing entries. (All the nominal accounts are included.)

P3-7. Financial information for three different corporations follows:

a. Net income	$ 45,600
Retained earnings at beginning of year	200,000
Dividends declared and paid	30,000
Retained earnings at end of year	?
b. Net Income	?
Retained earnings at beginning of year	320,000
Dividends declared and paid	40,000
Retained earnings at end of year	310,000
c. Net loss	10,000
Retained earnings at beginning of year	?
Dividends declared and paid	15,200
Retained earnings at end of year	530,000

Supply the missing figures.

P3-8. On August 1, Marley Plumbing Company Ltd. purchased $800 plumbing supplies on account.

On August 15, Marley Plumbing Company Ltd. paid $620 to its creditors on account.

P3-9. *(Accounting policy decision problem)* John Stewart decided to start business in May. Transactions for the month of May follow:

May 1 Issued capital stock for $15,000 in cash.
3 Paid $300 for the first month's office rent.
5 Purchased office equipment for $1,000. Paid $300 in cash and issued a note payable for the balance.
6 Paid $150 for a one-year insurance policy on the office equipment, effective May 1.
7 Paid $200 in cash for office supplies.
8 Billed $800 to clients for services rendered.
15 Received $300 cash on account from clients for services billed May 8.
18 Received $900 in cash for services rendered not previously billed.
31 Paid $410 for miscellaneous general expenses for May.

Required:

1. Journalize the transactions.
2. Suggest a chart of accounts.

P3-10. Riggsbee Tool Service and Repair Shop Ltd. was incorporated on June 1, Year 1, and capital stock was issued for $20,000 in cash. During the month of June, the corporation completed the following transactions:

June 1 Paid a $250 premium on a one-year comprehensive insurance policy, effective June 1.
1 Paid $400 for June rent.
2 Purchased shop equipment for $4,000 in cash.
2 Purchased $2,600 shop supplies on account.
5 Purchased an automobile for $3,500 giving $1,000 in cash and a note payable for the balance.
9 Received $800 in cash for servicing and repairing tools.
10 Paid $100 in cash for advertising space in the *Dawning Sun Paper.*
15 Paid cash for gas, oil, and other automobile expenses for two weeks, $70.
15 Paid $1,500 on account to creditors.
18 Received $600 in cash for repairing tools.
20 Paid $1,000 in cash on the note given for the purchase of the automobile.

21 Declared and paid a $500 dividend.

22 Paid $40 for telephone service.

23 Paid $36 for a new battery for the automobile (debit Automobile Expense).

24 Billed customers $950 for service and repair work:

25 Paid $25 for cleaning the shop.

25 Received $500 in cash for servicing tools.

26 Purchased $500 additional shop supplies on account.

27 Paid $60 for electric service.

28 Purchased a typewriter and an adding machine for $650.

29 Received $575 on account from customers.

30 Paid $65 for gas, oil, and other automobile expenses for two weeks.

30 Received $450 from customers for repair work not previously billed.

30 Paid $200 in cash for advertising space in a local magazine.

30 Received a promissory note for $100 for the balance due on an account.

Required:

1. Open the following accounts in the general ledger: Cash, 101; Accounts Receivable, 111; Notes Receivable, 115; Shop Supplies, 136; Prepaid Insurance, 140; Automobile, 201; Shop Equipment, 211; Office Equipment, 221; Accounts Payable, 301; Notes Payable, 304; Capital Stock, 351; Dividends, 352; Repair Service Revenue, 401; Advertising Expense, 518; Rent Expense, 503; Heat and Light Expense, 505; Telephone and Telegraph Expense, 509; Automobile Expense, 510; Miscellaneous General Expense, 512.
2. Record all the transactions in the general journal, including the issuance of capital stock.
3. Post to the appropriate ledgers.
4. Prepare a trial balance.

P3-11. The trial balance of Capitol Parking Lot Ltd. shows the following accounts, arranged in alphabetical order:

Account Title	*Debits*	*Credits*
Accounts Payable		$ 2,000
Accounts Receivable	$13,000	
Cash	43,600	
Capital Stock, 4,000 shares issued and outstanding		40,000

Dividends	1,900	
Equipment Maintenance Expense	2,400	
Heat and Light Expense	1,600	
Interest Earned		1,200
Land	10,000	
Notes Payable		4,000
Notes Receivable	3,000	
Parking Fees Earned		39,300
Salaries Expense	9,000	
Retained Earnings, January 1		2,500
Supplies on Hand	1,400	
Supplies Used	2,900	
Telephone Expense	200	
Totals	$89,000	$89,000

Required:

1. Prepare a trial balance in proper chart-of-accounts sequence.
2. Prepare an income statement, a statement of retained earnings, and a balance sheet.
3. Journalize the closing entries.

P3-12. The following statements have been prepared for Morton Company Ltd.:

MORTON COMPANY LTD.
Balance Sheet
March 31

Assets			*Liabilities and Shareholders' Equity*		
Current Assets			Current Liabilities		
Cash	$2,000		Accounts Payable		$ 600
Repair Parts	1,000		Shareholders' Equity		
Total Current Assets		$ 3,000	Capital Stock	$6,000	
Plant and Equipment			Retained Earnings	3,400	
Land	$2,000		Total Shareholders' Equity		9,400
Building	5,000				
Total Plant and Equipment		7,000	Total Liabilities and		
Total Assets		$10,000	Shareholders' Equity		$10,000

MORTON COMPANY LTD.
Income Statement
For the Month Ended March 31

Revenue		
Storage Fees		$ 4,970
Expenses		
Office Rent Expense	$ 600	

Salaries Expense	2,000	
Miscellaneous Expenses	670	3,270
Net Income		$ 1,700

During March, the company declared and paid a dividend of $200.

Required: Prepare a statement of retained earnings for Morton Company Ltd. for the month of March and the closing entries as of March 31.

P3-13. The Atwater Plumbing Company Ltd. completed the following transactions during January:

Jan. 2 Issued capital stock for $5,000 in cash.
3 Paid $150 rent for the month of January.
4 Purchased $1,150 plumbing supplies on account.
6 Purchased from the Porter Motor Company a used truck for $3,500, giving $500 in cash and a note payable for the balance.
9 Paid $800 in cash for shop equipment.
10 Paid $210 in cash for a one-year insurance policy on the shop equipment and truck, effective January 2.
14 Received $450 for a completed plumbing job.
18 Paid $350 to creditors on account.
20 Paid a cash dividend of $300 to shareholders.

Use the following account numbers and titles:
101 Cash
111 Accounts Receivable
121 Plumbing Supplies
131 Prepaid Insurance
241 Truck
245 Shop Equipment
301 Accounts Payable
306 Notes Payable
351 Capital Stock
352 Dividends
401 Rental Revenue
402 Plumbing Revenue
501 Rent Expense
502 Telephone and Telegraph Expense

Required:

1. Journalize the transactions.
2. Post to the appropriate ledger accounts.
3. Take a trial balance.

P3-14. The following transactions occurred during March at Durham Roof Repair Company Ltd.:

Mar. 1 Issued 1,500 shares of capital stock for $15,000 in cash.
5 Paid $150 for two days' rental of a derrick and pulley assembly used on a repair job.
6 Purchased Canada Savings Bonds for $5,000 in cash.
11 Collected $1,400 on completion of roofing repair work.
20 Signed an agreement with Guilford College to repair dormitory roofs for $4,500. The work is to be completed during April and May.
25 Paid a cash dividend of $400 to shareholders.
28 Paid $650 for repair materials used on jobs during the month.
30 Paid $2,500 in salaries and wages.
31 Completed roofing repair work for Thomas Rockness in the amount of $1,850. Rockness promised to pay for the work on April 10.

Use the following account titles and numbers:

101 Cash
109 Marketable Securities
111 Accounts Receivable
351 Capital Stock
352 Retained Earnings
353 Dividends
401 Repair Service Revenue
501 Salaries and Wages Expense
502 Repair Materials Expense
503 Rental Expense
600 Income Summary

Required:

1. Journalize the transactions.
2. Post to general ledger accounts.
3. Take a trial balance.
4. Prepare an income statement, a statement of retained earnings, and a balance sheet.
5. Prepare and post the closing entries.
6. Rule the accounts that have no balances.
7. Take a postclosing trial balance.

P3-15. The following information is taken from the books of Kutz Company Ltd.

KUTZ COMPANY LTD.
Statement of Retained Earnings
For the Year Ended December 31

Retained Earnings, January 1	$100,000
Add Net Income	200,000
Total	$300,000
Deduct Dividends	70,000
Retained Earnings, December 31	$230,000

The expenses for the year were: salaries expense, $95,000; advertising expense, $19,000; office expense, $16,000; and miscellaneous expense, $28,000. The revenue came from only one source, commissions earned.

Required: Prepare a formal income statement for Kutz Company Ltd. Show your computations of the amounts that are not given.

4

The End-of-Period Process

A complete but simple service company illustration, the transactions of Nelson Garage Ltd., was used in Chapter 3. A similar but more complex illustration is used in this chapter to introduce and review the following elements: (1) two accounting methods, (2) *adjustments*—continuous transactions that, for convenience, are not recorded until the end of the period, (3) the *work sheet*—an orderly method of collecting information for the preparation of formal financial statements, (4) a review of the accounting cycle, and (5) split entries.

TWO ACCOUNTING METHODS

Two accounting methods are found in practice: the cash basis and the accrual basis.

CASH BASIS

Under the cash basis of accounting, revenue is recognized when the cash is received, and the revenue is recorded at that time. Expenses are recognized in the period of payment. Recognition of revenue and expenses during an accounting period is based on an inflow and outflow of cash—a matching of cash receipts and cash disbursements to determine operating results during an accounting period. This method of accounting is obviously simple in application; but in most cases *it does not* properly measure net income, because, for example, it does not recognize uncollected revenue items as being earned and unpaid expense items as being incurred until actual payment is made. Hence, it matches only some of the revenues and expenses for a given period. There are instances, however, particularly in small professional and service businesses, in which the cash basis of accounting is used with acceptable results. Hybrid systems, or modifications of the cash-basis system, are often found in practice.

ACCRUAL BASIS

The accrual basis of accounting is founded on the principle that, if the net income of a business for a given period is to be measured properly, all the revenue earned during that period and all the related expenses of earning that income assignable to the period must be considered. Revenues are recognized at the time of sale, and expenses are usually recognized at the time the services are received and used in the production of revenue.

This process of matching the revenue of a period with the expenses of that period, regardless of when, whether, or how much cash has been received or paid, is the central goal of the accrual basis of accounting and underlies all the discussions in this text.

The difference in net income resulting from the use of each method is best illustrated by an example. The Louise Hale Company, which does landscape gardening, performed work during August for which it charged $1,000. It received $600 on August 15 and $400 on September 10. Wages (the only expense) of $550 were paid on August 31. No work was performed during September.

	Cash Basis		**Accrual Basis**	
	August	*September*	*August*	*September*
Revenue	$600	$400	$1,000	$-0-
Expense	550	-0-	550	-0-
Net Income	$ 50	$400	$ 450	$-0-

The accrual basis of accounting gives more useful results, because revenue is reflected in the period to which it properly belongs, that is, the period in which it was earned. Net income is the difference between revenue earned and expenses incurred during the accounting period—the difference between the results achieved and the efforts expended. The accrual method, by matching expenses incurred with revenue earned for the period, presents the better measurement of net income. Since the accrual basis of accounting results in more useful financial statements, most businesses keep their books on this basis.

ADJUSTMENTS

NEED FOR ADJUSTING ENTRIES

During the accounting period, regular business transactions are recorded as they occur. At the end of the period, the accountant may find that the ledger accounts are incomplete: some new accounts must be brought into the books and other accounts must be brought up to date. The journal entries necessary to accomplish this are referred to as ***adjusting entries.***

Periodic adjustment of the ledger accounts is indispensable if the financial statements are to reflect the realistic position of the company—its assets and equities—as of the end of the period, and the results of its operations—revenue earned and expenses incurred—during the period.

It is impractical and sometimes impossible to record the day-to-day changes in certain accounts. For example, when the premium payment is made on an insurance policy, the asset Prepaid Insurance is debited. At the end of the accounting period, however, only part of the balance of the Prepaid Insurance account represents an asset. The amount that has expired with the passage of time is an expense, because it represents the cost of insurance protection. At the end of the accounting period, therefore, Prepaid Insurance contains both an asset and an expense element. An adjustment is necessary to record the correct amount of Insurance Expense and to reduce Prepaid Insurance. This type of adjusting entry is referred to as a *short-term cost* apportionment adjustment.

An adjusting entry may be required to record previously unrecorded data. Assume, for example, that a company paid wages on March 28 for the two-week period that ended on that date. However, the employees worked on March 29, 30, and 31. If March 31 is the end of the accounting period, recognition must be given to this unrecorded but incurred expense as well as to the corresponding increase in liabilities, so that the financial statements may show the liability and the proper assignment of the expense to the period. This type of adjustment is referred to as an *accrued expense* adjustment.

A distinction is usually made between adjusting entries and entries that record regular business transactions. Regular business transactions start and complete their cycles within an accounting period. Adjusting entries deal with the transactions that transpire continuously and may be termed *continuous transactions.* It is neither feasible nor necessary to record these continuing changes during the period; rather, they are recorded at the end of each accounting period by means of *summary* adjusting entries. The nature of the adjusting entries varies. The adjusting entry for wages, for example, records a change that has already taken place—the increase in a liability incurred—but is unrecorded. The adjusting entry for Insurance Expense, on the other hand, recognizes the partial consumption of an item that was recorded in an asset account at the time of acquisition.

Adjusting entries may be entered initially in the work sheet with formal recording in the journal deferred until the closing entries are made, or they may be recorded in the journal first and then applied to the work sheet.

PROCESS OF RECORDING ADJUSTMENTS

Connolly Trucking Company Ltd. started business on June 1, 19XX. As a convenience in illustrating the end-of-period procedures, it is assumed that the books are closed on June 30 (books are customarily closed annually). The trial balance taken from Connolly Trucking Company Ltd.'s general ledger is shown in Figure 4-1.

Figure 4-1
Trial Balance

CONNOLLY TRUCKING COMPANY LTD.
Trial Balance
June 30, 19XX

Acct. No.	*Account Title*	*Debits*	*Credits*
101	Cash	$ 5,250	
111	Accounts Receivable	550	
112	Notes Receivable	1,440	
131	Office Supplies	230	
141	Prepaid Insurance	2,160	
142	Prepaid Rent	1,500	
201	Office Equipment	1,400	
211	Trucks	13,000	
301	Accounts Payable		$ 200
302	Notes Payable		8,000
321	Unearned Rent		600
401	Capital Stock		12,000
404	Dividends	500	
501	Trucking Revenue		7,465
601	Heat and Light Expense	40	
602	Maintenance and Repairs Expense	375	
603	Telephone and Telegraph Expense	95	
604	Gas and Oil Expense	525	
605	Wages Expense	1,200	
	Totals	$28,265	$28,265

The adjusting entries are journalized and posted to the accounts. The separate discussion of each adjusting entry is identified by the letter used to cross-reference the debit and credit adjustments in the Adjustments columns of the *work sheet*, shown in Figure 4-4.

The various kinds of continuous transactions, or adjustments, may be summarized in the following five groups:

1. Short-term cost apportionments: recorded cost that must be apportioned between current and later accounting periods, which could be a month, a quarter, but usually a year. Examples: supplies, prepaid insurance, and prepaid rent.

2. Short-term revenue apportionments: recorded revenue that will be apportioned between current and later accounting periods. Examples: rent collected in advance and magazine subscriptions collected in advance.

3. Long-term cost apportionments: a type of adjustment similar to short-term cost apportionment except that the recorded cost will usually be apportioned between three or more accounting periods. Example: the cost of a building.

4. Accrued expenses: unrecorded expenses incurred in the current period. Example: wages earned by employees after the last pay day in an accounting period.

5. Accrued revenues: unrecorded revenues earned in the current period. Example: interest earned on a note receivable held for thirty days in the current period but not due until sometime in the next period.

Short-Term Cost Apportionment Adjustments—a, b, and c

There are three steps in adjusting the mixed account involving a short-term cost apportionment.

1. Determining the balance of each account to be adjusted
2. Determining the amount of the asset and expense elements in each account
3. Recording the adjusting entries

(a)

On June 1, Connolly Trucking Company Ltd. paid $1,500 in cash for three months' rent.

Step 1. The general ledger shows the following balance in the account:

Prepaid Rent (mixed) Acct. No. 142

1,500	

The information in the foregoing ledger account (and other similar illustrations in this chapter) is reproduced from the original ledger and includes folio references for the original data.

Step 2. The amount of expense applicable to June is $500 = ($1,500 ÷ 3 months). On June 30, therefore, Prepaid Rent is a mixed account consisting of an expense element and an asset element.

Prepaid Rent (mixed) Acct. No. 142

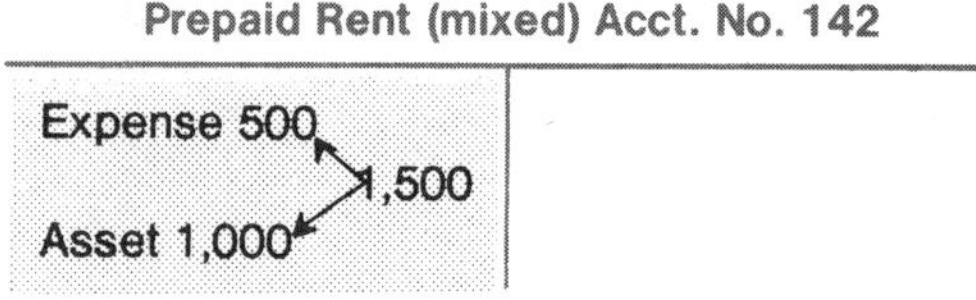

Step 3. As stated previously, the timing of the journalizing of the adjustments is optional; it may be delayed until the formal financial statements are prepared and presented to management for its use. Here, however, as a basic teaching device, the adjusting entries for Connolly Trucking Company Ltd. are made as each adjustment is explained.

The required adjusting entry is:

June	30	Rent Expense	606	500	
		Prepaid Rent	142		500
		To record rent expense for June.			

The expense element is thus removed from the mixed account, as shown by the following posting in the ledger accounts.

Rent Expense (expense) Acct. No. 606

Debit	Credit
500	

Prepaid Rent (asset) Acct. No. 142

Debit	Credit
1,500	
	500

Prepaid Rent ($1,000) is classified in the balance sheet as a current asset, and Rent Expense ($500) appears in the income statement as an expense.

(b)

Connolly Trucking Company Ltd. paid a premium of $2,160 for a comprehensive three-year insurance policy, effective June 1, 1976.

Step 1. Prepaid Insurance, before adjustment, shows a balance of $2,160. The title Prepaid Insurance classifies it as basically an asset account, but it is in fact a mixed account.

Step 2. An analysis of the account shows that the expense element for the month of June is $60 = ($2,160 ÷ 36 months), and that the unused portion of $2,100 is the asset prepayment benefiting future periods.

Step 3. The following adjusting entry is made:

June	30	Insurance Expense	607	60	
		Prepaid Insurance	141		60
		To record insurance expense for June.			

This information is shown in the following ledger accounts:

Insurance Expense (expense) Acct. No. 607

Debit	Credit
60	

Prepaid Insurance (asset) Acct. No. 141

Debit	Credit
2,160	
	60

(c)

Step 1. On the trial balance (Figure 4-1), Office Supplies has a debit balance of $230, representing a purchase made on June 6.

Step 2. The inventory taken on June 30 showed $60 worth of unused supplies; therefore, the expense element is $170 = ($230 − $60).

Step 3. The expense of $170 needs to be removed from the mixed account by the following adjusting entry, and the adjustment information is posted to the accounts shown below the journal entry:

June	30	Office Supplies Expense	608	170	
		Office Supplies	131		170
		To record supplies used during June.			

Office Supplies Expense (expense) Acct. No. 608

Debit	Credit
170	

Office Supplies (asset) Acct. No. 131

Debit	Credit
230	170

Office Supplies ($60) is classified in the balance sheet as a current asset and Office Supplies Expense ($170) appears in the income statement as an expense.

Short-Term Revenue Apportionment Adjustment—d

The same three steps are followed in making short-term revenue apportionments of amounts originally recorded in mixed liability accounts.

(d)

On June 1, Connolly Trucking Company Ltd. signed a contract for the use of its trucks on a part-time basis and received an advance payment of $600 for six months' rent. At that time, Cash was debited and a liability account, Unearned Rent, was credited for $600. On June 30, only the portion earned in the month of June is transferred from Unearned Rent to Rent Earned; the unearned portion remains in Unearned Rent as a liability, because Connolly Trucking Company Ltd. must provide the use of its truck on a part-time basis for another five months.

Step 1. The amount of the unearned rent liability as of June 1, 19XX, in the ledger T account is shown below:

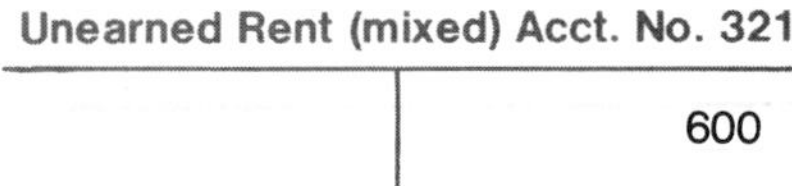

Step 2. The rent actually earned in June is $100 =($600 ÷ 6 mos.); on June 30, Unearned Rent is a mixed account and consists of a revenue element and a liability element.

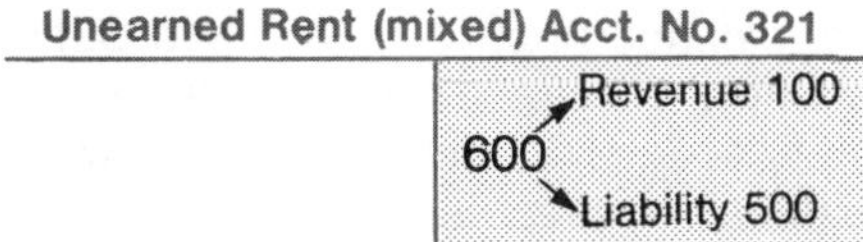

Step 3. The following adjusting entry is made:

June	30	Unearned Rent	321	100	
		Rent Earned	511		100
		To record revenue earned from rental of trucks during June.			

The revenue element is removed from the mixed account as follows:

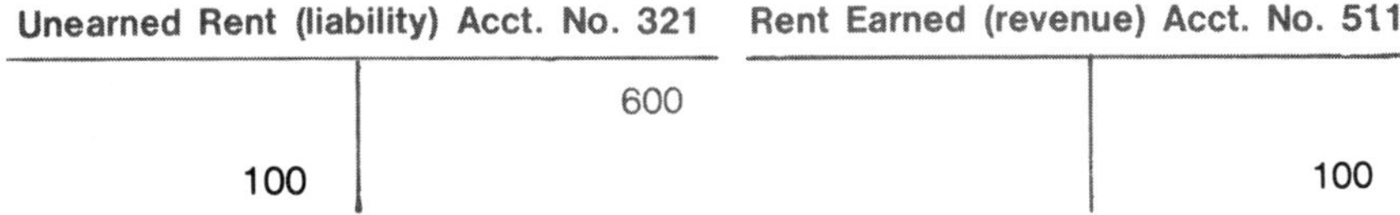

Rent Earned ($100) appears in the income statement as a revenue item, and Unearned Rent ($500) appears in the balance sheet as a current liability.

Long-Term Cost Apportionment Adjustment—Depreciation—e and f

Two of the remaining adjusting entries involve the recording of long-term asset cost expiration. Three steps similar to the short-term cost apportionments are followed.

(e)

Step 1. The trial balance, Figure 4-1, shows a balance of $1,400 in the Office Equipment account.

Step 2. The equipment, acquired on June 1, is estimated to have a useful life of ten years, or 120 months, and a *salvage value* of $200 at the end of that period. Salvage, or *residual,* value is the estimated price for which an asset may be sold when it is no longer serviceable to the business. In effect, the use of office equipment for ten years has been purchased at a net cost of $1,200 = ($1,400 − $200). A portion of this cost expires in each accounting period during the useful life of the equipment.

> This periodic expired cost, called ***depreciation expense,*** requires no periodic cash outlay, but nevertheless is a continuous expense of operating the business. The portion of the cost of an asset assigned to the accounting period is called ***depreciation.*** A number of methods may be used in calculating the periodic depreciation charge.

Depreciation expense for the month of June is computed in this case by using the *straight-line method,* in which a uniform portion of the cost is assigned to each period.

$$\frac{\text{Cost} - \text{Salvage value}}{\text{Estimated months of useful life}} = \text{Depreciation for month}$$

The depreciation expense for the office equipment in June is computed as $10.

$$\frac{\$1{,}400 - \$200}{120} = \$10$$

Step 3. The following adjusting entry is made:

June	30	Depreciation Expense— Office Equipment	609	10	
		Accumulated Depreciation— Office Equipment	201A		10
		To record depreciation for June.			

Both of the foregoing accounts are new accounts.

> The second is called an ***asset valuation*** account or ***contra-asset*** account, because its balance is deducted from Office Equipment to show the book value, or carrying value, of the asset.

Office Equipment could be credited directly, because the depreciation represents a decrease in the asset; but this procedure is undesirable because it fails to disclose information that is useful to management. Depreciation is an estimate; it is informative to keep asset costs separate from estimated reductions in cost. When separate accounts are used, the original cost and the accumulated depreciation can be determined readily. The June 30 adjusting information is shown in the following ledger accounts:

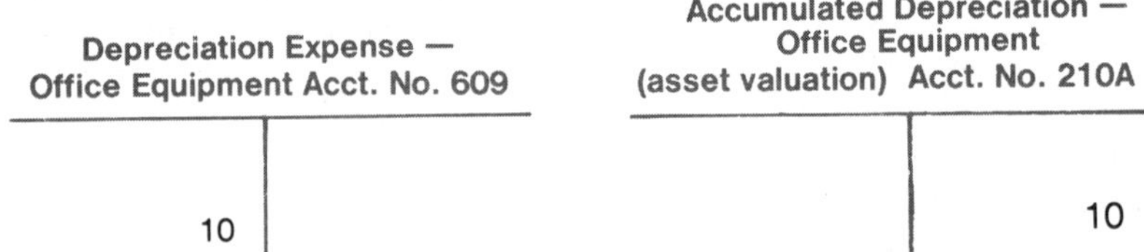

In the balance sheet (Figure 4-9), the asset valuation account, Accumulated Depreciation–Office Equipment, is deducted from Office Equipment; the remainder is the *undepreciated cost,* that is, the portion of the cost of the asset that is not yet charged to expense. Depreciation Expense–Office Equipment ($10) is shown in the income statement as an expense.

(f)

Step 1. On June 1, Connolly Trucking Company Ltd. purchased two trucks for business use, each costing $6,500. Because the useful life of the trucks is limited, a portion of the cost is allocable to the month of June. It is estimated that their useful life is five years, or 60 months, at the end of which time each truck will have a salvage value of $500.

Step 2. The computation and recording of the depreciation expense for the trucks is similar to that for the office equipment. The depreciation expense for June for the two trucks is calculated by the straight-line method as follows:

$$\frac{\text{Cost of \$6,500} - \text{Salvage value of \$500}}{\text{60 months}}$$

= $100 depreciation per month for each truck, or $200 for two trucks

Step 3. The following adjusting entry is made on June 30 and posted to the accounts shown below the journal entry:

June	30	Depreciation Expense—Trucks	610	200	
		Accumulated Depreciation—Trucks	211A		200
		To record depreciation for June.			

Depreciation Expense—Trucks (expense) Acct. No. 610	
200	

Accumulated Depreciation—Trucks (asset valuation) Acct. No. 211A	
	200

The classification of these accounts in the financial statements is shown in Figures 4-7 and 4-9.

The Accumulated Depreciation accounts are used to accumulate the periodic charges made to expense and to segregate the deduction for the asset valuation. Depreciation Expense shows the expired cost for the accounting period and is closed along with the other expense accounts in an entry that transfers the total expense to Income Summary. Assume that the same adjusting entry for trucks is made on July 31. After it is posted, the general ledger accounts for Trucks, Depreciation Expense—Trucks, and Accumulated Depreciation—Trucks appear as follows:

Trucks Acct. No. 211	
13,000	

Depreciation Expense—Trucks Acct. No. 610	
July 31 200	

Accumulated Depreciation—Trucks Acct. No. 211A	
	June 30 200
	July 31 200

The cost of the trucks and the accumulated depreciation are shown on the balance sheet at July 31 as follows:

Equipment		
Trucks	$13,000	
Deduct Accumulated Depreciation—Trucks	400	$12,600

Accrued Expense Adjustment—g and h

Accrued expenses are expenses that have been incurred in a given period but have not yet been paid. The accountant's job at the end of the accounting period is to record the expense in the proper period of incurrence and also to record the accompanying liability. The accrued expense adjustment described in (g) is that of unrecorded wages expense of $150.

(g)

Step 1. Wages Expense contains two debits of $600 each, representing wages paid biweekly to employees through June 27.

Step 2. The employees earned wages of $150 for work on June 28, 29, and 30, the last three days of the accounting period. Although the company will not pay the employees again until July 11, it has nevertheless incurred $150 of wages expense for these three days, and a $150 liability exists as of June 30.

Step 3. The following adjusting entry is made on June 30 and posted to the accounts shown below the journal entry:

June	30	Wages Expense	605	150	
		Accrued Wages Payable	311		150
		To record wages expense accrued during June 28–30.			

Wages Expense (expense) Acct. No. 605

Debit	Credit
600	
600	
150	

Accrued Wages Payable (liability) Acct. No. 311

Debit	Credit
	150

Wages Expenses ($1,350) is shown in the income statement as an expense; Accrued Wages Payable ($150) is shown in the balance sheet as a current liability.

(h)

Step 1. On June 12, Connolly Trucking Company Ltd. borrowed $8,000 from the bank and signed a 45-day, 6 percent interest-bearing note payable. This transaction was recorded in the general journal by debiting Cash and crediting Notes Payable for $8,000.

Step 2. The cost of the use of the $8,000—interest expense—continues throughout the 45 days because interest expense accumulates with the passage of time. The total interest expense plus the $8,000 principal amount will be paid to the bank on July 27, the *maturity,* or due, date. However, unpaid interest expense on an interest-bearing note payable for the 18-day period from June 12 through June 30 must be recognized by an adjusting entry debiting Interest Expense and crediting Accrued Interest Payable for $24.

The formula for computing interest is shown in Figure 4-2.

$$\text{Interest} = \text{Principal} \times \text{Interest rate} \times \frac{\text{Elapsed time in days}}{365}$$

Figure 4-2
Interest Formula

The unpaid interest expense accrued on June 30 is computed as follows:

$$\text{Interest} = \$8{,}000 \times 0.06 \times \frac{18}{365} = 24$$

The principle multiplied by the interest rate equals the total interest for one year (48,000 × 0.06 = $480); the interest for a year ($480) multiplied by the elapsed fraction of a year (18/365) is the interest expense for 18 days ($480 × 18/365), or $24. The use of 365 days in the formula is consistent with commercial practice, the primary reason being simplicity of calculation.

Step 3. The formal adjusting entry is made on June 30 and posted to the accounts indicated below.

June	30	Interest Expense	611	24	
		Accrued Interest Payable	303		24
		To record interest expense accrued during June 12-30.			

Interest Expense (expense) Acct. No. 611	
24	

Accrued Interest Payable (liability) Acct. No. 303	
	24

Interest Expense ($24) is reported as an expense in the income statement; Accrued Interest Payable ($24) appears as a current liability in the balance sheet. This entry gives rise to an *accrued liability.* This term refers to the liability for an expense incurred during one accounting period but payable in a future accounting period. Expenses incurred for which invoices have not yet been received—telephone, heat, light, water, and so on—are also in this category. These may be recorded by debits to appropriate expense accounts and a credit to Accrued Accounts Payable.

Accrued Revenue Adjustment—i

Accrued revenue items are items that have been earned in a given period but for which cash collections have not yet been received. The accountant's job at the end of the accounting period is to record the revenue in the proper period in which it is earned and also to record the accompanying receivable, an asset. The accrued revenue adjustment described in (i) is that of unrecorded earned interest of $4.

(i)

Step 1. Connolly Trucking Company Ltd. made a loan of $1,440 to one of its customers, who signed a 30-day, 5 percent interest-bearing note dated June 10. An entry was made debiting Notes Receivable and crediting Cash for $1,440.

Step 2. The company earned interest on the loan for 20 days in June (June 10 through June30); it will be received on the maturity date, July 10, when the amount due (principle plus total interest) is paid by the customer. Interest earned, like interest expense, accrues with the passage of time. The 20 days' interest earned by June 30 is recorded by an adjusting entry debiting Accrued Interest Receivable and crediting Interest Earned for $4. Using the formula shown in Figure 4-2, the computation of the interest is

$$\text{Interest} = \$1{,}440 \times 0.05 \times \frac{20}{365} = \$4$$

Step 3. The formal adjusting entry is made on June 30 and posted to the accounts indicated below.

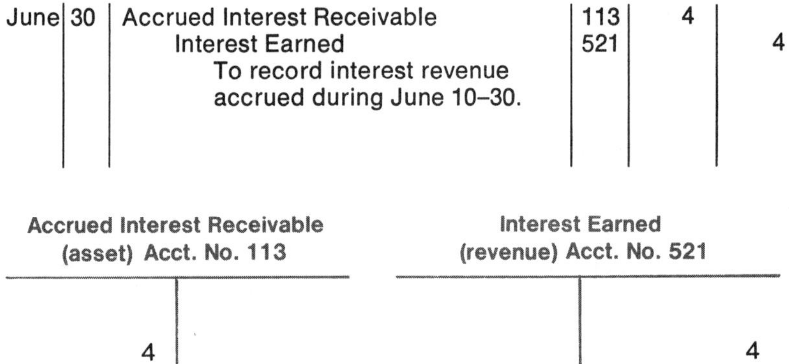

June	30	Accrued Interest Receivable	113	4	
		Interest Earned	521		4
		To record interest revenue accrued during June 10–30.			

Accrued Interest Receivable (asset) Acct. No. 113

Debit	Credit
4	

Interest Earned (revenue) Acct. No. 521

Debit	Credit
	4

Accrued Interest Receivable ($4) is a current asset in the balance sheet. Interest Earned is a revenue item in the income statement.

Income Tax Expense Adjustment—j

The income tax expense adjustment is similar to the accrued expense adjustment. A proprietor or a partner combines his net income from his proprietorship or partnership interest with his income from other sources and computes his tax as an individual taxpayer. A corporation, however, is taxed as a separate entity, and its financial statements must show the tax and the liability for the tax.

(j)

Step 1. It is difficult to determine precisely the tax related to the taxable income for the month of June, because the annual taxable income, on which the tax is based, is not yet known. Nevertheless, the business must make the best possible estimate.

Step 2. Connolly Trucking Company Ltd. estimates its income taxes for the month of June to be $1,900.

Step 3. The income tax estimate is journalized on June 30 and posted to the accounts indicated below the general journal.

June	30	Income Tax Expense	612	1,900	
		Income Taxes Payable	331		1,900
		To record estimated taxes for June.			

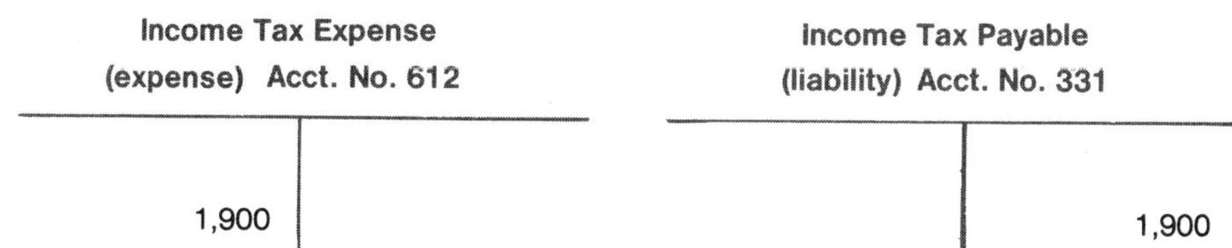

The income tax expense of $1,900 appears in the income statement; it is deducted from the net income before income taxes to determine net income after income taxes (Figure 4-7); Income Taxes Payable appears in the balance sheet as a current liability.

THE WORK SHEET

The work sheet is a device used by the accountant to facilitate the preparation of the formal financial statements; it is not a substitute for the financial statements. Although the work sheet is not indispensable, it would be difficult in most instances to prepare the statements directly from the journals and ledgers, since that would often require consolidating material from books, cards, and other documents. The work sheet bridges the gap between the accounting records and the formal statements and serves as a convenient device to calculate the effect of the adjustments and to determine the net income, or net loss, before the adjustments are formally entered in the books and posted to the ledger. It furnishes the accountant with a preview of the final statements. Many businesses do not formally close their books at the end of every accounting period; thus, the work sheet substitutes for the formal procedure of recording and posting the usual adjusting and closing entries.

PREPARATION OF THE WORK SHEET

Preparation of the work sheet consists of four steps.

Step 1. The work sheet is headed to show the name of the company, the name of the statement, and the accounting period; the column headings are entered; the trial balance account titles and amounts are entered either directly from the general ledger or from a prepared listing, if available. The account titles are entered in the space provided and the amounts are entered in the first pair of money columns. The work sheet of Connolly Trucking Company Ltd. after completion of step 1 appears in Figure 4-3.

Figure 4-3 Work Sheet, Step 1: Trial Balance Entered

CONNOLLY TRUCKING COMPANY LTD.
Work Sheet
For Month Ended June 30, 19XX

Acct. No.	Account Title	Trial Balance		Adjustments		Adjusted Trial Balance		Income Statement		Balance Sheet	
		Dr.	Cr.	Dr.	Cr.	Dr.	Cr.	Dr.	Cr.	Dr.	Cr.
101	Cash	5,250									
111	Accounts Receivable	550									
112	Notes Receivable	1,440									
131	Office Supplies	230									
141	Prepaid Insurance	2,160									
142	Prepaid Rent	1,500									
201	Office Equipment	1,400									
211	Trucks	13,000									
301	Accounts Payable		200								
302	Notes Payable		8,000								
321	Unearned Rent		600								
401	Capital Stock, 1,000 shares outstanding		12,000								
404	Dividends	500									
501	Trucking Revenue		7,465								
601	Heat and Light Expense	40									
602	Maintenance and Repairs Expense	375									
603	Telephone and Telegraph Expense	95									
604	Gas and Oil Expense	525									
605	Wages Expense	1,200									
	Totals	28,265	28,265								

Trial balance before adjustments.

Figure 4-4 Work Sheet, Step 2: Adjustments Entered

CONNOLLY TRUCKING COMPANY LTD.
Work Sheet
For Month Ended June 30, 19XX

Acct. No.	Account Title	Trial Balance		Adjustments		Adjusted Trial Balance		Income Statement		Balance Sheet	
		Dr.	Cr.	Dr.	Cr.	Dr.	Cr.	Dr.	Cr.	Dr.	Cr.
101	Cash	5,250									
111	Accounts Receivable	550									
112	Notes Receivable	1,440									
131	Office Supplies	230			(c) 170						
141	Prepaid Insurance	2,160			(b) 60						
142	Prepaid Rent	1,500			(a) 500						
201	Office Equipment	1,400									
211	Trucks	13,000									
301	Accounts Payable		200								
302	Notes Payable		8,000								
321	Unearned Rent		600	(d) 100							
401	Capital Stock, 1,000 shares outstanding		12,000								
404	Dividends	500									
501	Trucking Revenue		7,465								
601	Heat and Light Expense	40									
602	Maintenance and Repairs Expense	375									
603	Telephone and Telegraph Expense	95									
604	Gas and Oil Expense	525									
605	Wages Expense	1,200		(g) 150							
	Totals	28,265	28,265								
606	Rent Expense			(a) 500							
607	Insurance Expense			(b) 60							
608	Office Supplies Expense			(c) 170							
511	Rent Earned				(d) 100						
609	Depreciation Expense—Office Equipment			(e) 10							
201A	Accumulated Depreciation —Office Equipment				(e) 10						
610	Depreciation Expense—Trucks			(f) 200							
211A	Accumulated Depreciation —Trucks				(f) 200						
311	Accrued Wages Payable				(g) 150						
611	Interest Expense			(h) 24							
303	Accrued Interest Payable				(h) 24						
113	Accrued Interest Receivable			(i) 4							
521	Interest Earned				(i) 4						
612	Income Tax Expense			(j) 1,900							
331	Income Taxes Payable				(j) 1,900						
	Totals			3,118	3,118						

Letters are used to cross reference the debit and credit adjustments.

Additional accounts for the adjustments.

Adjustments are entered in these columns.

Step 2. The adjustments are entered on the work sheet generally before they are formally journalized. This procedure is followed partly to hasten the preparation of the formal financial statements.

The adjustments are keyed for identification (cross referencing) as they are entered in the Adjustments columns. Any additional accounts required by the adjusting entries are written in below the trial balance. In entry (a), for example, Rent Expense is debited for $500. Since this account does not appear in the trial balance, the title is written on the line immediately below the trial balance totals and the amount is entered directly in the Adjustments Debit column on the same line; the $500 is also entered in the Adjustments Credit column opposite Prepaid Rent. In this adjustment, only one of the accounts involved had to be written in below the trial balance. In entry (e), however, both the debited and the credited accounts had to be written in. After all the adjustments are entered, the Adjustments columns are added as a proof of their equality.

Figure 4-5 Work Sheet, Step 3: Adjusted Trial Balance Entered

CONNOLLY TRUCKING COMPANY LTD.
Work Sheet
For Month Ended June 30, 19XX

Acct. No.	Account Title	Trial Balance		Adjustments		Adjusted Trial Balance		Income Statement		Balance Sheet	
		Dr.	Cr.	Dr.	Cr.	Dr.	Cr.	Dr.	Cr.	Dr.	Cr.
101	Cash	5,250				5,250					
111	Accounts Receivable	550				550					
112	Notes Receivable	1,440				1,440					
131	Office Supplies	230			(c) 170	60					
141	Prepaid Insurance	2,160			(b) 60	2,100					
142	Prepaid Rent	1,500			(a) 500	1,000					
201	Office Equipment	1,400				1,400					
211	Trucks	13,000				13,000					
301	Accounts Payable		200				200				
302	Notes Payable		8,000				8,000				
321	Unearned Rent		600	(d) 100			500				
401	Capital Stock, 1,000 shares outstanding		12,000				12,000				
404	Dividends	500				500					
501	Trucking Revenue		7,465				7,465				
601	Heat and Light Expense	40				40					
602	Maintenance and Repairs Expense	375				375					
603	Telephone and Telegraph Expense	95				95					
604	Gas and Oil Expense	525				525					
605	Wages Expense	1,200		(g) 150		1,350					
	Totals	28,265	28,265								
606	Rent Expense			(a) 500		500					
607	Insurance Expense			(b) 60		60					
608	Office Supplies Expense			(c) 170		170					
511	Rent Earned				(d) 100		100				
609	Depreciation Expense—Office Equipment			(e) 10		10					
201A	Accumulated Depreciation—Office Equipment				(e) 10		10				
610	Depreciation Expense—Trucks			(f) 200		200					
211A	Accumulated Depreciation—Trucks				(f) 200		200				
311	Accrued Wages Payable				(g) 150		150				
611	Interest Expense			(h) 24		24					
303	Accrued Interest Payable				(h) 24		24				
113	Accrued Interest Receivable			(i) 4		4					
521	Interest Earned				(i) 4		4				
612	Income Tax Expense			(j) 1,900		1,900					
331	Income Taxes Payable				(j) 1,900		1,900				
	Totals			3,118	3,118	30,553	30,553				

Balances from the trial balance, adjusted by the amounts in Adjustments columns, are extended here.

Step 3. The amounts extended to the Adjusted Trial Balance columns result from combining the amounts in the Trial Balance columns with the amounts in the Adjustments columns.

On completion of Step 3, the adjusted trial balance figures will be the same as the balances of the accounts in the general ledger after the adjusting entries have been journalized and posted. Each line on the work sheet represents a general ledger account and functions in the same manner as to the debit and credit position. For example, after adjustment, the Prepaid Rent account appears in the general ledger as follows:

Prepaid Rent Acct. No. 142

June 1 1,500	June 30 500

The new balance is a debit of $1,000, which is the amount shown opposite Prepaid Rent in the Adjusted Trial Balance Debit column of the work sheet.

Figure 4-6 Work Sheet, Step 4: Remaining Extensions Made

CONNOLLY TRUCKING COMPANY LTD.
Work Sheet
For Month Ended June 30, 19XX

Acct. No.	Account Title	*Trial Balance*		*Adjustments*		*Adjusted Trial Balance*		*Income Statement*		*Balance Sheet*	
		Dr.	*Cr.*	*Dr.*	*Cr.*	*Dr.*	*Cr.*	*Dr.*	*Cr.*	*Dr.*	*Cr.*
101	Cash	5,250				5,250				5,250	
111	Accounts Receivable	550				550				550	
112	Notes Receivable	1,440				1,440				1,440	
131	Office Supplies	230			(c) 170	60				60	
141	Prepaid Insurance	2,160			(b) 60	2,100				2,100	
142	Prepaid Rent	1,500			(a) 500	1,000				1,000	
201	Office Equipment	1,400				1,400				1,400	
211	Trucks	13,000				13,000				13,000	
301	Accounts Payable		200				200				200
302	Notes Payable		8,000				8,000				8,000
321	Unearned Rent		600	(d) 100			500				500
401	Capital Stock, 1,000 shares outstanding		12,000				12,000				12,000
404	Dividends	500				500				500	
501	Trucking Revenue		7,465				7,465		7,465		
601	Heat and Light Expense	40				40		40			
602	Maintenance and Repairs Expense	375				375		375			
603	Telephone and Telegraph Expense	95				95		95			
604	Gas and Oil Expense	525				525		525			
605	Wages Expense	1,200		(g) 150		1,350		1,350			
	Totals	28,265	28,265								
606	Rent Expense			(a) 500		500		500			
607	Insurance Expense			(b) 60		60		60			
608	Office Supplies Expense			(c) 170		170		170			
511	Rent Earned				(d) 100		100		100		
609	Depreciation Expense—Office Equipment			(e) 10		10		10			
201A	Accumulated Depreciation—Office Equipment				(e) 10		10				10
610	Depreciation Expense—Trucks			(f) 200		200		200			
211A	Accumulated Depreciation—Trucks				(f) 200		200				200
311	Accrued Wages Payable				(g) 150		150				150
611	Interest Expense			(h) 24		24		24			
303	Accrued Interest Payable				(h) 24		24				24
113	Accrued Interest Receivable			(i) 4		4				4	
521	Interest Earned				(i) 4		4		4		
612	Income Tax Expense			(j) 1,900		1,900		1,900			
331	Income Taxes Payable				(j) 1,900		1,900				1,900
	Totals			3,118	3,118	30,553	30,553	5,249	7,569	25,304	22,984
	Net Income for Month							2,320			2,320
	Totals							7,569	7,569	25,304	25,304

The difference between the Income Statement columns is net income.

Net income is transferred to the Balance Sheet Credit column.

Step 4. The amounts in the Adjusted Trial Balance columns are extended either to the Income Statement columns or to the Balance Sheet columns, depending on their statement classification. Expense and revenue accounts are entered in the Income Statement columns; asset, liability, and shareholders' equity accounts are entered in the Balance Sheet columns. The four columns are then totaled. The difference between the totals of the Income Statement columns is the net income, or net loss, for the period; a net income is indicated if the total of the Credit column exceeds the total of the Debit column. The excess is entered in the Income Statement Debit column and in the Balance Sheet Credit column just below the column totals. This procedure records on the work sheet the increase in the shareholders' equity resulting from an excess of revenue over expenses during the period. A net loss is indicated if the total of the Income Statement Debit column exceeds that of the Income Statement Credit column. A loss is shown on the work sheet in the Income Statement Credit column and the Balance Sheet Debit column just below the column totals. The designation Net Income, or Net Loss, for the month, whichever is pertinent, is entered in the Account Title column on the same line. Following the completion of step 4, the work sheet is illustrated in Figure 4-6.

If the difference between the Income Statement Debit and Credit columns (net income) and the Balance Sheet Debit and Credit columns are not the same, an error has been made. The totaling and ruling of the last four columns of the work sheet (step 4) is illustrated in Figure 4-6. Note that balancing the last four columns provides only a limited proof of the accuracy of the work sheet—proof that the equality of debits and credits has been maintained throughout its preparation. The extension of the Cash account debit into the Income Statement Debit column, for example, would not destroy the debit-credit relationship of the work sheet, although statements prepared from that work sheet would be inaccurate. Note also that the total of the Balance Sheet Debit column need not correspond with the total assets reported in the statement. Accumulated Depreciation—Trucks, for example, is extanded to the Balance Sheet Credit column because it represents a balance sheet account with a credit balance. It is neither an asset nor a liability, but rather a deduction from Trucks, which is extended into the Balance Sheet Debit column. Since plus and minus symbols are not used on the work sheet, a deduction from an amount in a Debit column is effected by positioning the item to be deducted in the Credit column.

The work sheet may be varied in form—particularly with respect to the number of columns—to meet specific needs of the user. In Figure 5-3 for example, the columns for the adjusted trial balance are omitted.

Preparation of Financial Statements from the Work Sheet

The income statement is prepared from the amounts in the Income Statement columns of the work sheet; the balance sheet and the statement of retained earnings are prepared from the amounts in the Balance Sheet columns of the work sheet. In the preparation of financial statements, care should be taken to use each amount just once and in its proper debit and credit relation. The debit-credit relationship is not emphasized by the statements, but it is present. In the balance sheet, for example, Accumulated Depreciation—Trucks, with a credit balance of $200, is deducted from Trucks, which has a debit balance. Net income (or loss) appears in both the income statement and the statement of retained earnings.

The financial statements of Connolly Trucking Company Ltd. for June are shown in Figures 4-7, 4-8, and 4-9.

Figure 4-7
Income Statement

CONNOLLY TRUCKING COMPANY LTD. Income Statement For the Month Ended June 30, 19XX		
Revenue		
Trucking Revenue		$7,465
Interest Earned		4
Rent Earned		100
Total Revenues		$7,569
Expenses		
Heat and Light Expense	$ 40	
Maintenance and Repairs Expense	375	
Telephone and Telegraph Expense	95	
Gas and Oil Expense	525	
Wages Expense	1,350	
Rent Expense	500	
Insurance Expense	60	
Office Supplies Expense	170	
Depreciation Expense—Office Equipment	10	
Depreciation Expense—Trucks	200	
Interest Expense	24	
Total Expenses		3,349
Net Income before Income Taxes		$4,220
Income Tax Expense		1,900
Net Income after Income Taxes		$2,320

Figure 4-8
Statement of Retained Earnings

CONNOLLY TRUCKING COMPANY LTD. Statement of Retained Earnings For the Month Ended June 30, 19XX	
Net Income for Month of June	$2,320
Deduct Dividends	500
Retained Earnings, June 30	$1,820

Since the company was organized on June 1, 19XX, it had no beginning balance in the Retained Earnings account; therefore, this item does not appear in the statement.

Figure 4-9 Balance Sheet

CONNOLLY TRUCKING COMPANY LTD.
Balance Sheet
June 30, 19XX

Assets			
Current Assets			
Cash		$ 5,250	
Accounts Receivable		550	
Notes Receivable		1,440	
Accrued Interest Receivable		4	
Office Supplies		60	
Prepaid Insurance		2,100	
Prepaid Rent		1,000	
Total Current Assets			$10,404
Equipment			
Office Equipment	$ 1,400		
Deduct Accumulated Depreciation	10	$ 1,390	
Trucks	$13,000		
Deduct Accumulated Depreciation	200	12,800	
Total Equipment			14,190
Total Assets			$24,594

Liabilities and Shareholders' Equity		
Current Liabilities		
Accounts Payable	$ 200	
Notes Payable	8,000	
Accrued Interest Payable	24	
Accrued Wages Payable	150	
Unearned Rent	500	
Income Taxes Payable	1,900	
Total Current Liabilities		$10,774
Shareholders' Equity		
Capital Stock	$12,000	
Retained Earnings	1,820	
Total Shareholder' Equity		13,820
Total Liabilities and Shareholders' Equity		$24,594

UPDATING OF ACCOUNTS AFTER PREPARATION OF WORK SHEET

RECORDING ADJUSTMENTS IN THE GENERAL JOURNAL AND POSTING TO THE GENERAL LEDGER

If formal adjusting entries are not recorded in the general journal until after the financial statements have been prepared, the adjusting entries may be taken directly from the Adjustments columns of the work sheet and dated as of the last day of the accounting period. The caption "Adjusting Entries" is written in the general journal on the line following the last regular general journal entry. After the adjusting entries have been posted, the general ledger account balances will correspond with the amounts in the Adjusted Trial Balance columns of the work sheet. Although the adjusting entries for Connolly Trucking Company Ltd. have already been made as they were introduced, to add realism to the accounting job, they are collected and repeated in Figure 4-10. The account numbers in the folio column indicate that they have been posted.

When all the adjusting entries are recorded in the journal and posted to the general ledger, the mixed elements in the accounts have been eliminated.

Figure 4-10
Adjusting Entries

GENERAL JOURNAL **Page 4**

19XX					
		Adjusting Entries			
June	30	Rent Expense	606	500	
		Prepaid Rent	142		500
		To record rent expense for June.			
	30	Insurance Expense	607	60	
		Prepaid Insurance	141		60
		To record insurance expense for June.			
	30	Office Supplies Expense	608	170	
		Office Supplies	131		170
		To record supplies used during June.			
	30	Unearned Rent	321	100	
		Rent Earned	511		100
		To record revenue earned from rental of trucks during June.			
	30	Depreciation Expense—Office Equipment	609	10	
		Accumulated Depreciation—Office Equipment	201A		10
		To record the depreciation for June.			
	30	Depreciation Expense—Trucks	610	200	
		Accumulated Depreciation—Trucks	211A		200
		To record the depreciation for June.			
	30	Wages Expense	605	150	
		Accrued Wages Payable	311		150
		To record wages expense accrued during June.			
	30	Interest Expense	611	24	
		Accrued Interest Payable	303		24
		To record interest expense accrued during June.			
	30	Accrued Interest Receivable	113	4	
		Interest Earned	521		4
		To record interest revenue accrued during June.			
	30	Income Tax Expense	612	1,900	
		Income Taxes Payable	331		1,900
		To record estimated taxes for June.			

CLOSING ENTRIES MAY BE RECORDED DIRECTLY FROM THE WORK SHEET

The caption "Closing Entries" is written in the middle of the first unused line on the journal page under the adjusting entries. The closing entries are recorded (Figure 4-11) and are then posted to the general ledger. They are made directly from the work sheet in the following sequence.

GENERAL JOURNAL **Page 5**

		Closing Entries			
June	30	Trucking Revenue	501	7,465	
		Rent Earned	511	100	
		Interest Earned	521	4	
		Income Summary	902		7,569
		To close.			
	30	Income Summary	902	5,249	
		Heat and Light Expense	601		40
		Maintenance and Repairs Expense	602		375
		Telephone and Telegraph Expense	603		95
		Gas and Oil Expense	604		525
		Wages Expense	605		1,350
		Rent Expense	606		500
		Insurance Expense	607		60
		Office Supplies Expense	608		170
		Depreciation Expense—Office Equipment	609		10
		Depreciation Expense—Trucks	610		200
		Interest Expense	611		24
		Income Tax Expense	612		1,900
		To close.			
	30	Income Summary	902	2,320	
		Retained Earnings	403		2,320
		To transfer net income to Retained Earnings.			
	30	Retained Earnings	403	500	
		Dividends	404		500
		To close.			

Figure 4-11
Closing Entries

Entry 1.
Each account in the credit column of the Income Statement is debited and the total is credited to Income Summary.

Entry 2.
Each account in the debit column of the Income Statement column is credited and the total is debited to Income Summary.

Entry 3.
The balance in Income Summary is transferred to Retained Earnings.

Entry 4.
The balance of Dividends is closed to Retained Earnings.

THE POSTCLOSING TRIAL BALANCE

After posting the adjusting entries and closing entries to the general ledger, the general ledger balances are listed in a postclosing trial balance to check that all temporary accounts have been closed.

The postclosing trial balance of Connolly Trucking Company Ltd., taken from the general ledger, is shown in Figure 4-12.

Figure 4-12
Postclosing Trial Balance

CONNOLLY TRUCKING COMPANY LTD.
Postclosing Trial Balance
June 30, 19XX

Acct. No.	*Account Title*	*Debits*	*Credits*
101	Cash	$ 5,250	
111	Accounts Receivable	550	
112	Notes Receivable	1,440	
113	Accrued Interest Receivable	4	
131	Office Supplies	60	
141	Prepaid Insurance	2,100	
142	Prepaid Rent	1,000	
201	Office Equipment	1,400	
201A	Accumulated Depreciation—Office Equipment		$ 10
211	Trucks	13,000	
211A	Accumulated Depreciation—Trucks		200
301	Accounts Payable		200
302	Notes Payable		8,000
303	Accrued Interest Payable		24
311	Accrued Wages Payable		150
321	Unearned Rent		500
331	Income Taxes Payable		1,900
401	Capital Stock		12,000
403	Retained Earnings		1,820
	Totals	$24,804	$24,804

THE ACCOUNTING CYCLE

In this chapter and the preceding one, the complete *accounting cycle* of a service business concern has been presented. The cycle consists of a series of steps.

1. *Journalizing,* which consists of analyzing and recording transactions in chronological order in the journal.
2. *Posting,* which consists of transferring debits and credits to the appropriate ledgers and to the proper accounts in the ledgers.
3. *Preparing a trial balance,* or summarizing the general ledger accounts to test the equality of debits and credits.
4. *Preparing the work sheet,* or assembling and classifying information in columnar form to facilitate the preparation of financial statements.
5. *Preparing the financial statements* from the work sheet; these are the income statement, statement of retained earnings, and balance sheet.
6. *Adjusting the books,* or recording and posting the adjusting entries from the work sheet.
7. *Closing the books,* which consists of recording and posting the closing entries from the Income Statement columns of the work sheet.
8. *Taking a postclosing trial balance,* or totaling the open-account balances to prove the equality of the debits and credits in the general ledger.

SPLIT ENTRIES

PURPOSE OF SPLIT ENTRIES

The adjusting entries are recorded in the general journal and posted to the general ledger. Three of the adjusting entries—g, h, and i—involve the accrual of previously unrecorded revenue or expense items assignable to June and require a split form of entry in July, when the transaction cycle culminates in the receipt or payment of cash.

Paying the Accrued Wages Payable

The next regular pay day at Connolly Trucking Company Ltd. is on July 11. On July 1, Wages Expense had a zero balance as a result of the closing entries on June 30 but the Accrued Wages Payable account had a credit balance of $150 as a result of the adjusting entries. Assuming that the biweekly wages again amounted to $600, the entry on July 11 to record this payment is

July	11	Accrued Wages Payable		150	
		Wages Expense		450	
		Cash			600
		To record the payment of biweekly wages.			

The result of this entry is to split the biweekly wages of $600 so that $150, which was recognized as a June expense, is debited to Accrued Wages Payable and $450 is recorded as an expense in July. Accrued Wages Payable now has a zero balance.

Paying the Accrued Interest Payable

On the maturity date of the note payable, July 27 (45 days, including 18 days accrued in June), Connolly Trucking Company Ltd. pays the bank $8,060, the maturity value. The amount consists of $8,000 principal plus $60, which is 45 days' interest at 6 percent on $8,000, calculated as follows:

$$\text{Interest} = \$8{,}000 \times 0.06 \times \frac{45}{365} = \$60$$

The entry to record the payment to the bank is

July	27	Notes Payable		8,000	
		Accrued Interest Payable		24	
		Interest Expense		36	
		Cash			8,060
		To record the payment of a note payable.			

The adjusting entry on June 30 allocated 18 days' interest expense ($24) on the note to the month of June. The July entry splits the total interest of $60 so that the $24 liability applicable to June is canceled and the remaining $36 = ($60 − $24) is recorded as interest expense for 27 days in July.

Receiving the Accrued Interest Receivable

On the maturity date of the note receivable, July 10 (30 days, including 20 days accrued in June), Connolly Trucking Company Ltd. receives the maturity value, $1,446. The maturity value is determined by adding to the principal, $1,440, 30 days' interest at 5 percent, or $6, computed as follows:

$$\text{Interest} = \$1{,}440 \times 0.05 \times \frac{30}{365} = \$6$$

The entry to record the receipt from the customer is

July	10	Cash		1,446	
		Notes Receivable			1,440
		Accrued Interest Receivable			4
		Interest Earned			2
		To record the collection of a note receivable.			

On June 30, the adjusting entry accrued 20 days' interest earned on the note, or $4, in June. The total interest earned of $6 is split by the July entry so that the $4 asset, Accrued Interest Receivable, is canceled and the balance of $2 = ($6 − $4) is entered as interest earned in July.

GLOSSARY

Accrual Basis The accrual accounting basis assumes that revenue is realized at the time of the sale of goods or services irrespective of when the cash is received; and expenses are recognized at the time the services are received and utilized in the production of revenue irrespective of when payment for these services is made.

Accrued Expenses Expenses that have been incurred—for example, services received and used—in a given period but have not yet been paid or recorded.

Accrued Liability The liability that has accumulated for an expense that has been incurred but not yet paid or recorded.

Accumulated Depreciation The accumulated depreciation account reveals all past depreciation which has been taken on a depreciable plant and equipment item and charged against revenue; it is in essence a postponed credit to the applicable plant and equipment account.

Adjusting Entries Regular continuous entries postponed to the end of an accounting period, for the convenience of the accountant, and made to update revenue, expense, assets, liability, and shareholders' equity accounts as required by the accrual basis of accounting.

Apportionment The dividing of a cost or revenue among two or more periods.

Cash Basis The cash basis of accounting reflects the recognition of revenue at the time that cash is received for the sale of goods and services and the recognition of expenses in the period of the payment for the receipt of a service.

Contra Account A negative element of another account which is shown in a separate account; the contra account should always be shown immediately following the account of which it is a reduction.

Depreciation (Accounting Depreciation) Accounting depreciation is the system of allocation of a part of the cost of a plant and equipment item (that has a limited useful life) over the estimated useful life in a systematic and rational manner.

Long-Term Cost Apportionment Adjustment An adjustment requiring the apportioning of the cost of a long-lived asset between the current period and a future span of time of three or more years.

Materiality An item significant enough in size to influence decisions by statement users that it should receive separate and identified accounting.

Salvage Value The estimated scrap value or resale value that a plant and equipment item has at the end of the estimated life of the asset.

Short-Term Cost Apportionment Adjustment An adjustment which requires that a previously recorded prepaid item be apportioned between the current period and a future short period (usually a year).

Short-Term Revenue Apportionment Adjustment An adjustment which requires that a previously recorded liability involving an advanced collection of a revenue be apportioned between the current period and a future short period (usually one year).

Straight-Line Method of Depreciation A method that allocates the cost of a depreciable asset over the estimated useful life of the asset in equal amounts for each time period.

Work Sheet (Working Papers) A device used by the accountant to collect information rapidly and in an orderly manner for the preparation of the formal end-of-period financial statements.

QUESTIONS

Q4-1. (a) What are the essential differences between the cash basis of accounting and the accrual basis? (b) Under what conditions is it appropriate to use the cash basis? (c) Under what conditions is it inappropriate to use the cash basis?

Q4-2. (a) What purpose is served by adjusting entries? (b) What events make them necessary? (c) How do they affect the work of the accountant? (d) How does the time period covered by the income statement affect the adjusting entries? (e) How do adjusting entries differ from other entries?

Q4-3. Does the need to make adjusting entries at the end of a period mean that errors were made in the accounts during the period? Discuss.

Q4-4. (a) What is the purpose and function of the work sheet? (b) Can the work of the accountant be completed without the use of the work sheet? (c) Where do the amounts in the first pair of columns on the work sheet come from? (d) What determines the number of columns to be used in the preparation of a work sheet? (e) Why are the parts of each entry in the Adjustments columns cross-referenced with either numbers or letters? (f) How is the amount to be extended into another column determined? (g) What determines the column into which an amount is to be extended? (h) Is the work sheet foolproof? (i) Does the work sheet eliminate the need for formal financial statements?

Q4-5. "Prepaid items are not assets, since these amounts will become expenses in later periods." Comment on this statement.

Q4-6. (a) What is meant by the accounting cycle? (b) What are the steps in the complete cycle? (c) Is it possible for the accountant to vary the sequence in which he performs the steps of the cycle?

Q4-7. Is it possible to prepare the formal financial statements from a four-column work sheet consisting of the trial balance amounts and all the necessary adjustments?

Q4-8. (a) When would the amounts for Depreciation Expense and for Accumulated Depreciation in the adjusted trial balance be the same? (b) When would these amounts be different?

DEMONSTRATION PROBLEMS

DP4-1. (*Work sheet*) The general ledger of Center Bowling Lanes, Inc., showed the following balances at December 31, Year 1. The books are closed annually on December 31. The company obtains revenue from its bowling alleys and from a refreshment stand that is leased on a concession basis.

Cash	$29,000
Bowling Supplies	8,500
Prepaid Insurance	7,500
Prepaid Rent	6,800
Bowling Equipment	62,000
Mortgage Payable	30,000
Capital Stock	25,000
Retained Earnings	9,280
Dividends	5,000
Bowling Revenue	55,000
Concession Revenue	6,500
Wages Expense	14,500
Repair Expense	3,200
Heat and Light Expense	2,900
Telephone and Telegraph Expense	360
Miscellaneous Expense	1,020

Supplementary data:

a. Bowling supplies on hand based on physical count totaled $650.
b. The balance of the Prepaid Insurance account represents the premium on a 3-year insurance policy, effective January 1, Year 1.
c. Rent expense for the year was $4,800.
d. The bowling equipment has an expected useful life of 10 years and an estimated salvage value of $2,000. No equipment was acquired during the year.
e. Salaries earned by employees but unpaid on December 31 were $250.

Required:

1. Record the trial balance on a work sheet.
2. Complete the work sheet.
3. Why is the difference between the totals of the Income Statement columns and the totals of the Balance Sheet columns the same amount?

DP4-2. (*Adjusting entries*) Certain unadjusted account balances from the trial balance of Easter Company Ltd., a systems consulting firm, for the year ended December 31, are given below:

Account Title	*Debits*	*Credits*
Accounts Receivable	$40,000	
Notes Receivable	18,000	
Prepaid Insurance	2,160	
Office Supplies	1,240	
Automobiles	20,000	
Accumulated Depreciation —Automobiles		$ 4,000
Notes Payable		6,000
Revenue—Consulting Fees		480,000
Interest Earned		600
Rent Earned		2,400
Advertising Expense	1,800	
Rent Expense	40,000	
Salaries Expense	49,000	
Property Taxes Expense	3,350	
Heat and Light Expense	2,400	

Adjustment data on December 31 are as follows:

a. Office supplies on hand totaled $100.
b. Depreciation for the year was $2,000.
c. Estimated heat and light expense not recorded was $250.
d. Of the amount shown for Interest Earned, $200 was unearned as of December 31.
e. The balance of the Prepaid Insurance account consists of $720 for the premium on a 3-year policy dated July 1, and $1,440 for the premium on a 3-year policy dated January 1.
f. Advertising supplies on hand were $140.
g. The balance of the Notes Payable account represents a 9% interest-bearing note dated January 1, due July 1.
h. The rent is $4,000 a month.
i. Salaries earned but not paid were $1,300.
j. Property taxes accrued were $190.
k. On January 1, Easter Company Ltd. subleased a section of its rented space. The lease with the tenant specifies a minimum yearly rental of $2,400 payable in twelve installments at the beginning of each month. The maximum annual rental is 5% of sales. The rental adjustment, if any, is due on January 15. The tenant reported sales of $53,000.
l. Included in Revenue—Consulting Fees are advance payments of $15,000 by clients for services to be rendered the next year.

Required:

1. Record the adjusting entries.
2. Indicate the financial statement classification of each account in each entry.
3. Show the amount reported on the financial statements. Present the data in solution form as shown (Item a is done as an example):

Item	Adjusting Journal Entries December 31	Dr.	Cr.	Financial Statement Classification	Amount Reported on Financial Statement
a	Office Supplies Expense	1,140		Expenses	$1,140
	Office Supplies		1,140	Current Assets	100

DP4-3. *(Financial statements: closing entries)* Parker Decorators Ltd. adjusted trial balance, taken from the work sheet for the month ended October 31, was as follows:

Cash	$ 1,200	
Accounts Receivable	1,800	
Decorating Supplies	4,000	
Prepaid Insurance	2,400	
Land	6,000	
Building	20,000	
Accumulated Depreciation—Building		$11,400
Accounts Payable		4,000
Notes Payable		2,400
Bank Loan Payable—current		7,200
Capital Stock, $10 par value		3,000
Retained Earnings		1,380
Dividends	950	
Service Revenue		15,900
Heat and Light Expense	240	
Telephone and Telegraph Expense	80	
Wages Expense	1,600	
Decorating Supplies Expense	6,400	
Insurance Expense	320	
Depreciation Expense—Building	480	
Income Tax Expense	1,500	
Accrued Wages Payable		140
Interest Expense	50	
Accrued Interest Payable		100
Income Taxes Payable		1,500
Totals	$47,020	$47,020

Required:

1. An income statement.
2. A balance sheet.
3. A statement of retained earnings.
4. Closing entries.
5. The company needs additional cash to increase its volume of business. Suggest alternative means of raising money and the advantages and disadvantages of each alternative.

PROBLEMS

P4-1. Because of an impending paternity suit, the company's accountant quite unexpectedly quit; he took off for parts unknown just before the close of the company's accounting year. In his haste to leave he did not have a chance to discuss what adjusting entries would be necessary at the end of the year, December

31. Fortunately, however, he did jot down a few notes on his memo pad that provide some leads. These are his brief notes:

a. Depreciation on furniture and equipment for the year is $4,000.
b. Charge off $850 of expired insurance from prepaid account for the year.
c. Accrued interest at end of year on notes payable to bank is $1,500; make sure to pick up when adjusting entries are made.
d. No bill received yet from car rental agency for salesmen cars—should be about $1,200 for December.
e. Two days' salaries will be unpaid at year-end; weekly (5 days) total salary is $2,400.

1. On the basis of the available information given above, prepare for each adjustment that should be recorded a general journal entry with brief explanation.
2. What other normal or usual adjustments may have to be recorded in addition to the ones above? Briefly explain each one.

P4-2. Prepare adjusting entries from the following information pertaining to the accounts of Hyper-Video Control Corporation at the end of April.

a. Accrued rent receivable, $280.
b. Accrued interest payable, $75.
c. Accrued taxes payable, $120.
d. Accrued wages payable, $360.
e. A trenching machine was rented during April from the Rent-All Company at the rate of $20 an hour; the machine was used for a total of 80 hours during the month and the corporation had paid $500 to Rent-All Company for the rental of the machine. The $500 payment was debited to Prepaid Equipment Rental Expense.
f. Accrued interest on municipal bonds owned, $150.
g. As of April 30, the unbilled service fees for completed work amounted to $580.
h. The company signed an order form on April 30 to purchase a trenching machine for $11,500.

P4-3. Thomas Sparrow, an electrician, prepares monthly financial statements. The following transactions occurred during December.

Dec. 15	Billed customers $850 for services rendered this month.
17	Purchased $650 worth of electrical supplies on account.
31	Received $500 in cash from customers billed on December 15.
31	Paid $350 on account for electrical supplies purchased on December 17.

The electrical supplies inventory on December 31 was $150. Journalize the transactions, assuming that Sparrow keeps his books (a) on the cash basis; (b) on the accrual basis. What is the net income (c) on the cash basis? (d) on the accrual basis? Which method should Sparrow use? Why?

P4-4. On January 1, Year 1, the Angel Company purchased a truck for $4,900. It had an estimated useful life of four years and an estimated trade-in value at the end of that time of $500. (a) What is the depreciation expense for Year 1? (b) What is the balance in the Accumulated Depreciation—Delivery Equipment account at the end of Year 1? of Year 2? (c) What will the carrying value of the truck be in the statement of financial position of December 31, Year 1? of December 31, Year 2? (d) Why is depreciation expense credited to Accumulated Depreciation—Delivery Equipment rather than directly to Delivery Equipment?

P4-5. The trial balance of Castle Company Ltd. on December 31 included the following account balances before adjustments:

Prepaid Insurance	$1,800
Prepaid Advertising Supplies	1,600
Prepaid Rent	2,400
Office Supplies	3,000
Office Equipment	6,600

Data for adjustments on December 31 were:

a. On November 1, the company purchased a 2-year comprehensive insurance policy for $1,800.
b. Advertising supplies on hand totaled $450 on December 31.
c. On September 1, the company paid one year's rent in advance.
d. The office supplies inventory was $1,400 on December 31.
e. The office equipment was purchased on July 1, and has an estimated useful life of 10 years and an estimated salvage value of $600.

Make the adjusting entries.

P4-6. The Black Company employs three sales clerks at a weekly salary of $150 each. They are paid on Friday, the last day of a five-day work week. Make the adjusting entry, assuming that the accounting period ended on Thursday.

P4-7. The balance sheets of the Dempsey Company as of December 31, Year 1 and Year 2, showed Office Supplies at $1,600 and $1,800, respectively. During Year 2, office supplies totaling $2,600 were purchased. What was the office supplies expense for Year 2?

P4-8. The balances of the Prepaid Insurance account of the Parris Company were:

December 31, Year 1	$1,030
December 31, Year 2	620

The income statement for Year 2 showed insurance expense of $1,250. What were the expenditures for insurance premiums during Year 2?

P4-9. The Pictorial Magazine Company credited Subscription Revenue for $48,000 received from subscribers to its new monthly magazine. All subscriptions were for twelve issues. The initial issue was mailed during October. Make the adjusting entry on December 31.

P4-10. The income statement of the Walker Company for the 3-month period ended March 31, shows net income before income taxes of $140,000. Assuming an income tax rate of 48 percent, make the necessary adjusting entry.

P4-11. From the account balances given below, prepare the adjusting entries.

Account	*Account in Trial Balance*	*Balance After Adjustment*
Prepaid Insurance	$ 3,600	$ 1,200
Unearned Rent	1,400	400
Accumulated Depreciation—Building	14,000	20,000

Accrued Salaries and Wages Payable	-0-	900
Accrued Interest Receivable	-0-	220
Accrued Interest Payable	-0-	180

P4-12. Upon examining the books and records of the Gentry Company on December 31, Year 1, you find the following: (a) The inventory of office supplies on hand is $250; some partially filled cans of duplicating fluid valued at $3.75 were not inventoried. All purchases of office supplies were debited to Office Supplies Expense. (b) Included in Miscellaneous Expense was a charge of $600 for uninsured losses from a fire.
Indicate the adjustments, if any, that should be made and state why.

P4-13. On September 15 the Sampson Company received a 30-day, 9% note for $600 from a customer. On September 20 the company borrowed $2,400 from the bank on its own 30-day, 9% note. Make entries to adjust the books on September 30, and entries to record the collection and payment of the notes on their respective due dates.

P4-14. The Nabors Company issued to a supplier of merchandise a 60-day, 9% note for $1,000, dated July 1. On July 16 the company received from a customer a 30-day, 10% note for $800. Make the necessary adjusting entries on July 31.

P4-15. Lawton Company Ltd.'s adjusted trial balance, taken from the work sheet for year ended December 31, was as follows:

Cash	$ 25,700	
Accounts Receivable	21,400	
Machinery and Equipment	42,900	
Accumulated Depreciation		$ 22,000
Accounts Payable		4,040
Notes Payable		8,600
Capital Stock		54,360
Dividends	4,000	
Service Revenue		60,000
Heat and Light Expense	2,000	
Wages Expense	45,000	
Depreciation Expense	8,000	
Totals	$149,000	$149,000

Required:

1. Enter the adjusted trial balance on a work sheet.
2. Complete the work sheet.
3. Prepare an income statement, a balance sheet, a statement of retained earnings, and the closing entries.

P4-16. Selected transactions of the Brantley Sales Company follow:

Jan. 2 Purchased a 4-year insurance policy for $1,800, effective January 1.

July 1 Bought two trucks for $12,850. The trucks are expected to last four years, at the end of which time their salvage value will be $850 each.

Dec. 31 Paid $1,200 rent in advance for next year.

31 Purchased office supplies for $480.

Required:

1. Prepare journal entries to record the transactions.
2. Prepare the adjusting entries as of December 31. The company closes its books annually on December 31.
3. What adjusting entries would be made if the Brantley Sales Company were on the cash basis?

P4-17. Listed below are the account balances taken from the Trial Balance and Adjusted Trial Balance columns of the work sheet of Lasley Company Ltd. for the 12-month period ended June 30, the first year of operations.

Account Title	*Trial Balance*	*Adjusted Trial Balance*
Cash	$ 2,400	$ 2,400
Accounts Receivable	4,000	4,000
Office Supplies	3,500	1,000
Store Supplies	3,000	200
Prepaid Insurance	3,600	1,200
Prepaid Rent	4,800	1,200
Equipment	41,200	41,200
Accounts Payable	14,000	14,000
Capital Stock	39,300	39,300
Dividends	7,000	7,000
Service Revenue	31,000	31,000
Wages Expense	11,000	11,140
Miscellaneous Expense	3,800	3,800
Office Supplies Expense	–0–	2,500
Store Supplies Expense	–0–	2,800
Insurance Expense	–0–	2,400
Rent Expense	–0–	3,600
Depreciation Expense—Equipment	–0–	4,000
Accumulated Depreciation—Equipment	–0–	4,000
Accrued Wages Payable	–0–	140

Required: Reconstruct the Trial Balance, Adjustments, and Adjusted Trial Balance columns of the work sheet.

P4-18. *(Financial policy decision problem)* Following is the trial balance of Clawson Print Company Ltd. at October 31. The company began operations on September 1. Its fiscal year ends on October 31.

Account Title	*Debits*	*Credits*
Cash	$17,100	
Notes Receivable	12,000	
Accounts Receivable	13,400	
Office Supplies	1,750	

Printing Supplies	2,000	
Prepaid Rent	3,400	
Printing Equipment	22,000	
Accounts Payable		$13,600
Notes Payable		12,200
Capital Stock		27,000
Dividends	1,500	
Printing Revenue		23,635
Heat and Light Expense	180	
Telephone Expense	145	
Maintenance Expense	360	
Wages Expense	2,600	
Totals	$76,435	$76,435

Other data:

a. A physical count shows that office supplies on hand total $475 and that printing supplies on hand are $700.
b. The monthly rental is $680.
c. Printing equipment acquired on September 1 has an estimated useful life of five years and a salvage value of $2,000.
d. Wages of employees earned but not paid are $400.
e. The note payable is a 1-year note, signed on September 1, and bears interest at 9%.
f. The Notes Receivable account represents a 60-day, 8% interest-bearing note signed by a customer on October 1.

Required: Prepare adjusting entries.

P4-19 Certain account balances from the trial balance of the Jockey Ridge Company as of June 30, Year 1, the end of its fiscal year, are given below.

Account Title	*Debits*	*Credits*
Office Supplies	$ 900	
Prepaid Insurance	4,800	
Prepaid Advertising	4,400	
Unearned Rent		$1,200
Rent Expense	4,000	

Examination of the records as of June 30 shows the following:

a. Office supplies on hand totaled $250.
b. A 3-year comprehensive insurance policy was purchased on July 1, Year 1, at a premium cost of $4,800.
c. The monthly rent expense is $400.
d. Included in Prepaid Advertising is a payment of $300 for ads to appear during July, Year 2. The balance is for ads that appeared in prior months.
e. A portion of the floor space was subleased at $100 a month on September 1, Year 1. The tenant paid for a year's rent in advance on signing the lease.

Required: Record the adjusting entries as of June 30, Year 1. The books are closed annually.

P4-20. *(Accounting policy decision problem)* The bookkeeper for the Braxton Company Ltd. prepared the following condensed income statement for the year ber 31, and the condensed balance sheet as of that date.

Income Statement

Revenue from Services		$40,100
Operating Expenses		
Insurance Expense	$ 1,400	
Miscellaneous Expense	4,600	
Office Supplies Expense	800	
Wages Expense	20,000	26,800
Net Income		$13,300

Balance Sheet

Assets	
Cash	$ 4,600
Accounts Receivable	8,000
Equipment	40,000
Total	$52,600
Liabilities and Shareholders' Equity	
Accounts Payable	$ 9,800
Capital Stock	29,500
Retained Earnings	13,300
Total	$52,600

The following items were overlooked entirely by the bookkeeper in the preparation of the statements:

a. The depreciation of equipment (acquired January 1): estimated life, 10 years; no salvage value.
b. Wages earned but unpaid, $800.
c. Office supplies on hand, $260 (purchases were debited to Office Supplies Expense).
d. Unexpired insurance premiums, $400.
e. Heat and light invoices for December, $250.

Required:

1. What adjustments are needed?
2. Prepare revised financial statements.

P4-21. After an analysis of the accounts and other records of Pittsborough, Inc., the following information is made available for the year ended December 31:

a. The Office Supplies account has a debit balance of $720. Office supplies on hand at December 31 total $260.
b. The Prepaid Rent account has a debit balance of $7,200. Included in this amount is $600 paid in December for the succeeding January; $6,600 has expired.
c. The Prepaid Insurance account has a debit balance of $1,920. It consists of the following policies:

Policy No.	Date of Policy	Life of Policy	Premiums
A63210	January 1	3 years	$1,200
E4522	May 1	2 years	480
X3211	October 1	1 year	240

d. The Prepaid Advertising account has a debit balance of $2,400. Included in this amount is $400 paid to a local monthly magazine for advertising space in next year's issues.

e. At the close of the year three notes receivable were on hand:

Date	Face Value	Time of Note	Interest Rate
November 1	$6,000	90 days	9 percent
December 1	7,200	60 days	10 percent
December 16	4,000	30 days	none

f. At the close of the year two notes payable were outstanding:

Date	Face Value	Time of Note	Interest Rate
September 2	$ 6,600	180 days	8 percent
November 1	10,000	90 days	9 percent

g. Salaries and wages accrued totaled $2,000.

h. The Rent Earned account has a credit balance of $9,600. This amount represents receipt of payment on a one-year lease effective May 1.

i. The Store Equipment account has a debit balance of $13,500. The equipment has an estimated useful life of 10 years and a salvage value of $1,500. All store equipment was acquired prior to January 1.

j. The Truck account has a debit balance of $6,500. The truck was purchased on June 1, and has an estimated life of five years and salvage value of approximately $500.

k. Property taxes accrued were $1,400.

l. Estimated income taxes for the year were $4,650.

Required: Prepare the adjusting journal entries required at December 31.

P4-22. *(Accounting policy decision problem)* The closing entries and postclosing trial balance of the Village Realty Company Ltd. as of December 31, are given below. A yearly accounting period is used. On January 2 the company had issued capital stock for $36,000 cash.

GENERAL JOURNAL **Page 12**

		Closing Entries			
Dec.	31	Rental Revenue		11,000	
		Commission Revenue		43,200	
		Income Summary			54,200
	31	Income Summary		40,100	
		Rent Expense			3,600
		Insurance Expense			800
		Supplies Expense			300
		Commission Expense			33,000
		Depreciation Expense— Office Equipment			2,000
		Miscellaneous Expense			400

31	Income Summary		14,100	
	Retained Earnings			14,100
31	Retained Earnings		10,000	
	Dividends			10,000

VILLAGE REALTY COMPANY LTD.
Postclosing Trial Balance
December 31

Account Title	*Debits*	*Credits*
Cash	$10,600	
Office Supplies	300	
Prepaid Insurance	3,200	
Office Equipment	32,000	
Accumulated Depreciation—Office Equipment		$ 4,000
Notes Payable to Banks		2,000
Capital Stock		36,000
Retained Earnings		4,100
Totals	$46,100	$46,100

Required:

1. An income statement.
2. A statement of retained earnings.

P4-23. On October 1, Red Deer Corporation was formed. During October the following transactions were completed:

Oct. 1 Issued capital stock for $3,000.
2 Paid $185 for office supplies.
3 Purchased secondhand office equipment for $300 in cash.
4 Issued a check for $150 for October rent.
5 Paid a premium of $72 for an insurance policy on the equipment, effective October 1.
6 Purchased repair supplies on account to be used in repair work:

Amber Supply Company	$150
Carson Wire Company	200
Gaddy Supply Company	160
Ronson Repairs, Inc.	140
Total	$650

17 Received $1,250 for repair work completed.
20 Additional repair work was completed, and bills were sent out:

J. K. Blaine	$205
D. J. Dawson	80
H. H. Hooper	70
P. T. Peters	95
Total	$450

22 Paid $45 for the telephone service for the month.

25 Paid the following creditors:

Amber Supply Company	$ 50
Carson Wire Company	100
Gaddy Supply Company	60
Ronson Repairs, Inc.	40
Total	$250

27 Received cash from customers to apply on account:

J. K. Blaine	$105
D. J. Dawson	30
H. H. Hooper	20
P. T. Peters	35
Total	$190

31 Paid dividends of $400.

Supplementary adjustment data as of October 31:

a. The insurance premium paid on October 5 is for one year.
b. A physical count shows (1) that office supplies on hand total $65 and (2) that repair supplies on hand are $125.
c. The office equipment has an estimated useful life of five years with no salvage value.

Required:

1. Record all the transactions in the general journal, post to the appropriate accounts, and enter the general ledger account balances directly in the Trial Balance columns of the work sheet.
2. Enter the adjustment data in the Adjustments columns of the work sheet.
3. Complete the work sheet.
4. Prepare an income statement, a statement of retained earnings, and a balance sheet.
5. Prepare adjusting entries in the general journal.
6. Post the adjusting entries from the general journal to the general ledger.
7. Prepare closing entries in the general journal, post to the general ledger, and rule the nominal accounts that are closed.
8. Balance and rule the real accounts.
9. Prepare a postclosing trial balance.

5

Accounting for Merchandising Operations

Accounting for businesses that render a service to customers or clients has been discussed up to this point. In this and subsequent chapters, accounting for businesses that buy and sell *merchandise,* or goods, is examined. The principles developed thus far, however, apply to all classes of business enterprise, whether service, merchandising, or manufacturing.

ACCOUNTS FOR A MERCHANDISING BUSINESS

The principal difference in the accounts of a merchandising business from those of a service business is that a merchandising business has to account for the purchase of goods, their handling, and their sale; it has to account not only for operating expenses but also for the *cost of goods* that it has sold. The income statement for a merchandising business, therefore, shows an operating income only if the goods are sold for more than their cost plus all other expenses necessary in operating the business. Since a merchandising business is involved in many activities that are not found in service businesses, additional accounts are needed to report the financial position and operating results of the enterprise. The functions of the merchandising accounts and their classifications in the financial statements are discussed and illustrated in this chapter.

The Sales Account

A sale of merchandise, like a sale of service, is recorded by a credit to a revenue account as shown.

Transaction:
Sold merchandise for $200 on account.
Journal Entry:

Accounts Receivable	200	
Sales		200

The debit to Accounts Receivable (or to Cash if the sale is for cash) records an increase in an asset. The credit to Sales, a revenue account, records an increase in the shareholders' equity. This credit constitutes a recovery of the cost of the merchandise sold as well as a profit. However, each individual sale cannot be divided into a return of cost and a profit. To do so would require such extensive records as to make the accounting impracticable. Therefore, the entire sales price of the goods is recorded as revenue. The entire cost of goods sold becomes a deduction from revenue in the income statement. The result is called *gross margin.*

The Sales Returns and Allowances Account

A customer may return merchandise because it is not exactly what he ordered; or the customer may be entitled to a reduction of the price, or *allowance,* for defective or broken goods that he retains. The effect of the entry to record a return or allowance is the opposite of a sale. However, when Cash or the customer's account is credited, an account entitled Sales Returns and Allowances is debited. This contra account is used, rather than Sales, so that a record may be available of the amount of returns and allowances.

Transaction:
The customer returned $10 worth of the merchandise (see the previous transaction).
Journal Entry:

Sales Returns and Allowances	10	
Accounts Receivable		10

The Sales Discounts Account

The customer may be allowed a *discount,* or reduction in price, if he pays within a limited period. Since the effect of a discount is to reduce the amount actually received from the sale, Sales Discounts is debited for the amount of the discount. Sales Discounts is a contra account to Sales and is used for the same reason that prompts the use of Sales Returns and Allowances—to supply management with valuable information about the business. When discounts are offered, the customer is in fact being offered the choice of paying (1) the full amount of the invoice or (2) the full amount reduced by the amount of the discount. The seller, however, does not know at the time of the sale whether the customer is going to avail himself of the discount. The customer is charged, therefore, with the full amount of the sale. If the customer pays within the discount period, payment is recorded under the *gross price method* as shown below.

Transaction:
The customer (see the previous transactions) paid his invoice within the discount period, deducting the allowed 2 percent sales discount.
Journal Entry:

Cash	186.20	
Sales Discounts	3.80	
Accounts Receivable		190.00

Computation:

Gross sale price	$200.00
Merchandise returned	10.00
	$190.00
2% discount	3.80
Cash received	$186.20

An alternative procedure, the *sales discounts not taken method,* is discussed later in this chapter.

The following partial income statement of the King Corporation, whose accounts are used for illustrative purposes in this chapter, shows the classification of the Sales and contra Sales accounts.

KING CORPORATION
Income Statement
For the Year Ended December 31, 19XX

Sales Revenue		
Sales		$124,200
Deduct: Sales Returns and Allowances	$2,400	
Sales Discounts	1,800	4,200
Net Sales Revenue		$120,000

The Purchases Account

It is customary in a merchandising business to use a separate Purchases account for all merchandise bought for resale. The account is *not* used for the purchase of operating supplies, for example, or for store equipment used in operations. The Purchases account is debited for the cost of the goods bought, shown on the seller's *invoice,* and therefore provides a record of the cost of the goods purchased during the period—not a record of the goods on hand. During the year, Purchases will always have a debit balance; the credits to the account are to close the account or to correct errors requiring offsetting debits to some other account(s).

Transaction:
Purchased merchandise for $800 on account.
Journal Entry:

Purchases	800	
Accounts Payable		800

The Transportation In Account

The invoice price of goods may include the cost of transporting the goods from the seller's place of business to that of the buyer. If so, no separation is made, and the entire purchase price is debited to Purchases. If the cost of transportation is not included, the carrier is paid directly by the buyer, who debits the amount to Transportation In. This account is added to Purchases in the income statement to determine the *delivered cost of merchandise.*

The following terms are used in connection with the transportation of merchandise:

1. *F.O.B.* (free on board) *destination* means that the seller bears the freight cost to the buyer's location. (Sometimes the buyer pays the cost and deducts the amount from his payment to the seller.)
2. *F.O.B. shipping point* means that the buyer bears the freight cost from the point of shipment to the destination.

Transaction:
Freight charges of $50 were paid on delivery of merchandise (see the previous transaction); terms of the purchase were F.O.B. shipping point.
Journal Entry:

Transportation In	50	
Cash		50

The Purchases Returns and Allowances Account

Goods bought for resale may be defective, broken, or not of the quality or quantity ordered. Either they may be returned for credit, or the seller may make an adjustment by reducing the original price.

Transaction:
Returned to the vendor $100 worth of defective merchandise.
Journal Entry:

Accounts Payable	100	
Purchases Returns and Allowances		100

Purchases Returns and Allowances is a contra account to Purchases. The same result could be accomplished by crediting Purchases, but it is useful to management to have the books show total Purchases as well as total Purchases Returns and Allowances. Analysis of the Purchases Returns and Allowances account may indicate the need for changes in the procedures of ordering and handling merchandise.

The Purchases Discounts Account

The Purchases Discounts account is used to record deductions from the purchase price of goods for payment made within the discount period specified by the seller. At the time of the purchase, the buyer may not know whether he will avail himself of the discount; the account with the seller (Accounts Payable) is therefore credited for the gross purchase price. As in the case of merchandise sales, an alternative procedure, the *discounts lost method* or *net price procedure,* is discussed later in the chapter.

Transaction:
Paid for merchandise (see the previous transactions) within the discount period and deducted the allowed discount of 1 percent.

Journal Entry:

Accounts Payable	700	
Cash		693
Purchases Discounts		7

Computation:

Gross purchase	$800
Merchandise returned	100
	$700
1% discount	7
Cash paid	$693

Merchandise Inventory Account

The system of accounting for merchandise inventory described in this chapter is called the *periodic inventory method.* A different method which yields a continuously updated inventory balance, called the *perpetual inventory system,* is described in a later chapter.

Merchandise purchased is recorded at cost in Purchases; merchandise sold is recorded at selling price in Sales. Therefore, an account, called Merchandise Inventory, is needed to show the merchandise actually on hand at the end of the accounting period. The amount is determined by making a list of the goods on hand, usually based on an actual count showing physical quantities and their cost. This *ending inventory* is entered in the books and becomes the beginning inventory of the next period. The amount in the ledger account will not be changed until the end of the next accounting period, because the Merchandise Inventory account is not used during the period. Since the account remains open, its balance—the beginning inventory—appears in the trial balance at the end of the period and is transferred to Income Summary when the books are closed. Concurrently, the new ending merchandise inventory is entered as a debit to Merchandise Inventory and a credit to Income Summary. Thus, the amount of the beginning inventory has been eliminated and replaced by the amount of the ending inventory. After the closing entries are posted, the Merchandise Inventory account in the general ledger of the King Corporation appears as shown below.

Merchandise Inventory			Acct. No. 121
Jan. 1	❶ 15,400	Dec. 31 C.E.	❷ 15,400
Dec. 31 C.E.	❸ **11,480**		

1. The debit amount of $15,400 is the cost of the beginning inventory on hand at January 1.
2. The credit posting of $15,400 closes the account temporarily and transfers the balance to Income Summary at December 31.
3. The debit posting of $11,480 is the cost of the closing inventory on hand at December 31.

FUNCTIONS OF THE MERCHANDISE ACCOUNTS

The following T accounts define the functions of the merchandise accounts and their locations in the financial statements. The accounts are presented in their income statement sequence. The description *Balance* in each account refers to the balance before the closing entries have been posted. After the closing entries are posted, all the merchandise accounts, except Merchandise Inventory, are closed.

Sales	
Debited At the end of the accounting period to close the account.	*Credited* During the accounting period for the sales price of goods sold. *Balance* A credit representing cumulative sales for the period to date. *Statement Classification* In the income statement, the first item under sales revenue.

Sales Returns and Allowances	
Debited During the accounting period for unwanted merchandise returned by customers and allowances granted for defective or broken goods. *Balance* A debit representing cumulative sales returns and allowances for the period to date. *Statement Classification* In the income statement, a deduction from sales revenue.	*Credited* At the end of the accounting period to close the account.

Sales Discounts	
Debited During the accounting period for the amounts that the customers deduct from the gross sales price when payment is made within the period established by the seller. *Balance* A debit representing cumulative sales discounts taken by customers for the period to date.	*Credited* At the end of the accounting period to close the account.

Sales Discounts (Continued)	
Statement Classification In the income statement, a deduction from sales revenue.	

Merchandise Inventory	
Debited At the end of each accounting period for the merchandise actually on hand. *Balance* A debit representing the cost of goods on hand at the beginning of the period. *Statement Classification* 1. In the balance sheet, under current assets. 2. In the income statement, in the cost of goods sold section, the beginning inventory is added to purchases and the ending inventory is deducted from the cost of merchandise available for sale.	*Credited* At the end of each accounting period to remove the old inventory from the account (same figure as beginning debit).

Purchases	
Debited During the accounting period for the purchase price of goods bought for resale. *Balance* A debit representing cumulative purchases for the period to date. *Statement Classification* In the income statement, added to the beginning inventory under cost of goods sold.	*Credited* At the end of the accounting period to close the account.

Transportation In	
Debited	*Credited*
During the accounting period for delivery costs—freight or cartage—on merchandise purchases.	At the end of the accounting period to close the account.
Balance	
A debit representing cumulative costs for the period to date incurred by the buyer for the delivery of merchandise.	
Statement Classification	
In the income statement, in the cost of goods sold section, added to purchases.	

Purchases Returns and Allowances	
Debited	*Credited*
At the end of the accounting period to close the account.	During the accounting period for unwanted merchandise returned to the vendor or allowances received for defective or broken merchandise.
	Balance
	A credit representing cumulative purchases returns and allowances for the period to date.
	Statement Classification
	In the income statement, in the cost of goods sold section, as a deduction from the gross cost of merchandise purchased.

Purchases Discounts	
Debited	*Credited*
At the end of the accounting period to close the account.	During the accounting period for the amounts of discount from the gross purchase price of merchandise when payment was made within the period established by the seller.
	Balance
	A credit representing cumulative purchases discounts taken for the period to date.
	Statement Classification
	In the income statement, in the cost of goods sold section, as a deduction from the gross cost of merchandise purchased.

COST OF GOODS SOLD AND GROSS MARGIN ON SALES

> The *cost of goods sold* is the difference between the cost of the goods available for sale during a period and the cost of the unsold goods on hand at the end of the period.

The term does not identify an active account for the recording of transactions when the periodic inventory method is in use, but rather the result of adding and subtracting the balances of several accounts. The computation is shown as

$$\text{Cost of goods sold} = \text{Beginning inventory} + \text{Net cost of purchases} - \text{Ending inventory}$$

Cost of goods sold = $15,400 + 63,280 − 11,480 = $67,200

Net cost of purchases is the total cost of purchases, plus transportation in, less returns, allowances, and discounts.

The income statement of the King Corporation is shown in Figure 5-1. It was prepared from the work sheet in Figure 5-3.

The income statement of the King Corporation shows all the accounts needed to derive the cost of goods sold of $67,200.

The *gross margin on sales* of $52,800 is what is left after the cost of goods sold of $67,200 is deducted from the net sales revenue of $120,000. The term *gross* indicates that the operating expenses necessary to the conduct of the business must still be deducted to arrive at the *net operating margin.* If the gross margin on sales is less than the operating expenses, the difference is a net operating loss for the period.

THE OPERATING EXPENSE ACCOUNTS

Operating expenses include salaries, postage, telephone and telegraph, heat and light, insurance, advertising, and any other costs incurred for goods or services used in operating the business. The breakdown of operating expenses into a number of detailed accounts facilitates analyses and comparisons that aid in the management of the business. The amount of detail shown depends on the size and type of the business and on the needs and wishes of the management.

The operating expenses are often classified into *selling* and *general and administrative.* The expenses incurred in packaging the product, advertising it, making the sale, and delivering the product are classified as selling expenses. Salesmen's salaries, commissions, and supplies used in the Sales department are examples of expenses incurred in making the sale. Expenses of delivering the product include freight paid by the seller (transportation out) and the expense of operating delivery vehicles. Expenses such as rent, taxes, and insurance, to the extent that they are incurred in selling the product, are also classified as selling expenses. All other operating expenses are classified as general and administrative, including office expenses, executive salaries, and the portion of rent, taxes, and insurance applicable to the administrative function of the business. The expenses that are common to both selling and administrative functions may be apportioned on some equitable basis. If an apportionment is not practicable, the account should be classified under the function it serves most. In Figure 5-1, the operating expense accounts that are entirely related to selling are classified as such; all the others are classified as general and administrative. The total operating expenses of $41,400 are deducted from the gross margin on sales of $52,800 to arrive at the net operating margin of $11,400.

OTHER REVENUE AND OTHER EXPENSES

The Other Revenue and Other Expenses sections of the income statement serve a valuable function; they permit calculation of the net operating margin without it being distorted by nonoperating items and link the net operating margin for the period with the net income for that period.

Other Revenue

Some common examples of items classified as other revenue are gains from the sale of securities, dividends on shares of stock owned, and gains from the sale of plant and equipment. In Figure 5-1, the King Corporation shows

Figure 5-1 Income Statement

KING CORPORATION
Income Statement
For the Year Ended December 31, 19XX

Gross Sales Revenue				$124,200
Deduct: Sales Returns and Allowances			$ 2,400	
Sales Discounts			1,800	4,200
Net Sales Revenue				$120,000
Cost of Goods Sold				
Merchandise Inventory, January 1			$15,400	
Purchases		$63,580		
Transportation In		4,800		
Gross Delivered Cost of Purchases		$68,380		
Deduct: Purchases Returns and Allowances	$1,500			
Purchases Discounts	3,600	5,100		
Net Cost of Purchases			63,280	
Cost of Merchandise Available for Sale			$78,680	
Deduct Merchandise Inventory December 31			11,480	
Cost of Goods Sold				67,200
Gross Margin on Sales				$ 52,800
Deduct Operating Expenses				
Selling Expenses				
Salesmen's Salaries Expense		$12,000		
Transportation Out Expense		2,400		
Advertising Expense		3,000		
Total Selling Expenses			$17,400	
General and Administrative Expenses				
Rent Expense		$ 6,000		
Property Tax Expense		7,800		
Heat and Light Expense		2,160		
Miscellaneous General Expense		480		
Insurance Expense		1,920		
Supplies Expense		2,040		
Depreciation Expense—Machinery and Equipment		3,600		
Total General and Administrative Expenses			24,000	
Total Operating Expenses				41,400
Net Operating Margin				$ 11,400
Other Revenue				
Interest Earned		$ 125		
Rent Earned		300	$ 425	
Other Expenses				
Interest Expense		$ 75		
Loss on Sale of Equipment		100	175	250
Net Income Before Income Taxes				$ 11,650
Income Taxes				5,825
Net Income				$ 5,825

$125 in interest earned and $300 in rent earned under Other Revenue. These are additional examples; they are included under Other Revenue because they arose from a source other than the basic business purpose of King Corporation.

Other Expenses

Nonoperating expenses such as interest on money borrowed from the bank or on notes given to creditors for the purchase of merchandise, or losses from the sale of plant and equipment are shown under Other Expenses. In Figure 5-1, the King Corporation shows $75 in interest expense and $100 from a loss on a sale of equipment under this heading.

The King Corporation added $250, the excess of other revenue over other expenses, to the net operating margin. If other expenses exceed other revenue, the expenses are listed first and the excess is deducted from the net operating margin.

In the absence of other revenue or other expenses, net operating margin becomes net income and net operating loss becomes net loss.

COMPLETION OF THE WORK SHEET

The procedure for completing the work sheet of a merchandising business is similar to that of a service business, with the exception of the account for merchandise inventory.

At the end of the period, the balance of the Merchandise Inventory account, the beginning inventory of $15,400, is extended to the Income Statement Debit column of the work sheet because it is part of the cost of merchandise available for sale. The ending inventory, $11,480, is shown in the Income Statement Credit column because it is a deduction from the cost of merchandise available for sale, and in the Balance Sheet Debit column because it is an asset. This treatment preserves the equality of debits and credits in the work sheet, as shown in Figure 5-2.

Figure 5-2
Partial Work Sheet

KING CORPORATION
Partial Work Sheet
For the Year Ended December 31, 19XX

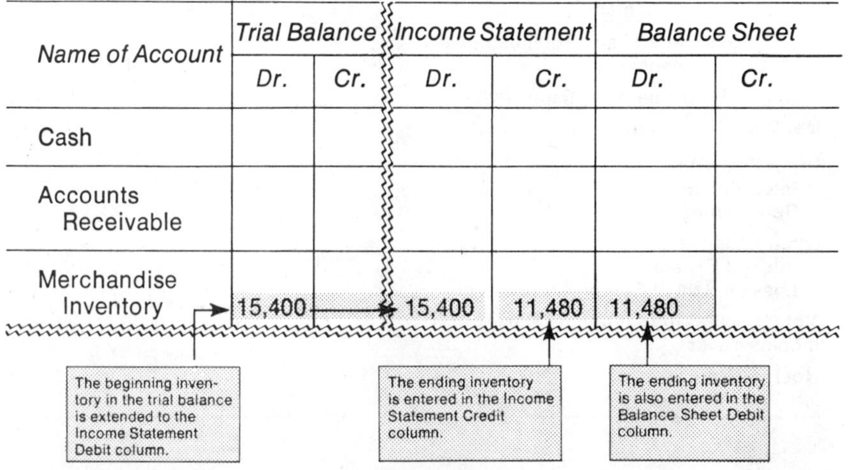

Name of Account	*Trial Balance*		*Income Statement*		*Balance Sheet*	
	Dr.	*Cr.*	*Dr.*	*Cr.*	*Dr.*	*Cr.*
Cash						
Accounts Receivable						
Merchandise Inventory	15,400		15,400	11,480	11,480	

Figure 5-3 Work Sheet

KING CORPORATION
Work Sheet
For the Year Ended December 31, 19XX

Acct. No.	Account Title	Trial Balance		Adjustments		Income Statement		Balance Sheet	
		Dr.	Cr.	Dr.	Cr.	Dr.	Cr.	Dr.	Cr.
101	Cash	7,200						7,200	
111	Accounts Receivable	39,800						39,800	
121	Merchandise Inventory	15,400				15,400	11,480	11,480	
131	Office Supplies	3,240			(b) 2,040			1,200	
141	Prepaid Insurance	3,740			(a) 1,920			1,820	
151	Machinery and Equipment	70,100						70,100	
151A	Accumulated Depreciation—Machinery and Equipment		7,200		(c) 3,600				10,800
201	Accounts Payable		17,700						17,700
202	Notes Payable		7,300						7,300
221	Mortgage Payable		20,000						20,000
301	Capital Stock		60,000						60,000
302	Retained Earnings		5,150						5,150
303	Dividends	1,000						1,000	
401	Sales		124,200				124,200		
402	Sales Returns and Allowances	2,400				2,400			
403	Sales Discounts	1,800				1,800			
501	Purchases	63,580				63,580			
502	Transportation In	4,800				4,800			
503	Purchases Returns and Allowances		1,500				1,500		
504	Purchases Discounts		3,600				3,600		
601	Salesmen's Salaries Expense	12,000				12,000			
602	Transportation Out Expense	2,400				2,400			
603	Advertising Expense	3,000				3,000			
701	Rent Expense	6,000				6,000			
702	Property Tax Expense	7,800				7,800			
703	Heat and Light Expense	2,160				2,160			
704	Miscellaneous General Expense	480				480			
801	Interest Earned		125				125		
802	Rent Earned		300				300		
821	Interest Expense	75				75			
822	Loss on Sale of Equipment	100				100			
		247,075	247,075						
705	Insurance Expense			(a) 1,920		1,920			
706	Office Supplies Expense			(b) 2,040		2,040			
707	Depreciation Expense—Machinery and Equipment			(c) 3,600		3,600			
708	Income Tax Expense			(d) 5,825		5,825			
709	Income Taxes Payable				(d) 5,825				5,825
				13,385	13,385	135,380	141,205	132,600	126,775
	Net Income for the Year					5,825			5,825
						141,205	141,205	132,600	132,600

The work sheet of the King Corporation is shown in Figure 5-3. There are a number of possible variations in the form; for instance, the Adjusted Trial Balance columns are omitted in this example. The combined Trial Balance and Adjustment column amounts are extended directly to the proper Income Statement or Balance Sheet columns.

COMPLETED FINANCIAL STATEMENTS

Figure 5-4 shows the statement of retained earnings and Figure 5-5 shows the classified balance sheet. These statements and the income statement (Figure 5-1) were prepared after the completion of the work sheet.

Figure 5-4 Statement of Retained Earnings

KING CORPORATION
Statement of Retained Earnings
For the Year Ended December 31, 19XX

Retained Earnings, January 1	$ 5,150
Add Net Income for the Year	5,825
Total	$10,975
Deduct Dividends	1,000
Retained Earnings, December 31	$ 9,975

Figure 5-5 Balance Sheet

KING CORPORATION
Balance Sheet
December 31, 19XX

Assets		
Current Assets		
Cash	$ 7,200	
Accounts Receivable	39,800	
Merchandise Inventory	11,480	
Office Supplies	1,200	
Prepaid Insurance	1,820	
Total Current Assets		$ 61,500
Plant and Equipment		
Machinery and Equipment	$70,100	
Deduct Accum. Deprec.	10,800	
Total Plant and Equipment		59,300
Total Assets		$120,800

Liabilities and Shareholders' Equity		
Current Liabilities		
Accounts Payable	$17,700	
Notes Payable	7,300	
Income Taxes Payable	5,825	
Total Current Liabilities		$ 30,825
Long-Term Liabilities		
Mortgage Payable		20,000
Total Liabilities		$ 50,825
Shareholders' Equity		
Capital Stock	$60,000	
Retained Earnings	9,975	
Total Shareholders' Equity		69,975
Total Liabilities and Equity		$120,800

CLOSING ENTRIES

The procedure for recording the closing entries in a merchandising business is essentially the same as that in a service business. The closing entries, including the closing of the beginning merchandise inventory, and the recording of the ending inventory, are shown in Figure 5-6. After the closing entries are posted, all the revenue and expense accounts have zero balances.

GENERAL JOURNAL **Page 12**

		Closing Entries			
Dec.	31	**Merchandise Inventory (12.31)**	**121**	**11,480**	
		Sales	401	124,200	
		Purchases Returns and Allowances	503	1,500	
		Purchases Discounts	504	3,600	
		Interest Earned	801	125	
		Rent Earned	802	300	
		Income Summary	901		141,205
		To record the ending inventory and to close the temporary credit balance accounts.			
	31	Income Summary	901	135,380	
		Merchandise Inventory (1.1)	**121**		**15,400**
		Sales Returns and Allowances	402		2,400
		Sales Discounts	403		1,800
		Purchases	501		63,580
		Transportation In	502		4,800
		Salesmen's Salaries Expense	601		12,000
		Transportation Out Expense	602		2,400
		Advertising Expense	603		3,000
		Rent Expense	701		6,000
		Property Tax Expense	702		7,800
		Heat and Light Expense	703		2,160
		Miscellaneous General Expense	704		480
		Interest Expense	821		75
		Loss on Sale of Equipment	822		100
		Insurance Expense	705		1,920
		Office Supplies Expense	706		2,040
		Depreciation Expense—Machinery and Equipment	707		3,600
		Income Tax Expense	708		5,825
		To close the beginning inventory and the temporary debit balance accounts.			
	31	Income Summary	901	5,825	
		Retained Earnings	302		5,825
		To transfer net income to Retained Earnings.			
	31	Retained Earnings	302	1,000	
		Dividends	303		1,000
		To close Dividends to Retained Earnings.			

Figure 5-6
Closing Entries

Entry 1
The ending inventory and each account in the credit column of the Income Statement is debited and the total is credited to Income Summary.

Entry 2
The beginning inventory and each account in the debit column of the Income Summary is credited and the total is debited to Income Summary.

Entry 3
The balance in Income Summary is transferred to Retained Earnings.

Entry 4
The balance of Dividends is closed to Retained Earnings.

INTERIM FINANCIAL STATEMENTS

Financial statements are prepared at least once a year, at which time the adjusting and closing entries are recorded and posted to the general ledger. The closing of the books at intervals of less than one year is not customary but has been assumed in this text as a convenience in illustrating the periodic summary. Financial statements, however, may be prepared at frequent intervals—monthly or quarterly—without the formal recording and posting of the adjusting and closing entries.

Financial statements may be produced at regular or intermittent intervals during the accounting period for external reasons, such as the establishment of credit for a bank loan, or for the internal use of managers and shareholders. They are referred to as ***interim statements*** and are prepared with the aid of the work sheet. The general ledger account balances as of the end of the interim period are entered on the work sheet, the adjustments are listed, the adjusted balances are extended to the appropriate Income Statement and Balance Sheet columns, and formal statements are prepared.

The amounts in the Trial Balance columns of the work sheet represent the cumulative general ledger totals for the year to date and the adjustments are for the same interval; hence, the amounts in the interim income statement are for the year to date. However, if monthly income statements are desired, the amounts on the statements for the previous months are deducted from the amounts on the current statement, thereby providing year-to-date figures as well as results of the current period. The amounts in the Balance Sheet columns of the work sheet are the correct amounts for the balance sheet as of the close of the current period.

The preparation of interim statements requires a determination of the cost of the merchandise on hand. Taking a detailed physical inventory, however, is costly and time-consuming and may not be necessary. Alternative methods of determining the ending inventory, such as the gross margin method of inventory valuation and the perpetual inventory system, are discussed in Chapter 8.

CASH DISCOUNTS—IMPLICATIONS TO MANAGEMENT

Cash discounts are computed on the net sales price; the conditions of payment are stated on the invoice. Typical cash discount terms are 2/10, n/30 and 1/10, n/60; the term n/30 means that the invoice must be paid without discount within 30 days (or 45 days if the term is n/45). The term of 2/10, n/30 means that if the buyer of merchandise pays within 10 days from the date shown on the invoice, he may deduct 2 percent from the invoice price, or he may take an additional 20 days, or 30 days in all, before paying the gross amount. It is important to recognize the magnitude of the discount offered. This can be done best if the discount is converted into its equivalent annual interest rate. Assuming terms of 2/10, n/30, the cost of the additional 20 days is high, because the loss of the 2 percent discount amounts to one-tenth of 1 percent per day (2% ÷ 20), or 36 percent per 365-day year (0.1% × 365). The prudent businessman should therefore take all cash discounts, even if he has to borrow the money to do so.

MANAGEMENT CONTROL—THE EXCEPTION PRINCIPLE

The control principle of management by exception involves isolating those amounts or accounts which indicate operating inefficiencies, and focusing attention on the areas that might require corrective action. Since only exceptions from the norm require such corrective action, management's task is simplified and expedited by separating from the mass of data the exceptional items for further study.

The alternative method for recording cash discounts, the *discounts not taken method,* illustrates the principle of management by exception. Under the *gross price method* discussed earlier in this chapter, the volume of discounts granted or taken is accumulated in the Sales Discounts and Purchases Discounts accounts. Management is interested primarily, however, not in the amount of discounts taken, since it assumes that all available discounts should be taken, but rather in the exceptions—that is, the discounts not taken.

Sales Discounts Not Taken

Assume that a $1,000 sale is made on April 1, with terms of 2/10, n/30, and that payment is received on April 10. The entries, recorded net of discount, are:

Apr.	1	Accounts Receivable	980	
		Sales		980
	10	Cash	980	
		Accounts Receivable		980

If the payment were received on April 25, the entry would be:

Apr.	25	Cash	1,000	
		Accounts Receivable		980
		Sales Discounts Not Taken		20

Sales Discounts Not Taken is classified as Other Revenue in the income statement.

Management should make a careful analysis of Sales Discounts Not Taken. A customer who does not take advantage of discount terms of 2/10, n/30, for example, is foregoing savings equivalent to an annual rate of 36 percent. This indicates an unwillingness or an inability to pay debts promptly, significant information in granting credit or evaluating possible losses from uncollectible accounts.

Purchases Discounts Lost Method

The rationale for the alternative method of recording purchases discounts under the purchases discounts lost method or net price procedure is the same as for the recording of sales discounts. Purchases are recorded at net of discount, and discounts lost are entered in a special account.

To illustrate the accounting for discounts lost by the purchases discounts lost method, assume that a purchase of $5,000 in merchandise is received on

July 1, with terms of 2/10 n/30, and that the invoice is paid on July 10. Purchases and Accounts Payable recorded *net of discount* are:

July	1	Purchases	4,900	
		Accounts Payable		4,900
	10	Accounts Payable	4,900	
		Cash		4,900

If the invoice were not paid until July 15, the entries would be:

July	1	Purchases	4,900	
		Accounts Payable		4,900
	15	Accounts Payable	4,900	
		Purchases Discounts Lost	100	
		Cash		5,000

Under the discounts lost procedure, the debit to Purchases is $4,900 whether or not the discount is lost, and the loss of $100 appears in a separate general and administrative expense account, isolating the amount for the detection of possible laxities in procedures. The loss of available discounts may indicate a weakness in the organization, such as lack of bank credit or slowness in processing invoices for payment. The cost of goods purchased is not increased when discounts are lost; the amount is classified under other expenses.

There are some disadvantages to recording purchases at the net price: (1) the amount of discounts taken is not reported separately in the income statement; (2) statements from creditors do not agree with the net amounts recorded in the accounts payable ledger; (3) the amounts entered on individual inventory record cards may not agree with the net amounts entered as purchases, since the inventory may be carried at invoice price; (4) the additional information may not justify the increased clerical costs and inconveniences; (5) an adjusting entry is needed at the end of the period to record lapsed discounts by debiting Purchases Discounts Lost and crediting Accounts Payable.

TRADE DISCOUNTS

Another class of discount is the *trade discount,* which, unlike the cash discount, is not recorded in the accounts. A trade discount is a percentage reduction from a list price. The seller prints a catalog in which the prices of the various articles are shown. The actual price charged may differ from the list price because of the class of buyer (wholesalers, retailers, and so on), the quantity ordered, or changes in the catalog. The granting of trade discounts eliminates the need for frequent reprinting of catalogs or printing different lists for different classes of buyers. If more than one discount is given—a so-called *chain discount*—each discount is applied successively to the declining balance to arrive at the invoice price. Thus, the actual price of an item listed at $300 less trade discounts of 20 percent, 10 percent, and 5 percent is $205.20. (Another way to compute the actual price is $\$300 \times .80 \times .90 \times .95 =$ $205.20.)

GLOSSARY

Cash Discount A reduction in price offered by terms of sale or purchase to encourage payment within the discount period.

Cost of Goods Sold A computation that appears on the income statement in a separate section. It is calculated by adding net purchases to the beginning inventory to derive the cost of goods available for sale and then deducting from this sum the ending inventory.

Exception Principle A principle of management that involves isolating amounts or accounts that indicate operating inefficiencies to focus attention on the areas that may require corrective action.

F.O.B. Destination The seller of merchandise bears the transportation cost to the buyer's location.

F.O.B. Shipping Point The buyer of merchandise bears the transportation cost from the point of shipment to the destination.

General and Administrative Expenses Amounts paid for goods or services generally reflecting the cost of supporting the marketing of the product other than the direct marketing cost.

Gross Margin The amount obtained by deducting the cost of goods sold from the net sales revenue.

Gross Price Method Accounting for cash discounts by accumulating the amount of the discount in Sales Discounts and in Purchases Discounts accounts.

Interim Statements Financial statements produced at regular or intermittent intervals during the accounting period for internal reasons.

Net Cost of Purchases The cost of all merchandise bought for sale including transportation in but reduced by purchases returns and allowances and purchases discounts.

Net Price Method A procedure illustrative of the principle of management by exception by requiring that purchases and sales be recorded at net of discount prices in anticipation of qualifying for the discount.

Operating Expenses Past or present expenditures for goods or services used or expired in operating the business.

Other Revenue and Other Expenses Extraneous items of ordinary revenue and expense that arise from a source other than the basic business purpose of the company.

Selling Expenses Direct expenses incurred in marketing the product.

Trade Discount A percentage reduction in a list price that, unlike the cash discount, is not recorded in the accounts.

QUESTIONS

Q5-1. What is the principal difference between the accounts of a merchandising business and those of a service business?

Q5-2. What is the procedure for entering and extending the merchandise inventory accounts on the work sheet of a merchandising business?

Q5-3. (a) What is the function of the Sales account? (b) the Sales Returns and Allowances account? (c) the Sales Discounts account?

Q5-4. (a) What is the function of the Purchases account? (b) the Purchases Returns and Allowances account? (c) the Purchases Discounts account? (d) the Transportation In account?

Q5-5. (a) What is the function of the Merchandise Inventory account? (b) How is its amount determined? In which columns of the work sheet is (c) the beginning inventory shown? (d) the ending inventory?

Q5-6. (a) How is the cost of goods sold determined? (b) Why is the cost of goods sold not recorded at the time of the sale? (c) What is the relationship between the cost of goods sold and the gross margin on sales?

Q5-7. Why is it desirable to show the following items separately on the income statement: (a) operating expenses and other expenses? (b) net operating margin and other revenue?

Q5-8. (a) How does the procedure of closing the books of a merchandising business differ from that of closing the books of a service business? (b) What advantage is gained by including merchandise inventory, beginning and ending, in the closing entries rather than in the adjusting entries? (c) List the various uses an accountant can make of the work sheet.

Q5-9. (a) What is the purpose of interim statements? (b) For whom are they prepared? (c) How are they prepared? (d) What special problems do they create?

Q5-10. Assume that a merchandise transaction was made on September 4. In each case determine the latest possible payment date to allow the discount deduction. (a) 1/10, n/30; (b) 1/10, n/60.

Q5-11. (a) Distinguish between a cash discount and a trade discount. (b) Why are trade discounts used in quoting prices? (c) What are the advantages, if any, of recording purchases of merchandise at the invoice amount less cash discount, or net, over recording the full, or gross, invoice amount? (d) Explain the term *2/10, n/30.* (e) Discuss and illustrate alternative income statement presentations of Purchases Discounts and Sales Discounts.

DEMONSTRATION PROBLEMS

DP5-1. (*Cash discounts: gross and net price procedures*) The following transactions were completed by the Hehre Company during June:

June 1 Sold merchandise on account to the Leib Company for $900; terms, 2/10, n/30.

5 Purchased merchandise from the Jean Company for $1,000; terms, 1½/10, n/30.

7 Purchased merchandise on account from the Faro Corporation for $850; terms, 1/10, n/30, F.O.B. shipping point.

7 Sold merchandise to the Mutual Corporation for $1,200; terms, 1/10, n/30.

10 Paid freight charges of $20 on the merchandise purchased from the Faro Corporation.

11 Received payment from the Leib Company, less the cash discount.

12 Received a $100 credit (gross amount) for defective merchandise returned to the Faro Corporation.

15 Paid the Faro Corporation.

25 Paid the Jean Company.

25 Received payment from the Mutual Corporation.

Required:

1a. Journalize the transactions, using the gross price method.
 b. Prepare the cost of goods sold section of the income statement. Assume the following inventories: June 1, $500; June 30, $850.
2a. Journalize the transactions, using the net price procedure.
 b. Prepare the cost of goods sold section of the income statement. Assume inventories as in 1b.
3. Under the net price procedure, how are Purchases Discounts Lost and Sales Discounts Not Taken classified in the income statement?

DP5-2. ***(Work sheet and financial statements)*** The trial balance of Duarte Company Ltd. is shown below.

Account Title	*Debits*	*Credits*
Cash	$ 84,200	
Accounts Receivable	366,300	
Merchandise Inventory	110,000	
Office Supplies	46,200	
Prepaid Insurance	50,900	
Store Equipment	479,100	
Accumulated Depreciation—Store Equipment		$ 77,500
Accounts Payable		125,000
Notes Payable		69,300
Capital Stock		570,500
Retained Earnings		132,000
Dividends	44,000	
Sales		1,098,300
Sales Returns and Allowances	22,000	
Sales Discounts	20,300	
Purchases	649,000	
Transportation In	33,000	
Purchases Returns and Allowances		13,200
Purchases Discounts		19,800
Salesmen's Salaries Expense	84,500	
Transportation Out Expense	10,600	
Advertising Expense	31,700	
Rent Expense	42,300	
Heat and Light Expense	15,900	
Miscellaneous Expense	15,600	
Totals	$2,105,600	$2,105,600

Supplementary data on December 31:

a. Merchandise inventory, $92,400
b. Unexpired insurance, $30,800
c. Office supplies on hand, $17,600
d. Depreciation on store equipment, $10,600
e. Estimated income taxes for the year, $52,800

Required:

1. Complete the work sheet.
2. Prepare an income statement.
3. Prepare a balance sheet.
4. Prepare a statement of retained earnings.

DP5-3. (*Closing entries*) The following account balances were taken from the Income Statement columns of John O'Brien's work sheet for the year ended December 31.

Account Title	Income Statement Debit	Income Statement Credit
Merchandise Inventory	23,760	25,650
Sales		62,370
Sales Returns and Allowances	745	
Sales Discounts	1,215	
Purchases	19,210	
Transportation In	1,015	
Purchases Returns and Allowances		610
Purchases Discounts		1,730
Selling Expenses	4,590	
General Expenses	9,720	
Totals	60,255	90,360
Net Income	30,105	
	90,360	90,360

The Balance Sheet Debit column showed a balance of $3,500 in the dividends account.

Required: Prepare closing journal entries.

PROBLEMS

P5-1. During the year, the Corvi Sales Company purchased merchandise costing $10,900. In each of the following cases, calculate (a) the total merchandise available for sale, and (b) the cost of goods sold for the year.

Case	Beginning Inventory	Ending Inventory
1	None	None
2	$ 9,000	None
3	12,000	$15,000
4	None	3,000

P5-2. From the following information taken from the books of the Walker Company, prepare a partial income statement through gross margin on sales:

Merchandise Inventory, January 1	$ 1,800
Merchandise Inventory, January 31	1,300
Sales	12,900
Transportation In	400
Purchases Discounts	330
Sales Returns and Allowances	210
Purchases	5,600
Sales Discounts	120
Purchases Returns and Allowances	100

P5-3. Prepare general journal entries to record the following transactions on the books of the Baez Company:

July 1 Sold merchandise to the Kane Company for $4,800, terms 2/10, n/30; F.O.B. destination. The Kane Company paid $275 freight on the shipment.

5 The Kane Company returned some unsatisfactory merchandise and received credit for $150.

10 The Kane Company mailed a check to the Baez Company for the net amount due.

P5-4. Prepare general journal entries to record the transactions in P5-3 on the books of the Kane Company.

P5-5. Prepare general journal entries to record the transactions in P5-3 on the books (a) of the Baez Company, and (b) of the Kane Company, assuming that the terms were F.O.B. shipping point.

P5-6. On June 5, Robert Bacon, who uses the net price procedure, purchased merchandise for $5,000; terms 2/10, n/30. The invoice was paid on July 1. (a) Record the purchase and the payment of the invoice. (b) Is the net cost of merchandise the same under both the gross and the net procedures? Show your computations. (c) Assume that Bacon takes advantage of all purchases discounts. Is there any advantage in his using the gross price method of recording the purchase of merchandise?

P5-7. Jean Gaylord, who uses the net price procedure, sold merchandise on May 1 for $6,000; terms 1/10, n/30. The customer paid the invoice on May 20. (a) Record the sale and the collection of the account receivable. (b) Would net sales revenue be the same under both the gross and the net procedures? Show your computations. (c) Compare and contrast the significance to management of the Sales Discounts Not Taken account and the Sales Discounts account.

P5-8. The Cordoza Company grants customer discounts on partial payments made within the discount period. On May 5, the company sold merchandise to Paul DeLobos for $5,000; terms 3/10, n/30. On May 15, the company received $2,500 to apply on account; on June 4, it received a check for the balance of the invoice. (a) Record the transactions for the Cordoza Company using (1) the net price procedure and (2) the gross price procedure. (b) Make the corresponding journal entries for Paul DeLobos.

P5-9. The following information is taken from John Rolando's books as of December 31:

Trial Balance		*Adjustments Data*	
1. Prepaid Insurance	$ 1,500	Expired Insurance	$1,000
2. Rent Expense	5,000	Rent paid in advance	1,200
3. Wages Expense	10,000	Accrued wages	500
4. Interest Expense	500	Accrued interest	100
5. Unearned Rent	4,000	Rent earned	2,500
6. Interest Earned	2,000	Unearned interest	600

For each account: (a) prepare the adjusting entry; (b) state the amount to be shown in the income statement; (c) state the amount to be shown in the balance sheet.

P5-10. The following items are taken from John Inge's trial balance on December 31. The books are closed annually on December 31. All the store equipment was acquired three years ago.

	Debits	*Credits*
Notes Receivable (90-day, 9% note, dated December 1)	$ 8,000	
Prepaid Insurance (1-year policy, dated Aug. 1)	720	
Prepaid Rent (payable one year in advance on Sept. 1)	1,800	
Store Equipment (10-year life; salvage value $500)	20,500	
Notes Payable (120-day, 10% note, dated November 1)		$4,000
Rent Earned (1-year lease commencing April 1)		4,400

Prepare the adjusting entries.

P5-11. A section of the work sheet of the Ada Nevson Company is presented below. Enter the beginning and the ending inventory amounts in the appropriate columns.

Account Title	*Trial Balance*		*Income Statement*		*Balance Sheet*	
	Dr.	*Cr.*	*Dr.*	*Cr.*	*Dr.*	*Cr.*
Cash	4,000				4,000	
Accounts Receivable	11,000				11,000	
Merchandise Inventory	9000		9000	13000	13000	
Beginning inventory	$ 9,000					
Ending inventory	13,000					

P5-12. Footings for the partially completed work sheet of the Cyril Corporation are shown below.

Income Statement		*Balance Sheet*	
Dr.	*Cr.*	*Dr.*	*Cr.*
15,650	20,200	43,100	38,550

Complete the work sheet.

P5-13. The Songin Company closes its books annually on December 31. An examination of its insurance policies show the following information:

Policy No.	*Unexpired Premium—January 1*	*Remaining Life—January 1*
3954	$630	21 months
4872	490	14 months
670	240	6 months

The following policies were purchased.

Policy No.	*Date of Policy*	*Life of Policy*	*Prepaid Premium*
65412	March 1	2 years	$ 720
8941	August 1	3 years	900
4624	November 1	5 years	2,100

a. What was the balance of the Prepaid Insurance account as of January 1? The Songin Company debits Prepaid Insurance for all purchases of insurance policies.

b. What was the adjusting entry necessary on December 31?

P5-14. On January 1, Year 1, the Matthew Company entered into a 10-year lease for the rental of a factory from the Seth Investment Corporation. The terms of the lease provided for a rental adjustment whereby the Matthew Company would pay the Seth Investment Corporation for any increase in real estate taxes in excess of a base assessment of $100,000 and a tax rate of $62 per $1,000 of assessed valuation. Make the adjusting entries for the Matthew Company for Year 1, Year 2, and Year 3, assuming the following:

Year	*Assessment*	*Tax Rate per $1,000*
1	$100,000	$65
2	100,000	68
3	105,000	70

P5-15. The balance sheet of the Stein Company at December 31, Year 1, showed:

Accrued Interest Receivable	$2,600
Unearned Interest Revenue	300

During Year 2, interested collected in cash amounted to $4,800. The balance sheet at December 31, Year 2, showed:

Accrued Interest Receivable	$2,280
Unearned Interest Revenue	195

Compute the amount of interest earned that should appear on the income statement for Year 2.

P5-16. The following information was taken from the records of the Mather Company at September 30, Year 2, the end of the fiscal year:

a. On April 1, $5,700 was collected as subscription revenue for one year; Unearned Subscription Revenue was credited.

b. On March 1, a 1-year, 10% note for $5,100 was received from a customer.

c. The company has an 8% mortgage note payable outstanding with a face value of $850,000; the interest on this note is payable semiannually on March 1 and September 1.

d. The store supplies inventory on September 30, Year 1, was $10,625; acquisitions of $31,550 for the year were charged to Stores Supplies; a physical count on September 30, Year 2, disclosed store supplies costing $14,450 on hand.

Make the adjusting entries.

P5-17. The accountant of the Jesson Corporation prepared the following trial balance at December 31.

Account Title	*Debits*	*Credits*
Cash	$ 2,850	
Accounts Receivable	92,500	
Prepaid Insurance	4,800	
Merchandise Inventory	104,500	
Store Equipment	57,800	
Accumulated Depreciation— Store Equipment		$ 11,400
Accounts Payable		17,000
Notes Payable		38,000
Capital Stock		95,000
Retained Earnings		20,900
Dividends	19,800	
Sales		345,800
Purchases	161,500	
Advertising Expense	7,000	
Miscellaneous Selling Expense	7,600	
Wages Expense	55,100	
Miscellaneous General Expense	11,200	
Rent Expense	4,600	
Interest Expense	900	
Interest Earned		750
Rent Earned		1,300
Totals	$530,150	$530,150

Additional data:

a. Included in Advertising Expense is a charge of $1,520 for space in next year's issue of a monthly periodical.

b. The Prepaid Insurance account consists of premiums paid on the following policies:

Policy No.	*Date of Policy*	*Life of Policy*	*Premium*
A938	January 1	6 months	$1,900
J672	September 1	3 years	2,300
N531	October 1	1 year	600
Total			$4,800

c. The Store Equipment account consists of the following acquisitions:

Purchase Date	Cost	Useful Life	Salvage Value
Prior to January 1	$41,800	10 years	$3,800
April 1	2,700	10 years	400
July 1	1,900	5 years	200
October 1	11,400	15 years	1,200
Total	$57,800		

d. A physical count of store supplies shows $475 worth on hand at December 31. At the time of purchase, Miscellaneous General Expense was debited.
e. On October 1, the Jesson Corporation rented some of its equipment to the Jere Company for eight months at $325 a month. A payment of $1,300 was received on October 1.
f. Wages earned by employees but unpaid on December 31 totaled $950.
g. Property taxes of $575 are unpaid.
h. An invoice of $575 from the Packing Materials Company, dated December 14, for shipping cartons is discovered and is to be recorded as a Miscellaneous Selling Expense.
i. Shipping cartons on hand at December 31 were worth $575.
j. The Notes Payable account consists of a 90-day, 9% note dated November 1, issued to a bank.
k. The merchandise inventory at December 31 was $85,500. Income taxes for the year were estimated at $21,850.

Required: In schedule form as in the example, show:

a. The adjusting entries.
b. The section of the balance sheet affected by the adjusting entries.
c. The section of the income statement affected by the adjusting entries.
d. The amount reported on the appropriate financial statement.

Item 1 has been entered as an example.

Item	*Explanation*	*Adjusting Entries*		*Financial Statement Classification*	*Amount Reported on Financial Statement*
		Dr.	*Cr.*		
1	Prepaid Advertising	1,520		Current Asset (PS)	1,520
	Advertising Expense		1,520	Selling Expense (IS)	5,480

P5-18. The following balances, arranged in alphabetical order, were taken from the Adjusted Trial Balance columns of the work sheet of the Beaver Corporation for the fiscal year ended December 31. The inventory on that date was $27,100.

Account Title	Amount
Accounts Payable	$ 9,775
Accounts Receivable	13,650
Accumulated Depreciation—Delivery Equipment	4,550
Advertising Expense	1,425
Capital Stock	53,700
Cash	3,900
Delivery Equipment	13,650
Delivery Expense	2,850
Depreciation Expense—Delivery Equipment	2,150
Dividends	3,900
Gain on Disposal of Temporary Investments	450
Heat and Light Expense	1,160
Income Tax Expense	2,800
Income Taxes Payable	2,800
Insurance Expense	2,240
Interest Earned	325
Interest Expense	210
Loss on Disposal of Land	4,560
Temporary Investments	28,380
Merchandise Inventory, January 1	29,100
Notes Payable	2,600
Office Supplies	920
Prepaid Advertising	1,170
Prepaid Insurance	1,850
Purchases	77,600
Purchases Discounts	940
Purchases Returns and Allowances	1,600
Rent Earned	2,350
Rent Expense	3,250
Retained Earnings	13,000
Sales	120,250
Sales Discounts	2,100
Sales Returns and Allowances	5,600
Salesmen's Salaries Expense	8,175
Transportation In	1,700

Required:

1. Prepare an income statement.
2. Prepare a statement of retained earnings.
3. Prepare a balance sheet.

P5-19. The following information was taken from the general ledger of the Helene Corporation on December 31.

Account Title	Amount
Cash	$ 18,200
Marketable Securities	48,400
Accounts Receivable	106,600
Notes Receivable	18,200
Accrued Interest Receivable	–0–
Merchandise inventory, January 1	130,000
Store Supplies	–0–

Advertising Supplies	–0–
Prepaid Insurance	6,500
Store Equipment	105,300
Accumulated Depreciation—Store Equipment	26,000
Accounts Payable	57,200
Notes Payable	59,800
Accrued Interest Payable	–0–
Accrued Wages Payable	–0–
Income Taxes Payable	–0–
Accrued Mortgage Interest Payable	–0–
Unearned Rent	–0–
Mortgage Payable (due 1990)	39,000
Capital Stock	130,000
Retained Earnings	39,000
Dividends	14,300
Sales	650,000
Purchases	367,900
Transportation In	6,500
Advertising Expense	12,700
Miscellaneous Selling Expense	19,500
Depreciation Expense—Store Equipment	–0–
Heat, Light, and Power Expense	13,000
Insurance Expense	–0–
Miscellaneous General Expense	22,900
Income Tax Expense	–0–
Rent Expense	12,500
Wages Expense	98,800
Interest Expense	3,900
Interest Earned	1,000
Rent Earned	3,200
Income Summary	–0–

Data for the end-of-period adjustments are as follows:

a. The Prepaid Insurance account consists of the following policies:

Policy Number	*Date of Policy*	*Life Policy*	*Premiums*
A648	January 1	3 years	$3,900
P832	July 1	2 years	2,600

b. The Notes Receivable account consists of a 60-day, 9% note dated December 1.

c. The Notes Payable consists of a 90-day, 9% note dated December 1.

d. Purchases of store equipment were as follows:

Purchase Date	*Cost*	*Useful Life*	*Salvage Value*
January 1 (5 years ago)	$57,200	10 years	$5,200
April 1	26,000	20 years	–0–
July 1	22,100	8 years	1,300

e. Wages earned by employees but unpaid as of December 31 totaled $1,000.
f. Income taxes for the year were estimated at $9,100.
g. On August 1, the Helene Corporation rented some store equipment to the O'Leary Company for 12 months and received a check for $3,200 representing the entire year's rental fee.
h. Interest on the mortgage payable is $2,100 a year, paid in semiannual installments on May 1 and November 1.
i. Inventories on December 31:

Merchandise	$93,000
Advertising Supplies	3,100
Store Supplies (the original debit was made to Miscellaneous General Expense)	800

Required:

1. Prepare a work sheet for the year ended December 31.
2. Prepare (a) an income statement, (b) a statement of retained earnings, and (c) a balance sheet.
3. Prepare the closing entries.

P5-20. The accounts and balances in the Income Statement columns of Thomas Cohen's work sheet for the year ended December 31 are given below.

Account Title	*Income Statement*	
	Dr.	*Cr.*
Merchandise Inventory	11,400	12,350
Sales		29,070
Sales Returns and Allowances	95	
Sales Discounts	665	
Purchases	13,300	
Transportation In	380	
Purchases Returns and Allowances		190
Purchases Discounts		950
Selling Expenses	3,420	
General Expenses	5,700	
Totals	34,960	42,560
Net Income	7,600	
	42,560	42,560

The Balance Sheet Debit column of the work sheet showed $1,900 for dividends.

Required:

1. Prepare an income statement.
2. Journalize the closing entries.
3. Show the Merchandise Inventory and the Income Summary accounts after the closing entries have been posted.

6

Accounting Systems

The system of recording, classifying, summarizing, and reporting accounting information discussed in the preceding chapters has been satisfactory for teaching the fundamentals of the accounting process, but a business of any size will usually find it necessary to modify the methods of capturing the flow of accounting data to meet the needs of the particular business firm. This chapter describes briefly how a simple system is designed for a business. A mini practice case, which can be completed by students in the space provided, is included at the end of the chapter.

DESIGN OF A RECORD SYSTEM

The transaction is the basic source of accounting data; it is central to the collection process. Before data processing by any system can begin, some evidence that a transaction has occurred must exist. Source documents providing this evidence, such as purchases invoices, sales invoices, and receiver's reports indicate the occurrence of transactions. The data must then be introduced into the system. Data can be captured and processed from these transactions by handwritten procedures, by accounting machines, punched-card equipment, electronic equipment, or by a combination of these methods. The similarity of these concepts of data collection, and that they all lead to the same results, is shown in Figure 6-1. The primary difference is in the methods of collection; however, the greater the volume and variety of information required, the more sophisticated, detailed, and elaborate is the collection process.

The information flow then is from input to output. It is the function of the

Figure 6-1
Information Flow Chart

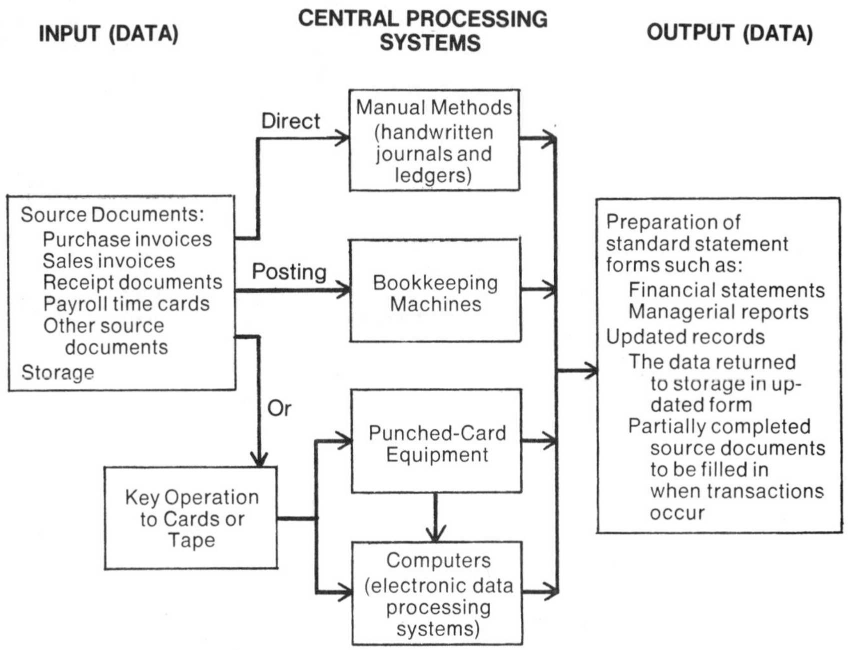

systems analyst to create a method of collecting these data that will permit management to measure and control its human and physical resources to its best advantage. This design requires a thorough examination of the company's table of organization, its personnel and job descriptions, the current forms in use, the procedures and policies of the organization, and the legal constraints on the business or industry, if the analyst is to gauge the integrity and accuracy of the measurement of the flow of information.

The development of the system will generally be in three stages: (1) *study and design,* (2) *implementation,* and (3) *operation.* The company's operation is studied and a method of collection is proposed for adoption. Once adopted it is put into operation for verification, for review for improvements and redesign, and for testing for effectiveness of the controls.

The next sections of this chapter describe the relationship between the general ledger and subsidiary ledgers, and the type of records that are usually found in an accounting system. A simple manual system is used for purposes of illustration; however, the concepts are as valid in mechanized and automated systems as they are in a manual system. A brief discussion of the use of bookkeeping machines and automated data processing in accounting concludes the chapter.

THE GENERAL LEDGER AND SUBSIDIARY LEDGERS

Accounts that are incorporated in the balance sheet and the income statement are kept in a separate book, or collection, called the ***general ledger.***

This ledger may actually be a loose-leaf binder, a bound book, cards in open trays, punched cards, or one of the several types of computer data storage devices. Accounts are usually arranged in the sequence in which they will appear in the financial statements—that is, assets, liabilities, shareholders' equity, revenue, and expenses. These accounts are referred to collectively as *general ledger accounts.*

Accounts Receivable Ledger

Many businesses have a large number of customers, and detailed information must be kept of transactions with each one. A separate account thus is required for each customer. If the general ledger were to include each customer's account, it would become too large and unwieldy. Consequently, only one account, Accounts Receivable, is maintained in the general ledger. This account shows the combined increases and decreases in the amounts due from all customers. The individual customer accounts are kept in a separate, or *subsidiary,* ledger called the *accounts receivable ledger.* The Accounts Receivable account, referred to as a controlling account, is a summary account in the general ledger of those individual customers' accounts which are relegated to the subsidiary ledger. After all the transactions for the period have been entered, the balance of the Accounts Receivable account in the general ledger should be equal to the sum of the individual account balances in the subsidiary ledger.

Accounts Payable Ledger

Many businesses have a large number of individual creditors. Consequently, only one account, Accounts Payable, is kept in the general ledger. This account shows total increases and decreases in amounts due to creditors. The individual creditors' accounts are kept in a subsidiary ledger called the *accounts payable ledger.* Accounts Payable, another controlling account, is a summary account in the general ledger of those individual creditors' accounts which are relegated to the subsidiary ledger. After all the transactions for the period have been entered, the balance of the Accounts Payable account in the general ledger should be equal to the sum of the individual account balances in the subsidiary ledger.

Controlling Accounts

As mentioned above, the Accounts Receivable and Accounts Payable accounts appearing in the general ledger are referred to as controlling accounts.

> A *controlling account,* by definition, is any account in the general ledger that controls or is supported by a number of other accounts in a separate ledger.

These accounts contain summary totals of many transactions, the details of which appear in subsidiary ledgers. The accounts receivable ledger is sometimes referred to as the *customers ledger;* the accounts payable ledger, as the *creditors ledger.* Other controlling accounts and their appropriate subsidiary ledgers may be established when enough homogeneous general ledger accounts are created to make it more efficient to relegate these accounts to a separate ledger.

Posting to the General Ledger and the Subsidiary Ledgers

To illustrate the method of posting from the general journal to the general and subsidiary ledgers, the following transaction is considered:

On August 3, Bookkeeping Services, Inc., billed the following clients for professional services performed.

Jay Johnson	$550
O. M. Omar	120
C. W. Wayne	230

This information is recorded and posted as indicated in Figure 6-2.

Entries to the Accounts Payable controlling account and the accounts payable ledger are handled similarly. An explanation of the encircled figures in Figure 6-2 follows:

❶ Figure 6-2 shows the total posting of the $900 debit to the Accounts Receivable account in the general ledger and detailed posting to the subsidiary ledger accounts. Each customer is debited for the amount shown in the explanation of the general journal entry; the balance is extended to the Balance column; the journal page number is entered in the folio (F) column; and the date is entered. After each posting has been completed, a check mark (√) is entered to the left of each amount in the Explanation column of the general journal to indicate that the amount has been posted to the proper subsidiary ledger account. A check mark is used rather than a page number because subsidiary accounts in the illustration are not numbered but are kept in alphabetical order.

It will be obvious to the reader that a business such as a department store that makes hundreds of credit sales daily does not list each one in the journal entry explanation; instead, postings to the subsidiary ledger accounts are made from the copies of the sales tickets. The principle, however, is the same, as illustrated in Figure 6-2.

After only a cursory study, it may seem that this dual accounting for accounts receivable would result in double debits that will be incorrectly reflected in the trial balance. Note carefully, however, that only one debit goes into the Accounts Receivable controlling account for later incorporation in the trial balance. The amounts entered in the accounts receivable ledger will not go in the trial balance, but the total of the uncollected balances at the end of a period will be compared with the single balance of the Accounts Receivable controlling account as a check on the accuracy of both the accounts receivable ledger and the Accounts Receivable controlling account in the general ledger.

❷ It should be observed that the balance form of ledger account is used for the accounts receivable ledger. This particular form is customarily used in subsidiary ledgers for two reasons: (1) The balances have to be referred to quite often. (2) The form is adaptable to machine accounting, which is frequently employed for subsidiary ledger accounting.

Figure 6-2 Posting to Control and Subsidiary Accounts

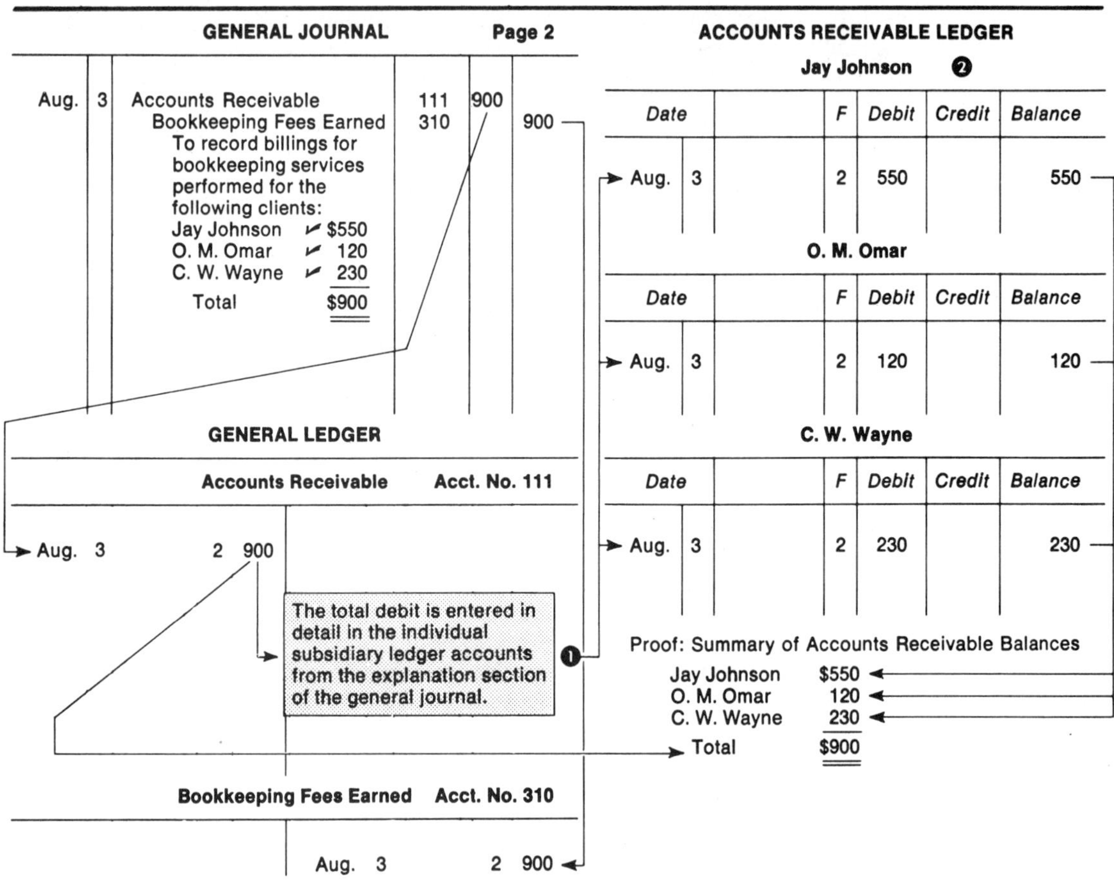

EXPANSION OF GENERAL JOURNAL: EVOLUTION OF A SIMPLE MANUAL SYSTEM

As the frequency of similar transactions increases, a more efficient means of processing the resulting data must be devised than the two-column general journal illustrated in the preceding chapters. With the use of this journal each entry must be posted individually to its general ledger accounts, and with the use of subsidiary ledger accounts each entry must be posted a second time. In essence, the data in the journal are repeated in detail in the ledger. In a large business, as thousands of transactions occur each day, some means of streamlining the method and accelerating the processing of these data must be developed.

The accounting records and procedures should be designed to meet the needs of the individual business firm. For example, for a small firm where one accountant records all the transactions, additional columns (each representing an account that receives repetitive entries) may be added to the general journal. As the number of transactions increases, however, and the processing becomes physically impossible for one accountant to perform, it will be necessary to group similar transactions into classes and use a special journal for recording each class of transactions. As a company grows and the volume of transactions further increases, it becomes necessary to use more (and perhaps more complex) accounting machines in the processing of the accounting data.

Special Journals

The manual system illustrated in the following pages saves time in recording the transactions and posting. This system also enables a business to divide the collection process among several employees. Small businesses, or those businesses with limited transactions, find this type of system or adaptations of it useful. Modifying some of the journals and subsidiary ledgers for use with mechanical equipment improves its utility.

The procedures in the preceding chapters can be modified principally by creating several journals for the purpose of recording special classes of transactions. Grouping transactions into classes and using a special journal to record each class offer the opportunity for the rapid and efficient processing of accounting data. The number and kinds of journals used are influenced by the type of business and the information desired. The model used in this text is shown in the following chart:

Journal	*Kind of Transaction*	*Symbol*
Sales Journal	Sale of merchandise on account	S
Purchases Journal	Purchase of merchandise on account	P
Cash Receipts Journal	Receipt of cash	CR
Cash Payments Journal	Payment of cash	CP
General Journal	All other transactions that are not grouped in the four classes above—for example, closing and adjusting entries, purchase of merchandise by note, purchase of equipment or supplies on account or by note, sales and purchases returns and allowances.	J

Special journals offer the following advantages:

1. Similar transactions are grouped in chronological order in one place. All credit sales of merchandise, for example, are entered in the sales journal.
2. The repeated writing of each account title—Sales, Purchases, Cash, and so on—is eliminated.
3. Postings are made from column footings in total only—rather than item by item—thereby reducing the volume of work. The general ledger is relieved of unnecessary detail, since fewer postings are made. As a

result of the fewer postings, the general ledger is more compact and easier to use, thus reducing the probability of error.

4. Bookkeeping duties may be divided by function. For example, one person may enter information regarding charge sales, taken from *sales* invoices, in the sales journal; a second person may post either from the sales journal or directly from the sales slips to the accounts receivable ledger; a third person may enter cash received from charge customers in the cash receipts journal and post to the accounts receivable ledger; and a fourth person may verify the accuracy of the work by comparing the accounts receivable ledger with the Accounts Receivable controlling account in the general ledger.

This division of responsibilities not only facilitates and accelerates the work flow but also creates some protection against errors and the misappropriation of assets.

An essential feature of *internal control*—the built-in safeguard for the protection of the assets of an enterprise—is the careful planning and supervision of the record keeping of a company and a division of the work so that no one employee has complete control both of an operation of the business and of the recording of that operation.

Sales Journal

All sales of merchandise on account are recorded in the sales journal.[1] To illustrate the use of the sales journal, assume that the following transactions took place at the Hayward Casuals during June:

June 3 Sold merchandise to Ella Gray, $400; terms 1/15, n/60, invoice No. 1
4 Sold merchandise to William Ramey, $600; terms 2/10, n/30, invoice No. 2
5 Sold merchandise to Arthur James, $300; terms 1/5, n/30, invoice No. 3
30 Sold merchandise to Byron Butts, $800; terms 2/10, n/30, invoice No. 4

When merchandise is sold on account, the transaction is recorded in the sales journal as follows:

1. The date of the transaction is entered in the Date column.
2. Sales invoices (or slips) are numbered in sequence; the numbers are entered in chronological order in the Sales Invoice No. column.
3. The name of the customer to whom the sale was made is entered in the Account Debited column.
4. The terms of the sale are listed in the Terms column.
5. If the subsidiary ledger account has a folio, or reference number, it is entered in the folio (F) column when posting is complete; otherwise, a check mark is entered.

[1] Despite the advantages of management by exception in the alternative methods of recording sales and purchases net of discounts (see Chapter 5), illustrations in Chapter 6 follow the gross procedure to simplify the examples.

6. The amount of the sale is entered in the Amount column.

A simple sales journal is illustrated in Figure 6-3, which shows the entries for the transactions of Hayward Casuals listed above. The posting to the general and subsidiary ledgers is also shown.

Figure 6-3
Sales Journal and the Posting Flow

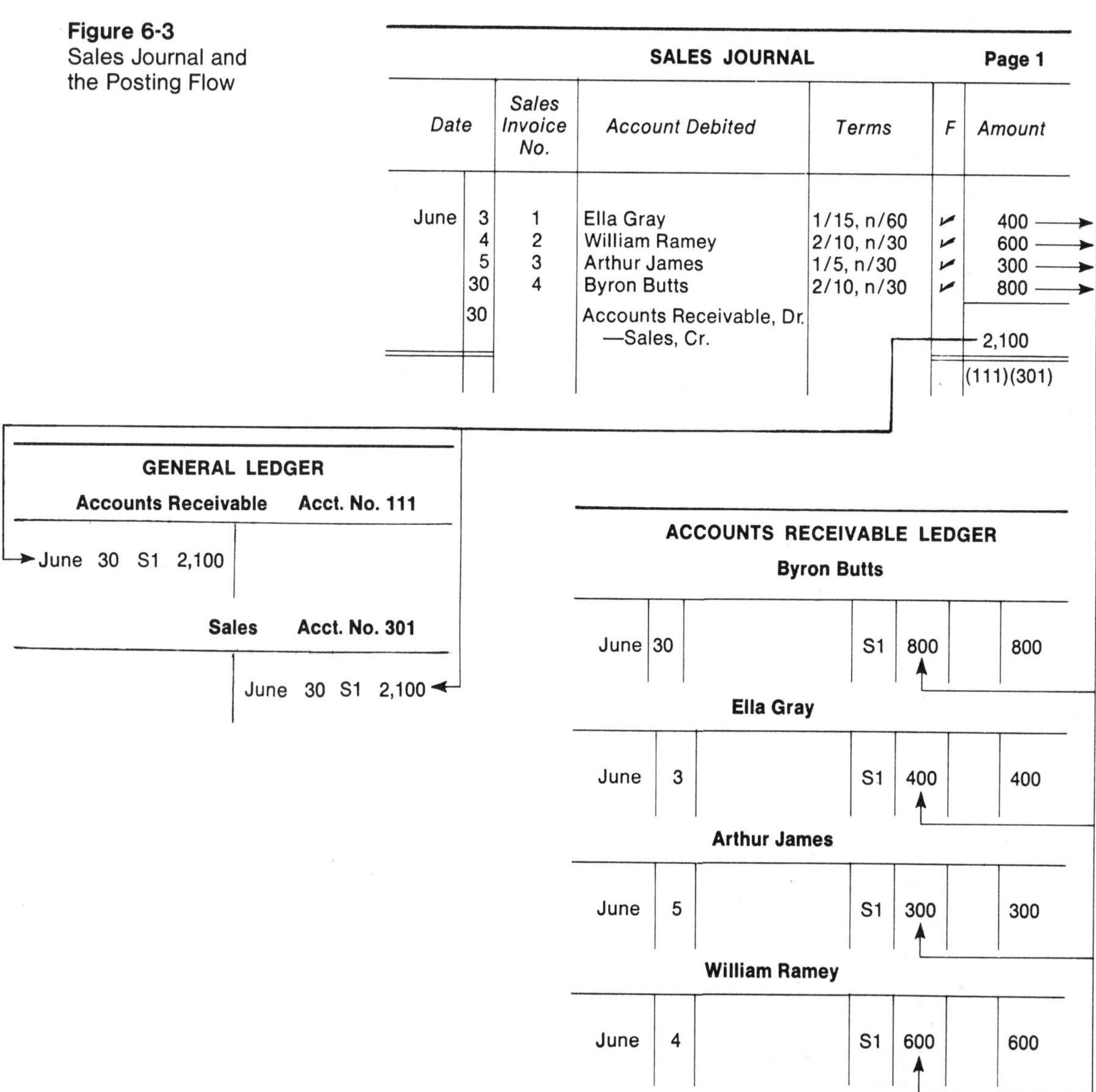

SALES JOURNAL — Page 1

Date		Sales Invoice No.	Account Debited	Terms	F	Amount
June	3	1	Ella Gray	1/15, n/60	✓	400
	4	2	William Ramey	2/10, n/30	✓	600
	5	3	Arthur James	1/5, n/30	✓	300
	30	4	Byron Butts	2/10, n/30	✓	800
	30		Accounts Receivable, Dr. —Sales, Cr.			2,100
						(111)(301)

GENERAL LEDGER

Accounts Receivable — Acct. No. 111

Debit	Credit
June 30 S1 2,100	

Sales — Acct. No. 301

Debit	Credit
	June 30 S1 2,100

ACCOUNTS RECEIVABLE LEDGER

Byron Butts

Date			F	Debit	Credit	Balance
June	30		S1	800		800

Ella Gray

Date			F	Debit	Credit	Balance
June	3		S1	400		400

Arthur James

Date			F	Debit	Credit	Balance
June	5		S1	300		300

William Ramey

Date			F	Debit	Credit	Balance
June	4		S1	600		600

Each entry in the sales journal is a debit to the Accounts Receivable account and to the customer's account in the accounts receivable ledger, and a credit to the Sales account. Expressed in the form of a two-column general journal entry, the entry for the sale made on June 1, for example, would be:

Accounts Receivable—Ella Gray	400	
Sales		400

The transaction is *not* actually recorded in both the general journal and the sales journal. It is shown in this manner only to illustrate the difference between the two forms.

Each amount is posted separately as a debit to the accounts receivable ledger, supporting the single debit that is posted at the end of the month to the Accounts Receivable controlling account in the general ledger. Posting to the subsidiary ledger accounts is usually done daily. It is important to have the up-to-date balance of each customer's account readily available so that requests for this information from the customer, the credit department, or others may be readily fulfilled.

The daily posting is usually done in the following sequence:

1. The amount of the sale is posted to the Debit column of the customer's account and is added to the balance, if any, in the Balance column.
2. The journal symbol and page number (S1) is written in the folio (F) column.
3. The date of the sale is recorded in the Date column.
4. A check mark is placed in the folio (F) column of the sales journal to indicate that the entry has been posted.

At the end of the month, the Amount column of the sales journal is totaled. The total, the date of the transfer, and the sales journal page number are then posted to the debit side of the Accounts Receivable controlling account and to the credit side of the Sales account in the general ledger. The general ledger account numbers are recorded in the sales journal immediately below the footing. To minimize errors, a systematic procedure should be followed in posting. The following sequence is suggested:

Debit posting:

1. The amount is posted to the Debit money column of the Accounts Receivable account in the general ledger.
2. The journal symbol (S1) is written in the folio (F) column of the account.
3. The date is recorded in the Date column.
4. The Accounts Receivable account number is written in parentheses below and to the left of the double rule in the Amount column of the journal.

Credit posting:

5. The same amount as the debit posting is posted to the Credit money column of the Sales account in the general ledger.
6. The journal symbol (S1) is written in the folio (F) column of the account.
7. The date is recorded in the Date column.
8. The Sales account number is written in parentheses below the double rule in the Amount column of the journal, to the right of the debit posting reference number.

Purchases Journal

The relationship of the purchases journal and the accounts payable ledger is similar to that of the sales journal and the accounts receivable ledger. All purchases of merchandise on account are recorded in the purchases journal. The transactions of the Hayward Casuals during June illustrate the use of this journal.

June 3 Purchased merchandise on account from Oakland Clothing Company, $900; terms 2/10, n/20.

8 Purchased merchandise on account from Southland Apparel, $400; terms 2/10, n/60.

16 Purchased merchandise on account from San Francisco Clothiers, $500; terms 3/5, n/30.

28 Purchased merchandise on account from the Dexter Custom Tailors, $700; terms 1/20, n/60.

Figure 6-4 shows how these transactions are recorded in the purchases journal and posted to the general and subsidiary ledger accounts.

Figure 6-4 Posting Flow from the Purchases Journal

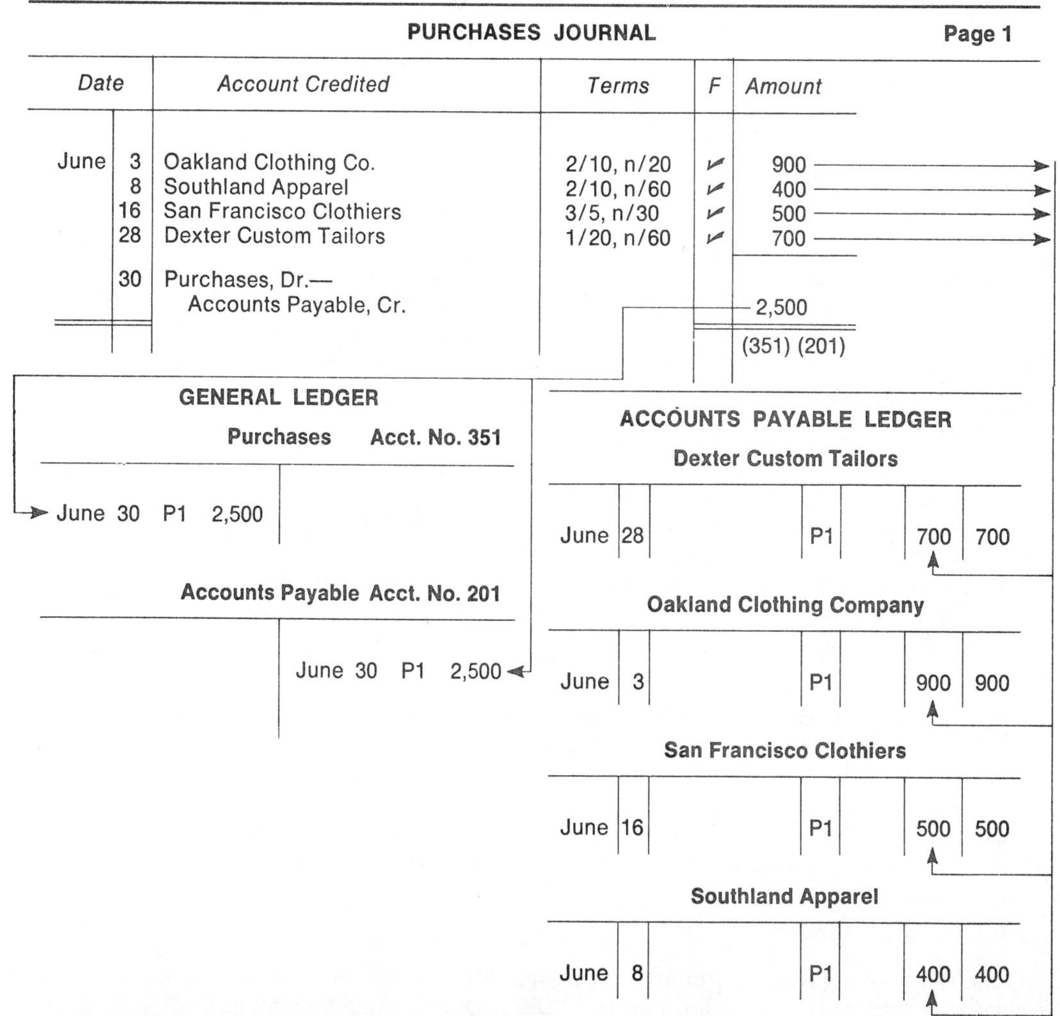

PURCHASES JOURNAL **Page 1**

Date		Account Credited	Terms	F	Amount
June	3	Oakland Clothing Co.	2/10, n/20	✓	900
	8	Southland Apparel	2/10, n/60	✓	400
	16	San Francisco Clothiers	3/5, n/30	✓	500
	28	Dexter Custom Tailors	1/20, n/60	✓	700
	30	Purchases, Dr.— Accounts Payable, Cr.			2,500
					(351) (201)

GENERAL LEDGER

Purchases Acct. No. 351

Debit	Credit
June 30 P1 2,500	

Accounts Payable Acct. No. 201

Debit	Credit
	June 30 P1 2,500

ACCOUNTS PAYABLE LEDGER

Dexter Custom Tailors

June	28		P1	700	700

Oakland Clothing Company

June	3		P1	900	900

San Francisco Clothiers

June	16		P1	500	500

Southland Apparel

June	8		P1	400	400

Expressed as a two-column general journal entry, the first entry in the purchases journal would be:

Purchases	900	
Accounts Payable—Oakland Clothing Co.		900

The transaction is *not* actually recorded in both the general journal and the purchases journal. It is shown in this manner to illustrate the difference between the two recording forms.

Each transaction is posted separately as a credit to the accounts payable ledger to support the credit posted at the end of the month to the Accounts Payable controlling account in the general ledger. Transactions are usually posted to the subsidiary ledger daily. The date of the entry in the subsidiary ledger account is the invoice date, which is significant in determining if a discount may be taken. At the end of the month, the Amount column of the purchases journal is footed. This total is posted to the Purchases account in the general ledger as a debit. The same total is posted to the Accounts Payable controlling account in the general ledger as a credit.

Cash Receipts Journal

All transactions involving the receipt of cash are entered in the cash receipts journal. A multicolumn form of cash receipts journal is illustrated in Figure 6-5. The column headings typically provide the flexibility necessary to record cash receipts from customers or any other source and to record sales discounts. The form may be varied, particularly in the number and headings of the columns, to meet the needs of the individual business.

Explanation of the various columns in the cash receipts journal follows.

1. The date of the transaction is entered in the Date column.
2. The explanation of the transaction is written in the Explanation column. Every transaction entered in this journal includes a debit to Cash.
3. There are three debit columns. Cash debits are entered in the first Debit column.
4. The Sales Discount Debit column is used for recording discounts granted to customers for paying within the discount period.
5. The Other Accounts Debit column is for debits to general ledger accounts for which no special columns have been provided.
6. There are three folio columns, two labeled (F), one, (✓); a posting symbol indicating that the amount has been posted to the general ledger or to the accounts receivable ledger is placed in the folio column.
7. The name of the general ledger or subsidiary ledger account to be credited is written in the Account Credited column.
8. When a charge customer makes a payment on account, an entry is made in the Accounts Receivable Credit column, the first of three credit columns. The amount entered is the actual amount of cash received plus any sales discounts properly taken by the customer.
9. Sales of merchandise for cash are entered in the Sales Credit column.
10. The Other Accounts Credit column is for credits to general ledger accounts for which no special columns have been provided.

Figure 6-5 Posting Flow from the Cash Receipts Journal

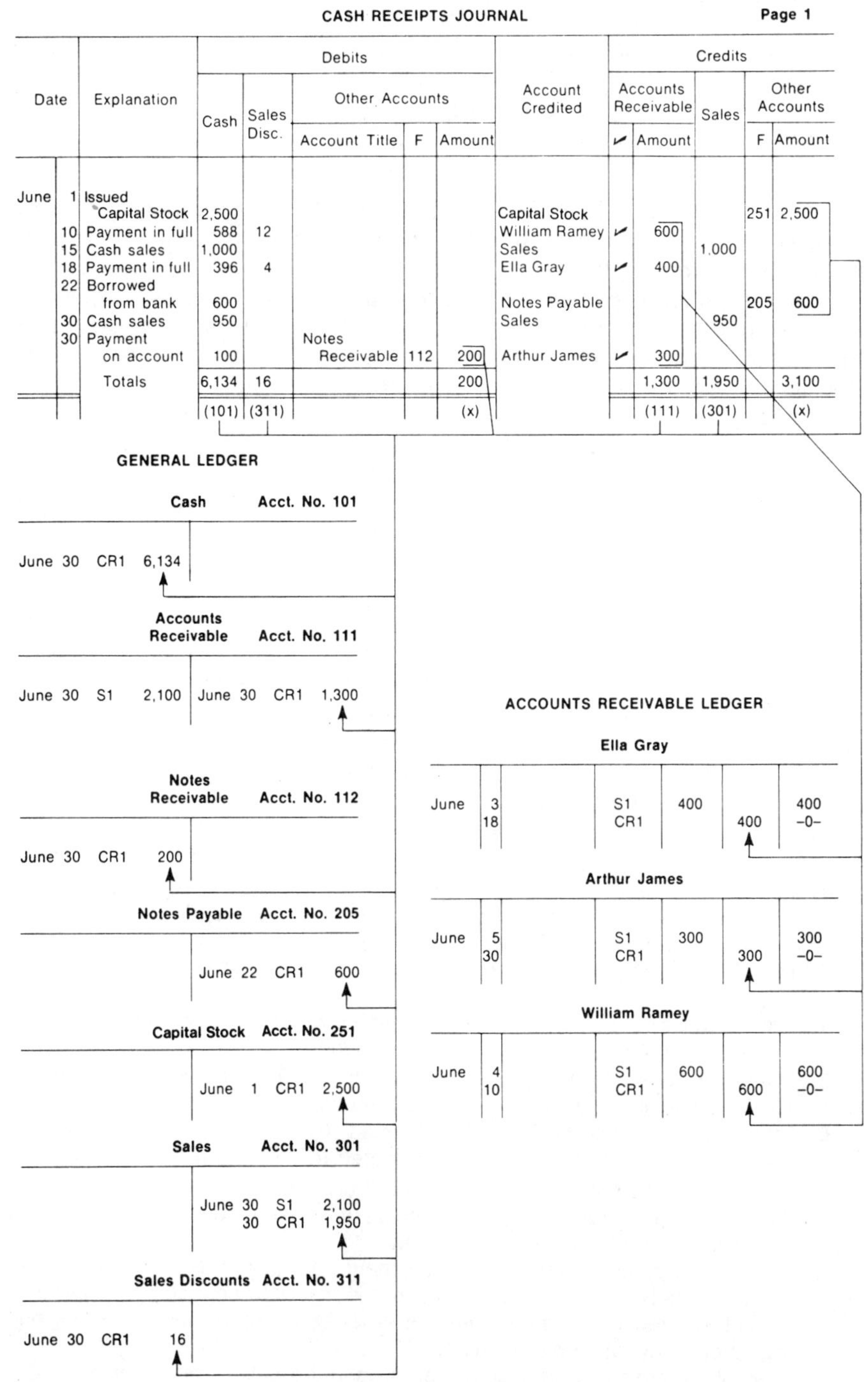

CASH RECEIPTS JOURNAL — Page 1

Date		Explanation	Debits: Cash	Debits: Sales Disc.	Debits: Other Accounts: Account Title	F	Amount	Account Credited	Credits: Accounts Receivable: ✓	Amount	Credits: Sales	Credits: Other Accounts: F	Amount
June	1	Issued Capital Stock	2,500					Capital Stock				251	2,500
	10	Payment in full	588	12				William Ramey	✓	600			
	15	Cash sales	1,000					Sales			1,000		
	18	Payment in full	396	4				Ella Gray	✓	400			
	22	Borrowed from bank	600					Notes Payable				205	600
	30	Cash sales	950					Sales			950		
	30	Payment on account	100		Notes Receivable	112	200	Arthur James	✓	300			
		Totals	6,134	16			200			1,300	1,950		3,100
			(101)	(311)			(x)			(111)	(301)		(x)

GENERAL LEDGER

Cash Acct. No. 101

Debit	Credit
June 30 CR1 6,134	

Accounts Receivable Acct. No. 111

Debit	Credit
June 30 S1 2,100	June 30 CR1 1,300

Notes Receivable Acct. No. 112

Debit	Credit
June 30 CR1 200	

Notes Payable Acct. No. 205

Debit	Credit
	June 22 CR1 600

Capital Stock Acct. No. 251

Debit	Credit
	June 1 CR1 2,500

Sales Acct. No. 301

Debit	Credit
	June 30 S1 2,100
	30 CR1 1,950

Sales Discounts Acct. No. 311

Debit	Credit
June 30 CR1 16	

ACCOUNTS RECEIVABLE LEDGER

Ella Gray

Date			Ref.	Debit	Credit	Balance
June	3		S1	400		400
	18		CR1		400	-0-

Arthur James

Date			Ref.	Debit	Credit	Balance
June	5		S1	300		300
	30		CR1		300	-0-

William Ramey

Date			Ref.	Debit	Credit	Balance
June	4		S1	600		600
	10		CR1		600	-0-

In previous chapters, transactions involving the receipt of cash were recorded in a simple two-column general journal. Similar transactions are recorded in a cash receipts journal in Figure 6-5. Although each transaction may be entered on a single line, the equality of debits and credits is still maintained through the use of multiple columns. The following is an analysis of the debit-credit relationship of the entries in Figure 6-5 to indicate their effect on the accounts. These transactions, however, are *actually recorded* only in the cash receipts journal, not the general journal.

Transaction:
June 1 Issued Capital Stock for $2,500.

Analysis of Debits and Credits:

Account	Debit	Credit
Cash	2,500	
Capital Stock		2,500

Cash is debited by entering the amount in the Cash Debit column. Since there is no special column for Capital Stock, the amount is entered in the Other Accounts credit column.

Transaction:
June 10 Received payment in full from William Ramey.

Analysis of Debits and Credits:

Account	Debit	Credit
Cash	588	
Sales Discounts	12	
Accounts Receivable		600

The sales journal shows that on June 4 merchandise with an invoice price of $600 was sold to William Ramey; terms 2/10, n/30. Since payment was made within 10 days, Ramey deducted $12 from the invoice price and paid $588. Entering the three amounts in the special columns as shown has the same effect on the general ledger as the explanatory debit and credit analysis does. The customer's name is entered in the Account Credited column for posting to the accounts receivable ledger. If cash receipts from charge customers are numerous, a daily total may be entered from an adding machine tape; posting to the subsidiary ledger is done from supporting documents.

Transaction:
June 15 Cash sales for the first half of the month were $1,000.

Analysis of Debits and Credits:

Account	Debit	Credit
Cash	1,000	
Sales		1,000

The word *Sales* is written in the Account Credited column to fill the space. However, it can be omitted, since both the debit and the credit amounts are entered in the special columns. Although a one-half month summary amount is used to simplify the illustration, cash sales *should be* recorded during each business day.

Transaction:
June 18 Received full payment from Ella Gray.

Analysis of Debits and Credits:

Cash	396	
Sales Discounts	4	
Accounts Receivable		400

The sales journal shows that on June 3 merchandise with an invoice price of $400 was sold to Ella Gray; terms 1/15, n/60. Since payment was made within 15 days, she deducted $4 from the invoice amount and paid $396.

Transaction:
June 22 Borrowed $600 from the bank on a note payable.

Analysis of Debits and Credits:

Cash	600	
Notes Payable		600

Since there is no special column for the Notes Payable account, the amount is entered in the Other Accounts credit column and the name of the account is written in the Account Credited column.

Transaction:
June 30 Cash sales for the last half of the month were $950.

Analysis of Debits and Credits:

Cash	950	
Sales		950

Transaction:
June 30 Received $100 from Arthur James on account and a promissory note payable in 30 days for the balance in his account.

Analysis of Debits and Credits:

Cash	100	
Notes Receivable	200	
Accounts Receivable		300

The sales journal shows that on June 5 merchandise with an invoice price of $300 was sold to Arthur James; terms 1/5, n/30. The Sales Discounts account is not involved in this partial payment because the discount period has expired.

At the end of the month, the columns in the cash receipts journal are footed. Since each line contains equal debits and credits, it follows that the total of the Debit column footings should equal the total of the Credit column footings. This equality should be proved for each special journal before the column totals are posted to the general ledger; otherwise, errors in the special journals may not be detected, the ledger will not have equal total debit and credit balances, and the trial balance will not balance. Moreover, the controlling accounts may not agree with their corresponding subsidiary ledgers. The cash receipts journal of the Hayward Casuals is proved as shown below.

	Debits		*Credits*
Cash	$6,134	Accounts Receivable	$1,300
Sales Discounts	16	Sales	1,950
Other Accounts	200	Other Accounts	3,100
Total	$6,350	Total	$6,350

Postings from the cash receipts journal of Hayward Casuals are shown in Figure 6-5.

Individual credit postings are made to the accounts receivable ledger to support the $1,300 credit posting to the Accounts Receivable controlling account in the general ledger. A check mark is entered in the folio (√) column of the cash receipts journal on the line of the entry to indicate that the item has been posted to the customer's account in the subsidiary ledger. The balance of each account is zero; however, any positive balance in an account would normally be a debit. Transactions have already been posted to these accounts from the sales journal.

The totals of the Cash Debit column ($6,134) and the Sales Discounts Debit column ($16) are posted to the respective general ledger accounts. The regular sequence for transferring an amount from a journal to a ledger is followed. The general ledger account number entered in parentheses below the double rule in each column shows that the total has been posted to that account.

The (X) below the Other Accounts Debit column means that the individual amounts contained in the column total have already been posted to the general ledger. The $200 debit to Notes Receivable was posted individually during the month. The account number of Notes Receivable (112) was entered in the folio (F) column of the journal at the time the posting was done.

The Accounts Receivable account is credited for $1,300 and the Sales account is credited for $1,950. These postings are also dated June 30. No posting symbol is used in the folio (F) column on the line of the entry for a cash sale because the item does not require individual posting.

The (X) below the double rule in the Other Accounts credit column indicates that the column total is not to be posted to the general ledger. The total is not posted because the $2,500 credit to Capital Stock, and the $600 credit to

Notes Payable were posted separately during the month. The ledger page numbers of these accounts were entered in the folio (F) column of the journal when the posting was done. Note that account numbers 251 and 205 are written in the folio column of the cash receipts journal in Figure 6-5. Postings from the Other Accounts Credit column are dated as of the date of the entry.

The Cash Payments Journal

All transactions involving the payment of cash are entered in the cash payments journal. Most cash payments should be made by check. When payments in currency are required, they may be made from a *petty cash* fund, for which procedures are discussed in Chapter 7.

A typical cash payments journal is illustrated in Figure 6-6. The columns provide for recording cash payments, either to creditors or for any other purpose, and for recording purchases discounts.

Explanation of the various columns follows.

1. The date of the disbursement of cash is entered in the Date column.
2. Detailed information is initially recorded on the check stub, which bears the same number as the check. Entries in the cash payments journal are then made from the check stub, and the check number is listed in the Check No. column.
3. An explanation of the transaction is entered in the Explanation column.
4. There are three credit columns; they are located to the left of the debit columns. In a special journal the sequence of columns need not follow the traditional placement. Cash is the first credit and will be used in each transaction entered in this journal.
5. The Purchases Discounts Credit column is used for recording discounts taken on invoices paid within the discount period.
6. Credits to general ledger accounts other than Cash and Purchases Discounts are recorded in the Other Accounts Credit column.
7. There are three folio columns, two labeled (F), one, (√); a posting symbol indicating that the amount has been posted to the general ledger or to the accounts payable ledger is placed in the folio column.
8. The name of the general ledger or subsidiary ledger account to be debited is written in the Account Debited column.
9. When a creditor is paid in full or on account, the amount is entered in the Accounts Payable Debit column. The amount entered is the actual amount of the check plus any purchases discounts taken.
10. The purchase of merchandise for cash is entered in the Purchases Debit column.
11. The Other Accounts Debit column is used for entries to general ledger accounts that have no special column.

The cash payments journal of Hayward Casuals is illustrated in Figure 6-6.

Although each transaction may be entered on a single line, such a practice is not an absolute requirement. Each new transaction entry should begin on a vacant line. The equality of debits and credits is maintained through the use of multiple columns. The transactions in Figure 6-9 are analyzed in terms of debits and credits to indicate their effect on the accounts. These transactions, however, are *not* actually recorded in both the cash payments journal and the general journal.

Figure 6-6 Posting Flow from the Cash Payments Journal

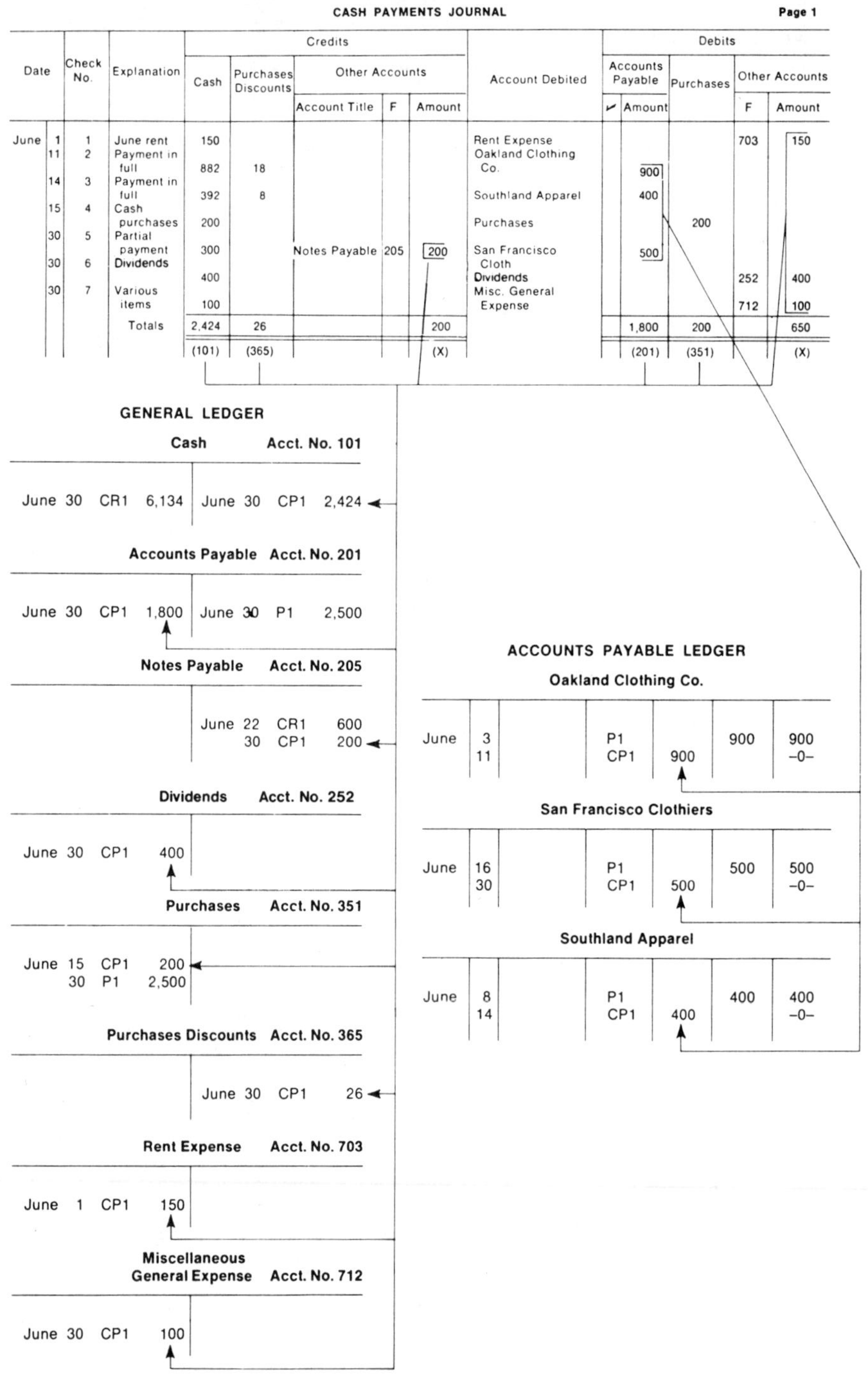

CASH PAYMENTS JOURNAL — Page 1

Date		Check No.	Explanation	Credits: Cash	Credits: Purchases Discounts	Credits: Other Accounts: Account Title	F	Amount	Account Debited	Debits: Accounts Payable: ✓	Amount	Debits: Purchases	Debits: Other Accounts: F	Amount
June	1	1	June rent	150					Rent Expense				703	150
	11	2	Payment in full	882	18				Oakland Clothing Co.		900			
	14	3	Payment in full	392	8				Southland Apparel		400			
	15	4	Cash purchases	200					Purchases			200		
	30	5	Partial payment	300		Notes Payable	205	200	San Francisco Cloth		500			
	30	6	Dividends	400					Dividends				252	400
	30	7	Various items	100					Misc. General Expense				712	100
			Totals	2,424	26			200			1,800	200		650
				(101)	(365)			(X)			(201)	(351)		(X)

GENERAL LEDGER

Cash Acct. No. 101

Debit	Credit
June 30 CR1 6,134	June 30 CP1 2,424

Accounts Payable Acct. No. 201

Debit	Credit
June 30 CP1 1,800	June 30 P1 2,500

Notes Payable Acct. No. 205

Debit	Credit
	June 22 CR1 600
	30 CP1 200

Dividends Acct. No. 252

Debit	Credit
June 30 CP1 400	

Purchases Acct. No. 351

Debit	Credit
June 15 CP1 200	
30 P1 2,500	

Purchases Discounts Acct. No. 365

Debit	Credit
	June 30 CP1 26

Rent Expense Acct. No. 703

Debit	Credit
June 1 CP1 150	

Miscellaneous General Expense Acct. No. 712

Debit	Credit
June 30 CP1 100	

ACCOUNTS PAYABLE LEDGER

Oakland Clothing Co.

Date			Ref.	Debit	Credit	Balance
June	3		P1		900	900
	11		CP1	900		-0-

San Francisco Clothiers

Date			Ref.	Debit	Credit	Balance
June	16		P1		500	500
	30		CP1	500		-0-

Southland Apparel

Date			Ref.	Debit	Credit	Balance
June	8		P1		400	400
	14		CP1	400		-0-

Transaction:
June 1 Issued check No. 1 in the amount of $150 for the June rent.

Analysis of Debits and Credits:

Rent Expense	150	
Cash		150

Transaction:
June 11 Paid Oakland Clothing Co. in full; check No. 2.

Analysis of Debits and Credits:

Accounts Payable	900	
Purchases Discounts		18
Cash		882

The purchases journal shows that on June 3 merchandise with an invoice price of $900 was purchased from Oakland Clothing Company; terms 2/10, n/30. Since payment was made within 10 days, a 2 percent discount, or $18, is taken, and a check for $882 is issued. Entering the three amounts in the special columns has the same effect on the general ledger as the explanatory debit and credit analysis does. The creditor's name is entered in the Account Debited column for posting to the accounts payable ledger.

Transaction:
June 14 Paid Southland Apparel in full; check No. 3.

Analysis of Debits and Credits:

Accounts Payable	400	
Purchases Discounts		8
Cash		392

The explanation for this entry is similar to that for the entry of June 11.

Transaction:
June 15 Purchased merchandise and issued a check for the full amount of the invoice; check No. 4.

Analysis of Debits and Credits:

Purchases	200	
Cash		200

Purchases of merchandise on account are entered in the purchases journal. A company may occasionally purchase merchandise for cash, probably from another company with which no credit relationship exists. These cash purchases are recorded directly in the cash payments journal. If cash purchases of merchandise occur frequently, a special Purchases Debit column may be provided in the cash payments journal.

Transaction:
June 30 Paid the San Francisco Clothiers $300 on account (check No. 5) and issued a promissory note for the balance, to be paid in 30 additional days.

Analysis of Debits and Credits:

Accounts Payable	500	
Cash		300
Notes Payable		200

Reference to the purchases journal shows that on June 16 merchandise with an invoice price of $500 was purchased from the San Francisco Clothiers; terms 3/5, n/30. Since the discount period has expired, no discount is taken.

Transaction:
June 30 The company paid dividends of $400.

Analysis of Debits and Credits:

Dividends	400	
Cash		400

Since there is no special column for dividends, the cash payment is entered in the Other Accounts Debit column. If such dividends are numerous, a special column with the heading Dividends Debit could be provided.

Transaction:
June 30 Issued check No. 7 in the amount of $100 for miscellaneous general expenses.

Analysis of Debits and Credits:

Miscellaneous General Expense	100	
Cash		100

The expense account is debited for various items purchased and consumed during the month.

Before the end-of-the-month postings are made, the columns of the cash payments journal should be footed, and the equality of debits and credits proved as shown below.

	Debits		Credits
Accounts Payable	$1,800	Cash	$2,424
Purchases	200	Purchases Discounts	26
Other Accounts	650	Notes Payable	200
Total	$2,650	Total	$2,650

The total debit and total credit postings from this journal to the general ledger are equal.

Posting from the cash payments journal of Hayward Casuals is also shown in Figure 6-6.

The individual debit postings to the accounts payable ledger support the $1,800 debit posting to the Accounts Payable controlling account in the general ledger. Each check mark in the folio (√) column of the cash payments journal indicates that a posting has been made to the supplier's account in the subsidiary ledger. Note that the balance of each account is either a credit or zero.

The Accounts Payable account is debited for $1,800 as of June 30. The total of the Purchases Debit column, $200, is posted to the Purchases account in the general ledger.

The total of the Other Accounts Debit column is not posted, because it is used to record debits to accounts for which no special columns have been provided; each amount must be posted separately. The numbers of these accounts—703, 252, and 712—are entered in the folio (F) column. The (X) below the double rule in the Other Accounts Debit column indicates that the column total is not posted to the general ledger.

The totals of the Cash Credit column ($2,424) and the Purchases Discounts Credit column ($26) are posted to the general ledger. The basic posting steps are followed. The general ledger account numbers are placed in parentheses below the double rules in the columns to indicate that the postings have been done.

The total of the Other Accounts Credit column is not posted, since each entry in the column has been individually posted at the time the entry is made in the journal. The folio (F) column indicates the account to which the entry was posted.

Combined Cash Receipts and Payments Journal

Many small entities use a combined cash receipts and cash payments journal sometimes called a *cashbook*. This journal is simply a combination of the cash receipts journal and the cash payments journal described earlier. The specialized debit and credit columns (except for cash) would be unique to the needs of the particular entity using it. In addition to small commercial enterprises, such a journal is appropriate to many not-for-profit organizations such as fraternities and sororities and civic clubs and to professional service organizations.

An outline of a simple combined cash receipts and payments journal is presented below.

Combined Cash Receipts and Payments Journal

Date	Explanation	Debits			Credits					Other Accounts			
		Cash	Purchases	Sales Disc.	Cash		Accounts Receivable	Sales	Purchases Discounts	Title	F	Debit	Credit
					Check No.	Amount							

Other Special Journals

Other special journals may be adopted as the need for them becomes apparent. Such a need is indicated if labor may be saved or if the special journal provides an element of flexibility in the accounting system. Examples of other special journals are ***sales returns and allowances journal, purchases returns and allowances journal, notes receivable register, notes payable register, check register,*** and *voucher register.* The voucher system, for example, uses a voucher register and check register for better cash disbursements control. This system is explained in the Appendix to this chapter.

THE GENERAL JOURNAL

Although special journals provide for recording frequently recurring transactions, a need for recording (1) unusual current transactions, (2) correcting entries, and (3) adjusting and closing entries remains. For these purposes, a simple two-column general journal is used in conjunction with the special journals.

Unusual Current Transactions. All the transactions that cannot be entered in the special journals are recorded in the general journal. Sales returns and allowances and purchases returns and allowances, for example, are entered in the general journal if special journals for these transactions are not maintained. Other typical current transactions recorded in the general journal include (1) credit purchases of assets other than merchandise inventory, such as plant and equipment or supplies, and the incurrence of liabilities for services; (2) notes received from customers to apply toward accounts receivable; and (3) notes issued to creditors to apply toward accounts payable. The recording of a typical general journal entry is shown below.

July	7	Notes Receivable	112	350	
		Accounts Receivable—S. Lee	111/✓		350
		To record receipt of 30-day note in full settlement of account.			

The amount of this entry, $350, is posted to the general ledger as a debit to Notes Receivable and a credit to Accounts Receivable. The other posting is to the subsidiary ledger to support the corresponding credit to the Accounts Receivable controlling account. A dual credit posting is necessary because the simple two-column general journal—unlike the special journals—does not have classified columns allowing end-of-period posting of column totals.

Note that the detailed explanation of the transaction, which is omitted from special journals (the type of special journal and a reference to an invoice date or number generally suffice to explain a special journal entry), is retained in the general journal because of the unusual nature of the transactions recorded there.

Correcting Entries. If it is discovered that an error has been made in the process of journalizing and posting, it may be corrected by a general journal entry. Erasures should be avoided, because they may create doubt in the minds of persons who examine the records regarding the reason for the erasure. This becomes particularly important when the records are audited, and in cases of litigation when the records may be offered as evidence.

Assume that the following entry, recording the payment of an invoice for repairs to machinery, has been posted (actually journalized in the cash payments journal but for simplicity is shown here in general journal form):

July 19	Machinery and Equipment	15	
	Cash		15

The debit should have been to an expense account; the error may be corrected by the following entry in the general journal:

July	26	Maintenance and Repairs Expense		15	
		Machinery and Equipment			15
		To correct entry of July 19 in cash payments journal.			

If an error in a journal entry is discovered before it is posted, it may be corrected by drawing a line through the incorrect account or amount and entering the correction immediately above it.

Adjusting and Closing Entries. Adjusting and closing entries are always recorded in the general journal. These entries were discussed and illustrated in Chapters 3 and 4.

Direct Posting from Business Documents

In many business firms, data can be processed more efficiently and rapidly by posting from the original documents—sales invoices, sales slips, purchase invoices, and so on—directly to the subsidiary ledgers instead of first copying the information in special journals and then posting to the accounts. For example, if sales slips are serially numbered, a binder file of duplicate slips arranged in numerical order could take the place of a more formal sales journal. Amounts from the individual slips could be posted daily to the accounts receivable ledger; at the end of a designated period—a week or a month—the sales slips in the binder file are totaled and the following general journal entry is made:

Aug.	31	Accounts Receivable Sales To record charge sales for the month of August.	120,000	
				120,000

A similar procedure may be used to record purchases on account.

If the postings are made from sales slips to the accounts receivable ledger, and if for any reason a special sales journal is still desired, a streamlined journal can be constructed by simply eliminating the Account Debited, Terms, and folio (F) columns, as shown below.

SALES JOURNAL

Date	*Sales Invoice Numbers*	*Amount*

Entries to such a sales journal may be made in batches; for example, a single line may read:

Aug. 12 13,500–13,599 18,329.21

A batch could represent a day's credit sales, or simply a predetermined quantity of invoices or sales slips. The use of *batch totals* is one means of checking the accuracy of posting to subsidiary ledgers.

These changes in procedure and the increasing use of direct posting from original documents are discussed here to add emphasis to a statement made earlier in this chapter: Accounting records and procedures should be designed to meet the needs of the particular business firm.

BOOKKEEPING MACHINE PROCESSING

The simple *posting machine* and similar electromechanical equipment can perform the two basic operations involved in the distribution of business transaction information to appropriate accounts: (1) *listing*—that is, writing such information as cross-reference, date, and amount, and (2) *adding* or *subtracting* amounts. Depending on the complexity of the machine—whether it has one or more *registers,* which allow it to accumulate amounts for further computation, and whether it has a built-in *program* (set of instructions for performing manipulations of data)—it may perform many additional tasks.

In a growing business, as the number of customers and credit transactions increases, the cost of hand posting to the accounts receivable ledger becomes excessive. It may be economical for such a company to buy or rent a simple posting machine that has a *horizontal register* (cross-footer) which can compute the difference between debits and credits on a single line. This type of machine can be used to post debits from sales invoices and credits from receipts to each customer's account in the subsidiary ledger. The operator punches into the machine the beginning balance and both debits and credits, if applicable, to the account, and the machine records this information and prints out a new balance automatically.

The typical ledger account used in machine accounting is the balance-form card shown in Figure 6-7.

A similar procedure is followed to post entries to the accounts payable ledger.

Many firms have accounting systems that permit posting by data-processing equipment to all ledgers, including the general ledger. Economies can be achieved by machine accounting when the volume of similar accounting routines is large enough to enable the bookkeeper to gain speed through repetitive motions that can eventually become habitual. Accuracy and legibility of accounting records are attained by the use of electromechanical and electronic equipment. These machines facilitate proofs of the accuracy of journalizing and posting. The more complex machines perform several stages of accounting—the preparation of specialized reports, journal entries, and ledger posting—in one operation.

Figure 6-7
Typical Machine Ledger Card

Date	*Explanation*	*F or Code*	*Debit*	*Credit*	*Balance*

OTHER ACCOUNTING SYSTEMS

As a business engages in a larger number of transactions of similar nature, it may be economical to acquire punched-card equipment. This equipment rapidly, accurately, and automatically completes the three basic stages of distributing the details of accounting transactions to the appropriate accounts and reports: (1) recording information on an input medium; (2) classifying the information according to the accounts affected; and (3) summarizing the resulting account balances. Punched-card equipment is also useful for recording, classifying, and summarizing nonfinancial statistical data that help management to make decisions.

Further expansion of the accounting system would lead to the development of electronic data-processing (EDP) systems, which offer the greatest speed, volume, and reliability, and consist of combinations of electronic equipment centered around digital computers. These machines are designed to receive a large mass of input data, perform basic arithmetic operations on the data, make comparison decisions regarding the data, update the previously stored data, almost immediately supply the information or output that results from these operations, and then store the data for later use.

MINI PRACTICE CASE

The following mini practice case is designed to help introduce the use of special journals and the process of posting to the subsidiary and general ledgers.

The Clarke Fishing Equipment Shop Ltd. made the following merchandise purchases during June. goods to be resold

June 1 From Herman Company Ltd. on account $500.
2 From Milton Company Ltd. on account $200.
5 From Queens Company Ltd. on account, $400.
13 From Thompson Supply Company Ltd. on account, $360.
17 From Uriah Company Ltd. on account, $240.
19 From Herman Company Ltd. on account, $280.
22 From Milton Company Ltd. on account, $210.
26 From Herman Company Ltd. on account, $180.
30 From Thompson Supply Company Ltd. on account, $215.

a. Record the transactions in the following purchases journal. The terms on all purchases of merchandise on account are 2/10, n/30.

P-1

PURCHASES JOURNAL **Page 1**

Date		*Account Credited*	*Terms*	F	*Amount*
June	1	Herman Co Ltd	2/10 n/30	✓	$ 500
	2	Milton Co Ltd	2/10 n/30	✓	$ 200
	5	Queens Co. Ltd	2/10 n/30	✓	$ 400
	13	Thompson Co Ltd	2/10 n/30	✓	$ 360
	17	Uriah Co. Ltd	2/10 n/30	✓	$ 240
	19	Herman Co Ltd	2/10 n/30	✓	$ 280
	22	Milton Co Ltd.	2/10 n/30	✓	$ 210
	26	Herman Co Ltd.	2/10 n/30	✓	$ 180
	30	Thompson Co Ltd	2/10 n/30	✓	$ 215
	30	Purchases, Dr.— Accounts Payable, Cr.			$ 2585
					(201) (351)

b. Post the accounts below from the purchases journal to the accounts payable subsidiary ledger.

Herman Company Ltd.

Date		Explanation	F	Debit	Credit	Dr or Cr	Balance
June	1	Herman Co	P1		500 —	Cr	
	19		P1		280 —	Cr	
	26		P1		180 —	Cr	

Milton Company Ltd.

Date		Explanation	F	Debit	Credit	Dr or Cr	Balance
June	2	Milton Co	P1		200 —	Cr	
	22		P1		210 —	Cr	

Queens Company Ltd.

Date		Explanation	F	Debit	Credit	Dr or Cr	Balance
June	5	Queens Co	P1		400 —	Cr	

Thompson Supply Company Ltd.

Date		Explanation	F	Debit	Credit	Dr or Cr	Balance
June	13	Thompson Co	P1		360 —	Cr	
	30		P1		215 —	Cr	

Uriah Company Ltd.

Date		Explanation	F	Debit	Credit	Dr or Cr	Balance
June	17	Uriah Co	P1		240	Cr	

c. Post the accounts below from the purchases journal to the general ledger.

Accounts Payable Journal Acct. No. 201

Date		Explanation	F	Debit	Credit	Dr or Cr	Balance
June	30		P1		2585 -	Cr	2585 -

Purchases Journal Acct. No. 351

Date		Explanation	F	Debit	Credit	Dr or Cr	Balance
June	30		P1	2585 -		Dr	2585 -

d. Prepare an accounts payable trial balance at June 30 from the subsidiary accounts payable ledger.

CLARKE FISHING EQUIPMENT SHOP LTD.
Schedule of Accounts Payable
June 30, 19XX

	$
Herman Company Ltd.	960
Milton Company Ltd.	410
Queens Company Ltd.	400
Thompson Supply Company Ltd.	575
Uriah Company Ltd.	240
	$2585

Note that the total of the schedule of accounts payable should agree with the balance in the general ledger control account, Accounts Payable.

APPENDIX The Voucher System

The accounting system must be designed not only to enable the recording of transactions and the preparation of financial statements but also to achieve other managerial objectives: (1) to furnish analyses and reports of past, current, and projected events and (2) to establish internal controls to protect the assets of the business against loss through errors or fraud. The achievement of these objectives goes hand in hand with the achievement of maximum operating efficiency and maximum earnings. A properly functioning voucher system plays a key role in establishing and maintaining effective internal control.

The voucher system is a method of accumulating, verifying, recording, and disbursing all the expenditures of a business. The system covers any transaction, except for payments out of petty cash, that will require the payment of cash, including the purchase of merchandise, services, supplies, and plant and equipment, and the payment of expenses. Expenditures are verified, classified, and recorded when they are incurred. All expenditures must be properly authorized and, except for petty cash transactions, are paid by check.

Reference has been made to the importance of having a built-in system to protect the assets of a business against loss through fraud or error. The voucher system is designed to achieve this internal control by distributing the duties of authorizing expenditures, reporting the receipt of goods or services, and signing checks. This division of duties prevents cash being disbursed from the business without proper approval and then only after verifications made by several members of the organization.

The Voucher

The *voucher* is a serially numbered form that is the written authorization for each expenditure. It is prepared from the seller's invoice or group of invoices or from other documents that serve as evidence of the liability. The voucher form is tailored to meet the needs of the particular business.

The voucher, not the invoice, is the basis for the accounting entry. The invoice, together with acknowledgments or approvals of the receipt of goods or services, and other supporting papers are the underlying documents for the voucher. The voucher form provides space for:

1. Summary of the invoice data
2. Accounts to be debited
3. Details of payment
4. Initials of persons who have checked accuracy of quantities, unit prices, extensions, and discount terms
5. Signature of the person who authorizes the payment
6. Signature of the person who records the voucher

The Voucher Jacket

The *voucher jacket* is a folded voucher form or envelope that serves both as a voucher and as a cover for the invoice, or group of invoices, from a particular vendor, and related documents. Space is provided on the outside of the jacket form for the details needed for the accounting entry.

Assume that during January 19XX Ajax Company Ltd. received ten invoices from a creditor, the Silver Company, with terms of 2/10, n/30. Upon receipt, the invoices are verified for quantities, prices, and extensions and are filed in a voucher jacket. The total price of the invoices, shown on the voucher jacket, is entered in the journal to record the liability and to classify the expenditures. It is then filed with other unpaid vouchers according to their due date so that payment will be made within the discount period. Another advantage of filing unpaid vouchers according to due date is that the amount of cash needed daily to pay vouchers due may be readily determined. Paid vouchers are filed alphabetically in a separate file.

The Voucher Register

The *voucher register* is an elaboration of the purchases journal. It is a journal for recording all liabilities approved for payment. The register is ruled in columns for the frequently used accounts to be charged or credited. The precise form of the register and the number and arrangement of the column headings vary with the needs of the particular business. A suggested outline of a voucher register is presented in Figure A6-1.

The function of the Vouchers Payable account is the same as that of the Accounts Payable account. It is a controlling account—its balance represents the total of the unpaid vouchers recorded in the voucher register. Unpaid vouchers may, therefore, be readily determined to be those without entries on the corresponding line of the Paid column or those in the *unpaid voucher* file. At the end of the period, a list of the unpaid vouchers in the file should be prepared for reconciliation with the balance of the Vouchers Payable account in the general ledger.

The voucher register is used for recording all transactions—of whatever category—that are due for payment. Each transaction is entered in the voucher register first, followed by an entry in the check register when payment is made. The vouchers are entered in the voucher register in numerical order. Transactions involving liabalities that are not initially credited to Vouchers Payable—notes payable and accrued expenses, for example—are usually not entered in the voucher register until payment is due. Vouchers are not prepared for accrued expenses; rather, a voucher is prepared for the full amount when the invoice is received or when payment is to be made.

Figure A6-1 Outlines of Voucher Register and Check Register

VOUCHER REGISTER — Page 8

			Paid		Credit	Debit							Other General Ledger Accounts			
							Selling Expense Control 600			General and Administrative Expense Control 700					Amount	
Date	Voucher No.	Name	Date	Check No.	Vouchers Payable 201	Purchases 351	Account No.	F	Amount	Account No.	F	Amount	Account	F	Debit	Credit

CHECK REGISTER — Page 6

				Debit	Credits	
Date	Voucher Number	Name	Check Number	Vouchers Payable 201	Purchases Discounts 365	Cash 101

An entry is made in the Credit Vouchers Payable column for the amount due on each voucher. The account or accounts to be debited are indicated on the voucher, and entries are made in one of the special debit columns or in the Other General Ledger Accounts column if no special column is available.

The Check Register

The check register is a book of original entry for all cash disbursements except petty cash; an outline of a check register is presented in Figure A6-1. No payment is made until a specific voucher has been prepared, recorded, and approved. Hence, each entry is a debit to Vouchers Payable, a credit to Cash, and a credit to Purchases Discounts, if any. No other columns are needed, because the transaction already has been classified under an appropriate heading in the voucher register. Checks are entered in the check register in numerical sequence, one line to each check. At the time that the check is entered in the check register, a notation must also be made in the Paid column of the voucher register showing the date of payment and the check number.

Use of the Voucher Register and the Check Register

The voucher register form must be tailored to meet the needs of the particular enterprise. The register provides columns for each general class of expenditure—Selling Expense Control and General and Administrative Expense Control, for example—with space to the left of each general column for the account number of the specific detail account to be debited. This gives the advantage of almost unlimited flexibility combined with economy of space.

The check register will include a Purchases Discounts column if the vouchers are recorded in the voucher register at invoice amounts. This register shows not only the serial number of the check but also the number of the voucher being paid.

Some companies prepare each voucher for the net amount due. This means that if payment is not made within the discount period, an additional voucher will be required, underscoring the expense for lost discounts. The entry in the voucher register for the additional voucher is a debit to Purchases Discounts Lost and a credit to Vouchers Payable. One check is made out for the full amount due as shown by the two vouchers.

Control of Unpaid Vouchers

The unpaid vouchers can be readily determined—they are the ones that have not been marked either "Paid" or "Canceled" in the Paid column. A schedule of unpaid vouchers is prepared at the end of the month; the total should correspond to the balance of the Vouchers Payable account in the general ledger. Thus, the unpaid vouchers file is a subsidiary ledger supporting the Vouchers Payable account.

Elimination of the Accounts Payable Ledger

When the voucher system is used, the subsidiary accounts payable ledger can be eliminated. Each numbered voucher is entered on a separate line in the voucher register and may be considered as a credit to a separate account. When the liability is settled and a notation is made in the Paid column, it is equivalent to a debit to that account. The file of unpaid vouchers replaces the accounts payable ledger. The total of the unpaid vouchers must agree with the total of the Vouchers Payable controlling account.

Advantages of the Voucher System

In a properly functioning voucher system, all invoices must be verified and approved for payment. As a result, responsibility is fixed and the possibility of error or fraud is reduced. The recording of all vouchers in a single journal (the voucher register) provides for prompt recognition and proper distribution of assets, liabilities, costs, and expenses. Economy in recording is effected by the elimination of the accounts payable ledger and by grouping invoices under a single voucher. The maintenance of a chronological unpaid voucher file facilitates the payment of invoices without loss of discounts. This file also enables management to determine its future cash needs for the settlement of liabilities. The systematic filing of paid vouchers provides a ready reference source for data and underlying documents for audit of all disbursements.

On the other hand, the voucher system has certain limitations. The difficulties in handling special transactions and the need for the preparation of separate vouchers or voucher jackets involve extra clerical and accounting work. The elimination of the accounts payable ledger results in a loss of valuable reference data, although this may be overcome by maintaining a file, arranged in alphabetical order by name of vendor, of copies of all vouchers.

GLOSSARY

Cash Payments Journal A special journal in which all cash payments are recorded.

Cash Receipts Journal A special journal in which all cash receipts are recorded.

Controlling Account One account in the general ledger that controls, and is supported by, a group of accounts in a separate subsidiary ledger.

Internal Control The built-in safeguards for the protection of the assets of an enterprise.

Purchases Journal A special journal in which only purchases of merchandise on account are recorded.

Sales Journal A special journal in which only sales of merchandise on account are recorded.

Schedule of Accounts Payable A listing of the individual creditors with amount owed to each and the total owed to all creditors at a given moment in time.

Schedule of Accounts Receivable A listing of the individual customers (debtors) with the amount owed by each and the total amounts receivable from all customers.

Source Document A business paper on which each individual transaction is recorded.

Subsidiary Ledger A group of accounts in a separate ledger that provides information in detail about one controlling account in the ledger.

Voucher A serially numbered form that is the written authorization for each expenditure prepared from the seller's invoice or a group of invoices or from other documents that serve as evidence of the liability.

Voucher Register A columnar journal for recording and summarizing all liabilities approved for payment.

Voucher System A method of accumulating, verifying, recording, and disbursing all the expenditures of a business. It covers all payments except those from the petty cash fund.

QUESTIONS

Q6-1. (a) What is the function of the systems analyst? (b) What are the considerations of the analyst in systems design? (c) In selecting the method or combination of methods of data collection, what criteria are used?

Q6-2. (a) What is the function of special journals? (b) What determines the types of special journals to be used? (c) Do the special journals entirely eliminate the need for a general journal? (d) How do special journals save time and labor? (e) Are there other advantages in using special journals?

Q6-3. What is the rule for entering a transaction (a) in the sales journal? (b) in the purchases journal? (c) in the cash receipts journal? (d) in the cash payments journal? (e) in the general journal?

Q6-4. What is the purpose of an Other Accounts section in a special journal? Describe the posting procedure for items recorded in the Other Accounts section.

Q6-5. Jetson Company Ltd. uses sales, purchases, cash receipts, cash payments, and general journals. State the journal in which each of the following transactions and events should be recorded:

1. Sale of merchandise on account
2. Purchase of store supplies on account
3. Return by a customer of a cash sale item for which the customer was given a refund check
4. Purchase of delivery equipment on account
5. Payment to a creditor
6. Sale of merchandise for cash
7. Adjusting entries
8. Purchase of merchandise on account
9. Note receivable issued by a customer in full settlement of his account
10. Return of a credit purchase for which the customer's account was credited
11. Payment of a dividend.
12. Closing entries
13. Payment of rent
14. Purchase of merchandise for cash
15. Note payable given to a creditor to apply on account

Q6-6. (a) When are postings made from the purchases journal (1) to the general ledger and (2) to the accounts payable ledger? (b) What is the relationship of the amounts posted? (c) How is it possible to trace postings from the journals to the ledgers? (d) What is the significance of the check mark in the folio (F) column of the purchases journal? (e) Would it be advisable to use code numbers as posting references for creditors' accounts rather than check marks?

Q6-7. The following questions relate to the cash receipts journal illustrated in this chapter: (a) What are the special columns? (b) Why is the journal cross-footed at the end of each month? (c) Explain the postings from this journal (1) to the general ledger and (2) to the accounts receivable ledger.

Q6-8. The column headings listed below might appear in one or more special journals.

1. Other Accounts—Debit
2. Purchases—Debit
3. Accounts Payable—Debit
4. Accounts Receivable—Credit
5. Office Supplies—Debit
6. Other Accounts—Credit
7. Accounts Payable—Credit
8. Cash—Credit
9. Accounts Receivable—Debit
10. Cash—Debit

The company maintains subsidiary ledgers for accounts receivable and accounts payable.

For each of the headings, state the special journal or journals in which it would be found and whether or not the amounts entered in the column would be posted as a total, or separately, or both as a total and separately.

DEMONSTRATION PROBLEMS

DP6-1. *(Special journals)* Quebec Company Inc. has been in operation for five years, selling merchandise for cash only. Beginning in January, it plans to start making sales on account. The general ledger of the company shows the following account balances on January 1.

101	Cash	$40,000
121	Accounts Receivable	-0-
122	Notes Receivable	-0-
131	Merchandise Inventory	60,000
141	Prepaid Insurance	-0-
201	Store Equipment	20,000
201A	Accumulated Depreciation—Store Equipment	8,000
301	Accounts Payable	-0-
302	Notes Payable	-0-
401	Capital Stock	100,000
402	Retained Earnings	12,000
501	Sales	-0-
502	Sales Returns and Allowances	-0-
503	Sales Discounts	-0-
601	Purchases	-0-
602	Purchases Returns and Allowances	-0-
603	Purchases Discounts	-0-
701	Salesmen's Salaries Expense	-0-

Transactions during the month of January:

Jan. 2 Sold merchandise to Thomas Armour on account, $900: terms, 2/10, n/30.

4 Sold merchandise to Billie Burton on account, $300: terms, 2/10, n/30.

6 Sold merchandise to William Canton on account, $600: terms, 2/10, n/30.

7 Sold merchandise to Dunlap Lawson on account, $400: terms, 2/10, n/30.

8 Purchased merchandise from the Milton Company on account, $2,000: terms, 1/10, n/30.

9 Purchased merchandise from the Naughton Company on account, $2,600, terms, 1/10, n/30.

10 Purchased merchandise from the Norton Company on account, $750: terms, n/45.

11 Purchased merchandise from the Rumbley Company on account, $1,200: terms, n/60.

12 Received a check from Thomas Armour for the amount due from the sale of January 2.

13 Issued additional capital stock for $10,000 in cash.

15 Cash sales of $9,000 were made.

16 Received a check from Billie Burton for $100 and a 60-day, 10% promissory note for the balance.

17 Received a check for $392 from William Canton in partial settlement of his account—$400 invoice price less $8 discount. Because the check was mailed before the expiration of the discount period, the discount was allowed.

18 Cash sales of $5,000 were made.

18 Purchased store equipment, $4,000, making a down payment of $1,000 and issuing a 120-day, 9% note payable for the balance.

18 Paid $480 for a comprehensive 2-year insurance policy, dating from January 1.

18 Paid the amount due the Milton Company for the purchases made on January 8.

19 Paid $1,485 in partial settlement of the amount due the Naughton Company: $1,500 invoice price less $15 discount.

20 Paid salesmen's salaries of $1,000.

20 Cash purchases totaled $4,760.

28 Issued a 90-day, 9% note to the Naughton Company in settlement of balance of account.

30 Returned merchandise to the Norton Company and received credit, $160.

31 Credited Dunlap Lawson for $120 for merchandise returned.

Required:

1. Open the necessary general and subsidiary ledgers.
2. Journalize all the charge sales in a sales journal and post them to the accounts receivable ledger. Provide invoice numbers starting with 0001. Summarize the sales journal and make the January 31 postings to the general ledger.

3. Journalize all the charge purchases in a purchases journal and post them to the accounts payable ledger. Summarize the purchases journal and make January 31 postings to the general ledger.
4. Journalize all the cash receipts in a cash receipts journal and post them to the accounts receivable ledger. Summarize and cross-foot the journal and make January 31 postings to the general ledger.
5. Journalize all the cash payments in a cash payments journal and post them to the accounts payable ledger. Provide check numbers starting with 4062. Summarize and cross-foot the journal and make January 31 postings to the general ledger.
6. Journalize any other transactions in a two-column general journal.
7. Prove the balances of the Accounts Receivable and Accounts Payable accounts by preparing a schedule of accounts receivable and a schedule of accounts payable.

PROBLEMS

P6-1. The numbers below indicate the corresponding columns in the cash receipts and cash payments journals of Brevard Company:

Journal	*Column Heading*	*Number*
Cash Receipts	Cash—debit	1
	Accounts Receivable—credit	2
	Sales—credit	3
	Other Accounts—credit	4
Cash Payments	Cash—credit	5
	Accounts Payable—debit	6
	Purchases—debit	7
	Other Accounts—debit	8

Indicate how the following transactions would be entered in the journals by designating the appropriate column numbers for the debits and the credits.

1. Payment to creditor on account
2. Payment of salaries
3. Collection from customer on account
4. Payment of insurance premium for two years
5. Issuance of common stock for cash
6. Cash sale
7. Cash purchase of merchandise

P6-2. Allison Company Ltd. made the following merchandise sales on account during May:

May 2 To A. B. Carson, $170.
3 To D. G. Dawson, $150.
4 To E. E. Eason, $300.
7 To J. K. Nelson, $420.
7 To A. B. Carson, $185.
12 To D. G. Dawson, $90.
20 To E. E. Eason, $65.
31 To J. K. Nelson, $175.

a. Record the transactions in a sales journal similar to the one illustrated in this chapter. The terms on credit sales are 2/10, n/30. Number the sales invoices, starting with 101.

b. Open accounts in the accounts receivable ledger for the customers.
c. Open the following accounts in the general ledger: Accounts Receivable 111 and Sales 301.
d. Post from the sales journal to the accounts receivable ledger and the general ledger.

P6-3. The Potter Corporation received its charter on March 1. During the month of March, it completed the following cash receipt transactions:

Mar. 1 Capital stock of $40,000 was issued at par for cash.
8 Received a check for $196 from Nelson Parker in settlement of a $200 sales invoice.
15 Cash sales for March 1 through 15 were $2,600.
17 Received $120 in cash from Bobo Farrell (no discount).
23 Borrowed $2,000 in cash from the Provincial National Bank and gave a note payable due April 23, 1976.
25 Received a check for $388 from Fred Eckel in settlement of a $400 sales invoice.
31 Cash sales for March 16 through 31 were $3,400.
31 Sold at cost a parcel of land purchased on March 1 for $5,500, receiving $2,500 in cash and a note receivable for the balance.

a. Record the transactions in a cash receipts journal similar to the one illustrated in this chapter.
b. Open the following general ledger accounts:
Cash 101
Accounts Receivable 111
Notes Receivable 115
Land 121
Notes Payable 205
Capital Stock 251
Sales 301
Sales Discounts 311

Post a debit of $890 to Accounts Receivable; date the posting March 31. This amount is from the sales journal.
c. Open the following accounts in the accounts receivable ledger and record the amounts given in the Debit and Balance columns (these are summary totals posted from the sales journal): Fred Eckel, $400; Bobo Farrell, $280; Nelson Parker, $210.
d. Post from the cash receipts journal to the accounts receivable ledger and the general ledger.
e. Prepare a schedule of accounts receivable.

P6-4. Copper Cliff Company Ltd. was organized on May 1. The following cash payments were made during the month:

May 1 Purchased land and building for $50,000. Paid $20,000 in cash and a note for $30,000. Land is appraised at $10,000; building, at $40,000.
10 Paid the Spragge Company $980 in settlement of a purchase made on May 2; the invoice price was $1,000.
15 Cash purchases for May 1 through 15 were $8,000.

May 17 Paid the Kagawong Company $2,000 on account (no discount).
20 Purchased office equipment for $3,000 in cash.
31 Paid the Providence Bay Company $700 on account (no discount).
31 Paid a 9%, 30-day note due this date. Face value of the note was $6,000; interest was $45.
31 Cash purchases for May 16 through 31 were $12,000.

a. Record the transactions in a cash payments journal similar to the one illustrated in this chapter.

b. Open the following general ledger accounts:

Cash 101
Land 201
Building 202
Office Equipment 203
Accounts Payable 301
Notes Payable 302
Purchases 401
Purchases Discounts 402
Interest Expense 501

Enter the following account balances:

1. Cash debit, $150,000—posted from the cash receipts journal.
2. Accounts Payable credit, $5,700—posted from the purchases journal.
3. Notes Payable credit, $6,000—posted from the cash receipts journal.

c. Open the following accounts in the accounts payable ledger and record the amounts given in the Credit and Balance columns (these are summary totals posted from the purchases journal): Kagawong Company, $2,400; Providence Bay Company, $1,800; Spragge Company, $1,500.

d. Post from the cash payments journal to the accounts payable ledger and the general ledger.

e. Prepare a schedule of accounts payable.

P6-5. Mattehorn Company Ltd. uses sales, purchases, cash receipts, cash payments, and general journals. On January 31, it had the following amounts in its general ledger after the books had been closed:

Cash

1	116,000	2	76,000

Accounts Receivable

3	120,000	4	40,000

Accounts Payable

5	16,000	6	39,000

Sales

7	156,000	8	120,000
		9	36,000

Purchases

10	39,000	12	51,000
11	12,000		

Purchases Returns and Allowances

13	3,600	14	3,600

On a sheet of paper, opposite numbers 1 through 14 corresponding to the numbers that appear in the folio columns of the accounts, indicate the most probable journal source for each posting. Use the abbreviations J, S, P, CR, and CP to identify the journals, as shown in the following example:

Number	*Journal Source*
1	CR

P6-6. During June, Builders' Hardware Supply Company Ltd. completed the transactions listed below:

June 1 Sold merchandise on account to Donald Baty, $2,300.
3 Sold merchandise on account to Robert Ludlow, $920.
7 Issued additional capital stock at par, $3,000.
10 Sold merchandise on account to Richard Mason, $560.
12 Sold merchandise on account to Donald Baty, $710.
13 Received a check from Robert Ludlow for the amount due.
15 Cash sales to date, $4,650.
18 Sold merchandise on account to Joseph Bateman, $380.
20 Borrowed $600 in cash from First Provincial Bank and gave a 30-day, 9% note for that amount.
23 Received a $200 check from Richard Mason to apply on account.
24 Received a check from Joseph Batemen for the amount due.
26 Sold merchandise on account to Robert Briant, $520.
27 Received a check from Donald Baty for the amount due.
28 Sold merchandise on account to Richard Mason, $200.
29 Received a check from Robert Briant for the amount due.
30 Cash sales from June 16 through 30 were $4,060.
30 Received $200 in rent on land for June.

Required:

1. Record the transactions in a sales journal and a cash receipts journal similar to the ones illustrated in this chapter. Terms of 2/10, n/30 apply to all sales on account. (Number the sales invoices, starting with 51.)
2. Open the following accounts in the general ledger: Cash, 101; Accounts Receivable, 111; Notes Payable, 205; Capital Stock, 251; Sales, 301; Sales Discounts, 311; Rent Earned, 351.
3. Open the customers' accounts in the accounts receivable ledger.
4. Post from the two journals to the accounts receivable ledger and general ledger.
5. Prepare a schedule of accounts receivable.

P6-7. Montreal Company Ltd. started operations on August 1. During August, the company used the following accounts:

Cash 101
Accounts Receivable 111
Notes Receivable 115
Prepaid Insurance 117
Office Supplies 118
Land 151
Store Building 154
Store Fixtures 156
Sales 401
Sales Discounts 402
Sales Returns and Allowances 403
Purchases 501
Purchases Discounts 502
Purchases Returns and Allowances 503
Transportation In 504
Salaries Expense 601

Office Equipment 158
Accounts Payable 201
Mortgage Payable 251
Capital Stock 301

Delivery Expense 611
Office Expense 621
Utilities Expense 631

The following transactions occurred during August:

Aug. 1 Issued for cash capital stock worth $30,000.
1 Purchased a store building and site for $60,000 of which $15,000 is considered land cost. Paid $10,000 in cash and issued a mortgage for the balance.
1 Purchased store fixtures from the Mebane Company for $6,800 on account; terms, n/60.
2 Purchased merchandise from Isaacs, Inc., on account, $4,000; invoice date August 1; terms, 2/10, n/60.
2 Purchased merchandise from Jacob Barstow on account, $8,000; invoice date, August 2; terms, 2/10, n/60.
6 Purchased a 3-year fire insurance policy for $720 in cash.
8 Purchased merchandise for $5,000 in cash.
9 Returned unsatisfactory merchandise to Isaacs, Inc., and received credit for $800.
13 Sold merchandise to Dunn Evanston on account, $8,200; invoice No. 1; terms, 1/10, n/30.
14 Paid Isaacs, Inc., and Jacob Barstow the amounts due.
15 Cash sales from August 1 through 15 were $3,400.
16 Sold merchandise to Hilton Keith on account, $4,700; invoice No. 2; terms 1/10, n/30.
16 Sold merchandise to Lamb Learner on account, $6,300; invoice No. 3; terms, 1/10, n/30.
16 Paid salaries for August 1 through 15 totaling $2,650.
19 Sold merchandise to Andrew Melbourne on account, $8,000; invoice No. 4; terms, 1/10, n/30.
21 Purchased merchandise from the Ramsey Company on account, $4,900; invoice date, August 21; terms, 1/10, n/30.
21 Received bill for $130 from the Saffelle Supply Company for items chargeable to Office Expense; terms n/30.
23 Received merchandise returned by Andrew Melbourne; issued credit memo No. 1 for $2,000.
23 Received cash from Dunn Evanston for invoice No. 1, less discount.
26 Received cash from Hilton Keith for invoice No. 2, less discount.
26 Purchased merchandise from Dunkirk, Inc., on account, $9,100; invoice date, August 24; terms, 3/10, n/30. Paid transportation charges of $90. The goods were shipped F.O.B. shipping point.
28 Received $1,300 cash from Lamb Learner and a 9%, 60-day note for the balance.
29 Sold merchandise to Nathan Waters on account, $4,000; invoice No. 5; terms, 1/10, n/30.
29 Paid $215 in cash for electricity.
29 Paid the Ramsey Company on the invoice of August 21, less discount.
29 Received cash from Andrew Melbourne for the balance of invoice No. 4, less discount.

31 Cash sales from August 16 through 31 were $1,950.

31 Paid salaries for August 16 through 31 totaling $2,850.

31 Received a bill for $96 from the Delivu Company for delivery service for the month.

31 Purchased two filing cabinets and a typewriter at a cost of $750 and various office supplies at a cost of $300; paid $350 in cash and issued $700 par value capital stock for the balance.

Required:

1. Record the transactions in a general journal, a cash receipts journal, a cash payments journal, a sales journal, and a purchases journal.
2. Indicate how the postings would be made from the journals by entering the appropriate posting references.

P6-8. (Appendix) Albie Company Ltd. prepares its vouchers for the net amount due. A section of the voucher register, showing the unpaid vouchers as of June 30, is given below.

Date		Vou. No.	Name	Paid		Credit Vou. Pay.	Debit Purch.	Debit Purch. Disc. Lost	Other General Ledger Accounts		
				Date	Ck. No.				Account	Debit	Credit
June	1	78	Robert Doyle			98					
	3	81	Bennett Co.			1,960					
	5	82	Gates & Son			392					

Among the company's July transactions are the following:

July 1 Issued check No. 110 in payment of voucher No. 78.

5 Issued voucher No. 83 payable to Gates & Son for $8 discount lost on the purchase of June 5.

6 Issued check No. 111 in payment of vouchers No. 82 and 83.

10 Issued voucher No. 84 to the Giles Company for $1,000 worth of merchandise; terms, 2/10, n/30.

14 Issued voucher No. 85 to Warren's, Inc., for $1,500 worth of merchandise; terms 1½/10, n/30.

16 By special arrangement with the Bennett Company the purchase of June 3 (invoice $2,000; terms, 2/10, n/30) is to be paid for in installments: $800 immediately and the balance on August 16. Issued voucher No. 86 for the purchase discount lost. Canceled vouchers No. 81 and 86 and issued vouchers No. 87 and 88. Issued check No. 112 in payment of voucher No. 87.

20 Issued check No. 113 in payment of voucher No. 84.

Required:

1. Enter the unpaid vouchers as of July 1 in a voucher register similar to the one shown above; record the July transactions in the voucher register and a single-column check register.
2. Enter the total amount of unpaid vouchers as of July 1 ($2,450) as a credit

to the Vouchers Payable general ledger account; post to a Vouchers Payable T account from the voucher register and the check register.

3. Prepare a schedule of unpaid vouchers.

P6-9. (Mini case) Dexter Distributors Inc. is a petroleum products dealership. It operates several trucks that are constantly on the road filling fuel tanks of customers who use fuel oil for home heating. For each such delivery a sales ticket is prepared. A meter on the truck automatically stamps the number of gallons delivered at each stop. These sales tickets are returned to the accounting department at the end of each day where they are priced so that invoices can be mailed to the customers. Customers are allowed a discount of one cent per gallon if they pay within ten days of billing date.

Fuel oil is stored in a large tank that is refilled about twice a week by tankers from the area distributor. Each time the area distributor's tanker delivers a load, a receiver's report is prepared and sent to the accounting department. The distributor requires payment monthly, and does not offer a discount.

The business has 32 employees. They are paid on the 15 and the last day of each month. Supplies and other expenses are billed to Dexter Distributors Inc. with almost all suppliers offering terms of 2/10, n/30.

You have been asked for your opinion on an accounting system for Dexter Distributors Inc.

1. Should it use a sales journal? Why or why not? If it should, what procedure should be used to record entries to it and get invoices mailed to customers as soon as possible after deliveries?
2. Does it need a purchase journal or could all purchases be recorded in the general journal? Explain.
3. Would a cash receipts journal be a good idea? (About 75 to 100 checks are received by mail per day.) If so, what special column should be included?
4. Is there any advantage to the use of a cash payments journal? Explain your answer.

Part Two

Income Measurement and Valuation Problems Related to Sources and Uses of Invested Capital

7

Cash and Receivables

Cash includes any item that a bank customarily accepts for deposit. Coins, *currency* (paper money), bank drafts, cashier's checks, money orders, and bank balances are included in the Cash account. Postdated checks and I.O.U.s are receivables, not cash; postage stamps are prepaid expenses.

Effective management and control of cash is of the greatest importance to a firm, because cash represents instantly available purchasing power and because nearly every transaction ultimately involves the exchange of cash.

Making sales and purchases on account has become standard business practice. Individuals and businesses alike buy and sell merchandise, invest in stocks and bonds, and even acquire plant and equipment on credit. Consequently, the increasing trend toward the extension of credit terms for transactions involving all types of goods and services has led to a greater need for control and analysis of receivables by management.

This chapter deals with the control of cash and the control and measurement of accounts receivable.

CONTROL OF CASH

INTERNAL CONTROL

One of the primary functions of management is to protect the assets of a business against avoidable loss. As a business grows in size and complexity, it becomes increasingly important to organize the supervision of the bookkeeping and accounting records to control the receipt of cash, to minimize or prevent the unauthorized disbursement of cash, and to eliminate errors. Employees must be carefully selected and trained, and their duties, responsibilities, and authority clearly defined. Adequate organization also requires the separation of duties, so that no one person is in complete charge of any business transaction. An error—whether intentional or not—is more likely to be discovered if a transaction is handled by two or more persons, so that, as far as possible, the work of each employee who records property is checked automatically by some other employee. It is customary business practice, for example, for one person to make the sale and prepare a sales slip and for another person to receive the cash or record the charge to the customer's account; one person may prepare the payroll and another person make the actual payments to employees; one employee may prepare the check for payment to a creditor, another employee or an officer may sign the check, and a third employee may post the debit to the creditor's account. Adequate organization also provides for a regular follow-up to see how well the accounting work is being done. This system of self-policing is referred to as *internal control.*

Cash Control

Cash is naturally vulnerable to theft or misuse. If cash is handled and controlled properly, both the employer and the employee benefit—the employer safeguards the asset and the employee avoids suspicion of inaccuracy or dishonesty. Embezzlers often begin their criminal careers by temporarily borrowing funds from the company, intending to replace the cash. The intention usually falters. It is to the advantage of both employer and employee to institute such safeguards as will deter employees from misappropriating funds. The safeguards must be designed to prevent the following:

1. Misappropriation of cash on receipt and failure to record the transaction in the cash receipts journal. For example, scrap and waste material may be sold by an employee for cash and not reported.
2. Delay in recording the receipt of cash (the cash being withheld during the interval), or recording false entries. For example, cash may be pocketed on receipt of a payment from a customer but his account may be credited with an offsetting debit to Sales Returns and Allowances.
3. The recording of fictitious charges to expense accounts or other accounts to cover fraudulent cash withdrawals. For example, a branch supervisor may carry a terminated employee's name on the payroll for several additional pay periods, forging the endorsement of the former employee on a fictitious payroll check.

Certain basic controls must be instituted to prevent the misuse of funds. The individual responsibility for each step in the flow of cash must be clearly established. An entry to record the receipt of cash must be made promptly. On receipt all checks should be rubber-stamped *For deposit only* to prevent their misuse. All cash receipts should be deposited intact daily; payments should be made by company check and not out of cash receipts. Mechanical accounting control devices should be used wherever possible.

The protection of cash against losses through fraud, error, and carelessness requires certain fundamental steps, including:

1. A clear segregation of duties and responsibilities.
2. Provision of the necessary facilities, such as cash registers.
3. Furnishing definite written instructions with respect to authorization for and the payment of cash.
4. Organization of the flow and recording of documents so that, whenever possible, the work of one employee is subject to automatic verification by another employee. The handling and recording of cash should be so planned that no one person both receives or disburses cash and records it in the cash journals.
5. Periodic testing to see if internal controls are operating effectively. For example, at unannounced times, a surprise cash count should be made to compare actual cash held with the records.

Petty Cash

For adequate internal control, all cash receipts should be deposited intact daily and all disbursements should be made by check. There are occasions, however, when payment by check is impractical, such as for postage, small contributions, express charges, carfare, and minor supplies. A special fund, called the *petty cash fund,* should be set up for these purposes. The fund is placed in charge of one person, and each payment should be supported by a signed receipt, called a *petty cash voucher,* that shows the purpose of the expenditure, the date, and the amount.

To set up the petty cash fund, a check is drawn to the order of the fund custodian and cashed for the amount to be placed in the fund. The journal entry is:

Petty Cash	50	
Cash		50

Safekeeping of the money and the signed vouchers is the responsibility of the custodian, who should be provided with a secure petty cash box or cash register.

When the cash in the fund approaches a stated minimum, or at the end of each month, the fund is replenished; the signed petty cash vouchers serve as evidence of the disbursements. The entry in the cash payments journal to record a check for $43 issued to replenish the petty cash fund for certain expenditures made is:

Postage Expense	12.00	
Telephone and Telegraph Expense	4.00	
Miscellaneous Selling Expense	14.50	
Miscellaneous General Expense	3.75	
Transportation In	8.25	
Cash Over and Short	.50	
Cash		43.00

The Petty Cash account in the general ledger remains at its original balance of $50. It does not change unless the amount of the fund itself is either increased or decreased. It is for this reason that the method described here is called the *imprest* (or fixed) petty cash system. The fund should be replenished at the end of each accounting period to record all the expenses incurred during the period and to bring the amount of cash on hand in the fund up to the balance of the Petty Cash account in the general ledger.

It will be noted that, in the foregoing journal entry, a cash shortage found at the time of replenishment was debited to an expense account, Cash Over and Short. Shortages considered unreasonable should be investigated. Unannounced inspections should be held at intervals to determine that the amount of cash in the fund plus receipted vouchers is equal to the fund amount.

The Bank Statement

It is customary for banks to send depositors a monthly statement together with the canceled checks and notices of bank charges and credits. The statement shows the activities for the month; it should list:

1. Beginning balance
2. Deposits received
3. Checks paid
4. Other charges and credits to the account
5. Ending balance

Hall Corporation's bank statement for September is shown in Figure 7-1.

Figure 7-1
Bank Statement

STATEMENT OF ACCOUNT
WITH
ONE CHARTERED BANK
EDMONTON, ALBERTA
Acct. No. 037–325079

Hall Corporation
Edmonton, Alberta

Checks and Other Debits			*Deposits*	*Date*	*Balance*
Balance forward from last statement.				Sept. 1	7,320.00
			450.00	Sept. 1	7,770.00
49.00	1,237.00			Sept. 2	6,484.00
			48.00	Sept. 3	6,532.00
175.00	1,300.00 CC			Sept. 6	5,057.00
14.00			1,650.00	Sept. 11	6,693.00
			762.00	Sept. 15	7,455.00
28.50	27.25	275.00	1,312.00	Sept. 18	8,436.25
2,000.00	367.00	2.00 DM	500.00 CM	Sept. 29	6,567.25
4.00 SC				Sept. 30	6,563.25

CC—Certified Check
NSF—Not Sufficient Funds
SC—Service Charge

DM—Debit Memo
CM—Credit Memo
OD—Overdraft

The letter combinations listed in the lower section of the bank statement form identify certain entries on the statement.

Certified Check (*CC*). When the depositor requests a check to be certified, the bank immediately deducts the amount of the check from the depositor's balance.

Not Sufficient Funds (*NSF*). Deposits generally include checks received from trade customers. A customer's check that has been deposited may not clear on presentation for payment because the customer's bank balance is less than the amount of the check. If so, the check is deducted from the depositor's balance, the entry is identified by the letters NSF, and the check is returned to the depositor.

Service Charge (*SC*). A service charge is a charge by the bank for acting as a depository for funds. The charge is based on the activity of the account in terms of number of items deposited and checks presented for payment.

Debit Memo (*DM*). A debit memo is a deduction from the depositor's account for additional services rendered (or an adjustment of an error); for example, the charge for collecting a note receivable is reported in a debit memo.

Credit Memo (*CM*). A credit memo is a credit, usually shown in the Deposits column, for items collected (or an adjustment of an error); for example, the collection of a note receivable left at the bank by a depositor is reported in a credit memo.

Overdraft (OD). An overdraft is the amount by which withdrawals exceed the depositor's available balance. The overdraft, if permitted, is usually preceded by a minus sign in the Balance column.

The Bank Reconciliation

The use of a checking account is essential to the control of cash. If all cash receipts are deposited intact and all cash payments are made by check, the records of the bank can be *reconciled* regularly with those of the depositor. The *bank reconciliation* underscores the reciprocal relationship between the bank's records and the depositor's. For each entry in the depositor's books, there should be a counterpart in the bank's books. All debits to Cash in the depositor's books should be matched by credit entries to the depositor's account in the bank's books; all credit entries to Cash in the depositor's books should be matched by debit entries to the depositor's account. For instance, cash received from a customer is recorded in the company's books by debiting Cash and crediting Accounts Receivable; the bank, on receiving the cash, credits the depositor's account. The company records a payment to a creditor by debiting Accounts Payable and crediting Cash; the bank debits the depositor's account.

The records of the depositor and of the bank will not normally agree at the end of the month because of items that appear on one record but not on the other. It is necessary, therefore, to reconcile the two balances and to determine the *adjusted,* or true, cash balance. Discrepancies between the balances may be due to the time lag in recording debits and credits, to special charges and credits of which either the depositor or the bank is unaware, or to errors and irregularities.

The Bank Reconciliation Procedure

A format for a bank reconciliation is given in Figure 7-2. Errors and adjustments in the Per Books section require entries in the general journal to correct the books; adjustments in the Per Bank section do not require entries.

The bank reconciliation is prepared as follows:

1. The deposits shown on the bank statement are compared with those entered in the cash receipts journal. Deposits made too late in the month to be credited by the bank on the current statement are referred to as *deposits in transit.* The bank reconciliation for the previous month should be inspected for any deposits in transit at the end of that period; they should appear as the initial deposits of the current period. Any items not on the statement should be investigated.

2. Checks paid and returned by the bank (*canceled checks*) are arranged in numerical order and compared with the entries in the cash payments journal. Checks that have not yet been presented to the bank for payment are called *outstanding checks.* The previous bank reconciliation should be inspected for outstanding checks.

3. Special debits and credits made by the bank—usually reported in debit or credit memos—are compared with the depositor's books to see if they have already been recorded.

4. Any errors in the bank's or the depositor's records that become apparent during completion of the prior steps are listed.

Hall's cash records for September show the following items:

		Cash Deposits	
Sept.	3		$ 48.00
	10		1,650.00
	14		762.00
	18		1,312.00
	30		1,050.00
			$4,822.00

		Checks Issued	
Sept.	2	702	$ 175.00
	5	703	1,300.00
	8	704	14.00
	15	705	82.50
	15	706	312.25
	18	707	27.25
	26	708	2,000.00
	26	709	367.00
	30	710	103.00
			$4,381.00

Figure 7-2
Format for a Bank Reconciliation

NAME
Bank Reconciliation
Date

Per Books

Cash Balance per Ledger, Date		$xxx
Add: (1) Any proper increases in cash already recorded by the bank that have not been recorded as yet by the firm		
Example: Collection of note by bank	$xx	
(2) Any error in the firm's books that failed to reveal a proper increase in cash or that improperly decreased cash		
Example: Check from customer for $90 entered as $70	xx	xx
Total		$xxx
Deduct: (1) Any proper decreases in cash already recorded by the bank that have not been recorded as yet by the firm		
Example: Bank service charges	$xx	
(2) Any error in the firm's books that failed to reveal a proper decrease in cash or that improperly increased cash		
Example: Check issued in payment to a creditor for $462 entered as $426	xx	xx
Adjusted Cash Balance, Date		$xxx

Per Bank

Cash Balance per Bank Statement, Date		$xxx
Add: (1) Any proper increases in cash already recorded by the firm that have not been recorded as yet by the bank		
Example: Deposits in transit	$xx	
(2) Any error by the bank that failed to reveal a proper increase in cash or that improperly decreased cash		
Example: Another depositor's check incorrectly charged to this depositor's account	xx	xx
Total		$xxx
Deduct: (1) Any proper decreases in cash already recorded by the firm that have not been recorded as yet by the bank		
Example: Outstanding checks	$xx	
(2) Any error by the bank that failed to reveal a proper decrease in cash or that improperly increased cash		
Example: Firm's deposit of $679 entered by bank as $697	xx	xx
Adjusted Cash Balance, Date		$xxx

The statement received from the bank (Figure 7-1) shows a balance of $6,563.25 as of September 30. The following items were received from the bank together with the bank statement:

Canceled checks:	*Check*	*Amount*
	680	$ 49.00
	694	1,237.00
	702	175.00
	703	1,300.00
	704	14.00
	705	28.50
	707	27.25
	708	2,000.00
	709	367.00
	Check of Frederick Hale	275.00

Memos:

Credit memo, $500, for a note receivable collected by the bank on September 29.

Debit memo, $2, dated September 29, for collection fee charged by bank.

Notification of a certified check for $1,300 deducted on September 6. (Even if the certified check, No. 703, had not been canceled by the bank during September, it would not be listed as outstanding, because it has been entered on both Hall's and the bank's records and would therefore not need to be reconciled.)

Service charge notification, $4, dated September 30.

The following points should be emphasized:

1. The beginning balance in the Per Books section is taken from the general ledger Cash account:

Cash balance per ledger, August 31	$ 6,400
Add deposits	4,822
Total	$11,222
Deduct checks issued	4,381
Cash balance per ledger, September 30	$ 6,841

2. Check No. 705 was incorrectly recorded in Hall's books as $82.50 instead of $28.50. The error overstated cash disbursements and therefore understated the ending cash balance by $54 = ($82.50 − $28.50).

3. The beginning balance in the Per Bank section is the last amount in the Balance column of the bank statement for the month of September (Figure 7-1).

4. The deposit of $1,050 made on September 30 was not credited on the bank statement because it was in transit.

5. While determining the outstanding checks, Hall discovered that the bank had deducted in error a check for $275 signed by another depositor, Frederick Hale. This resulted in an understatement of the bank balance on the bank statement. The bank was notified about this error.

6. Check No. 701 was listed as an outstanding check on the bank reconciliation of August 31. Since it has not yet been presented to the bank for payment, it continues to be listed as an outstanding check.

All the items that appear in the Per Bank section of the bank reconciliation for the previous month must be traced to the current month's bank statement.

The following items appear in the August bank reconciliation:

Deposit in transit		Outstanding checks	
		Check	*Amount*
August 31	450	680	$ 49
		694	1,237
		701	84

Following receipt of the bank statement, Hall prepares the bank reconciliation statement shown in Figure 7-3.

Figure 7-3
Bank Reconciliation

Per Books			
Cash balance per ledger, September 30			$6,841.00
Add: Customer's note collected by bank			500.00
Error in entering check No. 705:			
Entered as		$ 82.50	
Correct amount		28.50	54.00
Total			$7,395.00
Deduct: Bank service charge		$ 4.00	
Collection fee		2.00	6.00
Adjusted cash balance, September 30			$7,389.00
Per Bank			
Cash balance per bank statement, September 30			$6,563.25
Add: Deposit of Sept. 30 in transit to bank			1,050.00
Check of Frederick Hale deducted by bank in error			275.00
Total			$7,888.25
Deduct: Outstanding checks			
	Check	*Amount*	
	701	$ 84.00	
	706	312.25	
	710	103.00	499.25
Adjusted cash balance, September 30			$7,389.00

Required Journal Entries

All additions to, and deductions from, the balance per books must be entered on Hall's books to bring the general ledger Cash account balance into agreement with the adjusted cash balance. The Cash account balance of $6,841 should be increased by $548 = ($500 + $54 − $6) to show the actual cash balance of $7,389 as of September 30.

The required entries are shown below in general journal form:

Cash	498	
Bank Service and Collection Charges Expense	2	
Notes Receivable		500
To record collection of note receivable by bank and related charge.		
Cash	54	
Accounts Payable		54
To record correction of error in entering check No. 705 as $82.50 instead of $28.50.		
Bank Service and Collection Charges Expense	4	
Cash		4
To record bank service charge for September.		

These entries may be made in the cash journals for September if the journals have not been footed and posted, or the following compound entry may be made in the general journal:

Cash	548	
Bank Service and Collection Charges Expense	6	
Notes Receivable		500
Accounts Payable		54
To adjust the Cash account per bank reconciliation for September.		

After the entry is posted, Hall's Cash account appears as shown below. Note that the beginning balance for the new period (October) agrees with the adjusted cash balance in the bank reconciliation. Except for the word Balance on September 30 and October 1, the explanations would be omitted in an actual account. They are shown here in parentheses so that the reader may trace the source of each entry.

Cash **Acct. No. 101**

Sept.	1	(beginning balance)	6,400	Sept. 30	(checks issued)	4,381
	30	(cash deposits)	4,822			
	30	(adjustment)	548			
			11,770			4,381
Oct.	1	Balance	7,389			

Only the items from the reconciliation that either increase or decrease the balance per books need to be entered in the journal. The items that increase or decrease the balance per bank already have been recorded on the depositor's books. Any errors made by the bank should be brought to the bank's attention.

Cash Over and Short

The daily count of cash in the cash registers may differ from the cash register readings. If the records do not disclose a clerical error, it may be assumed that the overage or the shortage was caused by an error in making change. The discrepancy may be entered temporarily in the books as a debit or a credit to Cash Over and Short. To illustrate, assume that the cash register tape shows cash sales for the day of $100 but the count shows the cash on hand to be $101.50. The journal entry to record the cash sales and the cash overage is:

Cash	101.50	
Sales		100.00
Cash Over and Short		1.50

If the cash count showed $98.50, the entry would be:

Cash	98.50	
Cash Over and Short	1.50	
Sales		100.00

Cash Over and Short is classified on the income statement as general expense if a debit or other revenue if a credit.

ACCOUNTS RECEIVABLE MEASUREMENT

There are two classes of trade receivables: accounts receivable, which are claims against customers for sales made on open account, and notes receivable, which are claims against customers supported by written formal promises to pay. From a legal point of view, a note receivable is probably better security than an account receivable because it is a written acknowledgment of the debt; however, in Canada, the unsecured open account form of credit is well established. Nontrade receivables arise from money lent from deposits made, and from other sources.

The various claims should be properly recorded in several separate accounts, one possible classification of which appears below:

1. Accounts Receivable—Trade. This account represents claims against customers for goods sold or for services rendered.

2. Accounts Receivable—Nontrade. This group of accounts represents claims arising from sources other than normal trade transactions, including:
   a. Loans to employees, officers, directors and shareholders
   b. Deposits made on contract bids with public utilities or government agencies
   c. Claims against common carriers for loss or damage to goods in shipment, loss claims against insurance companies, and claims for tax refunds
   d. Amounts due from subsidiaries and other affiliated companies
   e. Amounts due or accrued from rentals, interest, and royalties

Notes are similarly classified as trade or nontrade receivables. Nontrade notes receivable should be carried in accounts specifically designated as to source (officers, affiliated companies, rental property) and properly classified on the balance sheet.

Receivables that are due and collectible within a year should be shown in the Current Assets section of the statement of financial position. The terms *Accounts Receivable* and *Notes Receivable,* if unqualified, should be understood to represent trade receivables collectible within one year or one operating cycle. Nontrade receivables that are not due or are not collectible within a year should be shown under Long-Term Investments.

The amount of loans made to directors or officers, other than in normal trade transactions, and repaid during the same financial period should be disclosed in the financial statements regardless of the fact that no receivable exists at the end of the financial period.[1]

RECOGNITION OF LOSSES ON UNCOLLECTIBLE ACCOUNTS

A basic principle in accounting is that the earned revenue of any accounting period and the actual expense incurred in realizing that revenue should be related.

The cost of the goods sold and all other expenses incurred during the period should be related or should be deducted from the revenue of that period. Hence, the cost of a machine is spread over the period during which the machine is used to arrive at a fair measure of the net income for each period. It would be inaccurate to charge the entire cost at the time of purchase or disposal of the machine.

Similarly, since the balance in the Accounts Receivable account represents uncollected amounts included in revenue, losses that may arise through failure to collect any of the receivables should be recognized as an expense of doing business during the period when the sales were made.

Recording the Bad Debts Adjustment

To illustrate the recording of a bad debts adjustment, assume that on December 31 the credit department of the Greene Corporation, having analyzed sales

[1]*CICA Handbook* (Toronto: Canadian Institute of Chartered Accountants), Section 3020.03.

during the year and past-due accounts, determines that out of the current year's sales, $550 will be uncollectible. This amount represents a bad debts expense to be shown in the General and Administrative Expenses section of the income statement as a deduction from revenue. The estimated losses pertain to accounts receivable resulting from sales of the current period; therefore, in accordance with the principle of the periodic matching of expenses and revenues, estimated bad debts losses should be charged against revenue.

The adjusting general journal entry recorded on December 31 and the posting of the entry to the general ledger are shown below.

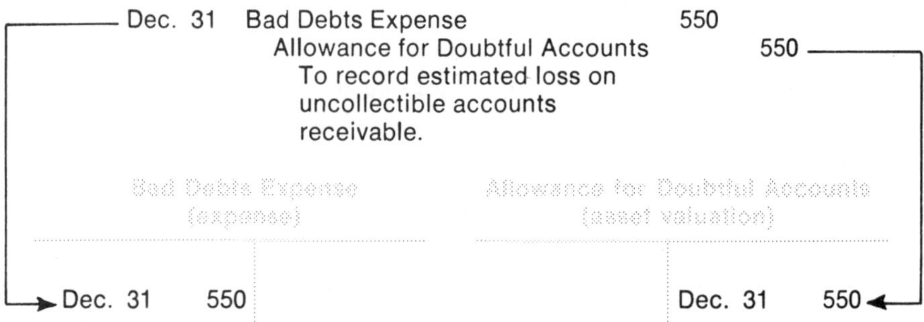

It is assumed that there was no balance before adjustments in Allowance for Doubtful Accounts and that no account receivable had been written off during the year. These complications are discussed in more detail later in this chapter.

Since the amount of $550 is an estimate and is not related to specific customers' accounts, the credit must be made to a contra (valuation) account. If the credit were to be made directly to Accounts Receivable without corresponding credits to subsidiary accounts, the equality of the controlling account and the subsidiary accounts would no longer exist. The use of the valuation account Allowance for Doubtful Accounts permits a reduction in the asset account without destroying this essential equality. Allowance for Doubtful Accounts is shown in the balance sheet as a deduction from the related asset account.

Assets		
Current Assets		
Cash		$1,210
Accounts Receivable	$6,945	
Deduct Allowance for Doubtful Accounts	550	6,395
Notes Receivable		1,000

The amount of $6,395 represents the anticipated net realizable value of the accounts receivable and may be shown as such without disclosing the amount of Allowance for Doubtful Accounts.[2]

[2] *Ibid.*, Section 3020.01.

Studies of financial reports prepared by leading Canadian corporations indicate that the number of companies referring to an allowance for doubtful accounts has continually declined.[3] As actual accounts receivable are determined to be uncollectible during subsequent accounting periods, Allowance for Doubtful Accounts is debited instead of Bad Debts Expense, with offsetting credits to the controlling account and the specific customers' accounts involved. This procedure is required because the expense already has been recognized by the bad debts adjusting entry. A debit to Bad Debts Expense at the time of write-off would cause the loss to be recorded twice.

Assume that on May 1 the Greene Corporation decides that a claim of $75 against John Landry for a sale made on March 1 is uncollectible.
The entry is:

May 1	Allowance for Doubtful Accounts	75	
	Accounts Receivable—John Landry		75

Estimating the Amount of Bad Debts Expense

It is necessary for management to make a careful estimate, based on judgment and past experience, of the amount of its uncollectible accounts. Accurate records must be kept and overdue accounts must be carefully analyzed.

There are two alternative approaches commonly used in estimating bad debts. In this text, these methods are referred to (1) as *the income statement **approach,*** based on the dollar volume of sales, and (2) as the ***balance sheet approach,*** based on the amount of receivables.

The Income Statement Approach. The income statement approach associates the bad debts expense directly with dollar volume of sales. Typically the estimate is based on a percentage of sales less sales returns and allowances. The percentage is based on information derived from the company's past experience. It may be desirable to establish the percentage on the basis of charge sales only, excluding cash sales, particularly if the proportion of cash sales to total sales fluctuates from year to year. The method is simple to apply and furnishes an equitable basis for distributing bad debts losses. Since the computation used in this method yields the amount of the bad debts expense for the year, any existing balance in the Allowance for Doubtful Accounts is ignored. A small error in the same direction over the years could accumulate to a large amount in the Allowance for Doubtful Accounts, since its balance is usually ignored in the adjustment process.

To illustrate the adjustment by this approach, assume that an examination of the accounts of a given company for the preceding five years shows that approximately one-half of 1 percent of credit sales have proved to be uncollectible. Assume further that credit sales for a particular year are $100,000 and that there is a credit balance of $85 in Allowance for Doubtful Accounts before adjustments are made. The bad debts expense for the year is $500 = (0.005 × $100,000), and in recording the adjustment, the $85 balance in the Allowance for Doubtful Accounts is ignored. The adjusting entry is

[3] ***Financial Reporting in Canada*** (Toronto: CICA, 1975), p. 85

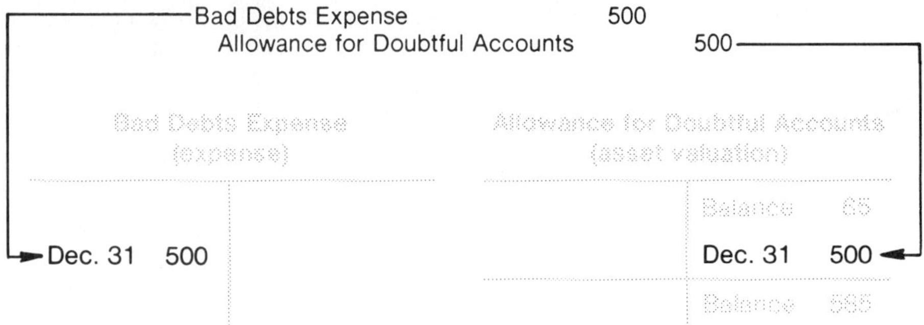

The Balance Sheet Approach. Under the income statement approach, any existing balance in the Allowance account is ignored in calculating bad debts expense; that is, the estimated amount of $500 is entered in the Allowance account as the bad debts expense for the year. The balance sheet approach requires an adjustment of the existing balance of Allowance for Doubtful Accounts to an amount that, when deducted from Accounts Receivable, will show accounts receivable at their net realizable value. In the balance sheet approach, the amount of accounts receivable rather than sales volume is used as the base for the adjustment. The necessary adjustment for the balance of Allowance for Doubtful Accounts is determined by either of two procedures: (1) the balance necessary to maintain the Allowance for Doubtful Accounts is established by *aging* the accounts receivable (that is, analyzing them by the amount of time they have remained unpaid) and adjusting the existing balance of Allowance for Doubtful Accounts to the proper amount, or (2) the balance of Allowance for Doubtful Accounts is adjusted to an amount equal to an estimated percentage of current accounts receivable. Aging the accounts receivable involves consideration of such factors as the date on which payment was due, the number of days that have elapsed since the due date, and any other available data of a financial nature that give some clue to collectibility of the accounts. A columnar work sheet like the one shown in Figure 7-4 is often used to facilitate the analysis of the Accounts Receivable account. It is sometimes referred to as an *aging schedule.*

Figure 7-4
Analysis of Accounts Receivable by Age

Customer's Name	*Total Balance*	*Not Yet Due*	*1–30 Days Past Due*	*31–60 Days Past Due*	*61–90 Days Past Due*	*Over 90 Days Past Due*
Walter G. Arnold	$ 880	$ 800	$ 80			
Allan Conlon	1,800	1,000	500	$ 300		
Charles Peacock.	50				$ 50	
Richard C. Smith	320	100	200	20		
Jerome Werther	960				900	$ 60
[Others]	51,990	27,220	15,460	5,280	730	3,300
Totals	$56,000	$29,120	$16,240	$5,600	$1,680	$3,360
Percent of Total	100	52	29	10	3	6

All the accounts in the subsidiary accounts receivable ledger with their corresponding account balances are listed in the Customer's Name and Total Balance columns. The component charges that make up each balance in the Total Balance column are then extended to the appropriate columns. The aging method yields a more satisfactory Allowance for Doubtful Accounts than does any other method, because the estimate is based on a study of individual customers' accounts rather than on a blanket percentage of a single general ledger account balance. Only a detailed analysis will disclose the accounts that are not past due but which may be uncollectible, and the long overdue accounts that may give indication of eventual collectibility. Yet, if recoveries of accounts receivable previously written off or the write-off in the current year of accounts receivable arising from prior years' sales are run through the Allowance for Doubtful Accounts without any designation of which of these items affect prior years' net income, the bad debts expense of the current year could be greatly distorted.

Management should also compare the current analysis of accounts receivable by age with those of earlier periods, especially the age-group percentages. Currently, 52 percent of the total accounts receivable are not yet due, 29 percent are past due from 1 to 30 days, and so on. When compared with earlier years, percentage increases in the lower age classifications with offsetting decreases in the older classes are favorable.

The analysis in Figure 7-4 may be used to determine the proper balance to be established in Allowance for Doubtful Accounts. To make this determination, companies may apply a sliding scale of percentages based on previous experience to the total amount shown in each column. The computation to determine expected losses for the Walter Carter Corporation is shown below.

	Amount	*Estimated Percentage Uncollectible*	*Allowance for Doubtful Accounts*
Not yet due	$29,120	2	$ 582.40
1–30 days past due	16,240	4	649.60
31–60 days past due	5,600	10	560.00
61–90 days past due	1,680	20	336.00
Over 90 days past due	3,360	50	1,680.00
Totals	$56,000		$3,808.00

On the basis of this summary, $3,808 of the outstanding accounts receivable on December 31 may become uncollectible. Consequently, an Allowance for Doubtful Accounts with a balance of $3,808 should be established. Before the adjusting entry is made, the existing balance in the account must be considered. The Walter Carter Corporation has a present credit balance in Allowance for Doubtful Accounts of $200, a provision remaining from earlier periods. The adjusting entry amount will be for $3,608 = ($3,808 − $200); when this amount is transferred to the allowance account, it will bring that account up to $3,808, the estimated probable uncollectible accounts. The adjusting journal entry is

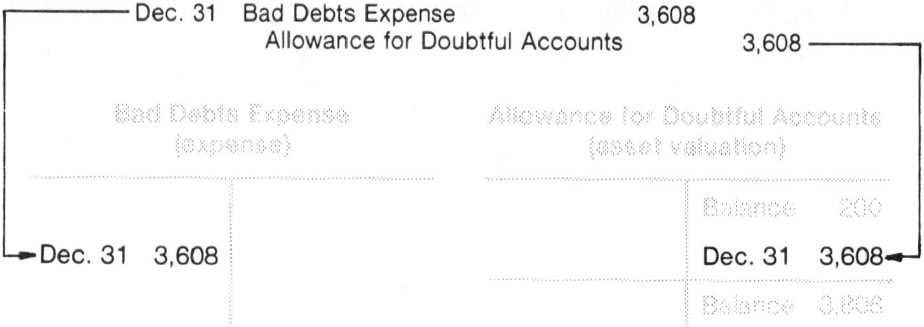

Under the balance sheet approach any existing balance in the Allowance account ($200) is taken into account in calculating bad debt expense for the year; that is, a total of $3,808 is required here as Allowance for this year. Since $200 remains from last year, only $3,608 is recorded as the bad debts expense for the year. This results in an Allowance of $3,808 at December 31.

End of Year	*Balance of Accounts Receivable*	*Total Losses from Uncollectible Accounts*
19X1	$20,000	$ 800
19X2	24,000	480
19X3	22,000	700
Totals	$66,000	$1,980

The average loss of the past three years has been 3 percent ($1,980 ÷ $66,000). Assume that at the end of 19X4 total accounts receivable are $25,000 and a credit balance of $150 is in the allowance account. Estimated uncollectible accounts at 3 percent of accounts receivable are $750 = ($25,000 × 0.03). The following adjusting entry at the end of 19X4 on the books of the Gnu Corporation increases the Allowance for Doubtful Accounts to the desired amount of $750.

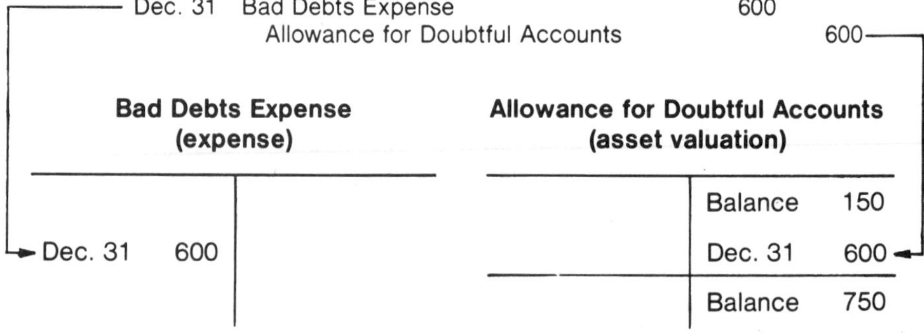

Writing Off Uncollectible Accounts

When it is decided that a customer's account is definitely uncollectible, the amount due should be written off. Assuming that on February 15 the Gnu Corporation definitely determined that the account of a customer, Joseph Sacks, is uncollectible, the entry to record the write-off is:

Feb. 15	Allowance for Doubtful Accounts	50	
	Accounts Receivable—Joseph Sacks		50

This entry has no effect on the net realizable value of the receivables; it only adjusts the balances of the two reciprocal accounts.

When the entry to write off Sacks's account is posted, the result is:

	Balances Before Write-Off	*Write-Off*	*Balances After Write-Off*
Accounts Receivable	$25,000	$50	$24,950
Allowance for Doubtful Accounts	750	50	700
Estimated Realizable Value	$24,250		$24,250

This points up the fact that since the loss was recorded in the period when the sale was made, the subsequent write-off does not change assets, liabilities, or shareholders' equity.

Recovery of Bad Debts

An account that is written off as uncollectible may later be recovered in part or in full. In that event, the entry that was made to write off the account is reversed to the extent of the amount recovered or expected to be recovered. Assuming that Joseph Sacks settles with his creditors for 50 cents on the dollar and that a check for $25 is received, the required journal entries are:

Nov. 15	Accounts Receivable—Joseph Sacks	25	
	Allowance for Doubtful Accounts		25
	To restore the collectible portion of the account previously written off.		
	Cash	25	
	Accounts Receivable—Joseph Sacks		25
	To record payment received.		

The debit and the credit to Accounts Receivable—Joseph Sacks cancel each other, but they are necessary if a complete record of all transactions with the customer is to be maintained. Such a record may be of considerable aid if further extension of credit to Joseph Sacks comes up for consideration at some future date.

Opposite Balances in Accounts Receivable and Accounts Payable

In the accounts receivable ledger, the customers' accounts normally have debit balances. Sometimes an overpayment, a sales return, a sales allowance, or an advance payment may convert the balance into a credit.

Assume that there is a net debit balance of $14,800 in an accounts receivable ledger consisting of 100 accounts, as follows:

98 accounts with a debit balance	$15,000
2 accounts with a credit balance	200
Net debit balance of 100 accounts receivable	$14,800

The debit amount of $15,000 and the credit amount of $200 should appear on the balance sheet as follows:

Current Assets		Current Liabilities	
Accounts Receivable	$15,000	Credit Balances in Customers' Accounts	$200

The controlling account balance of $14,800 should not be used because it would conceal the current liability of $200. Similarly, if the accounts payable ledger contains creditors' accounts with debit balances, the balance sheet should show the total credit balances and the total debit balances of the accounts payable. For example, if a company has a net balance in the Accounts Payable controlling account of $44,300, with certain subsidiary ledger accounts having debit balances that total $700, it should disclose this information as follows:

Current Assets		Current Liabilities	
Debit Balances in Creditors' Accounts	$700	Accounts Payable	$45,000

Direct Write-Offs in Period of Discovery

A company that uses the direct write-off method postpones recognition of a bad debts expense until the receivable is definitely known to be uncollectible. In this case, an Allowance for Doubtful Accounts is *not* used, and no end-of-period adjusting entry for estimated losses is made. The February 15 entry on the books of the Gnu Corporation to remove Joseph Sacks's account in full under the direct write-off method is:

Feb. 15	Bad Debts Expense	50	
	Accounts Receivable—Joseph Sacks		50

By this method, the loss is recognized in the period of write-off rather than in the period when the sale is made. This method, however, does not charge each accounting period with the losses arising out of sales made in that period and therefore violates the principle of matching expenses and revenue in each accounting period.

CORRECTION OF ERRORS IN ALLOWANCE FOR DOUBTFUL ACCOUNTS

Because of changing economic conditions and the fact that the percentage is based on past losses, errors can and do occur. Assume, for example, that the accountant of the Fountainhead Corporation, after analyzing sales and accounts receivable, determined the following information:

1. Correct bad debts expense, $4,000.
2. Actual balance in Allowance for Doubtful Accounts before adjustment, $1,000 debit balance.
3. Correct balance which should be in Allowance for Doubtful Accounts before adjustment, $100 credit balance.
4. Cumulative error as a result of past understatement of Allowance for Doubtful Accounts, $1,100.
5. Required balance in Allowance for Doubtful Accounts, $4,100.

The adjusting entry to record the bad debts expense and to record the error in the Allowance for Doubtful Accounts is:

Dec. 31	Corrections of Prior Years' Income	1,100	
	Bad Debts Expense	4,000	
	Allowance for Doubtful Accounts		5,100
	To correct a material underestimate of uncollectibles and to provide for an adequate allowance balance.		

After the foregoing information is posted to the Allowance for Doubtful Accounts, its balance will yield the estimated correct amount needed for future uncollectibles, $4,100. The correction account is deducted from the retained earnings' opening balance.

Allowance for Doubtful Accounts

Dec. 31	Balance before Adjustment	1,000	Dec. 31	Adjustment	5,100
			Dec. 31	Balance	4,100

INTERNAL CONTROL—ACCOUNTS RECEIVABLE

As in the case of cash, adequate safeguards must be established for accounts receivable. It is important that persons who maintain the accounts receivable records should not have access to cash. Recording of returns and allowances, discounts, and bad debts write-offs should be authorized by an officer and should be separated from the cash receipt and cash disbursement functions. Statements of account should be checked and mailed to customers by someone other than the accounts receivable bookkeeper. An independent check should be established to see that the statements sent to customers are in agreement with the accounts receivable records. Delinquent accounts should be reviewed periodically by a responsible official. Adequate control over receivables begins with the approved sales order and continues through the remaining stages in the credit sales process: approval of credit terms, recording of shipment, customer billing, recording of the receivable and its collection, and approval of subsequent adjustments.

APPENDIX Payroll Procedures

MANAGERIAL CONTROL OF PAYROLL

The payroll of a firm is a significant part of total expense, making continuous management control essential. The availability of machines and high-speed electronic equipment has facilitated the processing of payroll data and the establishment of effective controls at a reasonable cost. But the use of an electronic data-processing system for the payroll does not lessen the need for built-in self-policing internal control devices and procedures as part of the payroll system. Computer programs and data-processing systems can be manipulated to defraud the firm.

Effective managerial control of payroll requires that

1. Management has properly authorized the payroll payment.
2. Wages paid be correct and have been received by authorized employees; that is, for example, that no fictitious names or names of persons no longer employed have been listed on the payroll.
3. The numerous reports based on payroll information that are made to governmental agencies, union organizations, and employees be reliable.

Payroll Deductions

It is unusual for an employee to receive the full (*gross*) amount of salary or wages. Some deductions are required by law and must be *withheld* by the employer from the employee's regular pay. These include the following:

1. Federal and provincial income tax deductions.
2. Canada (or Provincial) Pension Plan deductions and, in some provinces, Health Insurance premiums.
3. Unemployment Insurance premiums.

Other deductions may be made for contributions to a registered pension plan; purchases of Canada Saving Bonds; group life, accident and private hospitalization insurance; and savings clubs. Deductions may also be required under union agreements or to settle other claims. The deductions are paid to the federal and provincial governments and other designated agencies. Adequate records must be maintained to account for the deductions and their related liabilities and to prepare the required reports to the agencies involved.

Recording and Paying the Payroll

Accurate payroll records are necessary to determine operating expenses and to report earnings information to employees and to federal, provincial, and other agencies. The records must show the names, earnings, and payroll deductions of all employees for each pay period. An individual record for each employee showing his earnings and deductions must also be kept. A general journal entry is made to record the payroll for the pay period. Assume that Burns Company Ltd. payroll entry for the week ended January 28 was as follows:

Salesmen's Salaries Expense	1,018.00	
Executive Salaries Expense	750.00	
Office Salaries Expense	320.00	
Income Tax Deductions Payable		507.50
Pension Plan Premiums Payable		35.70
Unemployment Insurance Premiums Payable		20.02
Salaries and Wages Payable		1,524.78
To record the payroll for the week ended January 28.		

The debits are to a selling expense account for $1,018 and to two general and administrative expense accounts for $1,070, or a total payroll of $2,088, of which the employees' *take-home* pay is $1,524.78.

Accrual of Salaries and Wages

If the end of the payroll period does not coincide with the end of the accounting period, an adjusting entry is made for salaries and wages earned but not paid. Assume that Burns Company Ltd. closes its books on March 31 and that the last payroll period ended on March 27 (Saturday). The entry to accrue the salaries for the partial pay period is

Salesmen's Salaries Expense	406	
Executive Salaries Expense	300	
Office Salaries Expense	128	
Accrued Salaries and Wages Payable		834
To record salaries and wages accrued from March 28 to 31.		

The entire credit for the accrued payroll is made to a single liability account rather than to separate liability accounts for the government and the employees. Amounts to be withheld from employees' earnings are based on the earnings for an entire payroll period and are not necessary in this case. Insofar as the employer is concerned, the total liability is $834; its breakdown into the several liability accounts does not provide additional useful information and may, therefore, be deferred until the date of payment.

GLOSSARY

Aging Schedule A columnar work sheet showing the individual receivables by age groups according to time elapsed from due date. The individual age groups are also totaled and a percentage analysis is computed to aid in determining the allowance for doubtful accounts.

Allowance for Doubtful Accounts A valuation account related to accounts receivable showing the amount of estimated uncollectible accounts as of a *given date*.

Bad Debts Expense The account showing the estimated uncollectible credit sales made in a given time period, that is, for one year if the accounting period is a year.

Bad Debts Recovered An account which is credited for the recovery of an account receivable previously written off under the direct write-off method.

Bank Reconciliation A statement which shows the specific items that account for the differences between the balance reported by the bank and the amount shown on the depositor's books.

Bank Statement A monthly statement sent by a bank to its depositors together with canceled checks and notices of bank charges and credits.

Cash Forecast Summary of projected cash receipts, cash disbursements, and resulting cash balances for the budgeted periods.

Cash Over and Short An account showing a discrepancy in the daily count of cash between actual cash receipts and cash disbursements and the cash register readings or other supporting documents.

Certified Check A depositor's check, payment of which is guaranteed by a bank by endorsement on the face of the check, the bank having previously deducted the amount of the check from the depositor's balance.

Check Register A book of original entry for all cash disbursements except petty cash.

Deck A set of cards each of which carries the same specified data related to a common subject.

Deposits in Transit Deposits made too late in the month to be credited by the bank on the current statement.

Internal Control A built-in system of self-policing for the effective control and safeguarding of cash and other assets.

Nontrade Receivable Claims against individuals or companies arising from money lent, from deposits made, and from other sources not involving the sale of merchandise or ordinary services.

Notes Receivable Claims against individuals or companies supported by formal written promises to pay. A notes receivable may be either a trade note or a nontrade note.

NSF Check A customer's check that has been deposited but did not clear on presentation for payment because the customer's bank balance was less than the amount of the check.

Outstanding Checks Checks sent to payees but not yet presented to the depositor's bank for payment.

Petty Cash A separate cash fund for the payment of relatively minor items when payment by check is impractical.

Trade Receivables Claims against customers arising from sales of merchandise or ordinary services.

Valuation Account A contra asset account; an account which is related to and offsets, in whole or in part, one or more other accounts. A contra asset account should be deducted from the asset to which it is related to determine a carrying or book value.

QUESTIONS

Q7-1. The Stenn Company employs an office manager, a cashier, an accounts receivable bookkeeper, two clerk-typists, and ten salesmen. The bookkeeper records all charge sales made to customers; she also opens the mail each day and credits the customers' accounts for remittances, turning the money over to the cashier. The monthly bank statement is received directly by the bookkeeper, who prepares the bank reconciliation.

Collections from cash sales are turned over by the salesmen to the cashier, together with a cash sales invoice. The cashier compares these invoices daily with the cash register tapes. Disbursements for petty cash items are made by the cashier out of cash receipts. The cashier fills out a petty cash slip, which is signed by the person receiving the cash. All other disbursements are by check, signed by either the office manager or the owner of the company. Entries in the cash receipts journal and in the cash payments journal are generally made by the office manager. In his absence, the cashier handles the cash receipts journal and the accounts receivable bookkeeper handles the cash payments journal.

(a) What is wrong with this system? (b) What basic internal controls are lacking? (c) Can the system be improved without increasing the present staff?

Q7-2. A company may pay its employees (a) in cash, (b) by checks drawn on the regular checking account, or (c) by checks drawn on a special payroll bank account. Discuss the advantages and disadvantages of each form of payment.

Q7-3. Why is it advantageous to deposit all cash receipts intact and to make all disbursements by check?

Q7-4. (a) What is a petty cash fund? (b) How does it operate? (c) Why should the petty cash fund always be replenished at the end of each accounting period?

Q7-5. Explain the reciprocal relationships between the cash records of the bank and those of the depositor.

Q7-6. Explain the following terms:

a. Certified check
b. Service charge
c. Not sufficient funds
d. Debit memorandum
e. Credit memorandum
f. Overdraft

Q7-7. Explain the effect, if any, on the bank statement balance of each of the following bank reconciliation items:

a. Outstanding checks total $323.
b. The bank recorded a $650 deposit as $560.
c. The service charge for the month was $7.
d. Deposits in transit total $800.
e. A note payable of $500 made to the bank by the depositor became due.

Q7-8. Discuss the general principle of the valuation of trade receivables.

Q7-9. (a) Explain the function of the Allowance for Doubtful Accounts account. (b) What methods may be used to estimate the allowance for doubtful accounts? (c) How is Allowance for Doubtful Accounts shown on the balance sheet?

Q7-10. Distinguish between the income statement approach and the balance sheet approach in estimating the bad debts expense.

Q7-11. The following entry was made to record the recovery of a bad debt:

Cash	450	
Allowance for Doubtful Accounts		450

Discuss the validity of this method of recording the recovery.

Q7-12. (a) Discuss the reasons for credit balances occurring in Accounts Receivable accounts. (b) How are such balances presented in the balance sheet?

Q7-13. (Appendix) (a) What two types of Federal taxes are most employers required to withhold from their employees' wages? (b) When do taxes withheld become liabilities to the employer? (c) When and in what manner is the employer required to pay to the Department of National Revenue the amounts withheld?

DEMONSTRATION PROBLEMS

DP7-1. *(Bank reconciliation)* The Cash account of the Tech Company showed a balance of $2,335.64 on March 31. The bank statement showed a balance of $2,533.23. Other differences between the information in the firm's Cash account and the bank's records are listed below.

1. A deposit of $130.46 made on March 31 was not recorded by the bank before the bank statement was issued.
2. The following items were returned with the bank statement:
   a. A credit memo for $123.53, the proceeds of a draft for $126.50 drawn on the George Company and accepted by the drawee 60 days ago. The bank deducted $2.97 from the total collected for the cost of collection.
   b. A debit memo for $5.28 for annual rental of a safety deposit box.
   c. A customer's check for $8.25 received on account, which the firm had included in its deposit on March 27, was returned marked NSF.
   d. A canceled check in the amount of $225.50 drawn by the Itek Company and charged by the bank against the account of the Tech Company by mistake. The check is being returned to the bank.
3. Check No. 298 was made out correctly for $19.44 in payment of office supplies, but was entered in the cash payments journal as $19.54.
4. Outstanding checks on March 31 totaled $443.45.

Required:

1. Prepare a bank reconciliation as of March 31.
2. Prepare the journal entries to adjust the Cash account as of March 31.

DP7-2. *(Use of Allowance for Doubtful Accounts)* The following transactions of the Faison Company occurred in 19X1, 19X2, and 19X3. The company uses the estimating procedure in accounting for bad debts.

19X1	
Dec. 31	Recorded bad debts expense of $5,600.
19X2	
Mar. 12	Wrote off N. O. Goode's account of $720 as uncollectible.
Nov. 8	Wrote off various other accounts of $3,850 as uncollectible.
Dec. 31	Recorded bad debts expense of $5,460.
19X3	
Feb. 9	N. O. Goode remitted $520 of the amount he owed the firm and agreed to pay the remainder in 30 days.

Required: Journalize the transactions.

DP7-3. *(Adjusting entries for bad debts)* The partial trial balance of the Ruth Company at December 31 before any adjustments are made, is given below:

	Debits	*Credits*
Accounts Receivable	$120,000	
Notes Receivable	45,000	
Allowance for Doubtful Accounts and Notes	900	
Sales		$163,750
Sales Returns and Allowances	3,750	

Required: Prepare the adjusting entries for the bad debts expense under the following assumptions: (a) Allowance for Doubtful Accounts and Notes is to be increased to 3% of trade receivables; (b) the bad debts expense is estimated to be 1.5% of net sales.

PROBLEMS

P7-1. (*Management policy decision problem*) The bookkeeper of the Kane Company, in need of money to pay off his debts, "borrows" $500 by pocketing some cash and checks mailed in by customers. He enters appropriate credits to each customer's account for payment made. Can this misappropriation be concealed for a short period? indefinitely? What measures should a company take to prevent the misappropriation of cash or other assets?

P7-2. On May 1, the Jay Company established a petty cash fund of $675. On May 31, the fund consisted of cash and other items as follows:

Coins and currency	$142.50
Postage stamps	141.00
Freight and express invoices	192.00
Salvation Army contribution receipt	75.00
Postdated check from an employee	124.50

Make the entries (a) to establish the fund; (b) to replenish the fund; (c) to increase the fund from $675 to $900 on May 31; (d) to reduce the fund from $675 to $450 on May 31.

P7-3. The George Company has an imprest petty cash fund of $1,500. On October 31 the fund consisted of cash and other items as follows:

Coins and currency		$ 795.00
Vouchers for:		
Transportation In	$337.86	
Telephone	32.25	
Postage Expense	324.48	
Stationery	1.50	696.09
Total		$1,491.09

Assuming that the petty cash fund was not replenished, make the necessary adjusting entry at October 31.

P7-4. The Olt Company's Cash account shows a balance of $20,818.47 as of April 30. The balance on the bank statement on that date is $23,334.27. Checks for $750, $533.46, and $126.54 are outstanding. The bank statement shows a charge for a check made out by the Olt Company for $75. The statement also shows a credit of $1,200 for a customer's note that had been left with the bank for collection. Service charges for the month were $19.20. What is the true cash balance as of April 30?

P7-5. From the following data prepare a bank reconciliation and entries to adjust the books of the Lans Company as of March 31.

Balance on bank statement	$6,153.50
Balance on books	5,704.02
Bank service charge	10.86
Credit for a customer's note collected by the bank (includes interest of $7.28)	169.78
Deposit made on March 31, not credited by the bank	330.33
Check No. 786 for $581 was entered in the cash payments journal as $518	
A customer's check for $16.77 was returned marked NSF on March 30.	
Outstanding checks:	

Check No.	*Amount*
817	$ 65.00
818	97.57
825	538.09

P7-6. According to the statement that John Fisher received from his bank as of March 31, his balance was $2,700. He noted the following discrepancies between the bank statement and his records:

a. A deposit of $500 that was made on March 31 was not shown on the statement.

b. Outstanding checks as of March 31 were: Nos. 652, $100; 689, $51; 701, $59; and 710, $86.

c. Check No. 655 for $350, issued on March 10 for advertising expense, was not recorded in the cash payments journal but was paid by the bank on March 16.

1. Determine the cash balance on the books before adjustments and prepare a bank reconciliation showing the true cash balances as of March 31.
2. Prepare the journal entries necessary to adjust the books.

P7-7. The following data are taken from the records of Hyde, Inc., and from the monthly bank statement furnished them by First Provincial Bank:

a. Balance per bank statement, June 30			$134,655.77
b. Balance per books, June 30			87,477.74
c. Outstanding checks, June 30			51,373.47
d. Receipts of June 30, deposited July 2			8,507.52
e. Service charge for June, per debit memo			6.16
f. Proceeds of bank loan, June 15 omitted from the company's books			15,600.00
g. Deposit of June 30, omitted from bank statement			4,627.86
h. Error on bank statement in entering deposit of June 25			
	Correct amount	$5,091.84	
	Entered as	5,090.84	1.00
i. Check of Heid, Inc., charged in error			4,304.00
j. Proceeds of a customer's note collected by bank on June 16, not entered in the company's books:			
	Principal	$3,200	
	Interest	32	
	Total	$3,232	
	Less collection fee	8	3,224.00
k. Error on bank statement in entering deposit of June 10			
	Entered as	$5,614	
	Correct amount	5,604	10.00
l. Deposit of Hide Corporation credited in error			2,880.00
m. Debit memo for noninterest-bearing note not recorded by the company			$8,000.00
n. A check from Black, Inc., was returned marked NSF; no entry has been made on the company's records			462.90

Required:

1. Prepare a bank reconciliation as of June 30.
2. Prepare the journal entries necessary to adjust the books of Hyde, Inc., as of June 30.

P7-8. The Hall Company prepared the following bank reconciliation as of March 31:

Balance per bank		$24,927.50
Less outstanding checks		
Check	Amount	
580	$4,051.00	
599	196.00	
600	6.80	4,253.80
Balance per books		$20,673.70

The bank statement for the month of April was as follows:

SECOND CHARTERED BANK
Statement of account with Hall Company

Checks			*Deposits*	*Date*	*Balance*
				April 1	24,927.50
4,051.00				2	20,876.50
196.00	24.00	230.00	1,570.00	6	21,996.50
200.00			390.00	11	22,186.50
124.46	397.00	6.80		16	21,658.24
2,220.00	180.00 NSF			21	19,258.24
1,720.00	30.80		5,000.00	26	22,507.44
5.50 SC			1,521.60	29	24,023.54

Cash receipts for the month:

Date	*Amount*
April 5	$1,570.00
10	390.00
23	5,000.00
28	1,521.60
30	1,000.00

Cash disbursements for the month:

Check	*Amount*	*Check*	*Amount*
601	$ 24.00	607	$1,364.42
602	1,720.00	608	99.80
603	230.00	609	40.00
604	200.00	610	1,520.00
605	2,220.00	611	124.46
606	287.00	612	397.00

The canceled checks returned by the bank included a check for $30.80 made out by the Hill Company and charged to the Hall Company in error. The NSF check had been received from a customer on account.

Required:

1. **Prepare the bank reconciliation as of April 30.**
2. **Make the necessary adjusting journal entries.**

P7-9. (*Management policy decision problem*) What specific safeguards will be provided by each of the following internal cash control procedures?

1. All cash receipts are deposited intact in a bank account daily.
2. Monthly bank statements are reconciled with the cash records.
3. Periodic unannounced counts are made of the petty cash fund.
4. Checks are issued only if supported by properly authorized vouchers.
5. The person who records cash receipts is not permitted to authorize cash disbursements or to sign checks.

6. The clerks who handle cash are not permitted to make entries in the cash records.
7. The person who approves vouchers for payment is not permitted to sign the checks for those payments.

P7-10. *(Accounting policy decision problem)* You have prepared the financial reports for the Cowan Corporation, which include the following amounts:

Cash balances:	
April 30, 19X2	$105,000
April 30, 19X1	66,000
Net income:	
For the fiscal year ended April 30, 19X2	165,000
For the fiscal year ended April 30, 19X1	180,000

John Cowan, the company's president, says that you must have made a mistake, because you report an increase in the cash balance of $39,000 although earnings for the fiscal year declined by $15,000 from the year before. (a) Is he right? Explain. (b) He asks you what the effect on the cash balance would have been if the company had reported a $15,000 net loss for the period?

P7-11. The Zeller Company, which uses an Allowance for Doubtful Accounts, had the following transactions involving worthless accounts in 19X1 and 19X2.

19X1

Dec.	31	Recorded bad debts expense of $2,650.

19X2

Mar.	6	Wrote off N. K. Garm's account of $610 as uncollectible.
Apr.	12	Wrote off J. J. Jones's account of $680 as uncollectible.
Sept.	6	Recovered $680 from J. J. Jones.

Journalize the transactions.

P7-12. The Tyrrell Trading Company had charge sales of $610,000 for the year and accounts receivable of $60,500 and a credit balance of $250 in Allowance for Doubtful Accounts at the end of the year.

Record the bad debts for the year, using each of the following methods for the estimate: (a) Allowance for Doubtful Accounts is to be increased to 4% of Accounts Receivable. (b) Bad debts expense is estimated to be 0.0045% of charge sales. (c) Allowance for Doubtful Accounts is to be increased to $3,700, as indicated by an aging schedule. Which method would you choose and why?

P7-13. The balance of the Accounts Receivable account of the Ramseur Company at December 31 was $74,460. Two customers' accounts in the subsidiary ledger show credit balances of $3,200 and $1,800.

Required:

1. What amount for Accounts Receivable would be shown under Current Assets?
2. How would the credit balances in the customers' accounts be disclosed?

P7-14. The accounts receivable ledger of the Saffelle Distributing Company shows the following data on December 31. The general ledger showed a $200 debit balance in Allowance for Doubtful Accounts before adjustments.

Name of Customer	*Invoice Date*	*Amount*
Monsanto Sand Company	May 2	$ 1,200
Naughton Company	August 15	671
Peters' Plants	December 8	385
	October 2	720
Temptation Seedling Company	March 3	565
Saundrin Company	November 11	825
Young Fruittrees Company	November 20	314
	September 4	484
	July 10	950
(Others)	December 5	40,000
Terms of sale are n/30.		

a. Prepare an analysis of accounts receivable by age.
b. Compute the estimated loss based on the following fixed percentages:

		Estimated Percentage Uncollectible
Accounts not due		1.0
Accounts past due:	1–30 days	1.5
	31–60 days	2.5
	61–90 days	8.5
	91–120 days	10.0
	121–365 days	30.0

c. Record the bad debts expense.

P7-15. The Allowance for Doubtful Accounts of the Biltmore Company showed a credit balance of $450 on December 31, 19X1, before adjustments were made. The bad debts expense for 19X1 is estimated at 3% of the charge sales of $200,000 for the year.
The following transactions occurred during the next two years:

19X2

May 1	Wrote off Gordo Durham's $945 account as uncollectible.
Oct. 15	Wrote off Bloke Gordon's account of $1,800 as uncollectible.
Nov. 30	Received a check for $200 in final settlement of Gordo Durham's account written off in May. He had been adjudged bankrupt by the courts.
Dec. 31	An analysis of accounts receivable by age indicated that accounts doubtful of collection totaled $4,650.

19X3

Aug. 21	Wrote off J. M. Tonto's $1,950 account as uncollectible.
Dec. 31	Estimated that uncollectible accounts receivable totaled $3,750.

Required:

1. Record in general journal form transactions and events including adjusting entry for December 31, 19X1.
2. Post to a T account for Allowance for Doubtful Accounts.

P7-16. On January 1, the balance of Allowance for Doubtful Accounts of the Ricky Company was $3,200. During the year uncollectible accounts totaling $3,900 were written off. The company collected $500 on one of these accounts after it had been written off. The balance of the Accounts Receivable on December 31, was $95,000.

Required: Make the journal entries (a) to charge off the worthless accounts, (b) to record the collection of the $500, and (c) to record the adjusting entry on December 31, for the bad debts expense. Assume that uncollectible accounts average 5% of the uncollected accounts receivable.

P7-17. The Accounts Receivable controlling account of the Warm Springs Corporation shows a balance of $370,500 on June 30. A summary of the analysis of accounts receivable by age shows accounts outstanding from the date of the invoice as follows:

Accounts not due		$300,000
Accounts past due:	1-30 days	25,000
	31-60 days	30,000
	61-150 days	12,500
	151 days and over	3,000
	Total	$370,500

On June 30, Allowance for Doubtful Accounts has a debit balance of $310 before adjustments. The adjustment of the Allowance account is to be based on the following schedule of percentages estimated uncollectible:

Accounts not due		½ of 1%
Accounts past due:	1-30 days	4%
	31-60 days	5%
	61-150 days	15%
	151 days and over	40%

Required: Prepare the necessary adjusting entry.

P7-18. On December 31, 19X1, David Jaye's trial balance showed the following:

Accounts Receivable	$82,500
Allowance for Doubtful Accounts (debit)	200

After an analysis of the accounts receivable, it was estimated that the accounts doubtful of collection would amount to $4,200.

During the year 19X2, the following transactions occurred:

a. Sales on account were $410,000.
b. Accounts written off as uncollectible totaled $4,010.
c. Collections from customers on account were $350,000. This amount included a receipt of $200 that had been written off during the year as uncollectible.

On December 31, 19X2, the accounts doubtful of collection were estimated at $3,650.

Required:

1. Journalize the above transactions.
2. Compute the bad debts expense for each year.

P7-19. The balance of the Accounts Receivable account of the Ramseur Company at December 31, was $74,460. Two customers' accounts in the subsidiary ledger show credit balances of $3,200 and $1,800.

Required:
1. What amount for Accounts Receivable would be shown under Current Assets?
2. How would the credit balances in the customers' accounts be disclosed?

P7-20. The following transactions of the Goodwin Corporation occurred during the year.

19X1	
Jan. 12	Wrote off B. E. Wiry's account of $319 as uncollectible.
Nov. 13	Wrote off I. M. Blokely's account of $219 as uncollectible.
20	Recovered the $319 from B. E. Wiry.
Dec. 13	Wrote off R. M. Saints' account of $560 as uncollectible.
19X2	
Mar. 10	Recovered the $219 from I. M. Blokely.

Required: Journalize the transactions.

P7-21. *(Accounting policy decision problem)* The sales revenue section of the annual income statements of four different companies are shown below.

	W Company	X Company	Y Company	Z Company
Sales	$600,000	$20,000,000	$12,000,000	$14,000,000
Deduct: Sales Discounts	$ –0–	$ 300,000	$ 960,000	$ 250,000
Sales Returns and Allowances	–0–	5,000,000	40,000	50,000
Bad Debts	–0–	–0–	–0–	120,000
Transportation Out	–0–	–0–	–0–	100,000
Total Offsets	$ –0–	$ 5,300,000	$ 1,000,000	$ 520,000
Net Sales	$600,000	$14,700,000	$11,000,000	$13,480,000

Required: Identify the unusual situations that you can discover in the four partial income statements. Briefly explain why you think each situation is unusual and whether you think the method of reporting is acceptable by current accounting theory.

P7-22. (Appendix) The payroll records of the Wilson Company for the week ended February 28 showed the following:

Total wages earned		$5,500.00
Deductions		
Income tax	$928.20	
Pension plan	90.78	
UIC	77.18	1,096.16
Net amount paid		$4,403.84

Assuming that a voucher system is used, record in general journal form: (a) total payroll, (b) payment of the payroll. Indicate the journal in which each entry would be properly reported.

P7-23. (Appendix) J. Handler pays his five employees weekly. The payroll summary for the week ended January 15 follows:

Total earnings		$2,100.00
Deductions		
Unemployment insurance	$ 12.95	
Income taxes	651.25	
Pension plan	36.60	
Total deductions		700.80
Net amount paid		$1,399.20

Required: Journalize the recording of the payroll.

P7-24. (*Management policy decision problem*)

a. The manager of a shoe department employing six salesmen has found on a number of occasions that the cash in the register at the end of the day is less than the amounts shown on the record of sales for that day. Each salesman rings up his own sales. What recommendations would you make to the manager?

b. How do the use of a petty cash system and the regular reconciliation of the bank account protect the company against mistakes and losses?

c. You note that the independent auditor, when making his examination, reconciles (1) total deposits shown on the bank statements with total receipts shown in the cash receipts journal, and (2) total disbursements shown on the bank statements with total checks drawn as recorded in the cash payments journal. Explain why the auditor makes these reconciliations.

d. It is essential for a business to establish internal controls to prevent the misappropriation of cash. Does management have other responsibilities relating to cash? Explain.

8

Inventory

Inventory in a wholesale or retail business—that is, a nonmanufacturing business—is generally understood to mean goods owned by the business for sale to customers. Alternative terms are *merchandise* and *merchandise inventory*. Up to this point in the text, the amount of the merchandise inventory was specified and, therefore, assumed to be correct. The factors involved in arriving at the value of the inventory—classification of items, determination of physical quantities on hand, and techniques of assigning costs—were not stated. These factors, however, are indispensable in valuing the merchandise inventory for the preparation of financial statements.

BASIS OF INVENTORY VALUATION

Inventories are recorded at cost.[1] For a nonmanufacturing business, the term cost "may be said to be laid-down cost."[2] Therefore, cost consists of the invoice price of the merchandise (less purchase discounts) plus transportation in, insurance while in transit, and any other expenditures made by the buyer to get the merchandise to his place of business. In the interest of simplifying the clerical task of prorating these other costs to the various items of inventory purchased, they are frequently carried in separate accounts, and the Purchases account shows only the invoice price. If these amounts are significant in relation to the invoice price of the merchandise, a proportionate part should be added to the cost of the goods on hand at the end of the period. The cost of the inventory may be determined in several different ways. The method used to determine cost should be the one "which result in the fairest matching of costs against revenues,"[3] with due regard to its usefulness as a measure of financial position and its effect on relevant balance sheet ratios, its effect on current and subsequent income statements, and possible impact on pricing and purchasing policies.

[1]*CICA Handbook* (Toronto: Canadian Institute of Chartered Accountants), Section 3030.01.
[2]*Ibid.*, Section 3030.02.
[3]*Ibid.*, Section 3030.09.

The term *value* is defined by the AICPA as "the amount at which an item is stated, in accordance with the accounting principles related to that item."[4] "Since accounting is predominantly based on cost, the proper uses of the word *value* in accounting are largely restricted to the statement of items at cost, or at modifications of cost."[5]

The accountant, therefore, usually expresses *value* in terms of *cost.*

There are, of course, other concepts of value; the accountant's valuation is *historical,* or prior, cost, which is objective, being subject to measurement. It is this objectivity which accounts for the predominance of historical cost as a valuation basis. The economist, on the other hand, relates value to current and anticipated prices for better comparability and matching of expired costs with revenue. The distinction between these two concepts is especially important during periods of rapidly rising prices with their concomitant effect on financial statement valuations. Many persons in and out of the profession question the usefulness of cost as a valuation concept when prices are unstable.

INVENTORY SYSTEMS

Two systems for determining inventory quantities on hand are in use: periodic (physical count) and perpetual (continuous record).

The total cost of goods available for sale must be allocated between the cost of goods sold and the cost of goods on hand. With the periodic inventory system, this allocation is made at the end of each accounting period; with the perpetual inventory system, it is made after each sale and each acquisition.

The process of assigning costs would be relatively simple if each item acquired could be marked and identified with a specific invoice cost. Such a procedure is possible in certain businesses in which the items are large or otherwise readily traceable. In most instances, however, specific identification of each inventory item is neither feasible nor practical, particularly when successive acquisitions are commingled in common storage facilities. The problem is complicated further because acquisitions of like items are usually made at fluctuating prices. Consequently, a method of assigning costs to merchandise items—with either a perpetual or a periodic inventory system—based on an *assumed* flow of goods and expired costs must be adopted and followed consistently for inventory valuation purposes and for matching costs with revenues. (The principle of consistency is discussed later in this chapter.)

Specific Identification Costing. The specific identification method of inventory valuation may be used if each item (automobiles, diamond rings, or other items) purchased can be identified specifically with the related underlying documents. Some businesses mark the specific cost in code on every unit so that each item of inventory as well as each unit sold may be valued.

[4]AICPA, *APB Accounting Principles,* vol. 2 (Chicago, Commerce Clearing House, Inc., 1973), p. 9509.

[5]*Ibid.*

In many instances, whether because of the volume of items involved or because the items are of a kind that make individual coding impossible, the method of specific identification is impracticable. Similar items acquired on different dates and at different prices may be commingled, or *fungible* (interchangeable) items—wheat in bins, coal in piles—might be matched with unrelated invoices, thereby misstating net income. Furthermore, some costs are common to groups of items—shipping, insurance, handling—and may not be readily identifiable with specific items.

To illustrate the various methods of assigning costs to inventories, the following information pertaining to a single inventory item, a steel lock, stock item number 7004 is used in the illustrations which follow.

April 1 Inventory on hand consisted of 20 units, purchased at $2.20 each.
5 Purchased 60 units at $2.60 each.
12 Sold 55 units.
15 Purchased 35 units at $2.80.
30 Sold 30 units.

For convenience, the data are rearranged as follows:

	Units	*Unit Cost*	*Total Cost*
Inventory, April 1	20	$2.20	$ 44
Purchases			
April 5	60	2.60	156
15	35	2.80	98
Goods available for sale	115		$298
Sales			
April 12	55		
30	30		
Total	85		
On hand, April 30	30	(115 − 85)	

PHYSICAL COUNT METHOD

Periodic Inventory

Inventory quantities on hand can be found by physical count. The inventory can then be valued by assigning the applicable cost per unit to calculate a total cost. The first-in first-out, last-in first-out and weighted average costing methods are used to illustrate how costs can be assigned to inventory after the physical count or periodic inventory method is explained.

Periodic Inventory. With the periodic inventory system, the value of the inventory for balance sheet presentation and for the determination of the cost of goods sold is determined at the end of each annual accounting period by a complete physical count and pricing of all inventory items. (Estimated gross margin rates described later in this chapter may be used to determine the cost of goods sold during interim periods.) Acquired goods not on hand are assumed to have been sold. Merchandise losses through misappropriation, breakage, or other causes are included in the cost of goods sold as a deduction from revenue, although these goods do not actually create revenue. Small retail businesses often use the periodic system as a matter of expediency, since it does not require a continuous record of inventory balances.

First-In, First-Out (FIFO) Costing. The FIFO method of determining the cost of goods on hand and the cost of goods sold is based on the assumption that the units are sold in the order in which they were acquired; that is, the oldest units on hand are sold first, the units acquired next are the next to be sold, and so on. This assumption relates only to the method of accounting and not to the actual physical movement of the goods although it may approximate the actual physical flow. What is significant, however, is the monetary value. The unsold units on hand at the date of the inventory are assumed to be the units acquired most recently. Consequently, for income measurement, earlier costs are matched with revenue and the most current costs are used for position statement valuation.

The periodic FIFO cost for the period, the inventory valuation, and the cost of goods sold are computed in Figure 8-1.

Figure 8-1 Periodic FIFO Costing

		Goods on Hand			–	*Goods Sold*			=	*Ending Inventory*		
		Units	*Unit Cost*	*Total Cost*		*Units*	*Unit Cost*	*Total Cost*		*Units*	*Unit Cost*	*Total Cost*
Inventory, April	1	20 ×	$2.20 =	$ 44		20 ×	$2.20 =	$ 44				
Purchases, April	5	60 ×	2.60 =	156		60 ×	2.60 =	156				
	15	35 ×	2.80 =	98		5 ×	2.80 =	14		30 ×	$2.80 =	$84
		115		$298		85		$214		30		$84

Ending inventory is assumed to consist of the most recently acquired units.

Last-In, First-Out (LIFO) Costing. LIFO costing is based on the assumption that the cost of goods sold should be based on prices paid for the most recently acquired units and that the inventory consists of the oldest units on hand. The major advantage claimed for this procedure is that during periods of continuously rising prices, the higher prices of the most recent purchases are included in the cost of goods sold, thereby reducing the gross margin on sales and the taxable income. It is further claimed that the cost of goods sold is more realistic, because LIFO costs most nearly approximate current replacement costs, thereby achieving a closer matching of costs with revenue.

The periodic LIFO cost for the period, the inventory valuation, and the cost of goods sold are computed in Figure 8-2.

Periodic LIFO Costing **Figure 8-2**

		Goods on Hand			−	Goods Sold			=	Ending Inventory		
		Units	*Unit Cost*	*Total Cost*		*Units*	*Unit Cost*	*Total Cost*		*Units*	*Unit Cost*	*Total Cost*
Inventory, April	1	20 ×	$2.20 =	$ 44						20 ×	$2.20 =	$ 44
Purchases, April	5	60 ×	2.60 =	156		50 ×	$2.60 =	$130		10 ×	2.60 =	26
	15	35 ×	2.80 =	98		35	2.80 =	98				
		115		$298		85		$228		30		$70

Ending inventory is assumed to consist of the oldest units acquired.

For income tax reporting, the use of the LIFO costing method is not permitted in Canada.

Weighted Average Costing. Under weighted average costing—not to be confused with moving average costing—the ending inventory is priced at the end of each accounting period at a unit cost computed by dividing the total cost of goods available for sale by the physical units available for sale. Similarly, all quantities sold are stated at a uniform price—the computed average price for the period (typically one month). The assignment of costs to goods sold during the month must be delayed until the end of the month so that the weighted average cost computation can be made.

The average cost for the period, the inventory valuation, and the cost of goods sold are computed as follows:

Figure 8-3
Periodic Weighted Average Costing

Date			*Units*	*Unit Cost*	*Total*
April	1	Beginning inventory	20	$2.20	$ 44.00
	5	Purchase	60	2.60	156.00
	15	Purchase	35	2.80	98.00
			115		$298.00

$$\text{Average unit cost} = \frac{\text{Cost of goods available for sale}}{\text{Units available for sale}} = \frac{\$298}{115} = \$2.5913$$

Units on hand, April 30	30
Inventory valuation (30 × $2.5913)	$77.74
Units sold	85
Cost of goods sold (85 × $2.5913)	$220.26

INVENTORY COSTING METHODS COMPARED AND ANALYZED

The most common periodic methods of inventory valuation have been discussed; others may be used in special circumstances. In a particular business, the method selected should be one that will best measure net income.

If there are no significant price changes in the merchandise handled during a given period and the quantity held does not change, FIFO, LIFO, and weighted average costing will produce approximately the same results. If, however, the prices of the goods acquired fluctuate significantly during the period and the inventory turnover is rapid, the method of inventory valuation used will have a direct effect on the financial statements. As shown before, the price of the item fluctuated from $2.20 to $2.80 during the month. To illustrate the comparative effect of rising prices on the financial statements under periodic FIFO, weighted average, and LIFO costing, the basic data for the preceding discussions are used again. Two additional assumptions are made: (1) The selling price of each unit is $5.50, and (2) the operating expenses for the month are $100. These computations of income are for a single inventory item. The effect of the different methods on net income would be proportionately increased with increasing volume and number of items. The effect of the three methods of allocating inventory cost and cost of goods sold under the stated assumptions is further highlighted in Figure 8-4 which is abstracted from the preceding income computations.

Figure 8-4
Summary Tabulation

	FIFO	*Weighted Average*	*LIFO*
Sales (85 units × $5.50)	$467.50	$467.50	$467.50
Cost of goods sold (see Figures 8-1, 8-2, and 8-3 for computations)	214.00	220.26	228.00
Gross margin on sales	$253.50	247.24	239.50
Deduct operating expenses	100.00	100.00	100.00
Net income	$153.50	147.24	139.50

	FIFO	*Weighted Average*	*LIFO*
Ending inventory	$ 84.00	$ 77.74	$ 70.00

During a period of rising prices, FIFO costing results in the highest ending inventory valuation, gross margin on sales, and net income and the lowest cost of goods sold. Given the same rising market conditions, the LIFO inventory method gives the opposite results: lowest ending inventory valuation, gross margin on sales, and net income and highest cost of goods sold. During a period of falling prices, FIFO results in the lowest ending inventory valuation, gross margin on sales, and net income and the highest cost of goods sold; LIFO gives the opposite results.

A major disadvantage of LIFO costing is that during inflationary periods LIFO costing results in a significant understatement of current assets, which limits the significance and usefulness of the balance sheet. LIFO's purpose is to match revenue with current cost, rather than with earliest cost, as is done under FIFO costing.

Figure 8-4 shows that the amounts for the income statement items listed under weighted average costing fall between the corresponding amounts for FIFO and LIFO costing. The same position would be maintained in a falling market. Weighted average costing reduces the effect of widely fluctuating prices and results in a valuation closer to FIFO than to LIFO.

The balance sheet classifies the ending inventory as a current asset; consequently, this statement as well as the income statement is affected by the method of inventory valuation used. The ending inventory is often the largest single item in the Current Assets section and has, therefore, a decided effect on financial statement analysis.

Historical cost is the primary basis used for inventory valuation. Some accountants recommend the use of replacement cost for inventory valuation. This may be defined as the current cost of replacing the inventory items at the inventory date, in the ordinary course of business, assuming access to the usual sources of supply and at volumes in which the goods are usually purchased. The accountants who criticize the use of historical cost argue that FIFO does not segregate gains from changing price levels and that LIFO eliminates the effects of changing price levels from income. Others recommend reporting parallel figures showing both historical cost and current costs, thereby providing the user with a better basis for evaluating past performance and for predicting future performance. The use of current costs would eliminate the need for a cost-flow assumption—LIFO, FIFO, average—and would result in a better matching of expired cost and revenue. The balance sheet valuation would also be more significant. "Where current value varies obviously and significantly from historical cost, the accountant should feel compelled to modify the recorded amount. Replacement cost may prove to be the most meaningful basis for modification of inventory and plant and equipment under some circumstances."[6]

According to the CICA, "if the method of determining cost has resulted in a figure which does not differ materially from recent cost, the simple term *cost* is considered to be suitable in describing the basis of valuation. Otherwise, the method of determining cost should be disclosed."[7]

CONTINUOUS RECORD METHOD

Perpetual Inventory

Inventory quantities on hand can be kept on cards for a continuous record of items on hand. The quantities can be assigned costs by the first-in first-out, last-in first-out, and moving average methods.

Perpetual Inventory. The perpetual inventory system provides for a continuous book inventory of items on hand; it is a method of record keeping. An

[6]Arthur Andersen & Co., *Accounting and Reporting Problems of the Profession*, 4th ed., p. 54.
[7]*CICA Handbook, op. cit.,* Section 3030.11.

inventory record card, often called a *stock record card,* or a record in a computer storage device is kept for each inventory item acquired; when units are purchased or sold, the inventory record for the item must be adjusted accordingly to show the quantity on hand at any time. The maintenance of continuous inventory records does not preclude the need for a complete annual physical inventory. Some companies that use the perpetual inventory system take physical counts of portions of the inventory during the course of the year to test whether the records are in agreement with quantities actually on hand. This practice may be followed, instead of taking a complete annual physical inventory.

First-In, First-Out (FIFO) Costing. A detailed perpetual inventory card illustrating the FIFO procedure for assigning costs is shown in Figure 8-5.

Figure 8-5 Perpetual Inventory Card (FIFO)

ITEM: LOCK, STEEL, NO. 7004 LOCATION S-5												
Date		Ref.	Received (or Purchased)			Issued (or Sold)			Balance			
			Quantity	*Unit Cost*	*Total Cost*	*Quantity*	*Unit Cost*	*Total Cost*	*Quantity*	*Unit Cost*	*Total Cost*	
April	1	Balance							20	2.20	44.00	
	5	P.O.* 673	60	2.60	156.00				20 60	2.20 2.60	200.00	
	12	S.T.† 401				20 35	2.20 2.60	135.00	25	2.60	65.00	
	15	P.O. 690	35	2.80	98.00				25 35	2.60 2.80	163.00	
	30	S.T.407				25 5	2.60 2.80	79.00	30	2.80	84.00	

* Purchase Order
† Shipping Ticket

As each shipment of goods is received, the quantity, unit cost, and total cost are recorded in the appropriate columns. When goods are issued, the unit cost of the oldest goods on hand is recorded in the Unit Cost column; this cost is then multiplied by the number of units, and the total is written in the Total Cost column. The balance on hand, unit cost, and total cost for each shipment from which units are assumed to remain are recorded in the Balance column.

The cost of the 55 units sold on April 12 is assumed to consist of the 20 units on hand on April 1 and 35 units from the April 5 purchase. The cost of the 30 units sold on April 30 is assumed to consist of the remaining 25 units from the April 5 purchase and 5 units from the April 15 purchase. Therefore, the 30 units on hand on April 30 are assumed to be from those purchased on April 15. The cost of the units sold may be summarized as follows:

Cost of goods available for sale (beginning inventory plus purchases)	$298
Cost of April 30 ending inventory (30 units at $2.80)	84
Cost of goods sold	$214

When FIFO costing is used, the amount of the ending inventory as well as the amount of the cost of goods sold is identical with either the periodic or the perpetual inventory system, because in each instance the goods on hand are assumed to consist of the most recently acquired units.

Last-In, First-out (LIFO) Costing. The application of LIFO costing is illustrated in Figure 8-6.

Perpetual Inventory Card (LIFO) **Figure 8-6**

ITEM: LOCK, STEEL, NO. 7004 LOCATION S-5

Date		Ref.	Received (or Purchased)			Issued (or Sold)			Balance		
			Quantity	*Unit Cost*	*Total Cost*	*Quantity*	*Unit Cost*	*Total Cost*	*Quantity*	*Unit Cost*	*Total Cost*
April	1	Balance							20	2.20	44.00
	5	P.O. 673	60	2.60	156.00				20 60	2.20 2.60	200.00
	12	S.T. 401				55	2.60	143.00	20 5	2.20 2.60	57.00
	15	P.O. 690	35	2.80	98.00				20 5 35	2.20 2.60 2.80	155.00
	30	S.T. 409				30	2.80	84.00	20 5 5	2.20 2.60 2.80	71.00

Sold goods are listed at the unit cost of the latest acquisition, up to the amount assumed to be still on hand. For instance, the 55 units sold on April 12 are assumed to have come from the units received on April 5. The balance on hand, unit cost, and total cost for each receipt from which units are assumed to be on hand are recorded in the Balance column.

The inventory on April 30 is assumed to consist of:

20 units at $2.20	=	$44
5 units at 2.60	=	13
5 units at 2.80	=	14
30 units		$71

The cost of goods sold is $227 (goods available for sale, $298, less ending inventory, $71). This figure is obtainable by adding the Total Cost column of the Issued (or Sold) section of the inventory card.

If the *periodic inventory system* were used, the 30 units in inventory on April 30 would be assumed to consist of the beginning inventory of 20 units and 10 units from the purchase of April 5 for a total cost of $70. The cost of the units sold would be $228:

Cost of goods available for sale (beginning inventory plus purchases)	$298
Cost of April 30 inventory	70
Cost of goods sold	$228

Note that, unlike FIFO costing, the valuations of the cost of goods sold and ending inventory under LIFO costing may be different, depending on whether the perpetual or the periodic inventory system is used. When LIFO costing is used with the perpetual inventory system, prices at the beginning of the period that would be reflected in the ending valuation with the periodic inventory system may be dropped from the running balance as goods are issued. When the inventory is taken only at the end of the period, the various dates of sales are ignored. The LIFO procedure may be used appropriately with either periodic inventories or perpetual inventories even though the results may be different; the system selected, however, should be followed consistently. The following tabulation illustrates the different results of LIFO costing with the perpetual and the periodic inventory systems:

	Perpetual Inventory	*Periodic Inventory*
Inventory, April 1	$ 44	$ 44
Purchases	254	254
Total goods available for sale	$298	$298
Inventory, April 30	71	70
Cost of goods sold	$227	$228

Moving Average Costing. Under moving average costing, the cost of each purchase is added to the cost of units on hand, and the total cost is divided by the total quantity on hand to find the average price. Units issued are priced at the average price until additional units are purchased; then a new average price is computed. This method tends to level off price fluctuations. The application of moving average costing is shown in Figure 8-7.

Figure 8-7 Perpetual Inventory Card (Moving Average Costing)

ITEM: LOCK, STEEL, NO. 7004 LOCATION S-5											
Date		Ref.	Received (or Purchased)			Issued (or Sold)			Balance		
			Quantity	*Unit Cost*	*Total Cost*	*Quantity*	*Unit Cost*	*Total Cost*	*Quantity*	*Unit Cost*	*Total Cost*
April	1	Balance							20	2.20	44.00
	5	P.O. 673	60	2.60	156.00				80	2.50	200.00 (a)
	12	S.T. 401				55	2.50	137.50	25	2.50	62.50
	15	P.O. 690	35	2.80	98.00				60	2.675	160.50 (b)
	30	S.T. 409				30	2.675	80.25	30	2.675	80.25

Computations

(a)		(b)	
20 at $2.20 =	$ 44.00	25 at $2.50 =	$ 62.50
60 at 2.60 =	156.00	35 at 2.80 =	98.00
80	$200.00	60	$160.50
Average $2.50		Average $2.675	

Stock Ledger Card

BALANCE SHEET DISCLOSURE

Studies of financial reports prepared by leading corporations show that LCM is the most commonly used basis of valuation for inventories, the only other common basis being cost.[8] Cost, of course, includes LIFO, FIFO, and weighted average valuations, by either the perpetual or the periodic inventory system. FIFO costing is the method most frequently used.[9] The LCM method of inventory valuation is discussed below.

LOWER OF COST AND MARKET (LCM)

The various methods of inventory valuation discussed thus far in this chapter are methods of arriving at the cost of the inventory.

However, a long-standing convention in accounting holds that inventories may be valued at the *lower of cost and market.*

"A departure from the cost basis of pricing the inventory is required when the utility of the goods is no longer as great as its cost. Where there is evidence

[8]Financial Reporting in Canada (Toronto: CICA, 1975), p. 59.
[9]*Ibid.*, p. 60.

that the utility of goods, in their disposal in the ordinary course of business, will be less than cost, whether due to physical deterioration, obsolescence, changes in price levels, or other causes, the difference should be recognized as a loss of the current period. This is generally accomplished by stating such goods at a lower level commonly designated as *market.*"[10] The term *market* generally means the cost of replacing the goods as of the date.

The CICA has recommended that "in view of the lack of precision in meaning, it is desirable that the term *market* not be used in describing the basis of valuation. A term more descriptive of the method of determining market, such as replacement cost, net realizable value, or net realizable value less normal profit margin, would be preferable."[11] This recommendation should be noted when financial statements are being prepared.

Application of Lower of Cost and Market

The process of valuing the inventory at LCM occurs at the end of the accounting period when financial statements are prepared. It may be applied (1) to each item individually, (2) to each major inventory category, or (3) to the entire inventory. On the basis of the inventory tabulations in Figure 8-8 (FIFO costing is assumed), the valuation under each procedure is as follows (Items A and B are assumed to constitute category X and the remaining items constitute category Y):

1. If each item is valued individually, the inventory is reported as $5,725 (column 6).
2. If the inventory is valued by major categories, it is reported as $5,925 (column 7).
3. If the inventory is valued in total, it is reported as $6,225 (column 8).

Evaluation of LCM

The reason for LCM inventory valuation is to avoid the anticipation of profits and to provide for all foreseeable losses. This practice was developed when the influence of the grantor of credit was paramount and when primary emphasis was on the balance sheet and on conservative asset valuations. It is based on the assumption that a drop in the purchase price of goods will be followed by a corresponding drop in the selling price of those goods, thereby reducing or eliminating the normal profit margin.

CONSISTENCY IN APPLICATION OF PROCEDURES

Different procedures may be used in different areas of accounting.

It is of paramount importance, therefore, that the selected method should be followed consistently from year to year.

[10] AICPA, *op. cit.*, p. 6015.
[11] *CICA Handbook, loc. cit.*

Figure 8-8 Application of LCM

Column Nos.	1	2	3	4	5	6	7	8
						Lower of Cost and Market Basis		
Item	*Quantity*	*Unit Cost*	*Unit Market Price*	*Total Cost*	*Total Market*	*Unit*	*Major Category*	*Total Inventory*
Category X:								
Item A	100	$10	$9.00	$1,000	$ 900	$ 900		
Item B	200	4	6.00	800	1,200	800		
Subtotal				$1,800	$2,100		$1,800	
Category Y:								
Item C	400	1	1.25	$ 400	$ 500	$ 400		
Item D	600	6	5.00	3,600	3,000	3,000		
Item E	250	3	2.50	750	625	625		
Subtotal				$4,750	$4,125		4,125	
Totals				$6,550	$6,225			$6,225
Ending Inventory-LCM						$5,725	$5,925	$6,225

Inconsistency in inventory pricing, cost allocations, and financial statement presentation would make year-to-year comparisons of operating results and financial position meaningless. Since such comparisons often serve as the basis for managerial decisions and decisions of external users of accounting information, the importance of consistency becomes evident.

The concept of consistency may be applied at several levels. Consistency is important not only in the matter of valuation procedures followed but also with respect to the classification of items in financial statements. Consistency in classification applies to the grouping of items within each statement as well as to year-to-year consistency. The principle of consistency does not preclude required changes properly made and fully disclosed. A change from FIFO to LIFO inventory costing, for example, requires an explanation accompanying the financial statements of the year of change, giving the nature of the change and its effect on the net income for the period.

PERPETUAL AND PERIODIC INVENTORY SYSTEMS COMPARED

With the periodic inventory system assumed in the preceding chapters, the beginning inventory is shown in a Merchandise Inventory account, and all purchases are entered in a Purchases account. The cost of goods sold does not appear as an account balance in the general ledger but is determined only after the physical inventory is taken at the end of the period. With the perpetual inventory system, however, the beginning inventory and all purchases are shown as debits in a Merchandise Inventory (asset) account. The cost of all goods sold is debited to a Cost of Goods Sold Account and credited to the Merchandise Inventory account. The balance of the Merchandise Inventory account is the cost of the goods remaining in the inventory, provided there have been no shrinkages or other losses. The Merchandise Inventory account is a controlling account supported by a subsidiary inventory ledger made up of inventory record cards for all items.

The entries in summary journal form for both systems are shown below.

Periodic Inventory		
(1)		
Purchases	254.00	
Accounts Payable		254.00
To record April purchases.		
(2)		
Accounts Receivable	467.50	
Sales		467.50
To record April sales of 85 units at $5.50 each.		
Perpetual Inventory		
(1)		
Merchandise Inventory	254.00	
Accounts Payable		254.00
To record April purchases.		
(2)		
Accounts Receivable	467.50	
Sales		467.50
To record April sales of 85 units at $5.50 each.		
(3)		
Cost of Goods Sold	214.00	
Merchandise Inventory		214.00
To record the cost of 85 units sold (amounts from Issued column, Figure 8-5).		

The Merchandise Inventory account shows a balance of $84, which is the cost of goods on hand.

Information on quantities on hand is useful for determining when and how much to order and for comparison with periodic physical counts for detecting discrepancies and errors.

GROSS MARGIN METHOD

Taking a physical inventory or maintaining perpetual inventory records is often costly and time-consuming. For some purposes—preparing monthly financial statements, checking the accuracy of a physical inventory, or estimating inventory value when an accurate valuation cannot be made, as in the case of a fire loss—the *gross margin* method of estimating the inventory is used.

Assume that during the previous three years Needham Company Ltd. has averaged a gross margin rate on sales of 30 percent, as shown below.

	Prior Years			
	1	*2*	*3*	*Totals*
Sales	$124,000	$142,000	$154,000	$420,000
Cost of Goods Sold	87,420	97,980	108,600	294,000
Gross Margin	$ 36,580	$ 44,020	$ 45,400	$126,000
Gross Margin Rate	29.5%	31%	29.5%	30%

For the current year, the following data are available from the records of the company:

Inventory—January 1	$ 20,000
Purchases	110,000
Sales	160,000

Under the gross margin method, the estimated inventory on December 31 would be computed as follows:

a. Sales − Gross margin = Cost of goods sold
$160,000 − (0.30 × $160,000) = $112,000

b. Beginning inventory + Net cost of purchases − Cost of goods sold = Ending inventory
$20,000 + $110,000 − $112,000 = $18,000

On the basis of the foregoing computations, the complete income statement is as follows:

Sales (given)		$160,000
Cost of Goods Sold		
Inventory, January 1 (given)	$ 20,000	
Purchases (given)	110,000	
Total	$130,000	
Estimated Inventory, December 31 (item b)	18,000	
Cost of Goods Sold (item a)		112,000
Gross Margin (Sales − Cost of Goods Sold)		$ 48,000

This method is based on the assumption that the rate of gross margin on sales is substantially the same in every period. It is accurate, therefore, only to the extent that the assumed gross margin rate reflects the experience of the current period.

RETAIL METHOD

Another method of estimating the ending inventory, commonly used by chain and department stores, is the *retail inventory* method. Its value is twofold: It serves as a means of computing the ending inventory without a physical count; it provides a method of centrally controlling inventories that consist of a variety of items dispersed over several departments or several branch stores. Goods are charged to the departments or branches at their selling price, records of both cost and selling price of goods purchased are kept centrally, and records of sales are kept in the usual manner. From these records, the inventory valuation may be prepared at any time. The estimated inventory at retail is derived by deducting the sales during the period from the total goods available for sale priced at retail. This amount is then converted to cost by applying the cost percentage (the ratio of the cost of goods available for sale to the retail price of those goods). This is illustrated in Figure 8-9.

Figure 8-9
Retail Inventory Method

	Cost	*Retail*
Inventory at beginning of period	$ 20,000	$ 30,000
Purchases during period	180,000	270,000
Total goods available	$200,000	$300,000
Cost percentage (ratio of cost to retail) $\frac{\$200{,}000}{\$300{,}000} = 66\frac{2}{3}\%$		
Sales during period		258,000
Inventory at retail		$ 42,000
Estimated inventory at cost (66⅔% of $42,000)	$28,000	

Changes in previously established retail prices by increases (called *markups*) or decreases (called *markdowns*) are often necessary. Depending on how these changes are applied in computing the cost-to-retail ratio, the ending inventory may approximate lower of cost and market, LIFO, FIFO, or replacement cost.

Both the gross margin method and the retail inventory method are based on a calculation of the gross margin rate. The gross margin method uses past experience as a basis; the retail inventory method uses current experience. The gross margin method is, therefore, less reliable, because past experience may be different from the current experience.

IMPORTANCE OF INVENTORY VALUATION

The proper valuation, or *costing,* of the merchandise inventory is of considerable importance for income measurement and balance sheet usefulness. The inventory is often large in proportion to the other items in the financial statements; a misstatement of the inventory will cause a misstatement of the cost of goods sold, gross margin on sales, and net income for the period in which the error occurred, and will also misstate current assets and shareholders' equity as of the end of that period. Furthermore, since the ending inventory of one accounting period is the beginning inventory of the next period, any overstatement or understatement will also misstate the cost of goods sold, gross margin on sales, and net income of the next period.

The following information is taken from the income statements of a retail store for 19X2 and 19X1 (amounts shown are in thousands):

	19X2				*19X1*			
	Incorrect		*Correct*		*Correct*		*Incorrect*	
Sales		$300		$300		$250		$250
Cost of Goods Sold								
Beginning Inventory	$ 90		$ 85		$ 80		$ 80	
Purchases	150		150		120		120	
Total	$240		$235		$200		$200	
Deduct Ending Inventory	105	135	105	130	85	115	90	110
Gross Margin on Sales		$165		$170		$135		$140
Expenses		130		130		120		120
Net Income		$ 35		$ 40		$ 15		$ 20

If it is assumed that the ending inventory for 19X1 should have been valued at $85,000 rather than $90,000, the effect of the error on the income statements is evident from the corrected statements. The $5,000 overstatement in 19X1 ending inventory resulted in the following errors of $5,000 in the two income statements.

	19X2	*19X1*
Cost of Goods Sold	Overstated	Understated
Gross Margin	Understated	Overstated
Net Income	Understated	Overstated

Since the misstatements cancel each other, the error has no overall effect on the two-year span covered by the statements. That fact, however, does not diminish the seriousness of an inventory valuation error. The interpretation and analysis of the income statement for each period may influence some basic management decisions. Since both income statements are in error, their reciprocal canceling effect does not cancel erroneous interpretations caused by reliance on two incorrect statements.

INVENTORY CONTROL

The principle of the separation of duties discussed in chapter 7 is equally applicable to merchandise. Internal controls must be established to protect against loss, theft, and misappropriation of inventory. The system for receiving, storing, issuing, and paying for the merchandise must provide for such records and supporting documents and for the assignment of individual responsibility and accountability as will safeguard the assets. Absence of control over inventories can be a serious detriment to the successful management of a business. An excessive inventory is expensive to carry. Studies made indicate that the costs of carrying an inventory—taxes, insurance, warehousing, handling, and inventory taking—may be as high as 25 percent of the original purchase price. This is exclusive of lost potential earnings (interest) on the funds tied up in inventories. On the other hand, sufficient items and quantities must be stocked to provide customers with good service.

Maintaining a proper balance, to avoid both shortages and excesses of inventory, requires organization and planning. Control plans must provide for day-to-day comparisons of projected inventory acquisitions with current sales volume. A reduction in sales volume will result in excess inventories unless adjustments are made.

Maximum and Minimum Levels

It is customary to establish maximum and minimum stock levels for inventory items, so that the purchasing agent is automatically notified when the balance on hand is at the minimum quantity and the item must be replenished. Minimum levels should be set to allow for anticipated sales requirements during the time required for placing the replenishment order and receiving the goods, with a margin for unforeseen delay. Maximum balances should be set, based on sales requirements, minimum stock point, and the most economical buying quantities.

Economical Buying Quantities

Deciding the quantity to purchase involves considering the cost of acquisition and the cost of carrying the items. Ordering large quantities often results in a lower unit purchase price and lower transportation costs per unit, but the saving is offset by the increased cost of carrying the inventory. Carrying cost includes taxes, insurance, storage, losses due to obsolescence and deterioration, interest on the investment, and other factors. The point at which the aggregate of all the cost elements—cost to order, carrying cost, and purchase cost—is lowest indicates the most economical quantity to order or the number of orders to place each year.

GLOSSARY

Consistency The concept that uniformity—with full disclosure for any departures—from year to year, especially in inventory pricing, cost allocation, and financial statement presentation, is essential to make comparisons meaningful.

FIFO A method of determining the cost of goods on hand and the cost of goods sold based on the assumption that the units are sold in the order in which they were acquired.

Gross Margin Method A method of estimating inventory value by deducting the cost of goods sold from the total cost of goods available for sale, the cost of goods sold being the product of the average gross margin percentage for prior periods applied to sales for the current period.

LIFO A costing method based on the assumption that the cost of goods sold should be calculated on prices paid for the most recently acquired units and that the units on hand consist of the oldest units acquired.

Lower of Cost and Market (LCM) An inventory valuation method by which units are valued at the lower of either original acquisition cost or at replacement cost (market) for those units in inventory whose replacement cost has fallen below original acquisition cost.

Moving Average An inventory costing method by which the cost of each purchase is added to the cost of units on hand, and the total cost is divided by the total quantity on hand to find the average unit price.

Periodic Inventory An inventory system of record keeping by which the value of the inventory for statement of financial position presentation and for the determination of the cost of goods sold is determined at the end of each annual period by a complete physical count and pricing of all inventory items.

Perpetual Inventory An inventory system of record keeping that provides for a continuous book inventory of items on hand.

Retail Method A method of estimating inventory value by applying the current gross margin ratio (the ratio of the cost of goods to the selling price) to net sales to derive the cost of goods sold which, when deducted from sales, equals the selling price of the inventory. The inventory valued at retail is then converted to cost by the application of the gross margin ratio.

Specific Identification An inventory costing method by which the unit cost is identified specifically with the related supporting acquisition document.

Weighted Average A costing method by which the ending inventory and the cost of goods sold are priced at the end of each accounting period at a unit cost computed by dividing the total cost of goods available for sale by the physical units available for sale.

QUESTIONS

Q8-1. Why is it important that the selected system of inventory valuation be applied consistently from year to year? Does strict compliance with the principle of consistency preclude a change from FIFO to LIFO?

Q8-2. Distinguish between the perpetual and the periodic inventory systems. Does the perpetual inventory system eliminate the need for a physical inventory count?

Q8-3. How do overstatements or understatements of inventory affect net income in the period when the error is made? in the following period?

Q8-4. What effect do the different methods of inventory valuation have on the financial statements?

Q8-5. Compare the gross margin method with the retail inventory method.

Q8-6. An audit of the records of the Shelley Corporation showed that the ending inventory on December 31, 19X1, was overstated by $7,600 and that on December 31, 19X2, the inventory was understated by$9,300. What was the effect of the errors on the income statement for each year? What was the overall effect for the two-year period?

Q8-7. The Cole Company maintains perpetual inventory cards for all merchandise items. An inventory is taken annually. Serially numbered perforated tags are placed on or alongside the various items. The inventory is taken by teams of two employees: One employee fills in the description and quantity of the item on each section of the tag; the other checks both the description and the count and removes the second half of the tag. The removed portions of the tags are then sent to the office, where the information is entered on inventory sheets and priced on the basis of lower cost and market.
Explain the purpose of each step of this procedure. Criticize the procedure followed. State what precautionary steps must be taken prior to the actual inventory count, during the count, and immediately following the completion of the count.

Q8-8. Explain the effect on the balance sheet valuation and on the income determination of the use of LIFO as compared with FIFO (a) if prices have risen during the year; (b) if prices have fallen during the year.

Q8-9. (a) Define the term *market* as used in lower of cost and market inventory valuation. (b) What is the rationale for LCM? (c) Does LCM always produce conservative financial statements?

Q8-10. (a) What is the relationship between the actual physical flow of goods in and out of inventory and the method used for inventory valuation? (b) What inventory valuation method should a company use if, as new shipments of inventory items are received, they are commingled with identical items on hand in storage bins?

DEMONSTRATION PROBLEMS

DP8-1. *(Accounting policy decision problem: Inventory valuation)* On January 1, the Fisher Company had an inventory of 500 units of a product that cost $27 each. January receipts and issues were as follows:

Received		Issued	
January 3	200 units at $28	January 2	100 units
January 10	300 units at 32	January 8	200 units
January 23	100 units at 29	January 17	300 units
		January 26	200 units

Required:

Compute the January 31 inventory using (a) FIFO based on a periodic inventory, (b) LIFO based on a periodic inventory, and (c) weighted average.

DP8-2. (*Management policy decision problem: Inventory valuation—retail inventory method*) The records of the Tarrasch Company show the following information on January 31.

	Cost	Sales Price
Merchandise Inventory		
January 1	$ 12,700	$ 18,100
Purchases during January	118,000	176,000
Transportion In	1,600	

Purchases Returns and Allowances	4,460	6,650
Sales		180,000

Required:

1. Find the cost of the January 31 inventory, using the retail inventory method.
2. The Tarrasch Company has had frequent inventory shortages in certain of its departments. What steps should management take to eliminate these shortages?

DP8-3. (*Accounting policy decision problem: Inventory valuation—gross margin method*) A fire destroyed the entire inventory of the Mannes Corporation on December 23, 19X2. The following information is available for the years 19X1 and 19X2 (to the date of the fire):

	19X2	*19X1*
Merchandise Inventory, January 1	$ 36,200	$ 34,450
Sales	142,800	136,600
Sales Returns and Allowances	2,750	3,100
Purchases	120,000	103,300
Purchases Returns and Allowances	6,350	7,300
Transportation In	4,800	5,460

Required:

1. Estimate the amount of the inventory destroyed by the fire.
2. How reliable is the estimate?

PROBLEMS

P8-1. The records of the Stack Company show the following data as of December 31.

a. Cost of merchandise on hand, based on a physical count	$50,000
b. Merchandise sold to a customer, but held for him pending receipt of shipping instructions (included in item a)	1,800
c. Merchandise shipped out on December 30, F.O.B. destination; expected delivery time is 8 days	2,200
d. Merchandise purchased on December 28, F.O.B. shipping point, delivered to a carrier on December 29; expected delivery date is January 5	750
e. Cost of spoiled merchandise (to be given away); not included in item a	200

What is the value of the inventory on December 31 for financial statement reporting purposes?

P8-2. The following items were included in the income statements of the Egypt Company for the years ended December 31, 19X2 and 19X1.

	December 31	
	19X2	*19X1*
Cost of goods sold	$ 69,000	$ 76,000
Gross margin	142,000	135,000
Net income	35,000	20,000

An audit of the records revealed that the merchandise inventory at December 31, 19X1 was understated by $4,000. What was the effect of the error on the amounts given?

P8-3. The year-end inventory of the Kidder Company consisted of the following groups of items, priced at cost and at market:

Item	*Cost*	*Market*
A	$60,000	$63,000
B	40,000	40,000
C	80,000	78,000
D	50,000	42,000

What inventory amount should be used in the financial statements? Why?

P8-4. The inventory of the Lear Company on January 1 and December 31 consisted of 21,250 and 31,250 units, respectively, of Commodity X-1. The beginning inventory was priced at $1,700. The following purchases were made during the year:

Date	*Quantity*	*Cost*
January 10	12,500	$1,125
April 15	21,250	1,800
July 5	30,000	2,850
October 2	7,500	750
December 15	20,000	1,600

Determine the cost of the December 31 inventory by each of the following methods: (a) LIFO; (b) FIFO; (c) weighted average. Assume that the periodic inventory system is used.

P8-5. The beginning inventory, purchases, and sales of an item by the Golemme Company for the month of July were as follows:

July 1 Inventory on hand consisted of 100 units at $3.15 each.
12 Sold 50 units.
15 Purchased 40 units at $3.00 each.
17 Purchased 60 units at $2.70 each.
19 Sold 30 units.
26 Purchased 50 units at $3.45 each.
29 Sold 40 units.

What was the value of the units on hand on July 31 (a) under the perpetual inventory moving average method and (b) under the periodic inventory weighted average method?

P8-6. The following information pertains to a stock item of the Dailey Corporation:

January 1	On hand	10,000 units at $9.00
February 14	Purchase	12,000 units at 9.75
June 12	Purchase	14,000 units at 9.00
November 12	Purchase	10,000 units at 9.50
December 31	On hand	12,000 units

The periodic inventory system is used. Compute the value of the inventory on December 31, (a) under FIFO and (b) under LIFO.

P8-7. The DeVey Company calculates its inventory by the gross margin method for interim statement purposes. The inventory on January 1 was $53,200, net purchases during January were $139,650, and net sales for the month were $199,500. The gross margin rate is estimated at 35% of net sales. What was the estimated inventory on January 31?

P8-8. The entire stock of the Knit Company was destroyed by fire on June 22. The books of the company (kept in a fireproof vault) showed the value of goods on hand on June 1 to be $40,000. Transactions for the period June 1 through June 22 resulted in the following amounts:

Sales	$98,780
Sales Returns	2,105
Purchases	79,800
Purchases Returns	1,815
Transportation In	1,475

The rate of gross margin on sales for the previous three years averaged 35%. Determine the cost of the inventory destroyed by the fire.

P8-9. The books of Hopper Department Store show the following data for the leather goods department for the first year of operations:

Purchases (at cost)	$4,900
Purchases (at original selling price)	8,650
Sales	8,175

Compute the inventory on December 31 by the retail method. (*Hint:* Include the markups but exclude the markdowns in the computation of the cost percentage.)

P8-10. (a) From the following data, compute the cost of the ending inventory:

Sales	$30,000
Beginning inventory (cost)	12,500
Beginning inventory (retail)	17,500
Purchases (cost)	17,500
Purchases (retail)	22,500

(b) Recompute the ending inventory, assuming the following additional items:

Transportation In	$ 750
Purchases Returns (cost)	500
Purchases Returns (retail)	750
Sales Returns	1,000

P8-11. (*Accounting policy decision problem*) Purchases and sales data for the first three years of operation of Andover Company Ltd. for a single item were as follows (purchases are listed in order of acquisition):

	19X1	*19X2*	*19X3*
Sales	19,200 units at $52	24,000 units at $62	29,000 units at $68
Purchases	6,500 units at $25	9,000 units at $35	11,000 units at $43
	10,000 units at $27	10,000 units at $37	7,500 units at $46
	8,000 units at $33	6,500 units at $40	8,000 units at $48

Required:

1. Compute the year-end inventories under the periodic inventory system for each of the three years, using (a) FIFO and (b) LIFO.
2. (a) As a manager, which method would you prefer, assuming that you are paid a bonus based on earnings? (b) Which method would you prefer if you were (1) a present shareholder; (2) a prospective shareholder?

P8-12. The following data are from the inventory records of a single item of the Lawn Corporation:

Purchases	*Sales*	*Balance*
		100 units at $1.10
200 units at $1.30		
100 units at 1.40		
	120 units at ?	
40 units at 1.50		
	60 units at ?	
	40 units at ?	
100 units at 1.60		

Required: Determine the ending inventory using:

1. FIFO and (a) the periodic inventory system, (b) the perpetual inventory system.
2. LIFO and (a) the periodic inventory system, (b) the perpetual inventory system.
3. Weighted average and the periodic inventory system.

P8-13. The Weir Machine Company buys and sells planers. Purchases and sales during March are shown below.

	Purchases	*Sales*
March 2	88 units at $300	
3		160 units
9	84 units at $375	
15	92 units at $340	
20		60 units
25	88 units at $360	
30		172 units

The inventory on March 1 consisted of 100 units at $450 each.

Required: Compute the ending inventory at the lower of cost and market, applied (a) to each item, (b) to each category, and (c) to the entire inventory.

P8-14. *(Accounting policy decision problem)* In October the Hodge Company began buying and selling a recently patented stamping machine. Transactions for the month follow:

Oct. 2 Purchased a machine at $9,900.
7 Purchased a machine at $10,500.
15 Sold a machine at $21,000.
20 Purchased a machine at $12,000.
28 Sold a machine at $21,000.
Operating expenses for October were $12,000.

Required:

1. Record the information on perpetual inventory records, using each of the following methods: (a) FIFO, (b) moving average, and (c) LIFO.
2. Assume that Hodge is about to purchase another machine before the end of the month but asks you first (a) how the purchase will affect the net income for the month, and (b) whether he should defer the purchase until early in November. The price will not change. What would you recommend?

P8-15. *(Accounting policy decision problem)* The inventory of the Kaufman Upholstering Company on December 31 consisted of the following items:

	Quantity	Unit Cost	Unit Market
Frames			
Type F-1	110	$14.25	$15.50
Type F-12	75	26.00	22.50
Type F-15	60	21.50	21.00
Springs (sets)			
Type S-1	760	7.28	8.50
Type S-12	625	10.50	11.50
Type S-15	340	8.60	6.00

Required:

1. Compute the ending inventory at the lower of cost and market, applied (a) to each item, (b) to each category, and (c) to the entire inventory.
2. What is the effect of each application of LCM on the gross margin in the current year? in the following year?

P8-16. *(Accounting policy decision problem)* The following data relate to an inventory item of the Cork Station Corporation:

	Units	Unit Cost
Beginning balance	180	$3.00
First purchase	300	3.00
Second purchase	600	3.30
First sale	525	
Third purchase	750	3.60
Second sale	825	
Fourth purchase	300	3.75
Third sale	150	

Required: Compute the cost value of the ending inventory under each of the following methods: (a) Weighted average—periodic, (b) FIFO—perpetual, (c) LIFO—perpetual, (d) FIFO—periodic, and (e) LIFO—periodic.

P8-17. The records of the Fair Boutique show the following information for the month of June:

Sales	$200,000
Transportation In	3,000
Purchases at cost	142,500
Purchases at retail	210,000
Inventory—June 1, at cost	52,500
Inventory—June 1, at retail	75,000

Required: Compute the June 30 inventory at cost using the retail inventory method.

P8--18. (*Accounting policy decision problem*) The Rook Company estimates its merchandise inventory when preparing monthly financial statements. The following information is available on April 30:

	Cost	*Retail*
Merchandise Inventory, April 1	$120,000	$ 195,000
Purchases during April (net)	975,000	1,650,000
Transportation In during April	6,000	
Sales during April (net)		960,000

Required:

1. Compute the estimated inventory on April 30, using the gross margin method. On the basis of past experience, Rook estimates a rate of gross margin of 40% for the current year.
2. Compute the estimated inventory on April 30, using the retail inventory method.
3. (a) Give the reason for the difference in the ending inventory under the two methods. (b) Which method is more reliable? Why?

P8-19. The Singer Company closes its books annually on December 31, at which time the merchandise inventory is determined by a physical count. For its monthly interim statements, however, inventory estimates based on the gross margin method are used. Condensed partial income statements follow:

	19X1	*19X2*	*19X3*
Sales	$437,500	$500,000	$550,000
Cost of Goods Sold	262,500	295,000	319,000
Gross Margin	$175,000	$205,000	$231,000

The merchandise inventory on December 31, 19X3 was $87,500. During January 19X4, sales were $55,000 and purchases were $50,000.

Required:

1. Compute the inventory on January 31, 19X4, based (a) on the gross margin rate for the prior three years and (b) on the average of the past three annual gross margin rates.
2. Which gross margin rate should be used? Why?

P8-20. *(Accounting policy decision problem)* On July 1, Seth Matthew established the Matthew Company with an investment of $20,000 in cash. Purchases and sales of an item during the month are shown below.

July 1 Purchased $2,880 units at $19.20.
10 Sold 1,680 units at $32.
13 Purchased 2,400 units at $20.40.
17 Sold 2,640 units at $32.
22 Purchased 3,600 units at $21.20.
30 Sold 2,160 units at $32.

Operating expenses were $22,400. Cash settlements on all transactions were completed by the end of the month.

Required:

1. Prepare perpetual inventory schedules, using (a) FIFO, (b) LIFO, and (c) moving average.
2. Prepare income statements and balance sheets based on each method of inventory valuation.
3. Explain why the different methods yield different results. Which method is correct?
4. What other factors should Matthew consider in his choice of a method of inventory valuation?
5. Which method would you recommend? Explain.
6. FIFO reflects price increases on goods on hand in net income but these are not real profits because, as the inventory is depleted, replacement costs will be higher. Do you agree? Explain.

9

Plant and Equipment

Industrial expansion often requires large expenditures for land, buildings machinery, and equipment. When such expenditures must be made in an economic environment marked by sweeping technological changes, inflation, and high levels of taxation, the accounting problems become both more complicated and more controversial. This chapter deals with the determination of and accounting for the cost of plant assets, the allocation of these asset costs to the appropriate accounting periods, the disposal or retirement of plant assets, and the accounting for other long-lived assets such as natural resources and intangible assets. The question of valuing these assets at historical cost is also discussed in this chapter.

The term ***plant and equipment*** denotes all assets of a tangible and relatively permanent nature, acquired for use in the regular operations of the business, not for resale, and whose use or consumption will cover more than one accounting period. This classification includes land, buildings, machinery, trucks, fixtures, tools, office machines, furniture and furnishings, patterns, and dies. The terms ***plant assets, capital assets, fixed assets, tangible assets,*** and ***noncurrent assets*** are often used as synonyms for plant and equipment.

Wasting assets such as timber, oil and gas, or minerals are accounted for in a manner similar to plant and equipment. The term ***intangible assets*** denotes nonphysical rights and expected benefits that come from ownership. Their use and value is dependent on and limited by the degree of legal protection (patents, copyrights, franchises), economic factors (goodwill), and the passage of time (leaseholds).

COST OF PLANT AND EQUIPMENT

The cost of plant and equipment includes the purchase price (less any discount) plus all other expenditures required to secure title and to get the asset ready for operating use. The cost of buildings includes permit fees, engineering fees, and remodeling costs. The cost of machinery includes transportation, installation, and all other costs incurred in preparing the machinery for operations.

Assume that a company purchases a machine for $5,000 at terms of 2/10, n/60, with freight to be paid by the buyer. Installation of the machine requires specialized electrical wiring and the construction of a cement foundation. All these expenditures are charged to the asset account. The total asset cost includes the following:

Purchase price	$5,000
Deduct 2% cash discount	100
Net purchase price	$4,900
Transportation	125
Cost of wiring	75
Construction of a special foundation	110
Total asset cost	$5,210

The entry for the purchase of the machine is the net cash paid on purchase.

Machinery	4,900	
Cash		4,900

The entry for the freight payment is:

Machinery	125	
Cash		125

The entry to record the payment for installation of the machine is:

Machinery	185	
Cash		185

When these entries are posted, the Machinery account shows a total cost for the machine of $5,210. An asset acquired in some manner other than by cash payment—for example, by gift or issuance of securities—is valued on the basis of the amount of cash that would be required for its acquisition (*fair market value*). When a used plant asset is acquired, all expenditures incurred in getting the asset ready for use—paint, replacement parts, and so on—are charged to the asset account.

The cost of land includes brokers' fees, legal fees, transfer taxes, as well as costs incurred in preparing the land for use, such as grading, clearing, and the removal of unwanted existing structures. Land is shown separately on the balance sheet, because it is not subject to depreciation. However, improvements to land—landscaping, lighting, parking areas, fencing—which deteriorate through usage, are subject to depreciation and should be classified in a separate account, such as Land Improvements.

CAPITAL AND REVENUE EXPENDITURES

The term ***expenditure*** refers to a payment or a promise to make a future payment for benefits received—that is, for assets or services. Expenditures made on plant and equipment assets during the period of ownership may be classified as ***capital expenditures*** or ***revenue expenditures.*** A capital expenditure results in an addition to an asset account; a revenue expenditure results in an addition to an expense account.

Capital expenditures are payments for asset alterations, additions, and replacements that are significant in amount and which will benefit two or more accounting periods; therefore, through the depreciation process, these expenditures are expenses of such future accounting periods. They prolong the useful life of the asset, make it more valuable, or make it more adaptable. Most commonly they are recorded as increases in plant and equipment; the expenditure is said to have been *capitalized.* Original purchases of land, buildings, machinery, and office equipment are also capital expenditures.

Expenditures for extraordinary repairs made to equipment during its life are also classified as capital expenditures if they extend the useful life or capacity of the asset or otherwise make the asset more serviceable (for example, replacing a manually operated elevator with a fully automated one). Some accountants view an extraordinary repair as a restorative process; they record the increase in the asset by debiting Accumulated Depreciation, thereby canceling past depreciation charges.

Revenue expenditures benefit a current period and are made for the purpose of maintaining the asset in satisfactory operating condition. A routine repair or the replacement of a minor part that has worn out is an expense of the current accounting period, to be deducted from the revenue for the period. These expenditures do not increase the serviceability of the asset beyond the original estimate, but rather represent normal maintenance costs.

Careful distinction between capital and revenue expenditures is one of the fundamental problems of accounting; it is essential for the matching of expenses and revenue and, therefore, for the proper measurement of net income. A capital expenditure recorded as a revenue expenditure—as, for example, a purchase of office equipment charged to Office Expense—causes an understatement of net income in that year. If the error is not corrected, net income for the following years will be overstated by the amount of depreciation expense that would otherwise have been recognized.

DEPRECIATION OF PLANT AND EQUIPMENT

Depreciation is not necessarily a measure of the decline in the value of an asset, but rather a recognition that depreciable assets used in the business have a predictable and limited service life over which asset costs should be allocated for income measurement. The emphasis is on the periodic charge to expense rather than the resulting balance sheet valuation.

Since most plant and equipment assets have a limited useful life, their cost is properly allocable as an expense to the accounting periods in which the assets are used.

Although the serviceable life of the asset cannot be definitely known at the time of its acquisition, the cost of the asset cannot be considered as an expense chargeable entirely either to the period of acquisition or to the period of disposal. It is better to make an estimation of the useful life of the asset for purposes of making the periodic charge to expense than to omit the charge on the grounds that there is no strictly scientific way of making such an estimation.

Several factors limit the serviceability of plant assets, chiefly wear and tear through ordinary use, accidental damage, inadequacy, level of repairs or maintenance, and obsolescence. Inadequacy may be due to changes in the nature of the business—method of manufacture, location, or type or design of product—that necessitate the disposition or replacement of plant assets. Obsolescence is due to technological advances that necessitate replacement of an existing asset with a new model.

Estimated Useful Life (EUL)

It is often difficult to predict the useful service life of an asset. The estimate is important, because the amount of cost assigned to each period (depreciation for a period) is deducted from current revenue, thereby affecting net income for the period. Past experience, standard operating policies, and equipment replacement policies may be used in estimating the period during which the asset can or will be used by the business.

Estimated Salvage Value

The amount of the asset to be depreciated is its acquisition cost minus the amount that is expected to be recovered when the asset is ultimately scrapped, sold, or traded in (salvage or residual value). If an expenditure will be required in dismantling or removing the asset, the estimated gross salvage value is reduced by the anticipated removal cost. It is frequently assumed that the salvage value will be offset by the removal cost; in this case, depreciation is computed on the total cost of the asset. Also, total cost may be depreciated when the salvage value is known to be negligible.

Methods of Computing Depreciation

A number of methods are used to calculate periodic depreciation charges; each may give a significantly different result. The method selected in any specific instance should be based on a careful evaluation of all the factors involved, including estimated useful life, intensity of use, rapidity of changes in the technology of the industry and of the equipment, and revenue-generating potential. The objective is to charge each period in proportion to the benefits received during that period from the total pool of expected benefits over the asset's useful life.

Straight-Line Method. Under the straight-line method, depreciation is considered a function of time, and a uniform portion of the cost is allocated to each accounting period. Degrees of use, age, or efficiency factors are not considered in determining the amount of depreciation to be assigned to each period. The straight-line method may be expressed as follows:

$$\frac{\text{Cost less salvage value}}{\text{Number of accounting periods in estimated useful life of asset}} = \text{Depreciation for each accounting period}$$

Assume that a machine costing $5,210, with an estimated service life of five years and an estimated net salvage value of $210, is purchased on January 2. The annual depreciation charge is:

$$\frac{\$5{,}210 - \$210}{5} = \$1{,}000$$

The straight-line method is popular primarily because it is simple to use. It assumes, however, level operating efficiency, repair and maintenance, and revenue contributions.

Declining-Balance Method. The use of a declining-balance method results in larger depreciation charges during the early years of asset life with gradually decreasing charges in later years.

Under the *declining-balance method,* a uniform depreciation rate is applied in each period to the remaining *carrying value* (cost less accumulated depreciation). This rate can be calculated at twice the straight-line rate *(double-rate declining balance),* at one-half times the straight-line rate *(150 percent declining balance),* or in any other manner which is most appropriate in the circumstances. For income tax purposes, the rate cannot exceed the maximum rate which is allowed by official regulations. The computation is made without an adjustment for salvage, even though the asset cannot be depreciated below a reasonable salvage value, presumably because the arithmetic of this formula is such that it will never reduce the asset balance to zero.

Assume that a machine costing $15,300 is purchased on January 2, the EUL is five years, and the estimated salvage value is $300. A 40 percent depreciation rate—twice the straight-line rate of 20 percent—applied to the carrying value remaining at the end of each year gives the following results for the five years (note that salvage value is ignored in the amount being depreciated).

Year	*Computation*	*Annual Depreciation*	*Accumulated Depreciation*	*Carrying Value*
1	40% of $15,300	$6,120	$ 6,120	$9,180
2	40% of 9,180	3,672	9,792	5,508
3	40% of 5,508	2,203	11,995	3,305
4	40% of 3,305	1,322	13,317	1,983
5	40% of 1,983	793	14,110	1,190

The entry to record the depreciation charge for Year 3 follows:

Depreciation Expense—Machinery and Equipment	2,203	
Accumulated Depreciation— Machinery and Equipment		2,203

The balance sheet presentation of the machine at the end of the year is as follows:

Plant and Equipment		
Machinery and Equipment	$15,300	
Deduct Accumulated Depreciation	11,995	$ 3,305

A comparison of the straight-line and declining-balance methods shows the following depreciation under each.

Year	*Straight Line*	*Double-Rate Declining Balance (40%)*
1	$ 3,000	$ 6,120
2	3,000	3,672
3	3,000	2,203
4	3,000	1,322
5	3,000	793
Totals	$15,000	$14,110

The double-rate declining-balance method results in the highest depreciation in the first year because of the higher rate and the higher base ($15,300 as compared with $15,000). However, an undepreciated amount of $1,190 = ($15,300 − $14,110) remains at the end of the fifth year. If the machine is to be kept in service, $890 = ($1,190 − $300) may be written off on a straight-line basis over the remaining period of use, or by an adjustment of $890 for the final period, or it may be continued to be reduced at 40 percent of the carrying value until it is retired from use. However, no depreciation is recorded by this method in excess of the $15,000 which will expire over the EUL.

For income tax purposes, depreciation is referred to as capital cost allowance. Depreciable assets are grouped into classes called pools, and can be depreciated at any rate up to a maximum rate which is allowed by official regulations. For example, automobiles and trucks can be depreciated at a maximum rate of 30% calculated on the undepreciated balance at year-end. Each class of assets is treated separately, and is subject to a specific maximum depreciation rate. This system minimizes disputes between the taxpayer and the income tax authorities regarding useful lives and salvage values of depreciable assets.

For income tax purposes, salvage value is disregarded in the calculation of depreciation which can be taken as long as a balance exists in the class of assets being depreciated.

Production Methods. Production methods relate depreciation to usage or to results rather than time, recognizing either working hours or units of output with each unit being charged with an equal amount regardless of decline in service effectiveness, decline in revenue generated, or level of repair and maintenance requirements.

The *working-hours method* requires an estimate of useful life in service hours instead of years. The charge to depreciation for an accounting period is determined as follows:

$$\frac{\text{Cost less salvage value}}{\text{Total estimated working hours}} = \text{Depreciation expense per hour}$$

$$\text{Depreciation expense per hour} \times \text{Working hours for the period} = \text{Depreciation expense for the period}$$

An alternative computation procedure is:

$$\text{Cost less salvage value} \times \frac{\text{Working hours for the period}}{\text{Total estimated working hours}} = \text{Depreciation expense for the period}$$

Assume, for example, that a machine costing $21,000 with a salvage value of $1,000 is expected to render 40,000 hours of service. If it is used for 5,000 hours during an accounting period, the computation for that period would be:

$$\frac{\$21{,}000 - \$1{,}000}{40{,}000 \text{ hrs.}} = \$0.50 \text{ per service hour}$$

$$\$0.50 \times 5{,}000 \text{ hrs.} = \$2{,}500 \text{ depreciation expense for the period}$$

Under the *production-unit method,* depreciation is computed on units of output, and therefore an estimate of total units of output is required. If the machine in the previous example had an estimated productive life of 10,000 units and if 1,500 units were processed during the current period, the charge to depreciation for the period would be:

$$\frac{\$21{,}000 - \$1{,}000}{10{,}000 \text{ units}} = \$2 \text{ per unit produced}$$

$$\$2 \times 1{,}500 \text{ units} = \$3{,}000 \text{ depreciation expense for the period}$$

The production methods allocate cost in proportion to the use that is made of the asset, the assumption being that there is a correlation between units of use and revenue generated. The straight-line method ignores use, emphasizing the fact that the asset is available; depreciation expense is regarded as a measure of such availability, irrespective of the extent of use.

Depreciation for Partial Accounting Periods

A consistent method should be followed for recording depreciation on assets acquired or retired during the accounting period. A variety of procedures are used. One that is popular because of its simplicity is to consider that a plant asset is purchased as of the beginning of the month of acquisition if it is purchased on or before the fifteenth of the month, and to consider that a plant asset is purchased on the first day of the following month if it is purchased on or after the sixteenth of the month, the minimum measurable unit of time for the depreciation expense charge being one month.

Assume that a machine costing $6,500 with an estimated life of ten years and salvage value of $500 was purchased on November 1. Depreciation on the machine for the calendar year using straight line, is:

$$\frac{\$6{,}500 - \$500}{10} \times \frac{2}{12} = \$100$$

The year-end entry to record depreciation on the machine for two months is:

Depreciation Expense—Machinery and Equipment	100	
Accumulated Depreciation—Machinery and Equipment		100

If the machine had been acquired on or after November 16, the amount in the entry would be $50. Depreciation may have to be recorded for a partial accounting period when an asset is sold, discarded, or exchanged for another asset. In these situations, depreciation must be recorded to the date of the event, assuming that the asset has not already been fully depreciated. The amount of depreciation to be charged for the month of disposal is based on the method followed for acquisitions. The rules must be applied consistently.

Group Rates and Composite Rates

Some companies simplify the computation of depreciation and charge depreciation uniformly to all service years including the final one by use of a *group* or *composite* rate, applied either to all the assets owned or to each major asset category. The term *group* refers to a number of homogeneous assets. When a group rate is applied to a number of nonhomogeneous assets, it is called a *composite* rate; it is a special application of the group rate. The group rate is especially useful if there are a large number of individual units with similar service lives and relatively low costs (for example, railroad tracks and ties, telephone poles and cables, and restaurant and hotel furniture).

Several methods may be used to develop a composite rate; one is illustrated below.

Asset	*Cost*	*Estimated Salvage Value*	*Depreciable Cost*	*EUL (Years)*	*Annual Depreciation (Straight Line)*
A	$20,000	$2,000	$18,000	6	$3,000
B	15,000	-0-	15,000	10	1,500
C	10,200	600	9,600	12	800
	$45,200	$2,600	$42,600		$5,300

The *composite life* for this group of assets is 8.04 years, computed as follows:

$$\frac{\text{Depreciable cost}}{\text{Annual depreciation}} = \frac{\$42,600}{\$5,300} = 8.04 \text{ years of average life}$$

A group rate may be used with either straight-line depreciation or a declining-balance method. Assumimg that the straight-line method is used, the annual rate to be applied is:

$$\frac{\text{Annual depreciation}}{\text{Total cost}} = \frac{\$5,300}{\$45,200} = 0.1172, \text{ or } 11.72\%$$

Total depreciation at a mean rate of 11.72 percent, applied each year for 8.04 years to the total cost of $45,200, will be $42,600 = ($45,200 × 0.1172 × 8.04, adjusted for rounding), the amount to be depreciated. The annual depreciation charge is $5,297.44 = ($45,200 × 11.72%).

When any unit in the group is disposed of, it is assumed that it has been fully depreciated and no gain or loss on disposal is recognized. Underdepreciation on items in the group used for less than their estimated useful lives is assumed to be offset by overdepreciation on items used longer than their EULs. Although accumulated depreciation records on the individual units in the group are not kept, a record of original costs is kept.

REVISION OF DEPRECIATION CHARGES

The periodic depreciation charge may require revision as the result (1) of a capital expenditure that does not prolong the useful life of the original asset and (2) of errors in the original EUL. In either case, the new depreciable cost is typically allocated over the remaining life of the property on which the expenditure was made. Assume, for example, that an additional wing costing $8,000 is added to a five-year-old factory building. The original cost of the building was $33,000, the estimated salvage value was $3,000, and the estimated useful life was twenty-five years. The straight-line method of depreciation has been used. The calculation of the revised annual depreciation charge is:

Original cost	$33,000
Deduct five years' accumulated depreciation ($30,000 × 0.04 = $1,200 per year × 5 years)	6,000
Carrying value	$27,000
Additional cost	8,000
New carrying value	$35,000
Deduct estimated salvage value	3,000
New depreciable cost	$32,000
New annual depreciation charge, based on a remaining useful life of 20 years ($32,000 × .05)	$ 1,600

If the improvement prolongs the life of the asset or increases its salvage value, the calculations must be altered to give effect to such changes. For example, if after the addition of the wing the remaining useful life was estimated to be twenty-four years and the estimated salvage value was $3,800, the revised annual depreciation charge would be determined as follows:

New carrying value	$35,000
Deduct estimated salvage value	3,800
New depreciable cost	$31,200
New annual depreciation charge, based on a remaining useful life of 24 years ($31,200 × 0.04167)	$ 1,300

DISPOSAL OF PLANT AND EQUIPMENT

An asset may be disposed of by sale, by being *traded in* as part of the purchase price of a replacement, or by simply being discarded. The accounting treatment of sales and of discards is similar; the treatment of *trade-ins* is somewhat different.

An asset may still be in use after it is fully depreciated—that is, when the balance of the Accumulated Depreciation account, assuming that the salvage value is zero, is equal to the cost of the asset. In this case, no further depreciation is taken and no further entries are required until the asset is disposed of. In the balance sheet, the plant and equipment amount may be followed by a notation of the portion that represents fully depreciated assets still in use.

Sale or Discard of Plant and Equipment

When an asset is sold or discarded, the entry for the transaction must remove the appropriate amounts from the asset and the accumulated depreciation accounts. Assume, for example, that a company acquires a truck on January 2, at a cost of $5,000. Depreciation is recorded on a straight-line basis at a rate of $1,000 annually (salvage value is assumed to be zero). Five possible situations, together with the methods of accounting for the disposal of the truck, are illustrated.

Example 1—*Discard of fully depreciated asset.* The truck is discarded on December 31 of the fifth year.

Accumulated Depreciation-Trucks	5,000	
Trucks		5,000

The purpose of this entry is to eliminate the accumulated charges from the Accumulated Depreciation account and to reduce the asset account by the original cost of the truck.

Example 2—*Sale of fully depreciated asset.* The truck is sold on December 31 of the fifth year for $50.

Cash	50	
Accumulated Depreciation-Trucks	5,000	
Trucks		5,000
Gain on Disposal of Equipment		50

Gains and losses on disposal of plant assets are measured by the difference between the carrying value of an asset and the proceeds from its disposal: a gain results when the proceeds are greater than the carrying value; a loss results when the proceeds are less than the carrying value. If the asset is fully depreciated, as in the example, the carrying value is zero and the gain is the full amount realized from the sale. A gain or a loss may be indicative of errors in estimating the asset's useful life, salvage value, or both, in which case the gain or loss is, in fact, a correction of prior years' earnings. Also, the carrying value of the asset and, therefore, the gain or loss on disposal are affected by the depreciation procedure used. Gain on Disposal of Equipment is shown in the income statement under Other Revenue. A loss would be shown under Other Expenses.

Example 3—*Sale of asset at a price equal to carrying value.* The truck is sold on July 1, Year 5, for $500. The first entry is to record the depreciation for the current year, up to the date of the sale.

July 1	Depreciation Expense-Trucks	500	
	Accumulated Depreciation-Trucks		500
	To record depreciation on trucks for the six-month period.		

The Accumulated Depreciation account now has a credit balance of $4,500, as shown below.

Accumulated Depreciation—Trucks

	Year 1	1,000
	Year 2	1,000
	Year 3	1,000
	Year 4	1,000
	Year 5	500

The entry to record the sale is:

July 1	Cash	500	
	Accumulated Depreciation-Trucks	4,500	
	Trucks		5,000

Example 4—*Sale of asset at a price above carrying value.* The truck is sold on July 1, Year 5 for $600. The entry to record the depreciation for the current year, up to the date of the sale, is the same as in Example 3 and is assumed to have been made. The following entry is made to record the sale:

July 1	Cash	600	
	Accumulated Depreciation—Trucks	4,500	
	Trucks		5,000
	Gain on Disposal of Equipment		100

The gain of $100 is computed as follows:

Cost of truck	$5,000
Deduct accumulated depreciation	4,500
Carrying value of truck	$ 500
Amount received	600
Gain on disposal	$ 100

Example 5—*Sale of asset at a price below carrying value.* The truck is sold on July 1, Year 5 for $400 in cash. Again, the entry to record the depreciation applicable to the year of sale is the same as in Example 3 and is assumed to have been made. The entry to record the disposal is:

July 1	Cash	400	
	Accumulated Depreciation—Trucks	4,500	
	Loss on Disposal of Equipment	100	
	Trucks		5,000

The loss of $100 is computed as follows:

Cost of truck	$5,000
Deduct accumulated depreciation	4,500
Carrying value of truck	$ 500
Amount received	400
Loss on disposal	$ 100

Loss on Disposal of Equipment is shown in the income statement under Other Expenses.

Trade-in of Plant and Equipment—Recognition of Gain or Loss

It is common practice to exchange, or trade in, used property when new property is acquired. If the trade-in allowance is not arbitrarily excessive (as a partial offset to an unrealistic list price of the new asset), it may be considered the proper selling price of the old asset, and the new asset is recorded at its list price. After the accumulated depreciation up to the date of the trade-in is recorded, the carrying value of the old asset is compared with its trade-in allowance. A gain is recognized if the trade-in allowance is greater than the carrying value, and a loss is recognized when the trade-in allowance is less than the carrying value. When the carrying value and the trade-in allowance are equal, however, there is no recognized gain or loss. If the list price or trade-in allowance is not realistic, the new asset should be recorded at its *cash market price,* or the cash payment plus the *fair market value* of the asset traded in. The gain or loss can then be measured by the difference between the cash market price of the new equipment and the total of the cash outlay and the carrying value of the old equipment.

Example 1—*Trade-in allowance greater than fair market value.* A truck with a cost of $5,000 and accumulated depreciation up to the date of the trade-in of $4,500 is exchanged for a new truck listed at $6,000. A trade-in allowance of $1,000 is granted on the old truck. The fair market value of the old truck, however, is only $600. The entry to record the trade-in is:

Truck (new)	5,600	
Accumulated Depreciation—Trucks	4,500	
Truck (old)		5,000
Cash		5,000
Gain on Disposal of Equipment		100

The new truck is recorded at its cash market price—the cash payment ($5,000) plus the fair market value ($600) of the old truck. The inflated list price is reduced by the excess ($400) of the trade-in allowance ($1,000) over the fair market value ($600) of the old truck, as shown below.

List price	$6,000
Deduct trade-in allowance	1,000
Cash payment	$5,000
Fair market value of old truck	600
Fair market price of new truck	$5,600

The gain on the trade-in is computed in either of the two following ways:

1. Cost of old truck		$5,000
Accumulated depreciation to date of trade-in		4,500
Carrying value		$ 500
Fair market value		600
Gain on trade-in		$ 100
2. Cash market price of new truck		$5,600
Cash outlay for new truck	$5,000	
Carrying value of old truck	500	5,500
Gain on trade-in		$ 100

The following three examples illustrate the possibilities involved in trade-ins when the trade-in allowance is *equal* to the fair market value of the truck traded in.

Example 2—*Trade-in allowance greater than carrying value.* A truck that cost $5,000 with accumulated depreciation of $4,500 up to the date of the trade-in is exchanged for a new one listed at $4,000; the trade-in allowance is $800. The fair market value of the old truck is $800. Again, the new truck is recorded at its cash market price—the cash payment plus the fair market value of the old truck. The transaction is recorded as follows:

Truck (new)	4,000	
Accumulated Depreciation—Trucks	4,500	
Cash		3,200
Truck (old)		5,000
Gain on Disposal of Equipment		300

The gain on disposal of the truck is computed as follows:

Cost of old truck	$5,000
Accumulated depreciation to date of trade-in	4,500
Carrying value—unrecovered cost	$ 500
Trade-in allowance	800
Gain on trade-in	$ 300

Example 3—*Trade-in allowance less than carrying value.* The old truck in Example 2 is traded in for an allowance of $400.

Truck (new)	4,000	
Accumulated Depreciation—Trucks	4,500	
Loss on Disposal of Equipment	100	
Cash		3,600
Truck (old)		5,000

The loss on disposal of the truck is computed as follows:

Cost of old truck	$5,000
Accumulated depreciation to date of trade-in	4,500
Carrying value—unrecovered cost	$ 500
Trade-in allowance	400
Loss on trade-in	$ 100

Example 4—*Trade-in allowance the same as carrying value.* The old truck in Example 2 is traded in for an allowance of $500.

Truck (new)	4,000	
Accumulated Depreciation—Trucks	4,500	
Cash		3,500
Truck (old)		5,000

There is no gain or loss in this case because the trade-in allowance is the same as the carrying value.

DISCLOSURE REQUIREMENTS

Disclosure requirements for property, plant, and equipment are stated in the *CICA Handbook.*[1] The CICA suggested that the valuation and accumulated depreciation should be disclosed on the balance sheet and that the accumulated depreciation should be deducted from fixed assets which preferably should be disclosed by major category.

The Income Statement should also disclose the amount of depreciation and the methods and rates used in its calculation according to the CICA. Where the amount of depreciation is significant, separate amounts for each class of fixed assets should be disclosed.

Studies of financial reports prepared by leading corporations show that there is increasing support for the segregation of fixed assets but not for the segregation of accumulated depreciation.[2]

REPORTING THE EFFECTS OF INFLATION

A generally accepted principle is that plant and equipment should be carried at original cost in the case of land and original cost less accumulated depreciation in the case of depreciable assets. However, most plant and equipment accounts

[1]*CICA Handbook* (Toronto: Canadian Institute of Chartered Accountants), Section 3060.
[2]*Financial Reporting in Canada* (Toronto: CICA, 1975), p. 74.

contain a commingling of dollars with different purchasing powers. As a result comparison within entities and between entities has become less useful; not only asset values, but also net income figures become distorted. There are two basic approaches to the solution of this problem. One would use the historical cost adjusted for price level change; the other would use replacement cost.

Historical cost adjusted for price level change would occur when financial statements are adjusted by a factor derived from index numbers representing the amount of inflation for each year. These adjustments would restate historical cost figures in terms of current dollars.

Replacement cost is the cost of replacing one asset with another asset of equivalent capacity. For plant and equipment, replacement cost is the amount that would be required to buy the same productive capacity. This does not necessarily mean buying the same model of a machine; in fact, one would probably acquire a more modern design. But it does mean the amount needed to buy the ***present productive capacity*** and is considered, in most cases, to approximate current economic value.

In March 1976, the Securities and Exchange Commission (SEC) of the United States issued Accounting Series Release 190 (AR 190) requiring that financial statements of large businesses show replacement cost information, as a supplement to historical cost, for inventories; plant and equipment; depreciation, depletion and amortization; and cost of goods sold. The purpose was to aid investors in developing an understanding of the impact of inflation on the current operations of the firm. Large Canadian corporations that file financial statements with the SEC are required to follow the requirements of AR 190 and readers of Canadian corportation financial statements can expect more replacement cost information to become available as a result of AR 190.

The CICA is currently studying the appropriate methods of disclosing the effects of inflation on financial statements. Although it appears certain that more information about the effects of inflation will be required in financial statements, a commonly accepted method of reporting has not yet been recommended by the CICA at this writing.

DEPLETION OF NATURAL RESOURCES

Natural resources, or wasting assets, such as oil wells, mines, or timber tracts, should be recorded in the asset account at cost. As the resource is extracted, its asset value is reduced. This reduction in value, or expiration of the cost, of the asset resulting from production is called *depletion* and may be recorded on the books by a debit to the Depletion Cost account and a credit to the Accumulated Depletion account. Or, theoretically, since the depletion cost item becomes part of the cost of the merchandise inventory, it may be debited directly to the inventory account. Thus, the depletion amount would become an goods are sold. In the balance sheet, accumulated depletion is deducted from the cost of resource.

The periodic depletion charge is usually calculated on an output basis similar to the production-unit method of recording depreciation. The cost of the wasting asset is divided by the estimated available units of output, to arrive at a per unit depletion charge. The number of units removed during the accounting period multiplied by the per unit depletion charge represents depletion for that period. For example, if the asset is a mineral measured in tons:

$$\frac{\text{Cost} - \text{Salvage}}{\text{Estimated tons to be mined}} = \text{Depletion per ton}$$

Assume that a mine costs $180,000 and contains an estimated 400,000 tons of ore. It is estimated that the net salvage value will be $20,000. The per unit depletion charge is:

$$\frac{\$180{,}000 - \$20{,}000}{400{,}000} = \$0.40 \text{ per ton}$$

If 10,000 tons are mined during an accounting period, the depletion charge is 10,000 × $0.40, or $4,000, and the entry to record the depletion for that period is:

Ore Inventory	4,000	
Accumulated Depletion—Mine		4,000

The Ore Inventory account should also be debited with the additional costs of the extraction process such as labor and overhead.

At the end of the accounting period, the amount of the recorded depletion cost remaining in the Ore Inventory account is the number of units on hand multiplied by the per unit depletion charge. Assume that 2,000 tons remain unsold at the end of the period. The entry required is a debit to Cost of Goods Sold for $3,200 (expired depletion) plus four-fifths of applicable labor and overhead, and a credit to the Ore Inventory account for this total amount.

The cost of goods sold is deducted in the income statement from the revenue realized from the sale of 8,000 tons of ore. The balance of the Ore Inventory account includes not only the allocated portion of mine depletion cost but also the proportionate amount of labor and other costs of extracting the ore (*overhead*). This is illustrated in the following T account flow chart:

Ore Inventory				Cost of Goods Sold	
Depletion	4,000	3,200	($3,200 plus proportionate amounts) →	xxx	
Other:					
Salaries	xxx	xxx			
Wages	xxx	xxx			
Overhead	xxx	xxx			

In the above example, a balance of $800 of the depletion cost and one-fifth of the labor and other costs remain in the Ore Inventory account. The other four-fifths (8,000 tons) is transferred to Cost of Goods Sold. For income tax purposes the depletion deduction for a tax year may also be figured as a percentage of the net income from the natural resource during the financial period. The intended purpose of the percentage depletion allowance is to encourage further exploration and development of natural resources.

APPENDIX Intangible Assets

Intangible assets are nonphysical rights that are of future value to the business because they shelter the firm from competition or provide other similar advantage to the owner. Some intangibles, whether purchased or self-developed, such as patents, copyrights, franchises, and leaseholds, can be readily identified and their cost measured. Others, such as goodwill, are not specifically identifiable or measurable.

The procedure for the amortization, or periodic write-off of a portion of the cost, of an intangible asset is the same as for computing and recording depreciation on a plant and equipment item by the straight-line method. The amount to be amortized annually is computed by dividing the asset cost by the legal life or the estimated useful life, whichever is shorter. The entry is a debit to an amortization expense account and a credit directly to the asset account. The straight-line method is generally used in view of the difficulties and uncertainties in estimating useful economic life and future benefits.

Difficulties and uncertainties arise from the uniqueness of intangibles. The estimated useful life may be limited by law (copyright), by contract, by legislation (franchise), or by the economic factors of demand and competition (patents). Other intangibles (goodwill, trademarks) have an unlimited or indefinite life. Furthermore, some can be separately identified (franchise), whereas others cannot be, because they relate to the total entity (goodwill); finally, some intangibles are purchased, while others are developed within the firm.

The CICA has recommended that "the major items among the intangible assets should be shown separately, e.g., goodwill, franchises, patent rights, copyrights, and trademarks,"[1] and that "the basis of valuation for each type of tangible asset should be disclosed. Where an intangible asset has been acquired other than through payment of cash or its equivalent, the basis of valuation should be fully disclosed."[2] The amount of amortization taken for the current period and the basis of amortization should also be disclosed.[3]

PATENTS

The federal government grants *patents*, or exclusive rights to the owners to produce and sell their inventions or discoveries for a period of seventeen years. All the costs involved in developing and acquiring a patent are included in the intangible asset Patents account. The cost of a patent may be large and should be capitalized and amortized over the economic useful life of the asset or seventeen years, whichever is shorter. The Patents account may be credited directly for the amortized portion; the account debited is called Amortization of Patent Cost or Patent Amortization Expense.

COPYRIGHTS

A *copyright* is an exclusive right to publish a literary or an artistic work, granted by the government. The copyright is recorded at cost and exists for the

[1] *CICA Handbook* (Toronto: Canadian Institute of Chartered Accountants, October 1974), Section 3080.01.

[2] *Ibid.*, Section 3080.02.

[3] *Ibid.*, Section 3080.04.

lifetime of the author and an additional fifty years after his death. If the copyright is obtained directly, the cost is small and is usually written off entirely in the first year. If it is purchased, the cost may be large enough to warrant periodic amortization. In practice, however, since revenues from copyrighted material are uncertain and are often limited to a relatively brief period, the cost of a copyright is added to the other costs of the first printing and enters into the inventory cost of the books or other printed materials.

FRANCHISES

A *franchise* is a monopolistic right granted by a government or an entity in the private sector to render a service or to produce a good. A right to operate a bus line or a railroad or the exclusive use of a television transmitting channel is a valuable asset to the owner. The cost of obtaining the franchise is amortized over its life. Franchises are also used in industry whereby a manufacturer grants a dealer the exclusive privilege to sell the manufacturer's product within a defined geographical area.

LEASEHOLDS AND LEASEHOLD IMPROVEMENTS

Leaseholds are rights to the use of land, buildings, or other property. They are frequently paid for in advance and should be classified as capital expenditures. Leasehold improvements, such as buildings, are sometimes constructed on leased property. Leaseholds and leasehold improvements should be amortized over the life of the lease or over the estimated useful life of the asset, whichever is shorter. With respect to lease commitments that have not been classified as capital expenditures, the AICPA Accounting Principles Board has stated that "financial statements of lessees should disclose sufficient information regarding noncapitalized lease commitments to enable users of the statements to assess the present and prospective effect of those commitments upon the financial position, results of operations, and changes in financial position of the lessees."[4]

GOODWILL

Goodwill is a general term embodying a variety of intangible factors relating to the reputation of a firm and its ability to realize above-normal net income returns on an investment. Such factors as favorable customer relations; loyal and competent employees; possession of valuable patents, franchises, or copyrights; a high-quality product; and efficient management all aid in the development of goodwill. Self-developed goodwill is not recorded on the books. However, if the assets and goodwill of one company are purchased by another, the purchased goodwill should be recorded as an asset at cost.

The amount to be paid for goodwill is usually a product of a bargaining process between the buyer and the seller. The debit to Goodwill is the excess of the cost (purchase price) over the amounts allocable to assets other than Goodwill.

[4] AICPA, *APB Accounting Principles,* vol. 2 (Chicago: Commerce Clearing House, Inc., 1973), p. 6818.

In the case of business combinations, the CICA has recommended that "the amount reflected as goodwill at the date of acquisition should be amortized to income by the straight-line method over the estimated life of such goodwill; however, such period should not exceed forty years. The period of amortization should be disclosed."[5]

RESEARCH AND DEVELOPMENT

In theory, current expenditures for research and development should be capitalized to the extent that they will benefit future periods whether in the form of new or better products, reduced costs, or other benefits; when future benefits are uncertain, research and development costs should be expensed. In practice, a number of alternatives have been used, varying from charging all expenditures to income when incurred to deferring all expenditures and amortizing them over the years of benefit.

Since future benefits from research are difficult to estimate—especially pure research, although less so for new or better product development—current practice favors expensing research and development costs when incurred. The FASB Standard No. 2 recently issued in the United States requires that most research and development costs be treated as expenses when incurred and that all costs capitalized at the effective date of the Standard be written off as a prior period adjustment. An exception to the foregoing general conclusion occurs when research and development is done on a contract basis for another company. These costs should be accounted for in accordance with accounting standards for contracts in general.

ORGANIZATION COSTS

This is an intangible asset resulting from expenditures made incidental to incorporation and is discussed further in Chapter 10.

GLOSSARY

Amortization Often used as a general term to cover write-down of assets; it is most commonly used to describe periodic allocation of costs of intangible assets.

Capital Expenditure A payment or a promise to make a future payment for asset acquisitions.

Depletion The process of estimating and recording the periodic charges to operations because of the exhaustion of a natural resource.

Depreciation—Composite Rate A charge for depreciation using a blanket rate applied to a number of nonhomogeneous assets.

Depreciation—Declining-Balance Method A depreciation method that results in larger depreciation charges during the early years of the asset life with gradually decreasing charges in later years.

Depreciation—Group Rate A charge for depreciation using a blanket rate applied to a group of homogeneous assets.

[5]*CICA Handbook. Ibid.,* Section 1580.58.

Depreciation—Production Methods Charges for depreciation based on usage or results rather than time (mileage, units of output).

Depreciation—Straight Line A depreciation method that allocates a uniform portion of the depreciable asset cost to each accounting period.

Goodwill A general term embodying a variety of intangible factors relating to the reputation of a firm and its ability to generate above-normal earnings.

Intangible Assets Nonphysical rights and expected benefits that come from the ownership of such assets.

Price-level Adjusted Cost The number of current dollars required for the amount of general purchasing power invested when the item was bought.

Replacement Cost The current cost of replacing one specific asset with another asset of equal capacity.

Revenue Expenditure Expenditure that benefits a current period and is made for the purpose of maintaining assets in satisfactory operating condition.

Salvage Value The amount of asset cost that is expected to be recovered when the asset is ultimately scrapped, sold, or traded in.

Tangible Assets Land, structures, and equipment of a tangible and relatively permanent nature, acquired for use in the regular operations of the business.

QUESTIONS

Q9-1. What does the term *plant and equipment* encompass?

Q9-2. (a) List some expenditures other than the purchase price that make up the cost of plant and equipment. (b) Why are cash discounts excluded from the cost of plant and equipment? (c) What problems in cost determination arise when used plant assets are acquired?

Q9-3. (a) What distinguishes a capital expenditure from a revenue expenditure? (b) What is the effect on the financial statements if this distinction is not properly drawn?

Q9-4. Student A maintains that if a plant asset has a fair market value greater than its cost after one year of use, no depreciation need be recorded for the year. Student B insists that the fair market value is irrelevant in this context. Indicate which position you support and give your reasons.

Q9-5. What are some of the factors that must be considered (a) when the depreciation method to be used is chosen? (b) when depreciation is recorded?

Q9-6. The basis for depreciation is generally original (historical) cost. Is there any other basis that could logically be used?

Q9-7. Since the total amount to be depreciated cannot exceed the cost of the asset, does it make any difference which method is used in calculating the periodic depreciation charges?

Q9-8. Describe the conditions that might require the use of each of the following methods of depreciation: (a) straight line, (b) production, (c) declining amount.

Q9-9. (a) Distinguish between the composite rate and the group rate of depreciation. (b) Give reasons to support the use of these procedures and state their underlying assumptions.

Q9-10. What procedures may be followed in recording depreciation on assets acquired during the accounting period?

Q9-11. What is the relationship, if any, between the amount of the annual depreciation charges on plant assets and the amount of money available for the new plant assets?

Q9-12. What accounting problems result (a) from the trade-in of one like plant asset for another? (b) from the sale of a plant asset?

Q9-13. (a) Distinguish between the terms *depreciation, depletion,* and *amortization.* (b) How is the periodic depletion charge determined?

Q9-14. (a) What are intangible assets? What factors must be considered (b) when the acquisition of intangibles is recorded? (c) when intangibles are amortized?

Q9-15. It has been argued that with proper maintenance certain equipment will last almost indefinitely, in which case depreciation is not necessary. Do you agree? Explain.

DEMONSTRATION PROBLEMS

DP9-1. (*Computing depreciation expense*) The St. Johns Company began business on July 1 with three new machines. Data for the machines are as follows:

Machine	*Cost*	*Estimated Salvage Value*	*EUL (years)*
A	$ 93,000	$ 9,000	12
B	126,000	14,000	10
C	34,000	6,000	7

Required: Compute the depreciation expense for the first two years by each of the following methods: (a) straight-line and (b) double-rate declining balance.

DP9-2. (*Asset sale; trade-in*) On January 2, the Lorne Corporation purchased a machine costing $20,000 with a useful life of 10 years and salvage value of $2,000. Assume that the double-rate declining-balance method is used to record depreciation.

Required: Give the journal entries to record the sale or trade-in of the machine, on the basis of each of the following assumptions:

1. Sale of the machine for $3,000 at the end of the sixth year.
2. Sale of the machine for $4,000 at the end of the fourth year.
3. Trade-in of the machine at the end of the sixth year for a new machine listed at $25,000. The corporation paid $15,000 in cash to acquire the new machine. (Recognize the gain or loss on the exchange.)

DP9-3. (*Accounting policy decision problem*) The Hopper Corporation has acquired depreciable plant and equipment items totaling $100,000. Using a 10-year life and no salvage value, calculate the effect on net income for the first three years for each of the following methods of depreciation:

a. Straight line
b. Double-rate declining balance.

Assume that the company is subject to an income tax rate of 50%.

DP9-4. (*Computing depreciation expense*) The Stang Corporation acquired a compressor on July 1, Year 1, at a cost of $25,000. The compressor had an estimated useful life of eight years and a salvage value of $2,500. Two years later the compressor was completely overhauled and rebuilt at a cost of $5,000. These improvements were expected to increase the estimated useful life of the compressor by four years from July 1, Year 3.

Required: Prepare all entries through December 31, Year 3. The company reports on a calendar-year basis and uses straight-line depreciation.

PROBLEMS

P9-1. For each of the following items, indicate the account to be debited:

a. Expenditure for installing machinery
b. Expenditure for trial run of new machinery
c. Expenditure for conveyor system for machinery
d. Payment of delinquent taxes on land (taxes were delinquent at the date of purchase of the land)
e. Expenditure for extensive plumbing repairs on a building just purchased
f. Sales tax paid on new machinery just purchased
g. Payment of incorporation fees to the province.
h. Expenditure for a major overhaul that restores a piece of machinery to its original condition and extends its useful life
i. Expenditure for an addition to a building leased for 20 years
j. Amount paid for a purchased business in excess of the appraised value of the net assets

P9-2. The Bhaby Company made the following expenditures on the acquisition of a new machine:

Invoice cost ($19,000) less 2% cash discount	$18,620
Transportation charges	570
Installation charges	950
Property insurance—premiums for three years	570
Materials and labor used during test runs	285

What is the cost of the machine?

P9-3. The Wildey Manufacturing Company acquired an old building for $48,000 and spent $15,000 to put it into usable condition. One year later, an additional expenditure of $1,200 was made for painting, plumbing, and electrical repair work. Record all the expenditures.

P9-4. The Fay Corporation purchased a machine for $10,000; terms, 1/10, n/60. Record (a) the acquisition of the machine and (b) payment of the invoice within the discount period.

P9-5. The Nitze Corporation solicited bids for a new wing for its factory building. The lowest bid received was $25,000. The corporation decided to do the work with its own staff, and the wing was completed for a total cost of $22,000. Record the expenditure.

P9-6. On April 1, Year 4, a calculating machine used in the office of the Andrea Company was sold for $400. The sale was recorded by a debit to Cash and a credit to Office Equipment for $400. The machine had been purchased on October 1, Year 1, for $1,200 and had been depreciated at the rate of 10% annually (straight-line method—no salvage value) through December 31, Year

3. The Andrea Company closes its books annually on June 30. Make an entry to correct the accounts as a result of the transaction.

P9-7. On February 1, Year 1, the Tyre Corporation acquired a truck costing $15,000 with an estimated useful life of five years and a salvage value of $1,000. On August 1, Year 4, the truck was traded in for a new one with a cash market price of $20,000. The dealer allowed $4,200 on the old truck, and the balance was paid in cash. Record the trade-in on the books of the Tyre Corporation, on the basis of recognition of gain or loss. The company uses the straight-line method to calculate depreciation.

P9-8. The Boston Corporation purchased a truck on January 2, for $12,500. It had an estimated useful life of six years and a trade-in value of $500. Compute the depreciation charge for the year under the following methods: (a) straight line, (b) double-rate declining balance, and (c) production, assuming an operating life of 100,000 miles and 18,000 miles of actual use the first year.

P9-9. On January 2, Year 1, the Fleet Company purchased land and an old building for $200,000. The land is appraised at $20,000; the building is estimated to have a useful life of 20 years and a salvage value of $10,000. After three years' use, the building was remodeled at a cost of $75,000. At this time, it was estimated that the remaining useful life of the building would be 25 years with a salvage value of $20,000. Using the straight-line method of depreciation, give the entries (a) for the purchase of the land and building, (b) for depreciation for Year 1, (c) for remodeling costs, and (d) for depreciation for Year 4.

P9-10. The Eybe Corporation acquired a building for $150,000 with an estimated useful life of 20 years and an estimated salvage value of $12,000. Five years later, an addition to the building was constructed at a cost of $30,000. Using straight-line depreciation, compute the annual depreciation charges before and after the construction of the addition to the building.

P9-11. The Phillips Company acquired three machines as follows:

		Machine	
	A	B	C
Cost	$95,000	$75,000	$89,000
Estimated salvage value	7,000	5,000	9,000
Estimated life (years)	11	10	8

Assuming that the straight-line method is used, compute (a) the composite life for the three machines and (b) the annual depreciation rate.

P9-12. The unadjusted trial balance of the Beatrice Company at December 31, includes the following accounts:

Patents (granted January 2	$30,000
Copyrights (acquired July 1)	7,800
Goodwill	6,750
Research and Development (new products)	12,500
Organization Costs	3,750

(a) What is the basis of valuation of each of these accounts? (b) What adjustments should be made on December 31? (c) What additional information is needed to complete requirement (b)?

P9-13. The Pauline Corporation reported a net income of $150,000 for the year. The president of the corporation noted that the beginning and ending inventories were $600,000 and $750,000, respectively, although the physical quantities on hand were relatively stable. She also noted that deductions for depreciation averaged 10% on plant and equipment costing $1,350,000, although the current dollar value of the assets is estimated at $1,800,000. The president suggests that the reported net income is erroneous. Comment.

P9-14. The Dune Company purchased a mine for $336,000. It was estimated that the land contained 1,120,000 tons of a recoverable mineral deposit, and that after recovery of the deposits the land would have a salvage value of $16,000. During the first year, 96,000 tons were recovered and 80,000 tons were sold. Labor and overhead costs were $160,000. Determine (a) the cost of goods sold and (b) the ending inventory valuation. (*Hint:* Depletion expense is prorated over the number of tons produced.)

P9-15. The condensed income statement of the Gail Company for the year ended March 31 was as follows:

Sales	$500,000
Cost of Goods Sold	300,000
Gross Margin	$200,000
Operating Expenses	
(includes depreciation expense of $20,000)	125,000
Net income	$ 75,000

(a) Assuming that beginning and ending Accounts Receivable, Accounts Payable, and Merchandise Inventory balances were approximately the same, how much cash was generated by operations? (b) Did the depreciation expense deduction result in a direct cash increase of $20,000? Explain.

P9-16. The Scollay Corporation purchased land and buildings for $450,000; the buildings were demolished at a cost of $17,000, salvaged materials were sold for $4,000, and a new building was constructed on the site for $4,000,000. The following additional expenditures were incurred during construction:

Fees for permits and licenses	$1,500
Interest on money borrowed for payment of construction costs	2,000
Architectural fees	25,000
Insurance	1,500
Real estate taxes	2,000
Land grading and leveling	10,000
Promotional literature describing the new facility	1,000
Trees, shrubs, and other landscaping costs	7,500

Required: Open T accounts for (a) Land, (b) Buildings, (c) Land Improvements, and (d) Operating Expenses. Post the transactions to the accounts.

P9-17. On January 2, a piece of machinery was acquired by Norbert, Inc., for $9,000. It was estimated to have an eight-year life and a salvage value at the end of that time of $750.

Required: Prepare tables showing periodic depreciation over the eight-year period, for each assumption listed:

1. Depreciation is to be calculated by the straight-line method.
2. Depreciation is to be calculated by the double-rate declining-balance method.
3. Repair charges are estimated at $400 for the first year and are estimated to increase by $200 in each succeeding year; depreciation charges are to be made on a diminishing scale so that the sum of depreciation and estimated repairs is the same over the life of the asset.

P9-18. The Vida Corporation purchased a machine on January 3, at a cost of $30,000. In addition, the corporation paid $500 to have the machine delivered and $2,500 to have it installed. The estimated useful life of the machine is six years with a trade-in value of $5,000 at the end of that time.

Required: Prepare four separate schedules, showing the annual depreciation charge for the six-year period under each of the following methods: (a) straight line; (b) production, assuming a total operating life of 40,000 hours with actual annual hours of use as follows: 5,000; 7,000; 9,000; 6,000; 6,000; 7,000; and (c) double-rate declining balance.

P9-19. On January 2, the Dolan Company purchased a new machine for $75,000 with an estimated salvage value of $5,000 and an estimated useful life of six years, or 9,000 machine-hours. The plant manager expects to use the machine for 2,200 hours for the first year, and 1,500 hours for the second year.

Required:

1. Compute the depreciation expense for each of the first two years by the following methods: (a) straight line, (b) production, and (c) double-rate declining balance.
2. Assume that the Dolan Company is in an industry in which rapid changes in technology have, in the past, made existing equipment obsolete. How does this affect the estimate of the asset's useful life?

P9-20. The following information was taken from the books of the Marjorie Corporation.

	Machine A	*Machine B*	*Machine C*
Date acquired	January 2, Year 1	January 2, Year 2	January 2, Year 3
Cash payment	$30,800	$8,800	$39,600
Estimated salvage value	2,000	2,400	4,400
Estimated useful life in years	—	6	7
Method of depreciation	Units of production	Straight line	Double-rate declining balance

Machine A is capable of producing a total of 15,000 units during its useful life. During Year 1, 5,000 units were produced.

On January 2, Year 2, machine A, with a cash value of $18,800, was traded for machine B, which listed for $28,000.

Required: Give all the necessary entries to record the transactions for the three years. The books are closed annually on December 31.

P9-21. The Gull Corporation acquired two factory buildings. Subsequently, major improvements were made to roofs and foundations, extending the useful life of each building. The following information was taken from the records:

	Building A	*Building B*
Date acquired	Jan. 2, Year 1	July 2, Year 1
Original cost	$46,000	$68,000
Estimated salvage value	$ 2,000	$ 5,000
Estimated useful life	10 years	20 years
Date improvements completed	July 2, Year 2	July 2, Year 2
Improvement costs	$5,000	$13,000
Revised estimated salvage value	$1,500	$ 3,500
Remaining estimated useful life	12 years	20 years
Method of depreciation	Straight line	Straight line

Required: Give the journal entries to record the transactions, including year-end adjustments for the first two years. The books are closed annually on December 31.

P9-22. (*Accounting policy decision problem*) The Brittany Corporation purchased a new machine at a cost of $55,000. The machine is expected to produce 20,000 units over its estimated useful life of five years as follows:

Year	*Number of Units*
1	3,000
2	4,000
3	6,000
4	5,000
5	2,000

Required:

1. Compute the annual depreciation charges under each of the following methods (assume $5,000 salvage value):
   a. Straight line
   b. Double-rate declining balance.
   c. Units of production
2. What factors should be considered in selecting a depreciation method?
3. Which method do you recommend? Why?

P9-23. The Globe Company purchased a tract of land at a cost of $200,000. It was estimated that the land contained 1,000,000 tons of a recoverable ore deposit and that after recovery of the deposits, the land would have a resale value of $25,000. Costs of clearing the area and drilling mine shafts was $300,000. During the first year of operations, 90,000 tons were recovered and 70,000 tons were sold for $8 a ton. Labor and overhead costs were $200,000, and general and administrative expenses were $50,000.

Required:

1. Prepare the income statement for the year.
2. Prepare a partial balance sheet showing how the foregoing would be reported as at December 31.

10

Shareholders' Equity

Shareholders' equity results from assets contributed by shareholders and from assets earned and reinvested in a business.[1] It is important that the sources of this equity be clearly distinguished. This chapter begins with a description of the characteristics of corporations followed by a description of the different classes of stock and the meaning of the different "value" terms used to measure capital stock. The recording of transactions is influenced by several factors including the laws of incorporation and the interests of shareholders. This is illustrated by a series of entries with resulting balance sheet classifications. Other sources of equity which result from donated surplus, revaluation of assets and retained earnings are also discussed. A complete illustration of shareholders' equity components with explanations of major items concludes this chapter. Stock subscriptions are reviewed in the Appendix to this chapter.

CHARACTERISTICS OF A CORPORATION

In a famous 1819 decision, John Marshall, Chief Justice of the United States, gave this classic definition of a corporation: "A corporation is an artificial being, invisible, intangible, and existing only in contemplation of law."

> The corporation is, from both the legal and the accounting points of view, a special and separate being, or separate *legal entity*, created by law.

That is the characteristic that makes it almost ideally suited to doing business. The weaknesses inherent in proprietorships and partnerships do not generally exist with the corporate form. The death or retirement of a proprietor or of a partner may terminate the business, whereas the corporate form continues indefinitely irrespective of changes in shareholders.

[1] The terms "shareholders" and "stockholders" are synonymous and are used interchangeably.

A corporate charter may place restrictions on the transfer of shares in a private corporation, the most common of which is the requirement of director approval. A shareholder in a public corporation may sell his stock whenever he chooses without the prior consent of other shareholders, with the corporation simply recording the change in ownership; a partner wishing to sell his interest must first get the consent of all the other partners. The purchase and sale of stock is a relatively simple matter because of the existence of stock exchanges (the Toronto Stock Exchange, for example). The sale and transfer of a block of stock from one holder to another is a private matter between the buyer and the seller. Except for a change of names and addresses in the shareholders' ledger, the transfer does not affect the issuing corporation.

Proprietors and general partners are fully liable to the firm's creditors. Their personal fortunes—in addition to their investments in the business—may have to be used. A shareholder, on the contrary, having paid for his stock in full, is not further liable either to the corporation or to satisfy the creditors' claims. For example, the possible losses of an investor who pays $500 to a corporation for ten shares of $50 par value stock is limited to $500. This is a distinct advantage to the investor in a corporation. It may also be a disadvantage, especially to the smaller corpration seeking credit. Since satisfaction of creditor claims is limited to the assets of the corporation, the extent of credit tends to be limited to the level of corporate assets.

Because the corporation is treated as a legal entity, separate and distinct from the shareholders who own it, it enjoys the same legal rights and privileges as do a proprietor and a partner, and may therefore engage in any type of business activity authorized by the charter. The corporate form of business organization is of great advantage for a large business because it may sell its stock to anyone willing to invest and is, therefore, able to raise large sums of capital. Most large-scale businesses are incorporated and do a much larger volume of business than all other forms of business organization. Many small businesses are also incorporated—frequently with only a few shareholders—because of the advantages that the corporate form offers.

The corporate form also has its disadvantages. Because it is an artificial legal being created by law, it must file reports with the government by which it was organized; it may engage in only that type of business for which it was chartered; it cannot distribute profits arbitrarily, as do partnerships, but must treat all shares of stock of the same class alike; and it is subject to special taxes and fees. Both the federal government and the provinces have the right to incorporate companies. Corporate laws vary and are often complex. The rights and obligations of corporations, directors, and shareholders are therefore often difficult to determine. The business corporation is taxed as a legal entity, and its pro rata distributions of earnings to shareholders (in the form of dividends) are also taxed as personal income of the recipient. A dividend tax credit and investment income exemption for dividends from Canadian corporations minimize this additional taxation. The earnings of proprietorships and partnerships, on the other hand, are taxed only once, as the personal income of the owners.

Ownership of Corporations

Ownership in a corporation is represented by shares of stock, which may be owned by individuals, or by other corporations, or by estates and trusts.

Each share of stock represents a fractional part of the ownership. Ownership of a corporation may be vested in a single individual who owns all the stock, in a family whose members own all the stock, or by hundreds of thousands of shareholders. The holders of stock in a corporation are entitled to certain rights, including the right to participate in the distribution of earnings and the right to vote at elections of members of the board of directors, thereby participating, albeit indirectly, in the management of the corporation.

Organizing a Corporation

A corporation may be organized for a number of reasons. The purpose may be to start a new business or to buy a previously existing proprietorship or partnership. It should be emphasized that the work of organizing a corporation must be done by competent lawyers, since it often involves complex legal matters.

To form a corporation it is first necessary for one or more incorporators to file a document known as "Articles of Incorporation" with the proper governmental authority. In some provinces, this document is called an Application for Letters Patent. This form sets forth the name and head office address of the proposed corporation; the classes and the maximum number of shares that the corporation is authorized to issue; the number of directors; and various other matters. Most provinces also require that the objects or nature of the business of the corporation be indicated. On approval of the application, a charter (known as the *certificate of incorporation* or the *letters patent*) is issued by the government.

The incorporators then hold the initial shareholders' meeting. Capital stock certificates are issued, the shareholders elect a board of directors, and a set of rules and regulations (known as *bylaws*) governing the internal activities of the corporation is approved. The directors in turn appoint the officers of the corporation, who execute the policies approved by the board of directors for the operation of the business.

Capital Stock

Ownership in a corporation is represented by its stock, which is divided into shares representing fractional ownership. There may be more than one class of stock, each in turn divided into shares. Each share in a class of stock must be treated like every other share in that class with respect to whatever rights and privileges attach to it.

Whenever there is more than one class of stock, one of the classes may enjoy the right to receive dividends, for example, before the other classes of stock. By the same token, certain restrictions, such as not having the right to vote, may be placed on a particular class of stock. If only one class of stock is issued, it is refered to as *common stock;* if two classes of stock are issued, they are usually referred to as common stock and *preferred stock.* There may be subclasses of stock within each major class, also with specific rights, privileges, and restrictive provisions.

The rights and privileges attached to common stock are:

1. The shareholders' right to sell or otherwise to dispose of all shares owned.
2. The right to vote.

3. The right to participate in dividend distributions when a dividend is declared.
4. The right to participate in a distribution of assets upon liquidation of the company.
5. Common and other voting shareholders are entitled to appoint auditors.

Stock Certificate. A *stock certificate* is a printed or an engraved serially numbered document issued to the stock purchaser as evidence of ownership of the stated number of shares of capital stock of the issuing corporation. Transfer of the shares from one person to another is accomplished by filling in the assignment section on the reverse of the stock certificate. The buyer sends the assigned stock certificate to the corporation or to its transfer agent, who records the transfer on the corporation's capital stock records, cancels the old certificate, and issues a new one to the new owner. Stock certificates are often bound with attached stubs in the same manner as checkbooks. The perforated stock certificate is removed, and the stub is filled in and retained by the corporation as a permanent record.

Classes of Stock

As previously stated, stock is usually issued in two classes, *common* and *preferred.*

Preferred Stock. One of the reasons for issuing two or more classes of stock is to endow one class with certain features that will make it more salable. The attractive feature of preferred stock is that, when a dividend declaration is made by the board of directors, the preferred shareholders must be paid at the stated rate and amount for the class of stock before payments are made to other shareholders. The same preference applies when a corporation is dissolved: assets remaining after satisfaction of creditor claims are used first to redeem the claims of preferred shareholders; the remainder of the assets, if any, are paid to the other shareholders. Preferred shareholders, on the other hand, are often restricted to a specific dividend rate and do not, therefore, benefit from extra earnings. A preferred shareholder is usually denied the right to vote.

Common Stock. If a corporation issues only one class of stock, then all shares are treated alike, and, there being no preferences, that class of stock is called common stock. If there is more than one class, the class that does not have preferences and that shares only in the remainder of earnings or assets distribution is known as common stock. This class of stock does have voting privileges.

Value of Stock

The term ***par value*** refers to a specific dollar amount per share and represents the minimum amount that must be paid to the issuing corporation by the original purchaser of the stock; otherwise the purchaser may be held liable for the ***discount,*** or difference, in case of future claims by the corporate creditors.

The use of par value stock used to be considered advantageous to the shareholder and the creditor, since it requires payment in full or the assumption of a liability for the discount. The market value of stock, however, is determined not by its par value but rather by the value of the corporation's net assets and by its earnings. Furthermore, in some cases, evasive schemes were evolved to by-pass the par value rule, and creditors also found it difficult to recover the stock discount from shareholders in a bankrupt company. The evasive schemes usually involved the issuance of ***watered*** stock—that is, the transfer of property or the rendering of services to the corporation for its capital stock at highly inflated values, thereby overstating the shareholders' equity.

Since par value was often misleading, *no-par value* stock began to be used widely in order to overcome some of the disadvantages of the par value stock. The use of no-par value stock made it unnecessary to resort to evasive schemes for by-passing the contingent liability arising from a sale of par value stock at a discount. The attempted evasion of the par value rule through over-valuation of assets or services would no longer be necessary. Differences of opinion can and do exist, however, with regard to the proper value to be placed on an asset in exchange for stock, and resort to the use of no-par value stock has not eliminated this problem.

The Canada Business Corporations Act (1975), recognizing the difficulties created by the use of par value stock, permits only the issuance of no-par value stock in companies incorporated after December 1975. Prior to this date, federally incorporated companies were permitted to issue both par value and no-par value capital stock.

Provincially incorporated companies are currently permitted to issue both par value and no-par value stock.

Corporate Name

The word *Limited, Incorporated,* or *Corporation* (or the abbreviation *Ltd., Inc.,* or *Corp.*) must be used as the last word of the name of a company incorporated in Canada depending on the legislation of the jurisdiction where incorporation takes place. Federally and provincially incorporated companies were formerly required to use the word *Limited* to indicate the limited liability of corporate shareholders in Canada. The Canada Business Corporations Act (1975) and the British Columbia Companies Act (1973) also permit the use of the words *Incorporated* or *Corporation* to indicate this limited liability. Companies incorporated in Ontario and Québec are permitted to use the word *Incorporated* in place of Limited.

CAPITAL STOCK TRANSACTIONS

In the following discussion, the provisions of the Canada Business Corporations Act (1975) will be used to introduce accounting for capital stock transactions and to explain various applications of its provisions. Subsequently, accounting for companies incorporated federally prior to December 1975 and for provincially incorporated companies will be presented.

INCORPORATION UNDER THE CANADA BUSINESS CORPORATIONS ACT (1975)

Stated Capital

The term *stated capital* is incorporated in the Canada Business Corporations Act (1975) for the purpose of indicating a restriction on the return of capital to the shareholders. The purpose of this restriction is to protect the creditors, because it prevents the shareholders from withdrawing their investment as dividends to the point where there may be insufficient funds left to satisfy creditors' claims. The creditors of a corporation do not have access to the personal resources of the shareholders; their only protection is in the corporate assets. Since there is a legal limit on shareholder withdrawls, creditors are assured that in the event of corporate losses the investors as a group will absorb the losses up to the amount of the stated capital.

Number of Shares

When a new corporation is organized under the Canada Business Corporations Act (1975), the charter granted at the time of incorporation permits the issuance of an unlimited number of shares in every class unless the company prefers to establish a designated number of shares of capital stock. If a designated number of shares, usually called ***authorized capital stock,*** is indicated in the charter then the amount of authorized shares is included as part of the Shareholders' Equity section of the balance sheet. The balance sheet presentation, when the charter establishes an authorized number of shares, is illustrated as follows.

Shareholders' Equity	
Common Stock, no-par value, authorized 1,000 shares, issued 500 shares	$50,000

Where a company prefers to have the option of issuing an unlimited number of shares and has incorporated this in its charter, the balance sheet presentation in Shareholders' Equity would be as shown below.

Shareholders' Equity	
Common Stock, no-par value, issued 500 shares,	$50,000

In the following examples and problem assignments, it is assumed that the charter of the company involved limits the number of shares that can be issued by designating an authorized number of shares unless otherwise indicated.

Recording Stock Transactions

As was indicated previously, the Canada Business Corporations Act (1975) permits the issuance of only no-par value stock. The following discussion illustrates the accounting for this stock.

Authorization and Issuance of No-Par Value Stock. The initial entry on a corporate set of books may be a simple narrative statement setting forth certain basic data taken from the corporate charter, including the name of the corporation, the date of incorporation, the nature of the business, and the number and classes of shares authorized to be issued. Assume that the following three transactions took place at the New Canada Corporation, which is organized as a wholesale hardware supply business with an authorized capital consisting of 10,000 shares without par value.

1. One-half the stock is issued for $100,000.

Cash	100,000	
Common Stock		100,000

2. A total of 900 shares is issued for $40,000 in cash plus land and buildings having a fair cash value of $10,000 and $40,000, respectively.

Cash	40,000	
Land	10,000	
Buildings	40,000	
Common Stock		90,000

3. A total of 100 shares is issued to the organizers of the corporation in payment for their services.

Organization Costs	10,000	
Common Stock		10,000

The Shareholders' Equity section of the New Canada Corporation balance sheet after the foregoing transactions shows the following:

Shareholders' Equity	
Common Stock, no-par value; authorized 10,000 shares, issued 6,000 shares	$200,000

Acquisition and Subsequent Issuance of Stock. The Canada Business Corporations Act (1975) permits a corporation to reacquire some of its shares (provided that the purchase does not cause insolvency) and subsequently to re-issue shares. The Act requires that the reacquired shares be restored to the status of authorized but unissued stock, and the appropriate stated capital account be reduced by the payment. Technically, the reacquired shares cannot be sold. However, the corporation can issue authorized stock of which the reacquired shares are a part. The New Canada Corporation example introduced previously is continued to illustrate the repurchase and subsequent re-issuance of shares. Assume that the 10,000 shares issued in (1) above are repurchased for the same amount they were originally sold for.

4. 5,000 shares issued for $100,000 are repurchased for $100,000.

Common Stock	100,000	
Cash		100,000

5. The reacquired shares are restored to the status of authorized but unissued stock.

The Shareholders' Equity section of the New Canada Corporation balance sheet after the foregoing transactions shows the following:

Shareholders' Equity	
Common Shares, no-par value, authorized 10,000 shares, issued 1,000 shares	$100,000

As permitted by the Act, the reacquired 5,000 shares are removed from the issued shares, and the stated capital account, Capital Stock, is reduced by $100,000 which is the amount for which the reacquired shares were originally sold.

6. At a later date, 5,000 shares are issued for $150,000.

Cash	150,000	
Common Stock		150,000

The Shareholders' Equity section of the New Canada Corporation balance sheet after the foregoing transaction shows the following:

Shareholders' Equity	
Common Shares, no-par value, authorized 10,000 shares, issued 6,000 shares	$250,000

ACCOUNTING FOR COMPANIES INCORPORATED UNDER LAWS OTHER THAN THE CANADA BUSINESS CORPORATIONS ACT (1975)

Companies incorporated federally prior to December 1975 and provincially incorporated companies are permitted to issue both par value and no-par value stock. The accounting for capital stock transactions of these companies is illustrated in this section.

Great care needs to be taken to record stock transactions in strict compliance with the corporate laws of the place of incorporation, keeping in mind the interests of the shareholders and the creditors. Enough accounts should be created, especially those arising from invested capital, so that the Shareholders' Equity section shows in adequate detail the sources of the corporate capital.

Issuance of No-Par Value Stock. The accounting for the issuance of no-par value stock for these companies is identical to that for companies incorporated under the Canada Business Corporations Act (1975). The first three transactions of the New Canada Corporation illustrated previously are recorded in the same manner here and are therefore not repeated in this section.

> The directors of companies incorporated in some provinces are permitted to establish a stated value per no-par value stock at the time of each issuance. This value becomes the basis for recording the stock on the corporate books, and the accounting is the same as for par value stock. The amount received in excess of the stated value is called ***distributable surplus.*** Federally incorporated companies are not permitted to establish distributable surplus.

Issuance of Par Value Stock at a Premium. Assume that a corporation is organized with an authorized capital of $100,000, consisting of 1,000 shares of $100 par value stock, which are issued for $108,000. The entry is:

Cash	108,000	
Common Stock		100,000
Premium on Common Stock		8,000

When capital stock is offered for sale, the price it will bring depends not only on the condition and reputation of the corporation, but also on the availability of funds for investment and other external factors. When stock is issued above its par value, the difference is credited to Premium on Common Stock or to Excess over Par Value of Common Stock. The account represents the excess of the issue price per share over the the par value per share. Although the premium appears in a separate account, it is part of the total capital paid in by investors. By use of a separate account for the excess over par value paid in on the stock, the par value may be shown readily in the balance sheet. If more than one class of stock has been issued at a premium, separate premium accounts should be kept. Issuance of stock in excess of par does not constitute earnings, and premiums therefrom should never be recorded in accounts showing corporate earnings. This premium on stock is sometimes referred to as *contributed surplus.*

Immediately following the issuance of the 1,000 shares for $108,000, the Shareholders' Equity section appears as shown below.

Shareholders' Equity		
Common Stock, $100 par value; authorized and issued 1,000 shares	$100,000	
Premium on Common Stock	8,000	
Total		$108,000

Issuance of Par Value Stock at a Discount. Assume that a corporation is organized with an authorized capital of $100,000, consisting of 1,000 shares of $100 par value stock, which are issued for $90,000. Assuming that the discount is legal, the entry is:

Cash	90,000	
Discount on Common Stock	10,000	
Common Stock		100,000

When the issue is for less than par value—that is, when the stock has been issued at a discount—the difference between the par value and the issue price of the stock is charged to Discount on Common Stock. Purchasers of stock at a discount may be contingently liable to the corporation's creditors for the amount of the discount. With few exceptions, par value stock may *not* be issued at a discount. The account appears as a deduction in the Shareholders' Equity section of the balance sheet and designates the existence and amount of the contingency as shown below.

Shareholders' Equity		
Common Stock, $100 par value; authorized and issued 1,000 shares	$100,000	
Discount on Common Stock	10,000*	
Total		$ 90,000

* Deduction.

The use of premium and discount accounts makes it possible to show in the balance sheet the par value as well as the amount actually contributed. Premiums and discounts shoula not be offset. If, for example, a corporation that is authorized to issue 1,000 shares of $100 par value common stock issues 500 shares at $105 a share and later issues 250 shares at $98 a share, separate premium and discount accounts should be set up. The balance sheet presentation would be as shown below.

Shareholders' Equity		
Common Stock, $100 par value; authorized 1,000 shares; issued 750 shares	$75,000	
Premium on Common Stock	2,500	
Discount on Common Stock	500*	
Total		$77,000

* Deduction.

If only the net excess of $2,000 ($2,500 premium less $500 discount) is reported, the existence of the discount liability is concealed from readers of the statement.

Acquisition and Subsequent Issuance of Stock. A company incorporated in Ontario or British Columbia is permitted in certain circumstances to reaquire some of its own stock. Such stock is known as ***treasury stock.*** The accounting for these reacquisitions and their re-issue subsequently is illustrated in the Appendix to Chapter 11.

SOURCES OF SHAREHOLDERS' EQUITY

It is important to distinguish between the sources of shareholders' equity because the law provides that earnings may be distributed to shareholders but that, both for the protection of corporate creditors and for the continued operation of the business, shareholders investments in stock must not be distributed. Hence, separate accounts should be kept for each of the following.

1. Each class of stock
2. The excess of issue price over par value of stock (by class) and donated surplus
3. Appraisal arising from revaluation of assets
4. Retained earnings

The various sources of shareholders' equity are outlined in Figure 10-1.

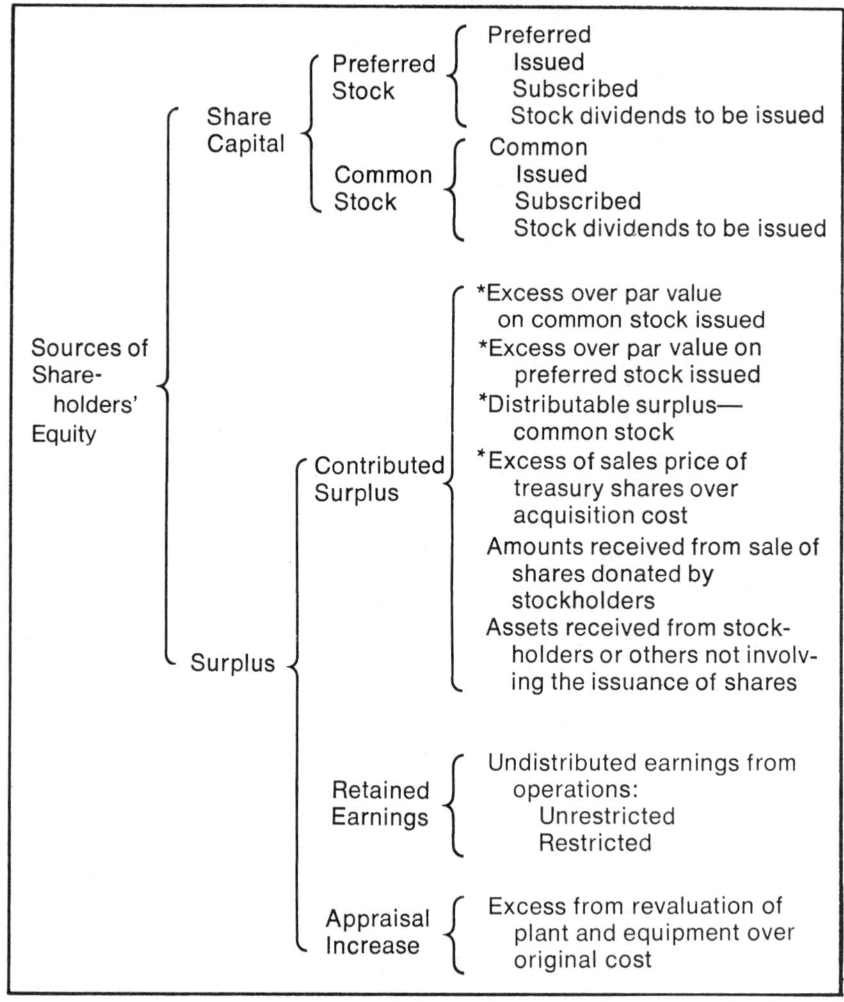

Figure 10-1
Sources of Shareholders' Equity

*These items do not apply to companies incorporated under the Canada Business Corporations Act (1975).

CONTRIBUTED SURPLUS

As stated above, shareholders' equity includes items other than the value of stock. Among these, in addition to premiums or discounts on par value stock in companies incorporated under legislation other than the Canada Business Corporations Act (1975), may be other capital donations.

Donations

A gift or donation to a corporation increases the assets and the shareholders' equity and is credited to Contributed Surplus—Donations. Gifts of land, buildings, or other facilities are sometimes made by a local organization to encourage a corporation to do business in the area. Sometimes donations of assets are made by the shareholders to a company in financial difficulties to enable it to raise funds.

A contribution of land and buildings by a town to a newly established firm is recorded by the receiving corporation at the fair market value of the assets contributed as shown below (the fair market values are assumed).

Land	80,000	
Buildings	20,000	
Contributed Surplus—Donations		100,000

To help a corporation in raising needed working capital, its shareholders instead of investing additional funds, may donate a portion of their fully paid stock to the corporation. Such stock is known as *treasury stock,* explained in the Appendix to Chapter 11. Sales of the donated stock for cash are recorded by a debit to Cash and a credit to Contributed Surplus—Donations.

APPRAISAL INCREASE

The upward revaluation of corporate assets, generally following a continuing increase in price levels, results in an increase in shareholders' equity. The practice of revaluing assets to reflect current market values is contrary to current practice, but the usefulness of historical cost amounts is limited when there is a wide disparity between original cost and market or replacement values.

The Canadian Institute of Chartered Accountants has stated that "the writing up of fixed asset values should not occur in ordinary circumstances."[2] Where an appraisal has been recorded, the Institute recommends that "subsequent charges against income for depreciation should be based on the new values"[3] and that the appraisal increase credit "should either remain indefinitely or be transferred to retained earnings in amounts not exceeding the realization of appreciation through sale or depreciation provisions. The basis of transfer, if any, should be disclosed."[4] Therefore, with an appraisal increase there is a corresponding increase in shareholders' equity that came neither from additional investment nor from earnings. Accordingly, it would be improper to report it as contributed surplus or as part of retained earnings. Instead, it should be credited to an appraisal capital account that carries a title descriptive of the event. (The debit is usually not made directly to the asset, but to an adjunct account such as Land—Appreciation in Value.)

[2] *CICA Handbook (Toronto: Canadian Institute of Chartered Accountants), Section 3060.01.*

[3] *Ibid.,* Section 3060.05.

[4] *Ibid.,* Section 3270.02.

RETAINED EARNINGS

Undistributed earnings from regular operating transactions are classified as *retained earnings.* These are sources of shareholders' equity other than transactions involving the company's own stock and revaluations. Such terms as *earned surplus, retained income, accumulated earnings,* and *earnings retained for use in the business* are also used to designate the earnings that have not been distributed to the shareholders as dividends.

> If cumulative losses and dividend distributions exceed earnings, the Retained Earnings account will have a debit balance and will be shown in the balance sheet as a deduction from shareholders' equity under the caption *Deficit.*

The creation of special Restricted Retained Earnings accounts indicates that a portion of the earnings of the corporation is not available for dividends. This does not mean that a special cash fund has been set up, nor does the restriction provide cash funds. The restrictions do not in any way alter the total retained earnings or the total shareholders' equity. The segregation of retained earnings is an accounting device by which a corporation, following a resolution of the board of directors, intentionally reduces the amount of earnings available for dividend distributions, thus indicating its intention to conserve corporate assets for other purposes. The restriction of retained earnings does not reduce the overall retained earnings but merely *earmarks,* or sets aside, a portion of the earnings in an account specifically designated to indicate its purpose. The same information can be communicated by a footnote or by a parenthetical notation.

The entry to record the creation of a special Restricted Retained Earnings account for bond redemption is illustrated as follows:

Retained Earnings	200,000	
Retained Earnings—Restricted for Bond Redemption		200,000

Each restricted account, although separated from the parent Retained Earnings account, is nevertheless a part of retained earnings and is so classified in the Shareholders' Equity section of the balance sheet. When the special account has served its purpose and the requirement for which it was set up no longer exists, the amount in the restricted account is returned to the Retained Earnings account.

The entry to return the restricted account for bond redemption to Retained Earnings is as follows:

Retained Earnings—Restricted for Bond Redemption	200,000	
Retained Earnings		200,000

This entry is made whenever the restriction's intended purpose has been accomplished and continuance of the restriction is no longer necessary.

Restrictions may be either voluntary or involuntary. A restriction for plant expansion, for example, may be set up by voluntary action of the board of directors. The purpose of this restriction is to show management's intention to retain cash or other assets for use in connection with a projected plant expansion program rather than to distribute them in the form of dividends. When cash dividends are paid, the assets of the corporation are depleted. To the degree, then, that dividend declarations are restricted, assets are retained for other business purposes such as plant expansion. Involuntary restrictions may be required either by statute, covered later in this chapter, or by contract. When a corporation enters into an agreement for a long-term loan, the terms of the contract may require periodic restrictions of retained earnings, accumulating over the term of the loan to an amount equal to the loan. The purpose of the restriction is to reduce the amount of cash earnings that might otherwise be distributed to the shareholders as dividends, and to improve the corporation's ability to make periodic interest payments and any other payments required under the terms of the loan. The restriction does not ensure the availability of working capital; it does, however, limit the use of working capital for dividend distributions.

BALANCE SHEET PRESENTATION

The shareholders' equity section of the balance sheet for Dwight Corporation Ltd. as of December 31 is shown in Figure 10-2. Each item in the statement is numbered and discussed in the following paragraphs. Dwight Corporation Ltd. is incorporated under a provincial statute.

❶ On the date of its organization, Dwight Corporation Ltd. issued 2,000 shares of preferred stock at $105 per share. The total par value of these shares (2,000 × $100 = $200,000) is labeled Preferred Stock. This amount represents part of the legal, or stated, capital. The excess ($5 × 2,000) over the par value of the preferred stock is reported separately as Premium on Preferred Stock under the Contributed Surplus heading.

❷ Dwight Corporation Ltd. also issued 5,000 shares of no-par value common stock at $50 per share. The province of incorporation permits the creation of distributable surplus and, accordingly, the directors have passed a resolution establishing a stated value per no-par value stock of $40 at the time of this issuance. As a result, $50,000 ($10 × 5,000 shares) is shown in the shareholders' equity as Distributable Surplus — Common Stock.

❸ A building site with an estimated cash market value of $50,000 was donated by the town of Needham as an inducement to Dwight Corporation Ltd. to establish itself there. This gift increased the assets and the contributed surplus.

❹ The beginning Retained Earnings balance represents undistributed earnings from prior years. An amount of $72,500 was restricted for specific purposes, and the remainder, $127,500, is unrestricted.

❺ The $10,000 increase in the Land account following an appraisal of the current market value of the land increased the assets and the shareholders' equity.

Figure 10-2 Partial Balance Sheet—Shareholders' Equity

DWIGHT CORPORATION LTD. Partial Balance Sheet December 31, 19XX				
	Shareholders' Equity			
	Share Capital			
❶	Preferred stock, 5 percent cumulative, nonparticipating, $100 par value, authorized 2,500 shares; issued 2,000 shares		$200,000	
❷	Common Stock, no par value; authorized 7,000 shares, issued 5,000 shares		200,000	
	Total Share Capital			$400,000
	Surplus			
	Contributed Surplus			
❶	Premium on Preferred Stock*	$10,000		
❷	Distributable Surplus — Common Stock *	50,000		
❸	Donation of Land by Town of Needham	50,000		
	Total Contributed Surplus		$110,000	
❹	Retained Earnings (of which $72,500 is restricted for anticipated plant expansion)		200,000	
❺	Appraisal Increase — Excess of Appraised Value of Land over Cost		10,000	
	Total Surplus			320,000
	Total Shareholders' Equity			$720,000

*These items do not apply to companies incorporated under the Canada Business Corporations Act (1975).

APPENDIX Stock Subscriptions

The descriptions of stock issuance transactions in the previous sections were based on the assumption that full payment for the stock was received and the stock certificates were issued at once. This condition normally exists for small or closely held corporations. In the following transactions, *subscriptions,* or pledges to buy the stock, are taken first, and payment is made later in single lump sums or in installments. The purchaser signs a formal, legally enforceable *subscription contract* in which he agrees to buy a certain number of shares of stock and to make certain specified payments. The stock certificates are not issued until completion of the payment.

The Subscriptions Receivable account is similar in nature and function to the Accounts Receivable account. It is a current asset and shows the amount due on stock that has been subscribed but has not been fully paid for. It is debited for the issue price, not necessarily the par value, of the stock and is credited for collections as they are received. Like the Accounts Receivable account, it is a controlling account with supporting detail kept in a subsidiary *subscribers ledger,* which contains the accounts of the individual subscribers. When more than one class of stock is issued, separate Subscriptions Receivable accounts should be kept for each class.

The Capital Stock Subscribed account is a temporary capital stock account. It shows the amount of stock that has been subscribed, but the stock certificates for the amount in the account have not been issued pending receipt of the payments still due on the stock as shown in the Subscriptions Receivable account. The account is credited for the par value of the subscribed stock and is debited for the par value when the stock is issued, with the permanent Capital Stock account being credited. If no-par value shares are issued, the Capital Stock Subscribed account is debited or credited for the full subscription price.

The subscriber to stock in some cases does not acquire full status of a shareholder with all rights and privileges until full payment is received. For example, under the Canada Business Corporations Act (1975), shares cannot be issued before being paid in full.

Issuance by Subscription at a Premium. Reed Corporation Ltd. is authorized to issue 6,000 shares of $100 par value common stock. On July 1, 5,000 shares are issued at a price of $105 a share for cash and subscriptions are received for 1,000 shares. A 60 percent down payment is received; the remaining 40 percent is payable in two installments of $21,000 each on August 2 and September 1. The journal entries are:

July 1	Cash	525,000	
	Common Stock		500,000
	Premium on Common Stock		25,000
	To record the issuance of 5,000 shares of $100 par value stock for cash at $105 a share.		
July 1	Subscriptions Receivable—Common Stock	105,000	
	Common Stock Subscribed		100,000
	Premium on Common Stock		5,000
	To record the receipt of subscriptions for 1,000 shares of $100 par value stock at $105 a share.		

			Debit	Credit
	1	Cash	63,000	
		Subscriptions Receivable—Common Stock		63,000
		To record the receipt of a 60% down payment on the stock subscription of July 1.		
Aug.	2	Cash	21,000	
		Subscriptions Receivable—Common Stock		21,000
		To record the receipt of the first 20% installment on the stock subscription of July 1.		
Sept.	1	Cash	21,000	
		Subscriptions Receivable—Common Stock		21,000
		To record the receipt of the second and final installment on the stock subscription of July 1.		
	1	Common Stock Subscribed	100,000	
		Common Stock		100,000
		To record the issuance of stock certificates for 1,000 shares of stock.		

When stock is subscribed at a premium, the entire excess over par value is credited to the Premium on Stock account at the time the stock is subscribed (see the first entry of July 1). The premium is recognized at the time of subscription—not proportionately as installments are collected. The amount of the entry for the issuance of the stock certificates is the par value of the stock; the existence of a premium or discount does not affect the amount recorded.

Partial balance sheets as of July 1 and September 1 are shown below.

July 1

Assets

Current Assets	
Subscriptions Receivable–Common Stock	$ 42,000

Shareholders' Equity

Common Stock, $100 par value; authorized 6,000 shares, issued 5,000 shares	$500,000
Common Stock, subscribed but not issued, 1,000 shares	100,000
Premium on Common Stock	30,000

September 1

Shareholders' Equity

Common Stock, $100 par value; authorized and issued 6,000 shares	$600,000
Premium on Common Stock	30,000

If Reed Corporation Ltd. was permitted to, and did, issue the stock at $95 a share, the entries on July 1 to record the issue and subscription would include debits of $25,000 and $5,000 to Discount on Common Stock. All other entries would be the same except that the amounts for the entries in Cash and Subscriptions Receivable—Common Stock would be reduced. The Discount on Common Stock account, like the Premium on Common Stock account, is recorded in full when the subscription is received and is not involved when the installment payments are received. The Discount on Common Stock account is reported in the balance sheet as a negative item in the Shareholders' Equity section.

If preferred stock is issued in addition to common stock, special accounts would be opened as required for Subscriptions Receivable—Preferred Stock, Preferred Stock Subscribed, Discount on Preferred Stock, and Premium on Preferred Stock.

GLOSSARY

Appraisal Increase The title of the account credited for the increase is shareholders' equity resulting from the upward revaluation of assets.

Capital Stock Shares representing fractional ownership in a corporation; may consist of several classes with varying rights and privileges.

Common Stock If only one class of capital stock is issued, it is called common stock.

Corporation From both the legal and the accounting points of view, the corporation is a special and separate being, or separate legal entity, created by law.

Organization Costs Expenditures necessary to bring the corporation into existence.

Par Value The nominal or face value printed on a stock certificate representing the minimum amount to be paid to the issuing corporation by the original purchaser.

Preferred Stock A class of capital stock having preferences as to dividends and as to assets upon liquidation.

Retained Earnings Undistributed earnings from regular operations and gains from sale of assets.

Retained Earnings—Restricted The portion of retained earnings not available for dividends.

Shareholders' Ledger A subsidiary ledger showing the account of each shareholder, the certificates issued or canceled, and the number of shares held.

Stated Capital The amount of capital that remains in the corporation for the protection of creditors, and which cannot be withdrawn by the shareholders.

Stock Certificate A printed or engraved serially numbered document issued to the stock purchaser as evidence of ownership of the stated number of shares of capital stock of the issuing corporation.

Stock Subscription A pledge to buy capital stock with payment to be made later in a single lump sum or in installments.

Stock Transfer Journal The journal in which are recorded the transfers or exchanges of stock from one person to another.

QUESTIONS

Q10-1. What is meant (a) by preferred stock? (b) by common stock? (c) by shareholders' equity? (d) by retained earnings?

Q10-2. What is the purpose and function of the following corporate records: subscription ledger, shareholders' ledger, stock transfer journal, minute book?

Q10-3. Distinguish between authorized and unissued stock and issued and outstanding stock.

Q10-4. Student A says that if he were buying stock, he would purchase only stock having a par value. Student B takes the opposite viewpoint. Discuss.

Q10-5. Student A says that Subscriptions Receivable is a current asset; student B argues that the account belongs in the Shareholders' Equity section. Discuss.

Q10-6. Define and give the significance of each of the following terms: (a) par value of stock; (b) market value of stock; (c) preferred stock; (d) corporation.

Q10-7. (a) What are the major subdivisions of the Shareholders' Equity section of the balance sheet? (b) Why must particular care be taken in subdividing the Shareholders' Equity section?

Q10-8. (a) What is the purpose of restricting retained earnings? (b) Is the restriction of retained earnings tantamount to the establishment of a special cash fund?

Q10-9. The following quotation is adapted from the notes to the financial statements of a large company, "Retained earnings of $28,500,000 are restricted from payment of cash dividends on common stock because of a promissory note agreement. Further restrictions of $1,700,000 are made to cover the cost of the company's own common stock reacquired."

What is the significance of this note (a) to a short-term creditor, (b) to a long-term creditor, (c) to a shareholder?

DEMONSTRATION PROBLEMS

DP10-1. (Appendix). *(Recording capital stock issuance; shareholders' equity)* Bechet Company Ltd. was organized on July 2, with authority to issue 50,000 shares of $50 par value preferred stock and 30,000 shares of no-par value common stock. The following transactions occurred during the year:

July 2 Issued for cash 24,000 shares of preferred stock at $51 a share
10 Issued for cash 16,000 shares of common stock at $20 a share.
15 Issued for cash 4,000 shares of preferred stock at $59 a share.
20 Received subscriptions for 8,000 shares of common stock at $17 a

share with a down payment of 50% and the balance due on September 30.

31 Received subscriptions for 12,000 shares of preferred stock at $51 a share; one-half the price was received on subscription, with the remainder due on September 30.

Aug. 2 Issued 100 shares of preferred stock to a lawyer in payment for services, valued at $5,000, rendered in organizing the corporation.

Sept.15 Issued 2,000 shares of common stock in exchange for land and a building appraised at $12,000 and $35,000, respectively.

30 Collected the installment due on the subscriptions of July 20 and July 31.

30 Net income from operations, after income taxes, for the period July 1 to September 30 was $50,000 (debit Other Assets).

Required:

1. Journalize the above transactions.
2. Prepare the Shareholders' Equity section of the balance sheet as of September 30.

DP10-2. ***(Recording capital stock transactions; Canada Business Corporations Act (1975))*** Following is the Shareholders' Equity section of the balance sheet of Willowdale Corporation as of December 31.

Common Stock, no-par value; issued and outstanding 50,000 shares	$600,000
Retained Earnings	450,000
Total	$1,050,000

The following transactions occurred during the year:

1. Acquired 7,500 shares of its own common stock at $12 a share.
2. Issued 4,000 shares at $17 a share.
3. One of the shareholders donated land and a building worth $25,000 and $75,000, respectively.
4. Paid a cash dividend of $1.50 a share.
5. Net income for the year after income taxes was $60,000 (make the closing entry).

Required:
1. Journalize the transactions.
2. Prepare the Shareholders' Equity section of the balance sheet as of December 31.

PROBLEMS

P10-1. The LePaz Corporation, organized on September 30, was authorized to issue 15,000 shares of $20 par value common stock.

Oct. 1 Issued 200 shares to a lawyer for services, valued at $4,000, in organizing the corporation.

25 Issued for cash 3,000 shares at $22 a share.

Nov. 10 Issued for cash 2,000 shares at $23 a share.

Record the transactions.

P10-2. (Appendix) Tilley Brunswick Ltd. was authorized to issue 30,000 shares of no-par value common stock and 10,000 shares of 10% preferred stock, $100 par value. At the end of one year of operations, Tilley Brunswick Ltd.'s trial balance included the following account balances:

Preferred Stock	$660,000
Common Stock	440,000
Subscriptions Receivable—Common	106,000
Subscriptions Receivable—Preferred	275,000
Preferred Stock Subscribed	330,000
Common Stock Subscribed	165,000
Distributable Surplus—Common Stock	77,000
Discount on Preferred Stock	44,000

How much cash has been collected from the stock transactions?

P10-3. Richard Powers Corporation Ltd. acquired the plant and equipment of the K. Raffol Company in exchange for 20,000 shares of its $25 par value common stock. Record the acquisition, assuming that if the assets had been acquired for cash, the purchase price would have been (a) $525,000; (b) $450,000.

P10-4. Spiller Corporation Ltd. is authorized to issue 15,000 shares of $50 par value common stock. The following transactions occurred:

1. Issued for cash 3,000 shares at par value.
2. Issued 100 shares to the promotors for services valued at $5,000.
3. Issued 100 shares to lawyers for services, valued at $5,000, in organizing the corporation and securing the corporate charter.
4. Issued 1,800 shares in exchange for a factory building and land valued at $85,000 and $12,000, respectively.
5. Issued for cash 1,500 shares at $55 a share.
6. Issued for cash 3,000 shares at $60 a share.

Record the transactions.

P10-5. India Corporation Ltd. was authorized to issue 5,000 shares of common stock. Record the issue of 4,000 shares at 7¼, assuming (a) that the shares have a $5 par value; (b) that the shares have no-par value; (c) that the shares have a stated value of $3.

P10-6. (Appendix). Zona Corporation Ltd. was authorized to issue 20,000 shares of no-par value common stock and 20,000 shares of $20 par value preferred stock. Organizers of the corporation received 3,000 shares of the no-par value common stock for services valued at $8,500. A total of 3,000 shares of the preferred stock was issued for cash at $22 a share, and 3,000 shares of common stock were issued for cash at $5 a share. A total of 4,000 shares of preferred stock was subscribed at $24 a share. One-half the subscribers paid in full. (a) Record the transactions in T accounts. (b) Prepare a balance sheet.

P10-7. (Appendix). The Shareholders' Equity section of Tout Corporation Ltd.'s balance sheet as of December 31, shows the following:

Common Stock, $100 par value; authorized 1,000 shares:	
subscribed but not issued 900 shares	$90,000
Premium on Common Stock	10,000

The Current Assets section shows:

Subscriptions Receivable $50,000

How much cash has been collected from the stock subscribers?

P10-8. *(Financial policy decision problem)* The annual report of M. H. Fish Limited includes the following note to its financial statements:

During the year the shareholders approved a change in the authorized capital stock of the company from 15,000 shares, $100 par value preferred stock to 500,000 shares, no-par value, and from 2,000,000 shares, $1 par value common stock to 3,000,000 shares, $1 par value common stock. (a) What was the effect of these changes on the company's financial statements? (b) What was the purpose of the changes?

P10-9. Murphy Corporation Ltd. entered into an agreement with the town of Tipton to build a plant there. The town donated land and buildings valued at $40,000 and $100,000, respectively. Record the transaction.

P10-10. Petow Corporation Ltd. was authorized to issue 50,000 shares of $1 par value common stock, all of which was issued to the principal incorporator in payment for machinery and equipment he sold to the corporation. Shortly thereafter, the incorporator donated 25,000 shares to the corporation. The shares were then reissued for cash at an average price of $1.50 a share.

a. Make all the necessary journal entries.
b. Prepare balance sheets immediately before and immediately after the re-issuance of the donated shares.

P10-11. Pamet Company Ltd. restricted retained earnings of $30,000 to cover a lawsuit by a customer. The lawsuit was ultimately settled for $15,000. Make all the necessary journal entries.

P10-12. The capital stock of Ville Marie Ltd. consists of no-par value common stock. Record: (a) the issuance of 750 shares at $10 a share, (b) the reacquisition of 200 shares at $9 a share, and (c) the re-issuance of the stock at $12 a share.

P10-13. January 1, the Grand Prairie Corporation was authorized to issue 25,000 shares of no-par value common stock and 2,000 shares of no-par value preferred stock. The following transactions occurred between January 1 and December 31.

1. Issued 6,000 shares of common stock at $25 a share and 1,500 shares of preferred stock at $102 a share.
2. Purchased the assets of the Willow Run Company at their fair cash value: the assets consisted of land worth $20,000, buildings worth $150,000, and plant and equipment worth $200,000. Issued 14,000 shares of common stock in payment.
3. Earnings through December 31 after income taxes were $90,000 (make the closing entry).

Required:

1. Journalize the transactions.
2. Prepare the Shareholders' Equity section of the balance sheet as of December 31.

P10-14. On December 31, the ledger of Knowles Company Ltd. included the following accounts:

Notes Receivable	$ 15,000
Merchandise Inventory	75,000
Marketable Securities—Canada Government Bonds	8,000
Common Stock ($100 par value)	300,000
Retained Earnings	100,000
Preferred Stock ($10 par value)	150,000
Goodwill	30,000
Organization Costs	20,000
Premium on Preferred Stock	12,000
Building	225,000
Premium on Common Stock	30,000
Cash	90,000
Research and Development Costs	110,000

Required: Prepare the Shareholders' Equity section of the balance sheet as of December 31.

P10-15. (Appendix). John Dill, an investor, and Richard Paris, an inventor, decided to form Hewlett, Inc., to manufacture and sell a product developed by Paris. The corporation is chartered by Ontario, with 10,000 shares of $100 par value common stock authorized.

a. Dill invests $200,000 and Paris invests $140,000 in cash for stock at par value. Paris is issued an additional $75,000 in stock at par value in payment for his patent on the product to be manufactured.
b. The corporation issues 200 shares of common stock at par value to each promoter as payment for promotion and incorporation fees.
c. Hewlett, Inc., sells stock on a subscription basis to five investors. Each investor subscribes to 200 shares of the common stock at $105 per share, making a down payment of 40% of the subscription price. The remainder is to be paid at a later date.
d. Four of the five subscribers pay the remaining installment.

Required: Journalize the transactions.

P10-16. (Appendix). Burns Corporation Ltd. was organized on January 2, with authority to issue 10,000 shares of $100 par value common stock. The following transactions occurred during the year:

Jan.	10	Issued for cash 150 shares at $102 per share.
Feb.	18	Issued for cash 150 shares at $108 per share.
Mar.	1	Issued 2,000 shares for land and a building with a fair market value of $200,000. One-eighth the total valuation was allocable to the land.
June	1	Received subscriptions for 1,000 shares at $104 per share, payable 40% down and the balance in two equal installments due on August 2 and October 1.
	10	Paid $5,000 for legal fees incurred in organizing the corporation.
July	5	Purchased equipment for $60,000 in cash.
Aug.	2	Received the installment due on the subscription of June 1.
Oct.	1	Received the installment due on the subscription of June 1.
Dec.	15	Received subscriptions for 1,000 shares at $107 a share payable 40% down and the balance in two equal installments due on February 15 and April 15.

31 Recorded the following entry, summarizing the net effects of the results of operations before income taxes for the year:

Cash	35,000	
Accumulated Depreciation—Building		6,000
Accumulated Depreciation—Equipment		3,000
Income Summary		26,000

31 Recorded the income tax liability of $4,500.

31 Closed the Income Summary account.

Required:

1. Journalize the transactions.
2. Prepare a balance sheet as of December 31.

P10-17. (Appendix). The following selected transactions occurred at the Love (Canada) Corporation recently incorporated under the Canada Business Corporations Act (1975):

July 1 Received a charter authorizing the issuance of 5,000 shares of no-par value preferred stock and 50,000 shares of no-par value common stock.

2 Issued 25,000 shares of common stock at $10 per share for cash.

2 Issued 500 shares of common stock to an incorporator for a patent that he had perfected.

3 Received subscriptions from four investors for 250 shares each of preferred stock at $52.50.

5 Received 60% down payments on the subscriptions from all four subscribers.

20 Received payment in full from three of the preferred subscribers, and issued the stock.

31 Received payment in full from the fourth preferred subscriber, and issued the stock.

Aug. 10 Received a subscription from Yok Lie for 500 shares of the preferred stock at $59 a share.

12 Collected 60% of Lie's subscription total. The balance is due on September 1.

Required: Journalize the transactions.

P10-18. Gander Corporation was organized on April 1, Year 1, with authority to issue 15,000 shares of no-par value common stock and 7,500 shares of no-par preferred stock. The following transactions occurred during the year:

1. Issued 750 shares of preferred stock at $56 a share.
2. Issued 6,000 shares of common stock for cash at $15 a share.
3. Issued 150 shares of common stock, in lieu of a $2,000 fee, to the corporation's lawyers for their services in drafting the articles of incorporation and a set of bylaws.
4. Acquired 300 shares of common stock for $3,500 from the estate of a deceased shareholder.
5. Reissued the 300 share at $15 a share.
6. Declared a $4.50 per-share dividend on preferred stock and a 30 cents-per-share dividend on common stock. The dividends are payable on January 10, Year 2, to shareholders of record on December 31, Year 1.

Required: Prepare the journal entries to record the transactions.

P10-19. The Shareholders' Equity of Skinners Inc. at December 31 is shown below (the company is incorporated under the Canada Business Corporations Act, 1975):

Common Stock, no-par value; issued 2,000 shares	$100,000
Retained Earnings	65,000
Total	$165,000

The following transactions occurred during the next twelve months:

1. Issued 1,000 shares at $80 per share.
2. Received, as a donation from the town of St. Paul, land and a building worth $20,000 and $115,000 respectively.
3. Acquired 200 shares at $75.
4. Net income for the year after income taxes was $50,000 (make the closing entry).

Required:
1. Journalize the transactions.
2. Prepare the Shareholders' Equity section of the balance sheet as of December 31 of the next year.

P10-20. *(Financial policy decision problem)* The annual report of Williams Canada Ltd. states in a note to its financial statements that "The terms of certain note agreements restrict the payment of cash dividends on common stock. The amount of retained earnings not so restricted on December 31, was approximately $122,000."

Required:

1. Of what usefulness is the statement regarding the amount of restricted retained earnings? the amount not restricted?
2. The cash dividend distributions were $14,908; net income for the year was $84,010. Do the shareholders have the right to dividends up to $14,908? up to $122,000?
3. Total shareholders' equity at December 31, was $860,703. Does this indicate what the shareholders would receive in the event of liquidation? of sale? Explain.

P10-21. *(Accounting policy decision problem)* The following information was taken from the ledger of Guay, Inc., as of September 30.

Cash	$ 60,000
Accounts Receivable	190,000
Cash Dividends Payable	55,000
Organization Costs	2,000
Common Stock, $5 par value	325,000
Preferred Stock, $10 par value	400,000
Premium on Preferred Stock	50,000
Premium on Common Stock	30,000
Retained Earnings	150,000

Retained Earnings—Restricted for Contingencies	20,000
Contributed Surplus—Donated	25,000
Allowance for Doubtful Accounts	12,000
Retained Earnings—Restricted for Plant Addition	50,000
Estimated Income Taxes Payable	30,000
Accumulated Depreciation—Building	20,000

Required: Prepare the Shareholders' Equity section of the balance sheet as of September 30.

11

Dividends and Retained Earnings

The components of shareholders' equity in a corporation were introduced in the preceding chapter. Transactions affecting these components are covered in this chapter. Emphasis is placed on the methods of dividend calculation, including cash and stock dividends, and the accounting for stock split-ups is also introduced. The meaning and computation of book value is discussed. The treatment of treasury stock transactions is explained in the Appendix to this chapter.

DIVIDENDS

The term *dividend* refers to the distribution of cash, stock, or other corporate property by a corporation to the shareholders. A dividend must be declared formally by the board of directors, a record of which should be entered in the minute book; the entry should indicate the date the dividend was declared, the ***record date*** to determine the eligibility of ***shareholders of record*** on that date, and the date of the payment. For a cash dividend distribution to be made, there must be accumulated unrestricted retained earnings and there must be assets available for distribution. If there are no accumulated earnings, the dividend becomes a reduction in contributed surplus, which is legal, or share capital, which is normally illegal. There may be adequate earnings but insufficient cash or other readily distributable type of assets. A corporation may have a good earnings record but no cash available for dividends because the cash may have been used to acquire other assets (land, buildings, machinery, or inventory), or funds are being accumulated for an anticipated expansion program or other corporate needs. Only the board of directors has the authority to determine whether a dividend is to be paid, to which classes of stock it is to be paid, and the time, manner, and form of payment. This applies to all classes of shareholders, preferred and common.

The board of directors is the ultimate authority in regard to dividend declaration. There have been court cases in which shareholders have attempted to force a dividend declaration that they felt was being deliberately withheld by the board of directors. Except in rare instances, courts have been reluctant to interpose and order dividend payments. Once formal action has been taken by the board, however, the declaration immediately becomes a current liability of the corporation. Federal and provincial corporation laws contain dividend provisions that must be observed by the board of directors. It is customary, for example, particularly for larger corporations with numerous shareholders, to make a public announcement of the dividend declaration in newspapers or magazines.

The term *dividend* is most often used to designate a cash distribution. A dividend may be paid in property other than cash; a company may, for example, distribute marketable securities or merchandise. A well-known distillery once declared a dividend and made a pro rata distribution of whiskey late in December. The term *stock dividend* is used to designate the distribution of additional shares of stock to existing shareholders. The term *liquidating dividend* refers to a distribution of assets by a company being liquidated. The term *ex-dividend* indicates that the quoted price of the shares is exclusive of a dividend declared and payable on a specified future date to shareholders of record as of a specified date prior to the payment date.

Declaration of a Dividend

The dividend may be stated as a percent of par or as a specified amount per share, as is the case in companies incorporated under the Canada Business Corporations Act (1975). Since there are no par-value shares under the new Act, dividends are stated at a specified amount per share.

Recording Cash Dividends

To illustrate the recording of a cash dividend, assume that on August 2, the board of directors of Magnetics, Inc., declared a quarterly dividend of $3,000 on 2,000 shares of $100 par-value 6 percent preferred stock, and a $2,000 dividend on 10,000 shares of $10 par-value common stock. The dividends are payable on September 1, to shareholders of record at the close of business on August 14. The entries to record the dividend declaration and the payment are as follows:

Aug.	2	Dividends—Common Stock	2,000	
		Dividends—Preferred Stock	3,000	
		Dividends Payable—Common Stock		2,000
		Dividends Payable—Preferred Stock		3,000
Sept.	1	Dividends Payable—Common Stock	2,000	
		Dividends Payable—Preferred Stock	3,000	
		Cash		5,000

Each Dividends account is closed out at the end of the accounting year to Retained Earnings. The use of a Dividends account has the advantage of segregating dividends declared during the year; it also keeps Retained Earnings clear of charges that would require analysis at the end of the year when the statement of retained earnings is prepared. The Dividends account is a temporary shareholders' equity account; it has a debit balance and represents a reduction in the shareholders' equity. It is shown on the statement of retained earnings as a deduction from the total of the beginning balance of Retained Earnings plus net income and other credits to Retained Earnings. Dividends Payable, on either common or preferred stock, is a current liability.

Dividends on Preferred Stock

As mentioned in Chapter 10, preferred stock enjoys certain dividend preferences. The right to a dividend of a preferred shareholder must await a formal declaration by the board of directors. On declaration, the preferred shareholders are entitled to a stated amount per share before any dividend distribution is made to holders of common stock.

If the preferred stock is *cumulative,* undeclared dividends are accumulated and must be paid together with the current dividend before any dividend payment is made on common stock. If the preferred stock is *noncumulative,* a dividend passed (not formally declared by the board of directors) in any one year is lost forever. Preferred stock may be either *participating* or *nonparticipating.* If the preferred stock is participating, it receives its specified dividend rate and a share of any additional dividends declared. The manner of determining the amount of the additional dividend depends on the terms of the stock contract. If the preferred stock is fully participating, it participates on a pro rata basis at the same rate based on par value with the common stock in dividend distributions after the common stock has received an amount equal to the stipulated preference rate on the preferred stock. The participation may be limited in the stock contract to a specified rate or amount per share. If the preferred stock is nonparticipating, it receives the stipulated rate only, and the balance of the dividend distribution, irrespective of amount, is paid to the common shareholders. Most preferred stock issues are cumulative and nonparticipating.

The extent to which preferred shareholders participate in distributions above the regular rates depends on the specific provisions of the corporate charter. The following examples illustrate the application of the dividend preference of preferred stock.

1. *Cumulative and Nonparticipating.* A corporation has outstanding 1,000 shares of 5 percent cumulative preferred stock and 2,000 shares of common stock, each with a par value of $100. Undistributed earnings are $75,000, there are no dividends in arrears, and a $27,000 dividend is declared. Assuming that the preferred stock is nonparticipating, the required journal entry for the dividend declaration is shown below.

Dividends—Preferred Stock	5,000	
Dividends—Common Stock	22,000	
Dividends Payable—Preferred Stock		5,000
Dividends Payable—Common Stock		22,000

2. *Cumulative and Fully Participating.* Assume the same facts as in example 1, except that the preferred stock is cumulative and fully participating—that is, the preferred stock shares at an equal rate with the common stock in the amount distributed in excess of the 5 percent preferred dividend and a comparable dividend on the common stock. The required journal entry is shown here.

Dividends—Preferred Stock	9,000	
Dividends—Common Stock	18,000	
Dividends Payable—Preferred Stock		9,000
Dividends Payable—Common Stock		18,000

The allocation is computed as follows:

	To Preferred	*To Common*
Current rate at 5%, or $5 per share:		
To preferred stock: 1,000 shares × $5	$5,000	
To common stock: 2,000 shares × $5		$10,000
Participation at 4%, or $4 per share:		
To preferred stock: 1,000 shares × $4	4,000	
To common stock. 2,000 shares × $4		8,000
Total distribution	$9,000	$18,000

Note that each shareholder receives $9 a share because the preferred stock is fully participating, and the common stock receives a current rate equal to the preference rate on preferred stock.

3. *Cumulative and Partly Participating.* Assume the same facts as in example 2, except that the preferred stock participates to a maximum of 2 percent, or $2 a share, above its preference rate; the allocation of the $27,000 is computed as follows:

	To Preferred	*To Common*
Current rate	$5,000	$10,000
Participation:		
Preferred stock: 1,000 shares × $2	2,000	
Common stock: remainder		10,000
Total distribution	$7,000	$20,000

Preferred stock participates at the stated maximum only if the proportionate distribution to the common stock—at a rate on the par value, or in an amount per share on no-par value stock—equals or exceeds the distribution to the preferred stock. In this example, the preferred rate per share is $7 and the common rate is $10. The amount actually received on participation may be less than $2 a share, as shown in the following example.

4. *Dividend Arrearage.* This example is based on the same facts as in example 3, except that there is a dividend *arrearage* (amounts owed from previous periods) on the preferred stock of $9,000. The dividend distribution is computed as follows:

To preferred stock:	
Arrearage	$ 9,000
Current year's preference dividend	5,000
Participation	1,000
Total to preferred	$15,000
To common stock:	
Remainder	12,000
Total distribution	$27,000

The distribution to the preferred stock due to the participation provision is computed as follows:

Total dividend		$27,000
Deduct: Arrearage payment	$ 9,000	
Current year's preference—preferred stock	5,000	
Current year's rate—common stock	10,000	24,000
Available for participation		$ 3,000
Number of shares outstanding		3,000
Rate per share on participation		$ 1
To preferred stock: 1,000 × $1		$ 1,000

Preferred stock may also be preferred in distributing assets; this means that if the corporation is liquidated, the preferred shareholders must be paid before any liquidating payments are made to the common shareholders. The manner of the preference application depends on the wording in the stock contract. The preference may be for the par value of the preferred stock, the par value and accumulated dividends, or some other stipulated amount. If the preferred stock is not preferred as to assets, then the assets are usually distributed to all classes of shareholders on an equal basis proportionate to the respective par values.

Stock Dividends

The term *stock dividend* refers to the issuance by a corporation of additional shares of its authorized stock without additional payment of any kind by the shareholders. There are various occasions for the declaration of a stock dividend, such as:

1. A large unappropriated retained earnings balance
2. A desire by the directors to reduce the market price of the stock
3. A desire to increase the permanent capitalization of the company by converting a portion of the retained earnings into capital stock
4. A need to conserve available cash

A stock dividend does not change the total shareholders' equity in the corporation; it simply effects a transfer of retained earnings to share capital. A cash dividend, on the other hand, decreases both the assets and the shareholders' equity. A stock dividend has no effect on either total assets or total shareholders' equity; the change is entirely within the Shareholders' Equity section (Retained Earnings decreases and Share Capital increases). To illustrate, assume that Truro Corporation Ltd., with $500,000 common stock, $100 par value, outstanding, and retained earnings of $80,000 declares a $50,000 stock dividend. The effect of the declaration on the shareholders' equity is shown below.

	Shareholders' Equity		
	Immediately before Declaration	*Immediately after Declaration*	*Immediately after Stock Issuance*
Shareholders' Equity:			
Common stock, $100 par value	$500,000	$500,000	$550,000
Stock dividends to be issued		50,000	
Retained earnings	80,000	30,000	30,000
Total Shareholders' equity	$580,000	$580,000	$580,000

The Stock Dividends To Be Issued account is part of the shareholders' equity. It is not a liability, because its reduction will result not in a reduction of a current asset but rather in an increase in capital stock. The account should therefore be shown under Capital Stock in the Shareholders' Equity section of the balance sheet.

It is evident that a stock dividend has no effect on the total shareholders' equity; the relative interest of each shareholder is, therefore, unchanged. For example, John Green, a shareholder with 100 shares before the stock dividend, will have 110 shares after the stock dividend. His proportionate holdings remain unchanged at 2 percent of the total stock outstanding. Hence, all his rights and privileges are unaltered, as shown below.

	Line	*Before Declaration*	*After Declaration*
Total shareholders' equity	1	$580,000	$580,000.00
Number of shares outstanding	2	5,000	5,500
Shareholders' equity per share (line 1 ÷ line 2)	3	$ 116	$ 105.45
Shares owned by John Green	4	100	110
Green's equity (line 4 × line 3)	5	$ 11,600	$ 11,600.00

A stock dividend, nevertheless, is significant to the shareholder. The dividend does not alter the recipient's equity in the company and is not, therefore, considered income. But there may be income tax on a stock dividend. If the stock dividend does not cause a significant decline in the price of stock, the shareholder's gain is equal to the market value of the new shares received. If, in addition, the corporation does not reduce the amount of its cash dividends per share, the shareholder gains the dividends on the additional shares. It is this aspect—the expectation of greater dividends as well as the availability of more shares for possible ultimate profitable resale—that creates a favorable reception for a stock dividend.

A stock dividend provides certain advantages to the corporation. Its earnings are capitalized (that is, earnings are transferred to capital stock accounts); there is no reduction in working capital; and the corporation may plow back its earnings for expansion or other purposes. The corporation also may wish to reduce the market price of its shares in order to attract more buyers; by issuance of more shares, the price per share will decrease. At the same time, a stock dividend makes possible larger total dividend distributions without a change in the regular dividend rate.

When there are two classes of shareholders. the stock dividend normally applies only to the common shareholders. Payment, however, may be in either preferred or common stock.

Small Stock Dividends. The AICPA has recommended that for small dividends—those involving the issuance of less than 20 or 25 percent of the number of shares previously outstanding—the corporation should transfer from Retained Earnings to Capital Stock and Contributed Surplus accounts an amount equal to the fair value of the additional shares issued.[1] To illustrate, assume that the market value of the shares issued by Truro Corporation Ltd. was $60,000 (500 shares at $120 a share) and that the board of directors, in authorizing the stock dividend, directed that the dividend be recorded at market value. The entries to record the declaration and stock issuance are:

Stock Dividends (or Retained Earnings)	60,000	
Stock Dividends To Be Issued		50,000
Contributed Surplus—Excess Over Par Value on Stock Dividends		10,000
Stock Dividends To Be Issued	50,000	
Common Stock		50,000

If the account Stock Dividends is used, it would be closed to Retained Earnings at the end of the year.

The AICPA's rationale with respect to small stock dividends is that since the market value of the shares previously held remains substantially unchanged and since "many recipients of stock dividends look upon them as distributions of corporate earnings and usually in an amount equivalent to the fair value of the additional shares issued"—that is, as a cash dividend—the accounting should be such as to show the amount of retained earnings available for future dividend distribution.

Large Stock Dividends. For large stock dividends—those involving the is-

[1] AICPA, *Accounting Principles,* vol. 2 (Chicago: Commerce Clearing House, Inc., 1973), p. 6024.

suance of more than 25 percent of the number of shares previously outstanding—the AICPA recommends that there is no need to capitalize retained earnings other than to the extent occasioned by legal requirements.[2] This means that for large stock dividends, the amount of retained earnings capitalized is represented by the par value of the shares issued. To illustrate, assume that Truro Corporation Ltd. declares a stock dividend of 2,500 shares, or 50 percent of the 5,000 shares previously outstanding. The entry to record the stock issuance is shown below.

Stock Dividends (or Retained Earnings)	250,000	
Common Stock		250,000
To record the issuance of 2,500 shares of additional common stock as a stock dividend.		

The rationale with respect to large stock dividends is that the effect is to reduce materially the share market value, and the transaction is "a split-up effected in the form of a dividend."

Stock Split-Ups

A corporation may wish to reduce the par value of its stock, or it may desire to reduce the price at which the stock is being issued to make it more salable. This is accomplished by a stock split-up whereby the shares outstanding are increased and the par value per share is reduced; there is no change, however, in the total par value of the outstanding shares. No journal entries are required, and *there is no change in retained earnings.* The capital stock ledger account headings are changed to show the new par value per share and the subsidiary shareholders' ledger is revised to show the new distribution of shares.

Assume, for example, that a corporation has outstanding 100,000 shares of $50 par value common stock. The current market price of the stock is $175 a share. The corporation, wishing to reduce this high market price to create a broader market for a forthcoming additional stock issue, reduces the par value from $50 to $25 and increases the number of shares from 100,000 to 200,000. This is called a "2-for-1 split-up," because the number of shares owned by each shareholder is doubled. The split in shares may be accomplished by calling in all the old shares and issuing certificates for new shares on a 2-for-1 basis or by issuing an additional share for each old share previously owned. This action is recorded either by a memorandum notation in the capital stock account or by the following journal entry:

Common Stock, $50 par value	5,000,000	
Common Stock, $25 par value		5,000,000
To record a 2-for-1 split-up, increasing the number of outstanding shares from 100,000 to 200,000 and reducing par value from $50 to $25.		

[2] *Ibid.*, p. 6025.

It may be assumed that the market price of the shares will now be reduced sufficiently to enhance the marketability of the new issue.

Both stock dividends and stock splits change the number of shares outstanding without changing the pro rata shares of ownership of each shareholder or total shareholder equity. A stock dividend, unlike a stock split, requires a transfer from Retained Earnings to Share Capital, and increases in capital stock account by the par value of the dividend shares. A stock split, unlike a stock dividend, changes the par value of the capital stock without changing the balances of any accounts.

Book Value of Capital Stock

The value of a share of stock may be expressed in terms of par, market, or book value. The book value of a share of stock, or the shareholders' equity per share, assuming that there is only one class of stock outstanding, is computed as follows:

	Line	*Amount*
Total shareholders' equity	1	$750,000
Number of shares outstanding	2	6,000
Book value per share (line 1 ÷ line 2)	3	$ 125

When more than one class of stock is outstanding, it becomes necessary to determine the liquidation claims of each class against the net assets of the corporation (assets minus liabilities). If, for example, the preferred stock is cumulative and nonparticipating and there are dividends in arrears, the shareholders' equity is divided between the two classes on the basis of the preferences accorded to the preferred stock. Assume that a corporation has the following capital structure:

Common stock, $100 par value; issued 1,000 shares	$100,000
Preferred stock (6%), $100 par value; cumulative, nonparticipating; issued 1,000 shares	100,000
Excess over stated value of no-par common stock	5,000
Retained earnings	45,000
Retained earnings—restricted for plant addition	10,000
Total shareholders' equity	$260,000

Dividends are in arrears for the preceding year and the current year. The book value of a share of preferred stock at the end of the year is computed as follows:

Preferred stock, $100 par value; issued 1,000 shares	$100,000
Dividends in arrears (2 years × $6,000)	12,000
Total equity of preferred shareholders	$112,000
Number of shares outstanding	1,000
Book value per share	$ 112

The book value of a share of common stock is computed as shown:

Total shareholders' equity	$260,000
Deduct equity of preferred shareholders	112,000
Total equity of common shareholders	$148,000
Number of shares outstanding	1,000
Book value per share	$ 148

If the preferred stock is participating, an additional portion of the retained earnings is allocated to the preferred shareholders' equity based on the participation provisions. Hence, in computing the book value of preferred stock, its preference rights—dividends in arrears, dividend participation rights, and preference in dividing the assets on dissolution—must be known.

The book value and the market value of a share of stock may be and usually are different in amount.

The market value of a share of stock—the price that a share of stock commands on the stock exchange—reflects price level changes; available investment funds; economic, political, and psychological factors; and so on.

Since these factors are not reflected in the accounts, there is often a disparity between book and market values. The book value per share is what each shareholder would receive for each share held in the theoretical event of liquidation after the assets are sold without gain or loss. Since the valuations on the books—especially for inventories and plant and equipment—do not necessarily reflect market conditions, the book value of a share of stock may be of little significance as an indicator of the resale value of the stock.

APPENDIX Treasury Stock

The Canada Business Corporations Act (1975) permits a corporation to reacquire some of its shares (provided that the purchase does not cause insolvency) and to subsequently re-issue shares. However, the treatment of these reacquired shares differs from the method of handling treasury stock described below. The Act requires that the reacquired shares be restored to the status of authorized but unissued stock, and the appropriate stated capital account be reduced by the payment. Technically, the reacquired shares cannot be sold. However, the corporation can issue authorized stock of which the reacquired shares are a part. This treatment should eliminate some of the confusion which can result with the issuance of treasury stock and should simplify the recording for reacquired shares.

A company incorporated in Ontario or British Columbia is permitted, in certain circumstances, to reacquire some of its own stock, preferred or common, either by purchase or gift or in settlement of a debt. Such stock is known as *treasury stock.* Treasury stock, if it has been fully paid for originally, may be issued at a price below par value without the assumption of the usual contingent discount liability by the purchaser of discount stock to the corporation's creditors for the amount of the discount. Treasury stock does not fall into the category of new issues; it is the corporation's own stock that has been issued and later reacquired. It is issued, but not outstanding, stock and therefore does not have voting or dividend rights.

A corporation may purchase some of its own stock, at or below the market price, to bolster a sagging market or to meet the needs under a plan whereby the company's own stock is distributed to its employees in lieu of other compensation. Sometimes the stock is purchased because it is available at a favorable price. Acquisition of treasury stock has the effect of reducing the assets and the shareholders' equity. The Treasury Stock account, therefore, should appear in the Shareholders' Equity section as a deduction from Shareholders' Equity. Since the acquisition of treasury stock results in a distribution of corporate assets to shareholders, the provinces have enacted restrictive provisions pertaining to this kind of stock to protect the corporate creditors. If a corporation faces financial difficulties, certain influential shareholders could have the corporation buy back their shares, thereby reducing the amount available for the creditors and other shareholders. The restrictive provisions specify that a corporation cannot purchase more treasury stock than the amount available in retained earnings for dividend payments. Subsequent to the purchase of treasury stock, a restriction of retained earnings may be made to the extent of the disbursement for the treasury stock. The purpose of the restriction is to indicate the amount of retained earnings which is not available for dividend payments. This restriction may also be indicated by footnote in the financial statements. The new British Columbia Companies Act (1973) also requires that the reacquisition of shares must be made by a pro-rata offer to all shareholders if the shares are not acquired on the open market.

Recording the Purchase of Treasury Stock

When a corporation reacquires shares of its own stock, the Treasury Stock account is debited for the cost of the shares acquired. To illustrate, assume that Lee Corporation Ltd. reacquires ten shares of its own stock at $55 a share. The entry is as shown below.

Treasury Stock—Common	550	
Cash		550

The purchase of the ten shares of stock reduces cash by $550 and the shareholders' equity by $550. It also reduces the number of shares outstanding. It does not reduce the amount of issued stock, because the purchase of the shares is recorded not by a debit to Common Stock but by a debit to a special Treasury Stock account, which is shown in the Shareholders' Equity section as a deduction from Total Shareholders' Equity.

Issuance of Treasury Stock—Above Cost

The reissuance of treasury stock is recorded by a credit to Treasury Stock for the cost of the shares. The difference between the cost and the issue price of treasury stock when it is issued above cost is credited to Contributed Surplus from Treasury Stock Transactions. To illustrate, assume that Lee Corporation Ltd. reissues five shares for $65 a share. The entry is shown here.

Cash	325	
Treasury Stock—Common		275
Contributed Surplus from Treasury Stock Transactions—Common		50

The Shareholders' Equity section of Lee Corporation Ltd.'s balance sheet after the reissuance of the five shares is shown below (other amounts are assumed).

Shareholders' Equity		
Common Stock, $50 par value; authorized and issued 1,000 shares of which five shares are held in treasury		$50,000
Contributed Surplus		
Premium on Common Stock	2,500	
From Treasury Stock Transactions	50	2,550
Total		$52,550
Retained Earnings		20,000
Total		$72,550
Deduct Cost of Treasury Stock—Common		275
Total Shareholders' Equity		$72,275

Issuance of Treasury Stock—Below Cost

The entry to record the issuance of treasury stock below cost depends on the existence of capital accounts that are not considered to be part of the stated capital. To illustrate, assume that Lee Corporation Ltd. issues the five remaining shares of treasury stock (which cost $275) for $225. The difference of $50 is charged to Contributed Surplus from Treasury Stock Transactions, as follows:

Cash	225	
Contributed Surplus from Treasury Stock Transactions	50	
Treasury Stock—Common		275

If the negative difference on the issue of the shares exceeds the amount in Contributed Surplus from Treasury Stock Transactions—Common, the excess is charged to any other Contributed Surplus account arising from the original issuance of the same class of stock (Excess over Par Value, for example). In the absence of such accounts, the difference between the cost and the selling price of the treasury stock is charged to Retained Earnings.

Treasury Stock Donated

One or more shareholders may donate a portion of their shares to the corporation for reissuance to raise needed cash. Shares acquired by donation do not affect the balance sheet, as there is no change in the assets, liabilities, or shareholders' equity. On acquisition, a memorandum is made in the Treasury Stock account indicating the date and the number of shares donated. When the shares are reissued, the proceeds are credited to Contributed Surplus —Donations. Assume that on May 1, 100 shares are donated to Lee Corporation Ltd. by its principle shareholder. The shares are reissued on June 15 at $45 a share. Upon receipt of the shares, the following memorandum is made in the Treasury Stock account:

Treasury Stock

May 1	100 shares donated	

The journal entry to record the reissuance is shown below.

Cash	4,500	
Contributed Surplus — Donations		4,500
To record the reissuance for cash of 100 shares of donated treasury stock.		

A memo entry should also be made in the Treasury Stock account to record the reissuance of the shares.

BALANCE SHEET PRESENTATION

The Shareholders' Equity section of Dwight Corporation Ltd.'s balance sheet as of December 31, shown previously in Chapter 10, is expanded to include additional items concerning treasury stock and is shown in Figure 11-1. Each new item in the statement is numbered and the new items are discussed in the following paragraphs.

❶ On July 10, Dwight Corporation Ltd. acquired 1,000 shares of its own common stock for $55 per share. On August 2, it sold 500 shares for $60 per share. The excess of the issue price over the cost is shown as Contributed Surplus from Treasury Stock Transactions.

❷ On July 10, Dwight Corporation Ltd. reacquired 1,000 shares of its own common stock for $55,000. The laws of the province in which it is incorporated limit the payment of dividends to the extent of the amount in the unrestricted Retained Earnings account. Since the effect of a purchase of treasury stock is similar to a cash dividend—a reduction in corporate assets and in the shareholders' equity—the limitation applies equally to dividend payments and to treasury stock acquisitions. A company with free retained earnings of $25,000, for example, may either reacquire treasury stock or declare cash dividends, or do both, provided the total disbursement is not over $25,000. Such a restriction prevents a corporation from bypassing restrictions on dividend distributions and improves the protection of the corporate creditors. The amount of $27,500 ($55,000 from the transaction of July 10 less $27,500 from the transaction of August 2) appears twice in the Shareholders' Equity section: (1) as a parenthetical note following retained earnings and (2) as a reduction in the shareholders' equity resulting from a distribution of $27,500 in cash to the shareholders from whom the stock was acquired.

Figure 11-1
Partial Balance Sheet—Shareholders' Equity

DWIGHT CORPORATION LTD.
Partial Balance Sheet
December 31, 19XX

Shareholders' Equity			
Share Capital			
Preferred Stock, 5 percent cumulative, nonparticipating, $100 par value, authorized 2,500 shares; issued 2,000 shares		$200,000	
Common Stock, no par value; authorized 7,000 shares, issued 5,000 shares of which 500 shares are held in treasury		200,000	
Total Share Capital			$400,000
Surplus			
Contributed Surplus			
Premium on Preferred Stock	$10,000		
Distributable Surplus—Common Stock	50,000		
❶ From Treasury Stock Transactions—Common	2,500		
Donation of Land by Town of Needham	50,000		
Total Contributed Surplus		$112,500	
Retained Earnings (of which $27,500 is restricted for treasury stock acquisitions and $45,000 for anticipated plant expansion)		200,000	
Appraisal Increase—Excess of Appraised Value of Land over Cost		10,000	
Total Surplus			322,500
Total			$722,500
❷ Deduct Cost of Treasury Stock—Common			27,500
Total Shareholders' Equity			$695,000

GLOSSARY

Book Value The net amount at which an account or an account group appears on the books. For capital stock, it represents the portion of the shareholders' equity assigned to a class of stock divided by the number of shares of that class of stock issued and outstanding.

Dividend A distribution of cash, stock, or other corporate property by a corporation to shareholders.

Stock Dividend The issuance by a corporation of additional shares of its authorized stock without additional payment by the shareholders.

Stock Split-up An increase in the number of shares of stock outstanding without a change in the total par or stated value of the outstanding shares.

Treasury Stock A company's own stock previously issued and outstanding but reacquired either by purchase or gift or in settlement of a debt.

QUESTIONS

Q11-1. What is meant by the term *book value?* How is book value computed? Has it any real significance as a financial measure of the worth of stock?

Q11-2. Preferred stock enjoys certain preferences. (a) What are these preferences? (b) How do they affect dividend distributions?

Q11-3. (a) What is a stock dividend? (b) What conditions prompt the declaration of a stock dividend? (c) How does a stock dividend affect (1) the total shareholders' equity, (2) the total assets, (3) the book value per share, (4) the taxable income of the recipient, (5) the market price per share?

Q11-4. (a) What is accomplished by a stock split-up? (b) How is it recorded? (c) How does it affect (1) the total shareholders' equity, (2) the book value per share, (3) the market price per share?

Q11-5. *Limited liability* is one of the distinguishing characteristics of the corporate form of organization. In federal and provincial corporation law, limited liability is recognized in a number of the provisions relating to financial aspects of the corporation. Indicate three such provisions that are relevant to the financial and accounting aspects of the shareholders' equity.

Q11-6. (Appendix). (a) What is treasury stock? (b) Why do corporations buy back their own shares? (c) How does the reacquisition of a company's own shares affect its financial position? (d) Why do some provinces place certain restrictions on treasury stock acquisitions? (e) How is the purchase of treasury stock recorded? (f) How is the issuance of treasury stock recorded? (g) How does the issuance of treasury stock affect the financial statements?

DEMONSTRATION PROBLEMS

DP11-1. *(Effect of cash and stock dividends)* The Shareholders' Equity section of Shute Corporation Ltd.'s balance sheet consists of the following accounts:

Common Stock, $100 par value; issued 500 shares	$50,000
Retained Earnings	35,000
Total Shareholders' Equity	$85,000

Required:

1. (a) Prepare the journal entries to record the declaration and the payment of an $8-per-share cash dividend. (b) Compute the book value per share of the common stock immediately before the declaration of the dividend and immediately after the payment of the dividend.
2. Assume that the corporation declares a stock dividend instead of a cash dividend, each shareholder to receive one dividend share for each 5 shares he now holds. Complete requirements 1a and 1b on the basis of this assumption.
3. John Vanden owns 50 shares of Shute Corporation Ltd. stock. What was his equity (a) before the stock dividend and (b) after the stock dividend?
4. Discuss the purpose, advantages, and disadvantages of a stock dividend from the viewpoint (a) of the shareholder and (b) of the issuing corporation.
5. Suppose the board of directors declared a 2-for-1 stock split, which the shareholders approved. How would this affect John Vanden? the Company's balance sheet? the earnings per share?

DP11-2. (*Computing dividend distributions*) Usher Corporation Ltd. has outstanding 4,000 shares of $100 par value common stock and 4,000 shares of $100 par value 10% preferred stock.

Required: Journalize the declaration of the cash dividend based on each of the following assumptions:

1. The preferred stock is cumulative and nonparticipating; dividends declared, $75,000.
2. The preferred stock is cumulative and fully participating; dividends declared, $75,000.
3. The preferred stock is cumulative and nonparticipating, and dividends have not been declared for the current year or for the two years preceding the current year; dividends declared, $150,000.
4. The preferred stock is cumulative and fully participating, and dividends have not been declared for the current year or the preceding year; dividends declared, $150,000.
5. Assume the same facts as in requirement 4 except that dividends declared were $40,000.

DP11-3. *(Recording corporate transactions; shareholders' equity)* Following is the Shareholders' Equity section of the balance sheet of Skelly Corporation Ltd. as of December 31.

Common Stock, no-par value; issued and outstanding 50,000 shares		$ 600,000
Retained Earnings		
Restricted		
For Lawsuit Damages	$ 50,000	
For Plant Expansion	250,000	

Unrestricted	150,000	450,000
Total Shareholders' Equity		$1,050,000

The following transactions occurred during the next year (restriction of retained earnings is required):

1. Paid $6,000 in settlement of the lawsuit for injuries.
2. One of the shareholders donated land and a building worth $25,000 and $75,000, respectively.
3. Paid a cash dividend of $1.50 a share.
4. Reduced the retained earnings restriction for plant expansion by $50,000.
5. Wrote off organization costs of $12,000.
6. Net income for the year after income taxes was $60,000.

Required:

1. Journalize the transactions.
2. Prepare the Shareholders' Equity section of the balance sheet as of December 31.

PROBLEMS

P11-1. Lind Corporation Ltd. has issued and outstanding 4,000 shares of $25 par value common stock and 2,000 shares of $50 par value 9% cumulative and nonparticipating preferred stock. Glenda Linnell owns 10 shares of the common stock, which she purchased at $50 a share; John Little owns 20 shares of preferred stock, which he acquired for $105 a share.

(a) What basic rights and privileges does Linnell have? (b) Little? (c) How are these shares reported on Lind Corporation Ltd.'s balance sheet?(d) How much will Linnell and Little each receive if over a three-year period the corporation distributes earnings of $8,000, $16,000, and $38,000? (e) How much would Little receive if the preferred stock were cumulative and fully participating?

P11-2. Pina Corporation Ltd. has issued and outstanding 3,000 shares of common stock and 1,500 shares of 8% preferred stock, each with a par value of $50. Retained earnings are $75,000, and the directors declare a $50,000 cash dividend. Record the dividend declaration, assuming (a) that the preferred stock is cumulative and nonparticipating and there are no dividends in arrears; (b) that the preferred stock is cumulative and participates up to $4 a share above the regular 8% rate; (c) that the preferred stock is cumulative and fully participating, and there was no dividend declaration during the previous year.

P11-3. Indicate the effect, if any, of each of the following transactions on total retained earnings of Pilgrim Mining Ltd.

1. The board of directors declared a stock dividend to be issued one month from the current date.
2. Issued the stock dividend declared in transaction 1.
3. Wrote off Accounts Receivable against the Allowance for Doubtful Accounts.
4. Paid accounts payable.
5. Collected accounts receivable.
6. Issued $50 par value common stock at $45 a share.
7. Restricted retained earnings for contingencies.
8. Issued $50 par value preferred stock at $55 a share.

9. Purchased machinery on open account.
10. Issued long-term notes and received cash in return.

P11-4. On July 31, Year 3, the directors of Sisk Corporation Ltd., after a successful year with its new products, declared $80,000 in dividends on all classes of stock. There are outstanding 5,000 shares of $40 par value, 8% cumulative preferred stock participating to 10%, and 25,000 shares of no-par common stock. Dividends on the preferred stock are in arrears for the preceding two years. Common stock also has not received any dividends for the preceding two years. The same number of shares of preferred stock was outstanding on July 31, Year 2; however, on July 31, Year 1, only 4,000 shares of preferred stock were outstanding. The Common Stock account has remained unchanged for more than three years. Compute the amount of dividends each class will receive as a result of the dividend declaration.

P11-5. The following is part of note 8 accompanying the August 31 balance sheet of Gordon Corporation Ltd.:

> Capital Stock
> Each holder of Class A Stock or Class B Stock has one vote per share. Each and all shares vote as one class except that they are entitled to vote separately by classes in cases of certain amendments to the certificate of incorporation affecting the rights of the capital stock, and except as may be required by law. The holders of the Class A Stock and the Class B Stock are entitled to receive dividends when and as declared by the Board of Directors. Cash dividends must be declared and paid on each class at the same time but dividends on Class B Stock shall be 5 percent (or 1/20th) per share of the dividends per share on Class A Stock. The holders of Class A Stock and Class B Stock participate equally share for share in any stock or liquidating dividends to shareholders. The shares of Class B Stock are convertible into Class A Stock at any time at the option of the holder on a share-for-share basis. On June 1, should any share of Class B Stock be outstanding, they shall each, without further action of the company or the holder thereof, become one share of Class A Stock.

Give some reasons why a company might issue more than one class of capital stock. What are the advantages to the shareholders? to the corporation?

P11-6. The unclassified balance sheet of Quality Corporation Ltd. is shown below.

QUALITY CORPORATION LTD.
Balance Sheet
December 31

Assets	
Cash	$ 15,000
Accounts Receivable	35,000
Merchandise Inventory	40,000
Other Assets	10,000
Total Assets	$100,000

Liabilities and Shareholders' Equity		
Liabilities		
Accounts Payable		$ 15,000
Notes Payable		5,000
Total Liabilities		$ 20,000
Shareholders' Equity		
Common Stock, $100 par value	$50,000	
Retained Earnings	30,000	80,000
Total Liabilities and Shareholders' Equity		$100,000

The members of the board of directors are considering several dividend distribution plans. They seek your advice with respect to these alternatives: (a) a cash dividend of 20%, (b) a stock dividend of 50%, (c) no dividend distribution. Discuss.

P11-7. (Appendix). The Shareholders' Equity section of Guild Company Ltd.'s balance sheet shows the following:

Common Stock, no-par value, issued 15,000 shares	$270,000
Retained Earnings	90,000
Total	$360,000

What is the cumulative effect on shareholders' equity of each of the following events, occurring in sequence: (a) the declaration of a 5% stock dividend; (b) the distribution of the dividend; (c) the acquisition of 200 shares of the company's own stock for $18 a share; (d) the issuance of these shares for $20 a share; (e) the declaration of a $1-per-share cash dividend; (f) the payment of the dividend.

P11-8. (Appendix). Depot Corporation Ltd., having 50,000 shares of $10 par value common stock authorized and issued, finds itself in need of working capital. The shareholders agree to donate 10% of their holdings to the corporation. The shares are then reissued at $12 a share. Record the transactions.

P11-9. (Appendix). The capital stock of Pierce Corporation Ltd. consists of no-par value common stock. Record: (a) the issuance of 750 shares at $10 a share, (b) the reacquisition of 200 shares at $9 a share (restriction of retained earnings is not required), (c) the reissuance of the treasury stock at $12 a share, (d) a reduction in the stated value to $3 a share, (e) a 2-for-1 stock split-up.

P11-10. On March 1, Saint Paul Corporation Ltd. was authorized to issue 25,000 shares of $25 par value common stock and 2,000 shares of 9% preferred stock, $100 par value. The following transactions occurred between March 1 and December 31.

1. Issued 6,000 shares of common stock at $25 a share and 1,500 shares of preferred stock at $102 a share.
2. Purchased the assets of the Willow Run Company at their fair cash value: the assets consisted of land worth $20,000, buildings worth $150,000, and plant and equipment worth $200,000. Issued 14,000 shares of common stock in payment.

3. Established a restriction on retained earnings for contingencies of 20,000.
4. Earnings through December 31 after income taxes were $90,000 (make the closing entry).
5. Declared a 75 cents-per-share dividend on the common stock and a $4.50 dividend on the preferred stock.

Required:

1. Journalize the transactions.
2. Prepare the Shareholders' Equity section of the balance sheet as of December 31.

P11-11. The Shareholders' Equity section of Wiggin Corporation Ltd.'s balance sheet as of June 30 is shown below.

Shareholders' Equity	
Common Stock, $50 par value; issued 2,000 shares	$100,000
Retained Earnings	65,000
Total Shareholders' Equity	$165,000

The following transactions occurred during the next twelve months:

1. Established a retained earnings restriction of $10,000 for a pending law-suit.
2. Received, as a donation from the town of Lenox, land and a building worth $20,000 and $115,000, respectively.
3. Declared a 2% stock dividend. The shares to be issued are currently quoted at $55 a share.
4. Issued the stock certificates for the stock dividend.
5. Net income for the year after income taxes was $35,000 (make the closing entry).

Required:

1. Journalize the transactions.
2. Prepare the Shareholders' Equity section of the balance sheet as of June 30.

P11-12. The condensed balance sheet of Glass Corporation Ltd. as of December 31 was as follows:

Total Assets	$1,450,000
Liabilities	$ 400,000
Preferred Stock, 9%, $50 par value; cumulative	200,000
Common Stock, no-par value (120,000 shares)	600,000
Premium on Preferred Stock	20,000
Distributable Surplus	30,000
Retained Earnings—Restricted for Plant Expansion	100,000
Retained Earnings	100,000
Total Liabilities and Shareholders' Equity	$1,450,000

Required:

1. Find the book value per share of common stock, assuming that there are no dividend arrearages. The liquidating value of the preferred stock is equal to the par value.
2. Find the book value per share of common stock, assuming that dividends on the preferred stock are in arrears for two years.
3. What is the significance of the book value per share?
4. What is the interrelationship between book value per share and market value per share?

P11-13. (*Accounting policy decision problem*) The following information is taken from the Shareholders' Equity section of Wiesel Corporation Ltd.'s balance sheet as of December 31.

Preferred Stock, 10%, cumulative and nonparticipating, $100 par value; authorized and issued 3,000 shares	$ 300,000
Common Stock, no-par value; authorized 40,000 shares; issued 20,000 shares	400,000
Distributable Surplus—Common Stock	840,000
Retained Earnings—Restricted for Plant Expansion	80,000
Retained Earnings—Restricted for Bond Redemption	40,000
Retained Earnings—Unrestricted	300,000
Total Shareholders' Equity	$1,960,000

Dividends on the preferred stock are in arrears for two years.

Required:

1. Compute the book value per share of the common stock.
2. Assume that the market value of Wiesel Corporation Ltd. common stock was one-half the book value per share. Does this indicate that faulty accounting principles or procedures were used? Give some reasons for the difference in book and market values per share.

P11-14. The following account balances were taken from the ledger of Whitney Limited as of December 31.

Excess from Revaluation of Building	$ 72,000
Premium on Preferred Stock	60,000
Contributed Surplus—Donated	144,000
Preferred Stock, 9%, $100 par value; issued 9,600 shares	960,000
Retained Earnings—Restricted for Plant Additions	192,000
Retained Earnings—Restricted for Contingencies	24,000
Common Stock, no-par value; issued 24,000 shares	480,000
Retained Earnings	396,000
Estimated Income Taxes Payable	115,000
Organization Costs	24,000

Required: Prepare the Shareholders' Equity section of the balance sheet as of December 31.

P11-15. The Shareholders' Equity section of Fitz Corporation Ltd.'s balance sheet as of December 31 was as follows:

Shareholders' Equity	
Capital Stock	
Preferred Stock, 10%, $50 par value; authorized and issued 5,000 shares	$ 250,000
Common Stock, $40 par value; authorized and issued 15,000 shares	600,000
Premium on Common Stock	75,000
Retained Earnings	300,000
Total Shareholders' Equity	$1,225,000

Transactions for the year:

1. Declared a $70,000 cash dividend for the year. (The preferred stock is cumulative and nonparticipating; there are no dividends in arrears.)
2. Paid the dividend declared in transaction 1.
3. Established a restriction on retained earnings of $15,000 for contingencies.
4. Earnings from operations for the year after income taxes were $225,000 (make the closing entry).
5. The principal shareholder donated to the corporation a warehouse valued at $40,000.

Required:

1. Prepare journal entries to record the transactions.
2. Prepare the Shareholders' Equity section of the balance sheet as of December 31.
3. Why do you think the principal shareholder donated his warehouse to the corporation?

P11-16. A listing of the balances of all the Shareholders' Equity accounts, taken from the balance sheet of Tesson, Inc., at December 31 is given below.

Preferred stock, $100 par value; 10% cumulative; entitled to $105 per share plus cumulative dividends in arrears in liquidation; authorized 5,000 shares, issued 4,000 shares of which 250 are held in treasury	$400,000
Premium on preferred stock	12,000
Common stock, no-par value; authorized 10,000 shares, issued 8,000 shares	320,000
Stock dividend, to be issued at $40, 2,000 common shares	80,000
Distributable Surplus	28,000
Contributed Surplus from stock dividend—common stock	8,000
Land donated by Lee County	20,000
Retained earnings	
Restricted	20,750
Unrestricted	50,150

Required:

1. Prepare a properly classified Shareholders' Equity section.
2. Compute (a) the amount contributed by the preferred shareholders, (b) the amount contributed by the common shareholders, (c) the book value per share of common stock, (d) the book value per share of preferred stock, assuming that one year's preferred dividends are in arrears.

P11-17. (Appendix). Guest Corporation Ltd. was organized on April 1, with authority to issue 15,000 shares of no-par value common stock and 7,500 shares of 9% preferred stock, $50 par value. The following transactions occurred that year.

1. Issued 750 shares of preferred stock at $56 a share.
2. Issued 6,000 shares of common stock for cash at $15 a share. Distributable Surplus of $12 a share is set by the board of directors for the common stock.
3. Issued 150 shares of common stock, in lieu of a $2,000 fee, to the corporation's lawyers for their services in drafting the articles of incorporation and a set of bylaws.
4. Acquired 300 shares of common stock for $3,500 from the estate of a deceased shareholder.
5. Reissued the 300 shares of the treasury stock at $15 a share.
6. Declared a 9% dividend on preferred stock and a 30 cents-per-share dividend on common stock. The dividends are payable on January 10, Year 2, to shareholders of record on December 31, Year 1. The board also authorized the restriction of retained earnings of $15,000 for plant expansion.

Required: Prepare the journal entries to record the transactions.

12

Proprietorship and Partnership Capital

The owner's equity of a business results from assets contributed by the proprietor, partners, or shareholders and from earnings reinvested in the business. The characteristics of and the accounting for shareholders' equity were presented previously. The characteristics of and the accounting for a proprietorship and a partnership are presented in this chapter. The entries for the regular operating transactions are the same for all forms of business organization; only the entries for the formation of the business, the withdrawal of funds, and the closing process are different. The accounts used for recording the capital in a proprietorship and a partnership are shown in Figure 12-1.

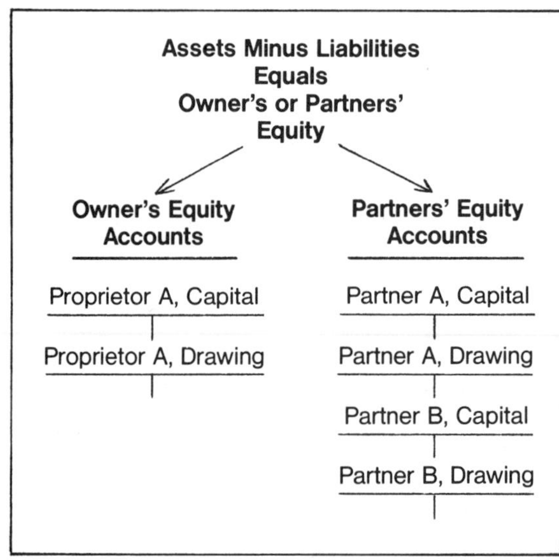

Figure 12-1
Accounts for Recording Proprietorship and Partnership Capital

PROPRIETORSHIPS

Many small service business are proprietorships. Among these are professional offices conducted by doctors, lawyers, accountants, and engineers or service stations and small retail outlets. The only difference between the proprietorship form of business organization and that of the corporation is the owner's investment and the withdrawl of drawings.

To illustrate the accounts used for recording the capital and other owner's equity items of a proprietorship, assume that on January 2, John Nelson formed the Nelson Garage with a cash investment of $30,000. This investment would be recorded in the journal as follows:

Jan. 2	Cash	30,000	
	John Nelson, Capital		30,000

The only other regular transaction that would be recorded differently in a proprietorship is the dividend paid by the corporation on January 31. A comparable situation in the case of the proprietor would be his withdrawal of cash (or some other asset) in *anticipation* of the net income that he expects to earn. If Nelson withdraws $300, the transaction would be recorded as follows:

Jan. 31	John Nelson, Drawing	300	
	Cash		300

A special account, *John Nelson, Drawing,* would be debited for all withdrawals in anticipation of income, and Cash would be credited; at the end of the period the drawing account would be closed to the central account.

All the other regular transactions of the Nelson Garage would be recorded in exactly the same manner for a proprietorship as for a corporation.[1] Assume for purposes of illustration that the following trial balance of Nelson Garage is taken from the January transactions of the business. In this trial balance, the balance sheet and income statement balances are listed in addition to proprietor drawings. In order to illustrate the closing process for a proprietorship from this trial balance, it is assumed that no adjustments are required.

NELSON GARAGE
Trial Balance
January 31, 19XX

Acct. No.	Account Title	Debits	Credits
101	Cash	$23,450	
121	Accounts Receivable	210	
131	Garage Parts and Supplies	375	
141	Prepaid Insurance	600	
201	Land	10,000	

[1] As indicated previously, a corporation must file income tax returns, and the income taxes payable would require accounting entries. No such entries are required in a proprietorship; its net income must be included in the personal tax return of the proprietor.

221	Automotive Tools and Equipment	4,000	
301	Accounts Payable		$ 350
302	Notes Payable		6,000
401	John Nelson, Capital		30,000
421	John Nelson, Drawing	300	
501	Garage Repair Revenue		5,020
601	Rent Expense—Garage Building	300	
602	Rent Expense—Automotive Tools and Equipment	80	
604	Salaries Expense	1,700	
608	Electricity and Water Expense	80	
609	Garage Parts and Supplies Used	275	
	Totals	$41,370	$41,370

The following closing journal entries illustrate the only other recording difference between the two forms of business organization. Revenue and expense accounts are closed in the same manner as previously illustrated in Chapters 3 and 4. These entries appear below:

Closing Entries

Jan.	31	Garage Repair Revenue	5,020	
		Income Summary		5,020
		To close revenue to summary account.		

> Entry ❶
> All the revenue accounts are debited and the total is credited to the Income Summary account.

❷

	31	Income Summary	2,435	
		Rent Expense—Garage Building		300
		Rent Expense—Automotive Tools and Equipment		80
		Salaries Expense		1,700
		Electricity and Water Expense		80
		Garage Parts and Supplies Used		275
		To close expenses to summary account.		

> Entry ❷
> All expense accounts are credited in a second entry and the total is debited to the Income Summary account.

After the revenue and expense accounts are closed, the Income Summary and John Nelson, Drawing accounts will appear as follows:

Income Summary

Expenses	2,435	Revenue	5,020
		Balance	2,585

John Nelson, Drawing

300	

Entries ❸ and ❹ are made to complete the closing process in the journal of the proprietorship (replacing entries ❸ and ❹ for the corporate form of business).

Entry ❸
After entries ❶ and ❷ are posted, a credit balance in the Income Summary account represents net income. The balance of this account is credited to John Nelson, Capital.

		❸		
Jan.	31	Income Summary	2,585	
		John Nelson, Capital		2,585
		To transfer net income to capital		

Entry ❹
The Drawing account is closed directly to John Nelson, Capital.

		❹		
	31	John Nelson, Capital		
		Drawings	300	300
		To close drawing to capital		

The effect of these entries is shown in the following T accounts:

John Nelson, Drawing

Withdrawal	300	Transfer to Capital	300
	300		300

Income Summary

Expenses	2,435	Revenue	5,020
Net Income	2,585		
	5,020		5,020

John Nelson, Capital

Drawings	300	Investment	30,000
		Net Income	2,585
	300		32,585
		Balance	32,285

Because there are no legal restrictions on the withdrawl of earnings of a proprietorship as there are on those of a corporation, the balance of the drawing account is usually closed into the proprietor's capital account at the end of the accounting period.

Because no Retained Earnings account is required for a proprietorship, a statement of retained earnings is not prepared; instead, a statement of owner's equity is prepared. The statement of owner's equity for the Nelson Garage as a proprietorship owned and operated by John Nelson is shown as

NELSON GARAGE
Statement of Owner's Equity
For the Month Ended January 31, 19XX

John Nelson, Original Investment, January 2	$30,000
Add Net Income for January	2,585
Total	$32,585
Deduct Withdrawals	300
John Nelson, Capital, January 31	$32,285

Since the owner's equity of the Nelson Garage has now been calculated, it is now possible to prepare the balance sheet as shown below.

NELSON GARAGE
Balance Sheet
January 31, 19XX

Assets			*Liabilities and Owner's Equity*		
Current Assets			Current Liabilities		
Cash	$23,450		Accounts Payable	$ 350	
Accounts Receivable	210		Notes Payable	6,000	
Garage Parts and Supplies	375		Total Current Liabilities		$ 6,350
Prepaid Insurance	600		Owner's Equity		
Total Current Assets		$24,635	John Nelson, Capital		32,285
Plant and Equipment					
Land	$10,000				
Automotive Tools and Equipment	4,000				
Total Plant and Equipment		14,000			
Total Assets		$38,635	Total Liabilities and Owner's Equity		$38,635

A statement of owner's equity for a proprietorship with a beginning balance and an additional investment during January is shown as

NANCY WOOTEN SECRETARIAL SERVICES
Statement of Owner's Equity
For the Month Ended January 31, 19XX

Nancy Wooten, Capital, January 1	$5,000
Add Net Income for January	1,000
Additional Investment	2,000
Total	$8,000
Deduct Withdrawals	500
Nancy Wooten, Capital, January 31	$7,500

PARTNERSHIPS

A partnership can be defined as an association of two or more persons to carry on, as co-owners, a business for their common profit. It is a contractual association whereby the partners pool their financial resources, services, skills, and knowledge and as a result hope to accomplish together what any one of them could not achieve individually. This association of two or more persons should be effected by a written contract called the *partnership agreement.* The law, however, does not require any written agreement and, in the absence of any evidence to the contrary, considers that the partners intend to share equally in profits or losses. Any other method of distributing profits or losses must be clearly agreed upon by all the partners.

The partnership form of business organization is the least common of the three principal forms. It is most often found in the professional fields, primarily medicine, accounting, and law, in which a personal responsibility exists.

Types of Partnerships

Most trading partnerships are *general partnerships.* In this type of association, the members are called *general partners.* They take an active part in the business, and each partner is subject to unlimited liability. If the partnership is unable to meet its obligations, the creditors may look to the personal assets of any of the partners for the full payment of the partnership debts.

The law may permit some partners, but not all, a limited personal liability equal to the amounts that they have agreed to contribute to the business. Once they have made the agreed contributions, neither the partnership nor the creditors can expect to receive any further financial aid from them. *Limited partners* cannot act as agents for the firm, and cannot withdraw any part of their agreed investment. *Silent partners* do not participate in the firm management and are not known to be members. They do have a financial interest in the partnership. *Secret partners* do participate in the management of the firm and have a financial interest, but their association with the firm is not revealed to persons outside the partnership. *Nominal partners* differ from general partners in that they have made no financial contributions. They take an active part in management and do not conceal their association with the firm. Silent, secret, and nominal partners incur the same liability status as general partners. Partnerships formed to accomplish a single objective are sometimes called *joint ventures.* The partnership is liquidated on completion of the objective.

Advantages of Partnerships

Some advantages of the partnership form of business are listed below.

1. The money, skill, and knowledge of two or more persons can be combined.
2. Partnerships can be formed easily and quickly.
3. Government regulations do not limit the sphere of activity of a partnership. Partnerships may change from one type of business to another at will or may expand without limitation, whereas a corporation is limited to the sphere of activity stated in its charter, although if stated broadly enough, it too may engage in multiple activities.

4. A partnership can act promptly as a business enterprise in all matters (withdrawal of funds, for example). A corporation may be restricted in its actions on certain matters by its charter, bylaws, or by statute.
5. Many of the formal government reports required of the corporation are not required of the partnership.
6. Income taxes are not levied against partnerships. The partners, however, report on their individual tax returns their distributive shares of partnership income. The partnership itself is not an income taxable entity.

Disadvantages of Partnerships

Some disadvantages of the partnership form are given below.

1. The liability of general partners is unlimited. They are jointly and severally liable for all debts of the partnership.
2. The life of the partnership is limited. Death, withdrawal, or admission of a partner; agreement to terminate; bankruptcy; and incapacity are all causes for the termination of a partnership relationship. By amending the existing partnership agreement, a new partnership can be brought into existence without cessation of the actual business carried on by the enterprise.
3. The general partnership is a mutual agency; that is, each partner may act in business matters as the agent of the partnership, and the remaining partners will be bound by his actions. If a partner purchases, in the name of the firm, merchandise used in the course of business, the other partners are also liable, although they may not have consented to or even been aware of the purchase.
4. The partners may find it difficult to cooperate, thus leading to dissolution of the partnership.
5. Partial or entire partnership interests may be difficult to transfer to another individual.
6. The ability of a partnership to raise funds is limited.

Nature of Partnership Accounting

The partnership form of business organization presents no new problems in accounting for assets, liabilities, expense, and revenue. The primary difference between a proprietorship and a partnership is that the accounts of the partnership must show the equities of each of the individual partners of the partnership.

Each partner's share of ownership is recorded in an equity account, and its balance is in turn reported on the statement of financial position. On formation of a partnership, the contribution of each partner is also recorded in that equity account. To illustrate, assume that Robert Walsh and John Snow form a partnership, each investing $8,000 in cash. The opening entry is shown below.

Cash	16,000	
Robert Walsh, Capital		8,000
John Snow, Capital		8,000
To record the investments of the partners in the Walsh and Snow Company.		

It is not necessary that each partner invest the same amount of cash. Assuming Walsh contributed $5,000 and Snow $10,000, the following entry is required:

Cash	15,000	
Robert Walsh, Capital		5,000
John Snow, Capital		10,000

Neither is it necessary that the original contributions be limited to cash. Assume that Walsh contributed land worth $3,000, a building worth $20,000, and merchandise costing $6,200, and that the partnership assumed his mortgage payable of $10,000 and $200 in interest accrued on the mortgage. Snow invested $15,000 in cash. The opening entry is shown below:

Cash	15,000	
Merchandise Inventory (or Purchases)	6,200	
Land	3,000	
Building	20,000	
Mortgage Payable		10,000
Accrued Mortgage Interest Payable		200
Robert Walsh, Capital		19,000
John Snow, Capital		15,000

Function of Partnership Equity Accounts. It is possible to record all equity changes in the partnership Capital accounts. However, since several individuals are involved, it is generally desirable to detail the reasons for equity changes in *capital subdivision* accounts, referred to as *personal, current,* or *drawing* accounts. The functions of partnership equity accounts are explained in the following paragraphs.

The following T account shows the recording of transactions in the Capital accounts:

Name of Partner, Capital
(separate account for each partner)

Debit	Credit
1. Withdrawals of permanent capital are recorded as debits. 2. A Drawing account debit balance is closed into this account at end of the period. 3. An income summary debit balance is closed into this account at the end of the period.	1. The original investment is recorded as a credit. 2. Additional permanent investments are also credited to this account. 3. An income summary credit balance is closed into this account at the end of the period.

After the closing entries have been posted, each Capital account normally has a credit balance showing the partner's equity in the net assets of the firm. A debit balance indicates a deficiency. An additional investment must be made by the partner to provide for the cumulative excess of his withdrawals and losses over his investments and profits.

The following types of transactions are recorded in the Drawing account:

Name of Partner, Drawing
(separate account for each partner)

1. Withdrawals in anticipation of profits earned during the period are debited to this account.	1. The balance in the drawings account is transferred to the partner's capital account.

The balance of the Drawing account is transferred periodically to the partner's Capital account. A partner's Drawing account is similar to the Drawing account of a proprietor.

Sharing of Profits and Losses. The allocation of profits and losses to the partners is based on mutual agreement. If no articles or other evidence of agreement exists, the law assumes that profits and losses are to be divided equally even when the factors of investment, ability, or time are unequal. Since allocation is based on mutual agreement, there are many ways to distribute profits and losses. The more common are:

1. Earnings are divided in an agreed ratio.
2. Interest is allowed on the capital investments and the balance is distributed in an agreed ratio.
3. Salaries are allowed to the partners, interest is allowed on capital investments, and the balance is distributed in an agreed ratio.

To illustrate these methods of sharing profits and losses, assume the following figures:

Robert Walsh, Capital

	Jan. 2 19,000
	July 1 6,000

John Snow, Capital

	Jan. 2 15,000
	July 1 5,000

Income Summary

	Dec. 31 12,000

1. *Agreed ratio.* The partners may agree to divide the net income in any ratio. If, for example, Walsh contributes twice as much time to the business as Snow, and if earnings are distributed accordingly, the entry to distribute the net income is:

Income Summary	12,000	
Robert Walsh, Capital		8,000
John Snow, Capital		4,000
To distribute the net income for the year in 2 to 1 ratio.		

2. *Interest and agreed ratio.* The partners may agree to allow for differences in capital investments as well as for differences in services rendered by allowing interest on capital balances and distributing the remainder in an agreed ratio. *Interest, as it is used here, is not an expense but rather a mechanism for dividing a portion of the earnings in the ratio of contributed capitals,* with the remainder divided in some other ratio. If 6 percent interest is allowed on opening capital balances, the division is as follows:

	Walsh	*Snow*	*Total*
Interest on opening capital			
6% of $19,000	$1,140		
6% of $15,000		$ 900	
Total interest			$2,040
Remainder: ⅔ and ⅓	6,640	3,320	9,960
Totals	$7,780	$4,220	$12,000

The entry to record this distribution of net income is:

Income Summary	12,000	
Robert Walsh, Capital		7,780
John Snow, Capital		4,220
To distribute the net income for the year divided 2:1 after allowing for 6% interest on opening capital balances.		

3. *Salaries, interest, and agreed ratio.* A part of the net income may be divided to recognize differences in capital balances, another part to recognize differences in the value of services rendered, and the remainder in an agreed ratio. Such a computation follows:

	Walsh	*Snow*	*Total*
Salary allowances	$4,000	$2,000	$ 6,000
Interest on opening capital			
6% on $19,000	1,140		
6% on $15,000		900	
Total			2,040
Remainder divided equally	1,980	1,980	3,960
Totals	$7,120	$4,880	$12,000

The entry to record the distribution is:

Income Summary	12,000	
Robert Walsh, Capital		7,120
John Snow, Capital		4,880
To distribute the net income for the year equally after allowing for salaries and interest on capital balances.		

In the absence of an agreement to the contrary, the salary and interest distributions must be made even though the net income is less than the total of such distributions. The excess is divided in the same ratio used for dividing an excess of net income over total salaries and interest. To illustrate, assume the same facts as in the previous example except that the net income for the year is $7,000. The computation is:

		Walsh	*Snow*	*Total*
Salary allowances		$4,000	$2,000	$6,000
Interest on opening capital				
6% on $19,000		1,140		
6% on $15,000			900	2,040
Totals		$5,140	$2,900	$8,040
Deduct excess of salary and interest allowances over net income				
Net income	$7,000			
Deduct allowances	8,040			
Excess divided equally		(520)	(520)	(1,040)
Distribution of net income		$4,620	$2,380	$7,000

The entry to record the distribution is:

Income Summary	7,000	
Robert Walsh, Capital		4,620
John Snow, Capital		2,380
To distribute the net income for the year.		

Partnership Financial Statements. The changes in partners' equity accounts during the year are shown in a statement of partners' equities. Its form is similar to the statement of owner's equity for a proprietorship and the statement of retained earnings for a corporation. It is a supporting statement for the total partners' equities reported in the balance sheet. Assume that Walsh and Snow each withdrew $3,000 during the year. The statement of partners' equities for the Walsh and Snow Company is shown as:

WALSH AND SNOW COMPANY
Statement of Partners' Equities
For the Year Ended December 31, 19XX

	Walsh	*Snow*	*Total*
Balances, January 2	$19,000	$15,000	$34,000
Add additional investments	6,000	5,000	11,000
Net income	4,620	2,380	7,000
Totals	$29,620	$22,380	$52,000

	Walsh	Snow	Total
Deduct withdrawals	3,000	3,000	6,000
Balances, December 31	$26,620	$19,380	$46,000

The entries to close the partners' Drawing accounts are as follows:

Robert Walsh, Capital	3,000	
Robert Walsh, Drawings		3,000
To close partner's drawing account		
John Snow Captial	3,000	
John Snow, Drawings		3,000
To close partner's drawing account		

The financial statements of a partnership are similar to those of a proprietorship. The allocations of net income to the partners may be shown below the Net Income line of the income statement or, if they are too numerous, in a supplementary statement. The balance sheet shows the individual capital account balances as of the end of the period and their total; or, if they are too numerous, the individual balances are shown in the supplementary statement of partners' equity.

Admission of a New Partner

The admission of a new partner technically dissolves the old partnership although, in the absence of complete dissolution or winding up, the business continues as before. A new partner either (1) may purchase his interest from one or more of the other partners or (2) may be admitted as a partner by making an investment in the partnership.

If the new partner buys his interest from one of the original partners, partnership assets are unchanged, because the transfer of assets is directly between the persons involved. The only entry on the partnership books is a transfer of the agreed share from the old partner's capital account to a capital account opened for the new partner. Assume that A and B are partners, each with capital balances of $50,000 and that A, with B's consent, sells one-half of his interest to C for $30,000. The entry required to record C's admission is:

A, Capital	25,000	
C, Capital		25,000

The amount paid by C to A has no effect on this entry, since there is no change in partnership assets or total capital. The $5,000 gain is a personal profit to A, which occurs outside the entity.

C may be admitted by making a contribution of cash or other assets directly to the firm, thereby increasing partnership assets and total capital. The amount credited to the incoming partner's capital account may be measured by the value of his investment. The admission of a new partner is often the occasion for recognizing goodwill—attributable to either the new partner or the old partnership—or a bonus may be allowed the old partners or the incoming partner. If the old partnership has been successful, the new partner may agree, as a condition, that part of his investment be considered a bonus from him to the old partners, or he may agree to the recognition of goodwill being credited to the old partners. On the other hand, if the old partners need additional resources—the funds, the skills, or both—that the new partner will contribute, they may agree to credit the new partner with an amount greater than his investment in the form of either a bonus or goodwill.

Assume that A and B are partners, sharing gains and losses equally, with capital account balances of $15,000 and $21,000. Some conditions under which C, a new partner, may be admitted, and the resulting journal entries, are illustrated below.

1. C is admitted to a one-third interest by investing $20,000, total capital to be $60,000.

Cash	20,000	
Goodwill	4,000	
A, Capital		2,000
B, Capital		2,000
C, Capital		20,000

Goodwill is recognized and is credited to the old partners in their profit-and-loss-sharing ratios.

2. C is admitted to a one-third interest by investing $24,000, total capital to be $60,000.

Cash	24,000	
A, Capital		2,000
B, Capital		2,000
C, Capital		20,000

C pays $24,000 but is credited with $20,000, the excess being credited to the old partners as a bonus.

3. C invests $15,000 for a one-third interest, total capital to be $51,000.

Cash	15,000	
A, Capital	1,000	
B, Capital	1,000	
C, Capital		17,000

In this illustration, the old partners provide a special inducement to C by crediting him with $2,000 more than his actual investment as a bonus.

Liquidation of a Partnership

A partnership may be terminated by selling the assets, paying the creditors, and distributing the remaining cash to the partners. This process is called *liquidation* of a partnership; conversion of assets to cash is called *realization*. Gains and losses resulting from the sale of assets must first be distributed to the capital accounts in profit-and-loss-sharing ratios before making any distribution of cash to the partners. If, after all gains and losses are distributed, a partner's capital account shows a debit balance, that partner must pay in the deficiency from his personal resources.

To illustrate, assume that A, B, and C, whose balance sheet is shown below, decide to sell their noncash assets, pay their creditors, and distribute the remaining cash to themselves.

A, B, AND C
Balance Sheet
August 31, 19XX

Assets

Cash	$ 25,000
Other Assets	125,000
	$150,000

Liabilities and Partners' Equities

Liabilities	$ 50,000
A, Capital	50,000
B, Capital	30,000
C, Capital	20,000
	$150,000

The noncash assets are sold for $140,000; profits and losses are shared equally. The summary below shows the liquidation sequence.

				Capital		
	Cash	Other Assets	Liabilities	A	B	C
Balances before realization	$ 25,000	$ 125,000	$ 50,000	$ 50,000	$ 30,000	$ 20,000
❶ Sale of assets at a gain	140,000	(125,000)		5,000	5,000	5,000
Balances	$ 165,000		$ 50,000	$ 55,000	$ 35,000	$ 25,000
❷ Payment of creditors	(50,000)		(50,000)			
Balances	$ 115,000			$ 55,000	$ 35,000	$ 25,000
❸ Cash distribution to partners	(115,000)			(55,000)	(35,000)	(25,000)

Amounts to be distributed to the partners ❸ are the balances in their capital accounts after each partner is credited with his share of the gain on the sale of the assets ❶.

Sale of assets at a loss in the process of liquidation may result in a capital deficiency in a partner's capital account. If the partner cannot cover the deficiency from his personal assets, it is normal practice in Canada to provide in the partnership agreement that the deficiency be allocated to the other partners, as an additional loss in the profit-and-loss-sharing ratio that exists between themselves. If, for example, the assets in the foregoing illustration are sold for $50,000, C's one-third share of the resulting loss of $75,000 =($125,000 – $50,000) is $25,000, or $5,000 more than the balance in his capital account. The payments to A and B must be such as to leave credit balances in their accounts that will exactly absorb each partner's share of C's $5,000 deficiency if C is unable to cover it. This is accomplished by treating C's deficiency as an additional loss and distributing it to A and B in their profit-and-loss-sharing ratio (which is now 1 to 1), or $2,500 to each partner.

A summary statement follows:

	Cash	*Other Assets*	*Liabilities*	*Capital A*	*Capital B*	*Capital C*
Balances before realization	$ 25,000	$ 125,000	$ 50,000	$ 50,000	$ 30,000	$ 20,000
Sale of assets at a loss	50,000	(125,000)		(25,000)	(25,000)	(25,000)
Balances	$ 75,000		$ 50,000	$ 25,000	$ 5,000	$(5,000)
Payment to creditors	(50,000)		(50,000)			
Balances	$ 25,000			$ 25,000	$ 5,000	$(5,000)
Cash distribution to partners	(25,000)			(22,500)	(2,500)	
Balances				$ 2,500	$ 2,500	$(5,000)

If C subsequently pays the $5,000 to the partnership, the amount will be distributed equally to A and B and all the accounts will be reduced to zero balances. Failing that, the $5,000 debit balance in C's account will be distributed to A and B and all accounts reduced to zero balances. If the partnership agreement does not provide for the method of distributing a deficiency in one partner's account to other partners, then the Garner v. Murray rule, from a 1904 English legal case, might be applied. According to this case, which may not be applicable in Canada today, the deficiency of one partner would be allocated to the remaining partners in the ratio of their capital accounts immediately prior to the date of liquidation. It may be assumed in completing the problem material in this text that the deficiency allocation would be in the profit-and-loss ratio.

GLOSSARY

Owner's Equity The owner's or owners' claims against assets of a business. As used in this text, owner's equity implies that the business is a proprietorship and, therefore, represents the proprietor's claims against assets of the proprietorship.

Partners' Equity The partners' claims against the assets of a partnership business.

Partnership An association of two or more persons to carry on, as co-owners, a business for their common profit.

QUESTIONS

Q12-1. (a) What are some of the distinct features of the partnership form of business organization? (b) What are its advantages? (c) What are its disadvantages?

Q12-2. Describe each of the following: (a) general partner, (b) limited partner, (c) secret partner, (d) nominal partner.

Q12-3. Compare the partnership form of business organization with the proprietorship and corporate forms.

Q12-4. Why should agreements reached in forming a partnership be in writing? What are some of the matters that should be specifically covered in a partnership agreement?

Q12-5. Can a partnership business continue after the death or retirement of one of the partners? Explain.

Q12-6. James Brown and Cedric Lee formed a partnership. Brown invested $10,000 in cash; Lee invested land and a building with a cash market value of $25,000. Five years later they agree to terminate the partnership, and Lee demands the return to him of the land and building. Is he justified in his demand?

Q12-7. D. Myers and S. Sacks agreed orally to form a partnership as of January 10, 19XX. They postponed formalization of their agreement pending the return of their lawyer, who was out of town. D. Myers invested $40,000 in cash; S. Sacks invested land and buildings worth $20,000 and $80,000, respectively. On January 11, the building was completely destroyed by an accidental explosion, and they terminated their partnership. Sacks claims that both the land and the $40,000 belong to him. Is he right? Explain.

Q12-8. Frank Fish and Homer Little are partners with capital account balances of $40,000 each. They share profits one third and two thirds, respectively. (a) Is this an equitable arrangement? (b) Assume that 10% interest on capital balances is agreed on. How will profits of $12,000 be distributed? (c) What account should be charged for the interest on the capital balances?

Q12-9. Douglas Evans and Stanley Byrd form a partnership by oral agreement. The matter of profit distribution is not discussed. Evans invests $15,000 and Byrd, $10,000. At the end of the first year, Evans contends that he should be credited with 60% of the profits of $10,000. Byrd disagrees. (a) Is Evans right? (b) How could this disagreement have been avoided?

Q12-10. What books and records do corporations have that are not necessary for proprietorships or partnerships?

DEMONSTRATION PROBLEMS

DP12-1. (*Recording partnership transactions*) The following selected transactions occurred in the partnership of Collins and Condin:

Jan. 2 Clark Collins and Daniel Condin formed a partnership on this date, making the following investments:

Collins invested $55,000 in cash. Condin contributed his equity in a building and lot. The partners agreed that the building was worth $90,000 and the land, $15,000. There was a mortgage on the land and building with a face value of $27,000; the mortgage carried an interest rate of 9%, and the interest was last paid on October 1, of last year. The partnership assumed all liabilities relating to the investment.

Mar. 1 Collins withdrew $800 cash in anticipation of income to be earned.

Apr. 1 Condin withdrew merchandise from the business. The merchandise cost $600 and had a selling price of $800. The firm uses the periodic inventory system.

Oct. 1 Collins was allowed to withdraw $12,000 in cash to pay a personal debt. This amount exceeds any anticipated income to be earned.

Required: Record the transactions.

DP12-2. (*Distribution of partnership profits and losses*) Edward Hand and Maurice Strong formed a partnership on January 1, with investments of $25,000 and $40,000, respectively.

On July 1 Strong invested an additional $10,000. On October 1, Hand and Strong withdrew $6,000 and $5,000 respectively, in anticipation of earnings.

Required: Make the appropriate journal entries to record the distribution of profits and losses on the basis of each of the following assumptions:

1. Net income is $12,000, profits and losses are shared equally.
2. Net loss is $5,000; the partnership agreement provides that profits are to be distributed 55% to Hand and 45% to Strong; the method of distributing losses was not specified.
3. Net income is $10,000, to be distributed in the ratio of capital balances as of December 31, 1976.
4. Net income is $20,000, to be distributed as follows: salaries of $10,000 to Hand and $12,000 to Strong; interest of 8% on ending capital balances; remainder to be distributed equally.

DP12-3. *(Proprietorship balance sheet)* The following alphabetical list of accounts is taken from the records of Jensen Company at December 31:

Accounts Payable	$125,000
Accounts Receivable	138,000
Building	300,000
John Jensen, Capital	78,000
Cash	14,000
Delivery Equipment	40,000
Land	15,000
Merchandise Inventory	70,000
Mortgage Payable (due July 1, 1993)	150,000
Notes Payable	110,000
Notes Receivable	18,000
Prepaid Insurance	12,000
Wages Payable	14,000

Required: Prepare a balance sheet.

DP12-4. *(Liabilities and partners' equity: partnership balance sheet)* Again refer to DP12-3. Assume that Jensen Company is a partnership owned and operated by David J. Jansen and John T. Jensen and that the two partners have equities as follows:

David J. Jensen	$410,000
John T. Jensen	204,000
Total	$614,000

Required: Show how the right side of the balance sheet would appear.

DP12-5. The following is an alphabetical list of the assets, liabilities, and owner's equity of the Michael Company, a proprietorship, as of December 31:

Accounts Payable	$ 16,000
Accounts Receivable	17,000
Building	150,000

Cash	60,000
Delivery Equipment	30,000
Land	25,000
Long-Term Notes Payable (due August 1, 2005)	80,000
Marketable Securities	5,000
Merchandise Inventory	32,000
Mortgage Payable (due March 1, 1985)	50,000
Notes Payable	6,000
John Michael, Capital	?
Prepaid Insurance	2,000
Salaries Payable	1,000

Required: Prepare a properly classified balance sheet.

PROBLEMS

P12-1. Enter the following transactions in appropriate T accounts:

a. Thomas Wojeck and James Lord form a partnership with cash investments of $25,200 and $19,800, respectively.

b. Wojeck and Lord withdrew $5,400 and $9,000.

c. Wojeck made an additional cash investment of $3,600, and Lord turned over to the partnership the title to a parcel of land with a fair market value of $10,800.

d. The net income for the period was $23,400 (profits and losses are shared equally).

P12-2. In their partnership agreement, Tom Jones and Ernest Raymond agreed to divide profits and losses as follows: (a) 10% interest on average capital balances, (b) salaries of $10,800 each, and (c) the remainder shared equally. Prepare a schedule showing the distribution of net income of $35,100, assuming average capital balances of $18,000 and $36,000 for Lones and Raymond, respectively.

P12-3. The following information relates to the partnership of A and B:

Average capital balances for the year	
A	$72,000
B	84,000
Net income for the year	9,600

The partnership agreement states that profits shall be divided as follows:

Salary allowances:
A $9,600
B 7,200
Interest allowance: 9% on average capital balances
Remainder:
A ¼
B ¾

Prepare the closing journal entries to distribute the net income in accordance with the partnership agreement.

P12-4. James Queene, owner of the Quality Store, asks you to determine his equity in the business at December 31, 19XX. You determine his net income for the year from the store to be $39,000. In addition, the following transactions occurred during the year:

Original investment	$45,000
Additional investment	6,000
Personal withdrawals	24,000

(a) Post the transactions to appropriate T accounts, and (b) prepare a statement of owners' equity.

P12-5. Paul Haley and John Galvin formed a partnership on June 8, 19XX. Haley contributed $10,000 in cash, land worth $6,000, a building appraised at $40,000 (the land and the building are encumbered by a mortgage of $8,000, which is assumed by the partnership), and a truck valued at $2,000. Galvin contributed $10,000 in cash.
(a) Make the entries to record the formation of the partnership. (b) Why may Haley be willing to enter into a partnership in which he contributes five times as much as his partner?

P12-6. C. Bunnell and R. Byrne form a partnership.

Required: Journalize their investments, based on each of the following assumptions:

1. Each partner invests $6,000 in cash.
2. Bunnell invests $7,000 in cash, and Byrne invests $9,000 in cash.
3. Bunnell invests $2,000 in cash, land worth $8,000, a building worth $20,000, and merchandise worth $3,000. Byrne invests $25,000 in cash.
4. Bunnell invests $3,000 in cash, land worth $5,000, and a building worth $20,000. The partnership agrees to assume a mortgage payable of $10,000 on the land and building. Byrne invests $3,000 in cash, store equipment worth $6,000, and merchandise worth $2,000.
5. Before the formation of the partnership, Bunnell and Byrne were competitors. They decide to form the partnership for their mutual advantage; the partnership assumes their existing assets and liabilities at book values as follows:

	Bunnell	*Byrne*
Cash	$ 6,000	$ 7,000
Accounts Receivable	13,000	16,000
Merchandise Inventory	30,400	22,200
Delivery Equipment (net)	7,000	10,400
Store Equipment (net)	12,000	20,000
Totals	$68,400	$75,600
Accounts Payable	$26,800	$24,400
Notes Payable	10,000	12,000
Bunnell, Capital	31,600	
Byrne, Capital		39,200
Totals	$68,400	$75,600

6. Assume the same facts as in assumption 5, except that the merchandise and equipment are to be recorded at their fair market valuations as follows:

	Bunnell	Byrne
Merchandise Inventory	$28,000	$22,000
Delivery Equipment (net)	8,000	10,000
Store Equipment (net)	10,000	14,000

P12-7. Arthur Dublin and Lowell Dworin form a partnership to operate a food brokerage business.

Required: Record their initial investments, on the basis of each of the following assumptions:

1. Dublin and Dworin each invest $10,000 in cash.
2. Dublin and Dworin invest $4,000 and $2,500 in cash, respectively.
3. Dublin invests $4,000 in cash, merchandise worth $7,500, a building worth $30,000, and land worth $9,000; Dworin invests $10,000 in cash, office equipment worth $6,000, and store equipment worth $10,000.
4. Dublin and Dworin transfer the following assets and liabilities to the partnership as their initial investments:

	Dublin	*Dworin*
Cash	$ 6,000	$ 4,500
Accounts Receivable	10,000	12,000
Merchandise Inventory	20,000	17,000
Delivery Equipment (net)	12,000	-0-
Store Equipment (net)	-0-	11,000
Accounts Payable	15,000	16,000
Notes Payable to Bank	13,000	15,000

P12-8. Barry Fuchs, John Galvin, and Tom Gee formed a partnership on May 1, 19X1, with investments of $15,000, $11,000, and $13,000, respectively. Profits and losses were to be shared equally. During the next twelve months, Fuchs and Galvin made additional investments of $5,000 each; Gee invested an additional $6,000 and withdrew $2,500. Net income for the period was $30,000.

Required: Prepare (a) a statement of partners' equities for the year ended April 30, 19X2, and (b) entries to close the partners' Drawing accounts.

P12-9. Peter Warg and Rae Burn formed a partnership on January 2. Certain relevant accounts are given as of December 31:

Peter Warg, Capital

Debit	Credit
Aug. 1 10,000	Jan. 1 80,000
	July 1 20,000

Rae Burn, Capital

Debit	Credit
	Jan. 1 100,000
	Dec. 1 12,000

Peter Warg, Drawing

Debit	Credit
Dec. 31 6,000	

Rae Burn, Drawing

Debit	Credit
Dec. 31 8,000	

The net income for the year was $10,000. The following provisions appeared in the articles of copartnership:

Net income shall be divided as follows:
Salary allowances: Warg, $6,000; Burn, $8,000
Interest allowances: 9% on beginning-of-year capital balances
Remainder: divided 55% to Warg and 45% to Burn

Required: Prepare the journal entries to distribute the net income to the partners' accounts and to complete the closing process.

P12-10. Assume that A and B are equal partners, each with a capital balance of $39,000. Record the admission of C under each of the following assumptions:

a. A sells his interest to C for $42,000.
b. C invests $39,000 for a one-fourth interest.
c. C invests $39,000 for a one-fourth interest, total capital to be $130,000.
d. C invests $39,000 for a one-third interest, total capital to be $117,000.
e. C invests $45,500 for a one-third interest, total capital to be $136,500.
f. C invests $26,000 for a one-third interest, total capital to be $117,000.
g. C invests $46,800 for a one-fourth interest, total capital to be $124,800.
h. C invests $46,800 for a one-half interest, total capital to be $124,800.

P12-11. A, B, and C, whose balance sheet information is shown below, have decided to liquidate their partnership. Their general ledger shows the following balances on March 31:

Cash	$10,000
Accounts Receivable	12,500
Inventories	50,000
Machinery	62,500
Accounts Payable	10,000
A, Capital	25,000
B, Capital	37,500
C, Capital	62,500

Proceeds from the sale of noncash assets were as follows:

Accounts Receivable	$ 7,500
Inventories	22,500
Machinery	12,500

Required: Prepare a schedule in good form showing the final distribution of the remaining cash following the sale of the assets and the payment of creditors.

P12-12. The accountant for Bruce and Thomas, interior decorators, prepared the following trial balance at December 31:

Cash	$ 4,850	
Accounts Receivable	12,600	
Supplies	3,800	
Prepaid Insurance	2,750	
Office Equipment	12,000	
Accumulated Depreciation—Office Equipment		$ 3,500
Building	80,000	

Accumulated Depreciation— Building		10,000
Accounts Payable		4,500
Accrued Salaries Payable		500
Mortgage Payable		20,000
Edward Bruce, Capital		25,000
Edward Bruce, Drawing	15,000	
Ray Thomas, Capital		20,000
Ray Thomas, Drawing	12,000	
Professional Fees		85,000
Supplies Used	3,000	
Depreciation Expense—Office Equipment	1,200	
Depreciation Expense— Building	4,000	
Utilities Expense	1,200	
General Expense	1,500	
Property Tax Expense	1,000	
Interest Expense	1,600	
Salaries Expense	12,000	
	$168,500	$168,500

Required:

1. Prepare an income statement for the year showing the distribution of net income to each partner. The partners have agreed to divide profits and losses as follows: (a) 10% interest on capital balances at the beginning of the year, (b) salaries of $15,000 each, and (c) the remainder equally. Each partner made an additional investment of $3,000 on July 1.
2. Prepare a statement of partners' equities for the year.
3. Prepare a balance sheet as of December 31.

P12-13. *(Financial policy decision problem)* Accounts included in the trial balance of the Karl Kutz Company as of November 30 were as follows:

Acct. No	*Account Title*	*Balance*
101	Cash	$ 25,200
111	Accounts Receivable	12,000
150	Office Suplies	1,500
200	Land	?
250	Building	?
300	Furniture and Fixtures	9,000
350	Machines	75,000
400	Delivery Equipment	3,500
600	Accounts Payable	4,000
650	Notes Payable	30,000
800	Karl Kutz, Capital	?

Land and building were acquired at a cost of $36,000. It was determined that one-third of the total cost should be applied to the cost of land.

The following transactions were completed during the month of December:

Dec. 2 Paid in full an open-account liability of $200 to the Duncan Company.

3 Collected in full an account receivable of $700 from the Papermoon Corporation.

4 Purchased office supplies from Boozier Corporation Ltd. for $500 on account.

8 Kutz made an additional investment of $20,000 in cash in the business.

10 Collected $1,500 from the Parker Company on account.

11 Purchased a machine from the Iber Business Machine Company for $25,000; paid $5,000 in cash, the balance to be paid within 30 days.

15 Paid in full an open-account liability of $600 to the Milton Company.

20 Paid $15,000 in cash to the Iber Business Machine Company in partial settlement of the liability of December 11. Issued a note payable for the balance.

31 Collected in full an account receivable of $400 from the Downy Company.

Required:

1. Journalize these transactions.
2. Enter the balances of November 30 in the ledger accounts, post the December entries, and determine the new balances.
3. Prepare a trial balance as of December 31.
4. Prepare a balance sheet.

P12-14. The following account numbers and titles were designed for the Herman Car Rental System, a proprietorship:

101 Cash
111 Accounts Receivable
201 Land
210 Building
215 Automobiles
220 Office Equipment
301 Accounts Payable
310 Notes Payable
400 Henry Herman, Capital

During the first month of operation the following transactions occurred:

Dec. 1 Herman deposited $100,000 in cash in a bank account in the name of the business, Herman Car Rental System, a proprietorship.

3 Purchased land for $10,000 and a building on the lot for $40,000. A cash payment of $20,000 was made, and a promissory note was issued for the balance.

4 Purchased 15 new automobiles at $3,000 each from the Foreign Motor Company. A down payment of $30,000 in cash was made; the balance was promised to be paid in 30 days.

5 Sold one automobile to Hilton Hertz, one of the company's employees, at cost. The employee paid $2,000 in cash and agreed to pay the balance within 30 days.

6 One automobile proved to be defective and was returned to the Foreign Motor Company. The amount due was reduced by $3,000.

11 Purchased a cash register and office desks for $2,500 for cash.

31 Paid $10,000 in cash to the Foreign Motor Company on account.

Required:

1. Journalize the transactions.
2. Post to T accounts (use account numbers provided).
3. Prepare a trial balance at December 31.
4. Prepare a classified balance sheet.

13

Debt Financing

The financial managers of modern corporations are constantly faced with the problem of how and where to get corporate capital for both short-term and long-term needs. The various alternative sources are outlined as follows:

1. Investments of the owners (discussed in Chapter 10)
2. Retention of earnings (discussed in Chapter 11)
3. Financing by creditors, which may create current or long-term liabilities (discussed in this chapter)
4. Other short-term financing devices (discussed in the Appendix to this chapter)

In this chapter detailed attention is paid to long-term debt financing instruments such as bonds payable, mortgages payable, and liabilities under pension contracts. Methods of short-term debt financing are discussed in the Appendix to this chapter.

REVIEW OF CURRENT LIABILITIES

As previously defined, current liabilities represent obligations, the liquidation of which requires the use of current assets or the creation of other current liabilities within a year or an operating cycle, whichever is the longer period. Various kinds of current liabilities are discussed elsewhere in this text, such as:

Bank overdrafts
Accounts payable, trade; or vouchers payable
Notes payable, trade
Maturing bonds payable
Current installments of serial bonds payable
Credit balances in customers' accounts
Accrued interest payable
Sales taxes payable
Income tax deductions payable
Unemployment insurance premiums payable
Pension plan deductions payable
Income taxes payable
Unearned subscriptions

Bonds payable, though they may have been originally issued with lives as long as fifty years or more, are classified as a current liability on the balance sheet prepared at the end of the fiscal year immediately preceding the year they mature. Unearned subscriptions are not liquidated by the use of current assets but are earned within the next year or the operating cycle; current assets are consumed in the earning process. Current liabilities are generally presented on the statement of financial position at their full maturity value.

All these current liabilities provide cash or some other asset, such as merchandise. They are significant to a financial manager, since payment or refunding must be accomplished; but the management of current liabilities may also influence decisions made in regard to long-term debt financing. For example, if the dollar amount of unsecured accounts payable outstanding is considerable, these short-term creditors may bring pressure to bear to prevent the issuance of long-term secured bonds payable, an act that would give prior claims on assets to the long-term debt instrument holders.

BONDS PAYABLE

One of the means used by businesses and governments to acquire funds that will not be repaid for many years is the issuance of bonds. A *bond,* or *bond certificate,* is a written promise under the corporate seal to pay a specific sum of money on a specified or determinable future date to the order of a person named in the certificate or to the order of the bearer. An example of a corporate bond is the 9¾% sinking fund debentures, due 1996, issued by Imperial Oil Limited.

Bonds are usually issued in denominations of $1,000 or $5,000 each; this variation enables the issuing company to obtain funds from many different classes of investors. Denominations smaller than $100 are used by the government in its Savings Bonds issues.

Bonds may be issued directly by the borrowing corporation or they may be transferred to banks, brokers, or other underwriting syndicates who, in turn, market the bonds through their own channels. *Bondholders* are creditors of the corporation; with the exception noted above, the Bonds Payable account is a long-term liability. Bonds contain provisions for interest to be paid at regularly stated intervals. Interest is usually paid semiannually on industrial bonds.

A bond, like a promissory note, represents a corporate debt to the lender, which must be satisfied from the assets of the corporation in preference to shareholders' equity claims. The main functional difference between bonds and promissory notes is that bonds are used in long-term financing, whereas promissory notes are used in short-term financing. The contract or covenant between the corporation and its bondholders is called a *bond indenture.*

BONDS COMPARED WITH CAPITAL STOCK

A better knowledge of bonds may be obtained if they and related concepts are compared with capital stock. The following parallel listing should help the reader understand more fully the nature of bonds.

Bonds	Capital Stock
Bondholders are creditors.	Shareholders are owners.
Bonds Payable is a long-term liability account.	Capital Stock is a shareholders' equity account.
Bondholders, along with other creditors, have primary claims on assets in liquidation.	Shareholders have residual claims on assets in liquidation.
Interest is typically a fixed charge; it must be paid or the creditors can institute bankruptcy proceedings against the debtor corporation.	Dividends are not fixed charges; even preferred dividends are at best only *contingent charges*.
Interest is a valid expense.	Dividends are not expenses; they are distributions of net income.
Interest is deductible in arriving at both taxable and business income.	Dividends are not deductible in arriving at taxable and business income.
Bonds do not carry voting rights.	All stock carries voting rights unless they are expressly denied by contract, as is usually the case with preferred stock.

CLASSIFICATIONS OF BONDS

There are many types of bonds, each tailored to meet the particular financial needs of the issuing corporation. Some common classifications of bonds are described in the following paragraphs.

Registered Bonds. Registered bonds are issued in the name of the bondholder. They require proper endorsement on the bond certificate to effect a transfer from one owner to another. The debtor corporation or its transfer agent, usually a bank or trust company appointed by the corporation, maintains complete ownership records. Large corporations (or their transfer agents) maintain computer records of bondholders. The file of records of registered bonds is updated in the same manner as the shareholders ledger; thus the computation of interest due on registered bonds and the actual writing of checks in payment simply require the execution of a computer program on each interest date. Bonds may be registered as to both principal and interest, in which case interest checks are issued only to bondholders of record. It is possible, however, to register the principal only (*coupon bonds*); the owner detaches *interest coupons* from the bond certificate and deposits them at the stated interest dates at his bank or at a designated bank.

Bearer Bonds. Bonds may be issued without being registered in the name of the buyer; title to them is vested in the *bearer.* The procedure for making interest payments is the same as with coupon bonds. This method is least burdensome to the issuing corporation, but the owner must take particular care against loss or theft of the certificates, or unauthorized removal of the coupons attached to the bonds.

Secured Bonds. A *secured* bond is one for which the issuing corporation pledges some part of the corporate property as security for the bond. The property pledged may consist of land and buildings (*real estate mortgage* bonds), machinery (*chattel mortgage* bonds), negotiable securities (*collateral trust* bonds), or other corporate property. Several loans may use the same property for collateral; this gives rise to *first mortgage* bonds and *second mortgage* bonds. The numbers indicate the order to be followed in satisfying the mortgage-holders' claims if the corporation does not meet its obligations under the *bond indenture*—the contract between the corporation and the bondholder. In the event of default, *foreclosure* and sale of the property follow. Second and third mortgage bonds necessarily carry a higher interest rate than first mortgage bonds because of the order of priority of payment in the event of a default; thus, they are not as marketable as first mortgage bonds and are more costly to the borrowing company. It is, therefore, desirable for the borrower to raise the required funds through a single, large first mortgage bond issue.

Unsecured Bonds. Unsecured bondholders rank as general, or ordinary, creditors of the corporation and rely on the corporation's general credit. Such bonds are commonly referred to as *debenture* bonds, or often simply as *debentures.* Sometimes debenture bonds are issued with a provision that interest payments will depend on earnings; such bonds are called *income* bonds.

Bonds may have other special features; for instance, the bonds may mature in serial installments (*serial* bonds), which means that specified portions of the outstanding bonds will mature in installments and will be paid at stated intervals. Sometimes the issuing corporation retains an option to call in the bonds before maturity (*callable* bonds); or, in other cases, the bondholder may be given an option to exchange his bonds for capital stock (*convertible* bonds). The bond indenture may require the issuing corporation to deposit funds, often to a trustee for the bondholders, at regular intervals to insure the availability of adequate funds for the redemption of the bonds at maturity (*sinking fund* bonds).

MANAGEMENT REASONS FOR ISSUING BONDS INSTEAD OF CAPITAL STOCK

Among the many factors influencing management in regard to the issuance of bonds instead of capital stock is that management may be enabled to tap another market source of creditor funds that it would not be able to tap by the issuance of stock. For example, many banks and other financial institutions are not permitted by law or regulation to buy stocks, but they are allowed to buy bonds.

A second factor is *leverage,* or *trading on the bondholders' equity.* This practice can be described simply: If funds can be borrowed at an interest rate of 6 percent and utilized in the business to earn 14 percent after taxes, then the additional earnings of 8 percent (14% − 6%) accrue to the common shareholders However, there is always the possibility of the opposite result: in other words, the borrowed funds may earn less than the cost of borrowing—an instance of unfavorable leverage.

A third reason why corporations decide to issue bonds instead of capital stock is that there is a high income tax rate on corporate net income. If a corporation pays at least half its net income in income taxes, it naturally considers the issuance of bonds as a means of effecting a considerable tax saving.

To illustrate the way that leverage and heavy income taxes affect financial decision making involving the choice of alternative methods of fund raising, assume that the Hunt Corporation, which has $100 par value common stock outstanding in the amount of $1,000,000, needs $500,000 to purchase additional plant and equipment. Three plans are under consideration: Plan 1 is to issue additional common stock at $100 par value; Plan 2 is to issue 8% preferred stock at $100 par value, cumulative and nonparticipating; Plan 3 is to issue 7% bonds.

	Plan 1	Plan 2	Plan 3
Common stock	$1,000,000	$1,000,000	$1,000,000
Additional funds	500,000	500,000	500,000
Total	$1,500,000	$1,500,000	$1,500,000
Net income before bond interest and income taxes	$ 350,000	$ 350,000	$ 350,000
Deduct bond interest expense	-0-	-0-	35,000
Net income after bond interest expense	$ 350,000	$ 350,000	$ 315,000
Deduct income taxes (assumed rate of 50%)	175,000	175,000	157,500
Net income after income taxes	$ 175,000	$ 175,000	$ 157,500
Deduct dividends on preferred stock	-0-	40,000	-0-
Available for common stock dividends	$ 175,000	$ 135,000	$ 157,500
Pro forma earnings per share on common stock (15,000 shares outstanding under Plan 1; 10,000 shares under Plans 2 and 3)	$11.67	$13.50	$15.75

All the plans assume that the securities will be issued at par value, that earnings of $350,000 annually before the bond interest expense is deducted will be maintained, and that an income tax rate of 50 percent will prevail.

Assuming that earnings per share on common stock is an accepted decision-making criterion, Plan 3 appears to be the most promising for the common shareholders, particularly if the annual earnings exceed $350,000, because the bond interest rate is fixed. If the annual earnings fall below $350,000, one of the other plans may become more advantageous. Since the securities market and corporate net earnings remain uncertain, there is no exact mathematical formula to solve this financial problem. The decision requires sound judgment based on past experience and projected future needs.

A fourth reason for the issuance of bonds instead of common stock is that bonds, and to a lesser extent preferred stock, aid in offsetting losses due to shrinkage in the purchasing power of the funds invested in assets. Bonds, for example, carry fixed contract maturity values in terms of the monetary unit at the maturity date. If the value of the dollar decreases before the bonds are paid, a gain resulting from the use of the more valuable money received at the time of borrowing accrues to the owners of the business.

A fifth factor is control. The issuance of additional common stock may result in a loss of management control, because the ownership of the corporation is distributed over a larger number of shareholders. Bondholders, on the other hand, are creditors and do not participate in managerial decisions, except in the rare instances when this is a specific provision of the bond indenture.

Other reasons may influence the decision of management to issue bonds; but these five factors indicate the scope of the problem.

AUTHORIZING THE BOND ISSUE

Even after management decides that bonds should be issued, it is faced with months of preliminary work before the bonds can actually be *floated,* or sold. For example, the exact amount to be borrowed, the *contract* or *nominal interest rate* (the rate on the bond certificate that applies to the face value), the maturity date, and the assets, if any, to be pledged must be determined. The provisions of the bond indenture must be chosen with extreme care. For instance, should the bonds be callable, and should they be convertible into some other form of security? Careful long-range financial planning helps to reduce the cost of securing the long-term funds. For example, if there is any chance that the company will need additional funds in the near future, management should not close the door on the possibility of marketing additional bonds by pledging the company's total mortgageable assets. In this case, management probably should seek authority for a bond issue large enough to meet all foreseeable needs.

The financial vice-president, working with other corporate officers, is responsible for finding answers to these and other questions. He prepares a written report for the board of directors, summarizing the proposed features of the bond financing and stating why the funds are needed, how they are to be used, and the means of ultimately retiring the bond issue. Various alternative methods of raising funds, such as those shown in the example of the Hunt Corporation, are presented to point up the financial advantage of issuing the bonds.

The board of directors studies this written report, along with the laws of the place in which the company is incorporated, the corporate charter, and the corporate bylaws, before passing a resolution recommending to the shareholders that bonds be issued; a record of the resolution is entered in the minute book of the corporation. Once this approval has been gained, the board of directors prepares a resolution instructing the proper corporate officers to issue the bonds and sign the necessary documents. The final step is the issuance of a formal certified statement that the approval of the board of directors has been obtained. The charter or bylaws of some corporations may also require shareholder approval of the bond issue.

ACCOUNTING FOR ISSUANCE OF BONDS

No formal journal entry is required to record the authorization of the bond issue by the board of directors, but a memorandum should be made in the Bonds Payable account indicating the total amount authorized. This information is needed when the balance sheet is prepared, since it should disclose the total authorization as well as the amount issued.

The issue price, usually stated as a percentage of the face value, is affected primarily by the prevailing market interest rate on bonds of the same grade. Bonds are graded by various financial institutions; the grade depends on the financial condition of the issuing corporation. The highest grade is AAA; the next, AA; and in descending order: A, BBB, BB, B. If, on the issue date, the stated interest rate applicable to the face value of the bonds—also called *contract,* or *nominal,* rate—is established at the prevailing market interest rate for the particular grade of bonds, the authorized bonds will sell at face value.

On the other hand, if there is a disparity between the contract bond interest rate and the prevailing market rate for that grade of bonds, the bonds will sell at a price above or below face value, that is, at a *premium* or a *discount.*

Bonds Issued at Face Value. The first example relates to the simple situation in which a corporation issues bonds at face value (sometimes called issuance *at par)* on an interest rate. The same sequence is followed in each of the first three examples. First, an entry is made to record the issuance of the bonds; next, any peculiarity of financial statement presentation is discussed; after this, the accounting procedure for interest payments is described; finally, the recording of the *retirement* of the bonds at the maturity date is shown.

Assume that on July 1, the Grogan Corporation is authorized to issue 8% debenture bonds with a face value of $200,000 and that these bonds mature in 20 years. Interest is paid semiannually on June 30 and December 31. All the bonds are issued on July 1, at 100, or face value, and the following entry is made:

Cash	200,000	
Debenture Bonds Payable		200,000

A balance sheet prepared after this transaction would report the bond issue as follows:

Long-Term Liabilities	
8% Debenture Bonds Payable, due June 30, 19XX	$200,000

The following entry records the payment of interest on December 31.

Bond Interest Expense	8,000	
Cash		8,000

A similar entry is made each June 30 and December 31 until the bonds are retired. It is possible for all the interest paid by the corporation to be recorded in a single Interest Expense account; however, in the present case, the interest on bonds payable is considered to be material enough to warrant a separate general ledger account.

At maturity, the bonds are retired by the payment of cash to the bondholders. The following compound entry is made on that date to record the last interest payment and the retirement of the bonds:

Debenture Bonds Payable	200,000	
Bond Interest Expense	8,000	
Cash		208,000

Bonds Issued at a Discount or a Premium. If the average effective market interest rate on bonds of any particular grade exceeds the contract interest rate of bonds of the same grade being issued, investors will offer less than the face value of the bonds in order to make up the difference between the rates. The difference between the issue price and the maturity value, plus receipts of the semiannual interest, will give the investors a return on their investments approximating the yield of similar amounts invested at the prevailing market interest rate. By the same token, if the stated interest rate is more favorable than the current market rate, investors will tend to offer more than the face value, because they know that the premium paid will, in effect, be returned to them to the extent that the periodic interest payments exceed the amount that they would otherwise receive on investments made at the current market rate.

Two examples are presented to emphasize the reasons for bonds selling at a premium or a discount. First, assume that Strong Company Ltd. has an AAA financial rating and is planning to issue debenture bonds. Assume also that all the AAA debenture bonds on the market have an effective average market interest rate of 8 percent. If Strong Company Ltd. issues debenture bonds with an 8 percent contract interest rate, it will receive the face value of the bonds; if it issues bonds with a 9 percent contract interest rate, it will receive an amount in excess of the face value; but even with its excellent credit rating, if it issues bonds with a 7 percent contract rate, it will receive an amount less than the face value.

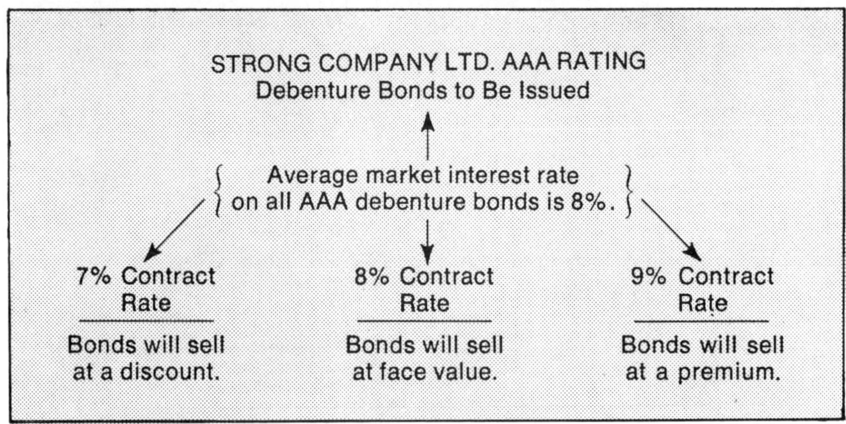

The second example will help to show that the financial condition of a company is not the basic determinant of the issue price of the company's bonds. Assume that Weak Company Ltd., with a BB financial rating, intends to issue first mortgage bonds. Further assume that the average effective market interest rate on BB first mortgage bonds is 9 percent. If Weak Company Ltd. issues its bonds with a 9 percent contract interest rate, it will receive the face value of the bonds. Even with its relatively poor credit rating, if it issues bonds with a 10 percent contract interest rate, is will receive an amount in excess of the face value; but if it issues bonds with an 8 percent contract interest rate, it will receive an amount less than the face value.

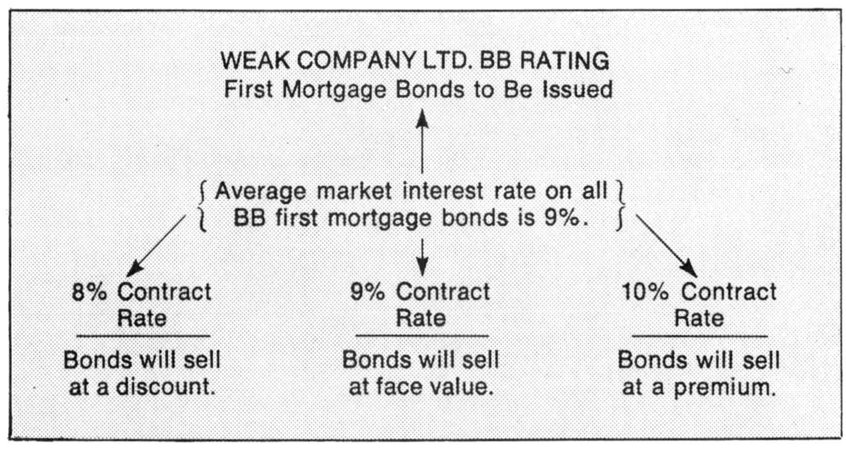

Accounting for Bonds Issued at a Premium

Assume that on July 1, the Hunt Corporation is authorized to issue 8% first mortgage bonds with a face value of $300,000 and that the bonds mature in 15 years. Interest is paid semiannually on June 30 and December 31. All the bonds are issued on July 1, at 103; that is, 103 percent of their face value; and the following entry is made:

Cash	309,000	
First Mortgage Bonds Payable		300,000
Premium on Bonds Payable		9,000

A balance sheet prepared on July 1 would show Bonds Payable and Premium on Bonds Payable as follows:

Long-Term Liabilities		
8% First Mortgage Bonds Payable, due June 30, 19XX	$300,000	
Premium on Bonds Payable	9,000	
Total Long-Term Liabilities		$309,000

The assets pledged as security for the bonds payable would be disclosed in the following footnote:

> Land and buildings costing $600,000 (market value $650,000) are pledged as security for the bonds payable.

This method of disclosure is consistent with the concept that the right side of the balance sheet describes the source of business funds. Of course, the Premium account will be reduced by periodic amortization and thus will be smaller on each subsequent statement; but, again, this procedure is consistent with the concept that when bonds are issued at a premium, each interest payment contains, in effect, a payment of the interest earned on the investment and also a partial return of the amount borrowed from the investor. If part of the $309,000 borrowed is repaid, a balance sheet prepared at a later date would naturally show a smaller amount. The footnote describing the assets pledged as security for the long-term debit is a disclosure of important information that may influence the decision of an investor to buy or not to buy the company's bonds.

The amount received from the issuance of the bonds is $9,000 greater than the amount that must be repaid at maturity. This amount is not a gain, for it is illogical to assume that revenue can result directly from the borrowing process. The premium arose because the contract rate of interest on the bonds issued was higher than the prevailing market rate on similar grade bonds; therefore, it is sound accounting practice to allocate part of the premium on bonds payable to each period as a reduction of the periodic bond interest expense. The straight-line method of allocation is most commonly used, and will be emphasized in this text; however, the compound interest method of premium and discount amortization is illustrated in the Appendix to this chapter. In summary, the total bond interest expense over the life of a bond issue is equal to the total amount of cash paid in interest reduced by the amount of the premium.

The bond interest expense of the Hunt Corporation is recorded on December 31, as follows:

Bond Interest Expense	11,700	
Premium on Bonds Payable	300	
Cash		12,000
To record the semiannual bond interest payment and amortization; the amount of the amortization is $\frac{1}{2} \times \frac{1}{15} \times \$9,000 = \$300$		

If the \$9,000 premium on the bonds payable represents a reduction in interest over the entire 15-year life of the bonds, it is evident that by the straight-line amortization method the reduction in interest for the six months ended December 31 is \$9,000 divided by 30 semiannual periods (calculated as $1/2 \times 1/15 \times \$9,000$ in the journal entry), or \$300.

This compound entry emphasizes that the \$12,000 constitutes the payment of effective bond interest expense of \$11,700 and a partial return of the amount borrowed, the \$300 amortized. (It is suggested that, for the problems in this text, premiums or discounts on bonds payable be amortized each time the bond interest expense is recorded to emphasize that this amortization is an adjustment of the bond interest expense.) Even though the compound entry is acceptable, two separate entries may be made: (1) one entry to record the payment of the semiannual bond interest, and (2) a separate entry to record the semiannual amortization of the premium.

Assuming the use of straight-line amortization of the premium on bonds payable, the validity of the \$11,700 semiannual bond interest figure can be established as follows:

Cash payments	
Face value of bonds at maturity	\$300,000
Total interest—8% × 15 years × \$300,000	360,000
Total cash payments	\$660,000
Cash receipts	
Bonds with face value of \$300,000 issued at 103	309,000
Net interest expense for 15 years	\$351,000
Net semiannual interest expense $\frac{\$351,000}{\text{30 semiannual periods}}$	\$ 11,700

Assume that the 8% first mortgage bonds payable are retired at maturity date. After the June 30 semiannual interest payment entry is made, the Premium on Bonds Payable account has a zero balance. The second entry, recording the retirement of the bonds at maturity, is similar to the one that records the retirement of Grogan Corporation bonds in the first bond example.

Bond Interest Expense	11,700	
Premium on Bonds Payable	300	
Cash		12,000

First Mortgage Bonds Payable	300,000	
Cash		300,000

Accounting for Bonds Issued at a Discount

Assume that on July 1, Ironson Company Ltd. is authorized to issue 7% debenture bonds with a face value of $400,000 and that these bonds mature in 10 years. Again, assume that interest is paid semiannually on June 30 and December 31. All the bonds are issued on July 1, at 97. The discount is caused by the difference in the prevailing market interest rate on similar grades of debenture bonds and the contract rate of interest on the bonds issued. In the case of Ironson Company Ltd.'s debenture bonds, their contract interest rate is lower than the prevailing market rate on a similar grade of securities. The issuance of these bonds may be recorded as follows:

Cash	388,000	
Discount on Bonds Payable	12,000	
Debenture Bonds Payable		400,000

A balance sheet prepared after the bond issuance on July 1 would disclose Bonds Payable and Discount on Bonds Payable as follows:

Long-Term Liabilities		
7% Debenture Bonds Payable, due June 30, 19XX	$400,000	
Deduct Discount on Bonds Payable	12,000	
Total Long-Term Liabilities		$388,000

Note the similarity of this method to the disclosure of a premium on bonds payable.

The following compound entry records the first semiannual interest payment by Ironson Company Ltd. and semiannual amortization of the Discount on Bonds Payable account.

Bond Interest Expense	14,600	
Cash		14,000
Discount on Bonds Payable		600
To record semiannual bond interest payment and amortization; the amount of amortization is $\frac{1}{2} \times \frac{1}{10} \times \$12,000 = \$600$		

This entry indicates that the effective semiannual interest expense is $14,600, not $14,000. Assuming that the straight-line method of amortization is used, the effective interest is equal to the cash interest payment plus a pro rata share of the discount, which is, in effect, a part of the total interest cost over the entire life of the bonds. This accounting procedure, therefore, recognizes the reason for the discount on the bonds—that the contract rate of interest was lower than the prevailing market interest rate on similar grades of securities.

Assuming the use of straight-line amortization of the discount on bonds payable, the proof of this semiannual bond interest expense can be established as follows:

Cash payments	
Face value of bonds at maturity	$400,000
Total interest—7% × 10 years × $400,000	280,000
Total cash payments	$680,000
Cash receipts	
Bonds with face value of $400,000 issued at 97	388,000
Net interest expense for 10 years	$292,000
Net semiannual interest expense $\frac{\$292,000}{\text{20 semiannual periods}}$	$ 14,600

At maturity date, the 7% debenture bonds payable are retired. After the June 30 semiannual interest payment entry is made, the Discount on Bonds Payable account has a zero balance. The second entry records the retirement of the bonds at maturity.

Bond Interest Expense	14,600	
Cash		14,000
Discount on Bonds Payable		600
Debenture Bonds Payable	400,000	
Cash		400,000

Amortization and End-of-Period Adjustments

The preceding examples emphasized the basic accounting procedures and the reasons for amortizing bond premiums and discounts. A more complex problem involving the issuance of bonds between interest dates is presented below.

Bonds may be authorized by the board of directors but not issued for several months or even years because market conditions are not favorable. Some of the bonds may be issued and the rest held until a specific need for the additional funds arises. Often, the time needed for clerical work delays issuance past an interest date. The interest on bonds issued between interest dates will have accrued from the last interest date to the date of issuance. Since the bonds carry an inherent promise to pay not only the face value at maturity but six months' interest at each interest date, it is customary in these cases for the investor to pay the issue price of the bonds plus an amount equal to the accrued interest. In turn, the first interest payment will be for one full interest period—six months' interest—thereby returning to the purchaser the accrued interest that he paid plus the interest earned from the date of purchase to the current interest date.

Assume that on April 1 Johnson Company Ltd. is authorized to issue 9% debenture bonds with a face value of $1,000,000 and that they mature in 102 months from the authorization date. The semiannual interest dates are April 1 and October 1.

The company holds the bonds until June 1 when bonds with a face value of $400,000 are floated at 105 plus accrued interest. The remaining life of the bonds from June 1 is now 100 months and the premium is amortized over this 100 months. The amount of cash that Johnson Company Ltd. receives is $426,000: $420,000 for the bonds plus $6,000 for accrued interest. Note that the promise to pay six month's interest is not retroactive beyond April 1, the interest date preceding the date of issuance.

Johnson Company Ltd. records the bond issuance as shown below.

Cash	426,000	
Debenture Bonds Payable		400,000
Premium on Bonds Payable		20,000
Accrued Bond Interest Payable		6,000

The accrued interest is credited to a current liability account, since it must be repaid on the next interest date.

On October 1, the purchaser of the bonds receives an interest payment of $18,000, although the interest on $400,000 at 9 percent from June 1 to October 1 is only $12,000. The payment includes a return of the $6,000 that the investor paid for accrued interest on June 1, as illustrated in Figure 13-1.

Figure 13-1
Accumulation of interest

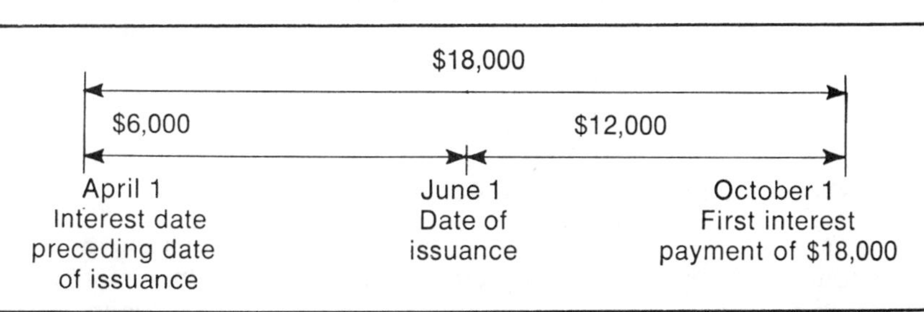

The entries to record the payment of semiannual interest and the amortization of bond premium are shown below.

Bond Interest Expense	12,000	
Accrued Bond Interest Payable	6,000	
Cash		18,000

The entry for the interest payment reflects the amount shown in Figure 13-1; that is, the semiannual cash payment includes a return of $6,000 for the accrued interest that was sold to the investor plus $12,000 for interest actually earned by the investor for the four months' use of his money.

Premium on Bonds Payable	800	
Bond Interest Expense		800
To record the amortization of the bond premium for four months: $20,000 ÷ 100 mos. × 4 = $800		

Note that amortization of the premium is made over the remaining life of the bonds from the date of issuance, that is, 100 months. Since the bonds were purchased on June 1, amortization is recorded for the four months from June 1 to October 1.

> The amortization covers only the period from the date of issuance to the maturity date.

The date of authorization and even the preceding interest date are not relevant to the start of the amortization period. For the bonds of Johnson Company Ltd., the amortization period begins on June 1, and ends 100 months later. The amount of bond premium to be amortized each month is $200 =($20,000 ÷ 100 mos.); the amount for four months is $800 =($200 × 4).

Assuming that Johnson Company Ltd. closes its books on a calendar-year basis, the following adjusting entries are made on December 31

Bond Interest Expense	9,000	
Accrued Bond Interest Payable		9,000
To record the accrual of bond interest for three months.		
Premium on Bonds Payable	600	
Bond Interest Expense		600
To record the amortization of bond premium for three months: 3 × $200 = $600		

The effect of the end-of-year adjustments is that the Bond Interest Expense account reflects the correct interest expense ($19,600) incurred for the seven months during which the bonds were outstanding (June 1 to December 31). The Bond Interest Expense account is closed to Income Summary. The Accrued Bond Interest Payable account is shown as a current liability on the balance sheet and remains on the books until the next regular interest date.

On April 1, the next regular interest date, the following entries are made to record the payment of interest and the amortization of the bond premium:

Bond Interest Expense	9,000	
Accrued Bond Interest Payable	9,000	
Cash		18,000
Premium on Bonds Payable	600	
Bond Interest Expense		600

Note that only three months' amortization of the bond premium is recorded. This coincides with the three months' bond interest expense incurred and recorded to April 1.

OTHER LONG-TERM LIABILITIES

Among long-term liabilities found on the balance sheet are those arising from the use of long-term financing devices such as secured or unsecured long-term notes and continuing obligations incurred under employee profit-sharing and pension plans and similar forms. Brief comments are made about each of these.

Instead of issuing bonds, a corporation may borrow from financial institutions, such as banks or insurance companies. A group of banks or insurance companies may jointly finance the transaction. By this arrangement, the corporation eliminates the need for dealing with many bondholders. The corporation issues long-term notes to the lending institutions. Such notes may also provide for a sinking fund and for a restriction on retained earnings. Notes are usually issued at face value; hence the accounting for these items is similar to that for short-term notes. They may be for a short period with optional renewal provisions. Renewable notes are often used when the bond interest rate is unfavorable.

Long-term financing may involve the pledging of specific assets. A corporation may, for example, acquire funds for plant expansion or other purposes by placing a mortgage on its plant and equipment. This creates a long-term liability—Mortgage Payable. Sometimes the lending institution advances funds for the construction of the plant and upon completion takes a mortgage on the newly constructed plant. This is known as a *construction mortgage payable.*

APPENDIX I Retirement and Refunding of Bonds Payable

The borrowing company may retire its outstanding bonds at the maturity date by paying the contract face value in cash. Even if the bonds were originally issued at a premium or a discount, the entry to record the retirement is a debit to Bonds Payable and a credit to Cash for the face value. Serial bonds are retired in serial installments. Assume, for example, a $500,000, 10-year serial bond issue, $50,000 to be retired at face value at the end of each year. The annual retirement entry is again a debit to Bonds Payable and a credit to Cash for $50,000. The retirement schedule is established by the issuing corporation and may provide for several retirement dates beginning a fixed number of years after the date of issue.

Other methods of retiring bonds include (1) the retirement of all or part of a bond issue by call, or purchase on the open market before the bonds are actually due, (2) the retirement of bonds by *refunding,* or refinancing by issuing new bonds on new terms, (3) the conversion of bonds payable into capital stock, and (4) the retirement of bonds with sinking fund assets and the attendant problem of accumulating the sinking fund.

Retirement of Bonds before Maturity. A corporation that has issued bonds may find itself with more cash than it expects to need for operations, thus permitting it to retire all or part of its outstanding bonded indebtedness prior to maturity date. Management may decide to retire the bonds immediately if the cash is available, if there appears to be no better alternative use now or in the future for the excess cash, and if it wishes to decrease the fixed charges for the bond interest. For bonds to be retired by a corporation before maturity, the indenture must contain a *call provision,* permitting the issuing corporation to redeem the bonds by paying a specified price, usually slightly above face value; or if the bonds are not callable, the issuing company may redeem them before the maturity date by purchasing them on the open market. Retirement of bonds below the carrying value adjusted to the date of retirement results in a gain; a loss is incurred if the purchase price exceeds the adjusted carrying value. Gains and losses on the retirement of bonds payable are classified in the income statement under Other Revenue or Other Expense.

Refunding. Bonds also may be retired by refunding, or refinancing by issuing new bonds on new terms. The proceeds from the new issue are specifically designated for the retirement of the old bond issue. The old bondholders may be given the option of exchanging their bonds for the new bonds at the call price. This procedure helps reduce the refinancing costs of the issuing corporation. A refunding decision may be warranted if it is possible to redeem bonds with a relatively high interest rate and to substitute bonds with a lower interest rate. Other reasons for refunding are to replace an issue about to mature with a new issue, thus extending the maturity date, or to retire outstanding bonds containing such stringent restrictive provisions as a closed mortgage lien or a requirement that funds be accumulated to retire the bonds.

In the accounting procedure for refunding, the retirement should be recorded in entries simila to those described in the preceding section. Accounting for the new issue is the same as described earlier in this chapter.

Conversion of Bonds into Common Stock. To make certain bonds more attractive to investors, and thus to increase their marketability, the bond agreement may give investors the option of exchanging bonds on a given interest date, or dates, for a certain number of shares of stock, usually common, of the issuing company. These securities, referred to as convertible bonds, have the advantage of offering the investor an initial fixed return on his investment combined with an opportunity to share in profitable operations of the issuing company by later conversion of the bonds to stock. The terms and conditions for conversion are designated in the bond indenture. Conversion is at the option of the bondholder, so that if earnings are unfavorable he does not need to exercise the conversion privilege and may retain the fixed return and greater security of the bonds. The conversion of bonds into stock changes the legal and accounting status of the security holder from creditor to owner. When conversion occurs, the generally accepted accounting procedure is to transfer the carrying value of the convertible bonds payable to share capital accounts, which probably will include both Common Stock and Premium on Common Stock.

Bond Sinking Fund. The borrowing corporation may agree in the bond indenture to accumulate funds to retire the bonds at maturity. Periodic cash payments are made to a sinking fund trustee, usually a bank or a trust company. These payments are ordinarily invested in revenue-producing securities. When the bonds mature, the sinking fund trustee sells the securities, and the proceeds are used to pay the bondholders. In some instances the corporation itself may act as trustee, thereby retaining control over the activities of the sinking fund.

To illustrate the operation of a simple nonactuarial sinking fund managed by trustee, assume that on the authorization date, January 1, Wells, Inc., issues 10-year sinking fund bonds with a face value of $500,000. The bond indenture provides that at the end of each year a deposit of $50,000—reduced by any net earnings of the funds from its investments—be made to the trustee. The entry to record the initial deposit with the trustee is shown below.

Bond Sinking Fund	50,000	
Cash		50,000
To record the initial sinking fund deposit with the trustee.		

The Bond Sinking Fund account is a controlling account. The trustee must invest all the available cash in the fund in revenue-producing securities. As a practical matter, it would not always be possible for the trustee to invest odd amounts of cash or to purchase securities immediately on the receipt of cash. Hence, the bond sinking fund is composed of a number of individual items, such as cash, securities, and accrued interest receivable. It is unnecessary for Wells, Inc., to maintain a separate general ledger account for each asset contained in the bond sinking fund.

If, at the end of the second year, the trustee reports net earnings of $1,500 from investments in bonds, the following entries record the second deposit:

Bond Sinking Fund	1,500	
Interest Earned		1,500
To record net earnings of the bond sinking fund per report of the trustee.		
Bond Sinking Fund	48,500	
Cash		48,500
To record the second sinking fund deposit with the trustee; the amount is $50,000 less earnings of $1,500, or $48,500.		

The following entry is made to record the retirement of the bonds at maturity by the payment of assets in the bond sinking fund:

	Debit	Credit
Sinking Fund Bonds Payable	500,000	
Bond Sinking Fund		500,000
To record the retirement of bonds by the trustee.		

The Bond Sinking Fund account is classified in the Assets section as a long-term investment on each balance sheet except the one prepared at the end of the year preceding the date of the retirement of the bonds. On this statement, Bond Sinking Fund should be shown as a current asset and Sinking Fund Bonds Payable should be disclosed as a current liability.

The actuarial method of accumulating a sinking fund provides for an equal sum to be deposited periodically with the trustee. It is assumed that these deposits, accumulating at compound interest, will equal the principal sum needed to retire the debt at maturity. This equal sum (in the Wells, Inc., case) is determined by dividing the required maturity amount of $500,000 by the amount of an ordinary annuity of 10 rents of $1 each at the estimated annual earning rate of the fund. If, at the retirement date, the accumulated funds exceed the required amount, the excess is returned by the trustee to the corporation; a shortage, on the other hand, requires an additional deficiency payment from the corporation.

Restriction on Retained Earnings for Bond Redemption. In addition to the requirement for sinking fund deposits, the bond indenture may require a restriction on retained earnings up to the amount in the sinking fund. The bondholders thus are provided with twofold protection: the sinking fund ensures the availability of adequate cash for the redemption of the bonds, and the restriction on retained earnings for bond redemption reduces the amount available for distribution as dividends to the shareholders. This restriction enhances the company's working capital position and its ability to meet its regular needs as well as its requirements for bond interest and bond sinking fund payments. An improved working capital position also is advantageous in enabling the company to meet its regular operational cash requirements and to maintain a favorable credit standing.

To illustrate, assume that the bond indenture of Wells, Inc., provides for a restriction of retained earnings. The entry at the end of each year is:

Date	Account	Debit	Credit
Dec. 31	Retained Earnings	50,000	
	Retained Earnings—Restricted for Bond Redemption		50,000
	To record the restriction of retained earnings equal to the annual increase in the bond sinking fund.		

Retained Earnings—Restricted for Bond Redemption is shown in the Shareholders' Equity section of the balance sheet under Retained Earnings. It should be noted that the provisions of the bond indenture may require (1) the creation of the bond sinking fund only, (2) a restriction on retained earnings until the bonds are redeemed only, or (3) both a sinking fund and a restriction on retained earnings. When the bonds are redeemed at maturity, the contractual restriction on retained earnings is removed. The journal entry to record the removal of the restriction is:

Jan.	1	Retained Earnings—Restricted for Bond Redemption	500,000	
		Retained Earnings		500,000
		To remove the restriction on retained earnings on retirement of the bonds.		

The unrestricted Retained Earnings account now has been increased by an amount equal to the maturity value of the bonds. The equivalent amount in funds may not be available for distribution to the shareholders, because it has been permanently committed to the operations of the business in the form of plant expansion or debt retirement. In essence, the shareholders have been contributing capital to the corporation through earnings retained in the business that might otherwise have been distributed as dividends. Formal recognition of this fact is often made in the form of a declaration of a stock dividend.

APPENDIX II Short-term Financing Devices

Business firms often find it more economical to use some means of short-term financing than to pay cash for various purchases. A popular form of short-term financing is the purchase of merchandise, supplies, and equipment on 30-, 60-, or 90-day open charge accounts. Cash terms—no carrying charges are assigned—are often extended for a period of ninety days or more. During this period, cash may be obtained from new sales and used to pay for merchandise obtained on the open charge accounts. This form of financing has already been discussed in Chapter 5. Several other short-term financing devices are considered in this appendix; they are:

1. Issuance of notes to trade creditors
2. Borrowing from banks on a company's own notes
3. Discounting notes receivable from customers

PROMISSORY NOTES

A *negotiable promissory note* may be defined as an unconditional written promise to pay a specified sum of money to the order of a designated person, or to bearer, at a fixed or determinable future time or on demand. The ownership of a negotiable promissory note is transferred simply by delivery if it is payable to the bearer; otherwise, it is transferred by endorsement and delivery.

Issuance of Notes for Merchandise. A business may use notes as a means of postponing payment for merchandise purchased for resale. For example, assume that on October 11, Able Company Ltd. purchases merchandise costing $1,800 from Baldwin Company Ltd. and issues a 9 percent, 45-day note to the creditor. The note and interest are paid on November 25. These transactions are recorded as follows:

Oct.	11	Purchases	1,800.00	
		Accounts Payable—Baldwin Company Ltd.		1,800.00
		To record merchandise purchased.		

			Debit	Credit
	11	Accounts Payable—Baldwin Company Ltd.	1,800.00	
		Notes Payable		1,800.00
		To record the issuance of a 9%, 45-day note to the Baldwin Company Ltd.		
Nov.	25	Notes Payable	1,800.00	
		Interest Expense	20.25	
		Cash		1,820.25
		To record payment of a note and interest to the Baldwin Company Ltd.		

NOTES RECEIVABLE FINANCING PROBLEM

Another financial device often employed to obtain short-term funds is discounting customers' notes receivable.

Receipt of a Note for a Sale

Assume that on March 5, Dawson Company Ltd. sells merchandise to John Roch and receives a 9 percent, 90-day note for $650. The following entries are made:

			Debit	Credit
Mar.	5	Accounts Receivable—John Roch	650	
		Sales		650
		To record sale of merchandise.		
	5	Notes Receivable	650	
		Accounts Receivable—John Roch		650
		To record the receipt of a 9%, 90-day note from John Roch.		

The first entry is made so that the customer's account in the subsidiary ledger will contain a complete record of all credit sales transactions. This information is useful to management in making decisions about collection efforts and further extension of credit.

On June 3, when Dawson Company Ltd. receives payment from John Roch, the following entry is made:

			Debit	Credit
June	3	Cash	664.63	
		Notes Receivable		650.00
		Interest Earned		14.63
		To record receipt of payment from John Roch for note and interest due today.		

The Interest Earned account is a revenue account. The balance of this account is closed at the end of the accounting period to the Income Summary account.

Dishonor of a Note Receivable by the Maker. If a note cannot be collected at maturity, it is said to be *dishonored* by the maker. Another term that is often used is *defaulting* on a note. Once the maturity date of a note passes without the note being collected, an entry should be made transferring the face value of the note plus any uncollected accrued interest to the Accounts Receivable account.

Assume that on June 1, Ronald Ronson issued a 9 percent, 90-day note for $2,000 to Dawson Company Ltd. At the maturity date, August 30, Ronson fails to pay the amount of the note and interest, at which time the following entry is made on the books of Dawson Company Ltd:

Aug.	30	Accounts Receivable—Ronald Ronson	2,045	
		Notes Receivable		2,000
		Interest Earned		45
		To record the dishonor by Ronald Ronson of a 9%, 90-day note.		

DISCOUNTING CUSTOMERS' NOTES RECEIVABLE

For a business that receives a large number of notes from customers, it may be economically advantageous to obtain cash by discounting these notes at a bank rather than hold them to maturity. If the credit rating of the firm is good, most banks will usually discount customers' notes receivable because, if the maker fails to pay the maturity value when it is due, the firm that has discounted the note—having previously endorsed it—must make payment to the bank.

This obligation is referred to as a *contingent liability.*

Assume that on April 19, Faison Company Ltd. receives from Edward Goodson a 9 percent, 60-day note for $2,000 in settlement of a past-due open account. This transaction is recorded as follows:

Apr.	19	Notes Receivable	2,000	
		Accounts Receivable—Edward Goodson		2,000
		To record receipt of a 9%, 60-day note from Goodson in settlement of a past-due open account.		

On May 1, Faison Company Ltd., needing short-term funds, decides to discount Goodson's note at a bank's rate of 8 percent. Calculation of the proceeds follows:

1. Maturity value of note (principal of $2,000 plus total interest of $30)		$2,030.00
2. Due date	June 18	
3. Period of discount:		
May 1–May 31 (not counting May 1)	30 days	
June 1–June 18 (including June 1)	18 days	
	48 days	
4. Discount at 8% for 48 days on the maturity value:		
Interest on $2,030 at 6% for 60 days	$20.30	
Less interest on $2,030 at 6% for 12 days (1/5 × $20.30)	4.06	
Interest on $2,030 at 6% for 48 days	$16.24	
Add interest on $2,030 at 2% for 48 days (1/3 × $16.24)	5.41	
Discount (or interest) on $2,030 at 8% for 48 days		21.65
Total cash proceeds		$2,008.35

Recording the Proceeds

The entry on Faison Company Ltd.'s books is:

May	1	Cash	2,008.35	
		Notes Receivable Discounted		2,000.00
		Interest Earned		8.35
		To record the discounting of Edward Goodson's 9%, 60-day note at the bank at 8%.		

The Notes Receivable Discounted account is used to indicate that Faison Company Ltd., having endorsed the note before turning it over to the bank, is now obligated to pay the bank if Goodson fails to do so; that is, Faison Company Ltd. would have to pay the $2,000 contingent liability plus the $30 interest at 9 percent for 60 days, plus any *protest fee* charged by the bank. The obligation assumed by Faison Company Ltd. is contingent on Goodson's payment, and the account is therefore referred to as a *contingent liability account.* This account brings the existence of the contingent liability to the attention of the reader of the statement of financial position.

Nonpayment of a Discounted Note

If Edward Goodson dishonors the note at the maturity date, the bank must follow a certain formal procedure to establish the legal basis for the collection of the full amount from Faison Company Ltd. Assuming that the bank charges a protest fee of $5, the following entries are made on Faison Company Ltd.'s books when the company pays the bank the face value of the note, the interest, and the protest fee.

June 18	Accounts Receivable—Edward Goodson	2,035	
	Cash		2,035
	To record payment of Edward Goodson's note, which was discounted and is now dishonored by Goodson:		

Protest Fee	$ 5
Interest	30
Face value	2,000
Total	$2,035

18	Notes Receivable Discounted	2,000	
	Notes Receivable		2,000
	To record the elimination of the contingent liability and Goodson's discounted and dishonored note.		

Note that Accounts Receivable, instead of Notes Receivable Discounted, is debited in the entry recording the cash payment. This procedure avoids the error of treating discounted notes as though they were actual liabilities; since payment is made as soon as the contingency is realized, no book liability need be recorded. The second journal entry is necessary to remove the contingent liability after the cash payment for the dishonored note is made.

The fact that a note is dishonored does not mean that it will be definitely uncollectible or that it should be written off to Allowance for Doubtful Accounts. Goodson, in this case, may pay at a later date, either voluntarily or on a court order. The account remains open in the accounts receivable ledger until it is settled or definitely determined to be uncollectible and written off.

APPENDIX III Compound-Interest Method of Premium and Discount Amortization

The exact price that an investor must pay for the bonds to yield a given effective rate can be determined by a compound interest computation or by reference to a *bond yield table.* To illustrate the compound interest computation, assume that a 10-year (20 semiannual periods), 8%, $1,000 bond with interest paid semiannually is to yield 6 percent (or 3 percent every six months). The issue price is calculated as shown below.

Present value of $1,000 for 20 periods at 3%:	
$1,000 × 0.553676	$ 553.68
Add present value of 20 interest payments of $40 each at 3%:	
$40 × 14.877475	595.10
Total price to yield 6% annually	$1,148.78

The computation by use of present value techniques of the exact price of an 8% 10-year $1,000 bond sold to yield 6 percent was determined to be $1,148.78 calculated above. If this bond were authorized and issued by the an 8% 10-year $1,000 bond sold to yield 6 percent was determined to be Edwards Corporation on January 1, Year 1, with a maturity date of December 31, Year 10, and with interest dates of June 30 and December 31, it would be recorded as follows:

Jan. 1	Cash	1,148.78	
	Bonds Payable		1,000.00
	Premium on Bonds Payable		148.78

An alternative to the straight-line method of amortization is the compound-interest method, sometimes called the *effective-yield* method of amortization. In other words, the interest expense is reported at the effective or yield rate multiplied by the carrying value of the bonds with the amount of amortization being the difference between the effective interest so computed and the nominal interest, calculated by multiplying the nominal interest rate by the face value of the bonds.

A formula for the approximation of effective interest rate (i) on bonds issued at a premium can be stated as follows:

$$i = I \div \left(F + \frac{P}{2}\right)$$

where I = annual absolute interest, adjusted for amortization of premium
F = face value of bonds
P = total premium (so that $\frac{P}{2}$ = average premium)

The effective interest rate on the Hunt Corporation bonds, mentioned on page 369, is approximately 7.68 percent [$23,400 ÷ ($300,000 + $9,000/2)]—that is, the absolute effective amount of annual interest divided by the average carrying value (face value plus unamortized premium) of the bonds issued. Exact effective rates may be determined readily from bond yield tables or by using compound interest techniques. The effective interest rate computation emphasizes the fact that the premium on the bonds results in a downward adjustment of the 8 percent contract rate to the effective rate.

The effective-interest calculation and attendant compound-interest amortization for the Edwards Corporation for June 30 and December 31 appear below.

June 30	Bond Interest Expense (3% × $1,148.78)	34.46	
	Premium on Bonds Payable ($40.00 − $34.46)	5.54	
	Cash		40.00
Dec. 31	Bond Interest Expense [(3% × ($1,148.78 − $5.54)]	34.30	
	Premium on Bonds Payable ($40.00 − $34.30)	5.70	
	Cash		40.00

A formula for the approximation of effective interest rate (i) on bonds issued at a discount can be stated as follows:

$$i = I \div \left(F - \frac{D}{2}\right)$$

where I = annual absolute interest, adjusted for amortization of discount
F = face value of bonds
D = total discount (so that $\frac{D}{2}$ = average discount)

It should be noted that the foregoing procedure will produce a constant yield on the carrying value of the bonds payable, face plus unamortized premium or face minus unamortized discount. Compare this with the results achieved with the straight-line method of amortization: a constant absolute interest amount related to bond carrying value that will be reduced over time will produce an "effective" interest rate that increases in subsequent years. The compound-interest method of amortization is superior to the straight-line method because of this peculiarity; but because of the complexity of the compound-interest calculation, the attendant effective-yield method of amortization is seldom used in practice.

GLOSSARY

Amortization of Premium or Discount on Bonds Payable The periodic writing off of the premium or discount on bonds payable as a decrease or an increase to interest expense; amortization can be accomplished by the straight-line method or by the compound-interest method.

Bearer Bond A bond issued without the owner's name being registered; the title to this kind of bond is deemed to be vested in the holder of the bond.

Bond A written promise under the corporate seal to pay a specified sum of money on a specified or determinable future date to the order of a person named in the bond certificate or to the order of bearer.

Bond Certificate Evidence that a loan has been made to a corporation; it contains the written promise under the corporate seal to pay a specific sum of money on a specified or determinable future date to the order of a person named in the certificate or to the order of bearer.

Bondholder A creditor who has lent money to a corporation or government and has received a bond certificate as evidence of the loan.

Bond Indenture A contract between the corporation issuing bonds and the bondholder; it will contain all privileges, restrictions, covenants, and other provisions, contained in this form of contract.

Bond Sinking Fund Segregation of assets for the purpose of retiring bonds usually at maturity.

Callable Bond A bond for which the issuing corporation retains an option to retire the bonds before maturity at a specified price on specific dates.

Carrying Value of Bonds Payable The face or principal amount of the bonds payable plus the unamortized premium, or face minus the unamortized discount on bonds payable.

Compound-Interest Method of Amortization Sometimes referred to as the effective-yield method of amortization; the periodic amortization is the difference between the nominal rate of interest computed on the face value of the bonds and the effective-yield rate of interest computed on the book value of the investment at the beginning of the current interest period.

Contingent Liability An amount that may become a liability in the future *if* certain events occur.

Contract or Nominal Interest Rate The rate of interest that is written in a bond indenture; it is the rate based on face or principal amount that will be paid on the stated periodic interest dates.

Convertible Bond A bond that contains a provision entitling the bondholder to exchange the bond for capital stock at the bondholder's option.

Coupon Bond A bond that has the periodic interest coupon attached to the bond certificate.

Current Liabilities Obligations the liquidation of which requires the use of current assets or the creation of other current liabilities within a year or an operating cycle whichever is the longer period.

Debenture Bond Often referred to as a debenture; it is an unsecured bond—one that carries no specific pledge of collateral.

Discount on Bonds Payable The amount by which the face value of bonds exceeds the price received for the bonds on issuance; it arises because the nominal (contract) rate of interest is lower than the going market rate of interest on similar grade bonds.

Discount on Notes Payable An account which discloses the amounts (or unexpired portion thereof) subtracted from the maturity value of notes payable to arrive at proceeds. As such, it represents future interest expense; it should be disclosed on the statement of financial position as a contra item to the applicable Notes Payable account.

Dishonored Note A note that has not been paid by the maker at the maturity date.

Effective-Yield Rate The constant rate of interest that, when applied to all future cash flows from an investment on a discount basis, will reduce those flows to the present market price or value of the investment.

Income Bond A bond with a provision that interest payments will depend upon earnings.

Leverage Usually refers to the practice of trading on the bondholders' equity; that is, the practice of borrowing money at a given rate of interest and utilizing the borrowed funds in the business to earn a higher rate of return than the borrowing rate.

Notes Payable A promissory note issued by an individual or a firm; it is a liability account of the issuing firm.

Notes Receivable A promissory note received from a customer or client; it represents an asset to the owner of the note.

Notes Receivable Discounted An account that discloses the contingent liability for customers' notes which have been discounted with others and endorsed either in blank or in full.

Premium on Bonds Payable The excess of the price received for bonds payable above face value; it arises because the nominal (contract) rate of interest is higher than the going market rate of interest on similar grade bonds.

Promissory Note An unconditional written promise to pay a specified sum of money to the order of a designated person, or to bearer, at a fixed or determinable future time or on demand.

Registered Bond A bond whose owner's name is recorded by the issuing corporation; for this bond to be transferred to another individual, it must be endorsed and a request must be filed to have the owner's name changed on the records of the issuing corporation.

Secured Bond A bond for which the issuing corporation pledges some part of the firm's property as security in case of financial difficulty.

Serial Bonds Bonds that mature in periodic installments and will be paid at stated intervals of time.

Trading on the Bondholders' Equity A practice of borrowing money at a given rate of interest and utilizing the borrowed funds in the business to earn a higher rate of return than the borrowing rate.

Unearned Interest An amount included in the face value of a note receivable; it represents future interest revenue, and should be disclosed on the statement of financial position as a contra item to Notes Receivable.

Unsecured Bond A bond for which there is no specific pledge of assets for security; these are also called debenture bonds.

QUESTIONS

Q13-1. Distinguish between *nominal* and *effective* interest rates on bonds.

Q13-2. On January 1, 19XX, Durham Sales Company Ltd. issued 20-year, 8% bonds having a face value of $2,000,000. Interest is payable semiannually on June 30 and December 31. The proceeds to the company were $1,900,000; that is, on January 1, 19XX, the bonds had a market price of 95% of face value. Explain the nature of the $100,000 difference between the face value and the market value of the bond on January 1, 19XX.

Q13-3. What is the difference (a) between a stock certificate and a bond? (b) between a bond and a promissory note?

Q13-4. Identify the following terms: (a) registered bonds, (b) bearer bonds, (c) secured bonds, (d) unsecured bonds, (e) serial bonds, (f) convertible bonds, (g) coupon bonds, (h) income bonds.

Q13-5. A corporation needs cash for the acquisition of plant and equipment. It is considering three alternative sources: additional common stock, 9% preferred stock, and 8% bonds. (a) What are some of the factors involved in this decision? (b) Will the decision affect the present common shareholders? Discuss.

Q13-6. (a) What are the general requirements for the approval of a bond issue? (b) Should the shareholders always approve a bond issue? Why?

Q13-7. (a) Why does the buyer of a bond purchased between interest dates pay the seller for accrued interest on the bond? (b) Is the accrued interest included in the stated purchase price of the bond?

Q13-8. Why are bonds not always issued at the prevailing interest rate, thereby eliminating bond discount or bond premium?

Q13-9. (a) What is the difference to the issuing corporation between common stock issued at a premium and bonds issued at a premium? (b) Does revenue result from either?

Q13-10. On December 31, 19XX, a corporation has serial bonds outstanding with a face value of $1,000,000. These bonds mature annually in $200,000 amounts, beginning June 30, 19X2. How will this be shown on the balance sheet as of December 31, 19X1, (b) December 31, 19X2, and (c) December 31, 19X3?

Q13-11. (Appendix II). The accountant for the Virgin Islands Limited recorded the receipt of a note on a sale to Joseph Sales as follows:

Notes Receivable	875	
Sales		875

State how you think the transaction should have been recorded and give your reason.

Q13-12. (Appendix II). The Saxon Limited negotiated with the First Bank a 90-day loan (reference l),which was paid on its due date (reference m).It arranged with the Second Bank for another 90-day loan (reference x), which was also paid when due (reference y).

Cash		Notes Payable to Bank		Interest Expense	
(l) 3,000	(m) 3,045	(m) 3,000	(l) 3,000	(m) 45	
(x) 2,955	(y) 3,000	(y) 3,000	(x) 3,000	(x) 45	

Describe the type of negotiable instrument used (a) by the First Bank; (b) by the Second Bank. (c) Which loan is more favorable to the Saxon Limited? Why?

Q13-13. (Appendix II). The following account balances appear in the general ledger of the Hobson Limited:

Notes Receivable		Notes Payable		Notes Receivable Discounted	
70,000			40,000		30,000

(a) What is the amount of customer notes outstanding? (b) What is the amount of customer notes in the Hobson Limited's possession? (c) What is the amount of discounted customer notes? (d) What is the Hobson Limited's contingent liability on discounted notes? (e) Do the accounts furnish enough data to compute the company's working capital position? (f) How would these accounts be shown in the balance sheet?

Q13-14. (Appendix II). Six transactions related to a sale to a customer are recorded in the T accounts below. Describe each transaction.

Cash		Accounts Receivable		Notes Receivable	
(c) 1,808	(d) 1,822	(a) 1,800	(b) 1,800	(b) 1,800	(e) 1,800
(e) 1,832		(d) 1,822	(f) 1,822		

Notes Receivable Discounted		Sales		Interest Earned	
(e) 1,800	(c) 1,800		(a) 1,800		(c) 8
					(f) 10

Q13-15. (Appendix II). (a) What is a contingent liability? (b) May there be more than one person contingently liable on a particular note? Explain. (c) What items must a person who is contingently liable on an interest-bearing note pay if the maker dishonors the note on its due date?

DEMONSTRATION PROBLEMS

DP13-1. (*Accounting for the issuance of bonds*) In each of the following cases, assume (a) 8% bonds with a face value of $1,000,000, (b) date of authorization, January 1, 19XX, (c) interest payable each January 1 and July 1,(d) the bonds mature in 10 years, and (e) year ends December 31.

	Case A	*Case B*	*Case C*	*Case D*	*Case E*
Date of issuance	Jan. 1	Jan. 1	Jan. 1	Mar. 1	Jan. 1
Issue price	100	102	97	101 plus accrued interest	at a price to yield 10%

Required:

1. For cases A, B, C, and D, prepare all journal entries, assuming the use of the straight-line amortization method.
2. For case E, prepare all journal entries for 19XX, assuming the use of the compound interest method of amortization.
3. For cases B and C, prepare a schedule proving the interest cost for 19XX by the straight-line amortization method.
4. For cases B and C, calculate the approximate effective interest rate.

DP13-2. (Appendix I: ***Retirement of bonds)*** on April 1, Year 1, Sanford Company Ltd. issued 8% bonds with a face value of $600,000 at 106 plus accrued interest. The bonds mature in 100 months, and interest is paid each February 1 and August 1. On December 1, Year 2, Sanford Company Ltd. purchased its own bonds with a face value of $200,000 on the open market at 102 plus accrued interest.

Required: Assuming that the books of Sanford Company Ltd. are closed each December 31, prepare all the entries relevant to the bonds for Year 1 and Year 2.

DP13-3. (Appendix I: ***Bond sinking fund)*** On the date of authorization, January 1, 19X1, the Pittsboro Corporation issued four-year sinking fund bonds with a face value of $800,000 at 100. The sinking fund indenture requires an annual contribution at the end of each of the four years to provide for the retirement of the bonds at maturity. As an added protection, the terms of the bond indenture require that retained earnings be restricted in an annual amount equal to the total addition to the sinking fund. The Pittsboro Corporation is to make a deposit to the Anytown Bank, which has been named trustee of the sinking fund, of amounts that when added to the sinking fund earnings will total $200,000 each year. The Anytown Bank guaranteed the Pittsboro Corporation a return of 8% annually. The bank will credit the Sinking Fund account with this return each December 31.

Required:

1. Record the issuance of the sinking fund bonds.
2. Give all the entries for the four years to record the deposits to the sinking fund and the related restrictions on retained earnings.
3. Record the retirement of the sinking fund bonds by the trustee on the maturity date and the removal of the retained earnings restriction.

DP13-4. (Appendix II: *Journalizing notes payable transactions)* The Watson Limited completed the following transactions:

Year 1

Jan.	2	Purchased $4,800 worth of merchandise from the Nunn Company; issued a 9%, 60-day note.
Mar.	3	Paid the Nunn Company the amount due for the note and interest.
	3	Issued a 9%, 45-day note for $3,600 to Cohoon, Inc., in settlement of an open account.
Apr.	17	Paid Cohoon, Inc., $2,600 on the March 3 note plus all the interest; issued a new 10%, 30-day note for the balance of the principal.
May	17	Paid Cohoon, Inc., for the April 17 note.
Dec.	1	Issued to the Queens Company a 9%, 90-day note for $6,000 in settlement of an open account.

Year 2

Mar.	1	Paid the amount due to Queens Company for the note issued on December 1.

Required: Journalize the transactions, including any necessary adjustment entries on December 31, of each year.

DP13-5. (Appendix II: *Journalizing notes receivable transactions)* The following were among the transactions of the Ranson Limited.

Year 1

Jan.	6	Sold merchandise worth $2,400 to Harry Geer and received a 9%, 45-day note.
Feb.	20	Collected the amount due from Harry Geer.
Mar.	1	Received a 9%, 75-day note for $3,600 from N. O. Ricardo in set-
June	1	Sold merchandise worth $3,000 to Gene Bettie and received a 90-day, non-interest-bearing note for the amount of the sale plus interest at 9%.
Aug.	30	Collected the amount due from Gene Bettie.
Nov.	16	Received a 9%, 120-day note for $4,800 from J. T. Tomkins in settlement of an open account.
Dec.	1	Received a 90-day, non-interest-bearing note from Janie Council in settlement of an open account of $4,000. Interest of $90 was included in the face value.

Year 2

Mar.	1	Received the amount due from Janie Council.
	16	Received the amount due from J. T. Tomkins.

Required: Journalize the transactions, including any necessary adjusting entries on December 31 of each year.

DP13-6. (Appendix II: *Journalizing notes discounted transactions)* Record in general journal form the following note transactions on the books of Ben Johnson, the maker, and Walter Hinton, the payee:

1. On July 1, Ben Johnson purchased $4,400 worth of merchandise on account from Walter Hinton.
2. Ben Johnson gave to Walter Hinton a 9%, 90-day note, dated August 21, in settlement of his account.
3. On August 31, Walter Hinton discounted Ben Johnson's note at the Bank of Vancouver at a discount rate of 9%.
4. On maturity date, Ben Johnson paid the bank the maturity value of the note.

PROBLEMS

P13-1. On the date of authorization, January 1, the Columbia Corporation issued 10-year, 9% bonds with a face value of $500,000 at 102. Interest is payable each January 1 and July 1.

1. Record the issuance of the bonds.
2. Record the first interest payment.
3. Record the accrued interest expense on December 31.

P13-2. On the date of authorization, January 1, the Columbia Corporation issued 10-year, 9% bonds with a face value of $500,000 at 102. Interest is payable each January 1 and July 1.

1. Record the issuance of the bonds.
2. Record the first interest payment and amortization of the premium by the straight-line amortization method.
3. Record the accrued interest expense and amortization of the premium on December 31.

P13-3. (Appendix III). On the date of authorization, July 1, Year 1, Baker Investment Company Ltd. issued 10-year, 8% bonds with a face value of $1,000,000 at a price to yield 10%. Interest is payable June 30 and December 31.

1. Compute the value of the bonds to yield 10% (that is, 5% each six months).
2. Record the issuance of the bonds on July 1, Year 1.
3. Record the December 31, and June 30, interest payments with accompanying amortization, using the effective-yield, or compound interest, method of amortization.
4. Briefly compare the reasons for using the effective-yield method of amortization as compared to the straight-line method of amortization.

P13-4. On the date of authorization, July 1, Year 1, the Carter Corporation issued 20-year, 8% bonds with a face value of $600,000 at 98. Interest is payable each January 1 and July 1.

1. Record the issuance of the bonds.
2. Record the accrued interest expense and amortization of the discount on December 31, Year 1.
3. Record the interest payment on July 1, Year 2, and amortization of the discount by the straight-line amortization method.

P13-5. On October 1, 19XX, the Myrtle Corporation issued 8% bonds with a face value of $500,000 at 103 plus accrued interest. The bonds mature in 92 months from date of issuance and interest is paid each June 1 and December 1. The straight-line amortization of premium is recorded each time bond interest expense is recorded. Prepare all the entries relating to the bond issue during 19XX.'

P13-6. (Appendix I). As authorized, January 1, Year 1, the Richey Corporation issued 10-year bonds with a face value of $2,000,000. Under the terms of the bond indenture, a sinking fund is to be maintained to provide for the retirement of the bonds at maturity. Deposits are to be made with a trustee at the end of each year in amounts that, when added to the sinking fund earnings, will total $200,000. Record (a) the deposit with the trustee on December 31, Year 1, (b) earnings of $17,500 during the second year, (c) the deposit with the trustee on December 31, Year 2, and (d) the retirement of the bonds at maturity by the trustee.

P13-7. (Appendix I). Assume the bonds in P13-6 require a restriction on retained earnings equal to the amount of the sinking fund. Record (a) the restriction at the end of Year 1 and Year 2 and (b) the removal of the restriction at the maturity date.

P13-8. On the date of authorization, January 1, 19X1, Wellon Company Ltd. issued 10-year 8% bonds. Interest is paid semiannually on January 1 and July 1. On July 1, 19X1, the accountant for Wellon Company Ltd. prepared the following journal entry to record the payment of bond interest and the straight-line amortization of the discount.

July 1	Bond Interest Expense	14,350	
	Cash		14,000
	Discount on Bonds Payable		350
	To record the bond interest expense for the preceding six months.		

From this information, reconstruct the journal entry that was made to record the issuance of the bonds. Show all your calculations.

P13-9. (Appendix I). On July 1, 19X1, Safetee Company Ltd. issued 10-year bonds with a face value of $1,000,000. As required by the indenture, a sinking fund is to be maintained to provide for the retirement of the bonds at maturity. The sinking fund will earn an annual return of 8% Beginning June 30, 19X2, ten annual, *equal* deposits are to be made to the sinking fund. Using the actuarial method—that is, appropriate compound interest techniques—compute the amount of the equal deposits to the sinking fund.

P13-10. (Appendix II). The following were among the transactions of the Trollingwood Limited.

Jan. 2	Purchased $5,000 worth of merchandise from the Biltmore Company, and issued a 9%, 45-day note.
Feb. 16	Paid note and interest due the Biltmore Company.
Mar. 15	Issued a 10%, 90-day note to the Melton Company in settlement of an open account of $4,000.
June 13	Paid the Melton Company $3,000 on principal and all the interest for the preceding 90 days; issued a new 9%, 60-day note for the balance of the principal.
Aug. 12	Paid the remaining amount due the Melton Company.
Dec. 1	Issued a 9%, 90-day note to the Donnan Company in settlement of an open account of $8,000.

Year 2
Mar. 1 Paid the amount due the Donnan Company.

Journalize the transactions, including any necessary adjusting entries on December 31, Year 1.

P13-11. (Appendix II). The following were among the transactions of the Easley Corporation.

Year 1
Apr. 19 Sold merchandise worth $900 to H. H. Nixon and received a 9%, 60-day note.
June 18 Collected the amount due from H. H. Nixon.
June 21 Received a 9%, 120-day note from A. C. Deece in settlement of an open account for $3,000.
Oct. 19 A. C. Deece dishonored his note.
Nov. 15 Received a 9%, 90-day note from I. M. Gooding in settlement of an open account of $4,000.
Year 2
Feb. 13 Collected the note and interest from I. M. Gooding.

Journalize the transactions, including any necessary adjusting entries as of December 31, Year 1.

P13-12. (Appendix II). On September 5, 19X1,the Best Limited sold $3,600 worth of merchandise to Bazley Limited on account and received a 9%, 60-day note. This note was discounted at 9% on October 20, 19XX, at the Foxboro Bank. At maturity date the note was dishonored by the Bazley Limited, and the Best Limited paid the maturity value plus a $3 protest fee. Journalize the transactions on the books of the Best Limited.

P13-13. On the date of authorization, March 1, 19XX, the Greensboro Corporation issued 10-year, 8% bonds with a face value of $600,000 at 103. Interest is payable each March 1 and September 1.

Required: Record the following transactions: (a) issuance of the bonds, (b) first interest payment and straight-line amortization of the premium, (c) accrual of interest on December 31 and amortization of the premium.

P13-14. On the date of authorization, April 1, 19XX, Boone Company Ltd. issued 20-year, 7% bonds with a face value of $500,000 at 97. Interest is payable each April 1 and October 1.

Required: Record the following transactions during 19XX: (a) issuance of the bonds, (b) first interest payment and straight-line amortization of the discount, (c) accrual of interest on December 31, 19XX, and amortization of the discount.

P13-15. On April 1, Year 1, the shareholders of the Samuel Corporation authorized the issuance of 20-year, 8% first mortgage bonds with a face value of $1,000,000. Interest is payable each April 1 and October 1.

Required: Make journal entries to record the following transactions:

Year 1
June 1 Issued bonds at 102 plus accrued interest.

Oct. 1 Paid the semiannual interest. (Assume that premium on bonds payable is amortized by the straight-line method each time bond interest expense is recorded.)

Dec. 31 Accrued the bond interest.

31 Closed the Bond Interest Expense account.

Year 2

Apr. 1 Paid the semiannual interest.

Oct. 1 Paid the semiannual interest.

Dec. 31 Accrued the bond interest.

P13-16. Selected accounts from three trial balances of the Cameron Corporation are presented.

	Adjusted		*Unadjusted*
	12/31/X1	12/31/X2	12/31/X3
Debits			
Bond Interest Expense	$ 7,100	$ 42,600	$ 31,950
Credits			
Accrued Bond Interest Payable	11,250	11,250	-0-
9% Bonds Payable—issued 11/1/X1	500,000	500,000	500,000
Premium on Bonds Payable	23,400	21,000	19,200

The data from the adjusted trial balances are correct. The bonds were issued between interest payment dates.

Required:

1. Compute the following:(a) original issue price as of November 1, 19X1, (b) maturity date, (c) semiannual interest payment dates.
2. Reconstruct the journal entry to record the issuance of the bonds on November 1, 19X1.
3. Prepare any required adjusting entries as of December 31, 19X3.

P13-17. (Appendix II). On July 1, Year 1, the Isaiah Corporation issued 10-year, 9% bonds with a face value of $1,000,000 at a price to yield 8%. Interest is payable June 30 and December 31.

Required: Prepare journal entries to record the following transactions, assuming that the compound interest amortization method (effective-yield method) is used.

Year 1

July 1 Issued all the bonds for cash.

Dec. 31 Paid the semiannual interest and recorded the proper amortization.

Year 2

June 30 Paid the semiannual interest and recorded the proper amortization.

Dec. 31 Paid the semiannual interest and recorded the proper amortization.

P13-18. On March 1, Year 1, the authorization date, Abraham Company Ltd. issued 10-year, 10% debenture bonds with a face value of $400,000 at 106. Interest is payable each March 1 and September 1. The company closes its books on

December 31. The following selected transactions and adjustments were made:

Year 1
Mar. 1 Issued all the bonds for cash.
Sept. 1 Paid the semiannual interest.
Dec. 31 Accrued the bond interest.

Year 2
Mar. 1 Paid the semiannual interest.

At maturity
Mar. 1 Paid the semiannual interest.
1 Paid the bonds outstanding at maturity.

Required: Record the foregoing transactions. (Assume that the premium is amortized by the straight-line method each time the bond interest expense is recorded.)

P13-19. (Appendix I). On January 1, Year 1, the Jacob Corporation authorized and issued 10-year, 8% sinking fund bonds with a face value of $1,000,000. It provided (a) for an annual deposit with a trustee at the end of each year of $100,000 less sinking fund earnings since the previous deposit and (b) for an annual restriction on retained earnings.

Required: Record the following selected transactions relating to the bond issue:

Year 1
Dec. 31 Made the initial deposit with the sinking fund trustee.
31 Made the restriction on retained earnings.

Year 2
Dec. 31 Received a report of sinking fund earnings of $7,600.
31 Made the deposit with the sinking fund trustee.
31 Made the restriction on retained earnings.

At maturity
Dec. 31 Paid the bonds at maturity.
31 Removed the contractual restriction on retained earnings.

P13-20. David Company Ltd. issued 10-year 8% bonds on September 1, at a certain price plus accrued interest. The bonds were authorized on June 1. Interest is paid each June 1 and December 1. The accountant for the company recorded the first semiannual bond interest payment as follows:

Dec. 1	Bond Interest Expense	6,274	
	Accrued Bond Interest Payable	5,314	
	Discount on Bonds Payable		960
	Cash		10,628
	To record the payment of semiannual bond interest and the straight-line amortization of the discount for three months.		

Required:

1. Compute the following: (a) face value of bonds issued, (b) original issue price and discount.

2. Reconstruct the journal entry to record the issuance of the bonds on September 1.

P13-21. (Appendix II). The Los Alto Limited completed the following transactions with Hoot Holton:

Jan.	10	Sold $2,000 worth of merchandise to Holton on account.
Mar.	1	Received a 9%, 60-day note in full settlement of the account.
	17	Discounted the note at 8% at the Branch Bank.
May	5	Received a notice from the bank that Holton failed to honor the note due on April 30.
	5	Paid the bank the maturity value of the note plus a protest fee of $3.50.
	19	Received a check from Holton for the full amount due, plus interest at 9% on the maturity value of the old note from the due date to the present.

Required: Record the transactions in general journal form on the books of the Los Alto Limited.

14

Investments

Most companies have excess cash available at times and invest this excess cash in shares and bonds of other companies on a temporary or long-term basis. Temporary investments are simply marketable securities that can and will be converted into cash in a relatively short period of time when there is a seasonal shortage of cash. Long-term investments that are capable of reasonably prompt liquidation can be classified as current assets on the balance sheet. Long-term investments that are not capable of reasonably prompt liquidation should be shown on the balance sheet as noncurrent assets.[1]

TEMPORARY INVESTMENTS IN MARKETABLE SECURITIES

Marketable securities include Canadian government bonds, widely traded industrial stocks and bonds that are listed on the various stock exchanges, as well as treasury bills, investment certificates, and call loans.[2]

TEMPORARY INVESTMENT IN BONDS

Assume that on March 1, 19XX, Owens Company purchases as temporary investments 6% bonds of Peters Company Ltd. with a face value of $30,000 at 102 plus accrued interest. Interest is paid on January 1 and July 1. The brokerage fee and other costs incident to the purchase are $60. This information is recorded as follows:

Mar.	1	Temporary Investment Bonds of Peters Company Ltd.	30,660	
		Accrued Bond Interest Receivable	300	
		Cash		30,960

[1] *CICA Handbook* (Toronto: Canadian Institute of Chartered Accountants), Section 3010.02.
[2] *Loc. cit.*

1. In accordance with the generally accepted principle of recording all assets at cost, Temporary Investments are recorded at full cost, including the brokerage fee and other incidental costs.

2. The transaction involves the purchase of two different assets: the bonds and the accrued bond interest. The amount of the accrued interest should be set up in a separate account since it is a different asset.

The receipt of semiannual interest on July 1, is recorded as follows:

July	1	Cash	900	
		Accrued Bond Interest Receivable		300
		Bond Interest Earned		600

1. The six months' interest represents a collection of the receivable that was purchased on March 1 and the amount of interest that was earned for the four-month period from March 1 to July 1.
2. Note that the premium element of the cost of the bonds is not amortized. Neither the premium element nor the discount element of the cost of bonds purchased as *temporary investments* is amortized, because the purchasing firm is uncertain about how long it will hold the temporary investments. On the other hand, the premium or the discount on bonds purchased as long-term investments *is amortized*.

To complete the cycle, assume that on August 1, 19XX, Owens Company found that it needed cash and decided to sell the bonds of the Peters Company Ltd. They were sold at 101¾ (net of brokerage fees and other costs) plus accrued interest; the transaction is recorded as follows:

Aug.	1	Cash	30,675	
		Loss on Disposal of Temporary Investments	135	
		Temporary Investments—Bonds of Peters Company Ltd.		30,660
		Bond Interest Earned		150

1. The computation of the loss on disposal of temporary investments is:

Original full cost of bonds	$30,660
Selling price of bonds ($30,000 × 101.75%)	30,525
Loss on disposal of temporary investments	$ 135

2. The cash received comes from two sources: the sale of the bonds, $30,525, and the sale of the accrued interest, $150.
3. The temporary investments account must be credited with the same amount, the cost, for which it was originally debited.

Loss on Disposal of Temporary Investments is shown in the income statement under Other Expenses. Management must consider this loss, along with the Bond Interest Earned, in evaluating the success of its decision to invest in the bonds of Peters Company Ltd.

TEMPORARY INVESTMENT IN STOCKS

To illustrate the recording of a purchase of stock as a temporary investment, assume that on April 1, 19XX, Arlex Company purchases 200 shares of Hurley Corporation Ltd. $100 par value preferred stock at $105 per share. Brokerage fees are $108. The entry to record the purchase is:

Apr.	1	Temporary Investments— Preferred Stock of Hurley Corporation Ltd.	21,108	
		Cash		21,108

1. The amount of the debit to the asset is the full cost. The par value is of no significance to the investor except as a possible base to measure the amount of dividends to be received when the dividend rate is stated as a percentage of par value.
2. Dividends do not legally accrue; therefore, no recognition is given to this feature even for preferred stock until the dividend is actually declared. If Hurley Corporation Ltd. had declared a dividend on its preferred stock, and Arlex Company had purchased the 200 shares between the declaration date and the dividend record date, then Arlex Company should divide the purchase price between Temporary Investments and Dividends Receivable. One important facet of stock market behavior should be mentioned. The market price of both common and preferred stock reflects investors' anticipation of the ultimate declaration of dividends. In other words, if all other variables were constant, the market price of stock on which dividends are regularly declared would go up gradually from one dividend date to the next in approximately the same manner that interest accrues on bonds. On the dividend record date, the market price per share would drop by the amount of the dividend per share.

Assume that on July 1, 19XX, a quarterly dividend of $1.50 per share is received on the 200 shares of Hurley Corporation Ltd. stock. The entry to record the dividend is:

July	1	Cash	300	
		Dividends Earned		300

Dividends Earned is classified under Other Revenue on the income statement.

Again, to meet a seasonal cash shortage, on September 15, 19XX, the preferred stock of Hurley Corporation Ltd. is sold for $106.50 per share (net of brokerage fees and other costs). The sale is recorded as follows:

Sept.	15	Cash	21,300	
		Temporary Investments— Preferred Stock of Hurley Corporation Ltd.		21,108
		Gain on Disposal of Temporary Investments		192

Gain on disposal of temporary investments is determined as follows:

Selling price of preferred stock (200 × $106.50)	$21,300
Original full cost	21,108
Gain on disposal of temporary investments	$ 192

Gain on Disposal of Temporary Investments is shown on the income statement under Other Revenue. Management must consider this amount, along with Dividends Earned, in evaluating the success of its decision to buy the preferred stock as a temporary investment.

VALUATION OF TEMPORARY INVESTMENTS

Ideally, all current assets should be shown at current market price on the balance sheet. However, this represents a departure from another generally accepted accounting standard, the use of historical cost. Only rarely do firms use the current market price because, in a rising market, writing up the temporary investments would mean recording an unrealized gain.

Temporary investments are therefore recorded in the accounts at cost and according to the CICA may also be represented on the balance sheet at cost. However the current market value of the securities should be disclosed on the balance sheet by a parenthetical notation as shown below.[3]

Assets		
Current Assets		
Cash		$ 562,000
Temporary Investments (shown at cost; current market price, $175,000)		158,000
Accounts Receivable	$200,000	
Deduct Allowance for Doubtful Accounts	8,000	192,000
Merchandise Inventory		300,000
Prepaid Insurance		2,000
Total Current Assets		$1,214,000

Studies of financial reports prepared by leading corporations show that cost is the most commonly used basis of valuation for temporary investments, the only other common basis being lower of cost and market. A majority of firms disclose the market value of these investments.[4]

Where the market value of temporary investments has declined significantly below cost, the CICA recommends that these investments should be written down to recognize the loss. The lower of cost and market method is often used to recognize these declines in market value.[5]

[3] *Ibid.,* Section 3010.05.
[4] *Financial Reporting in Canada* (Toronto: CICA, 1975), p. 51.
[5] *Ibid.,* Section 3010.06.

Until 1976, the typical method of valuing all temporary investmentsin the United States was also cost. However, because of a substantial decline in the value of many equity securities (ownership securities such as common stocks) during the immediately preceding years, the Financial Accounting Standards Board (FASB) concluded that temporary investments in equity securities should be treated as a single asset item, a single portfollio item, and be shown on the balance sheet at the lower of total cost and total market of these temporary investments.

To illustrate, assume that this method is applied to the securities owned by Duncan Limited as of December 31, and that this is the first year of securities ownership.

Temporary Investments	*Cost (at time securities were acquired)*	*Market (December 31)*
Preferred Stock of Anison Limited	$12,550	$12,000
Preferred Stock of Bassom Limited	16,470	16,200
Bonds of Connors Limited	20,000	20,500
Totals	$49,020	$48,700

If the lower of total cost and total market method is applied to these three securities, the amount to appear in the balance sheet for temporary investments is $48,700, which represents the December 31 market price of these securities.

Current Canadian practice is to reduce the book value of temporary investments only when they have declined significantly below cost. When this has occurred, the accounting for the decline is similar to that illustrated above.

The unrealized gains or losses arising from the valuation (in the above illustration, an unrealized loss of $320-$49,020 less $48,700) is included in their determination of net income for the period in which they occur. The loss of $320 would be shown in the income statement under Other Expenses. It is called an unrealized loss because no sale has taken place.

The adjusting entry necessary to give recognition to the valuation is shown below.

Dec. 31	Net Unrealized Loss— Temporary Investments	320	
	Loss in Value of Temporary Investments		320

The balance sheet then shows the following:

Assets		
Current Assets		
Temporary Investments	$49,020	
Deduct Valuation Loss in Value of Temporary Investments	320	
Temporary Investment at Lower of Cost and Market		$48,700

The account Net Unrealized Loss—Temporary Investments is closed to the Income Summary, and the $320 loss is reported on the income statement under Other Expenses.

The accounting for this method of valuation for subsequent years to the year of temporary investment acquisition is complex and is discussed in detail in most intermediate texts.

LONG-TERM INVESTMENTS

In addition to its primary operational activities, a firm may make investments in stocks, bonds, and other securities that are expected to contribute to the success of the business largely by making independent contributions to business revenue. These investments may be temporary or long term. As suggested in the preceding section, investments are called *temporary investments* and are classified as current assets only when they are capable of reasonably prompt liquidation. Investments that do not qualify as *temporary investments* are classified as long-term investments on the balance sheet.

INVESTMENT IN STOCKS

A company may buy stock in another company specifically for the dividend revenue, or it may acquire control of another company—a *subsidiary*—thereby expanding and diversifying its operations and gaining a more prominent competitive position, possibly accompanied by a steady supply of merchandise or the creation of sales outlets. The acquisition of a controlling interest in one or more subsidiary corporations frequently leads to the combining of the financial statements of the affiliated companies into single consolidated statements.

Stock may be acquired directly from the issuing company, but it is more likely to be purchased through a broker on the Toronto Stock Exchange, the Montreal Stock Exchange, or other exchange in this or other countries. If shares of stocks are not listed on an exchange—that is, sold through securities dealers—they are said to be sold *over the counter.*

The Cost Method of Recording and Valuation of Long-Term Investment in Stock

Portfolio investments in firms which are not subsidiaries or effectively controlled companies are initially recorded at full cost including brokerage fees and postage.[6] If cash is paid for the purchase of stock, there is no problem in establishing cost. In other cases, problems of valuation may arise. A sound accounting rule is to record the investment in stocks at the most objective measurement of the cash equivalent cost of the securities. Since dividends do not legally accrue, no recognition is given to the purchase of Dividends Receivable unless the issuing corporation has officially declared a dividend and the investing corporation purchases the stock between the dividend declaration date and the record date. Assume that on July 1, the Satterfield Company purchases 1,000 shares of $100 par value common stock of James Corporation

[6]*Ibid.*, Section 3050.

Ltd. at 105 with a broker's fee of $440. The investor's total cost is $105,440, and the following entry is made:

July 1	Investment in Stocks—Common Stock of James Corporation Ltd.	105,440	
	Cash		105,440

Observe that the asset Investment in Stocks is debited for the cost, not the par value, of the stock. The account title shows the general ledger controlling account, Investment in Stocks, and the subsidiary account title, Common Stock of James Corporation Ltd. The information about the specific stock is transferred to an investment register, which serves in place of a more formal subsidiary ledger.

Normally, for convenience, a cash dividend is not recorded until the cash is actually received. For example, if Satterfield Company receives a $0.60 per share quarterly dividend on the stock of James Corporation Ltd. on November 10, it records this information as follows:

Nov. 10	Cash	600	
	Dividends Earned		600

A necessary exception to the foregoing rule is the case of a dividend declared in one year and payable in another year.

> Sound accrual accounting theory dictates that the dividend revenue be recognized in the year in which the dividend is declared, not in the year in which it is paid.

In this case, an entry is made on or before the last day of the fiscal year in which the dividend is declared, debiting Dividends Receivable and crediting Dividends Earned. Then, when the dividend is actually received in the subsequent accounting period, an entry is made debiting Cash and crediting Dividends Receivable.

Today, frequent use is made of stock dividends and stock split-ups to reduce the market price per share and thus to put the stock in a more favorable price range. The additional shares received by an investing company are not revenue to the stockholder. Only a memorandum entry is necessary to record the increase in the number of shares owned. The unit cost is decreased, however, because of the larger number of shares held after the stock dividend is issued. For example, assume that James Corporation Ltd. declares a 100 percent stock dividend (a 2-for-1 split-up would be treated in the same way). The receipt of the additional 1,000 shares on December 12 by Satterfield Company is noted in the journal as follows (the original 1,000 shares had cost $105,440):

Dec. 12 Memorandum Entry—Today there was received 1,000 shares of stock of James Corporation Ltd. representing a 100% stock dividend. The cost per share of the stock is recomputed as follows:

Old number of shares	New number of shares
1,000	2,000
Total cost	**New cost per share**
$105,440	$52.72

The gain or loss per share on any subsequent sale of James Corporation Ltd. stock is determined by comparing the selling price with the adjusted cost of $52.72 per share.

If the investment is considered to be a permanent, nonmarketable item, and if it does not represent controlling interest in the company, then the generally accepted method of balance sheet valuation is *cost.* As with temporary investments, long-term investments are initially recorded at cost; therefore, there would be no valuation problems. Long-term investments would be disclosed on the balance sheet at the amounts which appear in the ledger accounts.

However, if the investment in these equity securities is considered to be an investment in long-term *marketable securities, FASB Standard Statement Number 12* requires that these equity securities be valued at the lower of total cost (of all such securities) and total market as explained in the preceding section *valuation of temporary investments.* The reader should be aware of this fact in the introductory course, but the process for accomplishing this valuation is complex and is not presented here.

INVESTMENT IN BONDS

A number of institutional investors are prohibited by law from buying common stock; others are restricted in the amount of common stock they may buy. Organizations such as banks, insurance companies, some trusts, and pension funds acquire bonds as sound investments. Industrial companies also frequently buy bonds, either for the interest revenue to be received or for reasons of business connection.

Accounting for the purchase of long-term bonds is practically the mirror image of accounting for the issuance of bonds, with one exception: *no premium or discount accounts are used when the bonds are purchased above or below face value.* To measure the bond interest revenue properly, the amount of the discount or premium is amortized, but the offsetting debits or credits are to the Bond Interest Earned account. An example is presented to illustrate the accounting for investment in bonds.

Example—*Boston Finance Limited Purchases Bonds from Aman Limited.* Assume that on May 1, Aman Limited places a 7%, $300,000 bond issue with Boston Finance Limited at 98. The interest is payable on May 1 and November 1 and the bonds mature in ten years. The entries on both the issuing company's and the investing company's books for the year are shown in Figure 14-1.

The discount accumulation (comparable to the discount amortization for the issuer) results in a debit to the asset account and a credit to the Bond Interest Earned account. For better measurement of periodic revenue from the securities, the discount on long-term investments on the investor's books is accumulated over the outstanding life of the bonds, starting with the date of purchase and ending with the maturity date. Otherwise, the amount of the discount would have to be recognized as a gain in the accounting period during which the bonds mature. Such a gain would reflect only the failure to adjust the Bond Interest Earned account in prior accounting periods.

The income statement of Boston Finance Limited for the current year ended December 31 includes Bond Interest Earned of $14,400 = ($14,000 + $400). Accrued Bond Interest Receivable of $3,500 is shown in the December 31 balance sheet under Current Assets. The Investment in Bonds is shown under Long-Term Investments on the balance sheet at $294,400 = ($294,000 + $400). At maturity, the investment account will have a balance of $300,000. It will have been increased by periodic discount accumulation entries to the $300,000 figure.

Figure 14-1 Entries for Bonds on Books of Issuer and Investor, Assuming the Use of the Straight-Line Amortization Method

Transaction	*Books of Aman Limited (Issuer)*			*Books of Boston Finance Limited (Investor)*		
May 1 Aman Limited issued the Bonds to Boston Finance Limited at 98.	May 1 Cash	294,000		May 1 Investment in Bonds—Aman Limited Bonds	294,000	
	Discount on Bonds Payable	6,000		Cash		294,000
	Bonds Payable		300,000			
Nov. 1 Aman Limited paid semiannual interest to Boston Finance Limited.	Nov. 1 Bond Interest Expense	10,500		Nov. 1 Cash	10,500	
	Cash		10,500	Bond Interest Earned		10,500
1 Amortized discount for six months. 6/120 × $6000 = $300	1 Bond Interest Expense	300		1 Investment in Bonds—Aman Limited Bonds	300	
	Discount on Bonds Payable		300	Bond Interest Earned		300
Dec. 31 Accrued interest for two months.	Dec. 31 Bond Interest Expense	3,500		Dec. 31 Accrued Bond Interest Receivable	3,500	
	Accrued Bond Interest Payable		3,500	Bond Interest Earned		3,500
31 Amortized discount for two months. 2/120 × $6000 = $100	31 Bond Interest Expense	100		31 Investment in Bonds—Aman Limited Bonds	100	
	Discount on Bonds Payable		100	Bond interest Earned		100

ACCOUNTING FOR INVESTMENT IN SUBSIDIARY

In the illustrations thus far, investments in other corporations have been carried at cost and revenue from these investments has been recognized only as dividends were declared. In cases where the investment has resulted in the other company becoming either a subsidiary or an effectively controlled company, the Canadian Institute of Chartered Accountants has recommended that the *equity method* should be used to account for the investment.[7]

[7] *Ibid.*, Section 3050.

Under the equity method, the initial purchase is recorded at cost. However, after the initial acquisition, the investment account of the parent company fluctuates in value to recognize income or losses and dividends declarations of the subsidiary. A simplified illustration of the effect of the equity method is as follows:

Investment in Common Stocks—Subsidiary S	
Increased by initial purchase of stock at cost Increased by proportionate share of subsidiary's reported net income (with an offsetting credit to a revenue account, Subsidiary Income)	Decreased by parent's share of dividend declarations. Decreased by proportionate share of subsidiary's net loss (with an offsetting debit to a loss account, Subsidiary Loss)

Using the equity method, a parent corporation recognizes an economic reality: income and losses of its subsidiary are also part of its own income and losses; dividends are simply a return to the parent of a portion of its investment—not income.

LONG-TERM INVESTMENT IN SECURED AND UNSECURED NOTES

Other types of long-term investments may be made, particularly by financial institutions. Notes secured by mortgages or deeds of trust and unsecured notes are typical. The accounting principles and procedures applicable to these investments are similar to those for investment in bonds. For example, mortgage notes are often acquired at a discount, in which case accounting theory dictates that the mortgage note be recorded at cost and the amount of the discount be accumulated (amortized) over the remaining outstanding life of the note. After the entry is made to record the periodic cash interest, the discount accumulation entry is made, debiting Investment in Mortgages and crediting Interest Earned.

APPENDIX Investment In Bonds—Compound Interest Amortization

The method of accounting for the amortization of the premium or discount elements involved in the investment in bonds described earlier in this chapter is referred to as the straight-line method. If an investor buys bonds to yield a given effective interest rate, he may want to reflect in his records this constant rate of return on the book value of the investment. In this case, he would use the compound interest or effective yield method of amortizing the premium or discount elements of the investment in bonds.

To illustrate this particular method of accounting, assume that on January 1, Harold Baskin purchased the one 8%, 10-year, $1,000 bond issued by Edwards Corporation described in Chapter 13 to yield 6 percent. Baskin would pay $1,148.78 for the bond. The purchase of the bond on January 1 and the compound-interest or effective-interest calculation and attendant compound-interest amortization for June 30 and December 31 appear below:

Jan. 1	Investment in Bonds—Edwards Corporation Bond	1,148.78	
	Cash		1,148.78
	To record the purchase of the Edwards Corporation bond to yield an annual rate of 6 percent.		
June. 30	Cash	40.00	
	Bond Interest Earned (3% × $1,148.78)		34.46
	Investment in Bonds—Edwards Corporation Bond ($40.00 − $34.46)		5.54
	To record the receipt of semiannual interest and the amortization of the premium element on a 6 percent annual yield basis.		
Dec. 31	Cash	40.00	
	Bond Interest Earned [3% × ($1,148.78 − $5.54)]		34.30
	Investment in Bonds—Edwards Corporation Bond ($40.00 − $34.30)		5.70
	To record the receipt of semiannual interest and the amortization of the premium element on a 6 percent annual yield basis.		

A similar procedure is used when the compound-interest method of amortization is applied to the investment in bonds purchased at a discount.

Two comments should be made about the foregoing procedure.

1. The procedure will produce a constant rate of return on the book value of the investment in bonds.
2. The accounting is essentially the mirror image of the accounting for the issuance of bonds described in Chapter 13 except that separate premium and discount accounts are not maintained; therefore, the amount of the premium amortization is credited to the Investment in the Bonds account and the amount of the discount accumulation is debited to the Investment in Bonds account.

GLOSSARY

Blue-Chip Stocks or Bonds High-grade stocks and AAA-rated bonds that are listed on one of the stock exchanges.

Conservatism The concept that adheres to the idea of recognizing all possible losses for a period without recognizing gains until fully realized through sales.

Investment in Secured Notes Purchased notes for which a pledge of specific assets has been made by the company issuing the secured notes.

Investment in Unsecured Notes Purchased notes of a given firm for which no pledge of specific assets has been made.

Long-Term Investments Investment in stocks, bonds, other securities, and certain other kinds of property that management intends to hold for a long period.

Lower-of-Cost-and-Market-Unit Method The lower value of the cost and the market for each security is determined; then the lower unit values are summed to determine the lower of cost and market value for marketable securities.

Marketable Securities High-grade, readily marketable securities purchased by a firm usually to be held for a short period; they are classified as current assets on the statement of financial position.

Realizable Cost The amount which could be obtained by the sale of investment securities is a measure of possible realizable cost when securities are not to be sold.

Subsidiary A company, the majority of whose voting capital stock is held by another company, referred to as the parent company.

Temporary Investments in Marketable Securities Investments in high-grade, blue-chip securities that management intends to hold for a relatively short period; these are classified as current assets on the balance sheet.

Valuation Allowance — Net Unrealized Loss in Value of Temporary Investment in Marketable Securities A valuation offset to Temporary Investments in Marketable Securities reflecting the difference between the total cost of the securities and the total market value of the temporary investments.

QUESTIONS

Q14-1. Generally speaking, the accounting for investment in bonds is the mirror image of the accounting for the issuance of bonds. Discuss: state the differences and similarities in the accounting for each. Be specific in regard to the account titles used and the accounting for temporary investments and long-term investments.

Q14-2. What are temporary investments? How are they classified on the balamce sheet?

Q14-3. List four types of investments that may qualify as temporary investments.

Q14-4. Name and discuss the methods of valuation of temporary investments.

Q14-5. Describe the two methods of recording and valuation of long-term investments in common stock.

Q14-6. Why do firms acquire stock as a long-term investment?

Q14-7. Do dividends legally accrue? Can a firm buy dividends receivable? Explain.

Q14-8. What is a stock split-up? Discuss the accounting for a stock split-up from the point of view of the investor. Would there be any difference in the accounting for a stock dividend as compared to the accounting for a stock split-up from the point of view of the investor?

Q14-9. Why is premium or discount amortized over the holding period of the bond and not over its life?

Q14-10. State the balance sheet classifications of (a) Bond Sinking Fund, (b) Accrued Bond Interest Receivable, (c) Accrued Bond Interest Payable.

DEMONSTRATION PROBLEMS

DP14-1. *(Accounting for temporary investments)* The Jim Goodfellow Company had the following transactions in temporary investments during the year:

Mar. 15 Purchased 500 shares of $100 par value, 8% preferred stock of Brown Corporation Ltd. at $104 a share. Dividends are paid semiannually on March 15 and September 15. Brokerage fees and other costs incident to the purchase were $102.

May 1 Purchased 8% bonds of Kaboodle Limited with a face value of $300,000 at 109 plus accrued interest. Interest is paid each May 1 and November 1. Brokerage fees and other costs incident to the purchase were $180. The bonds mature in 20 years.

Sept. 20 Received the semiannual dividends on the preferred stock of Brown Corporation Ltd.

Oct. 1 Sold bonds of Kaboodle Limited with a face value of $150,000 at 112 plus accrued interest.

Nov. 1 Received semiannual interest on the remaining bonds of Kaboodle Limited.

Dec. 31 Accrued the interest on the bonds of Kaboodle Limited.

Required: Journalize the transactions.

DP14-2. *(Valuation of temporary investments)* The Elton Parker Company had the following *temporary* investments as of December 31.

	Cost	Market Price at December 31
Bonds of Godwin Limited	$31,480	$32,050
Preferred stock of Hobson Limited	15,000	14,700
Preferred stock of Isaacs Limited	32,100	30,500

On February 1, of the next year the Elton Parker Company sold the preferred stock of Hobson Limited for $14,300 and the preferred stock of Isaacs Limited for $31,000.

Required:

1. Show how the investments should be shown on the end-of-period financial statement at December 31.
2. Record the sales of the temporary investments.

DP14-3. (*Accounting for long-term investment in stocks*) The Investment Company had the following transactions involving long-term investment in stocks:

Jan. 6 Purchased 4,000 shares of $100 par value common stock of Summer Limited at 108.

May 1 Received a $2.50 a share cash dividend from the Summer Limited.

June 1 Purchased 2,000 shares of $100 par value common stock of Summer Limited at 116.

Sept. 1 The Summer Limited split up its stock four for one. The Investment Company exchanged 6,000 shares of $100 par value stock for 24,000 shares of no-par value stock.

Oct. 10 The Investment Company sold 2,500 shares of the stock of Summer Limited for $41 a share.

25 Received a cash dividend on the remaining shares of stock of Summer Limited. The dividend was $1.20 per share.

Required:

1. Journalize the transactions.
2. Show how the long-term investment in stocks should be shown on the balance sheet at the end of the current year. Assume the shares are not readily marketable.

PROBLEMS

P14-1. On July 1, the Westminster Corporation purchased 8% AAA first mortgage bonds of the Goode Limited with a face value of $100,000 at 100 plus $68 brokerage fees. Interest is payable on July 1 and January 1.

1. If these bonds were purchased as a *temporary investment,* what account title(s) would be debited and for what amount(s).
2. If these bonds were purchased as a *long-term investment,* what account title(s) would be debited and for what amount(s).
3. Explain briefly the difference in accounting for the purchase of the bonds and the subsequent treatment of the investment as a temporary investment as compared to a long-term investment.

P14-2. The Marko Company had the following transactions in *temporary* investments during the year:

Jan. 1 Purchased 8% AAA bonds of Alpha Limited with a face value of $100,000 at 102. Interest is paid on Janauary 1 and July 1. Brokerage fees and other costs incident to the purchase were $65. The bonds mature in 20 years.

Apr. 10 Purchased 400 shares of $100 par value 8% preferred stock of Omega Limited at $105 a share. Dividends are paid semiannually on January 1 and July 1. Brokerage fees and other costs incident to the purchase were $125.

July 1 Received the semiannual interest from the Alpha Limited.

5 Received the semiannual dividends from the Omega Limited.

Aug. 1 Sold the bonds of Alpha Limited at 102½ plus accrued interest.

Journalize the transactions.

P14-3. The Grey Company had the following *temporary* investments as of December 31. This is the first year that the company has made investments.

	Cost	*Market Price at December 31*
Bonds of Charleton Limited	$40,000	$38,400
Preferred Stock of Deece Limited	20,000	20,200

Assuming the use of a valuation offset account, record the necessary adjusting entry under the lower-of-cost-and-market method as of December 31.

P14-4. The Neal Company had the following transactions in ***temporary investments*** in stocks during the current year:

Jan. 5 Purchased 3,000 shares of $100 par value common stock of Burlingraine Limited at 106.

20 Received a cash dividend from the Burlingraine Limited of $1 per share.

Mar. 10 Purchased 2,000 shares of $100 par value common stock of Burlingraine Limited at 110.

July 1 Received a $1.20 per share cash dividend from the Burlingraine Limited.

Dec. 1 The Burlingraine Limited split up its stock two for one. The Neal Company exchanged 5,000 shares of $100 par value stock for 10,000 shares of no-par value stock.

31 The Burlingraine Limited declared an $0.80 a share cash dividend.

Journalize the transactions.

P14-5. On January 1, the Barton Corporation Ltd. purchased as a *long-term* investment 9% bonds of Carson Corporation Ltd. with a face value of $400,000 at 102. The bonds mature in 10 years. Interest is payable each January 1 and July 1. Record (a) the purchase of the bonds by the Barton Corporation Ltd. and (b) all the necessary remaining entries for the year. Use the straight-line method of amortization.

P14-6. Assume that the Barton Corporation Ltd. (see P14-5) purchased the Carson Corporation Ltd. bonds at 99 instead of 102. Prepare all the required entries for the year. Use the straight-line method of amortization.

P14-7. On May 1, the Hobson Company purchased as a *long-term* investment 8% bonds of Potter Limited. Interest is paid semiannually on May 1 and November 1. The bonds mature in 12 years. On November 1 the accountant for the Hobson Company prepared the following entry to record the receipt of bond interest and the amortization of the premium:

Nov. 1	Cash	6,000	
	Investment in Bonds—Potter Limited Bonds		375
	Bond Interest Earned		5,625
	To record the receipt of bond interest from the Potter Limited and to amortize the premium for six months by the straight-line method.		

From this information, reconstruct the journal entry that was made to record the purchase of the bonds. Show all your calculations.

P14-8. (Appendix). On July 1, the Taylor Company purchased as a *long-term* investment 10%, 10-year bonds of Roughton Limited with a face value of $200,000 at a price to yield 8% (4% each six months). Interest is paid June 30 and December 31. The bonds mature in 10 years from the purchase date.

1. Compute the price paid for the bonds, using compound interest techniques.
2. Record the purchase of the bonds on the books of the Taylor Company and record the receipt of interest on December 31, and the amortization of the premium element, using the compound-interest method.

P14-9. The Sparks Company had the following transactions involving *temporary* investment during the year:

Jan. 1 Purchased 7% AAA bonds of Good-deal Limited with a face value of $150,000 at 101 plus accrued interest. Interest is paid each March 1 and September 1. Brokerage fees and other costs incident to the purchase were $140. The bonds mature in 116 months from the purchase date.

Mar. 1 Received semiannual interest on bonds of Good-deal Limited.

15 Purchased 500 shares of $50 par value, 8% preferred stock of Riggsbee Limited at $60 a share. Dividends are paid semiannually on February 15 and August 15. Brokerage fees and other costs incident to the purchase were $104.

Aug. 15 Sold 100 shares of preferred stock of Riggsbee Limited at $65 a share.

25 Received the dividend on the remaining preferred stock of Riggsbee Limited.

Sept. 1 Received semiannual interest on the bonds of Good-deal Limited.

Oct. 1 Sold the bonds of Good-deal Limited at 102 plus accrued interest.

Required: Journalize the transactions.

P14-10. On May 1, 19X1, the Slavino Limited purchased as a ***long-term*** investment 8% bonds of Albermarle Limited with a face value of $200,000 at 102. The bonds mature in 10 years and interest is paid each May 1 and November 1, The books are closed each December 31.

Required: Journalize all necessary entries on the books of the Slavino Limited for 19X1 and 19X2, assuming that proper straight-line amortization is recorded each time bond interest is recorded.

P14-11. The Parento Company had the following transactions involving *long-term* investment in stocks that are not readily marketable, during the year:

Jan. 4 Purchased 4,000 shares of $50 par value common stock of Sunny Limited at 58.

Feb. 10 Purchased 6,000 shares of $50 par value common stock of Sunny Limited at 62. On February 2, the Sunny Limited declared a $1.20 a share cash dividend payable February 26 to stockholders of record on February 21.

26 Received the cash dividend on the stock of Sunny Limited.

Mar. 2 Purchased 4,000 shares of $50 par value common stock of Sunny Limited at 64.

Sept. 10 The Sunny Limited declared a 100% stock dividend. The Parento Company received 14,000 additional shares of $50 par value common stock from the Sunny Limited.

Nov. 1 Sold 5,000 shares of the common stock of Sunny Limited at 36.

Dec. 31 The Sunny Limited declared a $0.65 a share cash dividend.

Required:

1. Journalize the transactions using the cost method.
2. Show how the long-term investment in stock should be shown on the balance sheet of the Parento Company as of December 31.

P14-12. On April 1, 19X1, the Brickhouse Company purchased as a ***long-term*** investment 9% bonds of Rock Limited with a face value of $500,000 at 98 plus accrued interest. The bonds mature on August 1, 19X8, and interest is paid each February 1 and August 1. On July 1, 19X5, the Brickhouse Company sold bonds with a face value of $200,000 at 100 plus accrued interest. The books are closed each December 31.

Required:

1. Journalize all necessary entries on the books of the Brickhouse Company for 19X1, assuming that proper straight-line amortization is recorded each time bond interest is recorded.
2. Assuming that the proper accounting is carried out in the years 19X2 through 19X4, prepare all the entries for the year 19X5, including the receipt of interest on February 1 and August 1, the proper discount accumulation, the sale of the bonds on July 1, and the accrual of interest and other necessary adjusting and closing entries at December 31.

P14-13. On June 1, 19X1, the Keller Company purchased as a ***long-term*** investment 9% bonds of Hinton Limited at a certain price plus accrued interest. Interest is payable semiannually on April 1 and October 1. The bonds mature in 232 months. On October 1, 19X1, the accountant for the Keller Company prepared the following entry to record the receipt of bond interest and the amortization of the premium:

Oct. 1	Cash	9,900	
	Investment in bonds—Hinton Limited Bonds		200
	Accrued Bond Interest Receivable		3,300
	Bond Interest Earned		6,400
	To record the receipt of semiannual bond interest from the Hinton Limited and to amortize the premium for four months by the straight-line method.		

Required:

1. Compute and state separately (a) the face value of bonds, (b) the original purchase price of bonds.
2. From the information given, reconstruct the journal entry to record the purchase of the bonds by the Keller Company.

P14-14. (Appendix). On March 1, 19X1, the Investure Company purchases as a *long-term* investment 7%, 20-year bonds of Whello Limited with a face value of $500,000 at a price to yield 8% (4% each six months). Interest dates are March 1 and September 1. The bonds mature in 20 years.

Required:

1. Compute the price Investure Company would pay for the bonds, using compound interest techniques.
2. Record the purchase of the bonds; the receipt of interest on September 1, 19X1, with the accompanying amortization, using the compound-interest method; and the accrual of interest receivable on December 31, 19X1, with the accompanying amortization using the compound interest method. (*Hint:* Figure the amortization of discount for a full six months and calculate two-thirds of this amount for a four-month period.)

P14-15. (*Financial policy decision problem*) John Gardner received an inheritance of $300,000. He plans to invest this amount in bonds which he contemplates holding for several years. After consulting with his broker and other advisers, he has narrowed his decision to the following four bonds:

1. 10%, 10-year, grade A debenture bonds of Alpha Limited, which are selling at 104.

2. 8%, 10-year, grade AAA first mortgage bonds of Beta, which are selling at 99.
3. 6%, 10-year, grade A debenture bonds of Kappa Limited, which are selling at 80.
4. 9%, 10-year, grade AAA debenture bonds of Delta Limited, which are selling at 100.

Required:

1. Compute the approximate effective interest yield on each $1,000 bond, and prepare a list indicating the order of yield from the highest to the lowest.
2. Which bond would be the safest? What criteria should you use? What additional information would be helpful in determining safety of principal and safety of interest? Discuss the method of rating bonds.
3. Which bond would you recommend that John Gardner buy? Give reasons for your answer.

Part Three

Financial Reporting:

Analysis and Interpretive Problems

15

Analysis and Interpretation of Financial Statements

The importance of financial reporting to outside groups has paralleled the growth of the corporate form of enterprise. Early Canadian corporations revealed very little financial information to anyone outside the internal management. Annual financial reports to shareholders were meager and consisted usually of the minimum information as required by law.

With the growth of corporations, stock exchanges and security commissions became interested in such information that was being furnished to shareholders. In 1898, for example, one exchange, in reviewing the application of a particular company for a listing of its stock, requested that the applicant present detailed statements to the shareholders prior to each annual meeting. This was the genesis of the detailed annual corporate reports made available today to the shareholders. These reports, in addition to a summary letter from the president or the chairman of the board of directors, contain detailed audited comparative balance sheets and income and other descriptive and analytic information about the present and future outlook for the corporation.

ANALYSIS AND INTERPRETATION OF FINANCIAL DATA

Before an individual can adequately understand and evaluate financial statement data, he must be acquainted with the tools of financial statement analysis. These tools are (1) ratio analysis, (2) comparative statements, (3) percentage analysis, and (4) a combination of the three. The central theme of any analysis is the evaluation of financial data through comparisons and measurement by some consistent standard to determine performance. Three types of standard have been proposed: (1) a company's past performance, (2) performance of companies in the same field, and (3) industry comparisons. In using each of these standards, the analyst should be aware of certain basic limitations. For example, if a company earned only $100 last year and earns $200 during the current year, it has improved 100 percent; yet it is still not a growth company. In a like manner, the performance of other companies the industry standards have similar pitfalls. Even with these difficulties, these standards of comparison can be extremely beneficial as a means of revealing improvements and regressions, and thus can be helpful in the interpretation of statement data. In the following discussion, emphasis is placed on ratio analysis to introduce the methodology for evaluation of financial statement data. Data are introduced at each stage of ratio analysis so that a proper understanding of the analysis results. Following this introduction, emphasis is placed on comparative statements.

RATIO ANALYSIS

Financial decisions cannot be based on any one ratio. Each ratio is effective only when used in combination with related ratios and other relevant information of current or past years. The following discussion centers on a number of different ratios that can be grouped as follows:

a. Measurements of short-run solvency
b. Measurements of long-run solvency
c. Measurements of earning power

MEASUREMENT OF SHORT-RUN SOLVENCY

External and internal users of financial statements are concerned with the measurements of short-run solvency, which indicate a firm's ability to pay debts as they become due and also the effectiveness of management decisions. The ratios discussed in this area include the current ratio, the acid-test ratio, and accounts receivable and inventory turnover.

To illustrate the computation of the current and acid-test ratios, the following information from the Murrow Clothing Store Ltd. is introduced.

Current Assets			Current Liabilities		
Cash	$ 325		Accounts Payable	$12,060	
Marketable Securities	1,900		Notes Payable	2,060	
Accounts Receivable	11,025		Accrued Wages Payable	970	
Notes Receivable	2,520		Total Current Liabilities		$15,090
Merchandise Inventory	14,750				
Prepaid Insurance	275				
Office Supplies	26				
Store Supplies	89				
Total Current Assets		$30,910			

Current Ratio

The relationship of current assets to current liabilities gives some indication of the firm's ability to pay its current debts as they mature. This relationship is called the *current ratio;* it is computed by dividing the current assets by the current liabilities.

The current ratio of Murrow Clothing Store Ltd. is computed below:

$$\frac{\text{Current Assets}}{\text{Current Liabilities}} = \frac{\$30,910}{\$15,090} = 2.05 \text{ to } 1$$

Murrow Clothing Store Ltd. has approximately $2.05 of current assets for every $1 of current liabilities. This means that even if the current assets of the company were to shrink in value by as much as 50 percent, the short-term creditors could still be paid in full.

In the past, as a rule of thumb, a current ratio of 2 to 1 was considered satisfactory. Analysts, however, generally agree that no one ratio is sufficient and that certain other factors must be considered, such as the nature of the business, the season of the year, the composition of the specific items in the current assets category, and the quality of the management of the company.

Grantors of credit emphasize the relative convertibility of the current assets into cash. To illustrate, assume that the Amber Company and the Battle Company have the following current ratios:

	Amber Company	*Battle Company*
Current Assets		
Cash	$ 500	$10,000
Accounts Receivable	700	14,000
Merchandise Inventory	28,800	6,000
Total Current Assets	$30,000	$30,000
Current Liabilities		
Accounts Payable	$15,000	$15,000
Current Ratio	2:1	2:1

Although each company has a current ratio of 2 to 1, the Battle Company is apparently in a far better position to meet its obligations. The Amber Company first must sell its $28,800 merchandise inventory and then convert the resulting receivables into cash; or it can sell its inventory for cash as a single lot, probably for less than the stated value. The Battle Company has $24,000 in cash and receivables and only $6,000 in merchandise inventory to be converted. The Amber Company thus may have a favorable current ratio but may be unable to pay its current liabilities because of an unfavorable distribution of the current assets.

An interesting comparison may be made regarding working capital analysis, assuming the following information:

	Line	*Carson Company*	*Dickinson Company*
Current Assets	(a)	$200,000	$800,000
Current Liabilities	(b)	100,000	600,000
Working Capital	(a − b)	$100,000	$200,000
Current Ratio	(a ÷ b)	2:1	1.33:1

The Dickinson Company has twice as much working capital as the Carson Company, but its debt-paying ability is not as satisfactory. The relationship between current assets and current liabilities may be more significant than their difference.

Acid-Test Ratio

A supplementary test of the ability of a business to meet its current obligations is the acid-test ratio, which is expressed as follows:

$$\text{Acid-Test Ratio} = \frac{\text{Quick Current Assets}}{\text{Current Liabilities}}$$

Quick current assets include only cash, readily marketable securities, and receivables. The acid-test ratio for Murrow Clothing Store Ltd. is computed as follows:

$$\frac{\text{Quick Current Assets}}{\text{Current Liabilities}} = \frac{(\$325 + \$1{,}900 + \$11{,}025 + \$2{,}520)}{\$15{,}090}$$

$$= \frac{\$15{,}770}{\$15{,}090}$$

$$= 1.05 \text{ to } 1$$

If the analyst is not satisfied with the current ratio as an indicator of liquidity, he may use the acid-test ratio, which excludes merchandise inventory and prepaid items. If the quick current assets are larger than the current liabilities (that is, if the acid-test ratio is better than 1 to 1), there is evidence of a strong short-term credit position and indication that the company is able to meet its currently maturing obligations.

Accounts Receivable Turnover

The manager of a business that sells on credit must watch carefully for past-due accounts and guard against possible losses. A detailed analysis of the due date of each customer's account is desirable and should be secured periodically by preparing an aging statement explained in Chapter 7. Two guides to the overall condition of the accounts receivable are the average collection period and the receivables turnover per year. If goods are sold on terms of 2/10, n/30, the amount of accounts receivable outstanding at any time should be less than the credit sales for the last 30 days, because many of the sales will have been paid within the discount period. If allowance is made for slow-paying accounts, the receivables may represent 30 to 35 days' sales. If the receivables exceed this limitation, a careful analysis of all the accounts should be made.

To illustrate the computation of the average collection period, or number of days' sales uncollected, and the receivables turnover per year, the following data for Morton Company Ltd. are assumed:

	Year 3	Year 2	Year 1
Credit sales for year	$183,600	$165,600	$160,000
Trade accounts and notes receivable (net) at end of year	$ 14,420	$ 17,200	$ 15,000

Only receivables (accounts and notes) arising out of sales of merchandise on account are used. The balance of Allowance for Doubtful Accounts is deducted in computing the average trade receivables balance.

	Year 3	Year 2
1. Net credit sales	$183,600	$165,600
2. Days in year	365	365
3. Net credit sales per day (line 1 ÷ line 2)	$503	$454
4. Average trade receivables [(balance at beginning of year + balance at end of year) ÷ 2]	15,810	16,100
Average collection period (line 4 ÷ line 3)	31 days	35 days
Receivables turnover per year (line 1 ÷ line 4)	11.6 times	10.3 times

If line 1 covered sales for a period of less than one year, then line 2 would be changed accordingly. Thus, if the sales were for a three-month period, line 2 would show 91 days (one-fourth of 365 days).

Average collection periods vary with the line of business. Wholesalers of shoes may average 45 days, compared with grocery wholesalers, whose average is approximately 15 days. In the illustration shown above, assuming that sales are on terms of 2/10, n/30, both years show a healthy situation, with Year 3 particularly good.

The receivables turnover per year or the ratio of credit sales to receivables is calculated by dividing net credit sales by the average balance of trade receivables. As illustrated, the receivables for the year Year 2 have been collected at a rate of approximately 10.3 times a year. For a standard of comparison, the preceding year's rate or the industry rate may be used. An increasing turnover of receivables indicates an improvement and reflects a decreasing relative amount of investment of working capital in receivables.

Inventory Turnover

The quantity of goods to be kept on hand is a major business decision. It is considered good management to carry as little as possible and to turn it over as rapidly as possible. Good management must guard against excessive inventories, the consequences of which could be an abnormal drain on working capital that could lead to financial difficulties. The greater the inventory, the greater the amount of money tied up, extra space required, and extra handling costs, as well as an increased possibility of loss through shrinkage, style changes, or other factors. Inadequate inventories, on the other hand, may result in higher costs due to buying in smaller quantities and the possible loss of business if the item the customer wants is out of stock. Good management, therefore, requires a careful evaluation of all these factors in establishing inventory levels.

One of the ratios used in inventory analysis is the inventory turnover—the relationship between inventory and cost of goods sold. Since the inventory is shown at cost, the ratio is computed by dividing the cost of goods sold rather than net sales by the average inventory. The figure used may be the average of the beginning and ending inventories of the period or, preferably, the average for the months involved, to minimize the effect of seasonal fluctuations. Although high turnover is usually a sign of good management, this ratio varies widely from one industry to another. A wholesaler of automobile parts and accessories may average five inventory turnovers per year as compared with thirty-five or more for a wholesaler of meat and poultry. Also, a high-volume, low-margin business would have to turn over its inventory more often than a similar business having a low-volume, high-margin policy. The average number of days' sales in inventory is also an overall guide to performance.

To illustrate the computation of the inventory turnover and the average number of days' sales for inventory, the following information for King Corporation is assumed (opening inventory was $15,400):

	Year 3
Cost of goods sold for year	$ 67,200
Inventory at end of year	$ 11,480

	Year 3
1. Cost of goods sold	$67,200
2. Days in year	365
3. Net cost of goods sold per day (line 1 ÷ line 2)	$ 184
4. Average inventory [(balance at beginning of year + balance at end of year) ÷ 2]	13, 440
Average sales period (line 4 ÷ line 3)	73 days
Inventory turnover per year (line 1 ÷ line 4)	5.0

The King Corporation sold and replaced its merchandise inventory five times during the year; that is, the cost of merchandise sold was five times greater than the average cost of merchandise on hand.

MEASUREMENT OF LONG-RUN SOLVENCY

The measurement of long-run solvency is of interest to internal and external users of a firm's financial statements. The ratios are grouped into four categories: investment in plant and equipment, equity ratios, number of times bond interest earned, and number of times preferred dividends earned.

Investment in Plant and Equipment Ratios

The investment by a company in plant and equipment assets may vary considerably, depending on the nature of the business. Manufacturing concerns require a greater investment in machinery and equipment than do retail or wholesale firms. The relationship of the plant and equipment to total assets and to sales should be in proper proportion for the industry If the amount invested in plant and equipment is too high, fewer funds are available for working capital purposes. Depreciation charges will also be high, resulting in either higher sales prices or lower profits. Finally, the long-term liabilities will be greater, resulting in greater interest costs and the need for funds to pay off debts as they mature.

The following ratios are used to determine whether there has been an overinvestment in plant and equipment:

1. Plant and equipment to long-term liabilities
2. Plant and equipment to shareholders' equity
3. Net sales to plant and equipment

To illustrate the computation of these ratios, the following data for St. John's Towing Equipment Corporation are assumed:

	Year 3	*Year 2*	*Year 1*
Plant and equipment (net)	210,000	160,000	100,000
Long-term liabilities	140,000	90,000	55,000
Shareholders' equity	200,000	220,000	175,000
Net sales	420,000	400,000	325,000

Plant and Equipment to Long-term Liabilities

The relationship of plant and equipment to long-term liabilities gives some indication of the adequacy of protection to long-term debtors. This ratio is obtained by dividing the total carrying value of the plant and equipment by the long-term liabilities.

	19X3	*19X2*	*19X1*
1. Plant and equipment (net)	210,000	160,000	100,000
2. Long-term liabilities	140,000	90,000	55,000
Ratio (line 1 ÷ line 2)	150%	178%	182%

This comparison is of particular significance to the long-term creditors if any of the plant and equipment has been mortgaged as security for loans. A reduced ratio reflects an increased dependence on long-term borrowing to finance plant and equipment acquisitions. In Year 1, the corporation owned $1.82 in plant and equipment for every $1.00 in long-term debt; in Year 3, only $1.50. It is obvious, therefore, that the increase in these assets were paid for by long-term borrowing since it owned less in 19X3 than in 19X1.

Plant and Equipment to Shareholders' Equity

The extent to which owner sources are being used to finance plant and equipment acquisitions is indicated by this ratio. This ratio is obtained by dividing the total carrying value of the plant and equipment by the shareholders' equity.

	Year 3	Year 2	Year 1
1. Plant and equipment (net)	210,000	160,000	100,000
2. Shareholders' equity	200,000	220,000	175,000
Ratio (line 1 ÷ line 2)	105%	73%	57%

In this case, Year 3 shows that a drastic increase in the plant and equipment investment has occurred during the year and that plant and equipment exceeds shareholders' equity. This indicates a possible overinvestment in plant and equipment, thus resulting in higher interest, taxes, maintenance expenses, and depreciation charges, and lower working capital. The heavy investment in land, buildings, and machinery greatly restricts the mobility of a company if a change in plant location or type of product manufactured is desirable.

Net Sales to Plant and Equipment

The ratio of net sales to plant and equipment, or plant and equipment turnover, is found by dividing net sales by the total carrying value of the plant and equipment.

	Year 3	Year 2	Year 1
1. Net sales	420,000	400,000	335,000
2. Plant and equipment (net)	210,000	220,000	175,000
Ratio (line 1 ÷ line 2)	200%	250%	325%

In Year 1, net sales were 325% of plant and equipment; that is, for every $1.00 of plant and equipment there were sales of $3.25. In Year 3, there were only $2.00 in sales for every $1.00 of plant and equipment. This ratio also underscores a possible overinvestment in plant and equipment in Year 2 and particularly in Year 3. Although sales have increased each year, the investment has increased at a larger rate.

These analyses, when based on historical cost, do not reflect the effect of changing economic and technological conditions and market price fluctuations. The Accounting Objectives Study Group of the AICPA concluded that different valuation bases are preferable for different assets and liabilities and that financial statements might contain data based on a combination of valuation bases. In addition to historical cost, the United States Securities and Exchange Commission (SEC) requires the disclosure of replacement cost information; others have proposed the use of current value accounting.

Equity Ratios

A significant measure of the stability of a business is the percentage relationship of the equities of the creditors and the owners in the total assets.

The following ratios are used to determine the amount of creditor and shareholder sources of total assets.

1. Creditors' Equity Ratio
2. Shareholders' Equity Ratio

To illustrate the computation of these equity ratios, the following information for Connolly Trucking Company Ltd. is assumed and used to calculate these ratios.

	Year 3
1. Total assets	24,594
2. Total liablities	10,774
3. Total shareholders'equity	13,820
Creditors' equity ratio (line 2 ÷ line 1)	43.8%
Shareholders' equity ratio (line 3 ÷ line 1)	56.2%

The creditors have an equity of 43.8 cents, and the shareholders have an equity of 56.2 cents, of each asset dollar. Many analysts consider the equity ratios equal in importance to the current ratio as indicators of credit strength and sound management. There are no universally accepted percentage relationships to serve as guides for the equity ratios, but it is generally felt that the larger the owner's equity, the stronger the financial condition of the business. A company may, for example, borrow money on a long-term note for working capital purposes. The loan increases the current assets and creates a more favorable current ratio; but it also reduces the shareholders' equity ratio, signaling a possible overdependence on outside sources for financial needs.

Investors' Ratio

In addition to the effective interest yield computations discussed in Chapter 13, another important ratio is used by investors in bonds—the *number of times bond interest expense is earned.* This ratio is of special interest to bond investors as a measure of the safety of their investment; it is an indication of a firm's ability to meet its annual bond interest requirement. To illustrate, assume that Analee Corporation Ltd. has bonds outstanding with a face value of \$500,000 and that in Year 3 it reports bond interest expense of \$40,000, income taxes of \$80,000, and net income (after income taxes) of \$80,000. Since bond interest expense is deductible in determining taxable income, the following formula seems appropriate:

Number of times bond interest expense is earned =

$$\frac{\text{Net income} + \text{Income tax expense} + \text{Annual bond interest expense}}{\text{Annual bond interest expense}}$$

Substituting the amounts given for Analee Corporation Ltd.,

Number of times bond interest expense is earned

$$= \frac{\$80,000 + \$80,000 + \$40,000}{\$40,000}$$

$$= 5 \text{ times}$$

A ratio of 5 times appears to be relatively safe for the investors holding bonds of Analee Corporation Ltd., although there are no established universal standards of safety. The safety margin depends in part on the type of collateral used, the type of business in which the firm is engaged, and the liquidity of the firm. Investors in a private utility with mortgageable plant assets, for example, may feel secure with a ratio of 2.5 times; whereas investors in other businesses without mortgageable assets may feel insecure with a ratio smaller than 5 times.

Another investor-oriented ratio similar to the foregoing one is the *number of times preferred dividends is earned.* This ratio is of particular interest to investors in preferred stock as a safety measure for their investment. To illustrate, assume that Analee Corporation Ltd. has 7% preferred stock outstanding with a par value of $1,000,000. Since preferred dividends are *not* deductible in determining taxable income, the following formula is appropriate:

$$\text{Number of times preferred dividends is earned} = \frac{\text{Net income (after taxes)}}{\text{Annual preferred dividends}}$$

Substituting the amounts given for Analee Corporation Ltd.

$$\text{Number of times preferred dividends is earned} = \frac{\$80,000}{\$70,000}$$

$$= 1.14 \text{ times}$$

The adequacy of this ratio must be interpreted in the same manner as that described for the number of times bond interest expense is earned; that is, the safety margin that is acceptable will depend in part on the type of business in which the firm is engaged, the liquidity of the firm, and other factors.

MEASUREMENT OF EARNING POWER

The measurement of earning power is of particular interest to investors and debtors. The ratios grouped into this category include net income per share, earnings and dividends yield rate, price earnings ratio, rates of return on total investment and shareholders' equity, net operating margin ratio, and operating ratio.

Per Share Profitability

Net income per share is generaly considered to be an excellent indicator of future profitability.

To illustrate the computation of net income per share assume that 3,000 common shares of Sakalas Blacksmiths Corporation are outstanding (assume there are no preferred shares) and that net income is $2,585. The net income per share, often called earnings per share is calculated as follows:

$$\frac{\text{Net income}}{\text{Outstanding common shares}} = \frac{2,585}{3,000} = \$0.86$$

The earnings per share in this case is $0.86

Where there are preferred shares outstanding, the calculation of earnings per common share is as follows:

$$\frac{\text{Net income - Annual preferred dividends}}{\text{Outstanding common shares}}$$

Of particular interest to investors are the ratios of earnings and dividends to the market value of shares, because it is the cash represented by the market value of the shares that can be put to other uses. These ratios are not a satisfactory substitute for a thorough financial analysis, but investors consider them key tools in their investment decisions. Three such ratios are:

$$\text{Earnings yield rate} = \frac{\text{Earnings per share}}{\text{Market value per share}}$$

$$\text{Dividend yield rate} = \frac{\text{Dividends per share}}{\text{Market value per share}}$$

$$\text{Price-earnings ratio} = \frac{\text{Market value per share}}{\text{Earnings per share}}$$

A careful analysis of the relationship and trend of these ratios indicates the profitability of the firm as related to the market value of its shares, its ability to pay dividends, and its growth prospects.

The book value and the market value of a share of stock may be and usually are different in amount.

> The market value of stock—the price that a share of stock commands on the stock exchange—reflects price level changes; available investment funds; economic, political, and psychological factors; and so on.

Since these factors are not reflected in the accounts, there is often a disparity between book and market values. The book value per share is what each shareholder would receive for each share held in the theoretical event of liquidation after the assets are sold without gain or loss. Since the valuations on the books—especially for inventories and plant and equipment—do not necessarily reflect market conditions, the book value of a share of stock may be of little significance as an indicator of the resale value of the stock.

Rate of Return on Total Investment

The relationship of the earnings of a corporation to its total resources is an important indicator of the effectiveness of management in generating a return to suppliers of capital, as well as a method of predicting future earnings.

To illustrate the computation of the rate of return on total investment, the following data are taken from the Melvin Company Ltd.

	Year 3	Year 2
1. Net income for the year	29,350	
2. Total liabilities	112,400	112,750
3. Average total liabilities for 19X3 [(112,400 + 112,750) ÷ 2]	112,575	
4. Total shareholders' equity	144,600	116,250
5. Average total shareholders' equity for 19X3 [(144,600 + 116,250) ÷ 2]	130,425	
6. Total average equities (line 3 + line 5)	243,000	
Rate of return on total investment (line 1 ÷ line 6)	12.1%	

Melvin Company Ltd. earned 12.1 cents for each dollar invested in the company—whether by outside creditors or by shareholders. Since total equities are equal to total assets, it may also be said that Melvin Company Ltd. earned 12.1 cents on each dollar of assets used in the business.

Rate of Return on Shareholders' Equity

The relationship between earnings and the shareholders' investment is a significant measure of the profitability of a business and is of particular interest to the corporate shareholders.

To illustrate computation of the rate of return on shareholders' equity the following data are taken from the Melvin Company Ltd.

1. Net income for the year	$29,350
2. Average shareholders' equity (above)	$130,425
Rate of return on shareholders' equity (Line 1 ÷ Line 2)	22.5%

The rate of return on the shareholders' equity is twice the rate of return on total investments. This means that the return to shareholders is well above the fixed rates on the mortgage payable and the notes payable, and the rate—if any—on the accounts payable. The difference of 9.3% = (22.5% – 13.2%) between the two rates is called the capital leverage factor. Melvin Company Ltd. is favorably "trading on the equity" of its shareholders by using that portion of total equities as a cushion or base from which to borrow from external sources at rates below those generated on shareholders' equity.

Net Operating Margin Ratio and Operating Ratio

The net operating margin ratio shows the relationship of the net operating margin to sales (other revenue and other expenses are excluded).

$$\frac{\text{Net operating margin}}{\text{Net sales revenue}} = \frac{\$\ 41{,}200}{\$197{,}000} = 20.9\%$$

The King Corporation earned 20.9 cents for each dollar of net sales. This ratio must be considered together with the rate of return on the shareholders' equity in appraising the earning power of a business. A high net operating margin ratio is not necessarily a favorable indication if it is accompanied by a low rate of return on the shareholders' equity.

The complement of the net operating margin ratio is the operating ratio (79.1 percent) or the amount of each sales dollar absorbed by operations.

Ratio Analysis—Limitations

A particular ratio may be satisfactory under one set of circumstances and entirely unsatisfactory under another set. Ratios are generalizations and reflect conditions that exist only at a particular time. The ratios change continually with the continuing operations of the business. Sole reliance on ratio analysis may at times give a misleading indication of financial condition. Often nonfinancial information, including the quality of the employees and employee-management relations, must be analyzed in order to get a realistic picture of the financial position of the business. Understanding and correct interpretation of ratios, however, reduce the area over which subjective judgment must be exercised and thus aid the analyst in making sound decisions.

The ratios and comparisons discussed in the preceding ratio analyses are valuable managerial aids, provided the user is aware of their limitations. For example, Murrow Clothing Store Ltd.'s current ratio of 2.05. to 1 shows the relationship between two groups of items as of a given moment of time only. The ratio may fluctuate considerably during the course of the year. Furthermore, the ratio may have little meaning unless it is related to the entire business unit. One small section of a painting has little meaning without the rest of the picture; or if one states, for example, that Paul Clifford is an excellent student, we know very little about him. If we are told that he is twenty-two years old, is in the upper 5 percent of his class, and is president of Beta Gamma Sigma and captain of the basketball team, we know a good deal more about him. Similarly, if we state that both the Atwater Company and the Excel Company each have current ratios of 2 to 1, it does not mean too much unless the acid-test ratio and specific composition of the current assets are known.

COMPARATIVE STATEMENTS

A study of the financial position of a company and the results of its operations for a period is more meaningful if the analyst has available the balance sheet and the income statements for several periods. Trends can be better ascertained when three or more financial statements are compared. It is not uncommon to find comparative statements for ten years in annual reports. One large corporation in its recent annual report showed comparative financial statements covering a period of fifteen years.

> **For effective analysis, the statements being compared must be based on the consistent application of generally accepted accounting principles over the period covered by the comparison. If there is an absence of comparability, it should be made known in the accountant's report.**

The effect on net income, for example, of a changeover from FIFO to LIFO in valuing inventories must be clearly disclosed in the report.

Comparative Balance Sheets. Successive balance sheets of a company may be given side by side, showing only the dollar amounts. These statements can be made more meaningful if the dollar amount of increase or decrease and the percentage of increase or decrease are also shown. This form of statement is illustrated in Figure 15-1, the comparative balance sheet of Melvin Company Ltd. In this illustration, Year 2 is the base year and represents 100 percent. Accounts Receivable increased by 30.8 percent ($8,000 ÷ $26,000) during Year 3; Notes Payable decreased by 5 percent ($1,000 ÷ $20,000); and Cash increased by

Figure 15-1 Comparative Balance Sheet

MELVIN COMPANY LTD.
Comparative Balance Sheet
December 31, Year 3 and Year 2

	December 31		*Amount of Increase or (Decrease) during Year 3*	*Percent of Increase or (Decrease) during Year 3*
	Year 3	*Year 2*		
Assets				
Current Assets				
Cash	$ 32,000	$ 16,000	$16,000	100.0
Accounts Receivable (net)	34,000	26,000	8,000	30.8
Inventories	45,000	36,000	9,000	25.0
Total Current Assets	$111,000	$ 78,000	$33,000	42.3
Plant and Equipment				
Land	$ 7,000	$ 7,000	$ -0-	-0-
Building (net)	116,000	119,000	(3,000)	(2.5)
Store Equipment (net)	23,000	25,000	(2,000)	(8.0)
Total Plant and Equipment	$146,000	$151,000	$ (5,000)	(3.3)
Total Assets	$257,000	$229,000	$28,000	12.2
Liabilities and Shareholders' Equity				
Current Liabilities				
Accounts Payable	$ 27,400	$ 24,750	$ 2,650	10.7
Notes Payable	19,000	20,000	(1,000)	(5.0)
Accrued Payables	11,000	8,000	3,000	37.5
Total Current Liabilities	$ 57,400	$ 52,750	$ 4,650	8.8
Long-Term Liabilities				
Mortgage Payable	55,000	60,000	(5,000)	(8.3)
Total Liabilities	$112,400	$112,750	$ 350	0.3
Shareholders' Equity				
Capital Stock	$109,000	$100,000	$ 9,000	9.0
Retained Earnings	35,600	16,250	19,350	119.0
Total Shareholders' Equity	$144,600	$116,250	$28,350	24.4
Total Liabilities and Shareholders' Equity	$257,000	$229,000	$28,000	12.2

$16,000, or 100 percent. The December 31, Year 3, cash balance is twice the December 31, Year 2, balance; Retained Earnings as of December 31, Year 3, are far more than twice the amount shown on December 31, Year 2. No additional plant and equipment assets are acquired; the decreases reflect the annual depreciation deductions.

The change that occurred during Year 3 for Melvin Company Ltd. is apparently favorable. Current assets increased by 42.3 percent, whereas current liabilities increased by only 11.1 percent. The total shareholders' equity increased by 24.4 percent; this is reflected by an increase in all the current assets. The favorable position of Retained Earnings, accompanied by an increase in work-

Figure 15-2 Comparative Statement of Income and Retained Earnings

MELVIN COMPANY LTD.
Comparative Statement of Income and Retained Earnings
For the Year Ended December 31, Year 3 and Year 2

	Years Ended December 31		*Amount of Increase or (Decrease)*	*Percent of Increase or (Decrease)*
	Year 3	*Year 2*	*during Year 3*	*during Year 3*
Sales (net)	$197,000	$151,000	$46,000	30.5
Cost of Goods Sold	123,000	92,000	31,000	33.7
Gross Margin on Sales	$ 74,000	$ 59,000	$15,000	25.4
Operating Expenses				
Selling Expenses				
Advertising Expense	$ 1,200	$ 1,100	$ 100	9.1
Sales Salaries Expense	18,300	17,900	400	2.2
Depreciation Expense—Store Equipment	2,000	2,000	–0–	–0–
Total Selling Expenses	$ 21,500	$ 21,000	$ 500	2.4
General Expenses				
Depreciation Expense—Building	$ 3,000	$ 3,000	$ –0–	–0–
Insurance Expense	675	650	25	3.8
Miscellaneous General Expense	425	350	75	21.4
General Salaries Expense	7,200	8,000	(800)	(10.0)
Total General Expenses	$ 11,300	$ 12,000	$ (700)	(5.8)
Total Operating Expenses	$ 32,800	$ 33,000	$ (200)	(0.6)
Operating Income	$ 41,200	$ 26,000	$15,200	58.5
Other Expenses				
Interest Expense	2,750	3,000	(250)	(8.3)
Net Income Before Income Taxes	$ 38,450	$ 23,000	$15,450	67.2
Income Taxes	9,100	5,750	3,350	58.3
Net Income After Income Taxes	$ 29,350	$ 17,250	$12,100	70.1
Retained Earnings, January 1	16,250	9,000	7,250	80.6
Total	$ 45,600	$ 26,250	$19,350	73.7
Dividends Declared	10,000	10,000	–0–	–0–
Retained Earnings, December 31	$ 35,600	$ 16,250	$19,350	119.0

ing capital, was accomplished without resort to long-term borrowing, because Mortgage Payable and Notes Payable have decreased during the period. Additional working capital was acquired by the sale of stock.

Comparative Income Statement. A single income statement is just one link in a continuous chain reporting the operating results of the business. Comparative income statements are required for an analysis of trends and for making decisions regarding possible future developments. An income statement showing the results of operations for a single year is inadequate for purposes of analyzing the significance of the changes that have occurred.

The comparative statement of income and retained earnings of Melvin Company Ltd. is shown in Figure 15-2. Year 3 figures are again used as the base year. Gross Margin on Sales increased by 25.4 percent; Net Income before Income Taxes increased by 67.2 percent; and Total Operating Expenses decreased by 0.6 percent. These favorable changes resulted primarily from an increase in sales. The provision for income taxes (which are assumed at 25 percent) increased by 58.3 percent because of the large increase in net income before income taxes.

There is a close relationship between the cost of goods sold, the volume of sales, and net income before income taxes. In periods of exceptionally high sales volume, net income before income taxes tends to rise (percentage of increase, 67.2) at a faster rate than do sales (percentage of increase, 30.5). In periods of declining sales volume, earnings fall more sharply than sales. This is because a significant part of the operating expenses are constant (or fixed)—they are not affected by the current sales volume. Such fluctuations in net income can be eliminated if unit sales prices are increased in periods of low sales volume and reduced in periods of high sales volume. Such a pricing policy, however, would be undesirable from the customers' viewpoint and impracticable from the company's viewpoint. It becomes important, therefore, that management know the volume at which profits begin. This figure, the *break-even point,* is that volume of sales at which the business will neither make a profit nor incur a loss.

Trend Percentages

Comparative financial statements for several years may be expressed in terms of trend percentages.

> Management can more readily study changes in financial statements between periods by establishing a base year and expressing the other years in terms of the base year. The base year, may be any typical year in the comparison—the first, the last, or any other years.

To illustrate, a partial comparative income statement is presented in Figure 15-3. The amounts in Figure 15-3 are converted into trend percentages with Year 1 as the base year, as shown in Figure 15-4.

Each item in the Year 1 column of Figure 15-3 is assigned a weight of 100 percent. All the amounts in other years are expressed as trend percentages, or

Figure 15-3
Partial Comparative Income Statements for Four Years*

	Year 1	Year 2	Year 3	Year 4
Sales (net)	$100,000	$95,000	$120,000	$130,000
Cost of Goods Sold	60,000	58,900	69,600	72,800
Gross Margin on Sales	$ 40,000	$36,100	$ 50,400	$ 57,200
Total Selling Expenses	$ 10,000	$ 9,700	$ 11,000	$ 12,000
Net Income before Income Taxes	$ 5,000	$ 3,800	$ 8,400	$ 10,400

* The years are listed in ascending order to facilitate analysis when data for three or more years are given. The reverse (descending order) is usually found in corporate annual reports.

Figure 15-4
Comparative Trend Percentages for Four Years*

	Year 1	Year 2	Year 3	Year 4
Sales (net)	100%	95%	120%	130%
Cost of Goods Sold	100	98	116	121
Gross Margin on Sales	100	90	126	143
Total Selling Expenses	100	97	110	120
Net Income before Income Taxes	100	76	168	208

* The years are listed in ascending order to facilitate analysis when data for three or more years are given. The reverse (descending order) is usually found in corporate annual reports.

percentages of the figures for the base year. Each base year amount is divided into the same item for the other years. Trend percentages for sales, for example, are calculated as follows: Year 2: $95.000 ÷ $100,000 = 95; Year 3: $120,000 ÷ $100,000 = 120; and Year 4: $130,000 ÷ $100,000 = 130. When the base year amount is larger than the corresponding amount in another year, the trend percentage is less than 100 percent; conversely, when the base year amount is the lesser of the two, the trend percentage is over 100 percent.

The trend percentage statement is an analytical device for condensing the absolute dollar data of comparative statements. The device is especially valuable to management because readability and brevity are achieved by substituting percentages for large dollar amounts, which in themselves are difficult to compare. Trend percentages are generally computed for the major items in the statements; minor amounts are omitted, the objective being to highlight the significant changes.

An evaluation of the trend percentages requires a careful analysis of the interrelated items. Sales, for example, may show increases over a four-year period leading up to a trend percentage of 150 percent for the fourth year. This is unfavorable if it is accompanied by trend percentages of 200 percent for cost of goods sold, 175 percent for selling expenses, and 95 percent for net income before income taxes. Other unfavorable trends include an upward trend in receivables and inventories accompanied by a downward trend in sales, and a downward trend in sales accompanied by an upward trend in plant and equipment. Favorable trends would be an increase in sales accompanied by a decrease in cost of goods sold and selling expenses or an increase in current assets accompanied by a decrease in current liabilities.

Trend percentages show the degree of increase and decrease; they do not indicate the causes of the changes. They do, however, single out unfavorable developments for further analysis and investigation by management. A marked change may have been caused by inconsistency in the application of accounting principles, by fluctuating price levels, or by controllable internal factors (for example, an unnecessary increase in merchandise inventory or a decrease in operating efficiency).

Common-Size Statements

Trend percentages provide for *horizontal statement analysis;* common-size statements provide for ***vertical analysis*** (see Figure 15-5). It is important for the analyst to compare changes on the financial statements that occur from period to period with certain base totals within those periods.

Thus total assets, total liabilities and shareholders' equity, and total sales are each converted to a base of 100 percent. Each item within each classification is expressed as a percentage of the base; each expense, for example, is expressed as a percentage of total expenses. Since these bases represent 100 percent in all the statements in the comparison, there is a common basis for analysis; therefore, the statements are referred to as "common-sized statements."

Comparisons can be made within the company, with other, companies in the same industry, or with entire industry figures. Thus, important relationships can be discerned even when comparisons are made with companies of unlike size; and any significant differences may indicate that a decision should be made. The common-size statement supplemented by additional analytical financial data are effective tools for a historical financial study of a business or industry.

If comparisons are to be made of one company with one or more other companies or with an entire industry, it must first be carefully established that the data in the comparison are based on reasonably uniform and consistent accounting methods and principles.

Common-Size Income Statement. The common-size income statement of Melvin Company Ltd. is shown in Figure 15-5. Examples of the conversion of income statement dollar amounts into common-size percentages are shown below.

$$\frac{\text{Gross margin on sales (Year 3)}}{\text{Net sales (Year 3)}} = \frac{\$74,000}{\$197,000} = 37.6\%$$

Gross margin on sales for Year 2 represents 37.6 percent of net sales; for each dollar of net sales there was a margin of 37.6 cents.

$$\frac{\text{Total operating expenses (Year 2)}}{\text{Net sales (Year 2)}} = \frac{\$33,000}{\$151,000} = 21.9\%$$

Figure 15-5
Comparative Common-Size Income Statement

MELVIN COMPANY LTD.
Comparative Common-Size Income Statement
For the Years Ended December 31, Year 3 and Year 2

	Year Ended December 31		*Common-Size Percentages Year Ended December 31*	
	Year 3	*Year 2*	*Year 3*	*Year 2*
Sales (net)	$197,000	$151,000	100.0	100.0
Cost of Goods Sold	123,000	92,000	62.4	60.9
Gross Margin on Sales	$ 74,000	$ 59,000	37.6	39.1
Operating Expenses				
Selling Expenses				
Advertising Expense	$ 1,200	$ 1,100	0.6	0.7
Sales Salaries Expense	18,300	17,900	9.3	11.9
Depreciation Expense—Store Equipment	2,000	2,000	1.0	1.3
Total Selling Expenses	$ 21,500	$ 21,000	10.9	13.9
General Expenses				
Depreciation Expense—Building	$ 3,000	$ 3,000	1.5	1.9
Insurance Expense	675	650	0.4	0.4
Miscellaneous General Expenses	425	350	0.2	0.2
General Salaries Expense	7,200	8,000	3.7	5.4
Total General Expenses	$ 11,300	$ 12,000	5.8	7.9
Total Operating Expenses	$ 32,800	$ 33,000	16.7	21.8
Net Operating Margin	$ 41,200	$ 26,000	20.9	17.3
Other Expenses				
Interest Expense	2,750	3,000	1.4	2.0
Net Income before Income Taxes	$ 38,450	$ 23,000	19.5	15.3
Income Taxes	9,100	5,750	4.6	3.9
Net Income	$ 29,350	$ 17,250	14.9	11.4

Total operating expenses for Year 2 represent 21.9 percent of net sales; for each dollar of net sales there were 21.9 cents of total operating expenses.

A comparison of the cost of goods sold for the two years shows an increase of 1.5 percent (62.4% −60.9%) and a corresponding decrease in the gross margin. This relatively modest change may indicate an increase in markdowns from original sales prices. Increases in amounts and percentages of inventories accompanied by a decrease in gross margin may indicate an overinvestment in inventories.

The change in total operating expenses is favorable. Sales increased by $46,000 = ($197,000 − $151,000), whereas total operating expenses remained approximately the same. Melvin Company Ltd. has increased the efficiency of its operations by increasing dollar sales without increasing its operating costs—a favorable development. The amount of increase in income taxes is at best a partially uncontrollable factor.

In addition to the analyses already illustrated, other ratios such as sales returns and allowances to sales revenue, sales discounts to sales revenue, purchase returns and allowances to purchases, and purchases discounts to purchases furnish information useful to management for controlling various activities, especially when they are compared from period to period.

FINANCIAL STATEMENT ANALYSIS—INFLUENCES

The techniques and procedures for the analysis of financial statements discussed thus far are useful tools for gaining an insight into the financial affairs of a business. The analyst must, however, evaluate many other influences that, although not specifically reflected in the statements, may nevertheless influence the future of the company. Careful evaluation must be made of the possible effect on the company of sudden changes in key management personnel, shifts in employee or customer loyalty, development of new competing products, as well as broad shifts in the social, political, or economic environment. Another factor that must be evaluated with care is the impact of changing price levels on the statements. Differences in financial statements may also be due to the wide variations that exist within the framework of generally accepted accounting principles and procedures—in the valuation of inventories, the selection of depreciation bases, the treatment of intangibles, and the method of disclosing extraordinary and nonrecurring items, for example.

Figure 15-6 Major Ratios

SIGNIFICANT RATIOS

Ratio	Computation of Ratio	Indicates
A. Short-Run Solvency Measurements		
Current Ratio	$\frac{\text{Current Assets}}{\text{Current Liabilities}}$	The ability of a business to meet its current obligations
Acid-Test Ratio (quick ratio)	$\frac{\text{Quick Current Assets}}{\text{Current Liabilities}}$	The ability of a business to meet quickly unexpected demands for working capital from assets readily convertible into cash
Average Number of Days' Sales Uncollected (Collection Period)	$\frac{\text{Average accounts receivable}}{\text{Net sales}} \times 365$	The rapidity with which the accounts receivable are collected; the average number of days elapsing from the time of sale to the time of payment
Accounts Receivable Turnover	365 ÷ Average collection period	
Average Number of Days' Sales in Inventory	$\frac{\text{Average Inventory}}{\text{Cost of Goods Sold}} \times 365$	
Merchandise Inventory Turnover	$\frac{\text{Cost of Goods Sold}}{\text{Average Inventory}}$	The number of times the merchandise inventory was replenished during the period, or the number of dollars in the cost of goods sold for each dollar of inventory

Figure 15-6 (continued)

SIGNIFICANT RATIOS (cont.)

Ratio	Computation of Ratio	Indicates
B. Long-Run Solvency Measurements		
Plant and Equipment to Long-Term Liabilities	Plant and Equipment (net) / Long-Term Debt	The adequacy of protection to long-term creditors
Plant and Equipment to Shareholders' Equity	Plant and Equipment (net) / Shareholders' Equity	The extent to which owner sources are being used to finance plant and equipment acquisitions
Sales to Plant and Equipment (Plant Turnover)	Net Sales / Average Plant and Equipment (net)	Dollar of sales per dollar of investment in plant and equipment assets
Creditors' Equity Ratio	Total Liabilities / Total Assets	The percent of creditor sources of total assets
Shareholders' Equity Ratio	Shareholders' Equity / Total Assets	The percent of owner sources of total assets
Number of Times Preferred Dividends Is Earned	Net Income / Annual Preferred Dividend	The primary measure of the safety of an investment in preferred stock—the ability of a firm to meet its preferred dividend requirement
Number of Times Bond Interest Is Earned	(Net Income + Income Taxes + Annual Bond Interest Expense) / Annual Bond Interest Expense	The primary measure of the safety of an investment in bonds—the ability of a firm to meet its bond interest requirement
C. Earning Power and Growth Potential Measurements		
Earnings Per Share of Common Stock	(Net Income minus Annual Preferred Dividend) / Outstanding Common Shares	The company's earning power as related to common shareholders' equity
Earnings Yield Rate	Earnings per Share / Market Value per Share	Earnings as related to market value of the shares
Dividends Yield Rate	Dividends per Share / Market Value per Share	Dividend payout as related to market value of the shares
Price-Earnings Ratio	Market Value per Share / Earnings per Share	Market value of each share as related to profitability of the firm
Return on Total Investment	(Net Income + Interest Expense) / Average Total Assets	The profitableness of the business expressed as a rate of return on total investments by both owners and creditors
Return on Shareholders' Equity	Net Income / Average Shareholders' Equity	The profitableness of the business expressed as a rate of return on the shareholders' equity
Operating Ratio	(Cost of Goods Sold + Operating Expenses) / Net Sales Revenue	The number of cents needed to generate one dollar of sales

Figure 15-6 (continued)

D. Financial Structure Measurements: These measurements can be determined from common-size statements of financial position, which shows the composition of items on each side of the position statement.

E. Asset Utilization Ratios: These are measures of asset turnover or the dollars of sales generated by each dollar of investment in total assets or in each individual asset.

F. Operating Performance Ratios: These are measures which show the relationship of each income statement item or groups of items to sales.

APPENDIX Disclosure Issues

ACCOUNTING POLICIES AND FOOTNOTES TO STATEMENTS

The proper purpose of footnotes is to furnish descriptive detail and explanatory support data for items quantified in the body of the statement. The Canadian Institute of Chartered Accountants has stated that "notes to financial statements, and supporting schedules to which the financial statements are cross-referenced, are an integral part of such statements."[1] Their purpose is to help the analyst to understand and to appraise the quantitative amounts in the statement proper. They should not be used as a substitute for a quantifiable amount or as a means of evading or avoiding a difficult or troublesome measurement decision. Footnotes are customarily used to disclose methods of inventory pricing, depreciation methods, terms and conditions of long-term debt, contingent liabilities, long-term lease provisions, and other items.

In recognition of the fact that financial statements are affected by the accounting policies used by a company, the CICA has recommended that "a clear and concise description of the significant accounting policies of an enterprise should be included as an integral part of the financial statements."[2] Disclosures should identify and describe the accounting standards selected from existing acceptable alternatives and any unusual or innovative applications of generally accepted accounting principles.

EXTRAORDINARY ITEMS AND PRIOR PERIOD ADJUSTMENTS

The treatment of these items has been surrounded by controversy about whether the income statement or the statement of retained earnings should be used to report such items as losses from fires or natural hazards, nonrecurring gains or losses on the retirement of bonds payable or the disposal of assets, and corrections of errors in the net income of prior periods. One group argued that if amounts of these items are substantial and if they are included in the income statements, they would distort net income: thus this group of advocates stated that these items should be disclosed in the statement of retained earnings. This view was referred to as the *current operating performance concept.* Opponents argued that all items affecting the calculation of net income should appear in the income statement. The foregoing items do affect the long-run income of a firm; thus many accountants argue that they should be disclosed in the income statement. This view was labeled the *all-inclusive income statement concept.*

[1] *CICA Handbook* (Toronto: Canadian Institute of Chartered Accountants, October 1972), Section 1500.03.

[2] *Ibid.*, Section 1505.04.

To illustrate the variation that could occur in net income under the two historical concepts, assume, for example, that Baxter Company Ltd. earns an ordinary income of $50,000 for each year for three years; in addition, in the first year, it sells for a gain of $100,000 a patent that it developed but did not use; in the second year, it sells other plant assets for a gain of $70,000; and in the third year, it experiences an uninsured fire loss of $50,000 in the plant. Under the current operating performance concept, the Baxter Company's net income would be reported as $50,000 each year. However, under the all-inclusive concept, the net income would be reported as shown below.

	Year 3	*Year 4*	*Year 5*
Ordinary Income	$ 50,000	$ 50,000	$50,000
Extraordinary Gain (loss)	100,000	70,000	(50,000)
Net Income before Income Taxes	$150,000	$120,000	$ –0–

Advocates of the current operating performance concept argued that under this theory, net income reflects what took place under normal business conditions and that the income statement comparability is thereby enhanced. On the other hand, adherents of the all-inclusive concept maintain that the periodic income statement should record the total income history of the company; that allowing the omission of extraordinary items from the income statement furnishes an opportunity to conceal pertinent information; and that the omission or inclusion of certain items in borderline cases may make possible the manipulation of reported net income.

The CICA states that all items of gain or loss recognized during the period with the single exception of "prior period adjustments" should be disclosed in the income statement. The extraordinary items, defined as "gains, losses, and provisions for losses which result from occurrences the underlying nature of which is not typical of the normal business activities of the enterprise, and are not considered as recurring factors in any evaluation of the ordinary operations of the enterprise"[3] should be segregated from the results of recurring, normal operations and disclosed separately in the income statement. Examples of occurrences giving rise to extraordinary items which are deducted from net income include disposal of part of the business, the sale of a plant, expropriation, and acts of God such as earthquakes. Other gains or losses which are large in size and caused by unusual circumstances "should be included in the income statement before 'income from extraordinary items' and should be disclosed as separate items or by way of a note." Bad debt and inventory losses are examples of this type of item.[4] These few items that qualify as "prior period adjustments" should be shown as adjustments of the opening balance of retained earnings in the statement of retained earnings. Prior period adjustments are limited to those adjustments which "(a) are specifically identified with and directly related to the business activities of particular prior periods, and (b) are not attributable to economic events, including obsolescence, occurring subsequent to the date of the financial statements for such prior periods, and (c) depend primarily on decisions or determinations by persons other than manage-

[3]*Ibid.*, Section 3480.04.
[4]*Ibid.*, Section 3480.12.

ment or owners, and (d) could not be reasonably estimated prior to such decisions or determinations."[5]

The CICA goes on to say, "Gains or losses which qualify as prior period adjustments are rare."[6] Examples of prior period adjustments include nonrecurring income tax reassessments and settlement of litigation from prior years.

Figure 15-7 shows the reporting of an extraordinary loss on a net after tax credit basis (loss of $12,000 reduced by a tax credit of $6,000).

Figure 15-7
Income Statement

Net Sales Revenue	$390,000
Cost of Goods Sold	200,000
Gross Margin on Sales	$190,000
Deduct Selling and General Expenses	60,000
Net Income Before Income Taxes	$130,000
Income Taxes (assuming 50%)	65,000
Net Income Before Extraordinary Items	$ 65,000
Deduct Extraordinary Item (net of applicable income tax reduction of $6,000)	
Loss from Riot Damages	6,000
Net Income	$ 59,000

Figure 15-8 illustrates the reporting of a prior period adjustment.

Figure 15-8
Statement of Retained Earnings

Retained Earnings, December 31, Year 2	$220,000
Adjustment of Prior-Years Income:	
Settlement of Year 1 damage suit	(7,500)
Adjusted Retained Earnings, December 31, Year 2	$212,500
Net Income per Income Statement	59,000
Total	$271,500
Dividends Declared	25,000
Retained Earnings, December 31, Year 3	$246,500

ACCOUNTING CHANGES

In another effort to improve reporting practices, the APB in Opinion No. 20 stated that an accounting principle, once adopted, should be changed "only if the enterprise justifies the use of an alternative acceptable accounting principle on the basis that it is preferable."[7] It stated further that the reason why the newly adopted accounting principle is preferable should be clearly explained, that the cumulative effect of the change should be shown in net income of the period of the change between "extraordinary items" and "net income."

Where a company has made a change in its application of accounting principles, the CICA has stated that "the change should receive the same treat-

[5]*Ibid.,* Section 3600.04.

[6]*Ibid.,* Section 3600.02.

[7]AICPA, *APB Accounting Principles,* vol. 2 (Chicago: Commerce Clearing House, Inc., 1973), p. 6689.

ment as that for a prior period adjustment, even though such a change does not have all four of the characteristics normally required of prior period adjustments."[8] It is important to recognize the different treatment of accounting changes recommended by the CICA and AICPA and the effect that each recommendation has on the net income figure reported in the financial statements.

THE AUDITOR'S OPINION

The primary purpose of an audit of his client's financial statements by the CA is to enable the auditor, in his role as an independent and objective examiner of the accounting records and other evidence, to express an opinion on the fairness of the presentation of the balance sheet and results of operations. Although management is primarily responsible for the integrity of the statements, the auditor assumes personal responsibility to those who rely on his opinion—investors, credit grantors, and others—about the fairness of management's representations. The auditor bases his opinion on his examination which includes "a general review of the accounting procedures and such tests of accounting records and other supporting evidence as considered necessary in the circumstances." The analyst must, therefore, be assured not only of the CA's technical competence but also of his integrity and judgment.

If the auditor is limited by his client or others in the scope of his examination, if the client's statements do not fairly present financial position and results of operations, or if they are not in accordance with generally accepted accounting principles, then the auditor will either qualify his opinion, deny an opinion, or give an adverse opinion. The reader is then put on his guard in making an appraisal of these financial statements.

GLOSSARY

All-Inclusive Concept The concept that extraordinary items should be disclosed in the income statement.

Auditor's Opinion The statement made by the auditor regarding his audit work and his opinion on the fairness of the presentation of financial position and results of operations.

Comparative Statements Successive financial statements of a company given side by side.

Current Operating Performance Concept The concept that extraordinary items should be disclosed in the statement of retained earnings rather than in the income statement.

Extraordinary Items Events and transactions that are of an unusual nature and that recur infrequently.

Intangible Assets Long-term assets, without physical form or substance, representing rights to future benefits which are without physical form or substance.

Trend Percentages An analytical device for condensing the absolute dollar data of comparative statements.

[8]*CICA Handbook, op. cit.*, Section 3600.11.

QUESTIONS

Q15-1. (a) What are some limitations of financial statements? (b) List and discuss some factors contributing to the development of financial reporting to outside groups.

Q15-2. Discuss the four basic devices that are commonly used to achieve interpretative statement presentation.

Q15-3. What major classifications may be applied (a) to assets, (b) to liabilities, and (c) to shareholders' equity items? Indicate the nature of the data that are reported within each classification.

Q15-4. How have the recommendations of the CICA altered the accountant's view (a) of the current operating performance concept of income reporting and (b) of the all-inclusive income statement concept?

Q15-5. "The financial statement analyst should have available comparative statements, showing changes in absolute amounts and percentage changes." Explain.

Q15-6. Comment on the significance of each of the following factors to the financial statement analyst:

1. A steadily increasing price level
2. An increase in inventory
3. An increase in plant and equipment
4. An increase in sales
5. An increase in sales and a decrease in accounts receivable
6. An increase in liabilities

Q15-7. Trend percentages are of limited usefulness (a) because they do not indicate whether the change is favorable or unfavorable, (b) because the change may be in relation to a year that is not typical or normal, and (c) because they do not measure the effectiveness of management. Discuss.

Q15-8. What are the advantages and limitations to the analyst of the following: (a) comparative statements, (b) trend percentages, and (c) common-size percentages?

Q15-9. Explain how each of the following would be determined:

1. A company's earning power
2. The extent to which owner sources have been used to finance plant and equipment acquisitions
3. The adequacy of protection to long-term debtors
4. The rapidity with which the accounts receivable are collected
5. The ability of a business to meet quickly the unexpected demands for working capital

Q15-10. What ratios or other analytical devices will help to answer the following questions?

1. Is there an overinvestment in plant and equipment?
2. Are the assets distributed satisfactorily?
3. Is there adequate protection for creditors?
4. How is the business being financed?
5. Are earnings adequate?
6. Is there a satisfactory relationship between creditor and owner financing?
7. Are costs and expenses too high? Are sales adequate?

Q15-11. (a) What knowledge must an analyst possess to enable him to evaluate financial statement data successfully? (b) What are some of the influences that are not specifically reflected in financial statements but which an analyst must evaluate to draw correct inferences from his analysis of financial statements?

DEMON-
STRATION
PROBLEMS

DP15-1. (*Comparative statements—trend percentages*) The following information is taken from the books of the Rockwood Company:

	Year 1	*Year 2*	*Year 3*	*Year 4*
Sales	$337,500	$368,750	$390,625	$421,875
Cost of Goods Sold	195,000	217,100	229,000	246,000
Accounts Receivable	50,000	57,500	61,000	67,000
Merchandise Inventory	87,500	101,500	107,625	114,625
Net Income	30,000	30,600	31,500	32,400

Required:

1. Calculate the trend percentages (Year 1 is the base year).
2. Point out the favorable and unfavorable tendencies.

DP15-2. *(Financial statement analysis)* The balance sheet of Rose Company Ltd. as of December 31 follows:

Assets

Current Assets			
Cash		$54,000	
Marketable Securities		27,000	
Accounts Receivable		54,000	
Notes Receivable		16,000	
Merchandise Inventory		108,000	
Prepaid Insurance		11,000	
Total Current Assets			$270,000
Plant and Equipment			
Store Equipment		$176,000	
Deduct Accumulated Depreciation		41,000	
Total Plant and Equipment			135,000
Total Assets			$405,000

Liabilities and Shareholders' Equity

Current Liabilities			
Accounts Payable	$ 51,300		
Notes Payable	43,200		
Accrued Wages Payable	13,500		
Total Current Liabilities		$108,000	
Long-Term Liabilities			
Mortgage Payable (due December 31, 1983)		189,000	
Total Liabilities			$297,000
Shareholders' Equity			108,000
Total Liabilities and Shareholders' Equity			$405,000

Additional data:

a. Shareholders' Equity, January 1	$ 81,000
b. Net sales	324,000
c. Net income	32,000
d. Cost of goods sold	162,000
e. Merchandise inventory, January 1	135,000
f. Total operating expenses	130,000

Required:

1. Compute the following (show all your computations): (a) current ratio, (b) working capital, (c) operating ratio, (d) acid-test ratio, (e) turnover of merchandise inventory, (f) net operating margin ratio.
2. Explain the significance of the ratios: (a) to Rose, (b) to the holder of the mortgage, (c) to the holder of the note payable.
3. What additional data are needed for a more comprehensive analysis of Rose's financial statements?

PROBLEMS

P15-1. The following information is given:

	Year 2	*Year 1*
Net Sales	$1,397,000	$1,122,000
Cost of Goods Sold	935,000	814,000
Selling Expenses	154,000	121,000
General Expenses	88,000	77,000
Other Revenue	4,000	7,000
Other Expenses	2,000	9,000
Income Taxes	134,000	66,000

(a) Prepare a comparative income statement with common-size percentages.
(b) Indicate the favorable and unfavorable changes.

P15-2. The following condensed information is taken from the statement of Muldoon Company Ltd.:

	December 31	
	Year 2	*Year 1*
Current Assets	$456,000	$340,000
Plant and Equipment (net)	580,000	600,000
Current Liabilities	260,000	244,000
Long-Term Liabilities	200,000	240,000
Capital Stock	450,000	400,000
Retained Earnings	126,000	56,000

Prepare a condensed comparative balance sheet, showing the dollar amounts and the percentages of increase or decrease during Year 2.

P15-3. In the left-hand column a series of transactions is listed; in the right-hand column, a series of ratios:

Transaction	*Ratio*
1. Declaration of a cash dividend	Current ratio
2. Write-off of an uncollectible account receivable	Receivables turnover
3. Purchase of inventory on open account	Acid-test ratio
4. Issuance of 10-year mortgage bonds	Rate of return on total assets

5. Issuance of additional shares of stock for cash	Creditor equity ratio
6. Issue of stock dividend on common stock	Earnings per share
7. Appropriation of retained earnings	Rate of return on shareholders' equity
8. Purchase of supplies on open account	Current ratio
9. Payment to short-term creditor in full	Acid-test ratio
10. Payment of accounts payable, taking the cash discount	Inventory turnover

State whether each transaction will cause the indicated ratio to increase, decrease, or remain unchanged. For the current ratio, receivables turnover, acid-test ratio, and inventory turnover, assume that the ratio is greater than 1:1 before each transaction occurred.

P15-4. The following condensed statement was prepared for Durham Company Ltd. as of December 31.

Assets	
Current Assets	$ 60,000
Plant and Equipment	200,000
Total Assets	$260,000
Liabilities and Shareholders' Equity	
Current Liabilities	$ 15,000
Long-Term Liabilities	60,000
Total Liabilities	$ 75,000
Shareholders' Equity	185,000
Total Liabilities and Shareholders' Equity	$260,000

1. Compute (1) the current ratio and (2) the working capital.
2. Explain the significance of each to management.

P15-5. *(Financial policy decision problem)* The following list contains all the current assets and current liabilities of the Lamplighter Company as of December 31, Year 1. The list also contains some noncurrent items.

Accounts Payable	$ 5,000
Accounts Receivable	13,000
Cash	6,000
Land	35,000
Marketable Securities	6,000
Merchandise Inventory	60,000
Mortgage Payable (due July 1, Year 20)	100,000
Notes Payable (due July 1, Year 2)	20,000
Prepaid Insurance	2,500
Salaries Payable	2,000

Required:

1. Compute the current ratio, the acid-test ratio, and the working capital.
2. Assume that you are the loan officer of a bank to which the Lamplighter Company has applied for a 90-day loan of $15,000. Would you grant the loan? Why? Assume that the loan is granted; compute the current ratio, the acid-test ratio, and working capital for the Lamplighter Company immediately following the receipt of the loan.

P15-6. The records of the Nabors Company show that amounts due from customers were $400,000 and $460,000 at the beginning and the end of the year, respectively, and that sales for that period were $3,500,000. What conclusions can be drawn regarding the collection of accounts receivable, assuming (a) that terms of sale are 2/10, n/30; (b) that terms of sale are 2/10, n/40; (c) that terms of sale are 2/10, n/40, and 25% of the sales are for cash?

P15-7. The Edenton Company sells on terms of 2/10, 1/20, n/60. Approximately 40% of its sales are for cash. The Accounts Receivable account shows an average balance of $62,768 for the year. The total sales for the year were $730,400. What is the average collection period?

P15-8. The balance sheet of Nelson Company Ltd. at December 31 shows the following totals:

Current Assets	$26,000
Total Assets	80,000
Current Liabilities	12,000
Total Liabilities	32,000

Prepare analyses that will make these summary totals more meaningful to a reader of the statement.

P15-9. (*Financial policy decision problem*) The following information was taken from the financial statements of the Gordon Company.

	December 31, Year 1	*December 31, Year 2*
Net income		$ 4,000
Cost of goods sold		48,000
Total operating expenses		36,000
Merchandise inventory	$12,800	11,000
Current assets	29,600	31,000
Sales		92,000
Sales discounts		2,000
Sales returns and allowances		2,000
Current liabilities	15,200	10,000

a. Compute the following:
   1. The operating ratio
   2. The net operating margin ratio
   3. The turnover of merchandise inventory
   4. The working capital turnover

b. As a bank officer, would you approve a request by the company for a 2-year loan for $10,000?

P15-10. The comparative financial statements of the Marjorie Corporation show the following information:

	Plant and Equipment	*Long-Term Liabilities*	*Shareholders' Equity*
December 31, Year 4	$154,000	$70,000	$210,000
Year 3	140,000	67,000	161,000
Year 2	119,000	60,000	147,000
Year 1	126,000	63,000	140,000

Sales:		
	Year 4	$420,000
	Year 3	308,000
	Year 2	280,000
	Year 1	252,000

1. Compute the appropriate ratios.
2. Evaluate the significance of the ratios.

P15-11. *(Management policy decision problem)* The annual report of the Fiske Engine Company, Inc., includes the following data:

	December 31	
	Year 2	*Year 1*
Net sales	$410,633	$366,489
Net earnings	18,350	13,153
Total shareholders' equity	130,205	115,762
Long-term liabilities	87,208	72,153
Property, plant and equipment at net book value	104,445	103,955
Total assets	278,065	251,342
Shares of common stock outstanding at end of year	6,045	5,475

Required:

1. Prepare such ratios as you consider useful by a present or prospective shareholder in evaluating the company.
2. On the basis of these ratios, (a) what is your assessment of the company? (b) why might these ratios be misleading? (c) why do you consider them useful?

P15-12. (*Management policy decision problem*) The board of directors of the Mainline Corporation, after reviewing the following data taken from the firm's records, is concerned about a possible overinvestment in plant and equipment.

	Year 1	*Year 2*	*Year 3*
Current Assets	$104,000	$118,000	$120,000
Plant and Equipment	40,000	64,000	88,000
Current Liabilities	52,000	58,000	68,000
Long-Term Liabilities	22,000	36,000	39,000
Capital Stock	32,000	32,000	54,000
Retained Earnings	38,000	56,000	48,000
Net Sales	130,000	160,000	168,000

Required:

1. You have been asked to prepare a report on this matter to the board of directors. Include appropriate analyses and computations to support your conclusions.
2. Assume you are a prospective shareholder. How would this report influence your evaluation of the company?

P15-13. The following information relates to three companies in the same industry:

Company	Dividends per Share	Earnings per Share	Latest Market Price
A	None	$11	$35
B	$4	5	40
C	6	10	80

On the basis of only the foregoing, which company represents the most attractive investment opportunity? Explain.

P15-14. The outstanding capital stock of Hague Corporation Ltd. consisted of the following:

9% preferred stock, par value $50 (6,000 shares)	$300,000
Common stock, par value $25 (18,000 shares)	450,000

Earnings from operations for the year were $110,000. Compute the earnings per share on the preferred and common stocks.

P15-15. L. Konrath Company Ltd. is considering giving credit to D. Hawk Company Ltd. As part of the analysis to determine whether or not Konrath should extend credit to Hawk, assume the ratios below were calculated from D.Hawk Company Ltd.'s statements. For each ratio indicate whether it is a favorable, unfavorable, or neutral statistic in the decision to grant Hawk credit. Briefly explain your choice in each case.

	Year 1	Year 2	Year 3
1. Rate of return on total assets	1.96%	1.12%	(.87)%
2. Return to sales	1.69%	.99%	(.69)%
3. Acid-test ratio	1.73/1	1.36/1	1.19/1
4. Current ratio	2.39/1	1.92/1	1.67/1
5. Inventory turnover (times)	4.41	4.32	4.52
6. Equity relationships			
Current liabilities	36.0%	43.0%	48.0%
Long-term liabilities	16.0	10.5	5.0
Shareholders	48.0	46.5	47.0
	100.0%	100.0%	100.0%
7. Asset relationships			
Current assets	77.0%	72.5%	69.5%
Property, plant & equipment	23.0%	27.5%	30.5%
	100.0%	100.0%	100.0%

Would you grant credit to D. Hawk Company Ltd.? Support your answer with facts given in the problem.

P15-16. (*Financial policy decision problem*) Certain financial information for Glazer Company Ltd. and Quaid Company Ltd. as of the end of June are shown below.

	Glazer Company Ltd.	Quaid Company Ltd.
Current Assets	$ 720,000	$ 660,000
Plant and Equipment	3,048,000	2,310,000
Accumulated Depreciation	(480,000)	(360,000)
Patents	12,000	-0-
Goodwill	-0-	30,000
Total Assets	$3,300,000	$2,640,000
Current Liabilities	$ 390,000	$ 204,000
Bonds Payable, 9%, due in 10 years	600,000	720,000
Preferred Stock, 10%, $100 par value	720,000	480,000
Common Stock, $25 par value	1,200,000	900,000
Retained Earnings	270,000	180,000
Retained Earnings Restricted for Contingencies	120,000	-0-
Premium on Common Stock	-0-	156,000
Total Liabilities and Shareholders' Equity	$3,300,000	$2,640,000
Analysis of Retained Earnings.		
Balance, beginning of year	$ 273,600	$ 148,800
Net Income for year	224,400	118,800
Dividends: Preferred	(50,400)	(33,600)
Dividends: Common	(57,600)	(54,000)
Additions to Retained Earnings—Restricted for Contingencies	(120,000)	-0-
Balance, end of year	$ 270,000	$ 180,000
Market price of common stock per share	$ 40	$ 40
Market price of preferred stock per share	110	107

Required: Under the assumption that the two companies are generally comparable, write a brief answer to each of the following questions. Use only the ratios that will most reasonably substantiate your answer and indicate why. Compute the amount of each ratio and percentage indicated (carry your computations to one place beyond the decimal point).

1. Since the market prices of the bonds are not given, what ratios would aid potential investors to determine which bonds would probably sell at the higher price and which bonds would probably yield the higher return?
2. What ratio(s) would aid potential investors in preferred stock to determine which company's preferred stock is the safer investment?
3. To what extent is each company benefiting from the leverage factor inherent in the existence of the bonds? of preferred stock?
4. What are the dividend yield rates and earnings per share for the common stock of each company?

P15-17. Statements for Wahtola Company Ltd. as of December 31 follow:

Gross Sales	$887,400
Sales Returns and Allowances	13,500
Net Sales	$873,900
Cost of Goods Sold	624,000
Gross Margin on Sales	$249,900
Operating Expenses	195,900
Net Income from Operations	$ 54,000
Interest on Mortgage Payable	2,400
Net Income before Income Taxes	$ 51,600
Income Tax Expense	18,600
Net Income after Income Taxes	$ 33,000

Assets

Current Assets			
Cash		$ 36,000	
Accounts Receivable	$285,000		
Deduct Allowance for Doubtful Accounts	18,000	267,000	
Inventory		240,000	
Total Current Assets			$543,000
Plant and Equipment			
Land		$ 60,000	
Building	$180,000		
Deduct Accumulated Depreciation	36,000	144,000	
Store Equipment	$ 45,000		
Deduct Accumulated Depreciation	21,000	24,000	
Total Plant and Equipment			228,000
Total Assets			$771,000

Liabilities and Shareholders' Equity

Current Liabilities		
Accounts Payable	$259,800	
Accrued Expenses Payable	87,000	
Total Current Liabilities		$346,800
Long-Term Liabilities		
Mortgage Payable		60,000
Total Liabilities		$406,800
Shareholders' Equity		
Preferred Stock, 6%, $100 Par Value	$ 60,000	
Common Stock, $100 Par Value	240,000	
Retained Earnings	64,200	
Total Shareholders' Equity		364,200
Total Liabilities and Shareholders' Equity		$771,000

On January 1, the inventory was $300,000 and the total shareholders' equity was $345,000.

Required: Compute the following (carry to two decimal places):
Current ratio
Acid-test ratio
Inventory turnover
Percent of year's net sales uncollected
Ratio of shareholders' equity to total assets
Ratio of net sales to shareholders' equity
Ratio of plant and equipment assets to long-term debt
Earnings per share of common stock
Percent of net income to average shareholders' equity
Number of times preferred dividends is earned
Number of times mortgage interest is earned

P15-18. (*Correcting errors*) Assume that you are hired as chief accountant of the Palmer Company as of December 31, Year 2, before the books are closed. To familiarize yourself with the accounting procedures, you review the records for the two preceding years and discover the following errors:

a. The depreciation on the building was recorded as $2,000 in Year 1; it should have been $4,000.
b. The December 31, Year 1, inventory was understated by $2,500.
c. The company purchased a typewriter on July 1, Year 1, at a cost of $500. This amount was debited to Office Expense. Normally, the Palmer Company depreciates office equipment by the straight-line method, using a five-year life.
d. The liability for a $3,000 purchase was not recorded as of December 28, Year 2, when the purchase was made, although the amount was correctly included in the December 31, Year 2, periodic inventory.

Required: Prepare correcting and adjusting entries as of December 31, Year 2.

P15-19. (*Comparative statements—trend percentages*) The following information is taken from the books of the Rockwood Company:

	Year 1	*Year 2*	*Year 3*	*Year 4*
Sales	$337,500	$368,750	$390,625	$421,875
Cost of Goods Sold	195,000	217,100	229,000	246,000
Accounts Receivable	50,000	57,500	61,000	67,000
Merchandise Inventory	87,500	101,500	107,625	114,625
Net Income	30,000	30,600	31,500	32,400

Required:

1. Calculate the trend percentages (Year 1 is the base year).
2. Point out the favorable and unfavorable tendencies.

P15-20. The following information is taken from the books of Paradise Company Ltd. on December 31, Year 2:

Retained Earnings, December 31, Year 1 (credit)	$ 26,000
Loss from Sale of Land	2,400
Sales	224,000
Loss from Flood	3,200
Cost of Goods Sold	112,000

Adjustment for Cost of Machinery Charged to Equipment Repairs	2,800
Income Taxes	34,000
Understatement of Depreciation in Prior Years	4,800
Selling and General and Administrative Expenses	36,000
Dividends Declared	20,000

Required: Prepare an income statement and a statement of retained earnings.

P15-21. The following information is available for Hamblin Company Ltd. as of December 31, Year 2:

Gain from sale of equipment	$ 30,000
Net sales revenue	900,000
Income taxes—Year 2	110,000
Selling and administrative expenses	225,000
Cost of goods sold	440,000
Loss on write-off of abandoned equipment	4,000
Uninsured loss through fire	5,000
Adjustment for cost of maintenance and repairs charged to plant and equipment	3,500
Retained earnings, Dec. 31, Year 1 (credit)	60,000
Dividends declared	50,000
Income tax refund for prior years	15,000

Required: Prepare (a) an income statement and (b) a statement of retained earnings for Hamblin Company Ltd. for the year ended December 31, Year 2.

P15-22. (*Financial policy decision problem*) Yee Company Ltd. presents the following comparative information as of December 31.

	Year 2	*Year 1*
Cash	$ 15,200	$ 14,000
Accounts Receivable	16,800	10,000
Notes Receivable	15,200	4,000
Inventories	26,000	28,000
Machinery and Equipment (net)	36,000	40,000
Land	16,000	16,000
Building (net)	40,000	48,000
Accounts Payable	22,000	18,800
Notes Payable (current)	6,000	11,600
Mortgage Payable (long-term)	28,000	40,000
Capital Stock ($100 par value)	100,000	80,000
Retained Earnings, January 1 (credit)	?	8,000
Sales (net)	154,000	120,000
Cost of Goods Sold	100,000	74,000
Operating Expenses	28,800	28,000
Income Taxes	13,600	9,200
Dividends Declared	12,000	7,200

Required:

1. Prepare comparative financial statements, including the amounts and the percentages of change during Year 2.
2. Write a report to management indicating the favorable and unfavorable financial and operating trends.

16

Statement of Changes in Financial Position

The income statement and the statement of retained earnings disclose the causes of part of, but not all, the changes that take place in the items appearing in the balance sheets at the beginning and the end of a given period. Businesses engage in a variety of financial transactions, the details of which are not disclosed in either the income statement or the statement of retained earnings. Information regarding the changes in working capital, cash, and/or other financial items are summarized in a fourth major statement entitled ***statement of changes in financial position.***

EVOLUTION OF CONTENT OF STATEMENT OF CHANGES IN FINANCIAL POSITION

Prior to 1974, a 'Statement of Source and Application of Funds' was usually presented in most annual reports. The concept of funds employed in most cases was that of *working capital*; that is, the statement explained sources and uses of working capital during a period of time.

In 1974, the Canadian Institute of Chartered Accountants recommended that the content of the funds statement be broadened to include "all aspects of the financing and investing activities" of an organization and not only those affecting working capital.[1] The objective of this statement was "to provide information as to how the activities of the enterprise have been financed and how its financial resources have been used during the period covered by the statement."[2] A change in the title of the statement to 'Statement of Changes in Financial Position' was suggested to highlight the broadened concept of the statement.[3] The concept of funds used was that of *working capital*, although it was acknowledged that "where working capital is not considered to be an

[1]*CICA Handbook* (Toronto: Canadian Institute of Chartered Accountants, August 1974), Section 1540.05.

[2]*Ibid.*, Section 1540.03.

[3]*Ibid.*, Section 1540.02.

appropriate definition of 'funds,' the term refers to either cash and cash equivalents or cash, cash equivalents, and such other assets less liabilities which constitute current resources."[4]

The Canadian Institute of Chartered Accountants recommended flexibility in the form, content, and terminology of this new statement and stated that "An enterprise should adopt the form of the statement presentation that discloses its financing and investing activities in a manner which is informative and appropriate for the particular industry (or industries) in which it is engaged."[5] The Institute also recommended that information about *sources and uses of working capital* be appropriately described, in addition to the inclusion of other financial information such as the issuance of bonds payable in exchange for land, the issuance of common stock to acquire plant and equipment items, the conversion of bonds into common stock, and other financial transactions that *do not affect* working capital.

The statement of changes in financial position has two broad purposes:

1. To strengthen financial planning by providing historical information on sources and uses of financial resources.
2. To help explain to financial statement users the causes of changes in financial position from one balance sheet prepared as of a given date to the one prepared as of the end of the next period.

Typically, in the preparation of a statement of changes in financial position, attention is *usually* focused first on working capital and then on those financing and investing activities not affecting working capital. It is therefore appropriate that we turn first to a careful consideration of working capital—specifically the preparation of a statement of changes in financial position on a working capital basis. After this narrower concept is carefully identified, the broader concept will be illustrated.

STATEMENT OF CHANGES IN FINANCIAL POSITION—WORKING CAPITAL BASIS

The chief sources of working capital are operations, additional investments by owners, long-term borrowing, and the sale of assets. The chief uses of working capital are to increase noncurrent assets, retire long-term debt, reduce the owner's or the shareholders' equity, and provide for the declaration of dividends. The statement of changes in financial position on a working capital basis emphasizes the interrelationship of the sources (inflows) and uses (outflows) of working capital. A chart of working capital inflows and outflows based on an analogy between the flow of working capital through a business and the flow of water into and out of a container is shown in Figure 16-1.

[4]*Ibid.*, Section 1540.06.
[5]*Ibid.*, Section 1540.14.

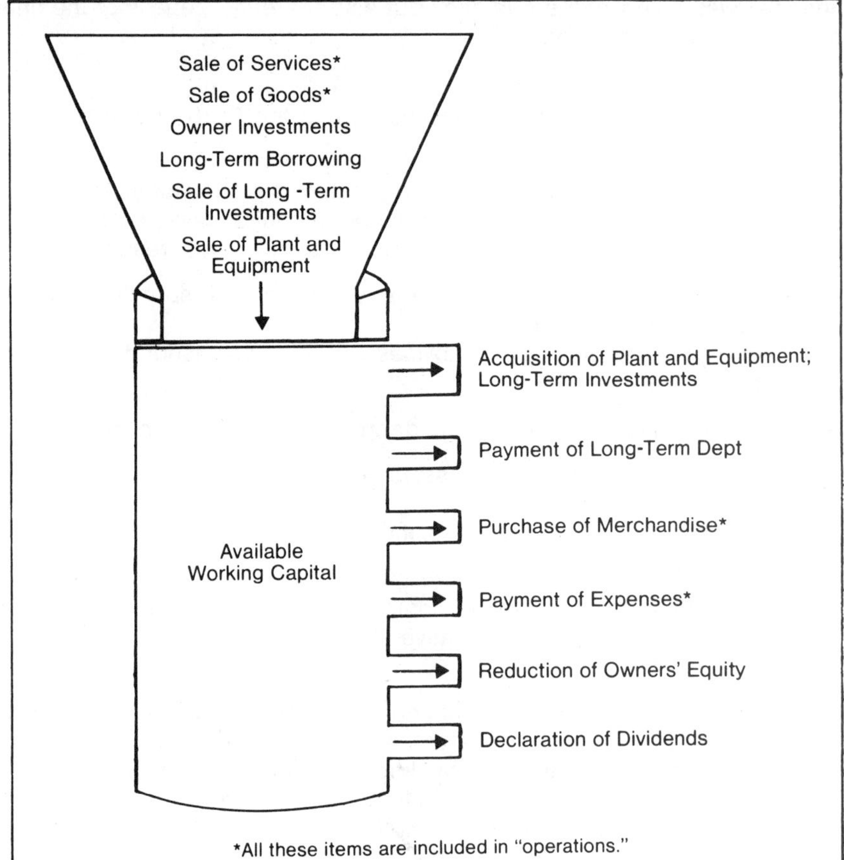

Figure 16-1
Working Capital Inflows and Outflows

Purpose of the Statement of Changes in Financial Position on a Working Capital Basis

It is often difficult for management and others to understand how the net income for a period was disposed of and the effect of the flow of working capital through the business. Readers of the conventional financial statements often ask such questions as: Where did the working capital come from? What was done with it? What happened to the various asset items during the period? Why did working capital decrease although earnings were favorable? Why were dividends not larger? Is the company solvent? Where did the working capital for replacement or expansion come from? What kind of financial decisions were made during the period? The statement of changes in financial position helps to answer these questions.

The smooth flow of working capital into and out of a business is the result of a continuing series of managerial decisions, often requiring a high level of skill and judgment. The statement helps the reader to understand not only the financial well-being of the company but also the effectiveness of the financial policies of its management.

Approaches to the Problem of Determining the Sources and Uses of Working Capital

In determining the information to be included in the statement of changes in financial position prepared under a working capital basis, a source of working capital—a cause of increase in working capital—must result:

1. In an increase in current assets without a corresponding increase in current liabilities, or
2. In a decrease in current liabilities without a corresponding decrease in current assets.

A use of working capital—a cause of decrease in working capital—must result:

1. In a decrease in current assets without a corresponding decrease in current liabilities, or
2. In an increase in current liabilities without a corresponding increase in current assets.

Since these sources and uses are compiled for a specific period, a month or a year, there are two possible alternative approaches to the solution of the problem.

1. An analysis of every transaction occurring during the period which affects a current asset or a current liability to determine the causes of changes in the working capital figure. This method would require much work, because many changes in both current assets and current liabilities *do not* change working capital—for example, the collection of accounts receivable.
2. An analysis of every transaction occurring during the period which affects a noncurrent account—long-term investments, plant and equipment, intangible assets, long-term liabilities, and shareholders' equity—to determine the causes of change in working capital. This approach is a shorter one; it can be used because every change in working capital must result in a change in one or more of the noncurrent accounts. This is the approach that is used in the following pages to determine the sources and uses of working capital that will be incorporated in the statement of changes in financial position—working capital basis.

Classification of Transactions

Since there is great variety in the transactions that enter into the inflow and outflow of working capital, it is helpful to classify them in distinctive categories, on the basis of their effect on working capital.

1. *Transactions that change a current and a noncurrent account.* For example, the acquisition of a tract of land for cash changes working capital and is, therefore, reported in the statement of changes in financial position—working capital basis.

2. *Transactions that change current asset or current liability accounts but have no effect on working capital.* For example, the purchase of merchandise on account and the settlement of an account receivable change the current accounts but do not change the amount of working capital; hence, they are not reported in the statement of changes in financial position—working capital basis. On the other hand, it should be noted that the purchases of merchandise and sales of merchandise are reported in the statement by being included in the overall category of "changes caused by operations" as illustrated in the following pages.

3. *Transactions that change noncurrent accounts only.* For example, the acquisition of a tract of land by a company in exchange for its own stock does not change working capital and is, therefore, not reported in the statement prepared on a working capital basis. Other transactions in this category include the conversion of bonds payable into common stock, and plant and equipment revaluations. It is apparent, however, that information about the acquisition of assets of a material amount by the use of nonworking capital items, should be shown on the statement of changes in financial position. The omission of this information is a definite weakness of the statement prepared on a rigid working capital basis.

Working Capital Provided by Operations

A primary source of working capital is the regular operating activities of the business. The determination of working capital from this source is complicated by the fact that the change in working capital may be greater than, or less than, the net income shown in the income statement. To illustrate, assume that the Cowan Company's income statement for the year ended December 31, is as follows:

COWAN COMPANY
Income Statement
For the Year Ended December 31, 19XX

Sales		$10,000
Cost of Goods Sold		7,000
Gross Margin on Sales		$ 3,000
Operating Expenses		
Depreciation—Plant and Equipment	$ 400	
Other	2,100	2,500
Net Income		$ 500

An analysis of this statement in terms of the change in working capital resulting from operations shows the following:

1. The recording of transactions that affect sales, cost of goods sold, and operating expenses—others change current asset and current liability accounts. That is, the recording of these transactions affects current accounts. Therefore, it is necessary to calculate the flow of working capital into the company from these transactions.

2. The recording of depreciation on plant and equipment does not affect the working capital from operations. Accordingly it is necessary to reduce net income for the year by all amounts that do not affect working capital.

For brevity, the required adjustment to net income to compute working capital from operations may be determined by working backward as follows:

Working Capital Provided by Operations	
Net Income (before extraordinary items)	$500
Add Nonworking Capital Charges to Income Summary:	
Depreciation Expense—Plant and Equipment	400
Working Capital Provided by Operations Exclusive of Extraordinary Items	$900

Section 1540.22 of the *CICA Handbook* requires that in disclosing the working capital provided by operations "net income before extraordinary items" be the starting figure. Since there are no extraordinary items in the Cowan Company illustration, the net income figure is also net income before extraordinary items. It must not be inferred from the mechanics of this procedure that the $400 depreciation expense increased working capital and is thereby a source of working capital. The deduction of depreciation expense merely decreased net income without effecting a corresponding decrease in working capital. Accordingly, the net income figure usually must be adjusted to determine working capital provided by operations. An income statement is likely to include several items of this kind—for example, depreciation, amortization of intangible assets, and loss on disposal of plant assets—representing costs and expenses that enter into income determination but do not affect working capital in the current period. The relevant expenditures either were made in a prior period or will be made in a future period. The recognition of depreciation is essential to income measurement, but it does not change the amount of working capital.

To illustrate the preparation of a simple form of the statement of changes in financial position on the working capital basis, the balance sheet of the Fairfield Company, Inc., is given.

FAIRFIELD COMPANY, INC.
Comparative Balance Sheet
December 31, Year 2 and Year 1

	December 31		
	Year 2	*Year 1*	*Increase or (Decrease)*
Assets			
Current Assets			
Cash	$ 30,000	$ 32,000	$ (2,000)
Accounts Receivable (net)	65,000	52,000	13,000
Merchandise Inventory	112,000	92,000	20,000
Unexpired Insurance	3,000	4,000	(1,000)
Total Current Assets	$210,000	$180,000	$ 30,000

Plant and Equipment	$470,000	$438,000	$ 32,000
Deduct Accumulated Depreciation	105,000	98,000	7,000
	$365,000	$340,000	$ 25,000
Total Assets	$575,000	$520,000	$ 55,000

Liabilities and Shareholders' Equity

Current Liabilities			
Accounts Payable	$ 60,000	$ 81,000	$ (21,000)
Bank Loans Payable (short term)	31,500	26,500	5,000
Accrued Payables	3,500	2,500	1,000
Total Current Liabilities	$ 95,000	$110,000	$ (15,000)
Shareholders' Equity			
Capital Stock	$410,000	$350,000	$ 60,000
Retained Earnings	70,000	60,000	10,000
Total Shareholders' Equity	$480,000	$410,000	$ 70,000
Total Liabilities and Shareholders' Equity	$575,000	$520,000	$ 55,000

Step 1 in preparing the statement of changes in financial position on a working capital basis is to determine the changes in working capital. Such an analysis is easily made as follows:

	December 31	
	Year 2	Year 1
Current Assets	$210,000	$180,000
Current Liabilities	$ 95,000	$110,000
Working Capital	$115,000	$ 70,000

Net Increase
in Working Capital
$115, 000 − 70,000 = $45,000

Step 2 is to analyze the changes in all the noncurrent accounts.

	(Debit) or Credit	Effect on Working Capital	
		Increase	Decrease
Plant and Equipment			
Balance, 12/31/Year 1	$(438,000)		
Acquisition during Year 2	(32,000)		$ 32,000
Balance, 12/31/Year 2	$(470,000)		
Accumulated Depreciation—Plant and Equipment			
Balance, 12/31/Year 1	$ 98,000		
Depreciation for Year 2	7,000	$ 7,000*	
Balance, 12/31/Year 2	$ 105,000		
Capital Stock			
Balance, 12/31/Year 1	$ 350,000		
Stock Issued	60,000	60,000	
Balance, 12/31/Year 2	$ 410,000		
Retained Earnings			
Balance, 12/31/Year 1	$ 60,000		
Net Income for Year 2	35,000	35,000	
Dividends declared	(25,000)		25,000
Balance, 12/31/Year 2	$ 70,000		
		$102,000	$ 57,000
Net Increase in Working Capital			45,000
		$102,000	$102,000

*Nonworking capital charge to Income Summary.

Step 3 is to prepare a statement of changes of financial position—working capital basis, as shown on the following page.

The T-Account Method

Although a statement of changes in financial position on a working capital basis can be prepared directly from a comparative balance sheet as in the preceding example, it becomes more difficult to prepare as the number of transactions and accounts to be analyzed increases. Some systematic method is needed to facilitate the analysis of the transactions required for the preparation of the formal statement. Several techniques may be used for this purpose, all of which lead to the same result. The technique known as the *direct,* or *T-account,* method is often used because of its relative simplicity and clarity. The basic steps are as follows:

Step 1. A schedule of changes in working capital is prepared.

Step 2. A T account is opened for each *noncurrent* balance sheet item and the amount of the net increase or decrease, obtained from the comparative balance

FAIRFIELD COMPANY, INC.
Statement of Changes in Financial Position—Working Capital Basis
For the Year Ended December 31, Year 2

Working Capital Was Provided by:		
Operations		
Net Income (before extraordinary items)		$ 35,000
Add Nonworking Capital Charges against Operations		
Depreciation of Plant and Equipment		7,000
Working Capital Provided by Operations Exclusive of Extraordinary Items		$ 42,000
Issuance of Capital Stock		60,000
Total Working Capital Provided		$102,000
Working Capital Was Used for:		
Purchase of Equipment	$32,000	
Declaration of Dividends	25,000	
Total Working Capital Used		57,000
Net Increase in Working Capital		$ 45,000

sheet, is entered in each account. Increases in assets and decreases in liabilities and shareholders' equity accounts are debit changes and are entered on the debit side; decreases in assets and increases in liabilities and shareholders' equity accounts are credit changes and are entered on the credit side. A single horizontal line is then drawn under each amount, across the account.

Step 3. Two additional T accounts, Working Capital Summary and Operating Summary, are opened. The Working Capital Summary account represents all the current asset and current liability accounts; the amount entered in this account is, therefore, the net change in working capital as determined in step 1: it is a debit if there is a net increase; a credit if there is a net decrease. The Operating Summary account is used to determine the amount of working capital provided by operations. No entry is made in this account at this point. The amounts entered in the T accounts are added to make sure that total debits equal total credits.

Step 4. The net changes entered in the T accounts in steps 2 and 3 represent, in summary form, all the transactions that occurred during the period. These transactions are now reconstructed by separate entries below the horizontal lines in the appropriate T accounts. An offsetting debit or credit to a noncurrent account may be to:

1. *Another noncurrent account.* Although such a transaction does not affect working capital, the entry is made so that all changes may be explained.
2. *Working Capital Summary.* This account is debited or credited for transactions other than revenue and expense that affect working capital and noncurrent accounts.

3. *Operating Summary.* This account is debited or credited for transactions affecting revenue, expense, and noncurrent accounts. It adjusts the net income figure to a figure representing working capital provided by operations.

Step 4 is completed only when the balance of the amounts below the horizontal line in each account is equal to the net change entered above the horizontal line in steps 2 and 3. This ensures that all the transactions that affect working capital have been accounted for. Each entry should be identified by a letter or number, together with a brief notation giving the source of the entry to facilitate the preparation of the formal statement.

Step 5. The balance of Operating Summary is closed into Working Capital Summary.

Step 6. The formal statement of changes in financial position on a working capital basis is prepared. Operating Summary shows the details of working capital provided by operations. Working Capital Summary contains details of sources and uses of working capital; the debit entries represent sources, the credit entries are uses.

The comparative balance sheet of Plymouth Corporation Ltd. and related supplementary data are used to illustrate the step-by-step T-account method for the preparation of a statement of changes in financial position—working capital basis.

PLYMOUTH CORPORATION LTD.
Income Statement
For the Year Ended December 31, Year 2

Sales		$125,000
Cost of Goods Sold		70,000
Gross Margin on Sales		$ 55,000
Operating Expenses		
Depreciation—Machinery	$12,000	
Depreciation—Building	3,000	
Amortization of Intangibles	1,000	
Other	20,675	36,675
Operating Margin		$ 18,325
Gain on Sale of Investments		1,000
Net Income		$ 19,325

PLYMOUTH CORPORATION LTD.
Comparative Balance Sheet
December 31, Year 2 and Year 1

	December 31		
	Year 2	*Year 1*	*Increase or (Decrease)*
Assets			
Current Assets	$ 66,600	$ 58,600	$ 8,000
Long-Term Investments (at cost)	$ 22,000	$ 19,000	$ 3,000
Plant and Equipment			
Land	$ 18,000	$ 18,000	$ -0-
Buildings	126,000	110,000	16,000
Accumulated Depreciation—Buildings	(38,000)	(35,000)	(3,000)*
Machinery	152,000	125,000	27,000
Accumulated Depreciation—Machinery	(37,000)	(25,000)	(12,000)*
Total Plant and Equipment	$221,000	$193,000	$28,000
Intangible Assets	$ 9,000	$ 10,000	$ (1,000)
Total Assets	$318,600	$280,600	$38,000
Liabilities and Shareholders' Equity			
Current Liabilities	$ 26,500	$ 23,000	$ 3,500
Long-Term Liabilities			
Mortgage Payable	32,000	35,000	(3,000)
Total Liabilities	$ 58,500	$ 58,000	$ 500
Shareholders' Equity			
5% Preferred Stock, $100 par value	$ 55,000	$ 50,000	$ 5,000
Common Stock, no-par value	125,000	110,000	15,000
Premium on Common Stock	13,000	10,000	3,000
Retained Earnings	67,100	52,600	14,500
Total Shareholders' Equity	$260,100	$222,600	$37,500
Total Liabilities and Shareholders' Equity	$318,600	$280,600	$38,000

*These items represent increases to contra asset accounts, which in turn represent decreases in assets.

An analysis of the income statement, the statement of retained earnings, and the changes in the noncurrent items discloses the following supplementary information:

1. Net income per statement $19,325
2. Depreciation
   a. Machinery 12,000
   b. Building 3,000
3. Amortization of intangible assets 1,000
4. Dividends declared and paid 4,825
5. Payment on mortgage payable 3,000
6. Investments costing $4,000 were sold for $5,000 (the gain of $1,000 was included in net income). Since investments increased by $3,000, additional investments costing $7,000 = ($4,000 + $3,000) must have been acquired.
7. Plant and Equipment
   a. No machinery was sold during the period. Acquisitions, therefore, must have cost $27,000.
   b. No buildings were disposed of during the period. Acquisitions, therefore, must have cost $16,000.
8. Issuance of Stock
   a. Preferred—50 shares at par value
   b. Common—1,500 shares at $12 per share

Step 1. A schedule of changes in working capital is prepared.

	December 31	
	Year 2	*Year 1*
Current Assets	$66,600	$58,600
Current Liabilities	$26,500	$23,000
Working Capital	$40,100	$35,600

Net Increase in Working Capital
$40,100 − 35,600 = $4,500

Step 2. A T account is opened for each noncurrent balance sheet item and the amount of change during the year is entered. A single horizontal rule is drawn under each amount. The accounts for Machinery and Common Stock are illustrated below.

Machinery

27,000	

Common Stock

	15,000

Step 3. Two additional T accounts are opened—Working Capital Summary and Operating Summary. The net change in working capital is entered in the Working Capital Summary account, and a rule is drawn.

Operating Summary

Working Capital Summary

4,500	
Increases in working capital	Decreases in working capital

Step 4. All the transactions for the year are reconstructed in separate summary entries and reflected below the horizontal rules of each account. The entries indicated by the changes in the comparative balance sheets and the supplementary data are made directly to the T accounts. They are shown in general journal form only to facilitate the explanation. They are posted to the T accounts only—*not to the regular general ledger accounts.*

(a)

Operating Summary—Net Income	19,325	
Retained Earnings		19,325

The amount of $19,325, the net income for the period, was originally recorded as a closing entry by a debit to Income Summary and a credit to Retained Earnings. In this entry, Operating Summary is debited in place of Income Summary. Since the balance of the Operating Summary account will show the amount of working capital provided by operations, this entry assumes a net increase in funds of $19,325 resulting from the revenue and expense transactions for the period.

(b)

Operating Summary—Depreciation of Machinery	12,000	
Accumulated Depreciation—Machinery		12,000

This entry represents the annual depreciation charge, the original debit being to Depreciation Expense—Machinery, an expense account. It is evident that the assumption made in entry (a), that all expenses decrease working capital, is not valid. Working capital is used to acquire machinery, but the periodic allocation of this cost as a deduction from revenue does not affect working capital. The debit in this entry will, therefore, be added to the debit from entry (a) in determining the amount of working capital provided by operations.

(c)

Operating Summary—Depreciation of Buildings	3,000	
Accumulated Depreciation—Buildings		3,000

The reason for this entry is the same as for entry (b). It is another of the required adjustments to net income to compute working capital provided by operations.

(d)		
Operating Summary—Amortization of Intangibles	1,000	
Intangible Assets		1,000

This entry represents the amortization of a cost incurred in a prior period. The reason for the entry is the same as for entry (b); another adjustment to net income.

(e)		
Retained Earnings	4,825	
Working Capital Summary—Declaration of Dividends		4,825

Dividends were declared and paid, resulting in a decrease in working capital. If the dividends were declared but not paid, the credit to Dividends Payable would increase current liabilities and decrease working capital. Entry (e) would, therefore, be the same.

(f)		
Working Capital Summary—Sale of Investments	5,000	
Long-Term Investments		4,000
Operating Summary—Gain on Sale of Investments		1,000

Securities that cost $4,000 were sold for $5,000. The gain on the sale is an ordinary item and is included in the reported net income of $19,325, and in Operating Summary through entry (a). But the effect of the sale was to increase working capital by a total of $5,000; hence, the debit to Working Capital Summary for $5,000 in entry (f). Furthermore, the increase in working capital resulting from the gain ($1,000) should be reported as an integral part of the total increase in working capital from sale of investments ($5,000) and not as a part of working capital provided by operations. The credit of $1,000 to Operating Summary, therefore, cancels a like amount included in Operating Summary through entry (a).

The T account for Long-Term Investments now appears as shown.

Long-Term Investments

Debit	Credit
3,000	
	(f) 4,000

Since the balance below the horizontal line must be the same as the balance above the line, a debit entry of $7,000 must be made. It may be assumed that securities costing $7,000 were acquired. In practice, reference would be made to the records to confirm this assumption.

(g)		
Long-Term Investments	7,000	
Working Capital Summary—Purchase of Investments		7,000
(h)		
Machinery	27,000	
Working Capital Summary—Purchase of Machinery		27,000

The explanation for entry (h) is the same as for entry (g). Since no machinery was sold during the period, it may be assumed that the net change represents acquisitions.

(i)		
Buildings	16,000	
Working Capital Summary—Acquisition of Building		16,000
(j)		
Working Capital Summary—Issuance of Preferred Stock	5,000	
5% Preferred Stock		5,000

Fifty shares of preferred stock were issued at par value.

(k)		
Working Capital Summary—Issuance of Common Stock	18,000	
Common Stock		15,000
Premium on Common Stock		3,000

Fifteen hundred shares of common stock were issued at $12 a share.

(l)		
Mortgage Payable	3,000	
Working Capital Summary—Payment of Mortgage Payable		3,000

The decrease in Mortgage Payable is assumed to be due to a cash payment.

At this point, the balance below the horizontal line in each noncurrent account is equal to the net change above the line, all the transactions affecting funds having been reproduced.

Step 5. The balance in the Operating Summary account is now $34,325, representing the working capital provided by operations. This balance is transferred to Working Capital Summary.

(m)		
Working Capital Summary—Working Capital Provided by Operations	34,325	
Operating Summary		34,325

The completeness and accuracy of the work is verified by the equality of the balances above and below the rule of the Working Capital Summary account.

Long-Term Investments

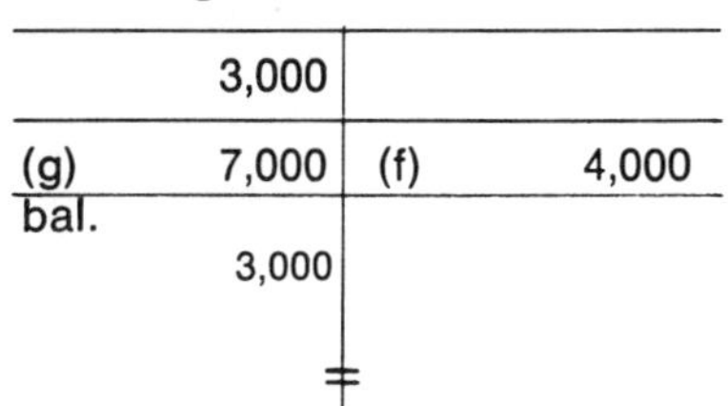

	3,000		
(g)	7,000	(f)	4,000
bal.	3,000		

Machinery

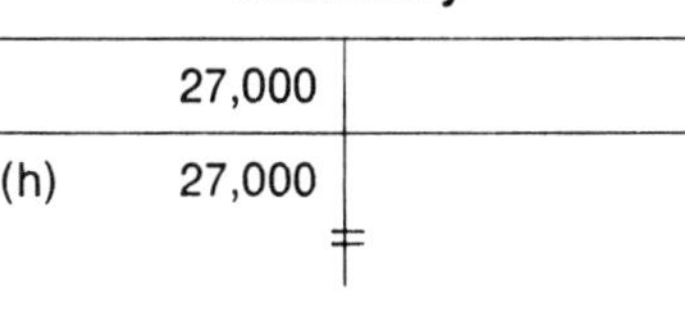

	27,000		
(h)	27,000		

Common Stock

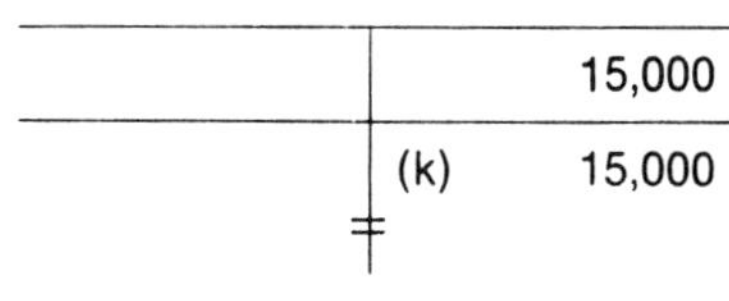

			15,000
		(k)	15,000

Buildings

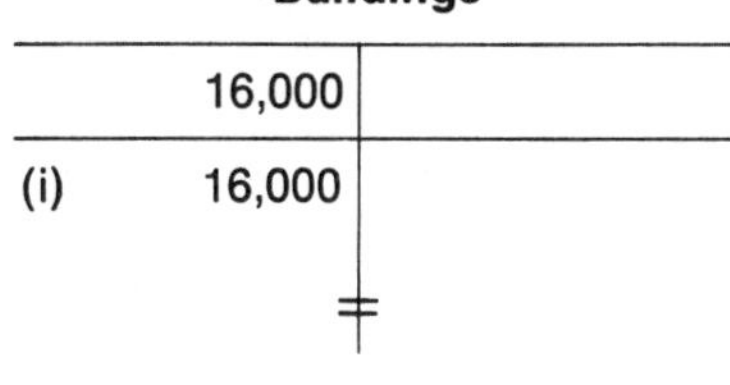

	16,000		
(i)	16,000		

Accumulated Depreciation —Machinery

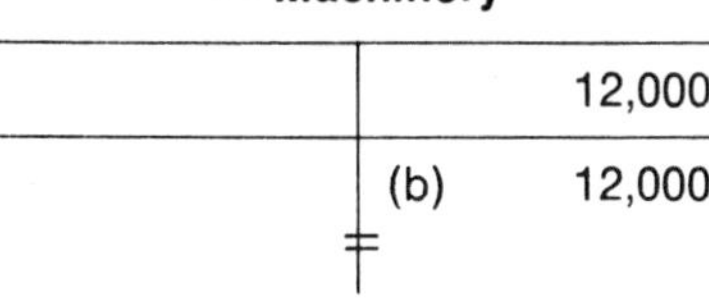

			12,000
		(b)	12,000

Premium on Common Stock

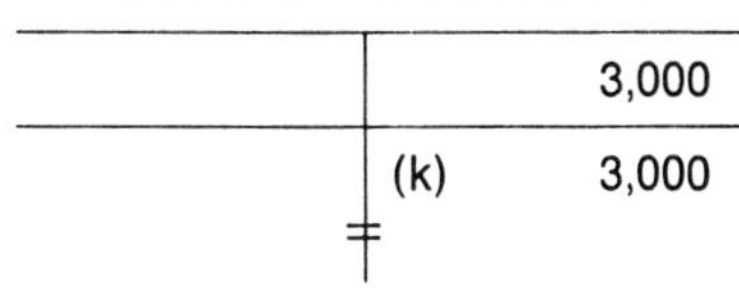

			3,000
		(k)	3,000

Accumulated Depreciation —Buildings

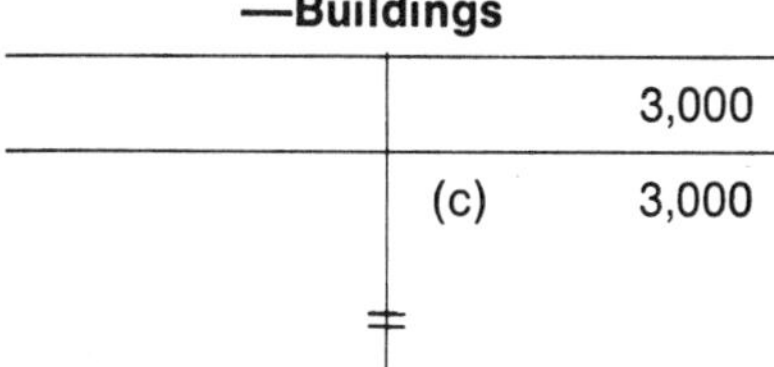

			3,000
		(c)	3,000

Mortgage Payable

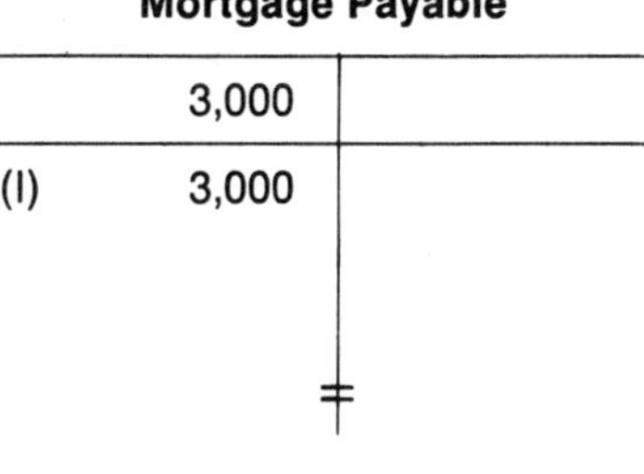

	3,000		
(l)	3,000		

Retained Earnings

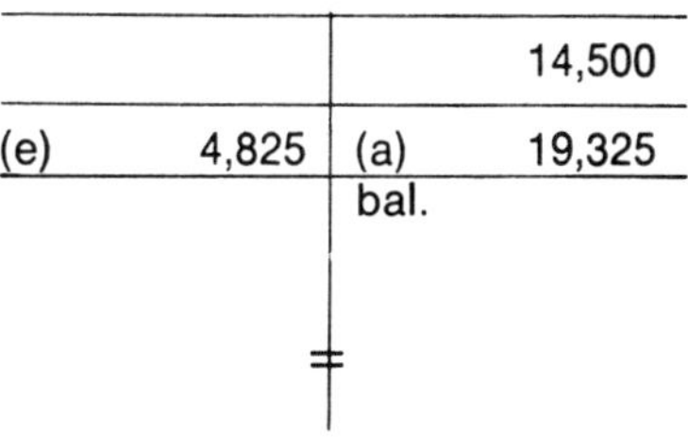

			14,500
(e)	4,825	(a)	19,325
		bal.	

Intangible Assets

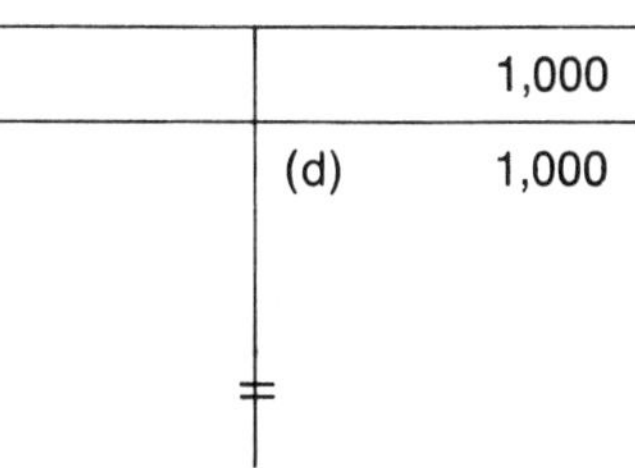

			1,000
		(d)	1,000

5% Preferred Stock

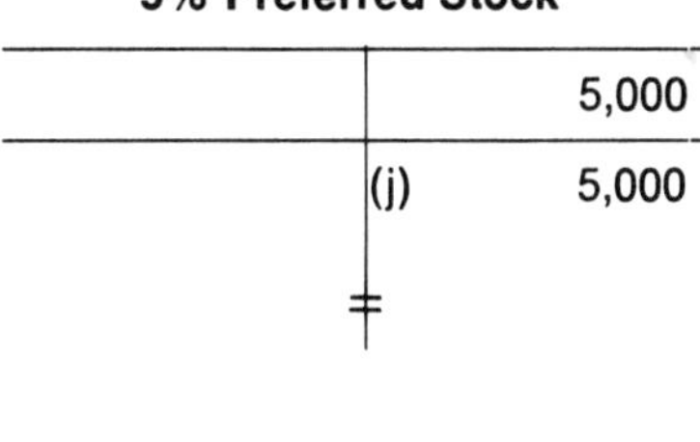

			5,000
		(j)	5,000

Operating Summary

(a) Net income	19,325	(f) Gain on Sale of investments	1,000
(b) Depreciation of machinery	12,000	(m) Working capital provided by operations	34,325
(c) Depreciation of buildings	3,000		
(d) Amortization of intangibles	1,000		
	35,325		35,325

Explanations are required.

Working Capital Summary

Sources		Uses	
	4,500		
(f) Sale of investments	5,000	(e) Cash dividends declared	4,825
(j) Issuance of preferred stock at par value	5,000	(g) Purchase of investments	7,000
(k) Issuance of common stock at premium	18,000	(h) Purchase of machinery	27,000
(m) Working capital provided by operations	34,325	(i) Purchase of buildings	16,000
bal. 4,500		(l) Payment on mortgage	3,000

Explanations are required.

Note that explanations are required for the last two summary accounts so that the formal statements can be prepared from these two accounts.

It is suggested that the accountant place some symbol in the noncurrent accounts to indicate that he has explained all the changes that have occurred in these accounts during the year. An equals sign (=) written across the vertical line of the T account is an excellent symbol to describe that the accountant has completed his task. When all the T accounts have an equals sign (=) written across the vertical line of the T, the accountant can quickly ascertain that he has completed the total work requirement on the T accounts. He can then proceed to step 6, the preparation of the formal statement.

Step 6. The formal statement of changes in financial position on the working capital basis can now be prepared directly from the Working Capital Summary and Operating Summary accounts: the debits represent sources of working capital; the credits represent uses of working capital. Supporting figures for working capital received from operations must be taken from the Operating Summary account.

PLYMOUTH CORPORATION LTD.
Statement of Changes in Financial Position—Working Capital Basis
For the Year Ended December 31, Year 2

Working Capital Was Provided by:	
Operations	
Net Income (before extraordinary items)	$19,325
Add Nonworking Capital Charges against Operations	
Depreciation of Machinery	12,000
Depreciation of Building	3,000
Amortization of Intangibles	1,000
Total	$35,325
Deduct Nonworking Credits to Operations	
Gain on Sale of Investments	1,000
Working Capital Provided by Operations Exclusive of Extraordinary Items	$34,325

Sale of Investments		5,000
Issuance of Preferred Stock		5,000
Issuance of Common Stock		18,000
Total Working Capital Provided		$62,325
Working Capital Was Used for		
Purchase of Investments	$ 7,000	
Purchase of Machinery	27,000	
Purchase of Buildings	16,000	
Declaration of Dividends	4,825	
Payment of Mortgage Payable	3,000	
Total Working Capital Used		57,825
Net Increase in Working Capital		$ 4,500

ALL-FINANCIAL RESOURCES CONCEPT OF FUNDS

The expanded concept of funds recommended by the Canadian Institute of Chartered Accountants includes not only items affecting working capital directly but also those financing and investing items which do not affect working capital.

Differences between Working Capital Concept and All-Financial Resources Concept

An interpretation of the information contained in the *CICA Handbook* indicates that the all-financial resources concept would include the following:

1. Sources and uses of working capital, plus
2. Sources and uses of other financial resources not affecting working capital, such as:
   a. Issuance of bonds payable or other long-term debt instrument in exchange for plant and equipment items.
   b. Issuance of capital stock in exchange for plant and equipment items.
   c. Conversion of bonds payable into common stock.
   d. Conversion of preferred stock into common stock.
   e. The exchange of one plant and equipment item for another plant and equipment item.

Each item listed in 2 above preferably would be shown both as a source of financial resources and as a use of financial resources.

Not all changes in balance sheet items are to be listed as sources and uses of financial resources. Specifically excluded are the following:

1. Stock dividends
2. Restrictions on retained earnings.
3. Asset appraisal adjustments.

These items are considered primarily to be accounting changes that do not alter the basic nature of financial resources.

Illustration of the All-Financial Resources Concept. Assume that Fundo Company Ltd. issued 9 percent bonds with a face value of $100,000 at 100 to Beaver Realty Corporation for land. This transaction consists of a financing item (issuance of bonds) and an investing item (purchase of land) both of which do not affect working capital. In analyzing the noncurrent accounts on the balance sheet—step 4—the following entries would be made:

Financial Resources Summary—Issuance of 9% Bonds Payable at 100	100,000	
9% Bonds Payable		100,000
Land	100,000	
Financial Resources Summary—Purchase of Land		100,000

Even though the bonds in this transaction are issued directly to the realtor for the land, the transaction must be disclosed both as a source of financial resources and as a use of financial resources. The two entries are suggested as a means of more carefully delineating this problem.

For the purpose of clarity the entries to the T accounts are presented in general journal form. The entries will be lettered to correspond to the letters preceding the additional information. Since the all-financial resources concept is being followed, the account equivalent to working capital summary has been renamed *Financial Resources Summary.* This change of name seems to be indicated because the new summary account will be used not only to record sources and uses of working capital, but also to record those sources and uses of financial resources that do not affect working capital.

In the above example the issuance and bonds and acquisition of land would be shown on the statement of changes in financial position as shown below.

Financial Resources Were Provided by Issuance of 9% Bonds Payable at 100	100,000
Financial Resources Were Used for Purchase of Land	100,000

Since the all-financial resources concept is being followed, the title equivalent to Working Capital Was Provided by is renamed ***Financial Resources Were Provided by*** and the title Working Capital Was Used for is renamed ***Financial Resources Were Used for.***

An illustrative formal statement of changes in financial position prepared under the all-financial resources concept is shown below.

THE FUNDO COMPANY LTD.
Statement of Changes in Financial Position
For the Year Ended December 31, 19XX

Financial Resources Were Provided by	
Operations	
Net Income (before extraordinary items)	$150,000
Add Nonworking Capital Charges to Operations	
Loss on Disposal of Machinery	10,000
Depreciation of Machinery	20,000
Total	$180,000

Deduct Nonworking Capital Credits to Operations		
Amortization of Premium on 9% Bonds Payable		1,000
Working Capital Provided by Operations Exclusive of Extraordinary Items		$179,000
Disposal of Machinery		80,000
Issuance of 9% Bonds Payable at 105		210,000
Issuance of 9% Bonds Payable at 100		100,000
Issuance of Common Stock		150,000
Total Financial Resources Provided		$719,000
Financial Resources Were Used for		
Declaration of Dividends	$ 50,000	
Purchase of Machinery	150,000	
Purchase of Land	100,000	
Retirement of Convertible Preferred Stock	150,000	
Total Financial Resources Used		450,000
Net Increase in Working Capital		$269,000

These items did not affect working capital.

STATEMENT OF CHANGES IN FINANCIAL POSITION—CASH BASIS

The specific content of the statement of changes in financial position will depend upon the purposes and objectives that users of this statement have in mind. For many short-run purposes, a statement based on cash is definitely of more importance than perhaps any other fund concept; such a statement is quite useful to management and analysts in budgeting and forecasting cash requirements. With the extremely high interest rates in effect today, the administration of cash is of paramount importance.

The basic logic of the analysis for a cash-basis statement of changes in financial position is the same as for a working-capital basis statement: an analysis of the relationships of the items in the financial statements. The causes of the changes in cash—the sources and uses of cash—are determined by analyzing the changes in all accounts other than Cash. Figures from the income statement are used to determine the changes in cash as a result of operations, and figures from the position statement together with supplementary data reveal the remaining causes for the changes in cash.

As with working capital provided by operations, a major problem is the determination of the cash generated by operations; this problem is complicated by the fact that the revenue and expense figures used for income measurement are different from cash receipts and cash disbursements. The time lag in the settlement of accounts with customers and creditors and the prepayment of certain expenses, for example, necessitate the conversion of accrual-basis revenue and expense amounts to the cash equivalent.

Thus in applying the T-account procedure for purposes of preparing a statement of changes in financial position on a cash basis, it is necessary to open a T account for every balance sheet account for which a periodic change is recorded, including an Operating Summary account and the Cash Summary account. The transactions causing changes in cash are reconstructed in summary form through a process of analyzing the changes in all accounts other than Cash and by reference to supplementary information. Since the procedural approach is similar to the preceding illustrations, an expanded example is not shown here.

GLOSSARY

All-Financial Resources A concept of funds which includes the disclosure of not only the sources and uses of working capital or cash, but also other financial and investment information that does not affect working capital.

Changes in Working Capital Working capital can be increased by transactions which increase current assets without increasing current liabilities or by transactions which decrease current liabilities without decreasing current assets; working capital can be decreased by transactions which decrease current assets without decreasing current liabilities or by transactions which increase current liabilities without increasing current assets.

Current Account Any current asset or current liability account.

Direct T-Account Method A method of determining the sources and uses of funds; T accounts for all noncurrent accounts are set up which show only the net change that has occurred during a year; then those transactions which cause these changes are reconstructed; and in this analytical process the sources and uses of funds are determined.

Financial Resources Summary A T account in the direct T-account method used to record on the debit side the sources of all financial resources and on the credit side the uses of all financial resources.

Funds In the context of the statement of changes in financial positions, funds usually refers to working capital. Other definitions of the term "funds" are also possible.

Noncurrent Account Any account on the statement of financial position *other than* current assets and current liabilities; specifically, a noncurrent account is any one of the long-term investments: plant and equipment, intangibles, long-term liabilities, or shareholders' equity accounts.

Operating Summary A T account in the direct T-account method used to record the working capital provided by or used in operations.

Statement of Changes in Financial Position A statement showing sources and uses of funds prepared in a manner to include all aspects of the financing and investing activities of an organization.

Working Capital Current assets less current liabilities, or that part of current assets not required to liquidate current liabilities.

Working Capital Summary A T account in the direct T-account method used to record on the debit side all sources of working capital and on the credit side all uses of working capital.

QUESTIONS

Q16-1. What is meant by the term *funds*?

Q16-2. The CICA recommended what concept of funds for typical presentation in annual reports?

Q16-3. The statement of changes in financial position may be a fourth major financial statement subject to the independent auditor's opinion. Secure an annual report (from your library) dated prior to 1974 and one dated after 1974 and compare the difference in location of the statement in the annual report and the difference in the title and content of the statement. Check to see whether the statement of changes in financial position prepared after 1974 conforms to the recommendations of the CICA.

Q16-4. What is the purpose of the statement of changes in financial position?

Q16-5. How may working capital provided by operations be determined?

Q16-6. What are the chief sources of working capital from operations? the chief uses of working capital for operations?

Q16-7. Certain transactions are eliminated from the statement of changes in financial position—working capital basis. Why? Give some examples.

Q16-8. How may the statement of changes in financial position—working capital basis be used to advantage by management? by investors? by others?

Q16-9. How may the statement of changes in financial position—cash basis be used to advantage by management? by investors? by others?

Q16-10. What are some of the sources of information for the preparation of the statement of changes in financial position—working capital basis?

Q16-11. What is the effect of a dividend declaration on working capital? of the payment of a dividend?

Q16-12. What is the effect of depreciation of plant and equipment (a) on working capital? (b) on cash?

Q16-13. The net income as shown on the income statement and the working capital provided by operations are different amounts. Why?

Q16-14. Which items are included in a statement of changes in financial position prepared under total financial resources concept that are not included on a statement prepared under the working capital concept?

Q16-15. Does the statement of changes in financial position eliminate the need for the balance sheet? for the income statement? Discuss.

Q16-16. What is the effect on working capital of a change to an accelerated method of depreciation?

Q16-17. In arriving at working capital provided by operations, certain items are added to net income and other items are deducted. Illustrate and explain.

Q16-18. The accounts receivable of a business totaled $30,000 at the beginning of the year and $24,000 at the end of the year. Accounts receivable written off as uncollectible during the year amounted to $2,600 and cash discounts allowed to customers amounted to $1,200. The sales for the year were $70,000. What were the cash receipts during the year from sales of the current and prior periods?

DEMONSTRATION PROBLEMS

DP16-1. *(Statement of changes in financial position—working capital basis)* The December 31, Year 2 and Year 1 balance sheets of Burley Company Ltd. carried the following debit and credit amounts:

	December 31	
	Year 2	*Year 1*
Debits		
Cash	$ 20,400	$ 25,200

Accounts Receivable (net)	70,200	65,800
Merchandise Inventory	170,400	172,800
Prepaid Expenses	3,000	3,600
Office Equipment	10,000	11,200
Store Equipment	59,600	56,600
Totals	$333,600	$335,200
Credits		
Accumulated Depreciation—Office Equipment	$ 5,000	$ 4,800
Accumulated Depreciation—Store Equipment	15,000	13,000
Accounts Payable	44,800	47,000
Notes Payable	20,000	10,000
Common Stock, $10 par value	220,000	200,000
Premium on Common Stock	13,000	11,000
Retained Earnings	15,800	49,400
Totals	$333,600	$335,200

Additional information:

a. The net loss for Year 2 was $3,800.

b. Depreciation expense on office equipment was $1,000; on store equipment, $3,400.

c. Office equipment that was carried at its cost of $1,200 with accumulated depreciation of $800 was sold for $600. The gain was credited directly to Retained Earnings.

d. Store equipment costing $4,400 was purchased.

e. Fully depreciated store equipment that cost $1,400 was discarded and its cost and accumulated depreciation were removed from the accounts.

f. Cash dividends of $8,000 were declared during the year.

g. A 2,000-share stock dividend was declared and issued. On the date of declaration, the common stock of the company had a fair market value of $11 a share.

Required: Prepare a statement of changes in financial position for Year 2 using the *working capital basis.* Use the direct T-account approach.

DP16-2. (*Statement of changes in financial position—total financial resources*) Kwick-Chango Corporation Ltd. reported the following information in regard to changes in financial position during Year 2.

THE KWICK-CHANGO CORPORATION LTD.
Comparative Balance Sheet
December 31, Year 2 and Year 1

	December 31		Change
	Year 2	*Year 1*	*Increase (Decrease)*
Cash	$ 787,500	$ 622,500	$165,000
Accounts Receivable (net)	135,000	120,000	15,000
Merchandise Inventory	889,500	600,000	289,500
Prepaid Insurance	9,000	7,500	1,500

Land	150,000	–0–	150,000
Machinery	675,000	600,000	75,000
Accumulated Depreciation on Machinery	(45,000)	(30,000)	15,000
	$2,601,000	$1,920,000	
Accounts Payable	$ 37,500	$ 30,000	7,500
Dividends Payable	75,000	15,000	60,000
9% Bonds Payable	450,000	–0–	450,000
Premium on 9% Bonds Payable	13,500	–0–	13,500
Convertible Preferred Stock	–0–	225,000	(225,000)
Common Stock, $10 Par	1,350,000	1,200,000	150,000
Premium on Common Stock	75,000	–0–	75,000
Retained Earnings	600,000	450,000	150,000
	$2,601,000	$1,920,000	

Additional information:

a. Net income for Year 2, $225,000.

b. A dividend of $75,000 was declared on December 12, Year 2, payable on January 16, Year 3.

c. On December 29, Year 2, the company traded in a machine which had cost $150,000 and had an accumulated depreciation of $15,000 for new machinery costing $225,000; the trade-in allowance, which was equal to fair market value of the old machine, was $120,000; the balance was paid in cash. The loss of $15,000 is an ordinary loss.

d. The annual depreciation expense on machinery was $30,000.

e. On January 1, Year 2, the company issued 9% bonds with a face value of $300,000 at 105 for cash. The bonds mature in 10 years.

f. On December 31, Year 2, the company issued directly to Orange Realty Company 9% bonds with a face value of $150,000 at 100 for land valued at $150,000.

g. The convertible preferred stock was converted during Year 2 into 15,000 shares of $10 par value common stock.

h. The annual amortization of premium on 9% bonds payable was $1,500.

Required:

1. Prepare a separate schedule of changes in working capital.
2. Prepare a statement of changes in financial position for Year 2 using the *total financial resources basis.* Use the direct T-account approach.

DP16-3. *(Statement of changes in financial position—working capital and cash basis)* The following data are taken from the books of Walker Corporation Ltd. (amounts are in thousands of dollars):

	December 31	
	Year 2	*Year 1*
Debits		
Cash	$ 630	$ 570
Marketable Securities	212	100

Receivables (net)	290	250
Inventories	190	140
Long-Term Investments	140	220
Machinery	1,000	700
Buildings	1,200	400
Land	70	70
Totals	$3,732	$2,450

Credits		
Accumulated Depreciation	$ 550	$ 300
Accounts Payable	200	150
Notes Payable	100	50
Mortgage Bonds Payable	1,000	500
Common Stock	1,100	800
Premium on Common Stock	110	-0-
Retained Earnings	672	650
Totals	$3,732	$2,450

WALKER CORPORATION LTD.
Income Statement
For the Year Ended December 31, Year 2

Sales		$1,200
Cost of Goods Sold		674
Gross Margin on Sales		$ 526
Operating Expenses		
Depreciation—Machinery	$100	
Depreciation—Buildings	160	
Other Expenses	200	460
Net Income from Operations		$ 66
Gain on Sale of Long-Term Investments—Ordinary		24
Total		$ 90
Loss on Sale of Machinery—Ordinary (proceeds were $30)		10
Net Income		$ 80

Required:

1. Prepare a statement of changes in financial position—working capital basis for Year 2.
2. Prepare a statement of changes in financial position—cash basis for Year 2.

PROBLEMS

P16-1. For each of the following transactions, state whether (a) it was a source of working capital, (b) it was a use of working capital, or (c) it had no effect on working capital:

1. Purchased government notes maturing in six months.
2. Issued a stock dividend to common shareholders.
3. Restricted retained earnings for anticipated plant expansion.

4. Issued common stock in exchange for a building.
5. Acquired machinery for $50,000; paid $20,000 in cash and issued a long-term note for the balance.
6. Reacquired some outstanding preferred stock for retirement.
7. Issued additional common stock at a premium for cash.
8. Issued bonds directly to preferred shareholders to retire preferred stock.

P16-2. Refer to P16-1 and state which of the transactions are a source or use of total financial resources yet are *not* a source or use of *working capital.*

P16-3. The Plant and Equipment section of the Seero Company comparative balance sheet shows the following amounts:

	December 31	
	Year 2	*Year 1*
Plant and Equipment		
Machinery	$275,000	$250,000
Deduct Accumulated Depreciation	125,000	120,000
Total Plant and Equipment	$150,000	$130,000

Acquisitions of new machinery during the year totaled $70,000. The income statement shows depreciation charges of $35,000 for the year and a loss from machinery disposals of $12,000.
Determine the original cost and accumulated depreciation of machinery sold during the year and the proceeds of the sale; prepare a partial statement of changes in financial position—working capital basis.

P16-4. For each of the following cases, compute the working capital generated by operations.

	a	b	c	d	e
Net income (loss) per income statement	$30,000	$(30,000)	$110,000	$90,000	$(40,000)
Depreciation of plant and equipment	4,000	4,000	9,000	6,000	2,000
Gain (loss) on sale of long-term investments			(2,000)	4,000	(1,000)
Periodic amortization of discount on bonds payable			2,000	1,000	500
Periodic amortization of patents				1,000	600

P16-5. During the year, the changes in the accounts of Miller Company Ltd. were as follows:

	Increases	*Decreases*
Cash		$20,000
Accounts Receivable	$ 12,000	
Merchandise Inventory	40,000	
Long-Term Investments	12,000	
Plant and Equipment	116,000	
Accumulated Depreciation	8,000	
Accounts Payable	15,000	
Taxes Payable		1,000
Mortgage Payable		12,000
Common Stock	92,000	
Retained Earnings	58,000	

Additional information:

a. Net income per income statement, $77,300
b. Dividends declared, $19,300
c. There were no disposals of plant or equipment during the year.

Prepare a statement of changes in financial position—working capital basis for the year

P16-6. The comparative statements of financial position of Tyrell Company Ltd., as of December 31, Year 2 and Year 1 disclosed the following:

	December 31	
	Year 2	*Year 1*
Debits		
Cash	$ 96,000	$ 126,000
Accounts Receivable (net)	117,600	99,600
Merchandise Inventory	170,000	130,000
Long-Term Investments	136,000	120,000
Machinery	700,000	600,000
Buildings	540,000	450,000
Land	100,000	100,000
Patents	36,000	40,000
Totals	$1,895,600	$1,665,600
Credits		
Accumulated Depreciation—Machinery	$ 80,000	$ 60,000
Accumulated Depreciation—Buildings	70,000	40,000
Accounts Payable—Trade	110,000	100,000
Notes Payable—Trade	16,000	20,000
Mortgage Payable	100,000	120,000
Common Stock	1,100,000	1,000,000
Retained Earnings	419,600	325,600
Totals	$1,895,600	$1,665,600

Additional information:

a. Net income for the year was $94,000.

b. There were no sales or disposals of plant or equipment during the year.

Required: Prepare a statement of changes in financial position using the ***working capital basis*** for Year 2.

P16-7. The following data of Morrison Company Ltd. are given in three parts (amounts are in thousands of dollars):

Part I

	December 31	
	Year 2	*Year 1*
Debits		
Current Assets	$210	$120
Plant and Equipment (net)	300	250
Totals	$510	$370
Credits		
Current Liabilities	$ 80	$ 40
Common Stock	300	300
Retained Earnings	130	30
Totals	$510	$370

Depreciation for period is $10.

Assume the same facts, except that Plant and Equipment cost and Accumulated Depreciation are itemized as follows:

Part II

	December 31	
	Year 2	*Year 1*
Debits		
Current Assets	$210	$120
Plant and Equipment	340	280
Totals	$550	$400
Credits		
Accumulated Depreciation	$ 40	$ 30
Current Liabilities	80	40
Common Stock	300	300
Retained Earnings	130	30
Totals	$550	$400

Part III

Assume the same debit and credit amounts as in Part II. Assume further that during the year a machine having an original cost of $20,000 and accumulated depreciation of $10,000 was sold for $14,000.

Required: For each part, prepare a statement of changes in financial position for Year 2 using the ***working capital basis.***

P16-8. Following is the comparative postclosing trial balance of Grand-Prix Company Ltd.:

	December 31	
	Year 2	*Year 1*
Debits		
Cash	$ 17,500	$ 25,000
Accounts Receivable (net)	47,500	40,000
Merchandise Inventory	130,000	97,500
Marketable Securities	–0–	55,000
Prepaid Expenses	2,000	1,250
Plant and Equipment	250,000	150,000
Patents	32,000	34,000
Totals	$479,000	$402,750
Credits		
Accumulated Depreciation—Plant and Equipment	$ 67,500	$ 50,000
Accounts Payable	50,000	30,000
Common Stock	250,000	250,000
Retained Earnings	111,500	72,750
Totals	$479,000	$402,750

Additional data:

a. Net income for the period was $62,500.
b. Dividends declared were $23,750.
c. The marketable securities were sold at a gain (included in a) of $7,500.
d. Equipment with an original cost of $10,000 and accumulated depreciation of $5,000 was sold at an ordinary loss (included in a) of $1,000.
e. Patents are being amortized over their legal life of 17 years.

Required: Prepare a statement of changes in financial position for Year 2 using the *working capital basis.*

P16-9. Data of Suskin, Inc., are given below.

	December 31	
	Year 2	*Year 1*
Debits		
Cash	$ 30,000	$ 22,500
Accounts Receivable	45,000	40,000
Merchandise Inventory	20,000	16,000
Investments (Long Term)	15,000	25,000
Machinery	20,000	12,500
Buildings	45,000	37,500
Land	5,000	5,000
Totals	$180,000	$158,500
Credits		
Allowance for Doubtful Accounts	$ 1,500	$ 1,000
Accumulated Depreciation—Machinery	3,750	1,500
Accumulated Depreciation—Buildings	9,000	6,000
Accounts Payable	20,000	16,500
Accrued Payables	2,250	1,750
Mortgage Payable	17,500	20,000
Common Stock	100,000	100,000
Retained Earnings	26,000	11,750
Totals	$180,000	$158,500

Additional data:

a. Net income for the year was $30,000.

b. Dividends declared during the year were $15,750.

c. Investments that cost $10,000 were sold during the year for $12,500. The gain is an ordinary one and is included in a.

d. Machinery that cost $2,500, on which $500 in depreciation had accumulated, was sold for $3,000. The gain is ordinary and is included in a.

Required: Prepare a statement of changes in financial position for Year 2 using the *working capital basis.*

P16-10. You are given the following information from the books of the Alberta Corporation:

ALBERTA CORPORATION
Statement of Financial Position Accounts
December 31, Year 2 and Year 1

	December 31		Change
	Year 2	*Year 1*	*Increase (Decrease)*
Debits			
Cash	$ 26,400	$ 31,200	$ (4,800)
Accounts Receivable	95,200	64,800	30,400

Merchandise Inventory	44,000	56,000	(12,000)
Machinery	164,800	174,800	(10,000)
Sinking Fund Cash	20,000	-0-	20,000
Totals	$350,400	$326,800	$ 23,600
Credits			
Allowance for Doubtful Accounts	$ 5,600	$ 5,000	$ 600
Accumulated Depreciation—Machinery	32,400	36,400	(4,000)
Accounts Payable	42,000	48,400	(6,400)
Dividends Payable	4,000	-0-	4,000
Bonds Payable	40,000	-0-	40,000
Premium on Bonds Payable	1,900	-0-	1,900
Capital Stock	200,000	200,000	-0-
Retained Earnings	4,500	37,000	(32,500)
Retained Earnings—Restricted for Sinking Fund	20,000	-0-	20,000
Totals	$350,400	$326,800	$ 23,600

ALBERTA CORPORATION
Statement of Retained Earnings
For the Year Ended December 31, Year 2

Balance, December 31		$37,000
Add: Net Income for year ended December 31		1,500
Total		$38,500
Deduct: Dividends Declared and Paid in Cash	$10,000	
Dividend Declared Payable January 15	4,000	
Appropriation for Sinking Fund	20,000	34,000
Balance, December 31		$ 4,500

ALBERTA CORPORATION
Income Statement
For the Year Ended December 31, Year 2

Sales		$170,900
Cost of Goods Sold		130,000
Gross Margin on Sales		$ 40,900
Operating Expenses		
Salaries Expense	$29,400	
Bad Debts Expense	600	
Depreciation of Machinery	7,000	
Taxes Expense	800	
Insurance Expense	600	38,400
Net Income from Operations		$ 2,500

Other Ordinary Expenses		
Bond Interest Expense	$2,100	
Deduct Amortization of Bond Premium	100	
Net Bond Interest Expense	$ 2,000	
Other Ordinary Revenue		
Gain on Sale of Machinery	1,000	1,000
Net Income to Retained Earnings		$ 1,500

Additional data:

a. Bonds payable in the amount of $40,000 were issued on April 30, Year 2, at 105.

b. Machinery that cost $14,000 and had accumulated depreciation of $11,000, was sold for $4,000 in cash.

Required: Prepare a schedule of working capital changes and a statement of changes in financial position—working capital basis for Year 2 by the T-account approach. Submit all supporting computations, including the T accounts.

P16-11. The comparative balance sheets of Rhodes Company Ltd. and related supplementary data are as follows:

	December 31	
	Year 2	*Year 1*
Assets		
Current Assets		
Cash	$ 50,000	$ 46,000
Marketable Securities	80,000	70,000
Accounts Receivable (net)	130,000	124,000
Merchandise Inventory	120,000	100,000
Total Current Assets	$ 380,000	$ 340,000
Investments (at cost)	$ 160,000	$ 20,000
Plant and Equipment		
Land	$ 100,000	$ 100,000
Buildings (net)	450,000	350,000
Machinery (net)	400,000	280,000
Total Plant and Equipment	$ 950,000	$ 730,000
Total Assets	$1,490,000	$1,090,000
Liabilities and Shareholders' Equity		
Current Liabilities		
Accounts Payable—Trade	$ 190,000	$ 180,000
Notes Payable—Trade	20,000	50,000
Total Current Liabilities	$ 210,000	$ 230,000
Long-Term Liabilities		
Mortgage Bonds Payable	150,000	50,000
Total Liabilities	$ 360,000	$ 280,000

Shareholders' Equity		
5% Preferred Stock, $100 par value	$ 200,000	$ -0-
Common Stock, $10 par value	700,000	700,000
Retained Earnings	230,000	110,000
Total Shareholders' Equity	$1,130,000	$ 810,000
Total Liabilities and Shareholders' Equity	$1,490,000	$1,090,000

Additional data:

a. Net income for the year, Year 2 was $140,000.
b. Dividends declared during year were $20,000.
c. Depreciation was: Machinery, $40,000; Buildings, $20,000.
d. There were no plant and equipment disposals during the year.
e. The Company issued 2,000 shares of 8% preferred stock at par value.
f. Investments costing $20,000 were sold for $28,000. The gain is an ordinary one and is included in Item a.

Required:

1. Prepare a separate schedule of changes in working capital.
2. Prepare a separate schedule of working capital provided by operations.
3. Prepare a statement of changes in financial position for Year 2 using the working capital basis. Use the direct T-account approach.

P16-12. You are given the following partial statement data and other information for Meade Company Ltd.:

	December 31	
	Year 2	*Year 1*
Balance Sheet Data		
Plant and Equipment	$550,000	$400,000
Credits		
Accumulated Depreciation	235,000	200,000
Bonds Payable	50,000	-0-
Premium on Bonds Payable	2,500	-0-

Income Statement Data	*Year 2*
Depreciation Expense	$ 60,000
Gain on Disposal of Plant and Equipment	4,000

Additional data:

a. Plant and equipment acquisitions during the year were $175,000.
b. Bonds payable were issued on December 31, Year 2, at 105 for a total of $52,500.

Required:

1. Set up T accounts for Plant and Equipment, Accumulated Depreciation, Bonds Payable, Premium on Bonds Payable, Operating Summary, and

Working Capital Summary. Place the net changes that occurred during Year 2 in the first four accounts.

2. Make all the necessary entries in the accounts to accumulate information for the statement of changes in financial position, using the working capital basis.

P16-13. Opry Company Ltd. revealed the following information regarding its changes in financial position during Year 2.

	December 31		*Change*
	Year 2	*Year 1*	*Increase (Decrease)*
Cash	$ 918,750	$ 726,250	$192,500
Accounts Receivable (net)	157,500	140,000	17,500
Merchandise Inventory	1,037,750	700,000	337,750
Prepaid Insurance	10,500	8,750	1,750
Land	175,000	–0–	175,000
Machinery	787,500	700,000	87,500
Accumulated Depreciation—Machinery	(52,500)	(35,000)	17,500
	$3,034,500	$2,240,000	
Accounts Payable	$ 43,750	$ 35,000	8,750
Dividends Payable	87,500	17,500	70,000
9% Bonds Payable	525,000	–0–	525,000
Premium on 9% Bonds Payable	15,750	–0–	15,750
Convertible Preferred Stock	–0–	262,500	(262,500)
Common Stock, $10 par	1,575,000	1,400,000	175,000
Premium on Common Stock	87,500	–0–	87,500
Retained Earnings	700,000	525,000	175,000
	$3,034,500	$2,240,000	

Additional information:

a. Net income for Year 2, $262,500.

b. A dividend of $87,500 was declared on December 19, Year 2, payable on January 14, Year 3.

c. On December 30, Year 2, the company traded in a machine which cost $175,000 and had an accumulated depreciation of $17,500 for new machinery costing $262,500; the trade-in allowance which was equal to fair market value of the old machine was $140,000; the balance was paid in cash. The loss of $17,500 is an ordinary loss.

d. The annual depreciation expense on machinery was $35,000.

e. On January 1, Year 2, the company issued 9% bonds with a face value of $350,000 at 105 for cash. The bonds mature in 10 years from issuance date.

f. On December 31, Year 2, the company issued directly to Lynch Realty Company 9% bonds with a face value of $175,000 at 100 for land valued at $175,000.

g. The convertible preferred stock was converted during Year 2 into 17,500 shares of $10 par value common stock.

h. The annual amortization of premium on 9% bonds payable is recorded by the straight-line method.

Required:

1. Calculate the change in working capital.

2. Prepare a statement of changes in financial position using the all-financial resources basis of funds.

P16-14. You are given the following information about certain items for two companies during a year:

Accounts Receivable—beginning of year	$ 54,000	$ 80,000
Accounts Receivable—end of year	70,000	76,000
Sales	210,000	300,000
Uncollectible Accounts Written Off	1,000	1,500
Cash Discounts on Sales	2,000	5,000

Required: For each company determine the amount of cash received from customers.

P16-15. You are given the following information about certain items for two companies during a year:

	1	*2*
Beginning Inventory	$ 24,000	$ 30,000
Ending Inventory	20,000	36,000
Purchases	150,000	170,000
Beginning Accounts Payable	20,000	28,000
Ending Accounts Payable	24,000	20,000
Discounts on Purchases	2,000	3,000

Required: For each company determine the amount of cash disbursements for merchandise.

Part Four

Cost Accumulation, Cost Control, and Financial Planning

17

Accounting for Manufacturing Operations

Up to this point, the accounting for only service and trading businesses has been considered. A trading business buys merchandise in finished form and sells it in the same form. A manufacturing company, on the other hand, buys materials that it converts into finished products by the application of labor and other factory costs. The accounting standards and procedures, however, are the same for both manufacturing and nonmanufacturing businesses. Additional accounts are opened to record the activities involved in the manufacturing process—the conversion of materials into finished goods. From these accounts the schedule of cost of goods manufactured may be prepared; this shows the cost of materials consumed, direct labor costs, and the other factory costs incurred in the manufacture of the finished product over a stated period.

This chapter describes procedures that are acceptable for financial accounting for a small general manufacturing business. It also introduces the general concepts and terms used in accounting for a manufacturing firm. These general manufacturing procedures, however, are not adequate to provide the information needed for effective managerial control. Such procedures are explained and illustrated in Chapter 18.

MATERIALS USED

All materials that are economically traceable to the finished product are referred to as *materials, raw materials,* or *direct materials.* Because many of these materials are fabricated by other manufacturers, the titles "materials" and "direct materials" are used here rather than "raw materials." The cloth used in the manufacture of a suit, for example, is classified as a "direct material." Some materials, although an integral part of the finished product, are not classified as direct materials because the cost or the quantity used is small or because it would be uneconomical to trace and determine the cost and amount of certain materials that are incorporated in the finished product. The thread used in manufacturing a garment, for example, may not be regarded as a direct material, although it can otherwise be clearly identified with the end product. The cost of the thread is an indirect factory cost. This and other indirect factory costs are discussed later in the chapter.

The cost of materials used during an accounting period in the manufacture of a product may be determined by the periodic inventory method in the same manner as is the cost of goods sold in a trading business. The procedure necessary to account for *materials, direct labor,* and *manufacturing overhead* in a manufacturing company may be illustrated by the following sequence of transactions.

(1)

Materials Purchases	79,500	
Accounts Payable		79,500
To record purchases of materials on account. Terms 2/10, n/30		

(2)

Transportation In on Materials Purchases	2,250	
Cash		2,250
To record freight charges on materials purchased.		

(3)

Accounts Payable	3,250	
Materials—Purchases Returns and Allowances		3,250
To record credit received for materials returned.		

(4)

Accounts Payable	76,250	
Materials—Purchases Discounts		1,525
Cash		74,725
To record payment of invoice of materials purchased.		

The Acme Manufacturing Company had materials on hand on January 1, costing $8,200.

Materials on hand on January 31 were $9,700. The Materials Used section of the schedule of cost of goods manufactured for the month of January is shown in Figure 17-1.

ACME MANUFACTURING COMPANY Schedule A-1 Partial Schedule of Cost of Goods Manufactured For the Month Ended January 31, 19XX			
Materials Used			
Materials Inventory, January 1			$ 8,200
Materials Purchases		$79,500	
Transportation In on Materials Purchases		2,250	
Gross Cost of Materials Purchases		$81,750	
Deduct Purchases Returns and Allowances	$3,250		
Purchases Discounts	1,525	4,775	
Net Cost of Materials Purchases			76,975
Cost of Materials Available for Use			$85,175
Deduct Materials Inventory, January 31			9,700
Cost of Materials Used			$75,475

Figure 17-1
Computation of Materials Used

DIRECT LABOR

The wages paid to employees performing operations directly on the product being manufactured are referred to as *direct labor.* Direct labor is the cost of wages paid for work involving the construction, composition, or fabrication of the end product.

The following journal entries demonstrate the recording of direct labor:

(5)		
Direct Labor	58,300	
Salaries and Wages Payable (and payroll tax withholding liabilities)		58,300
To record the direct labor costs incurred during January (payroll deduction details have been omitted).		

(6)		
Direct Labor	2,700	
Accrued Wages and Salaries Payable		2,700
To record direct labor costs accrued.		

The debit total of $61,000 = ($58,300 + $2,700) is the direct labor cost for the month. This amount is entered in the schedule of cost of goods manufactured on one line immediately following the amount for materials used.

MANUFACTURING OVERHEAD

All factory costs incurred in the manufacturing process other than the cost of materials used and direct labor are classified as *manufacturing overhead.* Other terms used for this group of costs are *indirect manufacturing costs* and *manufacturing burden.*

For a manufacturing company, manufacturing overhead, along with direct materials and direct labor, are product costs and not period expenses; that is, these costs are incorporated in the inventory of manufactured goods.

Selling expenses and general and administrative expenses are not considered manufacturing overhead, because they reflect the administrative and distributive functions of the business and are not part of the manufacturing function.

A separate account may be opened in the general ledger for each manufacturing overhead item; however, if these accounts are numerous, a subsidiary *manufacturing overhead ledger* may be set up. Its controlling account in the general ledger is Manufacturing Overhead.

The journals of the Acme Manufacturing Company showed the following additional entries (entry 7 was made during the month; the others represent end-of-period adjustments):

(7)

Factory Rent	2,000	
Heat, Light, and Power	12,000	
Indirect Labor	9,100	
Equipment Maintenance and Repairs	2,900	
Miscellaneous Factory Costs	2,950	
Accounts Payable (and payroll tax withholding liabilities)		28,950
To record overhead costs incurred during the month. (There was no accrued indirect labor, and payroll deduction details have been omitted.)		

Indirect labor is the labor cost for the workers whose efforts are not directly identified with the conversion of specific materials into specific finished products. Wages paid to employees who schedule and supervise the work of others, for example, would be classified as indirect labor. The term also includes the wages of repair and maintenance crews, guards, janitors, and cost accounting clerks assigned to the manufacturing function.

(8)

Depreciation—Machinery and Equipment	3,500	
Accumulated Depreciation—Machinery and Equipment		3,500
To record one month's depreciation of machinery and equipment.		

(9)

Factory Insurance	1,100	
Prepaid Insurance		1,100
To record the expiration of one month's insurance.		

(10)

Factory Property Tax	1,600	
Accrued Property Taxes Payable		1,600
To record property taxes accrued on the factory building.		

(11)

Amortization of Patents	950	
Patents		950
To amortize the patent cost for January.		

Amortization of patents represents that part of the cost of patents allocable to the current accounting period. It is assumed that these patents are for manufacturing processes. The cost of the patents should be amortized over the economically useful life or the remaining legal life of the asset, whichever is shorter. The Patents account may be credited directly for the amortized portion. The amortized portion is debited to Amortization of Patents, listed under Manufacturing Overhead. The unamortized balance of Patents is reported on the balance sheet as an intangible asset.

(12)

Small Tools Used	250	
Small Tools		250
To adjust the asset account to the inventory valuation.		

Small tools used represents the cost of special small tools used up by workmen during the accounting period. It is possible to depreciate small tools by methods similar to those used for machinery and equipment. This procedure is difficult, however, because of the great variety of tools used and their relatively small value. In addition, small hand tools are easily lost or broken, and their useful life is difficult to predict. To overcome this practical difficulty, small tools may be accounted for as follows: The acquisition cost is debited to the asset account Small Tools; at the end of each accounting period an inventory of tools on hand is taken and priced; the discrepancy between the balance in the asset account and the inventory count represents the cost of tools broken, discarded, or lost. The entry to adjust the Small Tools account to the inventory amount is a debit to Small Tools Used, a manufacturing overhead item, and a credit to Small Tools, a plant and equipment asset.

WORK-IN-PROCESS INVENTORY

The fabrication of a product is a continuing and repetitive process. At any time, therefore, partly finished products will be on hand in various stages of completion; they are known as *work in process* or *goods in process.* At the end of the accounting period, the work in process is inventoried and its value determined. Since the cost of these partly finished units is included in the total period manufacturing costs, the end-of-period work-in-process inventory is deducted from the total costs to arrive at the cost of goods manufactured. Work-in-Process Inventory is classified as a current asset in the balance sheet. The ending inventory of one period is the beginning inventory of the next period and enters into the cost of goods manufactured for that next period.

The Acme Manufacturing Company had a beginning work-in-process inventory on January 1 of $2,900. On January 31, the ending work-in-process inventory was $3,600. Note that the inventories include the cost of materials, labor, and overhead assignable to the unfinished product.

The completed schedule of cost of goods manufactured is shown in Figure 17-2.

Figure 17-2
Completed Schedule of Cost of Goods Manufactured

ACME MANUFACTURING COMPANY **Schedule A-1**
Schedule of Cost of Goods Manufactured
For the Month Ended January 31, 19XX

Materials Used			
Materials Inventory, January 1			$ 8,200
Materials Purchases		$79,500	
Transportation In on Materials Purchases		2,250	
Gross Cost of Materials Purchases		$81,750	
Deduct Purchases Returns and Allowances	$3,250		
Purchases Discounts	1,525	4,775	
Net Cost of Materials Purchases			76,975
Cost of Materials Available for Use			$ 85,175
Deduct Materials Inventory, January 31			9,700
Cost of Materials Used			$75,475
Direct Labor			61,000
Manufacturing Overhead			
Depreciation— Machinery and Equipment		$ 3,500	
Factory Insurance		1,100	
Factory Rent		2,000	
Factory Property Tax		1,600	
Heat, Light, and Power		12,000	
Indirect Labor		9,100	
Amortization of Patents		950	
Equipment Maintenance and Repairs		2,900	
Small Tools Used		250	
Miscellaneous Factory Costs		2,950	
Total Manufacturing Overhead			36,350
Total Period Manufacturing Costs			$172,825
Add Work-in-Process Inventory, January 1			2,900
Total			$175,725
Deduct Work-in-Process Inventory, January 31			3,600
Cost of Goods Manufactured			$172,125

TOTAL PERIOD MANUFACTURING COSTS

Total period manufacturing costs are made up of the costs of materials used, direct labor, and manufacturing overhead, as shown below.

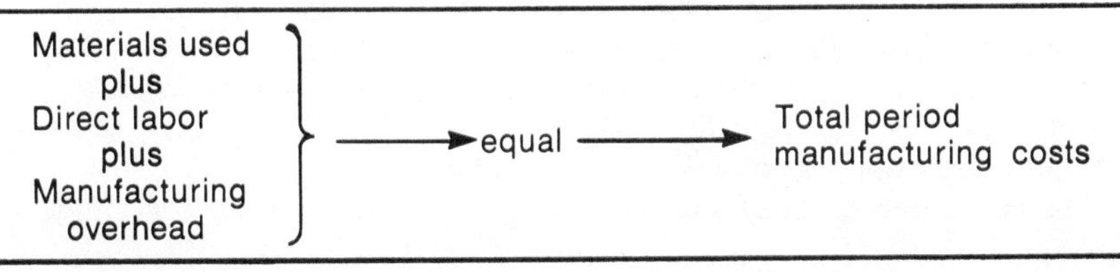

FINISHED GOODS AND COST OF GOODS SOLD

It is assumed in Figure 17-3 that the Acme Manufacturing Company had a beginning finished goods inventory of $12,100 and an ending inventory of $10,150. The term *finished goods* means the completed goods ready for sale and corresponds to the merchandise inventory of a trading business.

Cost of Goods Sold		
Finished Goods Inventory, January 1	$ 12,100	
Add Cost of Goods Manufactured (Schedule A-1)	172,125	
Cost of Finished Goods Available for Sale	$184,150	
Deduct Finished Goods Inventory, December 31	10,150	
Cost of Goods Sold		$174,075

Figure 17-3
Completed Schedule of Cost of Goods Manufactured

WORK SHEET FOR A MANUFACTURING COMPANY

There is only one essential difference between a work sheet for a manufacturing company and one for a merchandising company. In the work sheet for a manufacturing company, a pair of columns is added, headed Manufacturing, into which are extended the debit and credit account balances representing the elements of the cost of manufacturing—that is, all the accounts that enter into the preparation of the schedule of cost of goods manufactured. The difference between the totals of these columns is the cost of goods manufactured, which is then transferred to the Income Statement Debit column.

The function of the other work sheet columns is the same as in a merchandising company. The remaining illustrations and discussion in this chapter are based on the work sheet of Carol Manufacturing Company Ltd., shown in Figure 17-4. It should be observed that a different illustration is used here in order to add complexities that were not appropriate to the elementary illustration of the Acme Manufacturing Company.

ENDING INVENTORIES ON THE WORK SHEET

The ending inventories at December 31 are as follows:

Materials	$51,500
Work in Process	47,000
Finished Goods	19,600

All three amounts are entered as debits in the Balance Sheet columns. The two which affect manufacturing cost—Materials and Work in Process—are entered as credits in the Manufacturing columns. The Finished Goods is a part of the cost of goods sold computation and is entered as a credit in the Income Statement columns.

Entering the three inventories as debits in the Balance Sheet columns establishes them as the new end-of-year current asset value of inventories. Entering these same amounts as credits serves to reduce the cost of goods manufactured and the cost of goods sold because they offset the debits (including beginning inventory figures) that are extended to the Manufacturing columns and the Income Statement columns.

Allocation of Costs and Expenses on the Work Sheet

In the Trial Balance and Adjustments columns, there are certain accounts representing cost incurred partly in the manufacturing processes and partly in the selling and general and administrative functions. Assume that a study was made to find an equitable method for allocating these items. As a result of this study, the following bases for allocation were decided on:

Item	Basis for Allocation
Rent	Square footage of building space used
Heat, light, and power	Actual readings from meters in the factory, in the sales rooms, and in the general and administrative areas
Insurance	Cost of comprehensive policies covering the buildings allocated on the basis of square footage; other insurance costs charged directly to manufacturing, selling, or general and administrative expense

From these bases, converted to percentages, which are assumed for this illustration, the following allocations were made:

		ALLOCATION					
		Manufacturing		Selling		General	
Item	Total	%	Amount	%	Amount	%	Amount
Rent	$12,000	80	$9,600	15	$1,800	5	$600
Heat, light, and power	8,100	90	7,290	5	405	5	405
Insurance	1,500	70	1,050	20	300	10	150

On the line of the work sheet for each of these items, the total of the Trial Balance and Adjustments columns is extended to the appropriate column. The Rent debit balance of $12,000, for example, is distributed as follows: $9,600 = ($12,000 × 0.80) is extended to the Manufacturing Debit column; $1,800 = ($12,000 × 0.15) and $600 = ($12,000 × 0.05) are extended to the Income Statement Debit column. Note that the $9,600 is classified as manufacturing overhead under Factory Rent (Figures 17-4 and 17-5); the $1,800 is classified as a selling expense, Rent Expense (Figures 17-4 and 17-6). The $9,600 portion is carried as a product cost and not as an expense, because it is part of the cost of the finished product; it becomes an expense only when the product is sold. Until such time, overhead costs are assets; that is, they are part of either work in process (asset) or finished goods (asset). The $1,800 portion of the rent is classified as Rent Expense, because it does not enter into the cost of goods manufactured (finished goods) but is rather an expense of the period in which

Figure 17-4 Work Sheet for a Manufacturing Company

CAROL MANUFACTURING COMPANY LTD.
Work Sheet
For the Year Ended December 31, 19XX

Account Title	Trial Balance		Adjustments		Manufacturing		Income Statement		Balance Sheet	
	Dr.	Cr.	Dr.	Cr.	Dr.	Cr.	Dr.	Cr.	Dr.	Cr.
Cash	12,000								12,000	
Accounts Receivable	78,350								78,350	
Allowance for Doubtful Accounts		650		(a) 1,037						1,687
Materials Inventory	58,300				58,300	51,500			51,500	
Work-in-Process Inventory	31,725				31,725	47,000			47,000	
Finished Goods Inventory	23,200						23,200	19,600	19,600	
Prepaid Insurance	2,100			(b) 1,500					600	
Office Equipment	6,050								6,050	
Accumulated Depreciation—Office Equipment		2,000		(d) 605						2,605
Store Equipment	10,000								10,000	
Accumulated Depreciation—Store Equipment		4,000		(d) 1,000						5,000
Machinery and Equipment	51,000								51,000	
Accumulated Depreciation—Machinery and Equipment		10,000		(c) 10,200						20,200
Accounts Payable		29,200								29,200
Capital Stock		180,000								180,000
Retained Earnings		12,855								12,855
Dividends	10,000								10,000	
Sales		420,000						420,000		
Sales Returns and Allowances	5,200						5,200			
Sales Discounts	2,400						2,400			
Materials Purchases	91,000				91,000					
Materials—Purchases Returns and Allowances		2,800				2,800				
Materials—Purchases Discounts		2,650				2,650				
Direct Labor	98,530		(e) 3,500		102,030					
Indirect Labor	21,200		(e) 1,400		22,600					
Rent	12,000				9,600		1,800 S 600 G			
Heat, Light, and Power	8,100				7,290		405 S 405 G			
Advertising Expense	6,500						6,500			
Salesmen's Salaries Expense	50,000		(e) 5,100				55,100			
Executive Salaries Expense	60,500						60,500			
Office Salaries Expense	26,000						26,000			
	664,155	664,155								
Bad Debts Expense			(a) 1,037				1,037			
Insurance			(b) 1,500		1,050		300 S 150 G			
Depreciation—Machinery and Equipment			(c) 10,200		10,200					
Depreciation Expense—Office Equipment			(d) 605				605			
Depreciation Expense—Store Equipment			(d) 1,000				1,000			
Accrued Wages and Salaries Payable				(e) 10,000						10,000
Income Tax Expense			(f) 7,368				7,368			
Income Taxes Payable				(f) 7,368						7,368
			31,710	31,710	333,795	103,950				
Cost of Goods Manufactured						229,845	229,845			
					333,795	333,795	422,415	439,600	286,100	268,915
Net Income							17,185			17,185
							439,600	439,600	286,100	286,100

S = Selling expenses
G = General and administrative expenses

it is incurred. This distinction also applies to heat, light, and power and to insurance. All the overhead accounts and all portions of accounts allocated to manufacturing are product cost accounts.

The letters S and G after the amounts identify the specific income statement classifications of selling or general and administrative expenses. These letters may be further used for amounts extended as a lump sum in a single column to facilitate the precise classification of the accounts if the formal income statement is prepared directly from the work sheet.

FINANCIAL STATEMENTS

The Manufacturing columns of the work sheet contain all the amounts required for the preparation of the schedule of cost of goods manufactured in their proper debit or credit relationship; each amount is used once. The Schedule of Costs of Goods Manufactured follows:

Figure 17-5 Schedule of Cost of Goods Manufactured

CAROL MANUFACTURING COMPANY LTD. Schedule A-1
Schedule of Cost of Goods Manufactured
For the Year Ended December 31, 19XX

Materials Used			
Materials Inventory, January 1			$ 58,300
Materials Purchases		$91,000	
Deduct: Purchases Returns and Allowances	$2,800		
Purchases Discounts	2,650	5,450	
Net Cost of Materials Purchases			85,550
Cost of Materials Available for Use			$143,850
Deduct Materials Inventory, December 31			51,500
Cost of Materials Used			$ 92,350
Direct Labor			102,030
Manufacturing Overhead			
Indirect Labor		$22,600	
Factory Rent		9,600	
Heat, Light, and Power		7,290	
Factory Insurance		1,050	
Depreciation—Machinery and Equipment		10,200	
Total Manufacturing Overhead			50,740
Total Period Manufacturing Costs			$245,120
Add Work-in-Process Inventory, January 1			31,725
Total			$276,845
Deduct Work-in-Process Inventory, December 31			47,000
Cost of Goods Manufactured (to Exhibit A)			$229,845

The Income Statement columns of the work sheet contain all the amounts required for the preparation of the following Income Statement.

Figure 17-6
Income Statement

CAROL MANUFACTURING COMPANY LTD. **Exhibit A**
Income Statement
For the Year Ended December 31, 19XX

Sales Revenue			
Sales			$420,000
Deduct: Sales Returns and Allowances		$ 5,200	
Sales Discounts		2,400	7,600
Net Sales Revenue			$412,400
Cost of Goods Sold			
Finished Goods Inventory, January 1		$ 23,200	
Add Cost of Goods Manufactured (Schedule A-1)		229,845	
Cost of Finished Goods Available for Sale		$253,045	
Deduct Finished Goods Inventory, December 31		19,600	
Cost of Goods Sold			233,445
Gross Margin on Sales			$178,955
Operating Expenses			
Selling			
Rent Expense	$ 1,800		
Heat, Light, and Power Expense	405		
Advertising Expense	6,500		
Salesmen's Salaries Expense	55,100		
Insurance Expense	300		
Depreciation Expense—Store Equipment	1,000		
Total Selling Expenses		$ 65,105	
General and Administrative			
Rent Expense	$ 600		
Heat, Light, and Power Expense	405		
Executive Salaries Expense	60,500		
Office Salaries Expense	26,000		
Bad Debts Expense	1,037		
Insurance Expense	150		
Depreciation Expense—Office Equipment	605		
Total General and Administrative Expenses		89,297	
Total Operating Expenses			154,402
Net Income Before Income Taxes			$ 24,553
Income Tax Expense			7,368
Net Income After Income Taxes			$ 17,185

The balance sheet and statement of retained earnings are prepared from the Balance Sheet columns of the work sheet and are similar to the form illustrated in earlier chapters for other companies. Because the format of these statements are similar, they are not repeated here.

The closing inventory which consists of materials inventory, work-in-process inventory, and finished goods inventory are shown in the balance sheet as current assets. The presentation of these items is illustrated in the following partial balance sheet for the company.

Assets			
Current Assets			
Cash		$ 12,000	
Accounts Receivable	$78,350		
Deduct Allowance for Doubtful Accounts	1,687	76,663	
Materials Inventory		51,500	
Work-in-Process Inventory		47,000	
Finished Goods Inventory		19,600	
Prepaid Insurance		600	
Total Current Assets			$207,363

ACCOUNTING ENTRIES

After the work sheet has been completed and the statements prepared, the adjustments are recorded in the general journal and posted to the appropriate accounts. This process has been illustrated in earlier chapters for nonmanufacturing firms. There is no difference in journalizing and posting adjusting entries for a manufacturing firm.

In the closing process for a manufacturing firm a new account, Manufacturing Summary, is opened at the end of each accounting period. All account balances that enter into the computation of cost of goods manufactured are closed into the general ledger account, Manufacturing Summary. These account balances are the same figures that are found in the Manufacturing columns of the work sheet. The final balance of the Manufacturing Summary account is the cost of goods manufactured. It is closed into the Income Summary account. The remaining closing entries are the same as for a merchandising business.

The posting of closing entries and the preparation of a post-closing trial balance for a manufacturing firm do not differ from procedures illustrated for other businesses in earlier chapters. Upon completion of posting, all temporary accounts have a zero balance.

As mentioned in the introduction to this chapter, the procedures here use a *periodic* inventory system and are adequate to determine net income of a general manufacturing firm. They do not, however, provide the information needed for effective managerial control. If a manufacturing firm is to continue in business it should establish a cost accounting system using a manufacturing budget and a *perpetual* inventory system. These topics will be covered in Chapter 18.

GLOSSARY

Amortization of Patents The amount of patent cost applicable to a given time period; it is an element of manufacturing overhead for a manufacturing firm.

Cost of Goods Manufactured The cost of the units of finished products completed during a given period; it is calculated by adding the beginning work-in-process inventory to the three period manufacturing cost groups and deducting the ending work-in-process inventory.

Cost of Goods Sold for Manufacturing Firm Often referred to as cost of sales; it is computed by adding the beginning finished goods inventory to the cost of goods manufactured for the period and subtracting the ending finished goods inventory.

Direct Labor The cost of the wages paid to employees performing operations directly on the product being manufactured.

Finished Goods The inventory of finished products of a manufacturing firm.

Indirect Labor The labor cost of those workers whose efforts are *not* directly identified with the conversion of specific material into specific finished products; for example, the factory janitor's salary is an indirect labor cost.

Manufacturing Firm A firm which fabricates finished products out of basic materials by applying direct labor costs and other manufacturing costs to convert the basic materials into finished goods.

Manufacturing Overhead All factory costs incurred in the manufacturing process *other* than the cost of direct materials used and direct labor; examples are indirect labor, small tools used, factory insurance, and so forth.

Manufacturing Summary A summary account used in the closing process for a manufacturing firm to which all items used in the calculation of cost of goods manufactured are closed.

Materials The inventory, at cost, of material held for consumption in fabricating the finished product of a manufacturing firm; synonomous terms are *raw materials* or *direct materials.*

Materials Used The cost of the materials used in manufacturing during a given period; under the periodic inventory method the amount is the sum of beginning materials inventory plus cost of materials purchases less ending materials inventory.

Period Manufacturing Costs Those product manufacturing costs which are accumulated for a given period; these comprise direct materials used, direct labor, and manufacturing overhead items.

Work in Process The inventory of partly finished products in various stages of completion at any given time.

QUESTIONS

Q17-1. "The accounting standards and procedures are the same for both the manufacturing and the nonmanufacturing types of business." Justify this statement by showing that accounting in the two types of business is the same in regard to inventory items.

Q17-2. A manufacturing firm has three inventory controlling accounts and a fourth inventory account that is closely related to the other three. Name each of these accounts and describe briefly what the balance in each at the end of any accounting period represents.

Q17-3. Explain each of the following terms: (a) materials used, (b) direct labor, and (c) manufacturing overhead.

Q17-4. What are the criteria for distinguishing between direct labor and indirect labor?

Q17-5. Distinguish between total *period manufacturing costs* and *cost of goods manufactured.*

Q17-6. Describe the purpose and function of the Manufacturing columns in the work sheet. Where in the work sheet would the amounts normally contained in the Manufacturing columns be entered if the Manufacturing columns were eliminated?

Q17-7. During a given period the cost of materials used by a manufacturing firm was $50,000. The materials inventory increased by $5,000 during the period, and materials purchases returns amounted to $2,000. What was the delivered cost of materials purchased?

Q17-8. The books of the Brooks Corporation showed the following information:

Inventories	*12/31/19X2*	*12/31/19X1*
Finished goods	$24,000	$18,000
Work in process	17,250	10,500
Materials	15,900	19,050

Explain how each amount will be shown (a) in the work sheet, (b) in the schedule of cost of goods manufactured, (c) in the income statement, and (d) in the statement of financial position.

Q17-9. When a given cost is applicable partly to manufacturing and partly to the administrative or selling function, how is the amount allocated in the work sheet? Discuss a possible alternative method.

Q17-10. Identify some of the problems involved in the measurement of the periodic inventories of work in process and finished goods.

DEMONSTRATION PROBLEMS

DP17-1. (*Computation of materials used*) The following information is available from the records of the Hayes Manufacturing Company:

Materials inventory, December 31, 19X1	$ 19,125
Materials inventory, December 31, 19X2	15,000
Materials purchases, 19X2	300,000
Transportation in on materials purchases, 19X2	6,000
Materials purchases returns and allowances, 19X2	7,500
Materials purchases discounts, 19X2	5,250

Required: In schedule form, compute the cost of materials used in 19X2.

DP17-2. (*Computation of cost of goods sold*) The following information is available from the records of the Briley Company:

Finished goods inventory, December 31, 19X1	$ 37,500
Cost of goods manufactured in 19X2	450,000
Finished goods inventory, December 31, 19X2	45,000
Work-in-process inventory, December 31, 19X1	15,750
Work-in-process inventory, December 31, 19X2	18,975

Required: In schedule form, compute the cost of goods sold in 19X2.

DP17-3. (*Journal entries; schedule of cost of goods manufactured; analysis*) The Nanney Manufacturing Company uses a regular accounts payable system of recording liabilities for materials purchases. During the year, the firm completed certain transactions as follows:

1. Purchased materials on account for $125,500.
2. Paid transportation charges amounting to $4,100 on materials.
3. Received $5,500 credit for materials returned.
4. Issued checks for $100,500 in payment of liability for materials purchased for $102,500 (discounts taken were $2,000).
5. Paid direct labor wages of $75,000 (ignore payroll taxes).
6. Paid the following items: factory rent, $5,500; heat, light, and power, $6,800; indirect labor, $5,200; and miscellaneous factory costs, $1,200.
7. Made year-end adjusting entries to record expired factory insurance of $2,500; small tools costs of $1,500, and depreciation on machinery and equipment of $7,500.

Required:

1. Journalize the transactions and post to T accounts.
2. Prepare a schedule of cost of goods manufactured. Inventories were as follows:

	Beginning	Ending
Materials	$10,500	$8,500
Work in process	4,000	4,600

3. Journalize the entries to close the nominal manufacturing accounts.

DP17-4. (*Work sheet, statements, and closing entries*) The condensed adjusted trial balance of the Wentz Corporation on December 31, 19X2, after adjustment, consisted of the following:

Cash	$ 30,000
Accounts Receivable	21,000
Finished Goods, December 31, 19X1	18,000
Work in Process, December 31, 19X1	12,000
Materials, December 31, 19X1	15,000
Plant and Equipment	75,000
Accumulated Depreciation—Plant and Equipment	15,000
Accounts Payable	36,000
Common Stock ($100 par value)	75,000
Retained Earnings	27,000
Sales	126,000
Materials Purchases	45,000
Direct Labor	30,000
Manufacturing Overhead	24,000
Selling Expenses	6,000
General Expenses	3,000

Inventories on December 31, 19X2:

Finished goods	$15,000
Work in process	18,000
Materials	21,000

Required: Prepare (a) a manufacturing work sheet, (b) a schedule of cost of goods manufactured, (c) an income statement, (d) a balance sheet, and (e) the closing entries.

PROBLEMS

P17-1. The following data are taken from the books of the Sink Company:

Materials purchases	$150,000
Direct labor	300,000
Manufacturing overhead	300,000
Materials inventory change (amount of increase of ending inventory over beginning inventory)	45,000
Work-in-process inventory (net change—decrease)	30,000
Finished goods inventory (net change—increase)	15,000

Determine (a) the cost of goods manufactured and (b) the cost of goods sold.

P17-2. Manufacturing overhead is 20% of cost of goods manufactured. Direct labor is 30% of sales and 60% of cost of goods manufactured. Ending materials inventory is $8,000 more than beginning materials inventory. Sales totaled $200,000 for the year. Compute the net cost of materials purchased during the year. This company never has any work-in-process inventory at the end of each period.

P17-3. Compute the missing amounts in the following tabulation:

	Beginning Inventory of Materials	*Materials Purchases*	*Transportation In on Materials*	*Materials Purchases Returns And Allowances*
1.	$2,250	$12,900	$?	$450
2.	?	3,750	450	300
3.	5,250	?	1,050	300

	Materials Purchases Discounts	*Net Cost of Materials Purchases*	*Cost of Materials Available for Use*	*Ending Inventory of Materials*	*Cost of Materials Used*
1.	$225	$14,250	$?	$?	$12,750
2.	?	3,750	8,250	?	5,400
3.	600	?	29,850	7,500	?

P17-4. Compute the missing amounts in the following tabulation:

	Net Sales	*Beginning Inventory of Finished Goods*	*Cost of Goods Manufactured*	*Cost of Finished Goods Available for Sale*
1.	$61,500	$?	$45,000	$60,000
2.	?	37,500	?	?
3.	90,000	?	60,000	90,000

	Ending Inventory of Finished Goods	*Cost of Goods Sold*	*Gross Margin on Sales*
1.	$?	$ 38,250	$?
2.	15,000	121,500	30,000
3.	?	?	15,750

P17-5. Compute the missing amounts in the following tabulation:

	Cost of Materials Used	*Direct Labor*	*Manufacturing Overhead*	*Total Period Cost of Manufacturing*
1.	$ 15,750	$?	$ 18,000	$ 55,500
2.	?	75,000	90,000	203,250
3.	375,750	600,000	450,000	?

	Beginning Work-in-Process Inventory	*Ending Work-in-Process Inventory*	*Cost of Goods Manufactured*
1.	$ 7,500	$?	$52,500
2.	150,000	187,500	65,750
3.	150,000	225,000	?

P17-6. The Bumpus Corporation acquired certain patent rights for $180,000 and spent an additional $92,000 in further developing them.

1. Record the acquisition and development of the patents.
2. Record the patent amortization for one year on the basis of a full legal life.
3. Record the patent amortization on the basis of an assumed useful economic life of eight years.

P17-7. The following Small Tools account is from the books of the Huyett Corporation:

Small Tools

Jan. 1	Balance	20,800	
Aug. 3	Purchase	5,200	

The inventory of small tools on hand on December 31, was priced at $13,500, based on a physical count.

1. What part of the Small Tools account is allocated to the current accounting period?
2. Prepare the entry to adjust the Small Tools account.

P17-8. The adjusted trial balance of the Kincaid Corporation included the following items:

Rent	$7,000
Heat, light, and power	4,200
Insurance	2,400
Taxes	2,000
Depreciation	4,000

The accountant for the Kincaid Corporation determined the following allocation percentages:

	Manufacturing	Selling	General
Rent	80%	15%	5%
Heat, light, and power	90	3	7
Insurance (plant and equipment)	60	20	20
Taxes	70	20	10
Depreciation	75	10	15

Enter the account balances in the Adjusted Trial Balance columns of a manufacturing work sheet and, using the allocation percentages given, extend the items to the appropriate columns of the work sheet.

P17-9. The following information is from the books of the Wilson Company:

	Inventories		
	June 30, 19X1	*June 30, 19X2*	*Year Ended June 30, 19X2*
Materials	$ 30,000	$ 34,500	
Work in Process	44,700	43,050	
Finished Goods	110,250	106,350	
Materials Purchases			$413,250
Transportation In—Materials			20,550
Direct Labor			465,000
Manufacturing Overhead			394,500

Required:

1. Compute the total period cost of manufacturing.
2. Compute the cost of goods manufactured.
3. Compute the cost of goods sold.

P17-10. The following information is available for the Rosenberg Corporation:

	12/31/19X1	*19X2*	*12/31/19X2*
Inventories			
Materials	$18,000		$16,500
Work in Process	21,000		27,000
Finished Goods	33,000		32,250
Materials purchased during year		$55,000	
Direct Labor		33,000	
Manufacturing Overhead		25,500	

Required: Prepare a schedule of cost of goods manufactured for 19X2.

P17-11. Following are the Manufacturing columns of the work sheet of the Redfern Corporation for the year ended December 31:

	Manufacturing	
	Debits	*Credits*
Materials Inventory	$ 45,000	$ 43,500
Work-in-Process Inventory	30,000	37,500
Materials Purchases	105,000	
Direct Labor	52,500	
Indirect Labor	11,250	
Rent	4,800	
Heat, Light, and Power	3,600	
Depreciation—Plant and Equipment	4,500	
Miscellaneous Factory Costs	3,750	
	$260,400	$ 81,000
Cost of Goods Manufactured (40,000 units)		179,400
	$260,400	$260,400

Required: Prepare a schedule of cost of goods manufactured.

P17-12. The following accounts and amounts, arranged in alphabetical order, were taken from the completed work sheet of the Margeson Manufacturing Corporation:

Accounts Receivable	$ 42,750
Accumulated Depreciation—Machinery and Equipment	14,700
Advertising Expense	2,175
Allowance for Doubtful Accounts	900
Bad Debts Expense	825
Cash	3,825
Depreciation—Machinery and Equipment	1,650
Direct Labor	23,250
Factory Insurance	2,250
Factory Rent	4,500
Finished Goods Inventory, December 31, 19X1	35,250
Finished Goods Inventory, December 31, 19X2	31,800
Heat, Light, and Power—Factory	2,175
Indirect Labor	6,450
Machinery and Equipment	34,500
Materials Inventory, December 31, 19X1	27,750
Materials Inventory, December 31, 19X2	28,125
Miscellaneous Factory Costs	2,955
Prepaid Insurance	1,650
Purchases—Materials	69,225
Purchases Discounts—Materials	2,250
Purchases Returns and Allowances—Materials	1,800
Sales	222,750
Sales Discounts	3,150
Sales Returns and Allowances	2,100
Salesmen's Salaries Expense	20,250
Small Tools	9,300
Small Tools Used	975
Transportation In—Materials	1,125
Work-in-Process Inventory, December 31, 19X1	22,500
Work-in-Process Inventroy, December 31, 19X2	18,000

Required:

1. Prepare the schedule of cost of goods manufactured for 19X2.
2. Prepare a partial income statement through Gross Margin on Sales for 19X2.
3. Prepare the Current Assets section of the balance sheet.

P17-13. (*Accounting policy decision problem*) The Laffiteau Manufacturing Company produces a single commodity. A summary of its activities for 19X2 follows:

	Units	Amount
Sales	90,000	$900,000
Materials inventory, 12/31/19X1		48,000
Work-in-process inventory, 12/31/19X1		60,000
Finished goods inventory, 12/31/19X1	18,000	72,000
Materials inventory, 12/31/19X2		36,000
Work-in-process inventory, 12/31/19X2		75,000
Finished goods inventory, 12/31/19X2	24,000	?
Materials purchases		192,000
Direct labor		135,000
Manufacturing overhead costs		108,000

Required:

1. Prepare a schedule of cost of goods manufactured for 19X2. Indicate on the schedule the number of units completed for the year and the cost per unit of finished goods.

2. Determine the gross margin on sales for the year, assuming that the transfer of the cost of finished goods to cost of goods sold is on the last-in, first-out basis. Show all your computations.
3. Discuss the accounting concepts underlying the selection of the LIFO basis versus the FIFO basis. Which of these two methods should be chosen if sound accounting concepts are followed? Why?

P17-14. The adjusted trial balance of Markham Company Ltd. for the year ended December 31 is shown below.

	Debits	*Credits*
Cash	$ 24,450	
Accounts Receivable	59,835	
Allowance for Doubtful Accounts		$ 1,800
Materials Inventory	44,400	
Work-in-Process Inventory	2,385	
Finished Goods Inventory	18,150	
Prepaid Insurance	640	
Machinery and Equipment	67,950	
Accumulated Depreciation—Machinery and Equipment		30,480
Office Equipment	12,015	
Accumulated Depreciation—Office Equipment		5,700
Accounts Payable		21,900
Income Taxes Payable		5,250
Accrued Wages and Salaries Payable		8,250
Capital Stock, $100 Par Value		90,000
Retained Earnings		52,650
Sales		330,000
Sales Returns and Allowances	4,050	
Sales Discounts	1,875	
Purchases—Materials	68,700	
Purchases Returns and Allowances—Materials		2,065
Purchases Discounts—Materials		2,250
Direct Labor	76,605	
Depreciation—Machinery and Equipment	7,800	
Indirect Labor	16,350	
Rent	10,800	
Heat, Light, and Power	6,900	
Insurance	2,625	
Advertising Expense	5,700	
Salesmen's Salaries Expense	76,950	
Executive Salaries Expense	34,050	
Bad Debts Expense	1,650	
Depreciation Expense—Office Equipment	1,215	
Income Taxes Expense	5,250	
Totals	$550,345	$550,345

Additional data:

Ending inventories:

Materials	$18,790
Work in Process	1,690
Finished Goods	42,900

Allocation percentages:

Item	*Manufacturing*	*Selling*	*General*
Rent	70	20	10
Heat, light, and power	80	10	10
Insurance	70	15	15

Required: Prepare:

1. A schedule of cost of goods manufactured.
2. An income statement.
3. A balance sheet.

18

Cost Accounting Systems

A manufacturing company may accumulate costs under a general accounting system sometimes referred to as a noncost system, as described in the preceding chapter, or it may accumulate costs under a cost accounting system. The difference between the two systems is the method of cost determination and control. In a general accounting system for a manufacturing firm, the cost of goods manufactured in any particular period is determined by assembling appropriate account balances in a schedule of cost of goods manufactured. The shortcoming of this procedure is that the cost of each product, process, job, unit, or department—each *cost center*—is not known. Furthermore, the use of a periodic inventory does not provide as satisfactory a means of controlling the cost of materials used in manufacturing as does the perpetual inventory approach.

The flow of the product and its related costs through the factory can be determined by a historical *job order cost system* or a *process cost system.* The job order cost system is used when each unit maintains its identity and unit costs can be specifically associated with the physical units in the job order, as in job printing. A process cost system is used for manufacturing processes in which costs of any one unit cannot be distinguished from another unit and production is largely continuous, as in the petroleum industry. Accordingly, costs for the total output of a productive operation are determined over a time period, and the unit cost is determined by dividing the total cost by the number of units produced.

This chapter explains the nature and purpose of *job order* and *process cost* systems.

COST ACCUMULATION

Cost control accounts are controlling accounts used with a cost system. The function of the cost control accounts is the same as that of the controlling accounts in a general accounting system—Accounts Receivable and Accounts Payable, for example. Some commonly used cost control accounts and the related subsidiary ledgers or records are:

Cost Control Accounts	Subsidiary Ledgers or Records
Materials Inventory	Material perpetual inventory cards
Factory Payroll	Individual employee payroll records
Manufacturing Overhead	Manufacturing overhead ledger cost accounts
Work-in-Process Inventory	Job order cost sheets
Finished Goods Inventory	Finished goods perpetual inventory cards

Many forms and documents are used in conjunction with the flow and accumulation of costs. A job order cost sheet is shown in Figure 18-1.

Materials

Control of materials involves the recording, reconciling, efficient use, and verification of quantitative data; it is essential to effective management. The receipt of material is recorded from the approved vendor's invoice by a debit to Materials Inventory and a credit to Accounts Payable or Vouchers Payable; each different type of item purchased is entered on an individual *materials perpetual inventory card,* sometimes referred to as a *stores ledger card.* Transfer of materials from the storeroom is effected on receipt of an authorized materials requisition form, which shows quantity, stock and job numbers, unit price, and total price; a requisition for indirect materials refers to an identifying account in the manufacturing overhead ledger. Work-in-Process Inventory or Manufacturing Overhead is debited and Materials Inventory is credited for the transfers. On the subsidiary records, appropriate charges are made either to the job order cost sheet or to the manufacturing overhead ledger, with corresponding credits to the materials ledger cards. The pricing procedure used may be FIFO, moving average, or any other acceptable method.

The selected pricing method must be used consistently.

The reconciliation of material control is effected when the dollar balances of the individual materials ledger cards agree in total with the dollar balance of the Materials Inventory controlling account.

Under the perpetual inventory system for the control of materials, quantities of stock on hand may be determined readily from the records at any time; this eliminates the need for a complete physical inventory at the end of each accounting period. Verification by physical count of goods on hand and comparison with materials ledger cards can be a continuing process resulting in a minimum of interruption to plant operation.

Factory Payroll

Time cards, and *time tickets,* showing daily hours worked by employees are sorted by type of labor—direct and indirect. If an employee changes jobs during the day, a new time ticket is prepared. Time tickets serve as the basis for the distribution of employee wages either to job order cost sheets (direct labor) or to manufacturing overhead accounts (indirect labor, such as supervision, factory clerical, idle time, or overtime). At the end of each pay period, a summary entry of the total labor costs incurred is made, usually from the factory payroll register, debiting Factory Payroll and crediting Accrued Factory Wages Payable and other liabilities. Payroll details are entered regularly on individual employees' earnings record cards from the factory payroll register. The total debits to the Factory Payroll controlling account should agree with the total gross earnings on the individual employees' earnings record cards. A summary entry is also made at the end of the accounting period, debiting Work-in-Process Inventory for direct labor and Manufacturing Overhead for indirect labor and crediting Factory Payroll, to distribute the total factory payroll costs. The Factory Payroll account thus serves as a clearing account—all the charges to it are redistributed to other accounts.

Control accounts and subsidiary ledgers for Manufacturing Overhead, Work-in-Process Inventory, and Finished Goods Inventory are discussed individually in the job order and process cost sections that follow.

Figure 18-1 Job Order Cost Sheet

Quantity and Description 2 Type B Motors — ***Job. No.*** 53

Date Started January 2 — ***Date Completed*** January 19

For Stock

	Direct Materials		**Direct Labor**			
Date	*Requisition Number*	*Amount*	*Date*	*Time Ticket Number*	*Hours*	*Amount*
1/2	475	125.00	1/2	892	8	40.00
1/5	481	75.50	1/4	901	8	34.00
1/19	490	225.00	1/10	909	6	25.50
			1/11	915	8	40.00
			1/12	917	6	24.00
			1/15	920	8	34.00
			1/19	925	6	30.00
	Total	425.50		Totals	50	227.50

Summary

	Amount	*Per Unit*
Materials	$425.50	$212.75
Labor	227.50	113.75
Overhead 50 hours at $2.00	100.00	50.00
Totals	$753.00	$376.50

JOB ORDER COST SYSTEM

The Work-in-Process Inventory account and its subsidiary job order cost sheets accumulate production cost data for single items or a group of items. A job order cost sheet is kept for each job in process. During the accounting period, the costs of material, labor, and manufacturing overhead are entered on a cost sheet. Work-in-Process Inventory is a summary controlling account, the details of which are shown on the job order cost sheets. A job order cost sheet for the Wilson Company is shown in Figure 18-1 (the amounts are assumed). The amount of manufacturing overhead costs applied is explained later in this chapter.

The summary entry to record the data that are entered on the cost sheet in Figure 18-1 is:

Work-in-Process Inventory	753.00	
Materials Inventory		425.50
Factory Payroll		227.50
Manufacturing Overhead		100.00

The flow of costs into the Work-in-Process account is illustrated in Figure 18-2. As can be seen, the Work-in-Process account accumulates the cost for units started in production.

Figure 18-2
Flow Chart for Work-in-Process Cost Accumulation

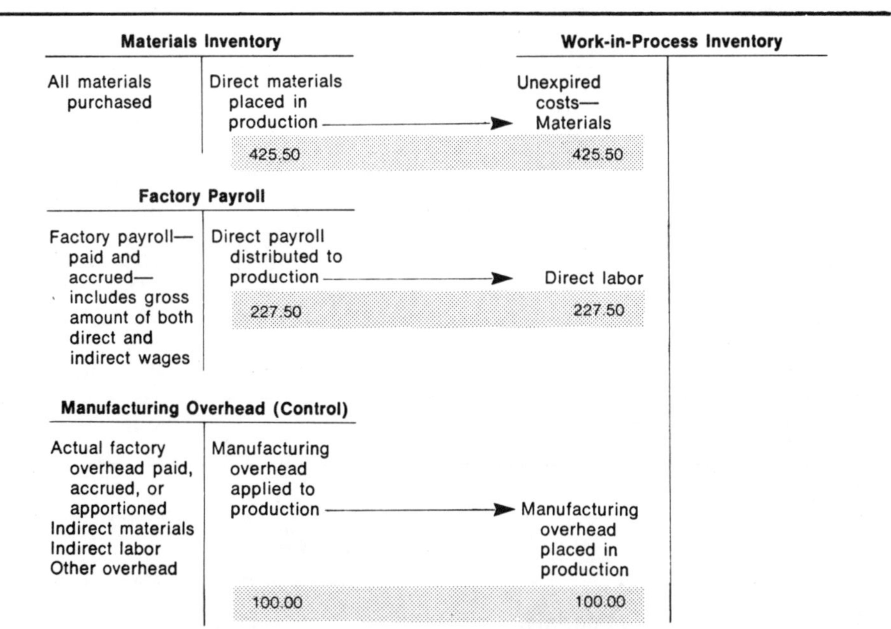

The balance of the Work-in-Process Inventory account should correspond to the total charges for materials, labor, and overhead entered on the job order cost sheets for all jobs started but not yet completed.

The job order cost sheet provides management with each element of the cost per unit. Once the variances between actual and budgeted costs and their causes are known, required remedial action may be initiated. In addition, the job order cost sheet may serve as a guide for future budgeting and pricing policies.

Finished Goods

The entry to record the transfer of work completed to the Finished Goods Inventory account is shown below (the items are two Type B motors at $376.50 each).

Finished Goods Inventory	753	
Work-in-Process Inventory		753

A corresponding debit entry for $753 for two motors is made on the subsidiary *finished goods perpetual inventory card* for Type B motors. When finished goods are sold, entries are made to record (1) the selling price and (2) the cost of goods sold. The entries to record the sale by the Wilson Company of one Type B motor for $750 are as shown below.

Accounts Receivable	750.00	
Sales		750.00
Cost of Goods Sold	376.50	
Finished Goods Inventory		376.50

The flow of costs to and from the Finished Goods Inventory account is illustrated in Figure 18-3. Corresponding entries would be made in the subsidiary finished goods ledger and the accounts receivable ledger.

Figure 18-3 Flow Chart Finished Goods Costs

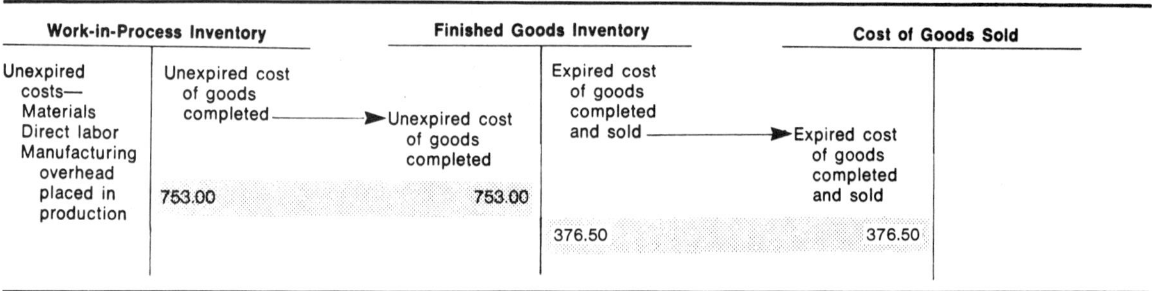

The perpetual inventory records for finished goods are of value to management in furnishing current inventory data and in inventory control. The availability of goods to fill telephone or across-the-counter orders, for example, may be determined without delay by reference to the perpetual inventory cards. The taking of a complete physical inventory at one time with its attendant interruption of normal operational activities is not necessary; the count of inventory items on hand may be compared with the finished goods ledger cards on a continuing basis.

THE MANUFACTURING OVERHEAD RATE

Manufacturing overhead includes all costs incurred in the manufacturing process other than the costs of materials and labor charged directly to job order cost sheets. All actual manufacturing overhead costs incurred are debited to the Manufacturing Overhead controlling account. At the same time individual overhead items—factory supplies used, indirect labor, depreciation of factory machinery, and others—are also debited to the various accounts in the subsidiary manufacturing overhead ledger. The accumulation of costs in manufacturing overhead (control) and the amount of overhead applied to work-in-process is shown in Figure 18-4.

Figure 18-4 Flow Chart for Manufacturing Overhead (control) Costs

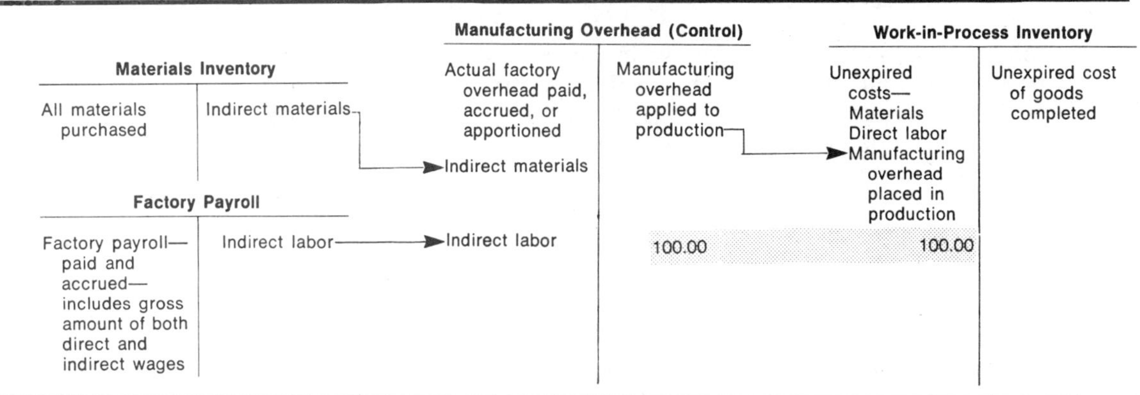

The job order sheet for the Wilson Company shown in Figure 18-1 indicated that manufacturing overhead for job No. 53 was $100 (50 hours × $2.00 per hour). This amount of $2.00 per hour is called a predetermined overhead rate. The need for calculating this rate and the methodology involved is discussed in the following sections.

The specific identification of the direct material and labor costs incurred on a given job order can be determined readily. Manufacturing overhead, however, cannot be economically identified with a specific job order. Some manufacturing overhead items—depreciation, insurance, rent, and property taxes, for example—are related to the passage of time and are not affected by production volume, whereas other manufacturing overhead costs—power, cutting oil, and small tools, for example—vary with the volume of production. If completed product costs are to be currently available to management, it becomes necessary to apply manufacturing overhead to job order cost sheets on a predetermined, or estimated, basis.

The calculation of a predetermined overhead rate is based (1) on expected manufacturing overhead based on budgeted production and (2) on an estimated cost factor related to expected future production.

A cause and effect, or high correlative, relationship should exist between the cost factor selected and the manufacturing overhead cost. To illustrate, assume that the Wilson Company estimates manufacturing overhead costs at

$800,000 and expects a production level of 400,000 direct labor hours for the year. In this plant, there is a close relationship between direct labor hours and manufacturing overhead. The predetermined overhead rate is calculated as follows:

$$\frac{\text{Estimated manufacturing overhead}}{\text{Estimated direct labor hours}} = \frac{\$800,000}{400,000} = \$2 \text{ per direct labor hour}$$

If a given job requires 50 labor hours, a charge of $100 (50 hours × $2) would be recorded on that job order cost sheet for overhead (see Figure 18-1). The entry in the controlling accounts would be:

Work-in-Process Inventory	100	
Manufacturing Overhead		100

If actual direct labor hours for the year are 400,000 as estimated, the Wilson Company will have charged $800,000 = (400,000 hours × $2) in manufacturing overhead costs to the various job order cost sheets. If, as is likely, a variance exists between the actual and the estimated amounts, there will be a balance in the Manufacturing Overhead account; a debit balance indicates overhead underapplied (overhead applied is less than actual overhead) and a credit balance indicates overhead overapplied (overhead applied is more than actual overhead). Although the under- or overapplied manufacturing overhead affects work in process, finished goods, and cost of goods sold, it generally, in practice, is treated as an adjustment to the largest of these items, the cost of goods sold and closed into that account. For example, if the actual manufacturing overhead amounted to $800,000 and the amount applied or charged to work-in-progress totaled $795,000, the following journal entry would be made:

Cost of Goods Sold	5,000	
Manufacturing Overhead		5,000

Other bases for applying manufacturing overhead are (1) direct labor dollars, (2) machine hours, (3) units of production, and (4) material cost. The computation of a predetermined overhead rate using any of these bases is the same as for direct labor hours. Assume that the Wilson Company selects the material cost basis and estimates the direct material cost to be $3,200,000 for budgeted production. The computation of the predetermined overhead rate based on material cost is as follows:

$$\frac{\text{Estimated manufacturing overhead}}{\text{Estimated material cost}} = \frac{\$800,000}{\$3,200,000} = 25\% \text{ of material cost}$$

The overhead to be applied to Job Order 53 (Figure 18-1) would be $106.38 (direct material cost of $425.50 × 0.25 predetermined overhead rate).

Selecting the Basis of Allocation. An important management decision is the selection of the proper basis for allocating overhead. The basis that should be selected is one that charges the job with an amount of manufacturing overhead most nearly corresponding to the actual manufacturing overhead costs incurred on the job. Each available basis—with due consideration for economy and practicability in application—has particular merits under particular circumstances. A detailed analysis should be made of all cost and production factors involved prior to the selection of a base, and should be continuously reconsidered. The direct labor hours method, for example, is used widely because it recognizes the causal relationship of time and overhead cost; an increase in direct labor hours on a job will result in a corresponding increase in the factory overhead charged to that job.

EVALUATION OF THE JOB ORDER COST SYSTEM

In some industries such as shipbuilding where direct materials and direct labor can readily be traced to a specific unit of product, job order costing is almost a necessity. In low-volume or high-unit-cost situations where the product is produced on a special "made-to-order" basis, the job order systems are appropriate. But, job order systems are expensive to maintain. The need to trace carefully the time of individual direct labor personnel to a product requires extra effort. Separate materials requisitions must be made for each job number even though a number of jobs may be underway in the same department.

Some companies use job order procedures for part of their operations and process cost accounting procedures for other parts. The following part of this chapter discusses process cost accounting procedures.

PROCESS COST SYSTEM

The process cost system is used by companies in which the manufacturing process is continuous and uniform—that is, where there is a continuous flow of units of a product through successive departments. Process costing is used by firms engaged in such diverse industries as pharmaceuticals, chemicals, petroleum, gas, electricity, plastics, and mining. Basic differences between job order costing and process costing are these: In job order costing, all costs are identified with specific jobs, and unit costs are computed when the job is completed; in process costing, there is a continuous flow of units of a product unrelated to specific jobs, and emphasis is placed on homogeneous output for a given period. Unit costs are computed for time intervals rather than for specific jobs.

The Cost Center

A process cost system makes it possible to accumulate costs for each department involved in the manufacturing process. Each department then becomes a *cost center.*

A cost center is the lowest level organizational unit in the company to which management has decided that specific costs will be directly identified as the responsibility of that unit's supervisor.

A Work-in-Process account is therefore required for each department in a process cost system. A cost sheet used in a job order system for specific jobs is replaced by a monthly ***departmental cost of production report*** in a process order system.

A production department may consist of two distinct operations—polishing and packaging. If cost can be identified directly with each operation, the finishing department (itself a cost center) could have two cost centers if it serves management's purpose best to accumulate costs for each of these two units. For each cost center, a separate Work-in-Process account is maintained. In the illustration of process cost accounting that follows each cost center is a production department.

Flow of Costs in a Process Cost System

The distinction between direct and indirect materials and labor in a process cost system may be different from that in a job order cost system. In many cases, what was an indirect cost in a job order cost system may now be a direct cost because it can be specifically identified with a particular department; if it cannot, the cost remains an element of manufacturing overhead.

The flow of costs in a process system begins with costs being recorded in Materials Inventory, Factory Payroll, and Manufacturing Overhead accounts. As work begins, the costs are transferred into each of the Work-in-Process accounts. The flow is first into the Work-in-Process Cooking Department. As the process in the Cooking Department is completed, the costs of the Cooking Department are transferred to Work-in-Process Finishing Department. Additional materials, labor, and overhead costs are then transferred to the Finishing Department so that the process can be completed. The finished goods are subsequently transferred to Finished Goods Inventory.

The flow of costs is illustrated in Figure 18-5. Since the recording of costs to Materials Inventory, Factory Payroll, and Manufacturing Overhead accounts is identical to that illustrated in Figure 18-2, Figure 18-5 shows the flow of costs after materials, labor, and overhead amounts have been transferred to each of the Work-in-Process accounts.

Figure 18-5 Flow Chart for Process Cost System

Work-in-Process—Cooking Department		**Work-in-Process—Finishing Department**		**Finished Goods Inventory**	
Materials Labor Overhead	Costs transferred to Finishing Department ——►	Costs from Cooking Department Additional Costs– Materials Labor Overhead	Cost of completed goods transferred to Finished Goods Inventory ——►	Cost of goods completed	Cost of finished goods sold

The accounting system for process costing follows the actual flow of resources through the production process, and records the costs in each department or cost center. The costs are then added to get the total cost of making the product. For example, the costs transferred from the Cooking Department are added to the materials, labor, and overhead and added to the process in the Finishing Department and the total cost is transferred to Finished Goods Inventory as the work-in-process is completed. As completed units are sold, the costs of the finished goods sold are transferred to Cost of Goods Sold.

The flow of costs illustrated in Figure 18-5 can be summarized in the following journal entries:

Work-in-Process—Cooking Department	xx	
Work-in-Process—Finishing Department	xx	
Manufacturing Overhead	xx	
Materials Inventory		xx
To record materials issued.		

Work-in-Process—Cooking Department	xx	
Work-in-Process—Finishing Department	xx	
Manufacturing Overhead	xx	
Factory Payroll		xx
To record the distribution of factory wages incurred during the period.		
Work-in-Process—Cooking Department	xx	
Work-in-Process—Finishing Department	xx	
Manufacturing Overhead		xx
To record the allocation of actual overhead to the producing departments.		
Work-in-Process—Finishing Department	xx	
Work-in-Process—Cooking Department		xx
To record the cost of goods transferred to the Finishing Department from the Cooking Department.		
Finished Goods Inventory	xx	
Work-in-Process—Finishing Department		xx
To record the cost of goods finished.		

Process Cost Accounting Illustration

The Atkins Chemical Company produces a single hypothetical product Bettergum, which is processed in two departments, Blending and Aging. On July 1, 19XX, there is no beginning work-in-process inventory in the Blending Department. During July, 50,000 units of Bettergum are started in the Blending Department; of this amount, 40,000 units are finished and transferred to the Aging Department. As of July 31, 100,000 units are still in the blending process–these are 100 per cent complete as to materials and 50 percent complete as to labour and overhead. The July costs added in the Blending Department are shown below.

Materials	$10,000
Labor	13,500
Overhead	11,250

In the Aging Department, there is a beginning (July 2) work-in-process inventory of 4,000 units, 75 percent complete as to labor and overhead; no materials are added in the Aging Department. During July, 40,000 units are received from the Blending Department. Of the 44,000 units of Bettergum to be accounted for in the Aging Department, 38,000 units are finished and transferred to Finished Goods Inventory, and on July 31, 6,000 units are in process, 33⅓ percent complete as to labor and overhead. The work-in-process inventory and costs added in July in the Aging Department are:

July 1 work-in-process inventory	$ 5,300
July costs	
Materials	–0–
Labor	14,800
Overhead	13,320

The flow of these resources through the production process is illustrated in Figure 18-6. Although beginning and ending work-in-process inventories are an important part of the computation of unit costs in each department, they are not shown here so that the flow of resources can be emphasized.

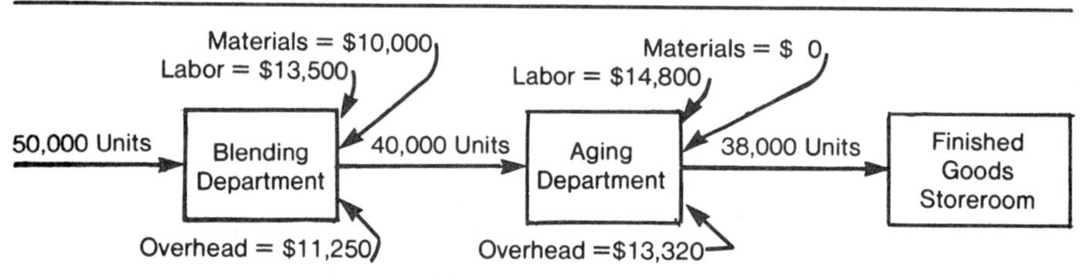

Figure 18-6
The Atkins Chemical Company—July Production

Quantity Schedule—Blending. A *quantity schedule* is prepared for each department, showing the number of units of the product processed during a given period. Such a schedule for the Blending Department is illustrated in Figure 18-7. The stage of completion for the July 31 work-in-process inventory is an average estimate; in other words, the Bettergum that has just entered the Blending Department has material added but no labor or overhead; the Bettergum that is almost ready to leave the department has almost all the labor and overhead absorbed; thus, the average work in process *in this case* has all the material cost and one-half the labor and overhead costs.

Figure 18-7
Quantity Schedule, Blending Department

	Units	
Quantity to be accounted for:		
Units in process at beginning of period	-0-	
Units started in process	50,000	
Total	50,000	
Quantity accounted for:		
Transferred to Aging Department	40,000	
Units still in process at end of period	10,000	(all material—½ L and O)
Total	50,000	

Schedule of Equivalent Production—Blending. Equivalent production is the finished unit equivalent of the units completely and partially processed in a given period; in other words, it is the finished number of whole units that could have been completed if all the effort and costs for the period had been applied only to wholly finished units. The conversion of work-in-process units to equivalent whole units is necessary when computing unit costs, because there may be a different number of units—called *equivalent production units*—for material, for labor, and for overhead. The schedule of equivalent production for the Blending Department is illustrated in Figure 18-8.

In the Blending Department, there is no beginning work-in-process inventory to complete; hence zeros are entered in the Materials column and in the L and O column (Figure 18-8). Units started and finished in this period (July) totaled 40,000 and are shown in both the Materials column and the L and O column. The ending work-in-process inventory consists of 10,000 units; its

Figure 18-8 Schedule of Equivalent Production, Blending Department

	Materials		*L and O*	
Beginning work-in-process inventory (to complete)	-0-		-0-	
Units started and finished (this period)	40,000		40,000	
Equivalent whole units contained in ending work-in-process inventory (stage of completion)	10,000	(10,000 × 100%)	5,000	(10,000 units × ½)
Equivalent production units	50,000		45,000	

stage of completion is such that all the materials have been received (10,000 is entered in the Materials column), and one-half labor and overhead has been absorbed (5,000 is entered in the L and O column). This is based on the assumption that the costs expended in completing one-half the work on 10,000 units are the same as the costs of completing 5,000 units.

Unit Cost Computation—Blending. Unit costs are computed for each element—materials, labor, and overhead. Each cost element in the Total Cost column is divided by the corresponding equivalent units produced, to derive the unit costs indicated in Figure 18-9.

Figure 18-9
Unit Cost Computation, Blending Department

Total Cost			
Element	*Amount*	*Equivalent Units*	*Unit Cost*
Materials	$10,000	50,000	$0.20
Labor	13,500	45,000	0.30
Overhead	11,250	45,000	0.25
Totals	$34,750		$0.75

Accumulated Cost Distribution—Blending. The total accumulated cost distribution of the Blending Department ($34,750) is accounted for by the $30,000 = (40,000 units × $0.75) transferred to the Aging Department and the $4,750 that appears in the ending work-in-process inventory; this is computed as follows:

Materials	10,000 units × $0.20	$2,000
Labor	10,000 units × ½ × $0.30	1,500
Overhead	10,000 units × ½ × $0.25	1,250
Work-in-Process Inventory—Blending Department (July 31)		$4,750

The same schedules and computations are now made for the second process in the Aging Department. Note that there is an added complication in this process, a beginning work-in-process inventory of 4,000 units.

Quantity Schedule—Aging. The quantity schedule for the Aging Department is shown in Figure 18-10.

Figure 18-10
Quantity Schedule, Aging Department

	Units*	
Quantity to be accounted for:		
Units in process at beginning of period	4,000	(¾ L and O)
Units received from Blending Department	40,000	
Total	44,000	
Quantity accounted for:		
Transferred to Finished Goods Inventory	38,000	
Units still in process at end of period	6,000	(⅓ L and O)
Total	44,000	

* No materials are added in the Aging Department.

Schedule of Equivalent Production—Aging. The 4,000 units in the beginning work-in-process inventory were three-fourths complete as to the elements of labour and overhead on July 1. Therefore, these 4,000 units receive one-fourth of their labor and overhead during this cost period (July); each should be equated with one-fourth of a unit of labor and of overhead. Consequently, 1,000 units (4,000 units x ¼) are entered in the L and O column, as shown in Figure 18-11. The number of units started and finished during this period is determined as follows:

[Units transferred to finished goods inventory]	–	[Units in beginning work-in-process inventory]	=	[Units started and finished]
38,000	–	4,000	=	34,000

These 34,000 units are recorded in the L and O column. Each unit in the ending work-in-process inventory of 6,000 units received one-third of its labor and overhead this month. The stage of completion of the ending work-in-process inventory, expressed in terms of whole units, is 2,000 (6,000 units × ⅓); this figure is recorded in the L and O column. The total of the L and O column (37,000 units) represents equivalent production units for the month of July.

Figure 18-11
Schedule of Equivalent Production, Aging Department

	Materials	L and O	
Beginning work-in-process inventory (to complete)	-0-	1,000	(4,000 units × ¼)
Units started and finished	-0-	34,000	
Equivalent whole units contained in ending work-in-process inventory (stage of completion)	-0-	2,000	(6,000 units × ⅓)
Equivalent production units	-0-	37,000	

Unit Cost Computation—Aging. Since no materials are added in the Aging Department, the departmental unit cost is computed by dividing the cost of labor and overhead added in July by the equivalent production for July. This computation is shown in Figure 18-12.

Figure 18-12
Unit Cost Computation, Aging Department

Total Cost

Element	*Amount*	*Equivalent Production*	*Unit Cost*
Labor	$14,800	37,000	$0.40
Overhead	13,320	37,000	0.36
Totals	$28,120		$0.76

It should be noted, however, that the total unit cost of goods started, completed, and transferred to the finished goods inventory during July is $1.51 (the unit cost of $0.75 from the Blending Department plus the unit cost of $0.76 from the Aging Department).

Accumulated Cost Distribution—Aging. The total cost to be accounted for in the Aging Department is shown below.

Work-in-Process Inventory, July 1 (beginning)	$ 5,300
Cost from the preceding department, the Blending Department, transferred to the Aging Department during July.	
40,000 units × unit cost of $0.75	30,000
Cost added to the foregoing units by the Aging Department during July (labor and overhead only)	28,120
Total cost for which an accounting must be made	$63,420

This cost is accounted for by the amount assigned to the 38,000 units finished and transferred to the storeroom and the amount assigned to the July 31 work-in-process inventory. The beginning work-in-process inventory and the new July production (started and finished) are typically recorded separately and are costed on the first-in, first-out basis; that is, the beginning work-in-process inventory is assumed to be completed before the new production is completed and costed. The cost of the completed 4,000 units which were in the July 1 (beginning) work-in-process inventory, the cost of the new production of 34,000 units which were started and finished during July, and the cost of the 6,000 units in the July 31 (ending) work-in-process inventory are shown below.

Accumulated Cost Distribution			
The completed cost of the 4,000 units in the beginning work-in-process inventory:			
Cost of the July 1 Work-in-Process Inventory, from June		$5,300	
Added July cost to complete these 4,000 units:			
Labor added 4,000 × ¼ × $0.40	$400		
Overhead added 4,000 × ¼ × $0.36	360	760	
Total cost of the 4,000 completed (unit cost, $1.515)			$ 6,060
The completed cost of the new production, the units started and finished during July:			
34,000 × $1.51			51,340

Total cost of the 38,000 units completed		$57,400
The cost of the Work-in-Process Inventory, July 31:		
Cost from the Blending Department 6,000 × \$0.75	$4,500	
Labor added during July 6,000 × ⅓ × \$0.40	800	
Overhead added during July 6,000 × ⅓ × \$0.36	720	
The cost of the Work-in-Process Inventory, July 31		6,020
Total Accumulated Cost Distribution		$63,420

It should be observed that the total cost of the first 4,000 units finished and transferred to finished goods is \$6,060, or \$1.515 per unit, and that these units have a different cumulative unit cost from the cumulative unit cost of \$1.51 for the new production which was started and finished during July. Thus there is a variation in the unit cost of the two groups of items. Also note that the total cost of the ending work-in-process inventory of \$6,020 added to the total cost of the 38,000 units finished of \$57,400 equals \$63,420, which is the accumulated cost to be distributed and for which an accounting must be made.

Cost of Production Report

The schedule of equivalent production, the quantity schedule, the accumulated costs, and the distribution of these for each department or process are combined into what is normally referred to as a *cost of production report.* The cost of production report is a valuable aid in controlling costs; it may be used for comparisons with prior company costs, current industry costs, and predetermined estimates. The report can be expanded to include the description and total cost of each item of material, each labor operation, and each item of overhead, together with corresponding unit costs. A careful study and analysis of day-to-day variations in unit costs as shown on daily cost reports may reveal losses or inefficiencies that might otherwise continue for an indefinite period. Because of its complexity, however, this report is not presented in this basic accounting text.

Flow of Process Costs—Summary Journal Entries

Summary entries to record the flow of costs for Atkins Chemical Company Ltd. are shown below (assuming that the same units manufactured were sold).

(a)		
Work-in-Process Inventory—Blending Department	10,000	
Materials Inventory		10,000
(b)		
Work-in-Process Inventory—Blending Department	13,500	
Work-in-Process Inventory—Aging Department	14,800	
Factory Payroll		28,300
(c)		
Work-in-Process Inventory—Blending Department	11,250	
Work-in-Process Inventory—Aging Department	13,320	
Manufacturing Overhead		24,570

(d)

Work-in-Process Inventory—Aging Department	30,000	
Work-in-Process Inventory—Blending Department		30,000

(e)

Finished Goods Inventory	57,400	
Work-in-Process Inventory—Aging Department		57,400

(f)

Cost of Goods Sold	57,400	
Finished Goods Inventory		57,400

Work-in-Process Inventory—Aging Department has a debit balance on July 1 of $5,300, which is the value of the beginning work-in-process inventory. Entry (d) transfers costs from the Blending Department to the Aging Department. When the finished goods are sold, the costs are transferred to Cost of Goods Sold, entry (f), and the customers are billed for the sales.

It should be noted that the accountant of Atkins Chemical Company Ltd. was able to assign all materials and labor costs to the applicable department; hence, none of these costs had to be considered as manufacturing overhead.

COSTS USED IN COST ACCOUNTING SYSTEMS

The job order and process cost accounting systems described in the preceding sections use historical costs in the accounting process. Either historical costs or standard costs can be used for both job order and process cost accounting systems. Standard costs allow the accountant to record what costs ought to be as well as what costs actually are. Use of standard costs is not a third type of cost accounting systems; it is simply the application of predetermined costs in recording data in the accounts of either a job order or process system.

The use of standard costs is explained in Chapter 19.

GLOSSARY

Cost Center A subentity or segment within a firm for which costs are accumulated; examples are job, process, unit of product, department, or subdepartment.

Cost Control Accounts Controlling accounts used with a cost system such as Work-in-Process Inventory, Factory Payroll, Manufacturing Overhead, and others.

Cost of Production Report A report combining the schedule of equivalent production, the quantity schedule, the accumulated costs, the distribution, and the calculation of unit cost for each department.

Cost of Goods Sold Account An account used to accumulate the cost of products sold when a perpetual inventory system is employed.

Equivalent Production Units The number of equivalent whole units produced in a time period. It is the units started and finished during a period plus partial completions converted into equivalent whole units.

Expense A period expired cost that is utilized in the production of revenue.

Factory Payroll Account An account used in a cost accounting system to show on the debit side the gross direct and indirect labor cost for a period; the entire amount is cleared out or shifted out of the account to either a work-in-process inventory account or to the manufacturing overhead control account.

Historical Cost System A cost system established to record only actual or historical costs; the job order and process systems can be designed to record only historical costs.

Job Order Cost Sheet A subsidiary record used with a job order cost accounting system to record the direct materials used, the direct labor incurred, and the manufacturing overhead applied to the specific job.

Job Order Cost System A cost accounting system that is used when costs can be specifically associated with the physical units in the specific production or job order; most job order systems accumulate historical cost only but could be designed to accumulate some form of predetermined-type cost.

Perpetual Inventory Card A subsidiary record for each of the materials that will be used in production and for each item of finished goods.

Predetermined Overhead Rate A rate used to allocate manufacturing overhead to work in process to accomplish two basic objectives: accuracy and equitability; it should be calculated by relating the budgeted overhead cost to budget amount of some high correlative factors.

Process Cost System A cost system which is used for manufacturing processes in which costs cannot be traced to specific units and in which production is largely continuous, as in the petroleum industry; a process system can accumulate either historical costs or standard costs.

Producing Department A department engaged directly in the production of the product being manufactured.

Product Cost A cost incorporated in the inventories of work in process and finished goods; it is an asset.

Quantity Schedule A schedule showing the units of product processed during a given time period for a particular process.

Service Department A department that provides a service for other service departments as well as producing departments—for example, the heating plant of a factory.

Standard Cost System A cost system devised to accumulate both standard costs (predetermined cost based on a given philosophy of cost) and historical cost; any differences between the two costs are measured and recorded in variance accounts.

Time Ticket A record of the daily number of hours, hourly rate, and total wages maintained for a factory laborer for each job or process for different amounts of time spent on these respective jobs and processes.

Unit Cost The amount of cost of direct labor, direct materials used, and factory overhead that is incorporated in one unit of product.

QUESTIONS

Q18-1. Name two approaches to the various types of cost systems. Which produces more meaningful information for management? Explain.

Q18-2. What factors should be taken into account in deciding whether to use a job order cost system or a process cost system in any given manufacturing situation?

Q18-3. What subsidiary ledgers or records are controlled by each of the following general ledger accounts: (a) Work-in-Process Inventory; (b) Materials Inventory; (c) Factory Payroll; (d) Manufacturing Overhead; and (e) Finished Goods Inventory?

Q18-4. (a) What is the function of a job order cost sheet? (b) What documents may furnish direct material and direct labor costs for the job order cost sheet? (c) How is manufacturing overhead applied? (d) What controlling account in the general ledger controls the data on the job order cost sheets?

Q18-5. (a) Define the term *manufacturing overhead.* (b) What are the debit and credit functions of the Manufacturing Overhead controlling account? (c) Why is a predetermined overhead rate used in applying overhead to job order cost sheets? (d) Explain the causes and the significance of over- and underapplied overhead.

Q18-6. (a) How is a predetermined overhead rate computed? (b) What bases may be used in applying manufacturing overhead to job order cost sheets? (c) What are the objectives in distributing overhead to job order cost sheets?

Q18-7. (a) What types of industry are likely to use a process cost system? (b) What are the differences between a job order cost system and a process cost system? (c) Describe the accumulation of costs when a process cost system is used.

Q18-8. A given manufacturing cost may be indirect if a job order cost system is used, but may be direct if a process cost system is used. Explain and give two examples.

DEMONSTRATION PROBLEMS

DP18-1. (*Job order cost system*) The Barry Manufacturing Company completed the following transactions during the month of April:

1. Purchased materials for $75,000.
2. Requisitioned materials for production as follows:

Job 101	$18,000
Job 102	12,000
Job 103	7,500
Job 104	4,500
Total	$42,000

3. Requisitioned materials for general factory use, $6,000 (charge Manufacturing Overhead).
4. Paid the factory payroll totaling $72,000 (ignore payroll taxes). The direct factory labor cost was distributed as follows:

	Hours	*Amount*
Job 101	7,500	$15,000
Job 102	4,500	9,000
Job 103	10,500	23,625
Job 104	9,000	20,250
Total		$67,875

   Indirect labor used cost $4,125.
5. Incurred additional overhead costs of $64,125 (credit Accounts Payable).
6. Applied manufacturing overhead to job order cost sheets at the rate of $1.75 per direct labor hour.

7. Completed Jobs 101, 102, and 103 and transferred them to finished goods.
8. Sold Jobs 101 and 102 on account for $135,000.
9. Transferred the balance of Manufacturing Overhead to Cost of Goods Sold.

Required:

1. Prepare journal entries to record the transactions.
2. Post to a Work-in-Process Inventory T account.
3. Post to a T account for each of the four jobs.
4. Verify the ending work-in-process inventory.

DP18-2. (*Process cost system with a single process*) The Boone Manufacturing Company began operations on January 1. It plans to manufacture a single standardized product called Uno, which requires a single process.

During January it started and finished 12,000 units of Uno. There was no January 31 work-in-process inventory. The company's costs for January were:

Materials	$ 78,000
Direct labor	102,000
Manufacturing overhead	122,400
Total	$302,400

During February, the company started and finished 13,500 units of Uno; it had 600 units in process as of February 28, in the following stage of completion:

Materials	75%
Direct labor and manufacturing overhead	50%

Costs for February were:

Materials	$ 86,490
Direct labor	113,160
Manufacturing overhead	135,792
Total	$335,442

During March, the company completed 15,000 units, including the beginning work-in-process inventory. It had 750 units in process as of March 31 in the following stage of completion:

Materials	100%
Direct labor and manufacturing overhead	60%

Costs for March were:

Materials	$ 91,800
Direct labor	121,200
Manufacturing overhead	145,440
Total	$358,440

Required: For each month, where applicable, (a) prepare a schedule of equivalent production; (b) compute the unit cost of materials, direct labor, and manufacturing overhead; (c) compute the total cost to be accounted for; (d) compute the cost of completed units; and (e) compute the cost of the ending work-in-process inventory.

DP18-3. (*Process cost system with two processes*) The Braswell Company manufactures a product in two processes. In Process 1, all the material is added when the units of the product are started in process; in Process 2, materials are added as the last step in the processing. During July, the company started 12,000 units in Process 1; 9,000 units were completed and sent to Process 2. The remaining 3,000 were one-half complete in Process 1. There were 1,500 units three-quarters complete in Process 2 at the beginning of the month; at the end of the month 2,700 were on hand, two-thirds complete. The following costs were incurred:

	Process 1	*Process 2*
Beginning work-in-process inventory	$ -0-	$13,005
Materials	36,000	3,900
Labor	16,800	8,475
Manufacturing overhead	23,100	6,780

Required:

1. Calculate the equivalent units produced.
2. Calculate the unit cost of material, direct labor, and overhead for July.
3. Calculate the cost of the units completed and transferred.
4. Calculate the cost of the ending work-in-process inventory in each process.

PROBLEMS

P18-1. The information shown below was taken from the job order cost sheets used by the Tillery Manufacturing Company for the manufacture of its only product, Glub. Assume that all units of Glub manufactured prior to August 20 had been sold.

Job Order Number	*Balance, September 1*	*Production Cost in September*	*Remarks*
1062	$2,000		Completed 8/20
1063	2,500		Completed 8/30
1064	700	$1,950	Completed 9/8
1065	450	2,050	Completed 9/12
1066	350	2,100	Completed 9/18
1067		1,740	
1068		910	

Jobs 1062, 1063, and 1064 were sold and were delivered to customers in September. From the foregoing information, compute the following:

1. Work-in-process inventory at September 1
2. Finished goods inventory at September 1
3. Cost of goods sold during September
4. Work-in-process inventory at September 30
5. Finished goods inventory at September 30

P18-2. The following are among the transactions of the Jolly Manufacturing Company:

1. Issued $120,000 worth of materials for use on jobs and $6,000 for general factory use.
2. Distributed factory payroll, consisting of $150,000 of direct labor and $12,000 of indirect labor.
3. Applied manufacturing overhead at 60% of direct material cost.

4. Completed jobs that cost $144,000.

Prepare journal entries to record the transactions.

P18-3. The Work-in-Process Inventory as of the end of a period is as follows:

Work-in-Process Inventory

Direct materials	60,000	Finished goods	174,000
Direct labor	84,000		
Manufacturing overhead	42,000		

There is one job in process at the end of the month. The direct materials charged to this job total $3,000.

Determine the amount charged to this job for direct labor and manufacturing overhead. Assume that manufacturing overhead is applied to production on the basis of direct labor cost.

P18-4. The following account is from the ledger of the Williams Manufacturing Company:

Manufacturing Overhead (Control)

Actual	307,005	Applied	304,875

(a) Before this account is closed, three accounts are understated because of underapplied overhead. Name these three accounts. (b) Give the entry to close the Manufacturing Overhead account.

P18-5. Various cost data for the Bailey Company are given as follows:

Direct labor	$82,500
Direct material	30,000
Manufacturing overhead	83,325
Materials inventory	18,000
Work-in-process inventory	12,000
Finished goods inventory	22,500

(a) On the basis of direct labor cost, what was the manufacturing overhead rate? (b) If the direct labor cost in the finished goods inventory was $9,000, what did the direct materials cost?

P18-6. The following information is taken from the records of a firm that produces one standardized product in a single process:

a. Beginning work-in-process inventory: 1,500 units, 75% complete as to materials and 40% complete as to direct labor and manufacturing overhead.
b. Finished and transferred to finished goods inventory: 45,000 units during the period.
c. Ending work-in-process inventory: 750 units, 60% complete as to materials and 20% complete as to direct labor and manufacturing overhead.

Compute the equivalent production for each element of cost for the period.

P18-7. The following information is taken from the books of the Cornick Company in August:

Schedule of Equivalent Production

	Materials	L and O
Equivalent production of Zonker	15,000	12,000

The beginning work-in-process inventory consisted of 1,500 units, 70% complete as to materials and 40% complete as to direct labor and overhead. The August cost to manufacture was:

Materials	$ 45,000
Direct Labor	36,000
Manufacturing Overhead	30,000
Total	$111,000

Cost of the beginning work-in-process inventory was $8,400. There were 7,500 units of Zonker started and finished during August.

Compute the total cost of only the 7,500 units that were started and finished during August.

P18-8 The Andrews Chemical Company manufactures its product in a single processing department. The costs of production for 19X2 were:

Materials	$300,000
Direct labor	211,500
Manufacturing overhead	176,250

During the year, 150,000 units were started in process, of which 138,000 units were transferred to the finished goods inventory. On December 31, 19X2, 12,000 units were still in process, having received all materials and one-quarter of labor overhead. The finished goods inventory on December 31, 19X1, consisted of 30,000 units costing $4.95 each. On December 31, 19X2, there were 18,000 finished units on hand. There was no work-in-process inventory as of December 31, 19X1. The finished goods inventory is costed on the first-in, first-out basis.

Calculate the cost of the December 31, 19X2, inventories of finished goods and work in process.

P18-9. The Apple Manufacturing Company produces a single product requiring a single process. Following are data for the month of May:

a. Beginning work-in-process inventory: 18,000 units, 100% complete as to materials and 50% complete as to direct labor and manufacturing overhead; cost $27,000.
b. Started in process: 72,000 units.
c. Added within department during the period: materials, $216,000; direct labor, $72,000; overhead, $36,000.
d. Completed: 81,000 units.
e. Units in process on May 31, 9,000; all material, and one-third completed as to labor and overhead.

Compute (a) the unit cost of material, direct labor, and overhead for May; (b) the total cost to be accounted for; (c) the cost of completed units; and (d) the cost of the ending work-in-process inventory.

P18-10. The following ledger accounts show certain cost flows for a period:

Materials Inventory

Inventory	54,000	Returned to vendors	2,700
Purchases	66,000	Direct	105,000
Returned from jobs	6,000	Indirect	3,000

Factory Payroll

90,000	Direct	81,000
	Indirect	9,000

Manufacturing Overhead

Materials	3,000	
Labor	9,000	
Other	43,650	

Finished Goods Inventory

Beginning Inventory	0	
	218,430	

Manufacturing overhead is applied to production on the basis of 70% of direct labor cost.

Required: Reconstruct the journal entries affecting the Work-in-Process Inventory account and post to a Work-in-Process Inventory T account.

P18-11. The following were among the transactions completed by the Chapman Manufacturing Company during the month of December (assume that there was no work-in-process inventory on December 1):

1. Purchased materials for $108,000.
2. Requisitioned materials for production as follows:

Job 90	$24,000
Job 91	21,000
Job 92	27,000
Job 93	15,000
Total	$87,000

3. Requisitioned materials for general factory use, $9,000 (charge Manufacturing Overhead).
4. Paid the factory payroll for December of $126,000 (ignore payroll taxes). Direct labor was distributed as follows:

Job 90	$ 30,000
Job 91	27,000
Job 92	34,500
Job 93	22,500
Total	$114,000

Indirect labor cost $12,000.

5. Recorded additional actual overhead costs for December of $108,000 (credit Accounts Payable).

6. Applied manufacturing overhead to job order cost sheets at the rate of 150% of direct material cost.
7. Completed Jobs 90, 91, and 93 and transferred them to finished goods inventory.
8. Sold Jobs 90 and 93 on account for $210,000.
9. Closed the balance of Manufacturing Overhead into Cost of Goods Sold.

Required:

1. Journalize the transactions.
2. Post to a Work-in-Process Inventory T account.
3. Post to T accounts for each of the jobs.
4. Verify the ending work-in-process inventory.

P18-12. The Cherry Manufacturing Company completed the following transactions during August:

1. Purchased materials on account for $156,000.
2. Requisitioned direct materials totaling $90,000 for job orders.
3. Used indirect materials worth $9,000.
4. Returned to the vendor during August materials worth $3,000.
5. Returned materials to the storeroom: from job orders, $3,600; from indirect materials issued, $1,500.
6. Paid a total factory payroll of $195,000 for August (ignore payroll taxes).
7. Distributed the factory payroll as follows: direct labor, $192,600; indirect labor, $2,400.
8. Recorded additional actual overhead costs of $87,000 for August.
9. Applied manufacturing overhead to production at 50% of direct labor cost.
10. Completed jobs during the month costing $345,000.
11. Sold finished goods on account as follows: selling price, $555,000; cost of finished goods sold, $333,000.
12. Allowed credit for finished goods returned by customers, $4,500. These finished goods cost $2,700.
13. Closed out the over- or underapplied manufacturing overhead to Cost of Goods Sold.

Required: Journalize the transactions.

P18-13. (*Management policy decision problem*) The Crane Company uses a job order cost system for assigning manufacturing costs to its products. Management has decided to change from a system of allocating actual manufacturing overhead to jobs at the end of each month to a system of allocating overhead at a predetermined rate.

At the beginning of the year the following estimates of production costs for the year were made:

Direct materials	$375,000
Direct labor	450,000
Manufacturing overhead	675,000

There was no work in process on January 1. During the first three months of the year, actual production costs were:

	January	February	March
Direct materials	$15,000	$22,125	$22,275
Direct labor	20,250	24,375	30,375
Manufacturing overhead	30,000	37,500	45,000

Required:

1. The company uses the direct labor dollar method to allocate manufacturing overhead to the various jobs. On the basis of the estimated production cost for the year. What should the predetermined rate for allocating manufacturing overhead be? In light of the actual costs for the three months given, is this rate realistic? Support your answer by computations.
2. In summary form, record the materials requisitioned for the various jobs; the distribution of the direct labor payroll; and, using the rate derived in requirement 1, the assignment of manufacturing overhead to the various jobs for the month of January.
3. All goods worked on during the three-month period were completed except for Job 1062, which had accumulated direct materials costing $600 and direct labor costing $450. All goods completed during the period were sold except Job 1091, which had a total assigned cost of $1,500. Record, in general journal entry form, the completion of work during the period and the cost of goods sold during the period.

P18-14. (*Accounting policy decision problem*) The Eastwood Manufacturing Company prepared the following budgeted data for the year:

Manufacturing overhead	$450,000
Direct material cost	$225,000
Machine hours	900,000
Direct labor hours	150,000
Direct labor cost	$450,000
Units of production	1,350,000

Required:

1. Calculate the predetermined overhead rate for the company on each of the following bases: (a) direct material cost, (b) machine hours, (c) direct labor hours, (d) direct labor cost, and (e) units of production.
2. Data on Job 45, which was completed during the year, are as follows: direct materials cost, $480; direct labor hours, 1,020; direct labor cost, $3,330; machine hours, 1,995; units, 3,000. (a) Compute the cost of Job 45, using each of the bases from requirement 1. (b) Which method of applying overhead do you recommend? (c) Why?

P18-15. The Frazelle Oil Company produces a product in a single process. Following are data for the month of May:

a. In process as of April 30: 3,000 units, 60% complete as to materials and 10% complete as to direct labor and manufacturing overhead
b. Started in process during May: 39,000 units
c. In process on May 31: 4,500 units, 75% complete as to materials and 20% complete as to direct labor and manufacturing overhead

Required: Prepare a schedule in good form showing the equivalent units produced in May.

P18-16. Cost information for Department 3 of the Gardner Company for June is shown below (there was no beginning work-in-process inventory).

	Total Cost	Unit Cost
Production costs		
Costs from preceding department	$270,000	$ 1.80
Costs added during June within department		
Materials	$ 60,000	
Direct labor	82,800	
Manufacturing overhead	27,600	
Total costs added	$170,400	
Total costs	$440,400	

	Units
Quantity to be accounted for	
Units transferred from Department 2	150,000
Quantity accounted for	
Units completed and transferred to storeroom	132,000
Units unfinished at end of month	18,000
Total	150,000

The work in process in Department 3 at the end of June is complete as to materials and one-third complete as to direct labor and manufacturing overhead.

Required:

1. Compute the equivalent units produced in June.
2. Compute the unit cost of production in Department 3 for materials, labor, and manufacturing overhead added in Department 3.
3. Compute the total cost and unit cost of goods transferred to finished goods inventory.
4. Compute the cost of the work-in-process inventory in Department 3 at the end of June.

Show computations in good form.

P18-17. The Holland Company started manufacturing a new product on November 1; it required processing in two departments, Cooking and Drying. Total cost and unit data for the month were:

	Department	
	Cooking	Drying
Costs		
Materials	$138,240	$ –0–
Labor	75,048	168,370
Overhead	49,608	153,470
Totals	$262,896	$321,840

	Units	Units
Quantity to be accounted for		
Started in process	48,000	
Received from preceding department		41,000
Totals	48,000	41,000
Quantity accounted for		
Transferred to next department	41,000	36,000
Units in process (all materials added)		
⅕ complete as to labor and overhead	7,000	
¼ complete as to labor and overhead		5,000
Totals	48,000	41,000

Required:

1. Prepare a schedule of equivalent production for each department.
2. Compute the unit cost of production for each department for materials, labor, and manufacturing overhead.
3. Compute the total cost and unit cost of goods transferred out of each department.
4. Compute the cost of the November 30 work-in-process inventory for each department.

Show computations in good form.

P18-18. The Kerr Chemical Company manufactures a product in two processes: grinding and blending. Materials are complete when a unit is started in the Grinding Department, but are added continuously in the Blending Department. During September, the company started 36,000 units in the Grinding Department; at the end of the month 6,000 of them were in the work-in-process inventory, one-quarter complete. The others went to the Blending Department, where there were 9,000 units, one-third complete, at the start of the month, and 12,000 units, three-quarters complete, at the end. Costs were as follows:

	Department	
	Grinding	*Blending*
Work in process, August 31	$ -0-	$27,360
Direct materials	39,600	16,500
Direct labor	22,050	26,400
Manufacturing overhead	15,750	21,450

Required:

1. Prepare a schedule of equivalent production for each department.
2. Prepare a quantity schedule for each department.
3. Compute the unit cost of production for each department for materials, labor, and manufacturing overhead.
4. Compute the total cost and unit cost of goods transferred out of each department.
5. Compute the September 30 work-in-process inventory for each department.

Show computations in good form.

19

Standard Costs, Direct Costing, Responsibility Accounting

A historical cost system furnishes information that often becomes available too late for many decisions. If data are to be received in time for most decisions, a system must be designed to yield predetermined or precomputed costs, the output of a *standard cost system.* This chapter deals with the rudiments of standard costs, the question of direct costing, and an introduction to responsibility accounting.

STANDARD COSTS

Standard costs are based on engineering studies of material and labor requirements, and the judgment of management as to what overhead costs should be. For each product being produced, a *standard cost card* is developed showing what each product's cost should be. Standards are developed for materials, labor, and overhead. When actual costs incurred for the manufacturing process are compared with the standards used in calculating product costs, *variances* (or differences) are usually found. A variance caused by actual costs being greater than standard is an *unfavorable* variance. A variance caused by actual costs being less than standard is a *favorable* variance.

A company could develop standards and use them only for comparison with actual costs at the end of the period. Stronger managerial control results, however, when the standards are incorporated into the accounting system. The latter method is illustrated and explained in this chapter.

USE OF STANDARDS FOR BUDGETS

Standard costs are similar to budgets in that both are predetermined. Both standard costs and budgets aim at the same objective—managerial control. Standard costs are the anticipated costs of a product; to be useful to management they must be computed with great care.

Budgeted overhead is sometimes based on the assumption of a *fixed* or static budget; that is, it is based on a predetermined level of production. Such a budget is of limited use to management in its control-exercising function, because variations of actual costs from budgeted costs arise whenever the total number of units produced is different from that on which the budget was based.

FLEXIBLE MANUFACTURING OVERHEAD BUDGET

A budget that gives recognition to varying levels of production and to the costs that change with these levels, often called the *flexible budget,* overcomes the shortcomings of the fixed budget by providing management with a basis for analyzing—and, therefore, controlling—the variances between budgeted and actual costs. This is accomplished by comparing actual expenditures with previously established budgeted amounts, adjusted for varying levels of production. A series of budgets is prepared, showing estimated or standard costs at various levels of production. Since it is not practicable to set up budgets for every possible level of operation, interpolation may be necessary if, for example, the flexible budgets are at 5,000 unit intervals and actual production falls at a point between the intervals. The preparation of a flexible budget involves an analysis of the degree and extent to which each item of overhead cost is affected by changes in volume of production. The flexible budget, therefore, is essentially a series of fixed budgets. The preparation of any one budget in the series is the same as for a single fixed budget.

Cost Behavior Patterns. A prerequisite to this type of budget planning is a knowledge of the patterns of cost (cost behavior) within the various cost functions. Up to this point the assumption has been made that all costs are strictly fixed or strictly variable. This assumption does not hold true in a number of situations. In Figure 19-1 cost curves are given to illustrate diagrammatically four types of cost patterns. Some costs, for a given period, may be relatively fixed *in total,* regardless of changes in production. Depreciation, property taxes on factory buildings, and fire insurance are examples of these costs. As indicated previously, these are referred to as *fixed costs;* they produce a curve similar to that indicated in Figure 19-1a.

Other costs, such as supplies, may be relatively variable; that is, they vary *in total* in proportion to changes in output. These costs are referred to as *variable costs* and produce a curve similar to that indicated in Figure 19-1b.

Figure 19-1
Patterns of Cost Behavior

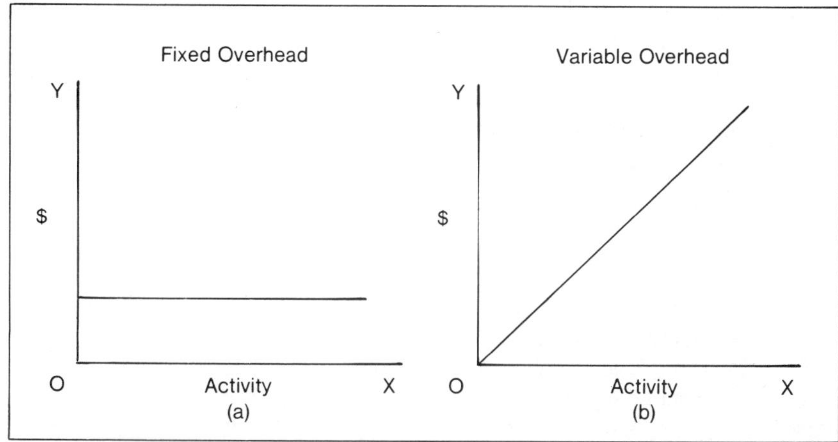

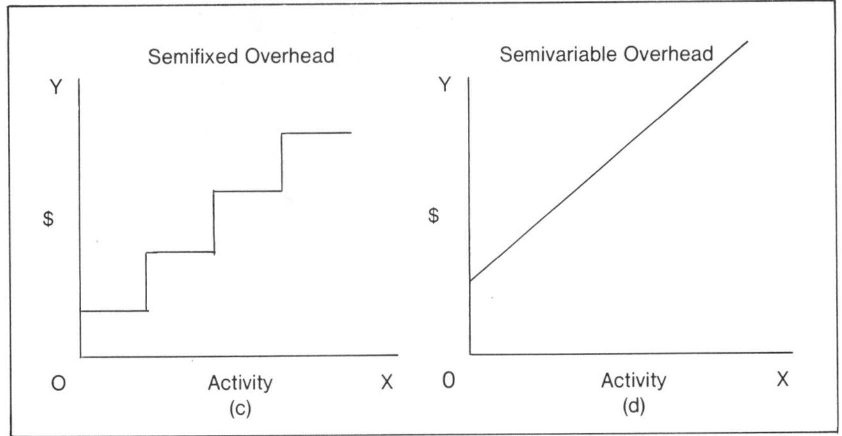

Certain other costs may change in total in the direction of changes in production, but these changes are not proportionate. Two examples of these kinds of costs are referred to as *semifixed costs* and *semivariable costs.* The semifixed costs vary in steps. For example, one inspector of finished goods may be needed for outputs of 0 to 10,000 units; two inspectors may be needed for outputs of 10,001 to 20,000 units, and so on. The salaries of the inspectors would be a *semifixed cost* (see the cost curve in Figure 19-1c). On the other hand, assume that a foreman receives a base salary of $10,000 plus a bonus of 2 percent of the revenue produced by sales of products made by his department. His salary would contain both a fixed component—the base salary—and a variable component—the bonus based on sales generated by his department. This kind of cost is referred to as a *semivariable cost* and produces a cost curve as indicated in Figure 19-1d.

Illustration of Flexible Budget. When the flexible budget is prepared, the fixed and variable components of each semivariable cost must be resolved.

Figure 19-2
Flexible Manufacturing Budget

	90%	95%	100%	105%
Direct Labor Hours	27,000	28,500	30,000	31,500
Fixed costs				
Depreciation—factory building	$ 3,000	$ 3,000	$ 3,000	$ 3,000
Factory property taxes	200	200	200	200
Insurance—factory building	300	300	300	300
Other costs	16,500	16,500	16,500	16,500
Total fixed costs	$20,000	$20,000	$20,000	$20,000
Variable costs				
Factory supplies	$ 450	$ 475	$ 500	$ 525
Light and power	720	760	800	840
Indirect labor	540	570	600	630
Other costs	7,290	7,695	8,100	8,505
Total variable costs	$ 9,000	$ 9,500	$10,000	$10,500
Total costs	$29,000	$29,500	$30,000	$30,500

Moreover, the production range of the *semifixed* costs must be known so that the amounts may be indicated as being fixed for only that particular range. For example, indirect labor may remain constant for the 85 and 90 percent production capacity, but it may be indicated at a higher fixed amount for the 95 and 100 percent production capacity. The range over which cost behavior is predictable is known as the *relevant volume range*.

To illustrate the flexible budget, assume that the Stetson Manufacturing Company produces a single, uniform product, and that its costs can be resolved into fixed and variable components. The flexible manufacturing overhead budget for the month of July is shown in Figure 19-2.

The 100 percent of capacity level used in Figure 19-2 is not intended to indicate the maximum plant capacity. Rather, it is the level at which it is considered theoretically sound to charge all fixed overhead costs to the finished products; in other words, no part of the fixed overhead costs should be considered as idle time cost. Hence, the Stetson Manufacturing Company may select 90 percent, 95 percent, or some other actual level as the standard level of output on which to base its predetermined overhead rate and the point from which to measure overapplied or underapplied overhead. It may be assumed that the level of 30,000 direct labor hours or 10,000 units of output represents the company,s practical operating capacity over a relatively long period.

Figure 19-2 indicates (1) that fixed costs are constant at all four levels of capacity, (2) that overhead is to be applied with direct labor hours as a basis, and (3) that variable costs are in direct proportion to capacity levels. This is evident from the following computations relating to the 100 percent and 95 percent columns:

30,000 direct labor hours × 95% = 28,500 hours
$500 in factory supplies × 95% = $475
$10,000 in total variable costs × 95% = $9,500

The Stetson Manufacturing Company produces 10,000 units at its 100 percent of capacity level. Each unit requires three hours of direct labor.

Illustration of Standard Cost Accounting

A standard cost accounting system is illustrated by the continuation of the activities of the Stetson Manufacturing Company for the month of July.

Standard Cost Card. The accountant working with engineers develops standards usually based on a given concept of standard cost, which may be the cost of the average performance of laborers working under normal operating conditions or average attainable standards. The standard cost card of the Stetson Manufacturing Company reveals the following standard cost per unit:

Materials: 2 pieces of Material K-12 at $5	$10
Labor: 3 hours at $3	9
Overhead: 3 hours at $1 (See Figure 19-2)	3
	$22

The predetermined overhead rate for the month of July, based on the 100 percent column (from Figure 19-2), is shown in Figure 19-3.

Figure 19-3
Predetermined Overhead Rate

$$\text{Variable cost per hour} = \frac{\text{Variable costs}}{\text{Total hours}} = \frac{\$10{,}000}{30{,}000} = \$0.33\tfrac{1}{3}$$

$$\text{Fixed cost per hour} = \frac{\text{Fixed costs}}{\text{Total hours}} = \frac{\$20{,}000}{30{,}000} = \$0.66\tfrac{2}{3}$$

Predetermined overhead rate (per hour) $1.00

The hourly rate also may be computed as follows:

$$\frac{\text{Total budget manufacturing overhead}}{\text{Total budgeted direct labor hours}} = \frac{\$30{,}000}{30{,}000} = \$1 \text{ per hour}$$

Flow Chart of a Standard Cost System. Figure 19-4 shows the flow of standard costs through the Stetson Manufacturing Company. Each of these indicated steps is illustrated and discussed in conjunction with the accounting for the activities and transactions described below.

July Cost Information for the Stetson Manufacturing Company. During July, 10,000 units were started and 9,880 units were completed; the beginning work-in-process inventory consisted of 80 units, which had received all the material and one-fourth of the labor and overhead; there were 200 units in the ending work-in-process inventory, which had received all materials and one-fifth of the labor and overhead. These data may be expressed in schedule form, as shown in Figure 19-5.

Figure 19-5
Quantity Schedule for July

	Units	
Quantity to be accounted for:		
Units in process at beginning	80	(all material—¼ L and O)
Units started in process	10,000	
Total	10,080	
Quantity accounted for:		
Transferred to finished goods inventory	9,880	
Units still in process	200	(all material—⅕ L and O)
Total	10,080	

The equivalent production is computed as shown in Figure 19-6.

Figure 19-6
Schedule of Equivalent Production for July

	Materials	*L and O*	
Beginning work-in-process inventory	–0–	60	(80 units × ¾)
Started and finished this period	9,800	9,800	(9,880 units—80 units)
Unit still in process	200	40	(200 × ⅕)
Equivalent production units	10,000	9,900	

Figure 19-4 Flow Chart of a Standard Cost System

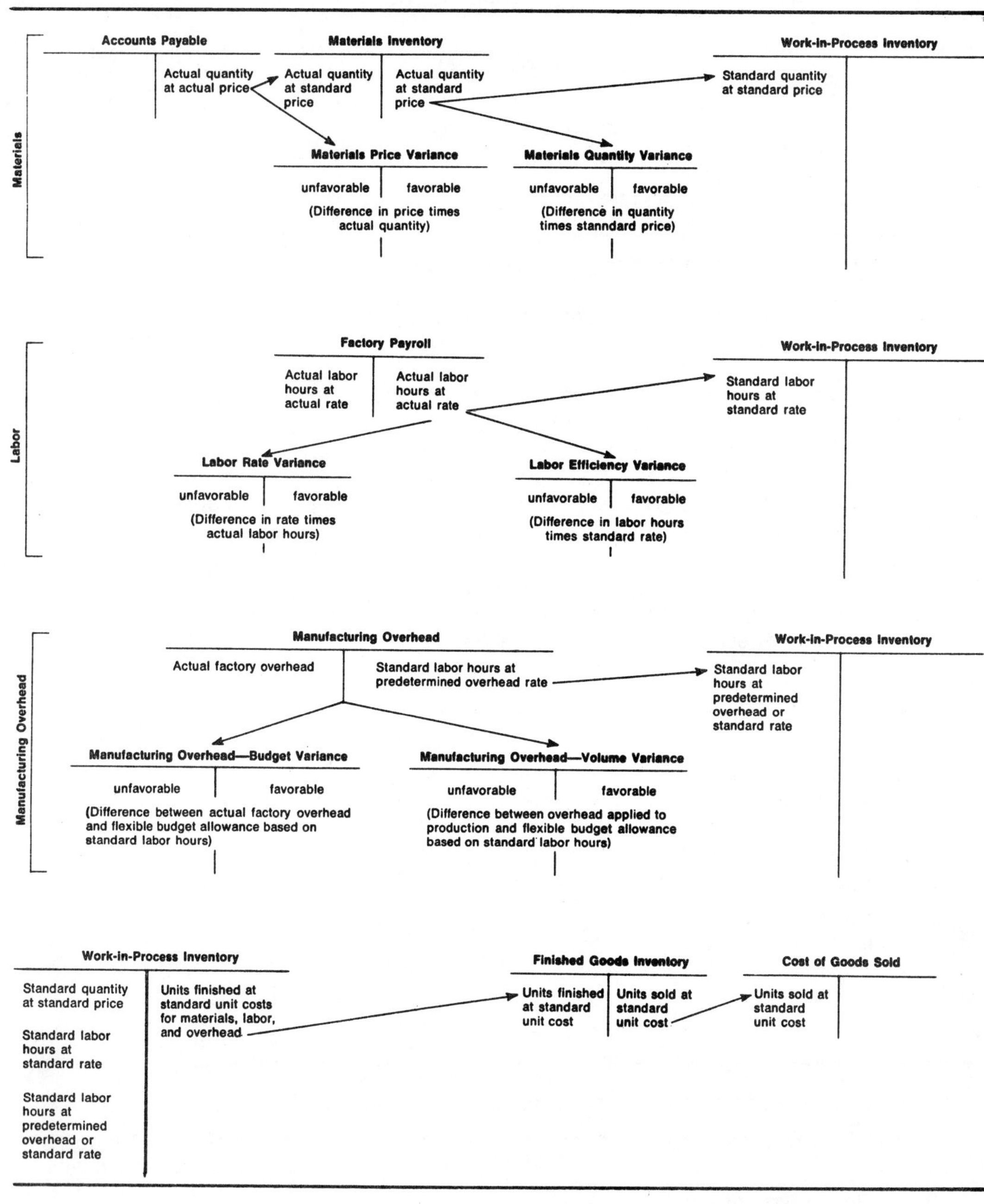

A summary of transactions for the month of July is given below.

1. Materials purchased: 20,200 pieces of Material K-12 at $4.98 each
2. Materials requisitioned for production: 20,100 pieces of Material K-12
3. Factory payroll incurred during July: 29,600 hours at $3.05 an hour
4. Direct labor applied: standard hours for 9,900 units of finished product times standard rate
5. Manufacturing overhead incurred: $29,850
6. Manufacturing overhead applied to production: $29,700 = (9,900 × $3)
7. Units finished: 9,880
8. Units sold on account: 9,500 at $30
9. Manufacturing Overhead controlling account closed and variances entered in budget and volume variance accounts

The entries to record the transactions for the month are given below.

(a)

Materials Inventory	101,000	
Materials Price Variance		404
Accounts Payable (or Vouchers Payable)		100,596

Quantity	*Price*	*Amount*
Actual: 20,200 ×	Standard: $5.00	$101,000
Actual: 20,200 ×	Actual: $4.98	100,596
Materials price variance (favorable)		$ 404

(b)

Work-in-Process Inventory	100,000	
Materials Quantity Variance	500	
Materials Inventory		100,500

Quantity	*Price*	*Amount*
Actual: 20,100 ×	Standard: $5.00	$100,500
Standard: 20,000 ×	Standard: $5.00	100,000
Materials quantity variance (unfavorable)		$ 500

10,000 equivalent production units (see Figure 19-6)
× 2 standard pieces per unit
20,000 standard units of material

(c)

Factory Payroll	90,280	
Salaries and Wages Payable (and other payroll deduction liabilities)		90,280

29,600 actual hours × $3.05 = $90,280

(d)

Work-in-Process Inventory	89,100	
Labor Rate Variance	1,480	
Labor Efficiency Variance		300
Factory Payroll		90,280

Rate Variance

Hours	*Rate*	*Amount*
Actual: 29,600 ×	Actual: $3.05	$90,280
Actual: 29,600 ×	Standard: $3.00	88,800
Labor rate variance (unfavorable)		$ 1,480

Efficiency Variance

Standard: 29,700 ×	Standard: $3.00	$89,100
Actual: 29,600 ×	Standard: $3.00	88,800
Labor efficiency variance (favorable)		$ 300

9,900 equivalent production units (see Figure 19-6)
× 3 standard hours per unit
29,700 total standard labor hours

	Debit	Credit
(e)		
Manufacturing Overhead	29,850	
Prepaid Insurance (and other accounts)		29,850
(f)		
Work-in-Process Inventory	29,700	
Manufacturing Overhead		29,700
29,700 standard labor hours × $1 per hour predetermined overhead rate = $29,700		
(g)		
Finished Goods Inventory	217,360	
Work-in-Process Inventory		217,360
9,880 completed units × $22 standard unit cost = $217,360		
(h)		
Cost of Goods Sold	209,000	
Accounts Receivable	285,000	
Finished Goods Inventory		209,000
Sales		285,000
9,500 units × $22 standard unit cost = $209,000		
9,500 units × $30 unit selling price = $285,000		
(i)		
Manufacturing Overhead—Volume Variance	200	
Manufacturing Overhead—Budget Variance		50
Manufacturing Overhead		150

The Manufacturing Overhead controlling account after entry (i) is posted appears as follows:

Manufacturing Overhead

Entry (e) 29,850	Entry (f) 29,700
	Entry (i) 150
29,850	29,850

The actual manufacturing overhead incurred ($29,850) exceeded the overhead applied ($29,700); therefore, the debit balance of $150 represents underapplied overhead. Further analysis indicates that the $150 is made up of a credit budget variance of $50 and a debit volume variance of $200. In deriving these two amounts, reference must be made to the flexible budget to determine the budget allowance based on standard labor hours for the actual work completed (29,700 units). Since a breakdown of the fixed and variable elements in the predetermined overhead rate is available, computations for the flexible budget allowances for 29,700 labor hours on work completed may be made as follows (see Figure 19-3):

Fixed costs	$20,000
Variable costs 29,700 hours × $0.33⅓	9,900
Flexible budget allowance	$29,900

If a breakdown of the fixed and variable elements is not available, the $29,900 may be derived directly from the flexible budget schedule (Figure 19-2):

$$\frac{\text{Standard labor hours for work done}}{\text{Budgeted direct labor hours}} = \frac{29{,}700}{30{,}000} = 99\%$$

The flexible budget allowance at this 99 percent level may now be interpolated as follows:

95% (28,500 hours)	$29,500
100% (30,000 hours)	30,000
5% difference	$ 500
1% difference	100
4%	$ 400

The flexible budget allowance at 99 percent level is:

95%	$29,500
4%	400
99%	$29,900

The underapplied overhead of $150 may be analyzed as follows:

1. Budget variance:	
Actual overhead incurred	$29,850
Flexible budge allowance for 99% capacity attained	29,900
Budget variance (favorable)	$ 50
2. Volume variance:	
Flexible budget allowance for 99% capacity attained	$29,900
Overhead applied during July (29,700 hours × $1)	29,700
Volume variance (unfavorable)	$ 200

The budget variance is favorable, because the actual overhead costs incurred are less than the flexible budget allowance at the 99 percent of actual capacity level. The volume variance is unfavorable, because a portion (1 percent) of the available plant facilities were not used, resulting in a loss of $200, computed alternatively as follows:

Budgeted hours	30,000
Standard hours for capacity attained	29,700
Idle capacity hours	300
Fixed overhead rate per hour	$ 0.66⅔
Cost of idle capacity	$ 200

The unfavourable volume variance, represents the portion of the fixed costs that was not asorbed because full production (30,000 hours) was not achieved. Had the volume of activity exceeded 100 percent (30,000 standard labor hours), an excess capacity, or favorable volume variance, would have resulted.

Practice varies with respect to the disposition of the variance accounts. Many accountants view standard costs as being realistic costs; therefore, they view the variances as losses, or, if they are favorable, as gains. They would close the variances to the Income Summary account. Another method is to treat the variances as costs of the period in which they are incurred—that is, to close all the variance accounts into Cost of Goods Sold. This may either be done monthly or be deferred until the end of the annual accounting period. Deferral may be practical if the variances tend to offset each other owing to seasonal volume fluctuations.

The standard cost of the 80 units (all material and one-quarter labor and overhead) in the beginning work-in-process inventory of the Stetson Manufacturing Company is comprised of the following cost elements:

Materials: 80 units × $10 standard cost =	$ 800
Labor: 80 units × ¼ × $9 standard cost =	180
Overhead: 80 units × ¼ × $3 standard cost =	60
Total	$1,040

The Work-in-Process Inventory ledger account appears as shown below.

Work-in-Process Inventory

Beginning balance	1,040	Entry (g) finished goods	217,360
Entry (b) materials	100,000		
Entry (d) labor	89,100		
Entry (f) overhead (2,480)	29,700		

The $2,480 debit balance in the account represents the standard cost of 200 units in the ending work-in-process inventory, which is verified as follows:

Cost Element	*Units in Process*	*Stage of Completion*	*Standard Unit Cost*	*Total Standard Cost*
Materials	200	100%	$10	$2,000 = (200 × $10)
Labor	200	20%	9	360 = (200 × ⅕ × $9)
Overhead	200	20%	3	120 = (200 × ⅕ × $3)
Total work in process				$2,480

MANAGERIAL INTERPRETATION OF VARIANCES

As a first step in the managerial interpretation of variances, it is necessary to identify who has primary responsibility for each of the variances. For example, the purchasing department is responsible, in part at least, for the materials price variance. Supervisory factory personnel, however, may have some influence on materials prices when these individuals specify certain brand-named materials or materials of certain grade and quality. Factory supervisory personnel have primary responsibility for the materials quantity and labor efficiency variances. The personnel department is partly responsible for the labor rate variance (although others in the factory may have some influence here—for example, hiring policies). Top factory heads are responsible for the overhead volume variance; those who acquire and use overhead items are responsible for the overhead budget variance.

When any variance is large enough, an investigation should be made to see if corrective action should be taken. For example, if the actual price of materials is substantially above the standard, a study should be made—possibly by the accountant working with the individual (or individuals) who has primary responsibility for the materials price variance—to see if this cost could be reduced by buying in larger quantities, by the substitution of other materials, or by taking other measures. The other variances are analyzed in a similar manner. It is important, moreover, to know what variances *are not* large enough to justify an investigation, as these studies may be extremely costly and hence, for small differences, unprofitable for management.

DIRECT COSTING

A primary purpose of cost accounting is to furnish management with meaningful accounting data for use in decision making. With this in view, a number of companies have adopted a cost method referred to as *direct cost-*

ing. Direct costing is contrasted with absorption, or conventional, costing. Under direct costing, all manufacturing costs are segregated into product costs and period expenses on the basis of the variability of costs with volume. For direct costing purposes, costs that vary with changes in volume are considered product costs; those which do not vary are treated as period expenses. The cost of goods sold and the cost of goods in inventory are valued on the basis of variable product costs alone—direct labor, direct material, and variable manufacturing overhead. Fixed manufacturing overhead costs are reported as expenses for the period and are deducted from the gross margin. Thus, the reported excess of revenue over variable costs and expenses, or *marginal income,* under direct costing reflects directly the effect of sales volume. Costs that are incurred to make a given level of plant productive facilities available—that is, costs that do not vary with the amount of work done but expire with the passage of time—are excluded in valuing both the cost of goods sold and the cost of goods on hand. Absorption costing, which treats *all* manufacturing costs as product costs, on the other hand, reflects the factors of both sales and production volume.

The ledger accounts under direct costing provide for the segregation of costs into their fixed and variable elements; the income statement is usually prepared to show *marginal income*—sales minus variable costs—from which fixed costs are deducted to arrive at net income. This is in contrast to absorption costing, under which the fixed and variable elements are mingled within the individual accounts. The separation of costs into their fixed and variable elements enables management to analyze the effect of volume changes on these cost elements and on net income. Under direct costing, fixed costs are deducted in the period when they are incurred, whereas under absorption costing, a portion of the fixed costs remains in inventory; hence the reported net income will differ under the two systems. When production exceeds sales, a portion of the fixed costs will remain in inventory under the absorption costing method, cost of goods sold will be less, and net income will be higher than under the direct costing method. The results are reversed when sales exceed production. Reported earnings under absorption costing may, therefore, rise with falling sales volume if production volume is increased, and fall with rising sales volume if production falls.

The difference between direct costing and absorption costing is illustrated by the operational data for the Directo Manufacturing Company. During 19XX, the company produced 40,000 units of a new product and sold 32,000 units at $25 each. Cost of production and operating expenses are as follows:

Direct materials	$120,000
Direct labor	80,000
Manufacturing overhead—fixed	200,000
Manufacturing overhead—variable	240,000
Selling and administrative expenses—fixed	60,000
Selling and administrative expenses—variable	40,000

Thus the product unit cost figures under each cost concept is:

$$\text{Absorption costing: } \frac{\$640{,}000 \text{ Total manufacturing costs}}{40{,}000 \text{ Units produced}} = \$16$$

$$\text{Direct costing: } \frac{\$440{,}000 \text{ Total variable manufacturing costs}}{40{,}000 \text{ Units produced}} = \$11$$

The company did not have a beginning finished goods or work-in-process inventory, because the product is new; also assume that it did not have a work-in-process inventory at December 31, 19XX. Two abbreviated income statements, distinguishing between the two costing concepts, are shown below.

DIRECTO MANUFACTURING COMPANY
Income Statement—Absorption Costing
For the Year Ended December 31, 19XX

Sales	$800,000
Cost of Goods Sold	512,000*
Gross Margin on Sales	$288,000
Selling and Administrative Expenses	100,000
Net Income	$188,000

* *Calculation:* $16 per unit × 32,000 units sold = $512,000.

DIRECTO MANUFACTURING COMPANY
Income Statement—Direct Costing
For the Year Ended December 31, 19XX

Sales		$800,000
Cost of Goods Sold		352,000*
Gross Margin on Sales		$448,000
Variable Operating Expenses		
Selling and Administrative Expenses		40,000
Marginal Income		$408,000
Fixed Operating Expenses and Costs		
Manufacturing Overhead	$200,000	
Selling and Administrative Expenses	60,000	
Total Fixed Operating Expenses and Costs		260,000
Net Income		$148,000

* *Calculation:* $11 per unit × 32,000 units sold = $352,000.

Since there was no beginning finished goods inventory, the $40,000 variation in net income results solely from the amount of fixed costs contained in the ending finished goods inventory ($5 × 8,000 units = $40,000).

Certain comparative operational results under direct costing and absorption costing are summarized below.

1. In any given year when units produced are greater than units sold, reported net income under direct costing is less than under absorption costing.

2. When units produced are less than units sold, reported income under direct costing is greater than under absorption costing.

3. When units sold and units produced are the same, reported income is the same under both methods.

4. Under direct costing, increases and decreases in units sold result in proportionate increases and decreases in marginal income because only variable costs are assigned to the cost of units produced.

5. Under direct costing, the emphasis is on the number of units sold, and the net income or net loss will, therefore, move in the same direction as the sales volume. Net income or net loss cannot increase or decrease, however, in direct proportion to sales volume because unit fixed costs do not stay constant. Under absorption costing, emphasis is on both production and sales, and the net income and net loss do not, therefore, show the expected relationship to sales.

6. Under direct costing, inventory valuations are determined with fixed costs excluded and are always smaller than inventory valuations computed under absorption costing, which includes fixed manufacturing overhead costs. Therefore, working capital (current assets less current liabilities) reported on the statement of financial position under the direct costing method will always be smaller.

In conclusion, note that the difference between the results under direct costing and absorption costing stems from the amount of fixed manufacturing costs allocated to finished goods and work-in-process inventories. The advocates of direct costing argue that these fixed costs are not a part of the cost of goods manufactured during a given period. Rather, these are the costs of having the capacity to produce; hence, they are expenses and should be charged against revenue irrespective of physical production. Proponents of absorption costing argue that fixed manufacturing costs are as essential to the production of goods as are variable costs and certainly add an element of economic utility to the finished product. Moreover, net income from the sale of any unit of a product does not emerge until after the total cost of bringing that product to the point of sale has been recovered.

Unquestionably, the delineation of costs into their fixed and variable components is useful to management in studying cost-volume-income relationships. To include only variable costs in finished goods and work-in-process inventories however, leaves some doubt about the validity of the valuation of those items for such purposes as securing loans and issuing capital stock. Moreover, the undervaluation of inventories leaves some doubt about the validity of subsequent income measurement. For these reasons, direct costing has not attained the status of a generally accepted accounting procedure. Some firms, however, have set up their records on a direct costing basis; then for financial reporting and tax purposes they convert their statements to an absorption costing basis.

RESPONSIBILITY ACCOUNTING

Planning and controlling functions of management have already been described briefly to illustrate an important managerial use of accounting information. Another approach is to examine the various cost accumulation techniques from the viewpoint of a responsibility accounting of the planning and control functions.

> *Responsibility accounting* traces cost, expense, and revenue measurements to specific segments of the organization (usually a department, division, or section thereof). Periodic comparisons of actual figures with budgeted, planned figures can then provide a basis for the evaluation of performance of each such organizational element and for corrective action where needed (controlling).

At the very outset, it should be pointed out that responsibility accounting does not require a separate set of accounting records. The accounts for developing product costs described in Chapters 17, 18, and this chapter must be classified or subdivided by areas of organizational responsibility. For each area of organizational responsibility, it is necessary that cost control accounts be further broken down into controllable and noncontrollable costs and that they be classified and coded in the same manner as are the budget categories. Although the design of such an information system is complex, its operation is relatively simple after the systems application work is completed. The system can be designed so that the actual data processing can be done by a computer.

Fundamental to responsibility accounting is the budget for the operating period. In actual practice, a company's budget consists of a hierarchy of budgets and supporting schedules which culminates in projected financial statements. A simplified budget structure is graphically presented on the next page.

The starting point in preparing a budget for a business is usually planned or projected sales. Once the sales summary (see budget structure on p. 558) is determined, other forecasts and budgeted schedules will be determined on the basis of the projection of sales. Thus it is extremely important that the best possible estimate of future sales be made. The several techniques of preparing the sales budget and other accompanying summaries and schedules are covered in cost accounting and managerial accounting textbooks; thus they are not discussed here.

It should be observed, however, that the work of behavioral scientists in recent years has made clear that the reduction of the budget formulation process to a mechanical routine—especially if imposed upon the organization without participation of those whose work is directly effected—often leads to results that are contrary to overall organizational goals.

Before illustrating briefly a generalized approach to a responsibility accounting system, let us restate Figure 19-2 on a responsibility basis for 30,000 direct labor hours as shown on the next page.

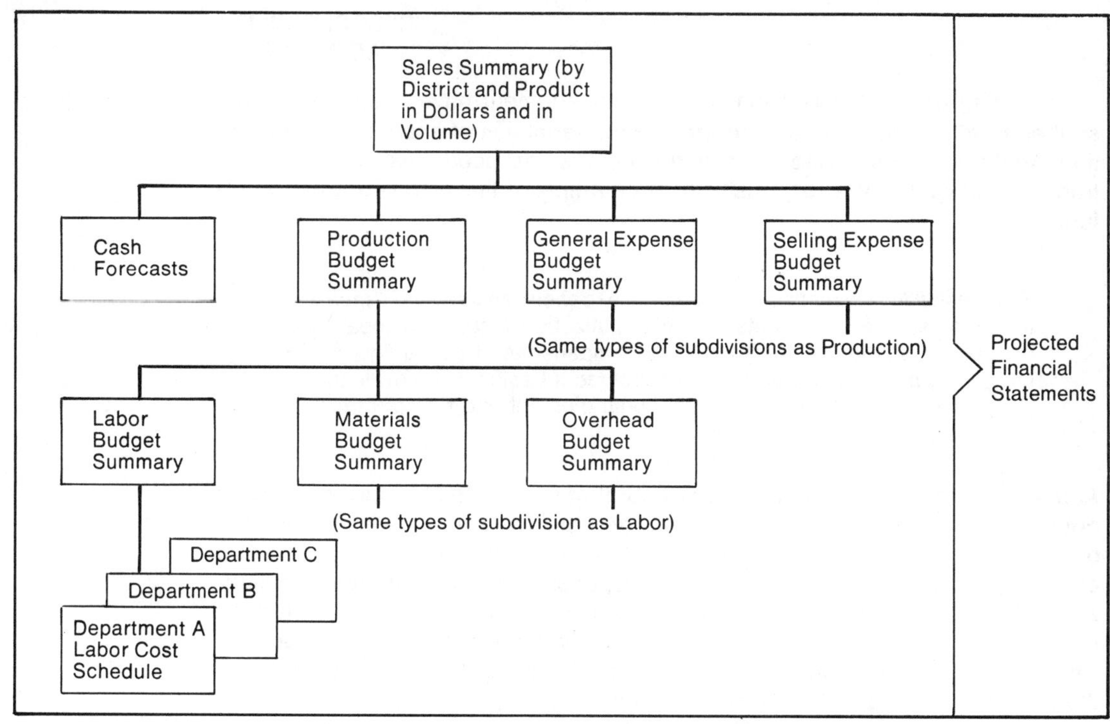

STETSON MANUFACTURING COMPANY
Manufacturing Overhead Budget—30,000 Direct Labor Hours
Month of July 19XX

	Producing Departments		*Service Departments*		*Total All Depts.*
	Dept. A	*Dept. B*	*Dept. X*	*Dept. Y*	
Fixed costs (not controllable)	$ –0–	$ –0–	$ –0–	$ –0–	$20,000*
Variable costs.					
Factory supplies	300	200	–0–	–0–	500
Light and power	400	220	80	100	800
Indirect labor	350	200	25	25	600
Other costs	4,000	3,000	600	500	8,100
Total costs	$5,050	$3,620	$ 705	$ 625	$30,000

* These costs are not controllable; for responsibility performance measurement, they are not budgeted to the various departments.

Assuming that the Stetson Company attained this level in July, a performance report could be produced from the accounting records and the budget shown as follows:

STETSON MANUFACTURING CORPORATION
Department A—Manufacturing Overhead
Planned versus Actual Performance—July, 19XX

	Expenditures		
Budget Item	*Budget*	*Actual*	*Variance**
Factory supplies	$ 300	$ 295	$ 5F
Light and power	400	410	10U
Indirect labor	350	500	150U
Other costs	4,000	3,975	25F
Totals	$5,050	$5,180	$ 130U

* F indicates a favorable variance;
U indicates an unfavorable variance.

Similar reports are issued for other departments for the overhead budget and for each other schedule in the budget structure. Managers at all levels are responsible for explaining the variances from planned results and for initiating corrective action where indicated. Note, for example, that indirect labor in Department A has exceeded budget by more than 40 percent.

Responsibility accounting is not limited to commercial enterprises; the concept can also apply to government or not-for-profit organizations. The major difference is that, for these latter groups, there is greater focus on cost control, since the generation of revenue does not involve continuous effort, as it does in a business firm.

GLOSSARY

Absorption Costing A cost system whereby direct materials, direct labor, and all factory overhead including both fixed and variable components are assigned to the units of products manufactured.

Average Attainable Standards Standards or predetermined costs of manufacturing a unit of product based on the use of average laborers working under average normal factory conditions.

Budget A financial plan for a future period developed in organizational detail.

Controlling The management function which consists of monitoring actual versus planned activity and taking corrective action where appropriate.

Direct Costing A cost system whereby only direct materials, direct labor, and *variable* overhead are assigned to the units of products manufactured; the fixed elements of overhead are treated as period expenses.

Engineering or Ideal Standards Standards or predetermined costs of manufacturing a unit of product based on the use of the most efficient laborers working under the most ideal conditions possible.

Fixed Budget A budget based on one specific predetermined level of production.

Fixed Costs Costs that, without change in present productive capacity, are not affected by change in volume of output.

Flexible Budget A budget that gives recognition to varying levels of production and to the costs that change with these levels; a series of fixed budgets at different levels of production.

Flexible Budget Allowance for Overhead The amount of budgeted overhead for the capacity that is actually attained.

Idle Capacity The cost of *not* fully utilizing the machinery, plant, and other fixed factors of production; an unfavorable manufacturing overhead volume variance is one measure of cost of idle capacity.

Labor Efficiency Variance. The difference in actual and standard labor hours multiplied by the standard rate.

Labor Rate Variance The difference in actual and standard rate of direct labor multiplied by the actual hours of direct labor.

Manufacturing Overhead Budget Variance The difference between the actual factory overhead and the flexible budget allowance based on production attained.

Manufacturing Overhead Volume Variance The difference between overhead applied to production and the flexible budget allowance based on production attained.

Marginal Income Excess of revenue above variable cost of goods sold and other variable operating expenses.

Materials Price Variance The difference between the actual and the standard price of materials multiplied by the actual quantity purchased.

Materials Quantity Variance The difference between the actual and the standard quantity of materials used multiplied by the standard price.

Planning The function that defines the goals and objectives of the organization.

Relevant Volume Range The range of production capacity over which cost behavior is predictable.

Responsibility Accounting Tracing of cost, expense, and revenue to specific segments of the organization, with periodic comparisons of actual versus planned performance.

Semifixed Costs Costs that vary in steps; they are not affected by changes in volume of output within a short range of output.

Semivariable Costs Costs that include both a fixed and a variable component.

Standards A philosophy or concept adapted for creating predetermined costs of materials, labor, and overhead incorporated in the unit of product manufactured.

Standard Cost Card The document which describes the standard quantity and standard price of materials, labor, and overhead that should be incorporated in each unit of product manufactured.

Standard Costs Predetermined costs of a unit of product based on a given standards concept.

Variable Costs Costs that are affected in total by changes in the volume of output; costs that vary proportionately with the changes in some base such as production.

QUESTIONS

Q19-1. (a) What is the difference between a fixed budget and a flexible budget? (b) Why is it desirable to establish the variable and fixed factors of the predetermined overhead rate?

Q19-2. (a) What is meant by the average attainable standard cost of a unit? (b) Why is a standard cost system an effective means of cost control? (c) Identify and explain six variance accounts used in a standard cost system.

Q19-3. (a) What is meant by "budget allowance based on standard costs"? (b) How may the budget and volume variances be analyzed? (c) When should the standard costs be changed?

Q19-4. Standard cost as discussed in this text applies to a manufactured product; is it possible to extend the general principle of standard cost to the cost of services? Explain and give examples.

Q19-5. What is the basic difference between an income statement based on direct costing procedures and one based on the absorption costing method?

Q19-6. Give the advantages and the disadvantages of direct costing to management.

Q19-7. On January 1, 19XX, the Duda Company had on hand 2,000 units of a given product; it manufactured 20,000 units and sold 12,000 units. Which costing method—direct or absorption—will produce the smaller net income for 19XX? Explain the reason for the difference.

Q19-8. "All costs are controllable at one time or another in the life of a firm." In the basic format of responsibility accounting, discuss this statement.

Q19-9. If responsibility accounting does not require a separate set of accounting records, how is it implemented?

DEMONSTRATION PROBLEMS

DP19-1. (*Standard cost accounting with a flexible budget*) The Berta Objects Company used a standard cost system and a fixed manufacturing overhead budget last year as follows:

Direct labor hours	80,000
Fixed costs	
Depreciation—factory building	$ 32,000
Factory taxes	2,400
Depreciation—machinery and equipment	64,000
Other costs (item data omitted)	141,600
Total fixed costs	$240,000
Variable costs	
Light and power	$ 8,000
Factory supplies	4,000
Other costs (item data omitted)	68,000
Total Variable Costs	$ 80,000
Total manufacturing overhead	$320,000

This year, management decided to prepare a flexible overhead budget at 80, 90, 100, and 110 percent of capacity levels of production. Last year, budget represents a normal capacity of 100 percent. The standard unit cost of the product is

Materials: 1 piece of Material Y-37	$ 6
Direct labor: 2 hours at $5	10
Manufacturing overhead: 2 hours at $4	8
Total	$24

Production data for this year:

1. There was no beginning work-in-process inventory.
2. 39,600 units started in production.
3. 38,000 units completed.
4. 800 units in process (all materials added and one-quarter labor and overhead).

Condensed transactions for this year:

1. Materials purchased totaled 40,000 pieces at $6.04.
2. Materials requisitioned for production were 39,620 pieces.
3. Direct labor was 77,000 hours at $4.96 an hour.
4. Manufacturing overhead totaled $308,800.
5. Manufacturing overhead was applied to production on the basis stated.
6. Units finished were 38,000.
7. Units sold were 37,600 at $44 each.
8. Manufacturing Overhead control account was closed and variances were entered in budget and volume variance accounts.

Required:

1. Construct the flexible budget.
2. Record the transactions.
3. Post to a Work-in-Process Inventory T account and prove the ending balance.
4. Prepare a schedule analyzing the manufacturing overhead volume variance.

DP19-2. *(Absorption and direct costing)* The Directorium Manufacturing Company produced 80,000 units of a new product and sold 60,000 units at $50 each. Costs were as follows:

	Fixed Costs	*Variable Costs*
Direct materials		$200,000
Direct Labor		160,000
Manufacturing overhead	$440,000	320,000
Selling and administrative expenses	280,000	80,000

There was no ending work-in-process inventory.

Required:

1. Prepare comparative income statements for the year using (a) the absorption cost method and (b) the direct cost method.
2. Give the reasons for the difference in reported net income or net loss in requirements 1(a) and 1(b).

DP19-3. (*Responsibility accounting*) Prince Edward Company, a distributor of art objects, offers a cash discount of 2% to customers paying their accounts within 10 days of sale, but charges 18% a year or 1½% a month on all accounts not paid within 30 days of sale. Each department decides which of its customers will be allowed to buy on credit. The net sales of each department are computed by subtracting the cash discount actually taken on department sales. Interest revenue from finance charges is allocated to the departments on the basis of credit sales made during the current month. A summary of these monthly transactions follows:

	Total	*Dept. A*	*Dept. B*	*Dept. C*
Cash sales (net of cash discount)	$300,000	$ 40,000	$120,000	$140,000
Cash discounts on credit sales collected within 10 days	4,700	1,800	2,600	300
Total sales	670,000	140,000	280,000	250,000
Interest revenue on credit sales not collected in 30 days	15,600	4,216	6,746	4,638

Required:

1. Discuss the method of allocating cash discounts and the revenue from interest charges for responsibility accounting purposes.
2. Compute the net revenue due to credit sales, assigning the discounts and interest revenue in a manner which you believe would produce more useful results for management use.

PROBLEMS

P19-1. Select the correct answer:

1. Which of the following statements is true for a firm that uses "direct" (variable) costing?
   a. The cost of a unit of product changes because of changes in number of units manufactured.
   b. Profits fluctuate with sales.
   c. An idle facility variation is calculated by a direct cost system.
   d. Product costs include "direct" (variable) administrative costs.
   e. None of the above.

2. When a firm prepares financial reports by using absorption costing, it may find that:
   a. profits will always increase with increases in sales.
   b. profits will always decrease with decreases in sales.
   c. profits may decrease with increased sales even if there is no change in selling prices and costs.
   d. decreased output and constant sales result in increased profits.
   e. none of the above.

(*IMA adapted*)

P19-2. Ten pounds of a given material at $1.30 a pound are standard for the production of a given product manufactured by the Larson Company. During August, 28,000 pounds of the particular materials were purchased at $1.32 a pound; 24,000 pounds were put into process; 2,470 equivalent units of the finished product were produced.

Determine the materials price and quantity variances.

P19-3. Six gallons of a given material at $2.20 a gallon are standard for the production of a given product manufactured by the Elliot Company. During March, the following transactions (in summary form) took place:

1. Materials purchased were 34,000 gallons at $2.16 a gallon.
2. Materials requisitioned for production totaled 31,530 gallons.
3. Equivalent production for March was 5,250 equivalent units of the finished product.

Journalize the transactions involving materials, including the materials price and quantity variances.

P19-4. The Taylor Company's standard cost card for one of its products showed the following direct labor charge:

4 hours at $5.50 an hour

Standard direct labor hours for production for the month of April were 4,800; actual direct labor hours were 4,720 at a total cost of $26,432.

Determine (a) the labor rate variance and (b) the labor efficiency variance.

P19-5. The Hoffman Company's standard cost card for its product, Chemtide, showed the following direct labor charge:

7 hours at $4 an hour

The following were among the transactions that occurred during June:

1. Factory payroll incurred during June was 60,920 direct labor hours, at a total cost of $242,460.
2. The standard direct labor cost was assigned to 8,680 equivalent finished units.

Journalize the transactions involving direct labor, including the labor rate variance and the labor efficiency variance.

P19-6. The Wooten Company maintains a standard cost system and a flexible overhead budget, as shown below.

	70%	*80%*	*90%*	*100%*
Standard direct labor hours	140,000	160,000	180,000	200,000
Variable costs	$28,000	$32,000	$36,000	$40,000
Fixed costs	50,000	50,000	50,000	50,000
Total costs	$78,000	$82,000	$86,000	$90,000

Normal capacity is budgeted at the 100% level of 200,000 direct labor hours; the standard overhead rate is 45 cents an hour. During the period, the company worked 196,000 actual direct labor hours. Overhead was applied to production on the basis of 197,000 standard hours. Actual overhead incurred was $88,000.

Determine the manufacturing overhead (a) volume variance and (b) budget variance. (c) Prove the volume variance, using alternative computations.

P19-7. The Holmes Company produced 10,000 units of a new product; 8,000 units were sold at $25 each. Cost of production and operating expenses were as follows:

Direct materials	$30,000
Direct labor	20,000
Manufacturing overhead—fixed	50,000
Manufacturing overhead—variable	60,000
(there was no ending work-in-process inventory)	
Selling and administrative expenses—fixed	15,000
Selling and administrative expenses—variable	10,000

Prepare an income statement, using the direct costing method.

P19-8. The Sparrow Company had a finished goods inventory of 6,000 units of a given product as of January 1, 19X2, with a cost of $48,600 under the absorption costing method, or a cost of $30,000 under the direct costing method. There was no beginning work-in-process inventory.

During 19X2, the Sparrow Company manufactured 113,000 units of the particular product. The fixed manufacturing overhead cost totaled $339,000 during 19X2, and the variable unit cost was the same as in 19X1. The company sold 100,000 units of the product at $18 each and used the FIFO method of assigning costs to the cost of goods sold. There was no ending work-in-process inventory.

Operating expenses for the year were:

Selling and administrative expenses—fixed	$32,800
Selling and administrative expenses—variable	44,000

Prepare an income statement for 19X2 using (a) the direct costing method and (b) the absorption costing method.

P19-9. An important concept in management accounting is that of "responsibility accounting."

1. Define the term "responsibility accounting."
2. What conditions are necessary for effective responsibility accounting?
3. What benefits are said to result from responsibility accounting?
4. Listed below are three charges found on the monthly report of a division which manufactures and sells products primarily to outside companies. Division performance is evaluated by the use of return on investment. You are to state which, if any, of the following charges are consistent with the responsibility accounting concept. Support each answer with a brief explanation.
   a. A charge for general corporation administration at 10% of division sales.
   b. A charge for the use of the corporate computer facility. The charge is determined by taking actual annual computer department costs and allocating an amount to each user on the ratio of its use to total corporation use.
   c. A charge for goods purchased from another division. The charge is based on the competitive market price for the goods.

(*IMA adapted*)

P19-10. The budgeted data for the Hillsborough Company at 100 percent of capacity follow:

Direct labor hours	240,000
Variable overhead costs	$120,000
Fixed overhead costs	$180,000

Required:

1. Prepare a flexible overhead budget at 85%, 90%, 95%, 100%, and 105% of capacity.
2. Compute the overhead rate at each capacity.

P19-11. Following are the budgeted data for the Pittsborough Company for the first three months of the year, based on a normal capacity level of 100%.

Units	120,000
Direct materials	$360,000
Direct labor cost	$240,000
Direct labor hours	120,000
Fixed overhead costs	
Depreciation—machinery and equipment	$ 20,000
Factory taxes	8,000
Factory insurance	12,000
Miscellaneous	20,000
Variable overhead costs	
Light and power	10,000
Factory supplies	4,000
Miscellaneous	16,000

Required:

1. Construct a flexible manufacturing overhead budget at levels of 85%, 90%, 95%, 100%, and 105%.
2. Prepare standard cost cards for the product at each level of activity; compute separate variable and fixed cost rates per direct labor hour.

P19-12. The standard cost card for the Tarborough Company showed the following information on its commodity, Slinko.

Materials: 4 gallons of Slough at $4 each	$16
Direct labor: 6 hours at $6	36
Total materials and direct labor cost	$52

Production data for the year:

1. Beginning work-in-process inventory: 200 units, 60% complete as to materials and 40% complete as to direct labor and manufacturing overhead.
2. Completed during 1976, 40,000 units.
3. Ending work-in-process inventory: 4,000 units, 80% complete as to materials and 50% complete as to direct labor and manufacturing overhead.

Transactions involving materials and labor during the year:

1. Purchased 192,000 gallons of Slough at $4.04 a gallon.
2. Requisitioned 172,480 gallons of Slough for production.
3. Factory payroll incurred during the period was 247,680 hours at a total cost of $1,491,033.60 (ignore payroll taxes).
4. A standard direct labor cost was assigned to production on the basis of information contained on the standard cost card.

Required: Record the foregoing information in journal form, clearly establishing all material and labor variances in appropriate accounts.

P19-13. The Carrborough Company manufactures a single product in several styles, all of which are uniform as to material quantity and production time requirements. The standard cost sheet for all products is as follows:

Materials: 32 pieces at $4	$128
Direct labor: 40 hours at $6	240
Manufacturing overhead: 40 hours at $2	80
Total	$448

The standard cost was the same for July and August. Overhead distribution is based on direct labor hours. The condensed flexible overhead budget for August is:

	50%	*75%*	*100%*	*125%*
Direct labor hours	4,800	7,200	9,600	12,000
Variable costs	$4,800	$7,200	$9,600	$12,000
Fixed costs	9,600	9,600	9,600	9,600
Total costs	$14,400	$16,800	$19,200	$21,600

Production data for August:
1. Beginning work-in-process inventory: 20 units, 80% complete as to materials and 50% complete as to direct labor and manufacturing overhead.
2. Completed during the period, 244 units.
3. Ending work-in-process inventory: 12 units, 100% complete as to materials and 50% complete as to direct labor and manufacturing overhead.

Transactions for the month included the following:
1. Materials purchased totaled 8,200 pieces at $3.96.
2. Materials issued for production totaled 8,160 pieces.
3. Labor costs incurred were 10,040 direct labor hours at $5.90; standard labor cost was transferred to the work-in-process inventory.
4. Manufacturing overhead incurred was $20,800.
5. Manufacturing overhead was applied to production.
6. Recorded units completed.
7. Sold 260 units for $750 each.
8. Closed the Manufacturing Overhead controlling account and entered the variances in budget and volume variances accounts.

Required:

1. Give the journal entries for the month.
2. Post to a Work-in-Process Inventory T account and verify the ending balance.
3. Prepare a schedule to account for the manufacturing overhead volume variance.

P19-14. The Vanceborough Company manufactures a single product in several styles, all of which are uniform as to quantity of materials and production time requirements. The standard cost card for all products reveals the following quantities and costs:

Materials	12 pieces × $2	$ 24
Direct labor	16 hours × $8	128
Manufacturing overhead	16 hours × $8	128
Total		$280

The normal (100%) standard budgeted overhead costs consist of:

Direct labor hours	8,000
Variable costs	$16,000
Fixed costs	48,000
Total costs	$64,000

Production data for July (there was no June 30 work-in-process inventory):

1. Completed: 500 units.
2. In process as of July 31: 20 units, 40% complete as to materials and 30% complete as to labor and overhead.

Selected transactions for the month of July included the following:
1. Materials purchased were 6,400 pieces at $1.96.
2. Materials issued for production totaled 6,120 pieces.
3. Manufacturing overhead incurred was $65,600.
4. Manufacturing overhead was applied to production.
5. Closed the Manufacturing Overhead controlling account and entered the variances in budget and volume variance accounts.

Required:

1. Prepare the journal entries to record the transactions.
2. Prepare the end-of-period entries to close the four established variances.

P19-15. The standard cost card for the Greensborough Company shows the following information on its commodity, Dunker:

Materials: 8 pounds of Dinklo at $3.00	$24
Direct labor: 4 hours at $4	16
Total material and direct labor cost	$40

The schedule of equivalent production reveals the following figures:

Materials	*Direct Labor*
104,000 units	103,200 units

Selected transactions for the month of November 1976 included the following:
1. Purchased 862,400 pounds of Dinklo at $2.98 a pound.
2. Requisitioned for production 831,800 pounds of Dinklo.
3. Factory payroll incurred during the period was 412,400 hours at a total cost of $1,640,800 (ignore payroll taxes).
4. Standard direct labor costs were assigned to production at the standard rate.

Required:

1. Prepare the journal entries to record the transactions.
2. Prepare the end-of-period entries to close the four established variances.

20

Cost, Volume, and Income Analyses

Business decisions are made only after different courses of action have been considered. The mere act of considering possible courses of action is not very useful to the manager, however, unless information is also available on the consequences of those choices. In this chapter the relationships between (1) costs, (2) volume of business activity, and (3) income are discussed. Some ways that knowledge of these relationships can be used to make better decisions are illustrated and explained. However, before costs can be analyzed and interpreted for managerial use, the content and behavior of various costs must be known. Therefore, certain basic cost concepts are reviewed and discussed in the following section.

VIEWS OF COST

Fixed costs are the costs that, without change in present productive capacity, are not affected by changes in volume of output. For instance, rent on a factory building is a fixed cost because it does not change when productive volume increases or decreases.

Variable costs are costs that are affected in total by changes in the volume of output. The cost of materials, for example, is a variable cost because it increases in direct proportion to the increase in the number of units produced.

Semifixed costs are costs that vary in steps; they are not affected by changes in volume of output within a given range of output. For example, one inspector may be required for an output of 0 to 10,000 units; two may be required for outputs of 10,001 to 20,000 units; and so on. Semivariable costs are costs that include both a fixed and a variable component. An example is a foreman who receives a base salary plus a bonus determined by a percent of production.

Marginal costs (or *differential costs*) are the differences in cost between two levels of output, or the additional cost necessary to produce an additional unit.

Opportunity cost is the cost of foregoing one thing to get an alternative; for example, a company may make a large investment in plant and equipment, thereby giving up an opportunity to invest in bonds.

Out-of-pocket costs are costs that give rise to cash expenditures, such as wages, in contrast to depreciation, which requires no cash disbursement in the current period.

Sunk costs are costs that have already been incurred. They cannot be recovered if the project in which they were sunk is dropped. Accordingly, they are usually not a factor to consider in decisions affecting the future. An example is the purchase of a machine that stamps the company's brand label on boxes. The machine would have no resale value.

BREAK-EVEN ANALYSIS

The break-even point is the volume of sales at which the business will neither earn income nor incur a loss; it is the point at which expenses and revenues are exactly equal. At this volume of sales, net income is equal to zero. The break-even point can be expressed in terms of dollars of total sales or in terms of total units of a product sold. In each of these, it is the level of business at which total revenues will recover the exact amount of total costs and, therefore, the business will ***break-even.***

Computation of the Break-Even Point

In discussion of the flexible budget in Chapter 19, it was noted that costs could be identified as either fixed or variable. Some costs, for a given period of time, may be relatively fixed in ***total,*** regardless of how many units are produced. Fire insurance on buildings is an example. These are referred to as *fixed costs.* Other costs, such as materials used in production, increase or decrease depending on how much is produced. The total amount of these costs for a given period of time, depends on how much is produced, and they are referred to as *variable costs.*

In the following discussion, it is assumed that the cost accounting department has already identified all costs and expenses as either fixed or variable. Once this has been done, total cost is the sum of total fixed costs *(TFC)* and total variable costs *(TVC).* Since the break-even point is the volume of sales at which the business will earn zero profit, the following equation can be used to describe it.

$$S_{BEP} = TFC + TVC$$

where S_{BEP} is the dollar volume of sales at the break-even point and is an unknown in the foregoing equation.

Figure 20-1
Data for Break-Even Computation

	Fixed	*Variable*	*Budgeted Net Income Calculation*
Budgeted sales:			
20,000 units $15 each			$300,000
Budgeted costs	$105,000	$120,000	225,000
Budgeted Net Income			$ 75,000

Assume for illustration purposes the data for Jackson Corporation in Figure 20-1. As can be seen, the variable cost is $120,000. If the company is operating at the 100 percent capacity level, then the variable cost per unit at this production level is \$6 (\$120,000 ÷ 20,000 units). If each unit is sold for \$15, then each unit sold brings in \$9 of revenue in excess of variable cost. This \$9 is known as the *unit contribution margin.* If total fixed costs are \$105,000, then the company must sell 11,667 units to cover its total fixed costs and thereby break-even (\$105,000 ÷ \$9 = 11,666.67 or 11,667 units).

Since variable costs per unit *(VC)* divided by selling price *(SP)* is a fraction representing the percentage of variable costs in each sales dollar, the term $1 - \frac{VC}{SP}$ represents the percentage of contribution that each sales dollar makes toward paying off fixed costs.

The percent of variable costs to sales for the Jackson Corporation can be calculated as follows, where selling price is \$15 per unit:

$$\frac{VC}{SP} = \frac{\$6}{\$15} = 0.40$$

The break-even point in dollars can be computed by dividing total fixed costs by the above calculated contribution margin percentage as follows:

$$\frac{\$105{,}000}{1 - 0.40} = \frac{\$105{,}000}{0.60} = \$175{,}000$$

If unit costs are not known, the variable cost percentage can be computed by using the total figures as follows:

$$\text{Variable cost percentage} = \frac{\text{Total variable costs}}{\text{Total sales}} = \frac{\$120{,}000}{\$300{,}000} = 0.40$$

Thus, 40 percent of sales is required to cover the variable costs.

	Percent
Break-even sales	100
Variable costs	40
Fixed costs at break-even point	60

Then 60 percent of each sales dollar (the *contribution margin percentage*) is available to cover the fixed costs.

$$S_{BEP} = \frac{\text{Fixed costs}}{\text{Contribution margin percentage}} = \frac{\$105{,}000}{0.60} = \$175{,}000 =$$

Volume of sales at break-even point

Proof of this solution follows:

Break-even sales		\$175,000
Costs		
Variable (40%)	\$ 70,000	
Fixed (60%)	105,000	175,000
Net income		\$ -0-

The Break-Even Chart

One effective means of presenting the relationship of fixed and variable costs to sales at different volume levels is the *break-even chart.* The two charts shown (Figures 20-2 and 20-3) are based on data in Figure 20-1. It is assumed that the total quantity produced can be sold at $15. Total sales are measured on the 45 degree line rising from the origin in both charts. In Figure 20-2, the vertical line (*Y* axis) represents dollars from which both total sales and various costs can be read; the horizontal line (*X* axis) represents sales unit volume and percent of plant capacity.

The fixed costs, assumed to be unaffected by volume changes, are, therefore, represented by a horizontal line running parallel to the *X* axis. Total costs, which are affected by volume changes, are represented by a straight line starting at the fixed cost intersection on the *Y* axis and rising to the right of the chart. The point at which the total sales and total cost lines meet is the break-even point; at this point costs equal sales so that there is neither income nor loss. The spread between the lines above the intersection measures the amount of income; the spread between the lines below the intersection measures the amount of loss.

In Figure 20-2, the fixed costs line is below the variable costs line. In Figure 20-3, an inverted break-even chart, the fixed costs line is above the variable costs line to show clearly the portion of the fixed costs remaining to be recovered (loss area) before income is realized. The break-even point in the two forms is, of course, the same.

Both charts show the *relevant volume range,* which is the operating range span over which all costs are likely to be predictable as fixed or variable. This range excludes extremely high and low levels of volume where the probability of the cost behavior patterns would most likely be different from those indicated for the output of the relevant volume range; for example, semifixed costs are lower at the lower volume range and are higher at the higher volume range. The information contained in the relevant volume range of the chart is, thus, more reliable for decision making than is the information contained in the nonrelevant range area of the chart.

The charts are based on certain assumptions regarding the relationship between prices and costs and the relative proportions of the various products sold. Further assumptions are that costs are either fixed or variable, that variable costs are affected proportionately by volume changes, and that beginning and ending inventories, price levels, product mix, and technical plant and labor efficiency will remain essentially unchanged. The degree and the effect of these factors on actual and assumed conditions must be carefully balanced and evaluated in break-even analysis. Break-even charts may be prepared from budgeting data as a forecast of costs and income, or they may be based on data taken from the books as a historical presentation of cost-volume-income relationships.

The break-even point in terms of units or in terms of percentage of plant capacity used may be determined from the *X*-axis scale. The amounts at the break-even point are as shown (see Figure 20-2):

Figure 20-2
Typical Break-Even Chart

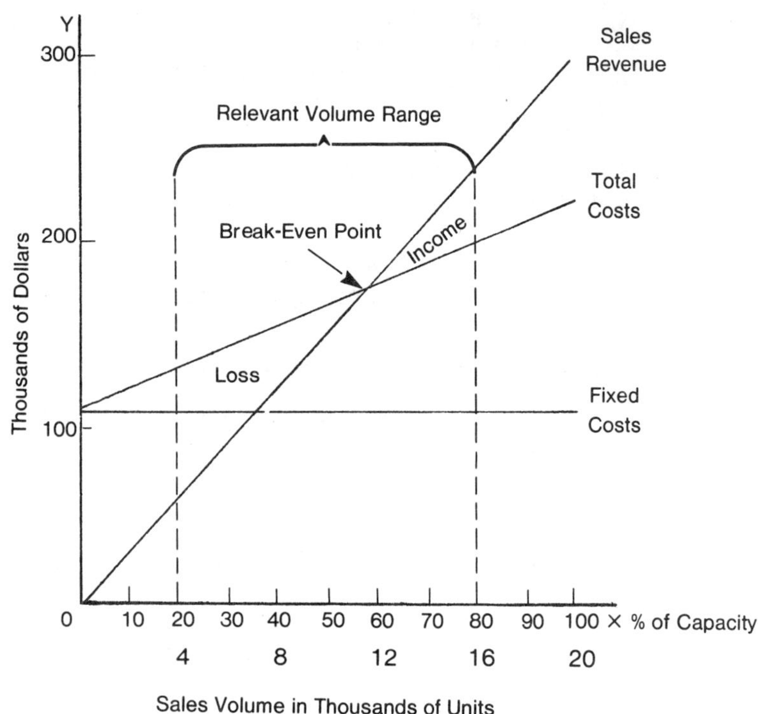

Figure 20-3
Inverted Break-Even Chart

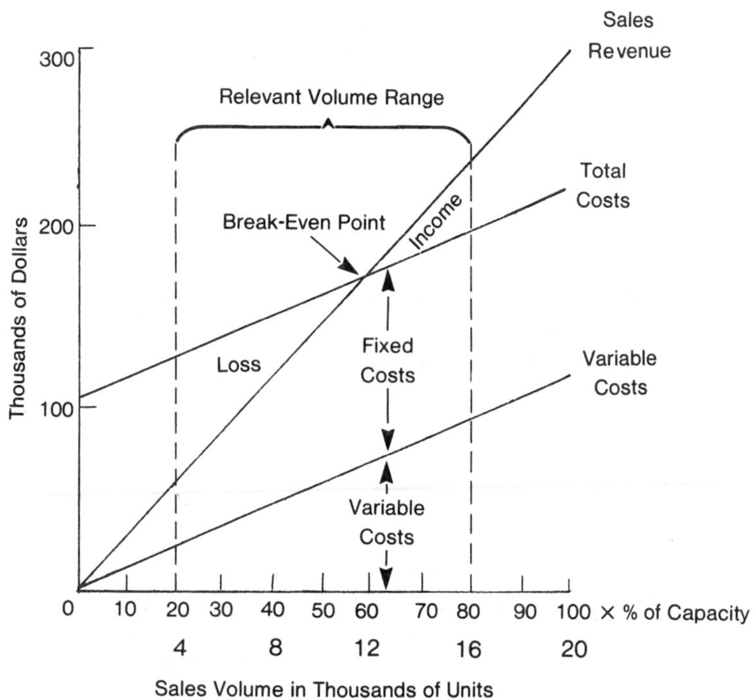

Break-even percent of plant capacity	58.3
Break-even units (assuming a single product or a constant mix)	11,667

The break-even percentage of operating capacity may also be verified mathematically as follows:

$$\frac{\text{Break-even sales volume}}{\text{Budgeted sales volume}} = \frac{\$175{,}000}{\$300{,}000} = 58.3\%$$

The break-even point in units is proved in the following equation:

$$\begin{aligned} x &= \text{number of units sold at break-even point at \$15 each} \\ \$15x &= \$15(0.4x) + \$105{,}000 \\ 9x &= \$105{,}000 \\ x &= 11{,}667 \end{aligned}$$

The same computation may be made in the following terms:

$$\text{Unit}_{BEP} = \frac{\text{Fixed costs}}{\text{Unit dollars contribution margin}} = \frac{\$105{,}000}{\$9} = 11{,}667 \text{ or,}$$

Line		
1	Unit sales price (see Figure 20-1)	$ 15
2	Unit variable cost (0.40 × $15)	6
3	Unit contribution (amount available for the recovery of fixed costs and profit)	$ 9
4	Fixed costs	$105,000
5	Unit break-even sales (line 4 ÷ line 3)	11,667

This is simply dividing the unit cost contribution into fixed cost to determine how many times it must be earned (units sold) to pay the fixed costs. The proof of this calculation is shown below.

Sales (11,667 × $15)		$175,000*
Costs		
Variable (11,667 × $6)	$ 70,000*	
Fixed	105,000	175,000
Net Income		$ –0–

* Adjusted for rounding.

As indicated, cost variability in break-even analysis has been based on the assumption that costs can be segregated into two groups—those which vary directly with volume and those which are unaffected by volume changes. This assumption is an oversimplification, and care must be taken against reaching possible erroneous conclusions, particularly for conclusions based on information outside the relevant volume range area. As shown in Chapter 19, the course of many costs is quite erratic in relation to volume. This is particularly true of second-shift costs, fringe benefits, and so on. Few, if any, costs are uniform in terms of units of output or time except within relatively limited volume ranges, referred to here as the *relevant volume* range.

Other limitations, in summary, are (1) if the break-even chart is based on data of only one or just a few periods, the results obtained may not be typical of the company's experience; and (2) the chart is not well designed for firms that sell a great variety of products, the proportions of which may change.

MARGINAL INCOME STATEMENTS

Marginal income, or contribution to fixed cost, is the excess of revenue over related variable costs and variable expenses. The marginal income statement, therefore, separates costs and expenses into their fixed and variable elements. It is a convenient means of presenting data to management when charts or other forms might not be as serviceable. The break-even sales volume can be calculated readily from such a statement. A marginal income statement and break-even computation for the Jackson Corporation is shown in Figure 20-4 (see Figure 20-1 for supporting data).

Figure 20-4
Marginal Income Statement

Sales (net): 20,000 units × $15 each	$300,000
Variable costs and expenses	120,000
Marginal income	$180,000
Fixed costs and expenses	105,000
Net income	$ 75,000
Marginal income (or contribution) percentage	60%
Break-even dollar volume: $105,000 ÷ 0.60	$175,000
Break-even point in units: $\frac{\$105,000}{\$15 - 0.4\ (\$15)}$	11,667

From information shown in Figure 20-4, the following basic equations may be derived:

Sales − Variable costs = Marginal income
Marginal income − Fixed costs = Net income
Marginal income ÷ Sales = Marginal income percentage or contribution margin percentage
Unit selling price − Unit variable cost = Contribution per unit

Fixed costs ÷ Contribution margin percentage = Break-even point in sales dollars

Fixed costs ÷ Contribution per unit = Break-even point in units

A marginal income statement is prepared to emphasize the contribution of each sales dollar toward the recovery of fixed costs and toward net income. Marginal income must equal fixed costs if the firm is to break even; marginal income must exceed fixed costs if a net income is to be realized. Thus, in Figure 20-4, 60 cents out of each sales dollar contributes toward the recovery of fixed costs up to sales of $175,000; out of each dollar of sales thereafter, 60 cents contributes to net income. Note that a marginal income statement used for decision making in a manufacturing firm requires the application of direct-costing techniques (see Chapter 19).

MARGIN OF SAFETY

The *margin of safety* is the dollar volume of sales above the break-even point, or the amount by which sales may decrease before losses are incurred. The margin of safety for the Jackson Corporation is

Sales	$300,000
Deduct break-even sales	175,000
Margin of safety	$125,000

A loss will not be incurred unless sales decrease by more than $125,000. The *percentage of safety* is computed as follows:

$$\frac{\text{Margin of safety}}{\text{Net sales}} = \frac{\$125{,}000}{\$300{,}000} = 0.4167$$

Any decreases in sales up to 41.67 percent can be absorbed before a loss is incurred.

There is a relationship between the contribution percentage and the percentage of safety. It is:

Contribution percentage × Percentage of safety = Profit as a percent of sales

For the Jackson Corporation at a sales level of $300,000:

$$0.60 \times 0.4167 = 0.25, \text{ or } 25\%$$

Note that 25 percent of $300,000 = $75,000, which is the net income shown in Figure 20-4.

MARGINAL INCOME PLANNING

The effect of any prospective changes in operations can be determined rapidly when data on costs are divided between the fixed and variable elements. This kind of evaluation and analysis is demonstrated in the following two cases.

Case 1. The Excel Manufacturing Company is considering the possibility of expanding its present plant facilities at a time when the plant is operating at full capacity. Two important factors that must be known before the decision is made are the sales volume required with the planned expansion to earn the current income and an appraisal from the marketing department of whether this figure can be reached and exceeded.

Assume the following data for the Excel Manufacturing Company:

	Under Present Plant Facilities		*Under Proposed Plant Facilities*	
Sales		$600,000		$800,000
Variable costs	$180,000		$240,000	
Fixed costs	350,000	530,000	462,000	702,000
Net income		$ 70,000		$ 98,000

The following basic formula (expanded from the break-even formula) is appropriate to determine the sales volume required with the planned expansion to earn a specified amount of income:

$$S = VC_S + FC + I,$$

where S = dollar volume of sales to attain I
VC_S = variable costs at the specifically required sales volume
I = specified income

Thus, the formula can be stated:

$$S = \frac{FC + I}{1 - \dfrac{TVC}{TS}}$$

The data for the company may be substituted in the foregoing formula to determine the volume of sales needed to maintain current net income:

$$S = \frac{\$462{,}000 + \$70{,}000}{1 - (\$240{,}000/\$800{,}000)} = \$760{,}000$$

This is verified in conventional income statement form as follows:

Sales (S)		$760,000
Variable costs (0.30S)	$228,000	
Fixed costs	462,000	690,000
Net income (currently being earned)		$ 70,000

It is assumed in this illustration that the variable cost rate will continue to be 30 percent of sales. It is possible that the additional facilities may permit an increase in the productivity of labor or purchasing economies, thus causing a decrease in the variable cost rate. Other factors must be considered in determining whether the proposed expansion is warranted. The acquisition of additional plant and equipment involves long-term investments, possible long-term financing, and increased taxes, insurance, maintenance, and other costs. Management should be reasonably assured that it will be able to make sustained use of the added facilities.

Case 2. A corporation is considering the purchase of some special machines. Management will buy the machines if their cost can be recovered in three years—that is, if the marginal income (less out-of-pocket related fixed costs other than depreciation) generated by these machines over a three-year period is equal to their cost. Assume the following facts:

1. The machines cost $180,000.
2. The annual revenue generated by the machines will total $200,000.
3. The variable cost is 60 percent of sales.

The marginal income is $80,000 a year, computed as follows:

$$[(1.00 - 0.60) \times \$200{,}000] = \$80{,}000$$

If the annual fixed cost on these machines other than depreciation—property taxes, insurance, and so on—amounts to $6,000 a year, then the remainder, or $74,000 = ($80,000 − $6,000) a year, is recovery of the cost of the machines. At this rate, the cost of the machines will be recouped in approximately 2.4 years, determined as follows:

$$\frac{\$180{,}000}{\$74{,}000} = 2.4 \text{ years}$$

If this is the only variable on which the decision rests, then the special machines should be purchased.

PRICING OF SPECIAL ORDERS

A decision with which management is often confronted is whether or not to accept a special order involving the production of additional units beyond outstanding commitments. An analysis of preexisting cost patterns will not necessarily furnish the required data for such a decision. Each new situation requires a new cost analysis. The probable effect of the additional order on fixed manufacturing costs, selling and administrative expenses, selling price, and possible reduction in direct material costs resulting from increased volume buying must be analyzed carefully.

If the price of the special order exceeds its marginal costs—which will equal variable costs if unused capacity is available and if there are no alternative uses for this available capacity—the offer should be accepted. To illustrate, assume the following total unit cost data for the Jason Company, based on a budgeted annual production of 60,000 units:

Manufacturing costs		
Direct materials	$	2.00
Direct labor		2.50
Variable overhead costs		1.50
Total variable costs	$	6.00
Fixed overhead costs ($180,000 ÷ 60,000 units)		3.00
Total unit cost	$	9.00
Fixed selling and administrative expenses		$100,000.00

The Jason Company has been offered a long-term contract for 20,000 additional units annually at a unit price of $8.50. Since the purchaser is to attach his own label to the product, the Jason Company's established price of $15 each will not be affected. Because fixed costs are not affected by the volume of production, fixed manufacturing overhead, fixed selling expenses, and fixed administrative expenses, $280,000 in this case, will not be increased by the new order. Therefore, since the special offer price of $8.50 exceeds the unit variable cost of $6, which is also the unit marginal cost, the regular sales are not affected, and a gain of $50,000 is realized on the additional order, the offer should be accepted. The comparative budget data sheet shown below verifies this conclusion.

JASON COMPANY
Budgeted Comparative Income Statement
For the Year Ending December 31, 19XX

	Budgeted Production	*Additional Order*	*Totals*
Sales			
60,000 units at $15.00	$900,000		
20,000 units at 8.50		$170,000	$1,070,000
Variable Manufacturing Costs			
60,000 units at $ 6.00	360,000		
20,000 units at 6.00		120,000	480,000
Marginal Income	$540,000	$ 50,000	$ 590,000
Fixed Costs*	280,000		280,000
Net Income	$260,000	$ 50,000	$ 310,000

* Includes fixed manufacturing overhead cost of $180,000 and selling and administrative expenses of $100,000, which are assumed to be fixed costs.

The data also indicate the possibility of developing a new market through price reductions made possible by the absorption of fixed costs in the regular volume of business. This may be particularly effective when a product is sold in a foreign market or in any decisions involving levels of output or the cost of additional volume.

PRODUCT PRICING

An intricate relationship exists between the factors of price, cost, and volume. An understanding of this relationship is imperative, because it underlies virtually every decision confronting management. It is essential, therefore, that management make continuing analyses of its selling prices, particularly for competitive products.

One of the knottiest problems is calculating the effect of price on the volume of sales in terms of both short-run and long-run effects. The cost analyst plays a significant role in pricing-policy decisions by projecting the effect on costs and income of the sales volumes that may be expected at different prices.

The method of accumulating costs to arrive at total costs has been discussed in previous chapters. Total costs consist of direct costs (direct materials and labor), variable manufacturing overhead (power, supplies, maintenance), and fixed manufacturing overhead (insurance, taxes, depreciation). The process of establishing a predetermined overhead rate involves an allocation of the fixed manufacturing overhead on some arbitrary basis as well as an estimated volume factor that becomes the denominator in the overhead rate formula. The pricing of the product on this total cost basis is often considered unsatisfactory (1) because the allocation of overhead items is inherently imprecise, (2) because the projected volume on which the overhead rate is based is also imprecise, and (3) because total cost is not relevant to short-run decisions.

In general, however, the unit price that yields the greatest marginal income is the price that should be used for a particular product. Following this approach, therefore, a schedule should be prepared based on variable costs only, such as the one in Figure 20-5 showing the probable volume of sales and the marginal income that will result at each of the several price levels under consideration. It may be assumed that the volume-price relationships are estimated from the results of a market survey based on test sales in selected areas and from questionnaires.

Figure 20-5
Marginal Income at Various Prices

Sales Price per Unit	*Quantity*	*Projected Sales Volume*	*Variable Costs ($40 per unit)*	*Marginal Income*
$80.00	40,000	$3,200,000	$1,600,000	$1,600,000
78.00	45,000	3,510,000	1,800,000	1,710,000
75.00	55,000	4,125,000	2,200,000	1,925,000
72.50	57,000	4,132,500	2,280,000	1,852,500
67.00	65,000	4,355,000	2,600,000	1,755,000

A sales price of $75 a unit will provide the greatest marginal income—that is, $1,925,000. The $75 selling price does not provide the greatest margin on each unit sold; the unit marginal income is $35 compared with $40 at the $80 selling price. The increased sales volume at the lower price, however, results in a greater total marginal income.

When more than one product is priced, it is necessary to find a combination of price and volume that results in the greatest marginal income. Assume, for example, that the Baker Company manufactures two different products, X and Y, that require nearly identical production processes. Variable unit costs are $10 for product X and $10 for product Y. Facilities are available to produce a combined total of 11,000 units. The following schedule was prepared to aid management in its pricing policy:

Sales Price per Unit	*Quantity*	*Projected Sales Volume*	*Variable Cost*	*Marginal Income*
		Product X		
$22	4,000	$ 88,000	$40,000	$48,000
20	5,000	100,000	50,000	50,000
16	7,000	112,000	70,000	42,000
		Product Y		
$26	3,000	$ 78,000	$36,000	$42,000
23	5,000	115,000	60,000	55,000
22	7,000	154,000	84,000	70,000

A combination of 5,000 units of X and 7,000 units of Y results in the largest possible marginal income ($50,000 + $70,000 = $120,000). If, however, plant capacity cannot be efficiently expanded beyond the previously assumed level of 11,000 units, the most profitable combination is 4,000 units of X and 7,000 units of Y, for a total marginal income of $118,000 = ($48,000 + $70,000).

The establishment of prices based on marginal income is the customary practice in retailing. Prices are set on the basis of a percentage markup on cost. The markup must be delicately adjusted to gauge the responsiveness of consumer demand. Studies may be made to determine the percentage of change in revenue that results from each percentage price change (elasticity of demand) for products whose sales potential fluctuates inversely with changes in price.

In these examples, it is assumed that fixed costs remain the same at all the indicated sales levels and that net income is, therefore, maximized at prices that provide the greatest marginal income. Total unit costs (fixed and variable) depend, however, on total volume, and total volume in turn depends upon the price charged. It is for this reason that cost studies also should be made showing estimates of total cost and net income at the various sales levels. Such studies might indicate maximum net income at levels different from the marginal income studies. In the last analysis, a firm must recover total costs, not just variable costs. Long-term pricing based on marginal income might result in prices set too close to the marginal income point, possibly resulting in needless cutthroat competition within the industry.

Another factor is that the firm may not be motivated exclusively by the maximum income objective. In the long run, or even in the short run, a just price resulting in a reasonable income may prove ultimately to be the best price. A short-run price based on maximized income may operate adversely in the long run by depressing future demand. There is also the possibility that competing costs and prices are such as to permit setting a price above the level indicated by the marginal income analysis if the firm should so decide.

DECIDING TO MAKE OR TO BUY

Management must often decide whether to make or to buy a particular part, product, or plant asset. If the plant facilities have already been acquired, the capacity is available, quality can be assured, and there are no negative factors, the decision depends upon a comparison of marginal costs, which in this case are equal to variable costs, with the outside purchase price of the item. (If other fixed costs have to be added, then marginal cost would be larger than variable cost.) If the variable production cost of the item—the marginal cost—is less than the quoted purchase price, then the item should be manufactured; if the quoted purchase price is less than the variable cost of the item, it should be purchased.

Assume that the Ames Company manufactures a particular part at a unit cost of $6.80 and that this cost consists of the following:

Direct materials	$1.50
Direct labor	2.50
Variable overhead costs	1.20
Total variable costs	$5.20
Fixed overhead costs	1.60
Total unit cost	$6.80

The Ames Company can purchase this part from a reliable manufacturer for $6.05. If the available plant facilities represent sunk costs that cannot be recovered by some other use of the facilities (the fixed overhead unit cost of $1.60), then the firm should continue to make the part. The variable costs of $5.20 are less than the quoted purchase price of $6.05, and the difference might be used to defray part of fixed overhead costs. If, on the other hand, the Ames Company can make an alternative and profitable use of those facilities for other purposes, it should buy the part. Under this assumption, fixed overhead costs must be included in the total cost of the part, because the company is foregoing the opportunity of making an alternate use of the facilities. With fixed overhead costs included, the unit cost to make is greater than the cost to buy—that is, $6.80 compared with $6.05.

This involves a decision whether to continue making a product or to buy it. The parallel problem—to manufacture a part or a product that is currently being purchased—involves essentially the same factors for consideration, together with such other relevant factors as the effect of the change on inventories and on working capital, on net income before and after taxes, on the rate of return on capital employed, and on the rate of return on sales. Finally, intangible factors at the top management level would also enter into the decision to make or to buy.

DEPARTMENT, TERRITORY, OR PRODUCT ABANDONMENT

The decision whether or not to abandon a supposedly unprofitable department, territory, or product involves a careful analysis of the effect of the abandonment on the fixed and variable costs and the marginal income. If a department, territory, or product produces any marginal income, it should not be abandoned unless the newly created capacity—that is, a substituted new department, territory, or product—could be committed to a more profitable use.

The departmental income statement of the Stevens Clothing Company is shown in Figure 20-6. The accountant for the company has been asked by the management to study the probable effect on total costs if the Children's Department is eliminated. Management is aware that although closing the department will entirely eliminate sales, cost of goods sold, and gross margin, certain other costs currently chargeable to the department will continue.

Figure 20-6 Departmental Income Statement

STEVENS CLOTHING COMPANY
Income Statement
For the Year Ended December 31, 19XX

	Men's Department	*Women's Department*	*Children's Department*	*Combined*
Sales (net)	$78,910	$128,000	$34,400	$241,310
Cost of Goods Sold	53,656	90,444	26,630	170,730
Gross Margin on Sales	$25,254	$ 37,556	$ 7,770	$ 70,580
Deduct Operating Expenses				
Advertising Expense	$ 981	$ 1,590	$ 429	$ 3,000
Salesmen's Salaries	9,050	12,030	3,515	24,595
Commissions Expense	750	1,100	240	2,090
Rent Expense	2,160	3,600	1,440	7,200
Depreciation Expense—Store Equipment	400	500	100	1,000
Supervisor's Salary	2,603	5,196	1,301	9,100
Office Salary	1,158	2,313	579	4,050
Insurance Expense	480	600	120	1,200
Bad Debts Expense	75	175	50	300
Miscellaneous General Expenses	400	500	100	1,000
Heat and Light Expense	450	750	300	1,500
Total Operating Expenses	$18,507	$ 28,354	$ 8,174	$ 55,035
Net Operating Income or (Loss)	$ 6,747	$ 9,202	$ (404)	$ 15,545

A careful analysis shows the cost tabulation shown in Figure 20-7.

Figure 20-7
Effect on Costs of Elimination of Children's Department

	Operating Costs Charged to Children's Department	**Effect of Elimination of Children's Department** *Eliminated*	*Not Eliminated*
Variable Costs			
Advertising	$ 429	$ 429	
Salesmen's Salaries	3,515	3,515	
Commissions	240	240	
Insurance	120	120	
Bad Debts	50	50	
General	100	100	
Fixed Costs			
Rent	1,440		$1,440
Depreciation—Store Equipment	100		100
Supervisor's Salary	1,301		1,301
Office Salaries	579		579
Heat and Light	300		300
Totals	$8,174	$4,454	$3,720

As a result of this study, the effect of discontinuing the Children's Department can be reasonably forecast as follows:

Net operating income of all departments (Figure 20-6)		$15,545
Reduction in gross margin on sales (Figure 20-6)	$7,770	
Reduction in variable costs (Figure 20-7)	4,454	
Reduction in net operating income		3,316
Combined net operating income with Children's Department eliminated		$12,229

On the basis of this calculation, the Children's Department should not be eliminated even though it shows a net loss. The department contributed to the earnings of the company by absorbing a part of the fixed expenses. Elimination of the department will reduce net operating income by $3,316.

Children's Department fixed costs (Figure 20-7)	$3,720
Deduct net loss (Figure 20-6)	404
Reduction in net operating income	$3,316

If this department is discontinued, the other departments will have to absorb that part of the fixed cost which is now absorbed by the Children's Department, $3,316, which is the contribution to fixed costs or marginal income. This would result in a comparable decrease in the combined net income.

Another way of verifying this information is to compute the marginal income earned by the Children's Department: revenue of $34,400, less variable costs of $31,084 (cost of goods sold of $26,630 plus variable operating expenses of $4,454), equals $3,316, the advantage to the total firm of continuing the Children's Department.

In this example, the information used is net operating income (or income before income taxes and other expenses and revenue). Since a loss reduces income taxes, the value of the Children's Department to the total firm would really be larger than the $3,316 indicated. To simplify the problem, the effect of income taxes on the decision has been ignored. Of course, income taxes are pertinent to the problem, but their inclusion in this instance will not change the final decision.

There are, in addition, certain intangible factors that would result from the elimination of the Children's Department and which cannot be measured by an analysis of the income statement. This department brings in customers; business may be lost, because some customers will not be able to buy clothing for the entire family in one location. Furthermore, customers who intend to purchase children's clothing only are exposed to the displays of the other two departments, which may result in additional purchases from these other departments. Finally, the reduction in the volume of purchases may have a negative effect on the ability of the company to get quantity discounts.

GLOSSARY

Break-Even Point The volume of sales at which the business will neither earn income nor incur a loss.

Contribution Margin Percentage Marginal income divided by sales.

Fixed Costs Costs that, without a change in present productive capacity, are not affected by changes in volume of output.

Make-Buy Decision The decision whether to make a product or to buy it outside.

Margin of Safety The dollar volume of sales above the break-even point.

Marginal Costs The change in total cost that occurs with a small change in output.

Marginal Income The excess of revenue over related variable costs and variable expenses.

Opportunity Costs The cost of foregoing one thing—investment, operation, material, process, and so on—to get an alternative.

Out-of-Pocket Costs Costs that give rise to cash expenditures.

Percentage of Safety The margin of safety divided by net sales.

Relevant Volume Range The operating-range span over which all costs are likely to be predictable as fixed or variable.

Semifixed Costs Costs that are not affected by changes in volume of output within a given range.

Semivariable costs Costs that include both a fixed and a variable component.

Variable Costs Costs that are affected in total by changes in the volume of output.

QUESTIONS

Q20-1. Define the following terms: (a) sunk costs, (b) variable costs, and (c) out-of-pocket costs.

Q20-2. What is meant by the statement "Different costs for different purposes"? Illustrate, by explaining, how an element of depreciation, as a cost, might be treated differently for different purposes.

Q20-3. (a) Costs relevant to a decision must be present or estimated future costs. Explain. (b) Can past costs ever be relevant to a given decision?

Q20-4. (a) What is meant by the term *break-even point?* (b) How is it computed? (c) What are its practical applications? (d) What are its limitations?

Q20-5. Define the following terms: (a) operating capacity, (b) product mix, (c) margin of safety, and (d) marginal income statement.

Q20-6. Under what circumstances would it be advantageous for a manufacturer in Canada to accept a long-term contract for his product from a foreign buyer?

Q20-7. The sales price of a product should be the amount that will result in the largest marginal income. Comment.

Q20-8. Is maximum income the sole objective in determining the sales price of a new product?

Q20-9. (a) What use does management make of cost data in deciding to make or buy a certain part? (b) Should fixed costs enter into the decision?

Q20-10. (a) Is it possible for one of three departments in a retail store to show a net loss even though its elimination would decrease the total net income of the entire store? (b) What other intangible factors must be considered when deciding whether or not a certain department should be eliminated?

Q20-11. Cost-volume-earnings analysis (break-even analysis) is used to determine and express the interrelationships of different volumes of activity (sales), costs, sales prices, and sales mix to earnings. More specifically, the analysis is concerned with what will be the effect on earnings of changes in sales volume, sales prices, sales mix, and costs.

1. Certain terms are fundamental to cost-volume-earnings analysis. Explain the meaning of each of the following terms:
   - **a.** Fixed costs
   - **b.** Variable costs
   - **c.** Relevant volume range
   - **d.** Break-even point
   - **e.** Margin of safety
   - **f.** Sales mix

2. Several assumptions are implicit in cost-volume-earnings analysis. What are these assumptions?

(*AICPA adapted*)

DEMONSTRATION PROBLEMS

DP20-1. (*Break-even sales; income planning in conjunction with expansion of plant facilities*) The Heald Manufacturing Company is operating at full capacity. It has under consideration a plan for the expansion of its plant facilities. Current and projected income statement data are shown below.

	Under Present Plant Facilities		Under Proposed Plant Facilities	
Sales		$500,000		$750,000
Variable costs	$200,000		$300,000	
Fixed costs	240,000	440,000	360,000	660,000
Net income		$ 60,000		$ 90,000

Required:

1. What is the present break-even point?
2. What is the break-even point under the proposed plan?
3. What will be the amount of sales necessary to realize the current net income of $60,000 under the proposed plan?
4. Prepare an income statement to prove your answer to requirement 3.

DP20-2. (*Acceptance or rejection of an offer*) The Boot Shop is operating at 65% capacity, producing 225,000 pairs of men's fancy boots annually. Actual unit cost and selling price data for the year are as follows:

Direct materials	$10
Direct labor	6
Variable overhead costs	3
Total variable costs	$19
Fixed overhead costs ($1,800,000 ÷ 225,000)	8
Total unit cost	$27
Selling price	$51

The company has been offered a long-term contract to sell 80,000 pairs of men's boots annually to a Mexican importing firm at $23 a pair. This will not affect domestic sales. Fixed overhead costs of $1,800,000, as well as fixed selling and administrative costs of $1,600,000, will not be affected by the new order.

Required: Prepare comparative statements for management indicating whether or not this long-term contract should be accepted.

DP20-3. (*Product pricing*) After conducting a market survey of its new product, the Coolidge Company prepared the following estimates:

Sales Price per Unit	Estimated Sales (units)
$40	58,000
$38	74,000
$35	86,000
$34	93,000
$26	102,000

Variable costs are estimated at $8 a unit.

Required: Determine the price that will result in the maximum marginal income and the maximum net income.

DP20-4. (*Make or buy decision*) The Britten Manufacturing Company can produce a part at the following costs:

Direct materials	$7.20
Direct labor	9.60
Variable overhead costs	4.00
Subtotal	$20.80
Fixed overhead costs	6.40
Total unit costs	$27.20

The company can purchase the part for $22.40.

Required: Should the part be purchased: (a) if fixed overhead unit cost of $6.40 is a sunk cost? (b) if an alternative and profitable use can be made of those plant facilities now devoted to making the part?

DP20-5. *(Department abandonment)* The following condensed marginal income statement is available for the Reynolds Department Store for the current year:

	Department			
	A	*B*	*C*	*Total*
Sales (net)	$560,000	$480,000	$400,000	$1,440,000
Variable costs	288,000	432,000	192,000	912,000
Marginal income	$272,000	$ 48,000	$208,000	$ 528,000
Fixed costs	160,000	128,000	109,000	397,000
Net operating income (or loss)	$112,000	$(80,000)	$ 99,000	$ 131,000

Required:

1. Should Department B be eliminated? Explain.
2. Assume that none of the fixed costs can be eliminated if Department B is abandoned, and that next year's operational results for Departments A and C are the same as this year's. Prepare a condensed marginal income statement for next year, assuming that Department B is eliminated.

PROBLEMS

P20-1. The Musquodobit Corporation estimates fixed costs at $312,000 and variable costs at $2.10 a unit for the current year.

1. How many units must be sold to break even, assuming a unit sales price of $5.20?
2. Prepare an income statement to prove your answer.

P20-2. The Run Company has fixed costs of $704,000 a year. Its variable costs are $10.60 a unit and its sales price is $17.60 a unit. It is considering the purchase of machinery that will increase the fixed costs to $819,000 a year, but will enable the company to reduce variable costs to $7.75 a unit.

1. Compute the break-even point before and after the acquisition of the new machinery, giving it in both sales dollars and units of product.
2. If net income before the acquisition is $140,000, how many units will have to be sold after the machinery is acquired to maintain the net income?

P20-3. The fixed costs in the Eastern Company are now $1,175,000 a year. They are expected to increase to $1,225,000 next year. Variable costs will also go up from $7.05 to $7.70 a unit. Its product sells for $15.50 a unit.

How much sales revenue must be obtained to have a net income (before taxes) of $115,000 next year?

P20-4. A new machine costing $510,000 is under consideration. The product it makes sells for $16 a unit and requires materials costing $3.50, direct labor of $5.10, and other variable costs of $0.50 a unit. Sales of 65,000 units a year are assumed. Applicable annual fixed costs other than depreciation amount to $19,000.

Over what period would this investment be recovered?

P20-5. The Jackson Company manufactures and sells 2,500,000 units of its product annually. The selling price per unit is $32; variable costs are $13 a unit; and fixed costs are $16 a unit.

Should the company accept an additional order to sell 800,000 units abroad (a) at $12 a unit? (b) at $12.65 a unit; (c) at $14.40 a unit; (d) at $16.80 a unit? Explain your answer to each question.

P20-6. During the year the Medicine Hat Manufacturing Corporation produced 9,600 units and sold 8,960 units; costs for the year were:

Variable costs	
Direct materials	$34,560
Direct labor	46,080
Manufacturing overhead	55,200
Selling and administrative expenses	14,400
Fixed costs	
Manufacturing overhead	21,600
Selling and administrative expenses	9,600

The selling price per unit is $35.

1. Calculate the break-even point.
2. Prepare a marginal income statement.
3. Compute the margin of safety, expressed as a dollar amount.

P20-7. Roxby, Inc., can sell 35,000 units of its product at $13 a unit. The variable costs of this product are $5 a unit. However, a reduction in sales price to $10 a unit would increase units sold to 56,000. The greater volume of production would reduce variable costs to $4 a unit; fixed costs are expected to increase by $24,000.

Should Roxby reduce its selling price? Explain and support with computations.

P20-8. The Plymouth Company manufactures Exoze; unit costs are as follows:

Direct materials	$ 9.60
Direct labor	6.40
Variable overhead costs	3.20
Subtotal	$19.20
Fixed overhead costs	4.80
Total	$24.00

The company can purchase this part for $21.50.

Should Exoze be purchased: (a) if fixed overhead unit cost of $4.80 is a sunk cost? (b) if an alternative and profitable use can be made of the plant facilities now devoted to making Exoze?

P20-9. The following operational information is available for Lou's Department Store for 19X1:

	Department			
	1	*2*	*3*	*Total*
Net operating income or (loss)	$20,000	$40,000	$(10,000)	$ 50,000
Marginal income	44,000	75,000	4,000	123,000

1. Should department 3 be eliminated?
2. If department 3 is eliminated and the 19X2 operating results for departments 1 and 2 are the same as in 19X1, how much higher (or lower) will the 19X2 net operating income be?

P20-10. In a recent period Zero Company had the following experience:

	Fixed	*Variable*	
Sales (10,000 units @ $200)			$2,000,000
Costs:			
Direct material	$ -0-	$ 200,000	
Direct labor	-0-	400,000	
Factory overhead	160,000	600,000	
Administrative expenses	180,000	80,000	
Other expenses	200,000	120,000	
Total costs	$540,000	$1,400,000	1,940,000
Net income			$ 60,000

Each item below is independent.

1. Calculate the break-even point for Zero in terms of units and sales dollars. Show your calculations.
2. What sales volume would be required to generate a net income of $96,000? Show your calculations.
3. What is the break-even point if management makes a decision that increases fixed costs by $18,000? Show your calculations.

(*AICPA adapted*)

P20-11. The Fall Company estimates its costs at full capacity as follows:

Fixed	$336,000
Variable	192,000

Fixed costs are constant at all levels of operation; variable costs vary in direct proportion to sales. Sales at full capacity are estimated at $640,000.

Required:

1. Calculate the break-even point.
2. Determine the break-even percentage of operating capacity.
3. Prepare a marginal income statement, assuming full capacity sales.
4. Compute the margin of safety, expressed as a dollar amount.
5. Compute the margin percentage safety.

P20-12. The management of the Murrow Corporation prepared the following budgeted income statement for the year:

	Fixed	Variable	
Estimated sales (112,000 units at $25)			$2,800,000
Estimated costs			
Direct materials		$425,600	
Direct labor		224,000	
Factory overhead	$656,000	512,000	
Selling	128,000	65,600	
Administrative	96,000	32,800	
	$880,000	$1,260,000	2,140,000
Estimated net income			$ 660,000

Required:

1. (a) Compute the break-even point. (b) Prove the break-even point. (c) Compute the break-even point expressed as a percentage of operating capacity. (d) Compute the break-even point in units, assuming a constant product mix. (e) Compute the margin of safety, expressed both as a percentage and as a dollar amount.
2. Prepare a marginal income statement.
3. Prepare a break-even chart.

P20-13. The estimate of the Crown Manufacturing Company is that fixed costs will total $1,150,000 during the year and that variable costs will be $11 a unit.

Required:

1. At a selling price of $24 a unit, at what level of revenue will the company break even?
2. At a selling price of $26 a unit, at what level of revenue will the company break even?
3. In order to earn $800,000 before taxes, how many units will have to be sold at a price of $25?

P20-14. (*Management policy decision problem*) The East Company can sell 70,000 units of its product at $26 a unit. The variable costs of this product are $10 a unit. However, a reduction in sales price to $22 a unit would increase units sold to 80,000. The greater volume of production would reduce variable costs to $8 a unit; fixed costs are expected to increase by $96,000.

Required: Should the East Company reduce its selling price? Explain, showing supporting computations.

P20-15. The condensed income statement for Cyril, Inc., is given below.

CYRIL, INC.
Condensed Income Statement
For the Year Ended December 31, 19XX

Net Sales		$800,000
Deduct Costs and Expenses		
Variable	$400,000	
Fixed	240,000	640,000
Net Income		$160,000

The directors of Cyril are considering a plant expansion program from the present 100% sales capacity of $800,000 to $1,200,000. The expansion would increase annual fixed costs by $120,000. Variable costs would remain directly proportional to sales, and the expansion would not change the current relationship of variable costs to sales.

Required:

1. What is the current break-even point?
2. What will the break-even point be under the proposed plan?
3. What dollar amount of sales is required under the proposed plan to equal the current net income of $160,000?
4. Prepare an income statement to prove your answer to requirement 3.

P20-16. (*Management policy decision problem*) The Beane Corporation is considering whether to purchase some special machines. Management does not wish to buy the machines unless their cost can be recovered in three years. The following information is available:

1. Cost of the machines is $575,000.
2. Sales revenue generated by new machines is estimated to be $640,000.
3. Variable cost is 65% of sales.
4. Annual fixed costs other than depreciation total $20,000.

Required:

1. On the basis of the criterion of the three-year recovery period, should the special machines be purchased? Support your answer with a computation of the period required for the investment of $575,000 to be recovered.
2. Discuss briefly any other factors that should be considered by management in deciding whether to acquire the special machines.

P20-17. (*Management policy decision problem*) The Lane Company is currently operating at its full capacity of 200,000 units annually. Costs are as follows:

Direct materials	$640,000
Direct labor	320,000
Variable overhead	160,000
Fixed overhead	96,000
Variable selling and administrative expenses	64,000
Fixed selling and administrative expenses	48,000

The product is sold under Lane Company brand for $10. Humphrey Distributors, Inc., offers to purchase 80,000 units annually for the next five years at $6.60 a unit. This offer, if accepted, will not affect the current selling price, because Humphrey Distributors will sell under its own brand name. Acceptance of the offer will have the following results:

1. Labor costs on the additional 80,000 units will be 1½ times the regular rate.
2. Variable selling and administrative expenses will increase by 8 cents a unit on the additional units only.
3. The required additional materials can be purchased at a 5% volume discount.
4. All other cost factors will remain the same.

Required: Should Lane Company accept the offer? Show all your computations in support of your conclusion.

P20-18. The Flora Company has the facilities to produce two additional products, Horex and Borex, which require approximately the same production processes. The following data were made available to management to aid in establishing sales prices and product mix:

Horex		Borex	
Estimated Sales Units	*Sales Price per Unit*	*Estimated Sales Units*	*Sales Price per Unit*
9,600	$104	7,200	$122
11,600	98	12,000	112
16,400	75	16,800	104
Variable costs per unit are $40.		Variable costs per unit are $56.	

Required: What product mix of Horex and Borex will result in the largest marginal income?

P20-19. (*Management policy decision problem*) The Rail Company is presently purchasing a package of five parts used in the manufacture of its finished product. Comparative costs to manufacture the parts and to buy them outside are as shown:

Part No.	*Estimated Materials Labor, and Variable Overhead to Make*	*Cost to Buy*
1	$28.80	$32.00
2	13.60	12.00
3	10.40	8.80
4	8.00	11.20
5	14.40	16.00
Totals	$75.20	$80.00

The Rail Company has the capacity to produce these parts, and at the present time it has no alternative profitable use for the facilities. Making the parts will not increase fixed costs of $100,000.

Required:

1. What is the proper decision? The finished product sells for $140.
2. Assume that the Rail Company is presently purchasing 32,000 units of each part annually, that it can use the available plant facilities to make and sell annually 16,000 units of a new product without increasing fixed costs, and that this will result in an estimated marginal income of $10.40 a unit. What is the proper decision under these circumstances?

P20-20. (*Management policy decision problem*) The management of the Welch Company is considering the elimination of Department B. The departmentalized income statement follows:

WELCH COMPANY
Income Statement
For the Year Ended December 31, 19XX

	Dept. A	*Dept. B*	*Combined*
Sales (net)	$214,400	$72,000	$286,400
Cost of Goods Sold	108,800	48,000	156,800
Gross Margin on Sales	$105,600	$24,000	$129,600
Operating Expenses			
Advertising Expense	$ 6,720	$ 1,920	$ 8,640
Salesmen's Salaries Expense	16,000	9,600	25,600
Office Salaries Expense	5,600	2,720	8,320
Insurance Expense	1,440	960	2,400
Bad Debts Expense	1,600	800	2,400
Miscellaneous General Expense	2,880	1,440	4,320
Rent Expense	17,600	8,000	25,600
Depreciation Expense—Store Equipment	3,200	1,920	5,120
Total Operating Expenses	$ 55,040	$27,360	$ 82,400
Net Operating Income (Loss)	$ 50,560	$ (3,360)	$ 47,200

The following additional data have been submitted to management on the proposed elimination of Department B:

1. There will be a 15% decline in the sales of Department A. The cost of goods sold varies directly with the sales volume.
2. The operating expenses of Department A will decrease as follows:
   a. Insurance Expense by 4%
   b. Bad Debts Expense by 9%
   c. Miscellaneous General Expense by 12%
3. The elimination of Department B will have the following effect on the operating expenses of Department B:
   a. Advertising expense, salesmen's salaries, insurance expense, and bad debts expense will be eliminated.
   b. Of the apportioned miscellaneous general expense, 80% will not be incurred.
   c. Office salaries will be reduced by $1,500 through the dismissal of some part-time employees.
   d. There will be no reduction in rent expense or in depreciation expense—store equipment.

Required:

1. Prepare a statement showing the probable effect on operating costs if Department B is eliminated.
2. Prepare a statement showing the effect on net income if Department B is eliminated.

P20-21. (*Management policy decision problem*) The Tall Company has three sales territories, X, Y, and Z. Management is considering the elimination of Territory

X. The following condensed information has been prepared to aid in making this decision:

TALL COMPANY
Marginal Income Statement
For the Year Ended December 31, 19XX

	Territory			
	X	*Y*	*Z*	*Total*
Sales (net)	$350,000	$400,000	$600,000	$1,350,000
Variable Costs	210,000	160,000	240,000	610,000
Marginal Income	$140,000	$240,000	$360,000	$ 740,000
Fixed Costs	200,000	100,000	150,000	450,000
Net Operating Income (Loss)	$ (60,000)	$140,000	$210,000	$ 290,000

None of the fixed costs of Territory X can be eliminated.

Required: Prepare a report to aid management in deciding whether to discontinue Territory X.

P20-22. (*Management policy decision problem*) The Parham Oil Company operates a chain of service stations throughout the local area. Each station sells the usual service station products: gasoline, oil, tires, batteries, automobile accessories. All the products are purchased in bulk by the home office and delivered on a scheduled basis to each station. If a station manager foresees that the quantities he will need will vary by more than 5% from the scheduled quantities, he calls the home office at least twenty-four hours in advance of the anticipated delivery time and changes the standing order.

Being an astute businessman, Otis Lester, the president and major shareholder of the company, has the accountant prepare a separate income statement for each station. Also, he often asks for income statements by product line within each station. His main concern at this time, however, is the poor overall operating results of the station located in Johnson City. This station was once considered profitable, but since a nearby military base was closed, business has declined. The most recent income statement is typical of each of the past three years.

Sales		$177,000
Cost of Goods Sold		138,000
Gross Margin on Sales		$ 39,000
Operating Expenses (listed alphabetically)		
Advertising (Company-oriented and allocated equally to each station)	$ 1,520	
Attendants' Salaries (the number of attendants is adequate for the current volume)	16,800	
Depreciation—Building and Equipment	8,000	

Home Office Expenses (allocated to each station based on station sales)	7,200	
Insurance (fire and public liability)	1,120	
Interest on average book Investment (a book charge only; all long-term funds are provided by the stockholders)	7,680	
Local Property Taxes and Privilege Licenses	6,100	
Manager's Bonus	640	
Manager's Salary	7,700	
Payroll Taxes (attendants' salaries and manager's salary and bonus)	1,675	
Repairs and Maintenance (on building and equipment)	440	
Station Supplies	5,600	
Utilities (electricity, heat, telephone, and water)	500	
Total Operating Expenses		64,975
Net Loss		$ (25,975)

Required:

1. As a management consultant with the local chartered accountants firm, what would you recomend to Lester as the course of action regarding the station in Johnson City? Some possibilities are (a) to continue to operate as is, (b) to discontinue operation, (c) to initiate local advertising, and (d) to sell the station. If your recommendation is to sell the station, what is the minimum amount that Lester should accept?
2. Give the reason(s) for your recommendation.
3. What overall business objective will your recommendation help to achieve? Justify this objective.
4. Support your recommendation with appropriate computations.
5. Identify some nonaccounting factors that could influence a decision of this type.
6. Which accounting techniques, if any, do you think should be changed? How should they be changed? Why should they be changed?
7. If the division into variable and fixed costs remains as it is and current accounting procedures are continued, by how much must sales increase in order for this station to break even?
8. How much must sales be in order for this station to report a net income of $10,000?

P20-23. (*Management policy decision problem*) The Vernom Corporation, which produces and sells to wholesalers a highly successful line of summer lotions and insect repellents, has decided to diversify in order to stabilize sales throughout the year. A natural area for the company to consider is the production of winter lotions and creams to prevent dry and chapped skin.

After considerable research, a winter products line has been developed. However, because of the conservative nature of the company management, Vernom's president has decided to introduce only one of the new products for this coming winter. If the product is a success, further expansion in future years will be initiated.

The product selected (called Chap-off) is a lip balm that will be sold in a lipstick-type tube. The product will be sold to wholesalers in boxes of 24 tubes for $8 a box. Because of available capacity, no additional fixed charges will be incurred to produce the product. However, a $100,000 fixed charge will be absorbed by the product to allocate a fair share of the company's present fixed costs to the new product.

Using the estimated sales and production of 100,000 boxes of Chap-off as the standard volume, the accounting department has developed the following costs:

Direct Labor	$2.00/box
Direct Materials	3.00/box
Total Overhead	1.50/box
Total	$6.50/box

Vernom has approached a cosmetics manufacturer to discuss the possibility of purchasing the tubes for Chap-off. The purchase price of the empty tubes from the cosmetics manufacturer would be $.90 cents per 24 tubes. If the Vernom Corporation accepts the purchase proposal, it is estimated that direct labor and variable overhead costs would be reduced by 10% and direct material costs would be reduced by 20%.

Required:

1. Should the Vernom Corporation make or buy the tubes? Show calculations to support your answer.
2. What would be the minimum purchase price acceptable to the Vernom Corporation for the tubes? Support your answer with an appropriate explanation.
3. Instead of sales of 100,000 boxes, revised estimates show sales volume at 125,000 boxes. At this new volume, additional equipment, at an annual rental of $10,000, must be acquired to manufacture the tubes. However, this incremental cost would be the only additional fixed cost required, even if sales increased to 300,000 boxes. (The 300,000 level is the goal for the third year of production.) Under these circumstances, should the Vernom Corporation make or buy the tubes? Show calculations to support your answer.
4. The company has the option of making and buying at the same time. What would be your answer to requirement 3 if this alternative was considered? Show calculations to support your answer.
5. What nonquantifiable factors should the Vernom Corporation consider in determining whether they should make or buy the lipstick tubes?

(*IMA adapted*)

P20-24. (*Management policy decision problem*) Victor Calderone started a pizza restaurant in 19X1. He rented a building for $400 a month. Two women were hired to work full time at the restaurant and six college boys were hired to work 30 hours a week delivering pizza. An outside accountant was hired (at $300 a month) for tax and bookkeeping purposes. The necessary restaurant equipment and delivery cars were purchased with cash. Calderone has noticed that expenses for utilities and supplies have been rather constant.

Calderone increased his business between 19X1 and 19X5. Profits have more than doubled since 19X1. Calderone does not understand why his profits have increased faster than his volume.

The following projected income statement for 19X5 has been prepared by the accountant:

CALDERONE COMPANY
Projected Income Statement
For the Year Ended December 31, 19X5

Sales		$95,000
Cost of Food Sold	$28,500	
Wages & Fringe Benefits of Restaurant Help	8,150	
Wages & Fringe Benefits of Delivery Boys	17,300	
Rent	4,800	
Accounting Services	3,600	
Depreciation of Delivery Equipment	5,000	
Depreciation of Restaurant Equipment	3,000	
Utilities	2,325	
Supplies (Soap, Floor Wax, etc.)	1,200	73,875
Net Income Before Taxes		$21,125
Income Taxes		6,338
Net Income		$14,787

Note: The average pizza sells for $2.50. Assume that Calderone pays 30% of his income in income taxes.

Required:

1. What is the break-even point in number of pizzas that must be sold?
2. What is the cash flow break-even point in number of pizzas that must be sold?
3. If Calderone withdraws $4,800 for personal use, how much cash will be left from the 19X5 income producing activities?
4. Calderone would like an after-tax net income of $20,000. What volume must be reached in number of pizzas sold in order to obtain the desired income?
5. Briefly explain to Calderone why his profits have increased at a faster rate than his sales.
6. Briefly explain to Calderone why his cash flow for 19X5 will exceed his profits.

(*IMA adapted*)

21

Capital Budgeting Decisions

Capital budgeting refers to the allocation and commitment of funds to long-term capital investment projects. The amount of such investments or expenditures is usually large, and they are made in expectation of benefits to be received over a number of years. Capital budgeting concerns itself with the development, selection, and evaluation of proposals for plant expansion and modernization, equipment replacement, product development, and so on. The nature of these investments and their effect on the long-range welfare of a company make it imperative that they be analyzed and evaluated with the utmost care.

BUDGETING CAPITAL EXPENDITURES

Types of Capital Expenditure

The types of capital expenditure can perhaps best be illustrated by questions involving capital investment decisions, such as the following:

1. *Expansion.* Shall we buy additional equipment to supply the actual or anticipated increase in demand for our product? Shall we expand our facilities to produce new products? Shall we acquire the necessary facilities to make parts we are now buying from outside sources?
2. *Replacement.* Shall we replace present equipment with new and more efficient equipment? Shall we automate our production lines? Shall we buy machine A or machine B? Shall we lease the new equipment or shall we buy it?
3. *Other.* Some investments are made on noneconomic grounds. Expenditures for recreational facilities for use by employees, for example, are not made to reduce costs or increase revenue, but rather to improve employer-employee relations. An investment to eliminate sound nuisances or smoke hazards may be made in compliance with local ordinances; but even if it is not mandatory, a company may choose to make such an investment in acknowledgment of corporate social responsibility.

Rate of Return

Business people make investments to get a satisfactory return. What constitutes a satisfactory rate of return depends on a number of factors, including available funds, available investment opportunities, cost of obtaining funds, and degree of uncertainty and risk. In the long run, the rate of return must be adequate to attract new capital.

The choice of an appropriate rate of return is central to the capital budgeting decision, since it has a direct influence on the decision. The choice may be based on the *investment opportunity* concept, which is a subjective evaluation of the available investment opportunities and their respective earnings rates. The selected rate of return is the rate that the funds could earn if they were invested in the best available alternative project. Since funds used on project A, for example, are not available for use on project B, the amount that could have been earned on project B is sacrificed. The amount or rate so sacrificed constitutes an opportunity cost, or the minimum rate that must be earned on project A, the project chosen.

The choice of a cutoff rate may be based on a different concept, the *cost of capital.* The premise for the use of the cost of capital as the minimum rate of return is that the project should earn at least as much as the cost of the funds invested in the project, whether using available capital or new capital. A rate of return (or cost) on new capital investment that is less than the rate of return on old capital investment would have a dilutive effect and decrease the return to owner's equity. This, in turn, may decrease the market value of the firm's stock.

The minimum rate of return or the cost of capital is difficult to measure and varies with each company. Stated in its simplest terms, it represents a weighted average of the cost to the company of common stock equity capital as measured by the ratio of the market value of the stock to the dividend rate, and the cost of long-term debt as measured by the rate of interest on the debt. But other variables such as reinvested earnings, future dividend rates, and changes in the market value of the shares complicate the calculations. Furthermore, some argue that the cost of capital is independent of the firm's capital structure and depends only upon the riskiness represented by the investment and the stream of earnings that it generates.

Budgeting Decisions

The capital budgeting decision involves making a choice among alternatives. Available proposals usually exceed available funds, so that a system must be established for ranking the proposals and selecting the most desirable ones. Since the capital budgeting decision is an investment decision, it may be subjected to the same criterion that any prudent investor uses—that is, the gain or the rate of return to be realized on the investment. This, in turn, furnishes the rationale for the selection, once the desired minimum rate of return has been fixed.

Present Value Concept

The present value concept refers to the conversion of cash inflows and outflows over a period to a common point in time for purposes of comparing capital expenditures. The concepts of compound amounts and present values are used in this conversion process: Since dollar amounts can be moved forward in time by compounding or backward in time by discounting, direct comparisons can be made of cash flows occurring in different periods. If, for example, an investment in a piece of equipment will reduce operating costs by $100 a year for four years, and the company has opportunities to invest its funds in other projects yielding a return of 10 percent a year, it can afford to pay $316.99 for this piece of equipment and still realize a 10 percent rate of return on the investment. The factor comes from the 10 percent column for Period 4 (Appendix Table 4, Compound Interest Tables). The computation is as follows:

$$\$100 \times 3.169865 = \$317 \text{ (rounded)}$$

The company could pay $317 for the equipment even if it had to borrow the $317 at 10 percent interest. The fact that the company could repay the loan and interest with the funds derived from the annual $100 costs savings and still be as well off as it would be before the equipment was purchased is demonstrated by the following calculation:

Amount borrowed	$317.00
Interest for 1st year	31.70
Total	$348.70
First payment	100.00
Amount due at beginning of 2d period	$248.70
Interest for 2d year	24.87
Total	$273.57
Second payment	100.00
Amount due at beginning of 3d period	$173.57
Interest for 3d year	17.36
Total	$190.93
Third payment	100.00
Amount due at beginning of 4th period	$ 90.93
Interest 4th year	9.09
Total	$100.02
Fourth payment	100.02

The discrepancy of 2 cents is due to rounding. Payments are assumed to have been made at the end of each year. The assumed saving of $100 each year in operating costs enables the company to recover the loan or the investment of $317 plus annual interest of 10 percent on the unrecovered balance. Note that any residual salvage value of the equipment has been ignored.

Capital expenditures are subject to the same test as any other kind of investment, the earning of a satisfactory profit. Investments in government securities are, of course, qualitatively different from investments in machinery, because the element of certainty of return on the investment is greater. But the essential objectives of the two types of investment are the same, a satisfactory rate of return. Since sums moved forward or backward in time can be converted to a comparable basis by the application of present value factors, such application to the solution of capital budgeting problems follows logically. The formulas that apply to the analysis of financial investments apply equally to the analysis of capital expenditures.

COMPARING CAPITAL EXPENDITURES

Determining the Relevant Cash Flows. A capital investment generates a flow of cash into and out of the business over a period. A comparison of several investment projects from which the best choice is to be made involves a comparison of the expected cash flows under the several alternatives. The concern is with future, not past, costs and with relevant costs—that is, the costs that will be different. Clearly, a cost or a revenue amount that will be the same under all the alternatives from which a choice is to be made is not relevant, since it will not change the decision. The appropriateness for the emphasis on cash flow to the exclusion of valuations based on generally accepted accounting principles must be considered within the context of the capital budgeting problem. The measurement of revenue and expense—the measurement of net income—*is not* relevant to the timing of the related cash flows. The measurement of a rate of return on a specific investment proposal *is* affected by the timing of the cash flows due to the time value of money. There is no conflict between conventional income measurements and rate of return measurements; the goals and end-uses of each are different.

Present Value Method

Under the present value method, the cash flows are discounted to the present, using the firm's cost of capital as the discounting rate. If the present value of the inflows exceeds the present value of the outflows, the investment is desirable. If the present value of the outflows exceeds the present value of the inflows, the investment is undesirable. The measurement of a proposed capital expenditure by the present value method requires a determination of the following:

1. Net cash investment
2. Net cash inflows
3. Estimated useful life of the investment
4. Excess present value

For example, assume that the West Company is planning to buy a new press for $25,000, with an estimated useful life of 10 years. Freight and installation costs will be $1,500. The press being replaced originally cost $20,000, has a carrying value of $8,000 and a remaining life of 10 years, and can be sold for $4,000. The new press is not expected to change revenue but is expected to reduce labor costs, including fringe benefits, by $5,500, and to increase power costs by $1,000. Maintenance, taxes, and insurance will be unchanged. The advisability of the replacement is being questioned. The company's cost of capital is 14 percent.

Step 1: Net cash investment. The initial step in the measurement of the rate of return is to determine the net amount of the initial cash investment required by the specific capital expenditure proposed. This usually consists of the purchase price of the asset, transportation, installation, and any other costs incurred to prepare the asset for operation. If the project involves the replacement of an old asset, the proceeds from the sale of the old asset are deducted in arriving at the amount of the net investment.

The net cash investment for the West Company is computed as follows:

Purchase price of new press	$25,000
Freight and installation	1,500
Total	$26,500
Deduct proceeds from sale of old press	4,000
Net investment	$22,500

The carrying value of the old press is irrelevant, because it represents a past, or sunk, cost, not a future cost. Whatever the carrying value, the net investment is $22,500. What is relevant is the selling price of the old machine, because it represents a reduction of the cash investment.

Step 2: Net cash inflows. The West Company proposal falls into the cost reduction category. The relevant cash outflows are the costs that will be different—the *differential costs*—if the proposal is adopted. The expected change in annual operating cash flows will be as follows:

Cost decreases—labor	$5,500
Deduct cost increases—power	1,000
Net annual saving	$4,500

This step involves a careful analysis of all operating costs to determine which costs will be increased and which decreased. Only those cost changes which will change cash flows are relevant. Changes in costs due, for example, to changes in cost allocations without corresponding changes in cash flow are irrelevant for this purpose, even though they are essential to the accounting process.

Step 3: Estimated useful life. The rate of return on an investment project is directly affected by the estimated useful life of the project. The serviceable life of an asset cannot be definitely known at the time of its acquisition, and it may be difficult to estimate, but an approximation or judgment must be made. The estimate is based not on physical life but on economic life. The question to be answered is: How long will the project contribute earnings to the firm? A machine with an estimated physical life of 10 years may have to be replaced after only one year due to changes in the nature of the business—method of manufacture; location, type, or design of product; and so on. Advances in technology may necessitate replacement of an existing machine even if it is in perfect condition. The relevant factor is earning power, not necessarily physical life, the life used for financial reporting, or the life used for Federal income tax reporting.

Step 4: Excess present value. The relative desirability of an investment is indicated by the difference, at a common point of time, between the cost of the investment and the expected earnings from that investment discounted at the desired minimum rate. The greater the excess of the present value of the earnings over the net cash investment, the more desirable the investment. Using the West Company figures, the excess present value is calculated as follows:

Present value of earnings at 14% rate for 10 years:	
$4,500 × 5.216115	$23,472.52
Net cash investment	22,500.00
Excess present value	$ 972.52

Since the present value of the earnings exceeds the investment, the project is desirable. If, however, the desired minimum is increased to 16 percent, the present value of the earnings is less than the investment; at 16 percent, therefore, the investment is undesirable. The computation is as follows:

Net cash investment	$22,500.00
Present value of earnings at 16% rate for 10 years:	
$4,500 × 4.833227	21,749.52
Excess present value	$ 750.48

Excess Present Value Index. The excess present value index is the ratio of the present value of the earnings to the required investment. This ratio, or *profitability index,* is useful as a ranking device for investments varying in size and economic life. An index of 1.00 or more indicates that the earnings equal or exceed the desired minimum rate. The higher the index, the more desirable the project. The indexes for the West Company at 14 percent and 16 percent are shown below.

$$\frac{\text{Present value of earnings at 14\%}}{\text{Investment}} = \frac{\$23{,}472.52}{\$22{,}500.00} = 1.04$$

$$\frac{\text{Present value of earnings at 16\%}}{\text{Investment}} = \frac{\$21{,}749.52}{\$22{,}500.00} = 0.967$$

The index at 16 percent, being less than 1.00, indicates that the earnings are not high enough to earn a 16 percent return on the $22,500 investment.

Rate of Return Method

The net cash investment of the West Company ($22,500), the annual net cash earnings ($4,500), and the economic life (10 years) having been determined, these relationships can now be combined to compute a rate of return on the investment and, concurrently, the return of the investment. In the language of compound interest, the rate of return will be that rate—the *internal rate of return* or the *time-adjusted rate of return*—at which the present values of the cash inflows and outflows offset each other. This means that if the company were to borrow funds to finance the investment at that internal rate of return, it would recover its investment as well as the interest on the borrowed funds. The computation on page 601 shows, for example, that an investment of $317 now is exactly equal to a future inflow of $100 at the end of each year for four years at 10 percent interest; that is, the present value of the inflows exactly offsets the present outflow. This means that the rate of return on the $317 investment is exactly 10 percent.

The rate of return computation for the West Company involves finding a discount rate that, applied to the net cash inflows of $4,500 over the 10-year period, equals $22,500, the net cash investment. This can be found by the process of trial and error. When positive and negative present values are found, the exact rate can be drived by interpolation. However, when the cash flows are *uniform*, as in the West Company problem, the time-consuming trial-and-error method can be avoided. The predicted annual earnings of $4,500 must, in each of the 10 years, contribute to the recovery of a portion of the net cash investment of $22,500 and a return on the yet unrecovered portion of the investment. What is needed is a present value of an annuity of 1 factor, that, when applied to the annual cash inflows of $4,500, equals $22,500. This factor must be the net cash investment divided by the net cash inflow, or $22,500 ÷ $4,500 = 5.000000.

The quotient 5 is the ratio of the investment to the annual earnings. The factors in Appendix Table 4 are likewise ratios of investments to earnings: of an investment of $1 to various rates and lives of earnings. Since the problem is to find a discount factor that, when applied to the earnings, exactly equals the investment, that factor must be the investment (numerator) divided by the earnings (denominator).

Appendix Table 4 lists combinations of three elements: (1) economic life, (2) interest rate, and (3) discount factor. Given any two of these elements, the third element can be read off directly. Given the factor 5.000000 and the economic life, 10 years, the third element, the rate, can be read directly from the table.

The rate of return can now be found by referring to Appendix Table 4, in the row corresponding to the economic life, and for the factor closest to 5, the quotient of the investment divided by the earnings. The column heading under which this figure is found is the approximate rate. The factors in the 14 percent and 16 percent columns are 5.216115 and 4.833227. The rate may therefore be estimated at roughly 15 percent.

The trial-and-error method yields the same result. Assuming that the first rate tried was 14 percent and the next was 16 percent, the results would be as shown below.

Net cash investment	$22,500.00
Present value of earnings at 14% rate for 10 years:	
$4,500 × 5.216115	23,472.52

Difference	$ 972.52
Present value of earnings at 16% rate for 10 years:	$22,500.00
$4,500 × 4.833227	21,749.52
Difference	$ (750.48)

The positive difference at 14 percent indicates a rate above 14 percent; the negative difference at 16 percent indicates a rate below 16 percent; the true rate is therefore between 14 percent and 16 percent. If an investment of $22,500 is made today with an estimated life of 10 years, and if the required minimum rate of return is 15 percent, then the project will have to produce annual cash earnings of $4,500 to repay the investment.

Depreciation, Income Taxes, and Capital Budgeting

For financial and income tax reporting, the costs of plant and equipment assets are amortized over the useful lives of the assets; a portion of the cost of the assets is deducted from revenue in measuring net income. Such revenue deductions, although essential to the income measurement process, are irrelevant to the capital budgeting decision, because they do not represent actual cash outflows. The inclusion of the entire net cash investment as a cash outflow makes it unnecessary to allocate portions of the cost over the asset's useful life as revenue deductions. Only the actual acquisition of the asset, not its allocation to income, involves cash. But the periodic depreciation deduction does reduce net income and therefore the amount of the income tax, which does represent a cash outflow. Furthermore, the use of accelerated depreciation methods has a direct effect on the pattern of the income tax cash outflows and thereby influences the rate of return.

Assuming that the West Company is subject to an income tax rate of 50 percent, the loss on the sale of the old press will result in a $2,000 tax benefit as shown below.

Carrying value	$8,000
Selling price	4,000
Deductible loss	$4,000
Tax rate	0.50
Tax deduction	$2,000

Although the book loss is $4,000, the net after-tax effect of the sale is a loss of only $2,000, since, if the sale did not take place, the West Company's cash outflow for income taxes would be $2,000 greater. In this case, the net cash investment would be as shown here.

Cost of new press		$26,500
Proceeds from sale of old press	$4,000	
Tax deduction from loss on sale of old press	2,000	6,000
Net cash investment		$20,500

If the old press were sold at a gain, the tax on the gain would be deducted from the proceeds in computing the net cash investment.

The depreciation deduction and income taxes affect not only the net investment but also the net cash inflow. The change in the annual depreciation deduction changes taxable net income, which, in turn, changes the net cash earnings after taxes. The net cash earnings after taxes for the West Company, assuming the use of the straight-line depreciation method, is as follows:

Annual cash savings before taxes			$4,500
Deduct income taxes on applicable earnings:			
Annual cash savings before taxes		$4,500	
Increase in annual depreciation deduction			
on new press: 10% of $26,500	$2,650		
on old press: 10% of $20,000	2,000	650	
Increase in taxable net income		$3,850	
Income taxes: 50% × $3,850			1,925
Net cash earnings after taxes			$2,575

Irregular Cash Flow Patterns

The capital budgeting proposals discussed thus far involved a single present net cash investment and uniform savings over the entire life span. Some projects, however, produce irregular cash flow patterns. The present value of a stream of earnings is influenced directly by both the amount and the timing of the inflow. The rate of discount increases with time, so that cash inflows of early years have a higher present value than corresponding inflows of later years. The analysis must, therefore, identify both the amount and the time pattern by years. To illustrate, assume that a company makes an immediate investment of $100,000 in a plant for the manufacture of a new product. Earnings rise in the second year, as the market for the product is developed, then fall in the third year under the impact of competition. An additional investment is made in the third year for an intensive advertising campaign. Because of the uneven cash flow, each amount must be multiplied by the appropriate present value of 1 factor, as shown (assumed cost of capital is 20 percent).

Year	*Cash Inflow (Outflow)*	*Present Value of $1 Discounted at 20% (Appendix Table 2)*	*Present Value*
1	$40,000	0.833333	$ 33,333
2	50,000	0.694444	34,722
3	25,000	0.578704	14,468
	(10,000)	0.578704	(5,787)
4	45,000	0.482253	21,701
5	30,000	0.401878	12,056
Total			$110,493

The excess present value and index are computed as follows:

Present value of cash flows	$110,493
Present value of original investment	100,000
Excess present value	$ 10,493
Excess present value index: $110,493 ÷ 100,000	1.10493

The approximate rate of return may be found by trial and error. The cash flows are discounted, using different trial rates, until a rate is found at which the net present value is zero. At this rate, the net inflows equal the amount of the investment. The trial-and-error computation, using trial rates of 20 and 24 percent, follows:

		Present Value Factors		*Present Values of Cash Flows*	
Year	*Cash Inflow (Outflow)*	20%	24%	20%	24%
1	$40,000	.833333	.80645	$ 33,333	$ 32,258
2	50,000	.694444	.65036	34,722	32,518
3	25,000	.578704	.52449	14,468	13,112
	(10,000)	.578704	.52449	(5,787)	(5,245)
4	45,000	.482253	.42297	21,701	19,034
5	30,000	.401878	.34111	12,056	10,233
				$110,493	$101,910

The second trial rate of 24 percent shows present value inflows of $101,910, which, when compared with the net investment of $100,000, gives a rate of return larger than 24 percent; the actual rate would be approximately 25 percent.

Annual Cost of an Investment

Businessmen customarily think in terms of annual costs. Statements of financial position and earnings reports are in annual terms. Capital budgeting problems may also be expressed in terms of annual costs. This is useful not only because it is a customary way of thinking but also because it provides a common basis for the comparison of two projects with different economic lives. The decision is based on whether the annual earnings expected from the investment exceed the annual cost of the investment over the estimated life.

The annual cost of an investment may be found by dividing the net investment by the present value factor corresponding to the desired rate of return and estimated life. Returning to the West Company proposal, if the company used a cutoff rate of 16 percent, the annual cost, given the net investment of $22,500 and a useful life of 10 years, is:

$$\frac{\text{Investment}}{\text{Present value factor for } i = 16\%,\ n = 10} = \frac{\$22{,}500}{4.833227} = \$4{,}655 \text{ (rounded)}$$

Since the estimated savings are $4,500, the project will not earn the 16 percent rate. If, however, the desired minimum is 14 percent, the annual cost becomes

$$\frac{\text{Investment}}{\text{Present value factor for } i = 14\%,\ n = 10} = \frac{\$22{,}500}{5.216115} = \$4{,}314 \text{ (rounded)}$$

The annual cost at 14 percent is $4,314, which is less than the estimated annual earnings of $4,500. The project therefore meets the 14 percent minimum rate test.

Annual cost computations are useful for a variety of capital expenditure problems. To illustrate, assume that a company is considering the advisability of investing in data-processing equipment that will reduce annual clerical costs from $30,000 to $18,000. The equipment costs $60,000 and has an estimated useful life of 10 years. Assuming that the desired rate of return is 10 percent, the annual cost comparison is as shown below.

Present costs		$30,000
Proposed costs:		
Clerical	$18,000	
Equipment	9,765	27,765
Annual saving		$ 2,235

The computation of the annual cost of the equipment is as follows:

$$\frac{\text{Investment}}{\text{Present value factor for } i = 10\%,\ n = 10} = \frac{\$60{,}000}{6.144567} = \$9{,}765 \text{ (rounded)}$$

The annual saving indicates (1) that the rate of return is greater than 10 percent, (2) that the 10 percent rate of return can be realized even if proposed costs increase by $2,235 or (3) that the company could pay up to $73,735 = [($30,000 − $18,000) × 6.144567] for the equipment and still realize a 10 percent rate of return, as shown.

Present costs		$30,000
Proposed costs:		
Clerical	$18,000	
Equipment	12,000	30,000
Annual saving		$ –0–

In this situation, the computation of the annual cost of the equipment is as follows:

$$\frac{\text{Investment}}{\text{Present value factor for } i = 10\%, n = 10} = \frac{\$73{,}735}{6.144567} = \$12{,}000$$

Payback

Payback, or *payout,* is a method of measuring the desirability of a project in terms of a single criterion: How soon will the cash invested in the project be returned? It is a measure of the time required for the accumulated cash earnings from a project to equal the cash investment, or

$$\frac{\text{Investment}}{\text{Annual net cash flow}} = \text{Payback}$$

In theory, the shorter the payback time, the less the risk. The popularity of payback is due to its simplicity and to its effectiveness as an initial screening measure, especially for high-risk investments in which the useful life is difficult to project. It is also useful in evaluating projects of such obvious merit that refined analysis is not needed, and projects showing no financial merit. Its limitations are that it ignores (1) the useful life, (2) the amount and pattern of cash flows beyond the payback point, (3) disposal values, (4) the time value of money, and (5) the profitability of the investment. To illustrate, assume the following figures:

Project	*Net Investment*	*Annual Net Cash Savings*
A	$10,000	$ 5,000
B	20,000	10,000

The payback on both projects is two years; on this basis they are equally desirable. However, if it is further assumed that Project A has a two-year life and Project B a five-year life, it becomes obvious that these proposals are not equally desirable.

LIMITATIONS

Although the rate-of-return method and the present value method will often point to the same choice, in some situations the two methods yield conflicting results. Given two or more investments with only one to be undertaken, the rate-of-return method ignores the sizes of the investments. The rate of return on the incremental cash flows generated by the incremental investment may be below the acceptable rate. In such cases, the present value method yields the more accurate rate and should be used.

The primary objective is to present an approach to the quantification of capital expenditures. The concept of present values has theoretical validity and practicability in the capital budgeting process. It provides the basis for a systematic analysis of available alternative investment proposals. But sophistication and refinement of procedure cannot insure a best choice if the data are wrong. The data used are projections of expectations—often long range—involving revenue, costs, equipment life, human and material performance, and so on. Under such conditions of uncertainty, skillful managerial judgment is imperative. Finally, there are irreducible factors that cannot be quantified. An investment may have a direct or indirect effect on employee morale or on relations with the community, which, if not carefully judged, could cause irreparable harm. There is usually no single right answer. Sophisticated analytical procedures will not mitigate the effects of poor judgment as to market potential, available resources, and environmental factors—economic, political, and social.

GLOSSARY

Annual Cost of an Investment Net investment divided by the present value factor corresponding to the desired rate of return and estimated life.

Capital Budgeting The allocation and commitment of funds to long-term capital investment projects.

Cost of Capital A bench mark used in capital budgeting decisions; the minimum rate of return should be not less than the cost of the funds invested in the project.

Excess Present Value A bench mark used in capital budgeting decisions with the desirability of an investment indicated by the difference, at a common point of time, between the cost of the investment and the expected earnings from that investment discounted at the desired minimum rate.

Internal Rate of Return The rate at which the present value of cash inflows and outflows offset each other.

Investment Opportunity Concept The concept that, in a capital budgeting decision, the appropriate rate of return is based on the subjective evaluation of the available investment opportunities and their respective earnings rates.

Payback A method of measuring the desirability of a project in terms of how soon the cash invested in a project will be returned.

Present Value Method The conversion of cash inflows and outflows over time to the present, using the firm's cost of capital as the discounting rate, for purposes of comparing capital expenditures.

Time-Adjusted Rate of Return See *Internal Rate of Return.*

QUESTIONS

Q21-1. What is capital budgeting? Why are the principles of compound interest relevant to capital budgeting?

Q21-2. What is meant (a) by simple interest? (b) by compound interest? (c) by present value? (d) by compound discount? (e) by ordinary annuity amount? (f) by present value of an ordinary annuity?

Q21-3. What kind of investment problems lend themselves to rate-of-return measurement techniques?

Q21-4. What constitutes a satisfactory rate of return? How is a rate selected? How is it determined?

Q21-5. What is meant by the term *discounted cash flow?*

Q21-6. Why is it appropriate in making capital budgeting decisions to emphasize the relevant cash flows rather than revenue and expense valuations based on generally accepted accounting principles?

Q21-7. What are the steps to be taken in measuring the rate of return on a proposed capital expenditure?

Q21-8. How is the annual cost of an investment measured? Of what use is such a measurement?

Q21-9. What is meant (a) by excess present value? (b) by excess present value index?

Q21-10. What is the relevance of depreciation and income taxes to capital budgeting problems?

Q21-11. (a) Define *payback.* What are (b) its advantages? (c) its disadvantages?

Q21-12. What limitations are inherent in the application of present value to capital budgeting problems?

Q21-13. "The excess present value method is wrong because it ignores depreciation." Comment on this statement.

Q21-14. "The method of depreciation does not affect the capital budgeting decision." Comment on this statement.

DEMONSTRATION PROBLEMS

DP21-1. (*Payback; excess present value; internal rate of return*) Correy, Inc., plans to invest $200,000 in certain improved metal fabrication equipment that is expected to save $70,000 (net after taxes) annually for ten years. Additional working capital of $20,000 will be required. Assume a 50% income tax rate and straight-line depreciation with no salvage value.

Required:

1. Compute the payback period.
2. Compute the excess present value.
3. Compute the internal rate of return.

DP21-2. (*Payback, excess present value; rates of return*) The Cork Company is considering a proposal to add an electrozinc-plating unit for finishing work now being done by outside contractors at an average cost of $0.027 a pound. Annual requirements are 2,500,000 pounds. Two types are available.

	Semiautomatic	*Fully Automatic*
Purchase price	$25,000	$ 50,000
Operating costs per unit	$ 0.024	$0.01955
Economic life	8 years	8 years

Required: Determine which type of unit is preferable.

PROBLEMS

Note: For all problems, use an interest rate of 20% unless otherwise instructed.

P21-1. Students A and B have expressed contrary views to you regarding each of the following matters and ask your help in settling their differences:

1. The amount of $75 today is more valuable than $100 five years from today.
2. It is worthwhile to invest $4,500 now in a canteen operation that will earn about $1,200 a year for the next five years.
3. It is better to invest $6,000 in food vending machines that will earn about $2,500 a year for five years than to invest $9,200 in a similar business that will earn about $3,300 a year for five years.
4. An investment of $35,000 in a business that will earn $5,600 a year for ten years will not earn a 10% return.
5. To justify a $75,000 investment in a ten-year concession operation, earnings would have to be at least $18,000 a year.
6. Projects A and B each involve a $3,000 investment but the net cash proceeds for the first year are $2,900 and $2,500, respectively. Project A should therefore be selected.

P21-2. What is the approximate rate of return on an investment with an initial cash outlay of $20,000 and net cash inflows of $6,000 a year for five years?

P21-3. A machine that costs $20,000 will reduce present operating costs by $4,000 a year (net). What is the approximate rate of return if the life of the machine is (a) 10 years? (b) 20 years? (c) What must the minimum useful life of the machine be if the required rate of return is 16%?

P21-4. A company has an opportunity to make one of three possible investments, as follows:

	1	*2*	*3*
Investment	$48,000	$60,000	$70,000
Estimated net cash inflow			
Year 1	15,000	20,000	25,000
Year 2	23,000	30,000	35,000
Year 3	25,000	34,000	45,000

For each investment determine (a) the payback period, (b) the excess present value, (c) the excess present value index, and (d) the time-adjusted rate of return.

P21-5. The engineer for the Waibel Corporation has proposed the installation of certain equipment that he estimates will produce the following net after-tax savings over a five-year period:

Year	*Savings*
1	$1,800
2	2,200
3	2,500
4	2,800
5	2,800

What is the maximum amount that should be paid for the equipment? (Assume a minimum rate of return of 16%.)

P21-6. The Ventura Machine Company is considering replacing a machine presently in use and carried on the books at $12,000 with a new machine costing $25,000. The new machine will make possible cost reductions of $4,000 annually for 10 years. The old machine, which could otherwise be continued in use for another 10 years, can be sold for $5,200.

Assuming the use of straight-line depreciation, a desired rate of return of 20%, and an income tax rate of 50%, should the replacement be made?

P21-7. What is the maximum amount that should be paid for a business that will earn $15,000 a year for five years, at the end of which time it can be sold for about $40,000?

P21-8. Net cash earnings from the introduction of a new product are expected to be $90,000 for 10 years. An initial investment of $450,000 will have to be made. (a) What is the internal rate of return? (b) Should the investment be made if the cost of capital is 16%?

P21-9. A new design computer is being considered for the design engineering group of the automotive division of the Kelsey Manufacturing Company, Inc. The investment will have no effect on revenue but will reduce operating expenses by $1,000,000 a year for the next seven years.

The equipment will cost $3,000,000, has an estimated useful life of 6 years, and a salvage value of $600,000 at the end of the sixth year. Annual fixed costs are $100,000. These will not change. Should the investment be made, assuming a desired rate of return of 16%?

P21-10. The Renay Chemical Company is considering the advisability of buying a new reactor that can handle products at high temperatures. The reactor will make possible annual savings in labor and maintenance costs of about $12,000. Data regarding the new reactor are as follows:

Purchase price	$50,000
Salvage value	5,000
Estimated life	15 years

Required: Determine whether the reactor should be purchased.

P21-11. The Kahn Corporation owns 60 concrete block buildings that house certain metering and control equipment. To maintain good public relations with the residents and officials of the towns in which the buildings are located, it is necessary to paint the buildings regularly at an annual cost of $23,000. It has been proposed that the buildings be covered with aluminum siding at a cost of $70,000; this will eliminate all further maintenance. The guarantee period is 15 years.

Required: Determine whether the proposal should be approved.

P21-12. The B. G. Baker Company is planning to buy a continuous gelatin dryer to replace the hand nets currently used to perform the drying operation. The useful life of the dryer is ten years and its installed cost is $400,000. The old equipment has a carrying value of $75,000 and can be sold for $30,000.

The new dryer will reduce labor costs and fringe benefits by $100,000 annually and will eliminate the need for nets at a saving of $30,000 each year. Maintenance costs will increase by $20,000 annually. The new dryer is expected to improve the quality of the product and eliminate some presently existing sanitation problems.

The company uses the straight-line method of depreciation and is subject to income tax of 50%. The present equipment can be used for another ten years.

Required: Determine whether the dryer should be purchased to replace the old equipment.

P21-13. John Ford, the plant engineer for the Jones Company, has been asked to procure equipment that will improve the present method used by the company for shearing bar stock. He finds three different systems, each of which will improve present methods and reduce space requirements. The costs of the systems are as follows:

A	$ 60,000
B	90,000
C	100,000

The work to be done by the new equipment currently requires 3,300 hours annually at an hourly variable cost of $24.02. The new systems will do the same work in 1,100 hours at the following rates:

A	$29
B	26
C	21

The company plans to depreciate the new equipment over eight years, using the straight-line method, and is subject to a 50% income tax rate. No salvage value is expected.

The old equipment is fully depreciated and has no salvage value. The new system will not require increased working capital.

Required:

1. Compute the payback period.
2. Compute the internal rate of return.

P21-14. The Rosen Company is considering the replacement of conventional drilling equipment with a numerically controlled drilling machine. The purchase price of the machine, including controls, is $60,000. Freight and installation costs are $1,800. Other first-year expenses include a programmer at $15,000 and training fees of $2,000. The useful life of the machine is ten years. Projected annual savings are as follows:

Reduction in tooling costs	$13,857
Reduction in tool wear and tear	600
Reduced scrap and rework costs	494
Reduced floor space: 200 square feet × $3.00 per square foot	600
Reduced maintenance	600
Reduction in labor and fringe benefits	8,000

After the first year, the part-time services of a programmer will be needed at an annual cost of $3,500.

Required: Compute the internal rate of return, assuming no salvage value, a 50% income tax rate, and straight-line depreciation.

P21-15. The Crowell Company needs equipment to produce about 1,500 microcircuits a week for the next five years. Rapidly evolving microcircuit technology makes projections for any period longer than five years hazardous. Two methods are being considered, as follows:

	A	*B*
Investment for equipment	$30,000	$36,000
Variable costs per 1-inch microcircuit (exclusive of transistors and diodes)	0.83	0.80

The choice of method will not affect sales volume, because the microcircuits are incorporated into a larger piece of equipment. No salvage value is expected.

Required: Determine which investment should be made.

Discount Factors for 20% (rounded off)

Period	*Present Value of $1*	*Present Value of $1 a Period Received at End of Period*	*Accumulated Value of $1*	*Accumulated Value of $1 a Period Received at End of Period*
1	.83	.83	1.20	1.00
2	.69	1.52	1.44	2.20
3	.58	2.10	1.73	3.64
4	.48	2.58	2.07	5.37

APPENDIX I

Simple Interest and Compound Interest

In periods of high interest rates, it is extremely important for managers to know the rudiments of both simple interest and compound interest. This appendix discusses the basic rudiments of calculating both simple interest and compound interest because they are significant elements in accounting for the borrowing and lending of money. Furthermore, a knowledge of compound interest is essential in the solution of complex problems of calculating insurance probabilities, of determining investment values to yield expected interest rates, and of solving management problems involving the time value of future sums.

DEFINITIONS OF INTEREST

Interest

Interest is the price of credit, a payment made (or collection received) for the use of money or the equivalent of money. Because it is similar to the price of supplies used, interest to the maker—the debtor—is an expense; to the payee—the creditor—interest is a revenue.

Simple Interest versus Compound Interest

Simple interest is interest on the original principal of a note or a time draft, regardless of interest amounts that may have accrued on the principal in past periods, whereas *compound interest* is interest that accrues on unpaid interest of past periods as well as on the principal. In other words, compound interest is interest earned on a principal sum that is increased at the end of each period by the interest for that period.

SIMPLE INTEREST

Assume that Tanya Crayne gives Johnson Evers a 9 percent, 60-day note that has a principal amount of $2,000. The interest specified on a note or a draft, unless otherwise indicated, is an annual fraction or rate on the principal, or face amount, of the instrument. Thus, in Tanya Crayne's note, the price, or charge, for the use of $2,000 for one year, is $180 = ($2,000 × 0.09). Since the term of the note, however, is less than one year, the interest must be computed by multiplying the interest amount for one year by a fraction; the numerator is the term of the note in days and the denominator, the number of days in a year. The formula is

$$\text{Interest} = \text{Principal} \times \text{Rate} \times \text{Time}$$

This is usually stated as $I = PRT$. In Crayne's note, the interest calculation for the 60-day period is

$$I = \$2{,}000 \times 0.09 \times \frac{60}{360}$$

$$I = \$30$$

It is common commercial practice to assume that the year contains 360 days (or 12 months of 30 days each) in computing interest. This practice is followed here, but it should be understood that the amount of bias in the final interest calculation is 1/73, that is,

$$\frac{365 - 360}{365} = \frac{1}{73}$$

Short-Cut Methods for Calculating Simple Interest

Time can be saved through various short-cut methods of computing simple interest. Two of these are referred to as the *6-percent 60-day method* and the *6-percent 6-day method.* Since the interest at 6 percent for 60 days on any principal is 1 percent = (60/360 × 6%), interest at 6 percent for 60 days on any principal can be figured by moving the decimal point two places to the left in the principal, which is the same as multiplying the principal by 1 percent. Similarly, the interest at 6 percent for 6 days can be figured by moving the decimal point three places to the left in the principal. Either or both of these short methods may be used for note terms other than 6 or 60 days. The term of the note can be stated as a fraction or multiple of 6 or 60 days, and the interest may then be quickly computed.

Short methods can also be applied when the interest rate is other than 6 percent. The interest calculation is first made at 6 percent, then an adjustment is made for the difference between 6 percent and the particular rate.

The following two examples illustrate interest computation by the short methods.

1. Interest at 9 percent on $3,600 for 90 days:

Interest at 6% for 60 days	$36
Interest at 6% for 30 days (½ of $36)	18
Interest at 6% for 90 days	$54
Interest at 3% for 90 days (½ of $54)	27
Interest at 9% for 90 days	$81

2. Interest at 4½ percent on $4,800 for 30 days:

Interest at 6% for 60 days	$48
Interest at 6% for 30 days (½ of $48)	$24
Less interest at 1½% for 30 days (¼ of $24)	6
Interest at 4½% for 30 days	$18

An advantage of the short methods is that they often require relatively simple arithmetical computations, thereby reducing the possibility of error. This is true when interest rates and terms are such that the mathematical manipulations are obvious, but if rates and terms require elaborate adjustments for the use of these methods (for example, 4.25 percent for 27 days), the calculation time will not be reduced, but increased. In such cases it is better to use the basic interest formula, $I = PRT$.

COMPOUND INTEREST

For the purpose of quickly computing the information needed in helping to solve many modern business problems, it is important that the accounting student be familiar with the following four basic types of compound interest computations:

1. Amount of a single invested sum at compound interest
2. Present value of a single given sum due in the future
3. Amount of an ordinary annuity
4. Present value of an ordinary annuity

Amount of a Single Sum at Compound Interest

A simple illustration of the interest compounded annually on a single sum of $100 for four years at 6 percent a year is shown here.

(1) Year	(2) *Amount at Beginning of Year*	(3) *Annual Amount of Interest (Col. 2 × 0.06)*	(4) *Accumulated Amount at End of Year (Col. 2 + Col. 3)*
1	$100.00	$ 6.00	$106.00
2	106.00	6.36	112.36
3	112.36	6.74	119.10
4	119.10	7.15	126.25
Total		$26.25	

The principal of $100 at the beginning of year 1 has by year 4 grown to $126.25, the *compound amount.*

Each amount in column 4 is 106 percent of the corresponding amount in column 2; that is, $100 × 1.06 × 1.06 × 1.06 × 1.06 = $126.25. This means that 106 percent, or 1.06, has been used as a multiplier four times; thus 1.06 has been raised to the fourth power. The compound amount is, therefore, $100 multiplied by 1.06 to the fourth power, as shown below.

$(1.06)^4$	1.2625
Multiplied by principal	$ 100
Compound amount	$126.25

The compound amount of 1 for n periods is expressed by the following formula:

$$a = (1 + i)^n$$

where a = compound amount of 1 ($1, or any other monetary unit) at interest for n periods
n = number of periods
i = periodic interest rate

The difference between the compound amount and the original principal is the compound interest. The compound interest (I) on 1 for four periods at 6 percent is computed as follows:

$$\begin{aligned} I &= (1 + i)^n - 1 \\ &= (1 + 0.06)^4 - 1 \\ &= 1.2625 - 1 \\ &= 0.2625 \end{aligned}$$

The calculation of compound interest on $100 for four years at 6 percent compounded annually is

$$\$100 \times 0.2625 = \$26.25$$

Present Value

If $100 is worth $126.25 when it is left at 6 percent compound interest each year for four years, then it follows that $126.25 four years from now is worth $100 now; that is, $100 is the *present value* of $126.25. The present value is the amount that must be invested now to produce the known future value. In compound-amount problems, the future value of a known present value must be determined; in present value problems, the present value of a known future value must be determined. Since the amount of $100 invested at compound interest in the preceding section was in effect determined by multiplying $100 × 1.06 × 1.06 × 1.06 × 1.06 to arrive at the $126.25 figure, to calculate the present value of $126.25 we must reverse the process. That is, we must take the $126.25 and successively divide by 1.06 as follows:

Year	*Amount at End of Year*		*Divide by*		*Present Value at Beginning of Year*
4	$126.25	÷	1.06	=	$119.10
3	119.10	÷	1.06	=	112.36
2	112.36	÷	1.06	=	106.00
1	106.00	÷	1.06	=	100.00

Observing that the *present value of a single sum* is the reciprocal value of the *amount of a single sum,* the computation can be shortened as shown.

$$\frac{\$126.25}{(1 + 0.06)^4} = \frac{\$126.25}{1.2625} = \$100$$

The general formula for the present value (p) of a single given sum of 1 due in any number of periods is as follows:

$$p = \frac{1}{(1 + i)^n}$$

The present value of 1 at 6 percent interest compounded annually for four years is computed as shown.

$$p = \frac{1}{(1 + i)^n} = \frac{1}{(1 + 0.06)^4} = \frac{1}{1.2625} = 0.79208$$

If the present value of 1 is 0.79208, then the present value of \$126.25 is computed as follows:

$$\$126.25 \times 0.79208 = \$100$$

The principal sum that must be deposited at 6 percent interest compounded annually to amount to \$126.25 in four years is \$100.

Compound Discount

Compound discount (D) is the difference between the future value and the present value; it is expressed by the following formula:

$$D = 1 - \frac{1}{(1 + i)^n}$$

The compound discount on 1 at 6 percent interest, compounded annually, is

$$D = 1 - \frac{1}{(1 + i)^n} = 1 - 0.79208 = 0.20792$$

The calculation of compound discount on \$126.25 for four years at 6 percent compounded annually is \$126.25 × 0.20792 = \$26.25 (rounded).

Ordinary Annuity—Amount

An *ordinary annuity* is a series of equal payments or deposits, also called *rents,* at the end of equal intervals of time with compound interest on these payments. The value of the annuity at the end of the successive time periods is the *amount of the annuity.* The calculation of the amount of an ordinary annuity of four payments of \$100 each at 6 percent is shown in Figure A-1.

Figure A-1
Amount of an Ordinary Annuity

(1) Period	(2) Beginning Balance	(3) Interest Earned (6% × Col. 2)	(4) Periodic Payment	(5) Accumulated at End of Period (Col. 2 + Col. 3 + Col. 4)
1	$ -0-	$ -0-	$100	$100.00
2	100.00	6.00	100	206.00
3	206.00	12.36	100	318.36
4	318.36	19.10	100	437.46

The formula for finding the amount (*A*) of an ordinary annuity of 1 each is as follows:

$$A = \frac{(1 + i)^n - 1}{i}$$

Since the numerator of this equation is the compound interest (*I*), the equation may be restated as

$$A = \frac{I}{i}$$

The amount of an ordinary annuity of four rents of $100 each at 6 percent interest compounded annually may be computed directly as follows:

$$A = \frac{I}{i} = \frac{0.2625}{0.06} \times \$100 = \$437.50$$

Figure A-1 shows the amount to be $437.46. The $0.04 difference is due to rounding.

Ordinary Annuity—Present Value

The present value of an ordinary annuity is the present value of a series of payments to be made at equal intervals in the future; that is, it is the single sum that, if invested at compound interest now, provides for a stated series of payments or withdrawals at equal time intervals. The formula for the present value of four payments of $100 each at 6 percent is shown in Figure A-1.

$$P = \frac{1 - \frac{1}{(1 + i)^n}}{i} \quad \text{or} \quad P = \frac{1 - (1 + i)^{-n}}{i}$$

Since the numerator of this equation is the compound discount (D), the equation may be restated as shown.

$$P = \frac{D}{i}$$

The present value of an ordinary annuity of four payments of $100 at 6 percent is calculated as follows:

$$P = \frac{D}{i} = \frac{0.20792}{0.06} \times \$100 = \$346.53$$

The proof that the present value of an ordinary annuity of four payments of $100 at 6 percent is $346.53 is shown below.

Amount invested	\$346.53
Interest earned, 1st period (6% × \$346.53)	20.79
Amount at end of 1st period	\$367.32
Deduct 1st payment	100.00
Balance of investment at beginning of 2d period	\$267.32
Interest earned, 2d period (6% × \$267.32)	16.04
Amount at end of 2d period	\$283.36
Deduct 2d payment	100.00
Balance of investment at beginning of 3d period	\$183.36
Interest earned, 3d period (6% × \$183.36)	11.00
Amount at end of 3d period	\$194.36
Deduct 3d payment	100.00
Balance of investment at beginning of 4th period	\$ 94.36
Interest earned, 4th period (6% × \$94.36)	5.66
Amount at end of 4th period	\$100.02
Deduct 4th payment	100.00
Total (difference is due to rounding)	\$000.02

The four basic formulas may be summarized in chart form, using the abbreviated notations, as follows:

Present value ←	$p = \frac{1}{a}$	≺ Single payment ≻	$a = (1 + i)^n$	→ Future value
Present value ←	$P = \frac{D}{i}$	≺ Series of payments ≻	$A = \frac{I}{i}$	→ Future value

Since $p = 1/a$, $D = 1 - p$, and $I = a - 1$, then the formula for the amount of 1, $a = (1 + i)^n$ is the source for the derivation of the other formulas.

Use of Compound Interest Tables

Compound interest tables are available and are in common use in banking, industry, and elsewhere. Tables of *a, p, A,* and *P* of \$1 for different periods and at various interest rates are shown in the Appendix tables.

To illustrate how these tables are used, first refer to page 629, which shows the present value of \$1 (*p*). The figure in the 10 percent column for period 10 is 0.385543. This means that \$1 due at the end of 10 years, compounded annually at 10 percent interest, if discounted, has a present worth or present value of \$0.385543; that is, if \$0.385543 is invested today at 10 percent interest compounded annually, it would accumulate to \$1 in 10 years. The figures in the table are *discount factors* that produce the present value equivalent of any known future amount when multiplied by that amount. For example, to produce \$6,750 10 years from now at 10 percent interest compounded annually, \$6,750 × 0.385543, or \$2,602.42, must be deposited.

The table on page 631 shows the present values of series of payments (*P*) to be made at equal intervals in the future. For example, the figure in the 10 percent column for period 10 is 6.144567. This means that $1 due at the end of each year for 10 years, compounded annually at 10 percent interest, has a present value of $6.144567. The same result can be obtained by using the discount factors from the table on page 629 to accumulate each present value in the series. The table on page 631 shortens the process by giving a single discount factor for an entire series. The figures in the present value tables are discount factors that, when multiplied by any series of uniform amounts due at regular intervals in the future, produce the present equivalent of that series of amounts. For example, to produce $1,250 at the end of each year when 10 rents are deposited annually at 10 percent interest compounded annually, $1,250 × 6.144567, or $7,680.71, must be deposited.

The precomputed formula values for *a* and *A* as shown on pages 628 and 630 are used in a manner similar to that described for *p* and *P* above. Several illustrations of these calculations are given below.

Illustration of Computation of Amount of a Single Sum at Compound Interest. Assume that on December 31, Year 1, Benjamin Boykin plans to invest in a savings account $10,000 at 6 percent interest compounded annually. He would like to know how much he would have in the savings account on January 1, Year 11, when he plans to retire. The problem can be graphically portrayed as follows:

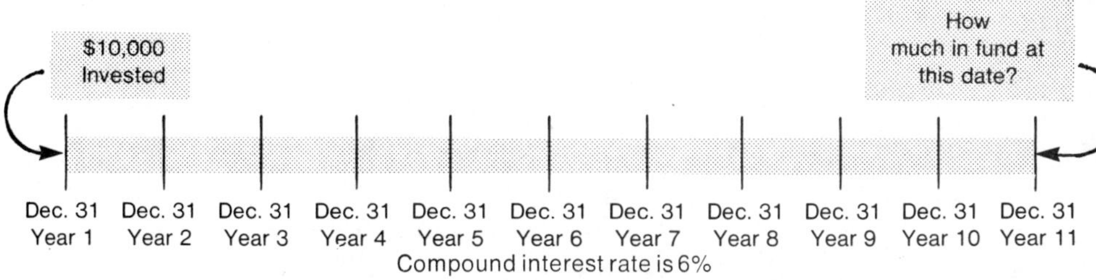

To solve the problem by the use of tables, we must look up the value of *a* for 10 periods at 6 percent on page 628. This value is 1.790848, which is the value of $(1.06)^{10}$. To obtain the answer, we must multiply the $10,000 by the 1.790848 as shown below.

1.790848 × $10,000 = $17,908.48

Illustration of Computation of the Present Value of a Given Sum. Assume that Elton Parker desires to have $50,000 in a given fund on December 31, Year 11. How much must he invest on December 31, Year 1, to produce $50,000 ten years later if the investment earns 6 percent interest compounded annually? Again, the problem can be shown graphically as follows:

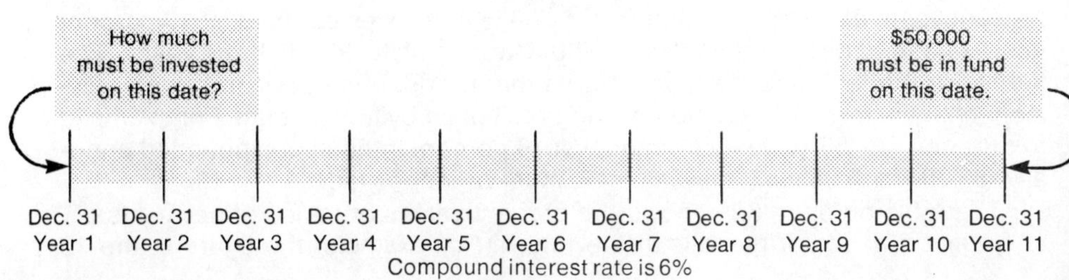

To solve the problem by the use of present value tables, we must look up the value of p for 10 periods at 6 percent on page 629. This value is 0.558395, which is $1/(1.06)^{10}$; then we must multiply the $50,000 by this discount factor, thus:

$$\$50{,}000 \times 0.558395 = \$27{,}919.75$$

On December 31, Year 1, Parker would have to invest $27,919.75 at 6 percent interest compounded annually to earn $50,000 by December 31, Year 11 (total 10 years).

Illustration of Computation of the Amount of an Ordinary Annuity at Compound Interest. Assume that John Gainsworthy receives a semiannual bonus of $10,000 on January 2 and July 2. He plans to deposit these bonuses in a savings account which earns interest at 6 percent a year compounded semiannually, or 3 percent each six months. If Gainsworthy starts investing his bonus on January 2, Year 1, how much will he have in the fund on July 2, Year 5? The problem can be illustrated graphically as follows:

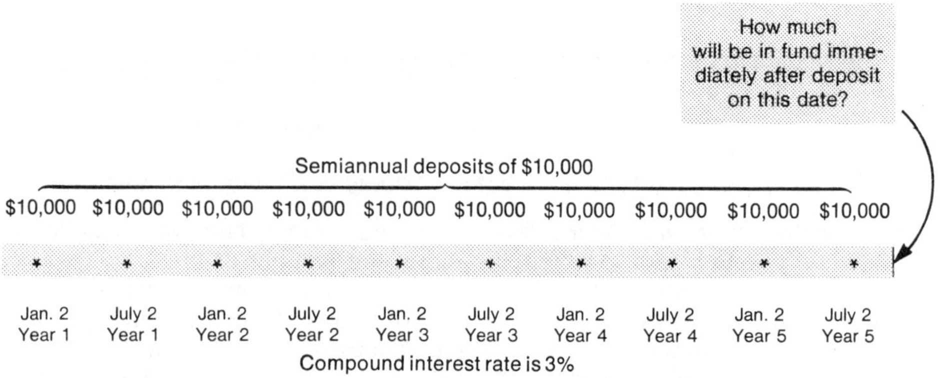

How much will be in fund immediately after deposit on this date?

Semiannual deposits of $10,000

$10,000	$10,000	$10,000	$10,000	$10,000	$10,000	$10,000	$10,000	$10,000	$10,000
*	*	*	*	*	*	*	*	*	*
Jan. 2 Year 1	July 2 Year 1	Jan. 2 Year 2	July 2 Year 2	Jan. 2 Year 3	July 2 Year 3	Jan. 2 Year 4	July 2 Year 4	Jan. 2 Year 5	July 2 Year 5

Compound interest rate is 3%

To solve the problem by the use of compound interest tables, we must look up the value of A for 10 rents of 1 each at 3 percent on page 630. This value is 11.463879, which is a precalculation of

$$\frac{(1.03)^{10} - 1}{0.03}$$

we must then multiply the semiannual deposits of $10,000 each by 11.463879, thus:

$$\$10{,}000 \times 11.463879 = \$114{,}638.79$$

Gainsworthy will have $114,638.79 in the fund on July 2, Year 5.

Illustration of Computation of the Present Value of an Ordinary Annuity at Compound Interest. Assume that Camilla Peate wishes to make 10 annual withdrawals of $1,000 each from a fund beginning December 31, Year 2. How much must she have invested on December 31, Year 1, if the balance of the fund will earn interest compounded annually at 6 percent? The problem can be shown graphically as follows:

How much must be invested on this date?

Annual Withdrawals

	$1,000	$1,000	$1,000	$1,000	$1,000	$1,000	$1,000	$1,000	$1,000	$1,000
	*	*	*	*	*	*	*	*	*	*
Dec. 31 Year 1	Dec. 31 Year 2	Dec. 31 Year 3	Dec. 31 Year 4	Dec. 31 Year 5	Dec. 31 Year 6	Dec. 31 Year 7	Dec. 31 Year 8	Dec. 31 Year 9	Dec. 31 Year 10	Dec. 31 Year 11

Compound interest rate is 6%

To solve the problem by the use of compound interest tables, we must look up the value of P for 10 rents of 1 each at 6 percent on page 631. This value is 7.360087, which is a precalculation of

$$\frac{1 - \dfrac{1}{(1.06)^{10}}}{0.06}$$

The amount to be invested on December 31, Year 1, is determined by multiplying $1,000 by 7.360087, thus:

$$\$1,000 \times 7.360087 = \$7,360.09.$$

Use of Tables to Determine Value of Rents in Annuity Problems

In the preceding annuity illustrations, the value of each rent was known, and the problem was to determine either the amount of the annuity or the present value of the annuity. The ordinary compound interest tables may be used to determine the value of each rent or deposit for either type of the foregoing annuity problems. For example, suppose that Thomas Merton had $100,000 to invest on December 31, Year 1, and he wanted to start making annual withdrawals on December 31, Year 2, and thereafter through December 31, Year 11; assume that the fund earns interest at 6 percent compounded annually. This is a present value of an ordinary annuity problem with the present value amount known and the value of each withdrawal or rent unknown. The problem can be graphically presented as follows:

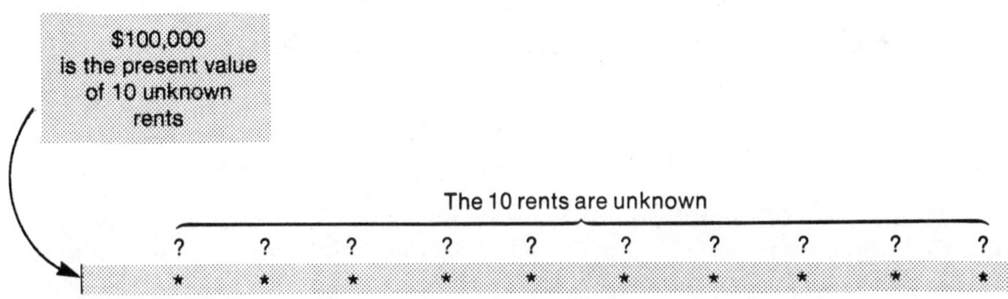

Interest is compounded annually at 6%

The problem can be solved by dividing $100,000 by *P* of 10 rents of 1 each at 6 percent. We must look up the value of *P* of 10 rents of 1 at 6 percent on page 631, which is 7.360087, and divide the $100,000 by this discount factor, thus:

$$\$100{,}000 \div 7.360087 = \$13{,}586.80$$

Merton can withdraw $13,586.80 on December 31, Year 2, and each December 31 thereafter through December 31, Year 11.

A similar problem could be solved for the amount of an ordinary annuity where the final amount is known, but the value of each rent is unknown. For example, suppose a firm must have $1,000,000 in 10 years to retire a debt. It wishes to make 10 annual payments in a fund earning 6 percent interest compounded annually; how much must be invested each year? The answer to the problem is $1,000,000 divided by *A* of 10 rents of 1 each at 6 percent, 13.180795, which is $75,867.96.

Uses of Compound Interest Techniques

To reiterate, compound interest must be used to solve complex problems of calculating insurance probabilities, to determine values of investments at given interest yield rates, and to equate the time value of future sums of many management decisions. Elementary problems involving compound interest are illustrated in Chapters 7, 13, and 14. Suggestions are made in several other chapters about how the compound interest techniques could be used.

Compound Interest Tables

TABLE 1. Compound Amount of 1 $a = (1 + i)^n$

	1½ %	2%	3%	4%	6%	8%	10%	12%	14%	16%	20%
1	1.015000	1.020000	1.030000	1.040000	1.060000	1.080000	1.100000	1.120000	1.140000	1.160000	1.200000
2	1.030225	1.040400	1.060900	1.081600	1.123600	1.166400	1.210000	1.254400	1.299600	1.345600	1.440000
3	1.045678	1.061208	1.092727	1.124864	1.191016	1.259712	1.331000	1.404928	1.481544	1.560896	1.728000
4	1.061364	1.082432	1.125509	1.169859	1.262477	1.360489	1.464100	1.573519	1.688960	1.810639	2.073600
5	1.077284	1.104081	1.159274	1.216653	1.338226	1.469328	1.610510	1.762342	1.925415	2.100342	2.488320
6	1.093443	1.126162	1.194052	1.265319	1.418519	1.586874	1.771561	1.973823	2.194973	2.436396	2.985984
7	1.109845	1.148686	1.229874	1.315932	1.503630	1.713824	1.948717	2.210681	2.502269	2.826220	3.583181
8	1.126493	1.171659	1.266770	1.368569	1.593848	1.850930	2.143589	2.475963	2.852586	3.278415	4.299817
9	1.143390	1.195093	1.304773	1.423312	1.689479	1.999005	2.357948	2.773079	3.251949	3.802961	5.159780
10	1.160541	1.218994	1.343916	1.480244	1.790848	2.158925	2.593742	3.105848	3.707221	4.411435	6.191736
11	1.177949	1.243374	1.384234	1.539454	1.898299	2.331639	2.853117	3.478550	4.226232	5.117265	7.430084
12	1.195618	1.268242	1.425761	1.601032	2.012196	2.518170	3.138428	3.895976	4.817905	5.936027	8.916100
13	1.213553	1.293607	1.468534	1.665074	2.132928	2.719624	3.452271	4.363493	5.492411	6.885791	10.699321
14	1.231756	1.319479	1.512590	1.731676	2.260904	2.937193	3.797498	4.887112	6.261349	7.987518	12.839185
15	1.250232	1.345868	1.557967	1.800944	2.396558	3.172169	4.177248	5.473566	7.137938	9.265521	15.407022
16	1.268986	1.372786	1.604706	1.872981	2.540352	3.425942	4.594973	6.130394	8.137249	10.748004	18.488426
17	1.288021	1.400241	1.652848	1.947900	2.692773	3.700018	5.054470	6.866041	9.276464	12.467685	22.186111
18	1.307341	1.428246	1.702433	2.025817	2.854339	3.996019	5.559917	7.689966	10.575169	14.462514	26.623333
19	1.326951	1.456811	1.753506	2.106849	3.025600	4.315701	6.115909	8.612762	12.055693	16.776517	31.948000
20	1.346856	1.485947	1.806111	2.191123	3.207135	4.660957	6.727500	9.646293	13.743490	19.460759	38.337600
21	1.367058	1.515666	1.860295	2.278768	3.399563	5.033833	7.400250	10.803848	15.667578	22.574481	46.005120
22	1.387564	1.545980	1.916103	2.369919	3.603537	5.436540	8.140275	12.100310	17.861039	26.186398	55.206144
23	1.408378	1.576899	1.973587	2.464716	3.819750	5.871463	8.954302	13.552347	20.361585	30.376222	66.247373
24	1.429503	1.608437	2.032794	2.563304	4.048935	6.341180	9.849733	15.178629	23.212207	35.236417	79.496847
25	1.450946	1.640606	2.093778	2.665836	4.291871	6.848475	10.834706	17.000064	26.461916	40.874244	95.396217
26	1.472710	1.673418	2.156591	2.772470	4.549383	7.396353	11.918177	19.040072	30.166584	47.414123	114.475460
27	1.494801	1.706886	2.221289	2.883369	4.822346	7.988061	13.109994	21.324881	34.389906	55.000382	137.370552
28	1.517223	1.741024	2.287928	2.998703	5.111687	8.627106	14.420994	23.883866	39.204493	63.800444	164.844662
29	1.539981	1.775845	2.356566	3.118651	5.418388	9.317274	15.863093	26.749930	44.693122	74.008515	197.813595
30	1.563081	1.811362	2.427262	3.243398	5.743491	10.062656	17.449402	29.959922	50.950159	85.849877	237.376314
31	1.586527	1.847589	2.500080	3.373133	6.088101	10.867669	19.194342	33.555113	58.083181	99.585857	284.851577
32	1.610325	1.884541	2.575083	3.508059	6.453387	11.737082	21.113777	37.581726	66.214826	115.519594	341.821892
33	1.634480	1.922231	2.652335	3.648381	6.840590	12.676049	23.225154	42.091533	75.484902	134.002729	410.186270
34	1.658997	1.960676	2.731905	3.794316	7.251025	13.690133	25.547670	47.142517	86.052788	155.443116	492.223524
35	1.683882	1.999890	2.813862	3.946089	7.686087	14.785344	28.102437	52.799620	98.100178	180.314073	590.668229
36	1.709140	2.039887	2.898278	4.103933	8.147252	15.968171	30.912681	59.135574	111.834203	209.164324	708.801875
37	1.734777	2.080685	2.985227	4.268090	8.636087	17.245625	34.003949	66.231843	127.490992	242.630616	850.562250
38	1.760799	2.122299	3.074783	4.438813	9.154252	18.625275	37.404343	74.179664	145.339731	281.451515	1020.674700
39	1.787211	2.164745	3.167026	4.616366	9.703507	20.115297	41.144778	83.081224	165.687293	326.483757	1224.809640
40	1.814019	2.208040	3.262037	4.801021	10.285718	21.724520	45.259256	93.050970	188.883514	378.721158	1469.771568

TABLE 2. Present Value of 1p $= \frac{1}{(1+i)^n}$

	1½ %	2%	3%	4%	6%	8%	10%	12%	14%	16%	20%
1	.985222	.980392	.970874	.961538	.943396	.925926	.909091	.892857	.877193	.862069	.833333
2	.970662	.961169	.942596	.924556	.889996	.857339	.826446	.797194	.769468	.743163	.694444
3	.956317	.942322	.915142	.888996	.839619	.793832	.751315	.711780	.674972	.640658	.578704
4	.942184	.923845	.888487	.854804	.792094	.735030	.683013	.635518	.592080	.552291	.482253
5	.928260	.905731	.862609	.821927	.747258	.680583	.620921	.567427	.519369	.476113	.401878
6	.914542	.887971	.837484	.790315	.704961	.630170	.564474	.506631	.455587	.410442	.334898
7	.901027	.870560	.813092	.759918	.665057	.583490	.513158	.452349	.399637	.353830	.279082
8	.887711	.853490	.789409	.730690	.627412	.540269	.466507	.403883	.350559	.305025	.232568
9	.874592	.836755	.766417	.702587	.591894	.500249	.424098	.360610	.307508	.262953	.193807
10	.861667	.820348	.744094	.675564	.558395	.463193	.385543	.321973	.269744	.226684	.161506
11	.848933	.804263	.722421	.649581	.526788	.428883	.350494	.287476	.236617	.195417	.134588
12	.836387	.788493	.701380	.624597	.496969	.397114	.318631	.256675	.207559	.168463	.112157
13	.824027	.773033	.680951	.600574	.468839	.367698	.289664	.229174	.182069	.145227	.093464
14	.811849	.757875	.661118	.577475	.442301	.340461	.263331	.204620	.159710	.125195	.077887
15	.799852	.743015	.641862	.555265	.417265	.315242	.239392	.182696	.140096	.107927	.064905
16	.788031	.728446	.623167	.533908	.393646	.291890	.217629	.163122	.122892	.093041	.054088
17	.776385	.714163	.605016	.513373	.371364	.270269	.197845	.145644	.107800	.080207	.045073
18	.764912	.700159	.587395	.493628	.350344	.250249	.179859	.130040	.094561	.069144	.037561
19	.753607	.686431	.570286	.474642	.330513	.231712	.163508	.116107	.082948	.059607	.031301
20	.742470	.672971	.553676	.456387	.311805	.214548	.148644	.103667	.072762	.051385	.026084
21	.731498	.659776	.537549	.438834	.294155	.198656	.135131	.092560	.063826	.044298	.021737
22	.720688	.646839	.521893	.421955	.277505	.183941	.122846	.082643	.055988	.038188	.018114
23	.710037	.634156	.506692	.405726	.261797	.170315	.111678	.073788	.049112	.032920	.015095
24	.699544	.621722	.491934	.390121	.246979	.157699	.101526	.065882	.043081	.028380	.012579
25	.689206	.609531	.477606	.375116	.232999	.146018	.092296	.058823	.037790	.024465	.010483
26	.679021	.597579	.463695	.360689	.219810	.135202	.083905	.052521	.033149	.021091	.008735
27	.668986	.585862	.450189	.346816	.207368	.125187	.076278	.046894	.029078	.018182	.007280
28	.659099	.574375	.437077	.333477	.195630	.115914	.069343	.041869	.025507	.015674	.006066
29	.649359	.563113	.424346	.320651	.184557	.107328	.063039	.037383	.022375	.013512	.005055
30	.639762	.552071	.411987	.308318	.174110	.099377	.057309	.033378	.019627	.011648	.004213
31	.630308	.541246	.399987	.296460	.164255	.092016	.052099	.029802	.017217	.010042	.003511
32	.620993	.530633	.388337	.285058	.154957	.085200	.047362	.026609	.015102	.008657	.002926
33	.611816	.520229	.377026	.274094	.146186	.078889	.043057	.023758	.013248	.007463	.002438
34	.602774	.510028	.366045	.263552	.137912	.073045	.039143	.021212	.011621	.006433	.002032
35	.593866	.500028	.355383	.253415	.130105	.067635	.035584	.018940	.010194	.005546	.001693
36	.585090	.490223	.345032	.243669	.122741	.062625	.032349	.016910	.008942	.004781	.001411
37	.576443	.480611	.334983	.234297	.115793	.057986	.029408	.015098	.007844	.004121	.001176
38	.567924	.471187	.325226	.225285	.109239	.053690	.026735	.013481	.006880	.003553	.000980
39	.559531	.461948	.315753	.216620	.103056	.049713	.024304	.012036	.006035	.003063	.000816
40	.551262	.452891	.306557	.208289	.097222	.046031	.022095	.010747	.005294	.002640	.000680

TABLE 3. Amount of an Annuity of 1 $A = \frac{(1+i)^n - 1}{i}$

	1½ %	2%	3%	4%	6%	8%	10%	12%	14%	16%	20%
1	1.000000	1.000000	1.000000	1.000000	1.000000	1.000000	1.000000	1.000000	1.000000	1.000000	1.000000
2	2.015000	2.020000	2.030000	2.040000	2.060000	2.080000	2.100000	2.120000	2.140000	2.160000	2.200000
3	3.045225	3.060400	3.090900	3.121600	3.183600	3.246400	3.310000	3.374400	3.439600	3.505600	3.640000
4	4.090903	4.121608	4.183627	4.246464	4.374616	4.506112	4.641000	4.779328	4.921144	5.066496	5.368000
5	5.152267	5.204040	5.309136	5.416323	5.637093	5.866601	6.105100	6.352847	6.610104	6.877135	7.441600
6	6.229551	6.388121	6.468410	6.632975	6.975319	7.335929	7.715610	8.115189	8.535519	8.977477	9.929920
7	7.322994	7.434283	7.662462	7.898294	8.393838	8.922803	9.487171	10.089012	10.730491	11.413873	12.915904
8	8.432839	8.582969	8.892336	9.214226	9.897468	10.636628	11.435888	12.299693	13.232760	14.240093	16.499085
9	9.559332	9.754628	10.159106	10.582795	11.491316	12.487558	13.579477	14.775656	16.085347	17.518508	20.798902
10	10.702722	10.949721	11.463879	12.006107	13.180795	14.486562	15.937425	17.548735	19.337295	21.321469	25.958682
11	11.863263	12.168715	12.807796	13.486351	14.971643	16.645487	18.531167	20.654583	23.044516	25.732904	32.150419
12	13.041211	13.412090	14.192030	15.025805	16.869941	18.977126	21.384284	24.133133	27.270749	30.850169	39.580502
13	14.236830	14.680332	15.617790	16.626838	18.882138	21.495297	24.522712	28.029109	32.088654	36.786196	48.496603
14	15.450382	15.973938	17.086324	18.291911	21.015066	24.214920	27.974983	32.392602	37.581065	43.671987	59.195923
15	16.682138	17.293417	18.598914	20.023588	23.275970	27.152114	31.772482	37.279715	43.842414	51.659505	72.035108
16	17.932370	18.639285	20.156881	21.824531	25.672528	30.324283	35.949730	42.753280	50.980352	60.925026	87.442129
17	19.201355	20.012071	21.761588	23.697512	28.212880	33.750226	40.544703	48.883674	59.117601	71.673030	105.930555
18	20.489376	21.412312	23.414435	25.645413	30.905653	37.450244	45.599173	55.749715	68.394066	84.140715	128.116666
19	21.796716	22.840559	25.116868	27.671229	33.759992	41.446263	51.159090	63.439681	78.969235	98.603230	154.740000
20	23.123667	24.297370	26.870374	29.778079	36.785591	45.761964	57.274999	72.052442	91.024928	115.379747	186.688000
21	24.470522	25.783317	28.676486	31.969202	39.992727	50.422921	64.002499	81.698736	104.768417	134.840506	225.025600
22	25.837580	27.298984	30.536780	34.247970	43.392290	55.456755	71.402749	92.502584	120.435996	157.414987	271.030719
23	27.225143	28.844963	32.452884	36.617889	46.995828	60.893296	79.543024	104.602894	138.297035	183.601385	326.236863
24	28.633521	30.421862	34.426470	39.082604	50.815577	66.764759	88.497327	118.155241	158.658620	213.977606	392.484236
25	30.063023	32.030300	36.459264	41.645908	54.864512	73.105940	98.347059	133.333870	181.870827	249.214024	471.981083
26	31.513969	33.670906	38.553042	44.311745	59.156383	79.954415	109.181765	150.333934	208.332743	290.088267	567.377300
27	32.986678	35.344324	40.709634	47.084214	63.705766	87.350768	121.099942	169.374007	238.499327	337.502390	681.852760
28	34.481479	37.051210	42.930923	49.967583	68.528112	95.338830	134.209936	190.698887	272.889233	392.502772	819.223312
29	35.998701	38.792235	45.218850	52.966286	73.639798	103.965936	148.630930	214.582754	312.093725	456.303216	984.067974
30	37.538681	40.568079	47.575416	56.084938	79.058186	113.283211	164.494023	241.332684	356.786847	530.311731	1181.881569
31	39.101761	42.379441	50.002678	59.328335	84.801677	123.345868	181.943425	271.292606	407.737005	616.161608	1419.257883
32	40.688288	44.227030	52.502759	62.701469	90.889778	134.213537	201.137767	304.847719	465.820186	715.747465	1704.109459
33	42.298612	46.111570	55.077841	66.209527	97.343165	145.950620	222.251544	342.429446	532.035012	831.267059	2045.931351
34	43.933091	48.033802	57.730177	69.857909	104.183755	158.626670	245.476699	384.520979	607.519914	965.269789	2456.117621
35	45.592088	49.994478	60.462082	73.652225	111.434780	172.316804	271.024368	431.663496	693.572702	1120.712955	2948.341146
36	47.275969	51.994367	63.275944	77.598314	119.120867	187.102148	299.126805	484.463116	791.672880	1301.027027	3539.009375
37	48.985109	54.034255	66.174223	81.702246	127.268119	203.070320	330.039486	543.598690	903.507083	1510.191352	4247.811250
38	50.789885	56.114940	69.159449	85.970336	135.904206	220.315945	364.043434	609.830533	1030.998075	1752.821968	5098.373500
39	52.480683	58.237238	72.234233	90.409150	145.058458	238.941221	401.447778	684.010197	1176.337806	2034.273483	6119.048200
40	54.267894	60.401983	75.401260	95.025516	154.761966	259.056519	442.592556	767.091420	1342.025098	2360.757240	7343.857840

TABLE 4. Present Value of an Annuity of 1 $P = \left[\dfrac{1 - \dfrac{1}{(1+i)^n}}{i}\right]$

	1½ %	2%	3%	4%	6%	8%	10%	12%	14%	16%	20%
1	.985222	.980392	.970874	.961538	.943396	.925926	.909091	.892857	.877193	.862069	.833333
2	1.955863	1.941561	1.913470	1.886095	1.833393	1.783265	1.735537	1.690051	1.646660	1.605232	1.527779
3	2.912200	2.883883	2.828611	2.775091	2.673012	2.577097	2.486852	2.401831	2.321631	2.245890	2.106482
4	3.854385	3.807729	3.717098	3.629895	3.465106	3.312127	3.169865	3.037349	2.913712	2.798181	2.588735
5	4.782645	4.713460	4.579707	4.451822	4.212364	3.992710	3.790787	3.604776	3.433080	3.274294	2.990613
6	5.697187	5.601431	5.417191	5.242137	4.917324	4.622880	4.355261	4.111407	3.888667	3.684736	3.325511
7	6.598214	6.471991	6.230283	6.002055	5.582381	5.206370	4.868419	4.563757	4.288304	4.038565	3.604592
8	7.485925	7.325481	7.019692	6.732745	6.209794	5.746639	5.334926	4.967640	4.638864	4.343590	3.837160
9	8.360517	8.162237	7.786109	7.435332	6.801692	6.246888	5.759024	5.328250	4.946372	4.606543	4.030967
10	9.222185	8.982585	8.530203	8.110896	7.360087	6.710081	6.144567	5.650223	5.216115	4.833227	4.192472
11	10.171118	9.786848	9.252624	8.760477	7.886875	7.138964	6.495061	5.937699	5.452733	5.028644	4.327060
12	10.907505	10.575341	9.954004	9.385074	8.383844	7.536078	6.813692	6.194374	5.660292	5.197107	4.439217
13	11.731532	11.348374	10.634955	9.985648	8.852683	7.903776	7.103356	6.423548	5.842361	5.342334	4.532681
14	12.543382	12.106249	11.296073	10.563123	9.294984	8.244237	7.366687	6.628168	6.002071	5.467529	4.610567
15	13.343233	12.849264	11.937935	11.118387	9.712249	8.559479	7.606080	6.810864	6.142168	5.575456	4.675473
16	14.131264	13.577709	12.561102	11.652296	10.105895	8.851369	7.823709	6.973986	6.265060	5.668497	4.729561
17	14.907649	14.291872	13.166118	12.165669	10.477260	9.121638	8.021553	7.119630	6.372859	5.748704	4.774634
18	15.672561	14.992031	13.753513	12.659297	10.827603	9.371887	8.201412	7.249670	6.467420	5.817848	4.812195
19	16.426168	15.678462	14.323799	13.133939	11.158116	9.603599	8.364920	7.365777	6.550369	5.877455	4.843496
20	17.168639	16.351433	14.877475	13.590326	11.469921	9.818147	8.513564	7.469444	6.623130	5.928841	4.869580
21	17.900137	17.011209	15.415024	14.029160	11.764077	10.016803	8.648694	7.562003	6.686957	5.973139	4.891316
22	18.620824	17.658048	15.936917	14.451115	12.041582	10.200744	8.771540	7.644646	6.742944	6.011326	4.909430
23	19.330862	18.292204	16.443608	14.856842	12.303379	10.371059	8.883218	7.718434	6.792056	6.044247	4.924525
24	20.030405	18.913926	16.935542	15.246963	12.550358	10.528758	8.984744	7.784316	6.835137	6.072627	4.937104
25	20.719611	19.523457	17.413148	15.622080	12.783356	10.674776	9.077040	7.843139	6.872927	6.097092	4.947587
26	21.398632	20.121036	17.876842	15.982769	13.003166	10.809978	9.160945	7.895660	6.906077	6.118183	4.956323
27	22.067618	20.706898	18.327031	16.329586	13.210534	10.935165	9.237223	7.942553	6.935155	6.136364	4.963602
28	22.726717	21.281272	18.764108	16.663063	13.406164	11.051078	9.306567	7.984423	6.960662	6.152038	4.969668
29	23.376076	21.844385	19.188455	16.983715	13.590721	11.158406	9.369606	8.021806	6.983037	6.165550	4.974724
30	24.015838	22.396456	19.600441	17.292033	13.764831	11.257783	9.426914	8.055184	7.002664	6.177198	4.978936
31	24.646146	22.937702	20.000429	17.588494	13.929086	11.349799	9.479013	8.084986	7.019881	6.187240	4.982447
32	25.267139	23.468335	20.388766	17.873551	14.084043	11.434999	9.526376	8.111594	7.034983	6.195897	4.985373
33	25.878955	23.988564	20.765792	18.147646	14.230230	11.513888	9.569432	8.135352	7.048231	6.203359	4.987810
34	26.481729	24.498592	21.131837	18.411198	14.368141	11.586934	9.608575	8.156564	7.059852	6.209792	4.989842
35	27.075595	24.998619	21.487220	18.664613	14.498246	11.654568	9.644159	8.175504	7.070045	6.215338	4.991535
36	27.660684	25.488843	21.832253	18.908282	14.620987	11.717193	9.676508	8.192414	7.078987	6.220119	4.992946
37	28.237127	25.969453	22.167235	19.142579	14.736780	11.775179	9.705917	8.207513	7.086831	6.224241	4.994122
38	28.805052	26.440641	22.492462	19.367864	14.846019	11.828869	9.732651	8.220993	7.093711	6.227794	4.995101
39	29.364583	26.902589	22.808215	19.584485	14.949075	11.878582	9.756956	8.233030	7.099747	6.230857	4.995918
40	29.915845	27.355479	23.114772	19.792774	15.046297	11.924613	9.779051	8.243777	7.105041	6.233497	4.996598

IS CURRENT VALUE REALLY PRESENT WORTH?

KEITH E. STEEVES, C.A.
Vice President–Finance and Treasurer

Bethlehem's annual reports for 1974 and 1975 stressed the need to recognize the effect of inflation in financial records and in taxing legislation. This year's balance sheet contains a restatement of accounts developed by applying current value accounting techniques which, it is felt, are more suitable than price level accounting as a method for demonstrating the effects of inflation on your company.

When reviewing the current value information, it should be borne in mind that a great degree of judgment has necessarily been exercised in assigning values to those areas where market information is not readily available. Assets not readily marketable are difficult to value, unlike such things as cash and traded securities. Mineral properties which are not currently in production or scheduled for production are good examples of assets which, being seldom traded, have no ready market.

Bethlehem's operating Iona and Jersey mines, equipment and support facilities can with assurance be assigned a present value by making arbitrary, but realistic, assumptions of metal prices and costs, and discounting to present dollar equivalents future cash flows to be produced by those assets. However, when placing a present value on the other ore reserves in Highland Valley which will eventually be processed through existing mill facilities, one must make assumptions about the timing of commencement of production. The date of commencement of Lake Zone production, though Bethlehem considers it to be presently economic, is dependent on a development decision by Valley Copper. While it is hoped that Lake Zone production will come sooner, it has been assumed for present valuing purposes that it will not occur until 1982. As in the case of the Iona and Jersey orebodies, the present value of the Lake Zone has been calculated by anticipating future metal prices, operating costs and the additional capital costs required to place the orebody into production and discounting to present dollars the resultant cash flows.

Recent studies based on block caving techniques indicate that the J-A orebody may be brought into production much sooner than previously anticipated although an actual production date is still uncertain. Existing mill capacity should be adequate if these studies confirm that the J-A can be brought into production upon exhaustion of the Iona and Jersey ore reserves. However, a decision by Valley to place the Lake Zone orebody into production would make it necessary for Bethlehem to expand the mill capacity to allow processing of ore from both Lake Zone and J-A when the Iona and Jersey Mines phase out. This would affect the present value of the J-A because the costs of developing it would then likely include some cost of mill expansion. Because of these uncertainties, the J-A has been assigned a present value limited to replacement cost. If there were an established market for ore reserves, which there is not, the best evidence of replacement cost would, of course, be the price required to purchase a similar orebody. The logical alternative used in these statements was to take actual J-A development costs and escalate them, by an appropriate factor, from the date expenditures were incurred to their present dollar equivalent. The weakness in this alternative is that it assigns the orebody no "discovery" value, an important factor when one considers the thousands of prospects that must be culled to find a mine.

Though somewhat more remote in development potential than the J-A, it is believed that the Maggie property will also be a producing mine at some future date. Accordingly, it was afforded the same current value treatment as the J-A.

Calculations have been limited to valuing the physical assets of the company, no attempt being made to assess the worth of so-called intangible assets, such as the trained work force, the technical expertise of management, the relationships with customers, suppliers and the financial community. All are recognized assets of the company.

Current values recorded in the balance sheet for this year have been prepared considering all these factors. As noted at the outset, one must remember that the current values have been based on management's best judgments formed under conditions existing at the time the statements were prepared. As economic conditions affect the assumptions used in preparing the calculations, the resultant current values will change. For this reason, it will always be difficult to compare current values for one year with those of another year even if assets remain the same.

Despite recognized shortcomings of current value calculations, it is believed the information provided will assist shareholders in making a realistic assessment of their company.

Consolidated Statement of Earnings
for the years ended December 31, 1976 and 1975

	(in thousands)	
	1976	1975 (Restated)
Revenues:		
Concentrate sales	**$ 24,374**	$ 22,800
Interest and investment income	**4,504**	4,461
	$ 28,878	$ 27,261
Expenses:		
Cost of sales and general and administrative	**$ 22,054**	$ 17,416
Depreciation	**3,241**	2,361
Exploration	**1,296**	936
	$ 26,591	$ 20,713
	$ 2,287	$ 6,548
Income and Resource Taxes (Note 7)	**896**	4,127
Earnings before extraordinary item	**$ 1,391**	$ 2,421
Extraordinary Item:		
Share of gain on sale of petroleum properties by an unconsolidated affiliate	**294**	—
Net Earnings (Note 2)	**$ 1,685**	$ 2,421
Earnings per Share (Note 8):		
Before extraordinary item	**$ .22**	$ .39
After extraordinary item	**$ .27**	$ .39

Consolidated Statement of Retained Earnings
for the years ended December 31, 1976 and 1975

	(in thousands)	
	1976	1975 (Restated)
Balance, Beginning of Year, as restated (Note 2)	**$ 57,489**	$ 58,819
Add: Net earnings (Note 2)	**1,685**	2,421
	$ 59,174	$ 61,240
Deduct: Dividends (Note 4)	**3,759**	3,751
Balance, End of Year	**$ 55,415**	$ 57,489

The accompanying notes to consolidated financial statements are an integral part of these statements.

Consolidated Balance Sheet

December 31, 1976 and 1975

ASSETS

CURRENT VALUE (in thousands) 1976 (Unaudited—Note 9)		(in thousands) 1976	1975 (Restated)
	Current Assets:		
$ 44,817	Cash and short-term deposits	**$ 44,817**	$ 53,509
9,849	Marketable securities, at lower of cost or market (market value $9,849; 1975—$7,156)	**8,870**	6,975
514	Accounts receivable	**514**	996
106	Income and other taxes receivable	**115**	—
	Inventories—		
5,380	Concentrate (Note 2)	**5,380**	2,865
4,146	Materials and supplies, at average cost	**3,776**	3,754
$ 64,812	Total current assets	**$ 63,472**	$ 68,099
$ 4,075	**Investments** (Note 3)	**$ 2,047**	$ 1,893
	Capital Assets, at cost:		
	Buildings, equipment and roads	**$ 38,230**	$ 31,808
	Less: Accumulated depreciation	**14,680**	11,936
		$ 23,550	$ 19,872
	Mineral claims	**334**	375
	Land	**2,472**	2,392
$ 85,637		**$ 26,356**	$ 22,639
$154,524		**$ 91,875**	$ 92,631

On behalf of the board:

J.A. McLallen, Director

P.M. Reynolds, Director

The accompanying notes to consolidated financial statements are an integral part of this statement.

LIABILITIES AND SHAREHOLDERS' EQUITY

	(in thousands)		CURRENT VALUE (in thousands)
	1976	1975 (Restated)	1976 (Unaudited—Note 9)
Current Liabilities:			
Accounts payable and accrued liabilities	**$ 7,245**	$ 4,166	$ 7,245
Income and other taxes payable	**—**	2,623	—
Total current liabilities	**$ 7,245**	$ 6,789	$ 7,245
Long-Term Liabilities	**$ 480**	$ 502	$ 337
Accumulated Provision for Future Income and Resource Taxes	**$ 3,139**	$ 2,486	$ 2,231
Shareholders' Equity:			
Share capital (Note 4)—			
Outstanding—			
6,471,297 shares without par value (1975—6,442,797 shares)	**$ 3,495**	$ 3,264	
Contributed surplus	**24,274**	24,274	
Retained earnings	**55,415**	57,489	
	$ 83,184	$ 85,027	
Less: 193,600 shares owned by the Company	**2,173**	2,173	
	$ 81,011	$ 82,854	$144,711
	$ 91,875	$ 92,631	$154,524

Notes to Consolidated Financial Statements

December 31, 1976 and 1975

1. SIGNIFICANT ACCOUNTING POLICIES

(a) Principles of Consolidation

The accounts of those subsidiary companies in which the Company holds at least a 50% ownership interest are consolidated in these statements. The Company's interest in affiliated companies, in which it has significant but not majority share ownership, is accounted for on the equity method.

(b) Currency Translation

Current assets in U.S. funds were translated into Canadian funds at the rate of exchange applicable at the balance sheet date.

(c) Exploration and Development Costs

Exploration and development costs are expensed until an orebody is considered to have economic feasibility, at which time all further costs are capitalized and written-off against future production revenue from that orebody.

(d) Depreciation

Depreciation of mine buildings, mill equipment and roads is on a straight-line basis over the estimated life of the ore reserves available to the mill. Mobile equipment is depreciated on a unit-of-use basis over its estimated productive life. Surface and mineral rights are recorded at original cost without amortization.

(e) Concentrate Sales

Prior to 1976, the Company recorded as revenue the net realizable value of concentrate when produced based on average metal prices for the month of production. The Company has revised its accounting policy to record revenue at the time of shipment to customers. Concentrate inventories are adjusted at the end of each accounting period to the lower of production cost or net realizable value. The comparative financial information for the year ended December 31, 1975 has been restated to conform to the present accounting policy.

2. RESTATEMENT OF 1975 CONSOLIDATED FINANCIAL STATEMENTS

The 1975 consolidated financial statements have been restated as follows:

	(in thousands)
Retained earnings—	
Balance, beginning of year, as previously reported	$ 58,885
Adjustment, net of taxes, for the change in the accounting policy for concentrate sales as set out in Note 1	(205)
Overprovision of the 1974 Mineral Land Tax	139
As restated	$ 58,819
Net earnings—	
As previously reported	$ 2,390
Adjustment for the change in accounting policy, as above	205
Adjustment, net of taxes, for additional smelter charges payable in accordance with an arbitration decision	(174)
As restated	$ 2,421

3. INVESTMENTS

The Company holds the following investments:

Investments in Unconsolidated Affiliates	Approx. Ownership	Recorded At	1976 (in thousands)	1975
Frio Oil Ltd.	36.5%	Equity	$ 474	$ 194
Minera Xitle S.A. de C.V.	49%	Equity	27	37
Other Investments				
Ionarc Smelters Ltd.	10%	Lower of cost or market	90	118
Valley Copper Mines Limited (N.P.L.)	5%	Cost	1,046	1,046
Other shares		Lower of cost or market	—	60
Employee housing agreements and property		Cost	301	330
Bonds, debentures and miscellaneous investments		Lower of cost or market	109	108
			$ 2,047	$ 1,893

The quoted value of marketable securities included above was $3,105,000 at December 31, 1976 and $4,442,000 at December 31, 1975.

4. SHARE CAPITAL

The authorized capital of the Company comprises 10,000,000 Class A and 10,000,000 Class B shares. The two classes of shares are freely inter-convertible and have the same rights in every respect. The Company distributes tax paid dividends on Class B shares by paying a 15% tax on certain surplus accounts of the Company from which the dividends are paid. The dividends on Class B shares are, therefore, 15% less than the dividends paid on Class A shares. As at December 31, 1976, 6,312,209 Class A shares (193,600 of which were owned by the Company) and 159,088 Class B shares were outstanding.

As at December 31, 1976, officers and employees held unexercised options to purchase a total of 155,000 shares exercisable in varying amounts to December 31, 1981, at prices ranging from $9.56 to $12.00 per share. Options for

28,500 shares were exercised during the year ended December 31, 1976, for a total cash consideration of $231,000. Options to purchase 145,000 shares at prices ranging from $11.14 to $12.00 per share were granted during the year.

Regulations made pursuant to the Anti-Inflation Act limit the amount of dividends which the Company may pay during the twelve months ending October 13, 1977, to a maximum of 86.4¢ per share.

5. REMUNERATION OF DIRECTORS AND SENIOR OFFICERS

The aggregate direct remuneration of directors and senior officers for the year ended December 31, 1976 amounted to $549,000 (1975—$547,000).

6. PENSION AND RETIREMENT PLANS

The Company has two voluntary pension plans for staff employees. The basic plan covers all staff employees who elect to participate and the executive plan provides supplementary pension benefits to 11 senior management personnel. Company policy is to currently fund all pension costs, including past service costs, and to update actuarial valuations once every three years. Actuarial valuations obtained as at December 31, 1974 indicated that pension plan assets exceeded vested benefits.

7. MINERAL LAND TAX ACT

The provisions of the British Columbia Mineral Land Tax Act, as they relate to the assessments based on the value of the Company's production, were rescinded effective January 1, 1976.

An action commenced in 1975 by the Company, together with 17 other mining companies, to challenge the constitutionality of the Act was discontinued. Subsequent to December 31, 1976, the Company commenced a separate action challenging the validity of the Regulations made pursuant to the Act, under which a total of $1,774,000 was paid in respect of the years ending December 31, 1975 and 1974.

8. EARNINGS PER SHARE

Earnings per share on Class A and Class B shares are based on the weighted average number of shares outstanding during the year. The exercise of the share options referred to in Note 4 would not have a dilutive effect on the earnings per share.

9. SIGNIFICANT ACCOUNTING POLICIES FOR CURRENT VALUE ACCOUNTS (unaudited)

The underlying principle in determining the current value of assets is to state them at their fair market value or replacement value.

The value of ore reserves considered economic under present conditions and the plant and equipment that will be used in exploiting the reserves has been determined by estimating future cash flows (net of future taxes) expected from such production and by discounting those cash flows to present dollar equivalents.

Mineral deposits not currently scheduled for production have been valued by restating the costs incurred in determining the reserves to present dollar equivalents. The methods used to determine the current values of ore reserves and related capital assets are described more fully on pages 8 to 11 and 16 of this annual report.

Marketable securities are stated at quoted market; materials and supplies at replacement cost; investments at appraised values; long-term liabilities and accumulated provision for future income and resource taxes at present dollar equivalents of future payments.

Auditors' Report

To the Shareholders,
BETHLEHEM COPPER CORPORATION:

We have examined the consolidated balance sheet of BETHLEHEM COPPER CORPORATION (a British Columbia company) and subsidiaries as of December 31, 1976 and 1975, and the consolidated statements of earnings, retained earnings and changes in financial position for the years then ended. Our examination was made in accordance with generally accepted auditing standards, and accordingly included such tests of the accounting records and such other auditing procedures as we considered necessary in the circumstances.

In our opinion, the accompanying consolidated financial statements present fairly the financial position of Bethlehem Copper Corporation and subsidiaries as of December 31, 1976 and 1975 and the results of their operations and changes in their financial position for the years then ended, in conformity with generally accepted accounting principles applied on a consistent basis after giving retroactive effect to the change in the timing of the recognition of concentrate sales, as explained in Note 1 to the consolidated financial statements.

The accompanying consolidated current value balance sheet of Bethlehem Copper Corporation as of December 31, 1976 has been prepared on the basis summarized in Note 9 to the consolidated financial statements and in pages 8 to 11 and 16 of this annual report. Because future developments could significantly change estimated values, there can be no assurance that estimates of values reflected in the current value balance sheet may not change. We have not audited the consolidated current value balance sheet and, therefore, express no opinion on it.

March 15, 1977
Vancouver, Canada.

ARTHUR ANDERSEN & CO.
Chartered Accountants

Five Year Summary

(all dollar amounts in thousands except per share figures)

OPERATIONS	**1976**	1975	1974	1973	1972
Concentrate sales	**$ 24,374**	$ 22,800	$ 40,001	$ 49,712	$ 23,382
Average price per lb. of copper—U.S. cents	**63.70**	56.02	93.41	80.00	48.36
Investment income	**$ 4,798**	$ 4,461	$ 4,865	$ 3,622	$ 2,331
Net earnings	**$ 1,685**	$ 2,421	$ 9,679	$ 20,352	$ 8,693
—per share	**$ .27**	$ .39	$ 1.52	$ 3.17	$ 1.36
Number of shares issued	**6,277,697**	6,249,197	6,241,697	6,422,897	6,397,797
Dividends on shares	**$ 3,759**	$ 3,751	$ 5,126	$ 4,491	$ 3,837
—per share	**$ .60**	$ .60	$ .80	$ .70	$ .60
Capital expenditures	**$ 6,999**	$ 4,215	$ 6,952	$ 937	$ 2,943
Employment					
—employment cost	**$ 7,252**	$ 6,197	$ 6,041	$ 5,077	$ 4,743
—number of employees	**402**	398	408	390	400
Exploration expense	**$ 1,296**	$ 936	$ 2,814	$ 5,445	$ 456
Income and resource taxes	**$ 896**	$ 4,127	$ 10,214	$ 10,422	$ 495
Production					
—dry tons milled (000)	**7,456**	6,465	6,346	6,339	5,965
—average head grade—%	**.44**	.47	.51	.58	.54
—pounds of copper produced (000)	**55,123**	54,630	57,089	67,086	58,244
FINANCIAL POSITION					
Assets employed:					
Current Assets	**$ 63,472**	$ 68,099	$ 68,190	$ 68,731	$ 38,823
Deduct: Current Liabilities	**7,245**	6,789	4,302	6,830	3,658
Working capital	**$ 56,227**	$ 61,310	$ 63,888	$ 61,901	$ 35,165
Capital assets	**26,356**	22,639	20,916	16,309	21,744
Investments	**2,047**	1,893	1,640	2,452	2,444
	$ 84,630	$ 85,842	$ 86,444	$ 80,662	$ 59,353
Represented by:					
Long-term debt	**$ 480**	$ 502	$ 440	$ 535	$ 623
Accumulated provision for future income and resource taxes	**3,139**	2,486	1,800	1,546	4,835
Shareholders' equity	**81,011**	82,854	84,204	78,581	53,895
	$ 84,630	$ 85,842	$ 86,444	$ 80,662	$ 59,353
Return on Assets employed	**2.0%**	2.8%	11.2%	25.2%	14.6%
Return on shareholders' equity	**2.1%**	2.9%	11.5%	25.9%	16.1%
Price range of shares traded on Toronto Stock Exchange	**$14¾-10⅜**	$13-8½	$16½-8½	$18-13	$23-14

Results for 1972 and 1973 have not been restated for the change in accounting policy for concentrate sales as set out in Note 1 to the financial statements. The cumulative effect has been included in the 1974 results.

MAJESTIC WILEY CONTRACTORS LIMITED
And Its Subsidiaries

CONSOLIDATED STATEMENT OF INCOME

FOR THE YEAR ENDED DECEMBER 31, 1976
(With 1975 figures for comparison)

	1976	1975
Revenues (Notes 1(b) and (f))	$125,093,000	$108,106,000
Cost of Operations (Note 1(f))	117,699,000	98,582,000
Gross Profit From Operations	7,394,000	9,524,000
General And Administrative Expenses	1,700,000	1,861,000
Income From Operations	5,694,000	7,663,000
Other Items:		
Other income and expenses, net	544,000	242,000
Interest on long-term debt	(240,000)	(695,000)
Total other items	304,000	(453,000)
Income Before Income Taxes	5,998,000	7,210,000
Provision For Income Taxes (Note 1(e))	3,179,000	3,676,000
Net Income	$ 2,819,000	$ 3,534,000
Earnings Per Share:		
On weighted average number of shares outstanding (1976 - 8,269,793 shares; 1975 - 8,262,375 shares)	34.0c	42.7c

The accompanying notes are an integral part of the consolidated financial statements.

CONSOLIDATED STATEMENT OF RETAINED EARNINGS

FOR THE YEAR ENDED DECEMBER 31, 1976
(With 1975 figures for comparison)

	1976	1975
Balance, Beginning of Year	$4,440,000	$ 906,000
Net Income	2,819,000	3,534,000
Balance, End of Year	$7,259,000	$4,440,000

The accompanying notes are an integral part of the consolidated financial statements.

MAJESTIC WILEY CONTRACTORS LIMITED
And Its Subsidiaries

CONSOLIDATED BALANCE SHEET

AS AT DECEMBER 31, 1976
(With 1975 figures for comparison)

Assets

	1976	1975
Current Assets:		
Cash, including certificates of deposit of $8,941,000 (1975 - $2,968,000)	$ 8,799,000	$ 2,784,000
Accounts receivable	3,294,000	4,649,000
Unbilled work (Note 1(b))	3,724,000	1,599,000
Equity in construction joint ventures including note receivable, at underlying book value (Note 1(f))	1,743,000	1,233,000
Prepaid expenses	127,000	559,000
Total current assets	17,687,000	10,824,000
Property And Equipment, at cost (Note 1(d)):		
Land	23,000	25,000
Buildings and improvements	907,000	815,000
Construction equipment	37,780,000	37,617,000
Other	196,000	201,000
	38,906,000	38,658,000
Less accumulated depreciation	22,909,000	19,690,000
Net property and equipment	15,997,000	18,968,000
Operating Authorities And Incorporation Expenses, at cost	193,000	193,000
	$33,877,000	$29,985,000

Approved by the Board:

J. M. Dawkins Director

V. N. Opadchuk Director

The accompanying notes are an integral part of the consolidated financial statements.

Liabilities and Shareholders' Equity

	1976	1975
Current Liabilities:		
Accounts payable	$ 448,000	$ 794,000
Accrued liabilities	812,000	737,000
Advance payment on contract in progress (Note 2)	1,374,000	—
Deferred contract revenue (Note 1(b))	1,194,000	349,000
Income taxes payable	5,843,000	3,190,000
Accrual for loss on contract in progress (Note 6(a))	—	349,000
Current portion of long-term debt (Note 3)	49,000	49,000
Total current liabilities	9,720,000	5,468,000
Long-Term Debt (Note 3)	3,116,000	5,209,000
Deferred Income Taxes (Note 1(e))	2,885,000	3,975,000
Shareholders' Equity:		
Capital stock (Note 4):		
Authorized - 20,000,000 shares without nominal or par value		
Issued and fully paid - 8,269,866 shares (1975 - 8,266,533 shares)	7,815,000	7,811,000
Contributed surplus	3,082,000	3,082,000
Retained earnings	7,259,000	4,440,000
Total shareholders' equity	18,156,000	15,333,000
	$33,877,000	$29,985,000

MAJESTIC WILEY CONTRACTORS LIMITED
And Its Subsidiaries

CONSOLIDATED STATEMENT OF CHANGES IN WORKING CAPITAL

FOR THE YEAR ENDED DECEMBER 31, 1976
(With 1975 figures for comparison)

	1976	1975
Source Of Working Capital:		
Net income	$2,819,000	$3,534,000
Depreciation	3,871,000	4,506,000
Deferred income taxes	(1,090,000)	55,000
(Gain) on disposal of property and equipment	(24,000)	(75,000)
Provided by operations	5,576,000	8,020,000
Disposals of property and equipment	283,000	502,000
Proceeds from stock options exercised	4,000	10,000
Working capital provided	5,863,000	8,532,000
Use Of Working Capital:		
Additions to property and equipment	1,159,000	1,936,000
Reduction of long-term debt	2,093,000	3,991,000
Working capital used	3,252,000	5,927,000
Increase In Working Capital	2,611,000	2,605,000
Working Capital, Beginning of Year	5,356,000	2,751,000
Working Capital, End of Year	$7,967,000	$5,356,000

The accompanying notes are an integral part of the consolidated financial statements.

AUDITORS' REPORT

TO THE SHAREHOLDERS OF
MAJESTIC WILEY CONTRACTORS LIMITED:

We have examined the consolidated balance sheet of Majestic Wiley Contractors Limited (an Alberta corporation) and its subsidiaries as of December 31, 1976 and 1975 and the related consolidated statements of income, retained earnings and changes in working capital for the years then ended. Our examination was made in accordance with generally accepted auditing standards, and accordingly included such tests of the accounting records and such other auditing procedures as we considered necessary in the circumstances.

In our opinion, the accompanying consolidated financial statements present fairly the financial position of Majestic Wiley Contractors Limited and its subsidiaries as of December 31, 1976 and 1975 and the results of their operations and the changes in their working capital for the years then ended, in conformity with generally accepted accounting principles consistently applied during the periods.

Calgary, Alberta
February 8, 1977.

ARTHUR ANDERSEN & CO.
CHARTERED ACCOUNTANTS

MAJESTIC WILEY CONTRACTORS LIMITED
And Its Subsidiaries

NOTES TO CONSOLIDATED FINANCIAL STATEMENTS

DECEMBER 31, 1976 and 1975

1. **SUMMARY OF ACCOUNTING PRINCIPLES**

a) Principles of Consolidation

The consolidated financial statements are expressed in Canadian dollars and include the accounts of Majestic Wiley Contractors Limited and its subsidiaries, all of which are wholly-owned; Falcon Transport Ltd., Specialty Construction & Equipment Ltd., J. L. Cox & Son, Inc., Liard Construction Company Limited, Norm Keglovic Contracting Ltd., Klondike Contractors Limited and D. K. Industries Ltd.

All significant intercompany transactions and balances have been eliminated in consolidation.

b) Method of Accounting for Income on Contracts

Profits from construction contracts are recognized on the percentage of completion basis. The percentage of completion is determined by relating the actual cost of work performed to date, to the current estimated total cost of the respective contracts. When the current estimated costs to complete indicate a loss, such losses are recognized immediately for accounting purposes. Income from claims is recorded in the periods such claims are resolved.

Unbilled work represents the excess of contract costs and profits recognized to date, on the percentage of completion accounting method, over billings to date on certain contracts. Deferred contract revenue represents the excess of billings to date, over the amount of contract costs and profit recognized to date, on the percentage of completion accounting method for the remaining contracts.

c) Current Assets and Current Liabilities

Current assets and current liabilities on the consolidated balance sheet are based on a one year operating cycle. A change was made during 1976 from a two year operating cycle to conform to industry practice. Such change (all of which relates to the current portion of long-term debt) has been applied retroactively and resulted in an increase in working capital used of $1,361,000 in 1976 and $1,366,000 in 1975 and an increase in the balance of working capital at December 31, 1974 of $2,776,000.

d) Depreciable Property and Equipment

Depreciation has been provided on the declining-balance method for approximately 75% of the depreciable property and on the straight-line method for the remaining 25%. The estimated lives used are as follows:

Buildings and Improvements	10 to 25 years
Construction Equipment	3 to 10 years
Other Equipment	10 years

e) Income Taxes

The tax effects of all income and expense transactions are included in each year's consolidated statement of income regardless of the year the transactions are reported for tax purposes.

The deferred income taxes arise primarily from the difference between the depreciation claimed for tax purposes and the depreciation recorded in the accounts.

f) Joint Ventures

Investments in joint ventures are accounted for on the equity basis whereby investments are carried on the consolidated balance sheet at cost plus the Company's share of income to date less cash distributions. Included in investment in joint venture is a 6% note receivable due December 29, 1977 from Perini Corporation, which note was received by the Company as a partial non cash distribution from the joint venture. Although the note is due on December 29, 1977, the Company will receive its share of cash distributions made prior to that date should funds become available in the joint venture. The Company's pro rata share of revenue and expenses and changes in working capital have been included in the consolidated statements under the proportionate consolidation method.

Included in the consolidated statement of income is the Company's share of revenue relating to the construction of Section 2 of the Trans Alaska Pipeline Project. The amounts so included are approximately 87% and 79% respectively for the years ended December 31, 1976 and 1975. The Company's participation in the construction of Section 2 has now been completed.

g) Foreign Exchange Accounting

Transactions with, and the Company's share of revenue and expenses and changes in working capital of a United States based joint venture, as well as some balance sheet accounts resulting therefrom, are included in the consolidated financial statements on the basis on one Canadian dollar being equal to one American dollar. Likewise, long-term debt, that is repayable in American funds, is included in the consolidated financial statements on the basis of the Canadian dollar and the American dollar being equal. This rate approximates the year end exchange rate and the average rate for the year.

2. ADVANCE PAYMENT ON CONTRACT IN PROGRESS

Under the terms of a contract with Engineering Projects (India) Ltd., the client advanced $1,600,000 prior to the commencement of work. Such advance payment is secured by an irrevocable letter of credit to the client in the amount of the advance. Both the advance payment and the amount of the letter of credit will be reduced on a proportional basis upon the payment of monthly progress billings by the client.

3. LONG-TERM DEBT

	1976	1975	Rate of Interest
Bank term loan, repayable at $683,333 U.S. per quarter beginning April 1, 1975 (principal only)	$ —	$2,045,000	1¼% over Royal Bank of Canada U.S. prime rate
Lease purchase contract, repayable at $4,909 U.S. per month (principal and interest)	111,000	153,000	13.32%
Convertible debenture, to Perini Limited, due March 1, 1980	3,000,000	3,000,000	7%
Mortgage payable, due in annual installments of $6,000 U.S. plus interest	54,000	60,000	8%
	3,165,000	5,258,000	
Due within one year	49,000	49,000	
	$3,116,000	$5,209,000	

The bank term loan was secured by a floating charge debenture on all of the Company's assets. Repayment of the funds was guaranteed by the parent company (Perini Limited) and could be made in advance of the due date without an early payment penalty. At December 31, 1975, $4,105,000 had been repaid in advance.

The lease purchase contracts are collateralized by the pledge of specific equipment (cost $219,000).

The 7% convertible debenture is convertible into 300,000 shares without nominal or par value at any time prior to March 1, 1980.

The mortgage payable is secured by the land and improvements of a subsidiary company (cost $90,000).

Payments on long-term debt over the next five years are as follows:

1977	$ 49,000
1978	49,000
1979	31,000
1980	3,006,000
1981	6,000
	$3,141,000

4. CAPITAL STOCK

Majestic Wiley Contractors Limited has a stock option plan whereby certain key employees have been granted options exercisable during the period of five years from the date of the grant at a rate of 20% of the total optioned shares per year on a partially cumulative basis. Following is a synopsis of transactions and events which affected the number of shares held under option agreements during the year ended December 31, 1976:

Date Option Granted	Price Per Share	Opening Balance	Options Exercised	Options Expired	Closing Balance
April 22, 1971	$2.625	6,930	—	6,930	—
May 4, 1971.	$3.325	6,270	—	6,270	—
May 1, 1974	$3.74	105,062	—	18,836	86,226
July 24, 1974	$3.69	6,800	—	1,200	5,600
December 9, 1974.	$1.148	13,333	3,333	—	10,000
October 27, 1975	$2.12	9,200	—	1,380	7,820
		147,595	3,333	34,616	109,646

As of December 31, 1976, the following shares of the Company have been set aside:

For possible future stock options	6,936
For possible conversion of 7% convertible debenture	300,000
	306,936

Exercise of all stock options and conversion of the 7% debenture would not significantly dilute earnings per share.

5. REMUNERATION OF DIRECTORS AND SENIOR OFFICERS

The aggregate direct remuneration paid to the Directors and Senior Officers for the years ended December 31, 1976 and 1975 is as follows:

	1976		1975	
	Amount	Number	Amount	Number
Directors who are not Senior Officers	$ 6,000	3	$ 4,000	4
Directors who are also Senior Officers	265,000	3	265,000	2
	271,000	6	269,000	6
Senior Officers who are not Directors	369,000	5	342,000	6
	$640,000	11	$611,000	12

6. CONTINGENCIES

a) In connection with the contract for which a provision for future loss has been provided in the accounts, legal counsel is of the opinion that because of revised project requirements, the Company is entitled to renegotiate the unit prices, or failing agreement on revised unit prices, to calculate the contract price on a "cost plus" basis. Although negotiations are continuing, the client has not agreed with the position advanced by management and as a result a substantial claim has been filed by the Company.

The Company and its joint venture partners are currently negotiating with a client relating to a completed project in Alaska. These negotiations could lead to a settlement which could result in a significant increase in revenues.

The amount of any additional revenue that may be received cannot be accurately determined at this time, and in accordance with the Company's application of generally accepted accounting principles, as described in Note 1 (b), no portion of any additional revenue has been reflected in the accounts.

b) The Company has a pension plan which covers certain executive, professional, administrative and clerical employees, subject to certain specified service requirements. At December 31, 1976, the unfunded past service liability is approximately $313,000 (1975 - $353,000) which will be paid and charged to operations in equal amounts over the next 13 years. In each of the years ended December 31, 1976 and 1975, the total cost of the pension plan, including current and past service costs, amounted to $107,000.

c) The Company has a deferred profit sharing plan and an incentive compensation plan for certain key employees which provide for payments to be made to or on behalf of such employees based on the profitability of the Company. As at December 31, 1976, an amount of $204,000 (1975 - $255,000) has been charged to income under the terms of these plans.

d) An action was filed in January, 1976 against a pipe manufacturer and the Company in the amount of $7,000,000 for alleged breach of contract relating to construction methods which allegedly did not produce a satisfactory quality of work.

Management is of the opinion that the suit is without merit and has instructed legal counsel to enter its defense accordingly. The insurers are defending the action up to a maximum coverage of $5,000,000.

e) Other contingent liabilities include the usual liability of contractors for performance and completion of both Company and joint venture construction contracts.

7. FEDERAL ANTI-INFLATION LEGISLATION

On October 14, 1975, the Canadian Federal Government announced extensive controls, to which the Company and its subsidiaries are subject, on wages, prices, and dividends. Initially, the controls will be in effect until December 31, 1978 for wages and prices.

Dividend payments are controlled under the guidelines for the period October 14, 1976 to October 13, 1977. During this period, dividends cannot exceed $883,000.

In the opinion of management, the Company has complied with all of the regulations of the legislation.

GLOSSARY OF TERMS

NET SALES: The Canadian dollar proceeds from the sale of products after deducting costs of delivery to customers.

OPERATING PROFIT: Profit realized from manufacture and sale of products after deducting all costs except interest charges, depreciation and income taxes. Applies to operations only; does not include investment or other income.

DEPRECIATION: The distribution on a yearly basis of the original cost of a fixed asset (defined below) over its estimated useful life, which is written off as a deduction from earnings.

NET EARNINGS: Total income less all costs; the net amount available from the year's operations to pay dividends or retain for use in the business.

CASH FLOW: Total funds generated by operations in a year. In our case, cash flow includes net earnings and charges not affecting working capital; principally depreciation and deferred income taxes.

RETAINED EARNINGS: Accumulated total of annual net earnings since the start of the company (1936) less dividends to shareholders during the same period.

CURRENT ASSETS: Assets which, in the normal course, will be converted into cash or consumed in operations within the following year.

FIXED ASSETS: Assets, such as land, buildings and machinery, held for long-term use rather than for sale or consumption in operations.

CURRENT LIABILITIES: Amounts owed (including a portion of long-term debt) due for payment within one year.

LONG-TERM DEBT: Amounts borrowed for a term of longer than one year.

SINKING FUND: Amounts paid to independent trustees of our bond issues, as stipulated in the trust deeds of these issues, to provide annual instalments for their redemption.

WORKING CAPITAL: Amount by which current assets exceed current liabilities, both as defined above. This is a measure of working or operating resources.

BALANCE SHEET: Statement of financial position at a year end showing what is owned (assets of all kinds) versus what is owed (liabilities of all kinds) and shareholders' equity; set forth in accordance with The Business Corporations Act (Ontario). The word "Consolidated" means that all subsidiaries are included to show position of the enterprise as a whole.

SHAREHOLDERS' EQUITY: Value of the shareholders' ownership or interest in the company. Consists of share capital plus retained earnings and is the amount by which assets exceed liabilities.

AUDITORS' REPORT TO THE SHAREHOLDERS

To the Shareholders of The Great Lakes Paper Company, Limited

We have examined the consolidated balance sheet of The Great Lakes Paper Company, Limited as at December 31, 1976 and the consolidated statements of earnings, retained earnings and changes in financial position for the year then ended. Our examination was made in accordance with generally accepted auditing standards, and accordingly included such tests and other procedures as we considered necessary in the circumstances.

In our opinion, these consolidated financial statements present fairly the financial position of the company as at December 31, 1976 and the results of its operations and the changes in its financial position for the year then ended in accordance with generally accepted accounting principles applied on a basis consistent with that of the preceding year.

Toronto, Ontario, February 2, 1977
except for Note 13 which
is dated February 17, 1977

THORNE RIDDELL & CO.
Chartered Accountants

EARNINGS

consolidated statement for years ended December 31 (thousands of dollars)

	1976	1975
Net sales: pulp and paper	$124,371	$100,508
building products	11,943	5,259
	136,314	105,767
Cost of sales	110,769	78,509
Selling and administrative expense	3,389	2,764
OPERATING PROFIT	22,156	24,494
Other income	222	59
	22,378	24,553
Interest (Note 9)	3,979	2,764
Bond issue discount and expense	–	812
Depreciation	9,635	9,162
EARNINGS before income taxes	8,764	11,815
Income taxes	3,897	5,388
NET EARNINGS for year	$ 4,867	$ 6,427
Net earnings per share (Note 7)	$ 1.35	$ 1.78

RETAINED EARNINGS

consolidated statement for years ended December 31 (thousands of dollars)

	1976	1975
Retained earnings at beginning of year	$ 57,004	$ 50,577
Net earnings for year	4,867	6,427
RETAINED EARNINGS at end of year	$ 61,871	$ 57,004

BALANCE SHEET

consolidated statement at December 31 (thousands of dollars)

Assets	1976	1975
CURRENT ASSETS		
Accounts receivable	$ 26,082	$ 2,055
Income taxes recoverable	402	2,706
Inventories:		
Finished goods	1,219	404
Pulpwood and sawlogs	17,562	16,142
Materials and supplies	9,512	8,583
Prepaid expenses	271	295
	55,048	30,185
FIXED ASSETS (Note 2)	356,391	284,242
Accumulated depreciation and depletion	118,813	109,381
	237,578	174,861
	$292,626	$205,046

Approved by the Board:

C. J. CARTER, *Director*

R. G. MEECH, *Director*

Liabilities	1976	1975
CURRENT LIABILITIES		
Bank indebtedness (Note 5)	$ 72,655	$ 27,138
Accounts payable and accrued charges	22,072	16,887
Sundry taxes payable	4,173	1,866
Current portion of long-term debt	4,630	590
	103,530	46,481
LONG-TERM DEBT (Note 6)		
First Mortgage Bonds		
8% sinking fund bonds, Series B, maturing 1989	17,060	17,650
11¼% sinking fund bonds, Series C, maturing 1995	35,000	35,000
Term loan	40,000	13,000
	92,060	65,650
Portion due within one year	4,630	590
	87,430	65,060
DEFERRED INCOME TAXES	37,045	33,751
Shareholders' Equity		
Common shares without par value (Note 7)		
Authorized 4,500,000 shares		
Issued 3,610,029 shares	2,750	2,750
Retained earnings	61,871	57,004
	64,621	59,754
	$292,626	$205,046

CHANGES IN FINANCIAL POSITION

consolidated statement for years ended December 31 (thousands of dollars)

	1976	1975
WORKING CAPITAL PROVIDED BY		
Net earnings	$ 4,867	$ 6,427
Charges not affecting working capital		
Depreciation	9,635	9,162
Increase in deferred income taxes	3,294	7,447
Bond issue discount and expense	–	812
GENERATED FROM OPERATIONS	17,796	23,848
Proceeds from issue of First Mortgage Sinking Fund Bonds, Series C	–	34,188
Term loan	27,000	–
Sale of fixed assets	47	72
	44,843	58,108
WORKING CAPITAL USED FOR		
Expenditures on fixed assets	72,399	76,540
Reduction of long-term debt	4,630	590
	77,029	77,130
DECREASE IN WORKING CAPITAL	32,186	19,022
WORKING CAPITAL(DEFICIENCY) at beginning of year	(16,296)	2,726
WORKING CAPITAL (DEFICIENCY) at end of year	$(48,482)	$(16,296)

NOTES TO CONSOLIDATED FINANCIAL STATEMENTS Year ended December 31, 1976

1. Summary of Significant Accounting Policies

PRINCIPLES OF CONSOLIDATION

The consolidated financial statements include the financial position and results of operations of The Great Lakes Paper Company, Limited and all its subsidiary companies.

FOREIGN EXCHANGE

Current assets and current liabilities in foreign currencies are translated into Canadian dollars at current rates of exchange at the date of the balance sheet. Fixed assets and items affecting earnings are converted at rates of exchange in effect at the dates of the transactions.

INVENTORIES

Inventories are valued at average cost which is less than net realizable value.

FIXED ASSETS AND DEPRECIATION

Fixed assets are recorded at cost. The cost and related accumulated depreciation of items disposed of are removed from the accounts and any gain or loss is included in earnings. Depreciation is based on the estimated economic lives of the assets, using the following methods and composite rates of depreciation:

Buildings and Machinery	
Pulp and paper	4½% straight line
Building products	10% straight line
Woodlands improvements and equipment	30% diminishing balance

No depreciation is charged on major improvements or expansions until construction has been completed.

DEFERRED INCOME TAXES

Income taxes are charged against earnings based on the items included within the determination of those earnings irrespective of any timing difference for the recognition of certain items under current tax legislation. The excess of the income taxes charged to earnings over the amount actually payable in any year is set aside as deferred income taxes to be drawn upon in future years when tax payments exceed the amount charged to earnings.

INTEREST

Interest on debt incurred to finance major expansion programs, less any interest earned on the temporary investment of the proceeds, is capitalized during the construction period.

FULLY DILUTED EARNINGS PER SHARE

Fully diluted earnings per share are determined on the assumption that warrants and options outstanding at the end of the year were exercised at the beginning of the year and the funds therefrom invested to produce a return at the average interest rate for 90-day bank certificates of deposit.

2. Fixed Assets (thousands of dollars)

	December 31, 1976 Cost	December 31, 1976 Net Value	December 31, 1975 Net Value
Land	$ 482	$ 482	$ 476
Buildings and machinery			
Pulp and paper	307,803	210,559	53,947
Building products	23,549	18,856	20,904
Woodlands improvements and equipment	20,612	7,681	4,074
Timber licences	3,945	–	–
Construction in progress	–	–	95,460
	$356,391	$237,578	$174,861

3. Expansion Program

The company's new kraft pulp mill, which is the major component of the expansion program, commenced trial production runs in November 1976. The period from this date to December 31, 1976, during which time the various areas of the mill were being completed by the construction forces and run in by operating crews, has been treated as part of the construction period and, accordingly, the operating loss has been capitalized. For financial reporting purposes construction has been regarded as completed on December 31, 1976. In accordance with the company's accounting policy, interest on debt incurred to finance the construction has been capitalized to December 31, 1976, and no depreciation has been charged against earnings.

4. Lease Commitments

The company has signed leases (with options to purchase) covering certain portable camp buildings and mobile equipment for terms of three to 11 years. The payments under these leases amounted to $3.2 million in 1976. Based on leases in effect at December 31, 1976 payments over the next five years will amount to approximately $3 million in each of the years 1977 and 1978, and $2 million in each of the years 1979, 1980 and 1981. In addition, under a 1974 agreement, the company has $7.6 million of lease financing available for the acquisition of woodlands camp buildings and mobile equipment over the next two years. The terms of these leases will be similar to those described above.

5. Bank Indebtedness

The bank indebtedness is partially secured by an assignment of accounts receivable and charges on inventory.

6. Long-Term Debt

The Term loan, which bears a floating rate of interest, is payable to Canadian Pacific Securities Limited, a wholly-owned subsidiary of Canadian Pacific Investments Limited, the majority shareholder in the company.

Payments required to meet sinking fund provisions of the First Mortgage Bonds and the Term loan over the next five years approximate $4.6 million in 1977, $9.3 million in 1978, $9.4 million in 1979, $9.5 million in 1980 and $9.7 million in 1981.

7. Warrants and Options

Common shares were reserved at December 31, 1976 for the following:

(a) 200,000 shares for the common share purchase warrants which accompanied the First Mortgage Sinking Fund Bonds, Series B. The warrants are exercisable at $33.00 per share until July 1, 1979.

(b) 100,000 shares for a purchase option granted to Canadian Pacific Investments Limited. The option is exercisable at $24.00 per share until January 1, 1982. Both the number of shares and the price per share are subject to adjustment in the event additional shares are issued, other than pursuant to the warrants described above, or other changes in the company's capital structure.

Exercise of the above warrants and options would not have resulted in any dilution of the 1976 net earnings per share.

8. Dividend Restrictions

The trust deeds securing the First Mortgage Bonds contain dividend restrictions. The most restrictive of these requires that, after any dividend is declared, working capital (which for these purposes is before the deduction of the current portion of long-term debt) must be over $10 million and shareholders' equity must be over $50 million.

A further dividend restriction is imposed by the Federal Anti-Inflation Legislation described in note 12.

9. Interest

Interest for the year amounted to $9.5 million ($6.8 million in 1975) on long-term debt and $4.5 million ($103,000 in 1975) on bank indebtedness. Of these amounts, $10 million ($4.1 million in 1975) has been capitalized as described in note 3.

10. Executive Remuneration

In 1976, directors' fees amounted to $48,000. The total remuneration, including directors' fees, received by the directors and senior officers amounted to $483,000.

11. Past Service Pension Costs

Past service pension costs, resulting from retroactive increases in benefits in prior years, are being funded and charged to earnings in equal annual instalments to 1989. Based on recent actuarial reports, the unfunded amount was $3.2 million at December 31, 1976.

12. Federal Anti-Inflation Legislation

The company is subject to the Anti-Inflation Act which provides for the restraint of profit margins on domestic sales and compensation until December 31, 1978. To the best of the company's knowledge, it has complied with the provisions of this Act.

The Act also provides for limitations on the amount of dividends which may be declared during this period. The impact of these limitations on the company can only be determined at the time of declaration of a dividend.

13. Subsequent Events

Subsequent to December 31, 1976 the company has undertaken a refinancing plan, the proceeds of which will be applied to reduce the existing short-term bank indebtedness. The plan comprises the following:

(a) On February 17, 1977 the company approved the terms of an agreement providing for the subscription by a European banking syndicate for $20 million (U.S. funds) of 8¾ percent debentures due 1984 to be issued by the company.

(b) On February 17, 1977, the company approved arrangements with its bankers under which the company will borrow $30 million (U.S. funds) for a term of two years with the interest rate to be determined when the funds are drawn down.

FINANCIAL SUMMARY: LAST TEN YEARS

Except as indicated, dollars are in thousands with 000 omitted	1976	1975	1974	1973	1972	1971	1970
SALES & EARNINGS							
Net sales: pulp and paper	124,371	100,508	110,977	92,237	69,433	71,010	71,822
building products	11,943	5,259	3,465	584	–	–	–
total	136,314	105,767	114,442	92,821	69,433	71,010	71,822
Operating profit	22,156	24,494	35,441	21,360	10,892	13,446	15,728
Interest expense	3,979	2,764	1,733	1,859	2,043	2,306	2,537
Depreciation	9,635	9,162	7,267	6,454	6,085	5,843	5,873
Earnings before income taxes	8,764	11,815	26,625	13,161	2,927	5,747	8,820
Income taxes	3,897	5,388	11,687	5,540	1,319	2,510	4,475
Net earnings	4,867	6,427	14,938	7,621	1,608	3,237	4,345
Net earnings per share	1.35	1.78	4.14	2.11	0.45	0.90	1.21
Dividends declared, total amount	–	–	–	–	1,081	2,342	3,603
Dividends per share; in cents	–	–	–	–	30	65	100
ASSETS & LIABILITIES							
Current assets	55,048	30,185	27,692	30,191	24,940	25,535	33,324
Current liabilities	103,530	46,481	24,966	16,001	11,790	13,124	12,718
Ratio of above assets to liabilities	.5	.6	1.1	1.9	2.1	1.9	2.6
Working capital (deficiency)	(48,482)	(16,296)	2,726	14,190	13,150	12,411	20,606
Inventories, described in balance sheet	28,293	25,129	15,761	10,874	10,260	9,753	9,279
Fixed assets, see notes to financial statements	356,391	284,242	207,999	158,378	147,718	143,808	132,877
Accumulated depreciation and depletion	118,813	109,381	100,444	93,423	87,892	82,242	76,630
Long-term debt	87,430	65,060	30,650	23,025	25,430	27,766	32,167
Above debt as percentage of capitalization	57.5	52.1	36.5	37.5	45.4	48.0	52.5
Deferred income taxes	37,045	33,751	26,304	17,731	16,963	16,155	15,525
Retained earnings, at year end	61,871	57,004	50,577	35,639	28,018	27,491	26,596
EQUITY & OTHER DATA							
Common shares outstanding, at year end	3,610,029	3,610,029	3,610,029	3,610,029	3,602,603	3,602,603	3,602,603
Number of shareholders	3,116	3,529	3,745	4,035	4,470	4,919	5,209
Percentage of shares held in Canada	97.6	96.9	96.9	97.0	96.0	95.5	95.3
Shareholders' equity, total	64,621	59,754	53,327	38,389	30,583	30,056	29,161
Shareholders' equity per share	17.90	16.55	14.77	10.63	8.49	8.34	8.09
Cash flow from operations	17,796	23,848	30,778	14,843	8,501	9,710	9,963
Cash flow per share	4.93	6.61	8.53	4.11	2.36	2.70	2.77
Net earnings percentage on net sales	3.6	6.1	13.1	8.2	2.3	4.6	6.0
Annual expenditures on fixed assets	72,399	76,540	49,997	12,137	4,455	11,191	7,446
Number of employees on payroll	3,471	3,110	3,013	2,778	2,441	2,527	2,768

All per share figures are based on shares outstanding at the end of the respective years.

1969	1968	1967
71,267	62,541	66,192
–	–	–
71,267	62,541	66,192
17,951	14,455	17,511
2,036	1,440	1,673
6,528	6,881	7,506
10,446	6,359	8,510
5,407	3,270	4,300
5,039	3,089	4,210
1.40	0.86	1.17
3,603	3,603	3,602
100	100	100
41,073	21,360	20,655
14,739	14,221	12,485
2.8	1.5	1.7
26,334	7,139	8,170
9,440	9,184	11,464
126,227	124,057	122,643
71,392	65,309	59,111
36,970	21,343	25,686
56.5	43.7	47.8
15,780	17,030	18,480
25,854	24,949	25,463
3,602,603	3,602,603	3,602,603
5,418	6,202	6,402
93.1	94.2	93.8
28,419	27,514	28,028
7.89	7.64	7.78
10,317	8,520	13,630
2.86	2.36	3.78
7.1	4.9	6.4
2,704	2,222	3,671
2,857	2,693	2,590

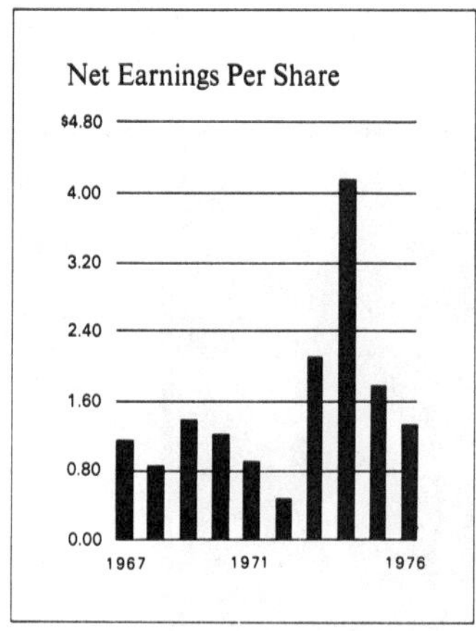

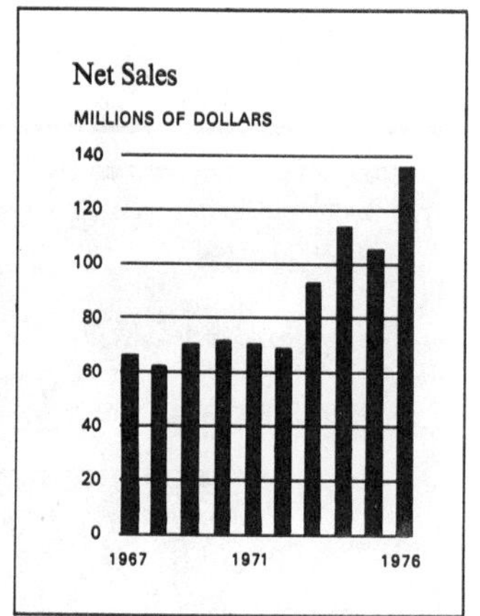

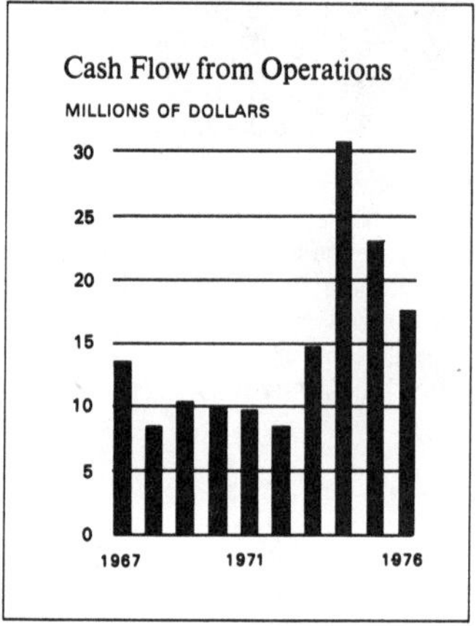

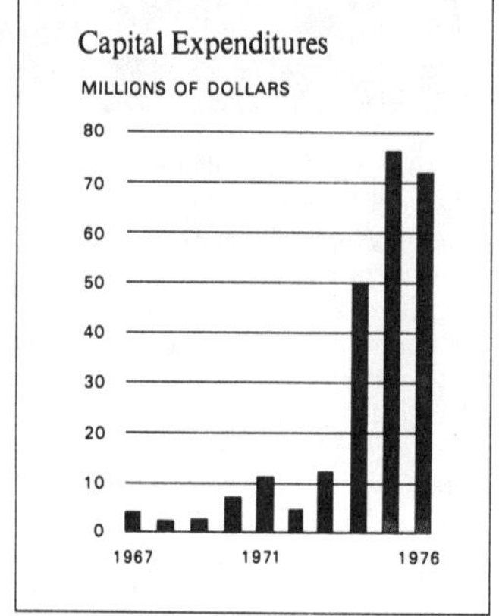

1976 Results by Quarters

Sales and Earnings '000 omitted

1976 Quarterly

Quarter	Net Sales	Oper. Profit	Net Earnings
First	$ 12,151	$(1,990)	$(3,193)
Second	41,027	7,688	2,510
Third	39,762	7,390	2,074
Fourth	43,374	9,068	3,476
	$136,314	$22,156	$ 4,867

Net Earnings Per Share

Quarter	1972	1973	1974	1975	1976
First	$(0.03)	$0.25	$0.99	$1.62	$(0.88)
Second	0.14	0.55	1.20	1.32	0.69
Third	0.14	0.52	1.59	0.33	0.58
Fourth	0.20	0.79	0.36	(1.49)	0.96
	$0.45	$2.11	$4.14	$1.78	$1.35

Inflation Accounting

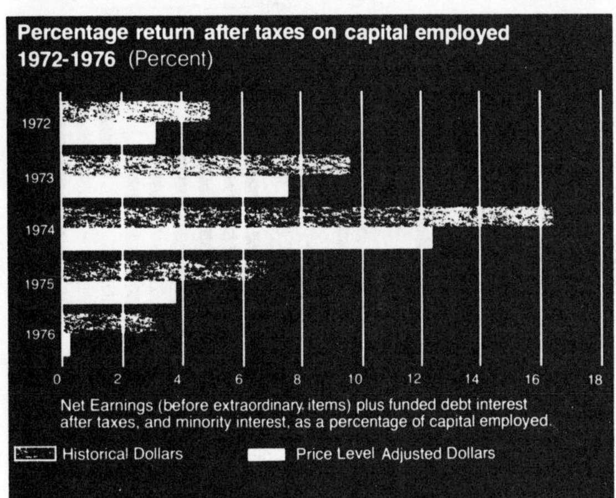

In 1976, inflation continued to be a significant factor in the Canadian economy even though it has declined from the levels of recent years. The methods to account properly for the impact of inflation are presently being examined in many countries including Canada. However, industry, the financial community and the accounting profession have not come to a consensus on a method of inflation adjusted accounting which should be adopted for financial reporting purposes.

The Company included supplemental statements in its Annual Report for the years 1974 and 1975 based on the general price-level concept. This concept was at that time accepted by the Canadian Institute of Chartered Accountants and endorsed by the Canadian Pulp and Paper Association as a method by which conventional historical cost financial statements could be amended to show the effects of inflation. General price-level restatement adjusts historical cost information for the decreases in general purchasing power. The deficiency of this concept relates to the use of a single measure of the change in the value of the monetary unit. Unless specific prices relating to a business have moved in an identical fashion, the use of a single measure of purchasing power change does not provide management with sufficiently precise information. Despite its limitations, the use of the general price-level concept recognizes in part the effect of changing prices and to that extent may be considered useful pending the development of a more meaningful concept.

Price-level adjusted figures have again been prepared for 1976 using the Consumer Price Index. In view of current developments which are directed towards the identification of more appropriate inflation accounting methods, particularly those which deal more specifically with current value measurements, the detailed summary of results and capital employed reported in prior years has been omitted from the Annual Report.

The application of price-level accounting concepts has the effect of restating the 1976 reported earnings of 68 cents per common share to a loss of 58 cents per common share.

A major impact of the application of price-level accounting as indicated on the graph is the reduction in the return on capital employed from 3.1% and 6.9% to 0.2% and 3.7% for 1976 and 1975 respectively.

Inflation accounting has become an issue of international concern. Exposure drafts, discussion papers and pronouncements have been issued by the professional accounting bodies in the major developed countries. In Great Britain, the Accounting Standards Committee has introduced proposals for inflation accounting which will require most stock exchange listed corporations to disclose current cost information in their annual financial statements by 1978.

In March, 1976, the Securities and Exchange Commission in the United States issued an Accounting Series Release which will require certain larger corporations which register with the Commission to provide financial disclosure of the current replacement cost of inventory and cost of sales, together with the replacement cost of productive plant and equipment and annual depreciation calculated on a replacement cost basis.

The Canadian Institute of Chartered Accountants recently prepared a discussion paper on current value accounting. A technical committee of the Institute, which includes representation from the Department of Finance of the Federal government, is now consulting widely on the practical problems of its implementation. The Company is actively participating in the work of this committee. The Province of Ontario has recently established a committee to study the impact of inflation on corporate finances and recommend a program of financial disclosure of the impacts of inflation in Ontario.

The Company is working closely with the Canadian Pulp and Paper Association to further research inflation accounting. Preliminary studies with the use of replacement values for fixed assets indicate a more significant adverse impact on earnings than the use of the general price-level concept. The Company is also committed to continue its participation with industry, government and professional bodies to develop a more meaningful profile of financial position during inflationary periods.

Domtar Limited and Subsidiary Companies

Consolidated Statement of Earnings and Retained Earnings

year ended December 31

	1976	1975
Revenue:		
Sales	**$886,768,907**	$815,221,364
Investment and sundry income	**9,608,165**	8,106,321
Gain on disposal of fixed assets	**1,612,051**	3,751,146
	897,989,123	827,078,831
Expenses:		
Cost of sales and selling and administrative expenses	**828,692,270**	725,548,977
Depreciation	**35,455,101**	31,695,409
Interest on funded debt	**13,292,673**	8,624,201
Interest on other indebtedness	**959,677**	913,330
	878,399,721	766,781,917
Earnings before income taxes and minority interest	**19,589,402**	60,296,914
Current income taxes	**3,730,000**	11,930,000
Deferred income taxes	**4,170,000**	11,970,000
Minority interest	**1,126,785**	1,109,400
	9,026,785	25,009,400
Net earnings	**10,562,617**	35,287,514
Retained earnings at beginning of year	**193,390,735**	182,362,092
	203,953,352	217,649,606
Dividends:		
Preference shares, $1 per share	**535,191**	535,191
Common shares, $1 per share (1975 — $1.60)	**14,827,300**	23,723,680
	15,362,491	24,258,871
Retained earnings at end of year	**$188,590,861**	$193,390,735
Earnings per common share	**$0.68**	$2.34

See accompanying summary of accounting policies and notes to financial statements

Domtar Limited and Subsidiary Companies

Consolidated Balance Sheet

December 31

Assets

	1976	1975
Current assets:		
Cash and short-term investments, at cost (approximates market value)	**$ 94,697,172**	$ 86,780,262
Receivables	**130,946,908**	112,058,539
Inventories	**145,892,291**	140,265,808
Prepaid expenses	**3,513,239**	2,661,706
	375,049,610	341,766,315
Investments and advances:		
Listed securities	**3,453,801**	3,453,801
Other investments and advances	**8,389,299**	10,849,181
	11,843,100	14,302,982
Fixed assets:		
Plant, machinery and facilities	**777,873,918**	743,466,245
Timber limits and land	**34,205,055**	28,447,942
	812,078,973	771,914,187
Less: Accumulated depreciation	**433,377,428**	407,608,849
	378,701,545	364,305,338
Intangible assets and deferred charges:		
Goodwill	**960,947**	—
Unamortized debt discount and expenses	**1,348,964**	993,795
	2,309,911	993,795
	$767,904,166	$721,368,430

APPROVED BY THE BOARD:

A. D. Hamilton, Director

M. C. G. Meighen, Director

Liabilities and Shareholders' Equity

	1976	1975
Current liabilities:		
Bank indebtedness	$ 7,765,135	$ 7,802,141
Payables	111,201,608	102,427,812
Income and other taxes	4,413,507	6,168,656
Dividends payable	3,193,446	6,175,067
Funded debt due within one year	512,000	—
	127,085,696	122,573,676
Funded debt	190,499,000	150,101,000
Deferred income taxes	102,542,500	97,747,000
Minority interest	13,865,298	12,235,208
Shareholders' equity:		
Capital stock—		
$1 cumulative redeemable preference shares, par value $23.50, redeemable at $25		
Authorized — 542,445 shares		
Outstanding — 535,191 shares	12,576,989	12,576,989
Common shares without nominal or par value		
Authorized — 25,000,000 shares		
Outstanding — 14,827,300 shares	132,743,822	132,743,822
Retained earnings	188,590,861	193,390,735
	333,911,672	338,711,546
	$767,904,166	$721,368,430

See accompanying summary of accounting policies and notes to financial statements

Domtar Limited and Subsidiary Companies

Consolidated Statement of Changes in Financial Position

year ended December 31

	1976	1975
Funds provided by:		
Net earnings	$ 10,562,617	$ 35,287,514
Gain on disposal of fixed assets	1,612,051	3,751,146
	8,950,566	31,536,368
Depreciation	35,455,101	31,695,409
Deferred income taxes	4,170,000	11,970,000
Minority interest	1,126,785	1,109,400
Other	85,679	—
Cash flow from operations	49,788,131	76,311,177
Issue of funded debt	48,854,152	49,006,205
Sale of investments	1,235,000	10,354,287
Disposal of fixed assets	2,983,300	3,869,109
	102,860,583	139,540,778
Funds used for:		
Fixed assets	42,946,960	56,932,267
Funded debt	8,897,000	7,986,000
Minority interest	1,058,672	1,122,161
Investments and advances	680,118	5,556,993
Dividends	15,362,491	24,258,871
Purchase of subsidiary companies, less $6,618,914 working capital at acquisition	5,144,067	—
	74,089,308	95,856,292
Increase in working capital	28,771,275	43,684,486
Working capital at beginning of year	219,192,639	175,508,153
Working capital at end of year	$247,963,914	$219,192,639
Changes in components of working capital:		
Receivables	$ 18,888,369	$ (18,594,117)
Inventories	5,626,483	(7,204,908)
Prepaid expenses	851,533	(130,778)
Payables	(8,773,796)	(7,099,455)
	16,592,589	(33,029,258)
Income and other taxes	1,755,149	35,843,310
Dividends payable	2,981,621	7,270
Funded debt due within one year	(512,000)	—
Net cash	7,953,916	40,863,164
Increase in working capital	$ 28,771,275	$ 43,684,486

See accompanying summary of accounting policies and notes to financial statements

Domtar Limited and Subsidiary Companies

Summary of Significant Accounting Policies

December 31, 1976

The Company follows the generally accepted accounting principles described below. These, together with the notes which follow, should be considered an integral part of the consolidated financial statements.

Principles of consolidation:
The accompanying financial statements include the accounts of Domtar Limited and all its subsidiary companies.

Translation of foreign currencies:
Current assets and current liabilities in foreign currencies are translated into Canadian dollars at current rates of exchange at December 31, 1976 or at rates related to forward exchange contracts. Fixed assets and related depreciation and other long-term assets and liabilities are translated at rates of exchange in effect at the dates of the transactions. Items affecting net earnings (other than depreciation) are translated at the average rates for the year.

Valuation of inventories:
Inventories of pulpwood, raw materials and operating and maintenance supplies are valued at the lower of cost and replacement cost. Finished goods, including work in process, are valued at the lower of cost and net realizable value.

Fixed assets and depreciation:
Fixed assets are recorded at cost. The cost and related accumulated depreciation of items retired or disposed of are removed from the books and any gains or losses are included in the consolidated statement of earnings. Depreciation is provided on the straight-line method using rates based on the estimated useful lives of the assets which are generally as follows:

Production machinery	12 — 16 years
Logging equipment	Up to 6 years
Automobiles	4 years
Buildings	Up to 40 years

Repairs and maintenance are charged against earnings as incurred.

Income taxes:
The Company provides for income taxes on the tax allocation basis. The Company follows the flow-through method of accounting for the 5% federal investment tax credit. The provision for deferred income taxes mainly arises as a result of depreciation being claimed for income tax purposes in excess of amounts of depreciation recorded for financial statement purposes.

Intangible assets and deferred charges:
Goodwill represents the excess of the cost of shares of acquired companies over the values attributed to the underlying net assets. The Company follows the policy of amortizing goodwill on a straight-line basis over periods not exceeding forty years.

Discount and expenses on funded debt are amortized over the terms of the related obligations.

Domtar Limited and Subsidiary Companies

Notes to Consolidated Financial Statements

December 31, 1976

1. Inventories:	**1976**	1975
Logs and pulp chips	**$ 20,699,483**	$ 24,393,487
Raw materials and operating and maintenance supplies	**60,021,808**	56,502,321
Finished goods including work in process	**65,171,000**	59,370,000
	$145,892,291	$140,265,808

2. Investments and advances:	**1976**	1975
Listed securities, at cost, quoted value $3,733,500 (1975 — $3,700,750)	**$ 3,453,801**	$ 3,453,801
Other investments and advances, at cost:		
Secured loans to the Trustees for employees under the Company's stock purchase plan	**$ 114,716**	$ 326,823
Municipal bonds	**—**	160,000
Loans, mortgages and debentures	**7,850,064**	7,987,206
Shares	**424,519**	2,375,152
	$ 8,389,299	$ 10,849,181

3. Fixed assets:

	Cost	**Accumulated depreciation**	**Net book value**
		(millions of dollars)	
December 31, 1976 —			
Plant, machinery and facilities —			
Pulp and paper	**$555.3**	**$293.5**	**$261.8**
Construction materials	**108.5**	**63.4**	**45.1**
Chemicals	**110.6**	**67.7**	**42.9**
Other	**3.5**	**2.8**	**0.7**
Timber limits and land	**34.2**	**6.0**	**28.2**
	$812.1	**$433.4**	**$378.7**
December 31, 1975 —			
Plant, machinery and facilities—			
Pulp and paper	$520.9	$269.6	$251.3
Construction materials	106.0	64.8	41.2
Chemicals	107.7	63.5	44.2
Other	8.9	4.7	4.2
Timber limits and land	28.4	5.0	23.4
	$771.9	$407.6	$364.3

Notes (continued)

	Maturity	1976	1975
4. Funded debt:			
Domtar Limited —			
Sinking fund debentures —			
5¼% Series "A"	1978	**$ 7,404,500**	$ 8,190,000
6¼% Series "B"	1980	**4,274,000**	4,741,000
5½% Series "C"	1982	**7,731,000**	8,845,000
5¾% Series "D"	1984	**10,244,000**	11,081,000
5⅝% Series "E"	1990	**28,046,000**	29,411,000
6¾% Series "F"	1987	**30,617,000**	32,166,000
11% Series "G"	1995	**50,000,000**	50,000,000
9⅝% Series "H" (U.S. $50,000,000)	1996	**49,295,000**	—
St. Lawrence Corporation Limited —			
First mortgage sinking fund bonds — 5% Series "C"	1978	**3,574,000**	3,792,000
Sinking fund debentures — 6¾% Series "A"	1980	**5,861,000**	6,711,000
		197,046,500	154,937,000
Less: Held for sinking fund		**6,035,500**	4,836,000
		191,011,000	150,101,000
Less: Due within one year		**512,000**	—
		$190,499,000	$150,101,000

Instalments due in each of the next five years:
1977 — $512,000 1978 — $10,562,000 1979 — $6,192,000 1980 — $11,050,000 1981 — $7,600,000

5. Acquisitions:

During the year, under agreements to purchase, the Company acquired directly or through subsidiary companies, a controlling interest in certain companies. These acquisitions were accounted for on the purchase method and their operating results have been included from the date of acquisition. The net assets acquired are recorded at fair value with any excess cost of acquisitions being recorded as goodwill.

The net assets acquired and consideration given for these acquisitions are as follows:

Net tangible assets acquired at book value	$ 7,294,054
Adjustment of net assets acquired to fair value	5,412,980
Excess of cost over fair value of net tangible assets	960,947
	$13,667,981

Net assets acquired for cash:	
Investments in prior year	$ 1,905,000
Controlling interest acquired during year	11,762,981
	$13,667,981

6. Minority interest:	1976	1975
Preferred share equity in subsidiary companies — St. Lawrence Corporation Limited — 70,933 5% preferred shares of $100 each, redeemable at $101 (after purchase for cancellation during the year of 4,292 shares)	**$ 7,093,300**	$ 7,522,500
Other	**411,450**	—
	7,504,750	7,522,500
Common share equity in subsidiary companies	**6,360,548**	4,712,708
	$13,865,298	$12,235,208

7. Pension plans:

The Company and its subsidiaries have pension plans for their employees. The cost charged against earnings in 1976 was $8,831,938 (1975 — $7,508,060). The liability for benefits in respect of past service remaining to be charged to operations approximated $24,638,000 at December 31, 1976. This cost will be charged to earnings over the next fourteen years.

8. Information on directors and officers:	Number		Remuneration	
	1976	1975	**1976**	1975
Directors	**13**	14	**$ 83,466**	$ 95,008
Officers	**24**	24	**1,576,372**	1,568,338
Officers who are also directors	**2**	2		

9. Sales by class of business:

	1976	1975
	(millions of dollars)	
Pulp and paper products	**$561.8**	$508.9
Construction materials	**172.0**	160.1
Chemicals	**153.0**	146.2
	$886.8	$815.2

10. Commitments and contingent liabilities:

The Company and its subsidiaries are contingently liable for $13,600,000 (1975 — $14,300,000) as guarantor of obligations of other companies and CMHC mortgages on employee homes.

Of the 1977 capital expenditure program the Company is committed for approximately $10,000,000 (1975 — $19,000,000).

There are outstanding lawsuits and claims against the Company as follows:

(a) Proceedings instituted by certain Cree Indians alleging that the mercury content of the environment has partly been caused by mercury discharges of the Company's chemical plant at Lebel-sur-Quévillon, Quebec, and that they have exclusive rights to a territory in Northern Quebec including the location of the Company's Lebel-sur-Quévillon pulp mill complex. They are claiming from the Company, jointly and severally with several other companies, an amount of approximately $5,200,000 in damages. In addition, they request that the Company be evicted from that area.

(b) Various sundry lawsuits and claims amounting to $7,000,000 in the aggregate.

The Company is contesting these lawsuits and claims and does not consider that their outcome will have a material adverse effect on the Company and its subsidiaries.

11. Anti-inflation program:

The Company and its Canadian subsidiaries are subject to controls on prices, profits, employee compensation and dividends under the federal anti-inflation program enacted on October 14, 1975. The Company is of the opinion that it has complied with this legislation.

12. The Companies Act of British Columbia:

These financial statements comply with the disclosure requirements of the act of incorporation (The Canada Corporations Act) and the securities legislation of certain provinces in Canada, but do not purport to comply with all disclosure requirements of the Companies Act of British Columbia.

Auditors' Report

To the Shareholders of
Domtar Limited:

We have examined the consolidated balance sheet of Domtar Limited as at December 31, 1976 and the consolidated statements of earnings and retained earnings and changes in financial position for the year then ended. Our examination was made in accordance with generally accepted auditing standards, and accordingly included such tests and other procedures as we considered necessary in the circumstances.

In our opinion, these consolidated financial statements present fairly the financial position of the Company as at December 31, 1976 and the results of its operations and the changes in its financial position for the year then ended in accordance with generally accepted accounting principles applied on a basis consistent with that of the preceding year.

PRICE WATERHOUSE & CO.
Chartered Accountants

Montreal, January 26, 1977

Index

Abandonment, 583-585
Absorption costing and direct costing
  compared, 554-556
Accounting
  changes, 442-443
  double-entry, defined, 3, 44
  external users, 4, 6, 8, 245, 420, 424
  historical perspective, 3
  internal users, 5, 6, 8, 420, 424
Accounting concepts
  accrual basis, 7
  asset valuation at cost, 234, 400
  comparability of data, 431
  conservatism, 7
  consistency, 7, 234, 244-245, 431
    436
  cost allocation, 264
  depreciation, 264
  entity, 6, 9,
  expenses and costs compared, 56
  extraordinary items, 440-442
  full disclosure, 7
  going concern, 6-7
  historical cost, 7
  income measurement, 68
  matching revenue and expenses,
    68-69, 89, 210-211
  materiality, 7
  objective evidence, 7
  other disciplines, 5-6
  periodicity, 7
  stable dollar, 7
  uniformity of data, 436
Accounting
  cycle, 110
  equation, 9-12, 21, 31, 38
    debit and credit rules and, 34, 54, 57
    expanded, 21-22, 58
  methods, 3, 6, 43, 87-89
  model, 9, 18-21
  principles, 6-7, 8, 210, 431, 436, 440,
    442, 602. *See also* Accounting
    concepts; Accounting procedures
  procedures
    adjusting entries, 89-90
    depreciation, 94-95, 96
    lower of cost and market, 243-244
    recognizing declared dividends,
    405
Accounting Research Committee, 8
Accounting sequence, 43-44, 64-74
  standards, 8, 402, 440. *See also*
    Accounting concepts
Accounts, 31
  and accounting equation, 31-32
  balance-form, 178
  balancing, 38, 41, 208-209
  chart of, 75
  closing, 71-73
  contra, 95, 128, 130, 211
  controlling, 5, 157-158, 163, 165, 169
    175-176, 211, 217, 246
    voucher system, 182
  debit and credit rules, 32-36, 39,
    57-64
  drawing, 338-340

Accounts (Cont.)
expense, 55, 56
footing, 37, 67
manufacturing. *See* Cost accounting
merchandise, 127-142, 136, 245, 246
mixed, 91, 92, 93, 107
nominal, 71-73
numbering, 37, 75, 76
operating expense, 127
purchases, 129-130, 233
permanent, 71
real, 71
revenue, 54, 127, 128
sales, 127-128
summary, 72
T, 31, 33, 34, 36, 41, 132
temporary, 64, 71-73, 109
three-column, 41
uncollectible. *See* Bad debts
valuation, 211, 274
Accounts payable, 10, 15, 19, 172, 173, 174, 361
accrued, 98
and balance sheet, 19-21
and bank reconciliation 203
and debit and credit, 35-36, 59-60, 61
notes to settle, 381
opposite balances, 217
and purchases journal, 163-165, 180, 181
Accounts payable ledger, 157
posting to, 157-158
from business documents, 176-177, 178
from cash payments journal, 172-174
from purchases journal, 163-165
and voucher systems, 183, 185
Accounts receivable, 10, 14, 20, 169, 175-176
aging, 213, 214, 215, 422
average collection period, 422-423
and bank reconciliation, 203
and balance sheet, 20-21
classification, 209-210
and debit and credit, 36-37, 63
internal control, 219
measurement, 209-219
nontrade, 210
notes to settle, 382
opposite balances, 217
ratio of credit sales to, 420
and sales journal, 162-163
trade, defined, 209
turnover, 422-423
uncollectible. *See* Bad debts
Accounts receivable ledger, 157
credit balances, 217
posting to, 157-158, 169
from business documents, 175-176
from cash receipts journal, 166, 169-170
from sales journal, 128, 162-163
Accrual basis, 7, 87-89
Accrued
expenses, 88, 89, 91, 97-98, 99, 111, 183, 220
interest payable, 15
bonds, 363, 366, 368, 370-371, 373, 376
notes, 97-98, 111
paying, 111
interest receivable, 99
marketable securities, 399-401
notes, 91, 98-99, 112
receiving, 112
liabilities, defined, 15, 98, 220
revenue, 88, 91, 92, 94, 98-99, 111
wages, 15, 89-90, 111, 220
Acid-test ratio. *See* Ratio
Adjusted trial balance. *See* Trial balance
Adjusting entries, 64, 89-112
Adjustments, 89-112
accrued expenses, 88, 89, 91, 97-98, 99, 111, 183, 220
interest, notes payable, 97-98, 111
interest, notes receivable, 91, 98-99, 112
revenue, 88, 91, 92, 98-99,111
bad debts, 210-212, 214
bank reconciliation, 203, 204
bonds payable, 373, 376
defined, 89
depreciation, 94-95
income taxes, 99-100
long-term cost apportionments, 91, 94-96
manufacturing work sheet, 498-504
need for, 89-90
notes payable, 97-111
notes receivable, 91, 383-384
office supplies, 91
posted, 90, 107, 110
prepaid insurance, 91
rent, 91
prior period, 440-442
recording of, 90-100
recorded in general journal, 107-108, 140, 175, 176
short-term cost apportionments, 89, 91-93, 94
revenue apportionments, 91, 93-94

Adjustments (Cont.)
unearned rent, 93-94
work sheet section, 100-103, 107, 109, 500, 504, 563
Aging accounts receivable, 213, 214, 215, 422
All-financial resources concept of funds, 472-474
All-inclusive concept, 440-442
Allowances
journal, 175
purchases, 130, 133
sales, 128
American Institute of Certified Public Accountants, 8-9, 278,426
comments on accounting changes, 442-443
stock dividends, 319
value, defined, 234
Amortization
bond investment, 406-407, 408-409
bonds payable, 370, 371, 373, 376, 384-386
income tax, 606
intangible assets, 277
patents, 497
Analysis
of debits and credits, 167-168, 172-174
of financial statements. *See* Financial statement analysis
Analyzing transactions, 58-64
Annual cost, 608-609
Annuities, 619, 621-623, 625-626
Application for letters patent, 289
Appraisal increase credit, 298
Articles of incorporation, 289
Asset valuation account, defined, 95
Assets, 10, 11, 12, 22, 33, 58
capital. *See* Plant and equipment
carrying value, 95, 265-266, 270-274, 377, 425, 426
current, 13-14, 15, 20, 75, 92, 93, 99, 210, 233, 249, 361, 362, 399, 402, 458
decrease of, 18, 20, 33-36, 58-64, 95
fixed. *See* Plant and equipment
gift of, 10, 298
increase of, 18-20, 33-36
intangible, 261, 277-279, 438, 458, 460, 583, 585
amortization, 277
on balance sheet, 15, 18-21, 31
net, 11, 291
plant and equipment. *See* Plant and equipment
quick, 422
revaluations, 298
trading, 422
valuation, 95, 96
on work sheet, 105
Association of Accountants in Montreal, 8
Auditor's opinion, 443
Authoritative bodies, 8-9
Average collection period, 422-423
inventory costing. *See* inventory

Bad debts, 210-219
adjustment, 210-212, 214
on balance sheet, 211, 217
comparison of methods, 212-213
errors in allowance account, 218
estimating, 212-215
recovery of, 216
writing off, 216, 217-218
Balance sheet, 9, 12-22, 31-45, 156, 455. *See also* Statement of changes in financial position
accounts payable, debit balances on, 19-21, 217
receivable, credit balances on 20-21, 217
analysis. *See* Financial statement analysis; Ratio analysis
asset valuation account, 95, 96
bad debts on, 211, 217
classification in, 12-16, 287
common-size, 436-438
comparative, 431, 432-434, 462, 464
contingent liabilities on, 382, 383
corporation, 293-296
current assets on, 13-14, 92, 93, 99
liabilities on, 15, 94, 98, 100, 362
debit and credit rules and, 32-36, 39, 57-64
depreciation on, 95, 96, 263, 266, 270, 274
dollar signs on, 12
equity ratios, 424, 426-427
intangible assets on, 15, 18-21, 31
and interim statements, 140
interrelationship with other statements, 71, 74
inventories on, 233, 235, 239, 243, 248, 497
long-term investments on, 15, 210, 399
liabilities on, 10, 31, 367, 368, 370, 372, 375, 376, 379, 380, 404, 405, 407
merchandising business, 136, 138
notes receivable discounted on, 383

Balance sheet (Cont.)
owner's equity on, 16-17, 341, 343
partnership, 343, 348, 350-351
percentage analysis, 434-438, 351
plant and equipment on, 266, 270
preparation of, 70-71
proprietorship, 16, 17, 338-339, 341
shareholders' equity on. *See* Shareholders' equity
stock premium discount on, 295
subscription on, 304
temporary investment on, 399, 402-403, 404, 405
treasury stock on, 325
from trial balance, 39
work-in-process inventory on, 497-498
work sheet section, 105, 110, 503
Balance-form ledger account, 178
Balancing accounts, 208-209
Bank
reconciliation, 203-209
service charge, 202
statement, 202-203, 204, 206, 207
Base
totals, 436
year, 434-435
Batch totals, 177
Bearer bonds, 363
Bond indenture, 362, 364
Bonds, 10, 14. *See also* Bonds payable
classification, 363-364
compared with capital stock, 362-363, 364-366, 376
at face value, 366-374
long-term investment in, 15, 362, 406-407
savings, 362
temporary investment in, 399-400, 408-409
times interest earned ratio, 424, 427-428
yield table, 384
Bonds payable, 16, 361, 362, 376
accounting for, 367-376
adjustments, 373-376
amortization, 373-376
compound-interest method, 370-371, 384-386, 408-409
straight-line method, 370-371, 373, 385, 386
authorizing, 366-367
conversion, 377-378, 472
issued at discount, 368-369, 372-373
at face value, 367-368
at premium, 368-372
long-term, 361, 362
reasons for issuing, 364-366
refunding, 376-380
retained earnings restricted, 376, 379-380
retirement, 367, 371, 373, 376-380
sinking fund, 362, 376, 377, 378-380
Book of final entry, 43
of original entry, 43
value. *See* Value, book
Bookkeeping, defined, 11
machines, 156, 177-178
Break-even analysis, 570-575
chart, 572-573, 575
margin of safety 576-578
marginal income statement, 575-576
percentage, 574
point, 434, 570-572, 574, 576, 577
computation, 570-571, 575, 576
British Columbia Companies Act (1973), 291, 323
Budgets. *See also* Capital budgeting; Investments
comparative, 579
defined, 5
fixed, 543, 544
flexible, 544-553, 570
manufacturing, 504
and responsibility accounting, 557-559
use of standards for, 543-544
Buildings, 10, 15, 18, 34-35. *See also* Plant and equipment
Business
documents, 155-156
posting from, 176-177
organization forms, 16-17
Bylaws, 289, 367

Callable bonds, 364, 366
Canada Business Corporations Act (1975)
corporate name, 291
issuance of no-par value stock, 291, 292-293, 294, 314
number of shares, 292
reacquisition of stock, 293-294, 322, 323
stated capital, 292
subscription to stock, 302
Canadian Institute of Chartered Accountants (CICA), 8. *See also* CICA
Cancelled checks, 204
Capital, 10. *See also* Working capital
accounts, partnerships, 337, 344-345, 346, 349-350
proprietorships, 337, 338, 340

Capital (Cont.)
assets. *See* Plant and equipment
budgeting, annual cost, 608-609
decisions, 599-611
defined, 599
depreciation and, 606-607
income taxes, 606-607
irregular cash flow, 607-608
limitations, 610-611
payback, 610
present value concept, 600-602, 610
rate of return, 600, 602, 610
corporations, 288, 361
expenditures
budgeting for, 599-602
comparing, 602-611
defined, 263
present value method, 602-604, 610
rate of return method, 604-606, 610
types, 599
invested, 294
legal, 292, 313
sources, 297
stated, 292
stock. *See* Stock, capital
Carrying value. *See* Value, carrying
Cash, 10, 13
basis, 87-88
book, 174
control, 199-209
debits and credits, 34-36, 58-63
discounts, 140, 141
allowance account, 130
purchases, 130-131
sales, 128-129
terms, 140
flow, 474-475, 600-601, 602-604, 605
determining, 602
irregular, 607-608
funds as, 474-475
overage, 201-202, 209
petty. *See* Petty cash
shortage, 201-202, 209
statement of changes in financial position, 18-21, 474-475
Cash payments journal, 160, 170-174, 175
error in, 204, 207-208
posting from, 172-174
posting flow from, 171
proving, 173-174
Cash receipts journal, 160, 165-170, 174, 175, 204
posting from, 167-170
posting flow from, 166
proving, 169
Certificate
bond, 362
of incorporation, 289
stock, 290, 301, 302, 303
Certified check, 203
Chain discount, 142
Charter, corporate, 288, 292, 294, 315, 367
Chartered accountant, 3, 8, 9,
Chart of accounts, 75
Check register, 175, 184
Checks
cancelled, 204
certified, 203
NSF, 203
outstanding, 204, 207
voucher, 182, 201
CICA Handbook, 8, 274
accounts receivable, 210, 212
business combinations, 279
change in application of accounting principles, 442-443
in financial position, 455
cost, defined, 233
disclosure of accounting policies, 274, 440
extraordinary items, 441
fixed costs, 274
general standards of financial statement presentation, 8
intangible assets, 477
inventory, 233, 239, 244
long-term investments, 402, 407
lower of cost and market, 244
marketable securities, 399, 402
notes to financial statements, 440
prior-period adjustments, 441
revaluation of fixed assets, 298
statement of changes in financial position, 455-456, 460, 472
Claims, primary and residual, 10
Closing entries, 72-73, 110, 111
journalizing, 175, 176, 460, 472
manufacturing business, 504
merchandising business, 131, 132, 139, 140
posting, 71-72, 109, 110
recorded from work sheet, 109, 110
Collection period, average, 422-423
Commercial paper, defined, 14
Common-size financial statements, 436-438
Common stock. *See* Stock, capital
Comparative financial statements, 419, 420, 431-438, 462, 464

Composite depreciation rates
268-269
Compound discount, 621
entry, defined, 44
interest. *See* Interest, compound; Bond, amortization
Conservatism, 7
Consistency, 7, 234, 244-245, 431, 436, 516
Contingent liabilities, 382-383
disclosure, 440
discounted notes receivable, 382-383, 384
stock discount, 295
Continuous transactions, 89, 91
Contra accounts, 95, 128, 130, 211
Contract rate, 366-369, 370
Contributed surplus, 295, 297-298, 313, 324, 325
Control, internal, 219
accounts receivable, 219
cash, 199-201
defined, 199
special journals and, 161
voucher system and, 182
Controlling accounts, 5, 157-158, 163, 165, 169, 175-176, 211, 217, 246, 550
cost system, 404-405, 517, 518, 521, 550
voucher system, 182
Convertible bonds, 364, 366
Copyrights, 261, 277, 278
Corporate name, 291
Corporations, 11, 288-304, 338
advantages, 16, 288
characteristics of, 287, 291
contributed capital, 295, 297-298
defined, 16, 17, 287
disadvantages of, 288
dividends. *See* Dividends
donations to, 297-298
income taxes, 99, 288
organization, 289
ownership, 288-289
stated capital, 292
Correcting entries, 175
Cost. *See also* Marginal cost
apportionments, 89-96
long-term, 91, 94-96
short-term, 89, 91-93, 94
behavior patterns, 544-546, 569, 572
of capital, 600
center, 515, 522-523
concepts, 600-602
curves, 544-545
data processing system and, 155
determination, 5
differential, 569
and expense distinguished, 56, 500-503
fixed, 544-546, 552, 554, 556, 569, 570-571, 572, 575-576, 578, 580, 582, 583, 584
flow of, 518-519, 523-524
historical 7, 234, 239, 261, 275, 298, 402, 426, 530, 543
idle time, 546
inventory, defined, 234
opportunity, 569
organization, 279
out-of-pocket, 569-570
semifixed, 546, 569, 572
semivariable, 546, 569
standard, 530
sunk, 570, 582
variable, 544-546, 552, 554, 556, 569, 570-571, 572, 575, 578, 582, 583
Cost accounting, 504, 515-530
accumulation, 515-517, 526-527, 528, 529, 557
controlling accounts, 515-516
direct labor, 516-517, 520, 521, 522, 523
finished goods, 516, 519
and general accounting compared, 515
job order, 515, 516-519
comprehensive illustration, 518-520
cost sheet, 516-517, 518, 519, 520, 521, 522
defined, 515
evaluation, 522
factory payroll, 516-517
finished goods, 516, 519
flow chart, 519
materials, 516
overhead, 516, 517, 518, 520-522
work in process, 516, 517, 518, 520-522
manufacturing summary, 504
materials, 493, 497, 498
overhead, 516, 517, 518, 520-522
process, 515, 522-530
comprehensive illustration, 524-529
cost of production report, 522, 529
defined, 522
equivalent production, 525-526, 527, 529
flow of costs, 523-524, 529-530
summary entries, 529-530

Cost accounting (Cont.)
unit cost computation, 526, 527-528, 529
responsibility accounting, 543, 557-559
standard, 530, 543-553
comprehensive illustration, 546-553
defined, 543
flow chart, 546-547
variances, 543, 544, 549-553
systems, 515
work in process. *See* Work in process
Cost of goods manufactured, 493, 497, 499, 500, 504, 515
Cost of goods sold, 127, 133, 134, 275, 276, 554
inventory, 233, 235, 236, 237, 238, 241, 242, 245, 246, 249, 424, 434, 437, 494, 554
manufacturing business, 498-499, 516, 523
Cost and market, lower of
inventory, 243-244
marketable securities, 402-403
Cost of production report, 522, 529
Cost sheet. *See* Cost accounting
Costing, direct, 543, 555-556, 576
and absorption compared, 554-556
Coupon bonds, 363
Credit, defined, 32
and debit rules, 32-36, 39, 57-64
memo, bank, 203, 204, 206
posting, 163
sales, ratio to accounts receivable, 422-423
in trial balance, 38, 39
Creditors' equity, 426-427
Creditors' ledger, 158
debit balances, 217
posting to, 158-159
from business documents, 176-177
from cash payments journal, 172-174
from purchases journal, 163-165, 180, 181
and voucher system, 185
Cumulative preferred stock, 315-316, 365
Current assets. *See* Assets, current
liabilities. *See* Liabilities, current
operating performance concept, 440-442
ratio, 420-422, 427
Customers' ledger, 157
credit balances, 218, 361
posting to, 158-159
from business documents, 176-177
from cash receipts journal, 167-170
from sales journal, 162-163
Cycle, accounting, 110
Data processing, 155
flow of information, 155-156
punched-card equipment, 155
system design, 155-156
Debentures, 364, 367, 368, 372, 373. *See also* Bonds payable
Debit, defined, 32
and credit rules, 32-36, 39, 57-64
memo, bank, 203, 204, 206
posting, 163
in trial balance, 38, 39
Declining balance. *See* Depreciation
Deductions, payroll, 219-220
Delivery equipment, 15
Depletion, 261, 275-276
Deposits in transit, 204
Depreciation, 56, 262, 263-275
adjustments, 94-95, 96
on balance sheet, 95, 96, 263, 266
and capital budgeting, 606-607
comparison of methods, 266-267
composite rates, 268-269
declining-balance method, 265-266, 269
defined, 94
disclosure requirements, 274, 440
and expenditures, 263
group rates, 266-269
in manufacturing, 520
methods, 264-267
for partial accounting periods, 267-268
production-unit method, 266-267, 275
and ratios, 425, 426
revision of rate, 269
of small tools, 497
straight-line, 94, 96, 265, 266, 267, 269, 270, 277, 279, 607
and trade-ins, 270, 272-274
and working capital, 460, 467
working-hours method, 267
Direct labor. *See* Labor, direct
materials, 493-495
posting, 175-176
Disbursements, defined, 56
Disclosure, issues, 440-443
Discounted notes receivable, 380, 382-384
Discounts
bonds, 367, 368-369, 372-376, 385,

Discounts (Cont.)
400, 406, 408-409
cash, 140, 141
flows, 602
purchases, 142
sales, 128-129
terms, 140
chain, 142
compound, 621
purchases, 130-131, 141, 172, 184
lost, 130-131, 141-142, 184, 262
sales, 128-129, 141, 165, 169
allowance account, 130
gross price method, 128-129, 141
not taken, 129, 141
stock, 295-296, 297
trade, 142
Dishonored notes receivable, 382
Distributable surplus, 294
Dividends, 53, 62, 70, 72, 73, 313-322, 363
arrearage, 316-317
declaration, 299-300, 313-314
defined, 16, 57, 313
large stock, 319-320
liquidating, 314
from long-term investments, 404-405
from marketable securities, 401-402
preferred, 289, 315-317
times earned, 424, 428
recognition, 405
recording, 58, 173, 299
small stock, 319
stock, 289, 317-321, 323
yield rate, 428-429
Documents. *See* Business documents
Dollar signs, 43
Donations
of assets, 297-298
capital, 297
of treasury stock, 325
Double-entry accounting defined, 3, 44
Doubtful accounts. *See* Bad debts
Drawing account
partner's, 345, 348
proprietor's, 338

Earning power, measurement of, 420, 428-431
Earnings
retained. *See* Retained earnings
per share, 428-429
yield rate, 427, 428-429
Economic unit, defined, 9
Effective interest bonds, 385-386, 408-409
yield amortization, 385-386
Electronic data processing, 155, 178, 219, 385
Entity concept, 6, 9
Equality of debits and credits, 38, 74, 105, 167, 173
Equation, accounting. *See* Accounting equation
Equipment. *See* Plant and equipment
Equity, creditors', 10, 424, 426-427
method of accounting for investments, 407-408
owners'. *See* Owners' equity
ratios, 424, 426-427
Equivalent production, 525-526
Errors
in allowances doubtful accounts, 218
bank, 204, 206, 207
in cash payments journal, 207, 208
correcting entries, 176
as extraordinary item, 440
in inventory, 249
not revealed by trial balance, 38
trial balance, locating, 38-39
on work sheet, 105
Estimated salvage value, 264, 265-270
useful life, 264, 265-271, 277, 602-603, 604, 608-609
Exception principle, 141-142
Ex-dividend, 314
Expenditures
capital. *See* Capital expenditures
defined, 263
revenue, 263
Expenses, 53, 57, 58, 59-61, 62, 64, 68, 71-72, 73
accrued, 88, 89, 91, 97-98, 99, 111, 183, 220
bad debts, 211, 212-215
and cash basis, 87-88
and costs distinguished, 56, 500-505
defined, 55-56
depletion, 275
depreciation, 95, 96, 263, 264
interest, 97-98, 99, 112
manufacturing overhead, 496
marginal income, 575, 579
matching revenue and, 68-69, 89, 210-211, 263, 275, 430-431, 434-435, 437
in mixed accounts, 91-92, 95
operating, 127, 134, 136
other, 134, 136
in proprietorships, 339
rates for recording, 56
variable, 575, 585

Expenses (Cont.)
wages, 86, 90, 91, 97
work sheet, 105
Extraordinary items, 440-442, 460

Face value. *See* Value, face
Factory costs, 493, 494
payroll, 516, 517, 523
Fair market value. *See* Value, fair market
FIFO. *See* Inventory
Final entry, book of, 43
Financial Accounting Standards Board (FASB), 9, 403
Financial Analysts' Federation, 8
Financial Executives Institute (FEI), 8
Financial position, statement of. *See* Balance sheet; Statement of changes in financial position
reports, 419. *See also* Financial statements
statements analysis, 419-443
horizontal, 436
influences, 438
percentage, 419
ratio. *See* Ratio analysis
tools, 419-420
trend percentages, 431, 434-436
vertical, 436-438
statements
common-size, 436-438
comparative, 419, 420, 431-438
and consistency, 7, 234, 244-245, 431, 436, 516
depreciation on, 274, 275
dollar signs on, 43
footnotes, 440
interim, 140
interrelationship, 74
inventory, 233, 245, 248
manufacturing business, 502-504
merchandising business, 127, 132, 138, 140
partnership, 347-348
prepared from work sheet, 100-107, 110
preparing, 65, 66, 69-72
and voucher system 182
Finished goods, 493, 499, 500, 504, 516, 519
on work sheet, 500
First-in, first-out. *See* Inventory
Fixed assets. *See* Plant and equipment
costs. *See* Costs, fixed
liabilities. *See* Long-term liabilities
Flexible budget. *See* Budget, flexible
Flow. *See also* Cash flow
job cost, 515, 518-519
process cost, 523-524, 529-530
standard cost, 546-547
working capital, 456, 457
Flow charts
information, 156
job order cost system, 515, 519, 520
posting. *See* Posting flow
process cost system, 523
standard cost system, 546-547
F.O.B., defined, 130
Folio column, 66, 73, 91
Footing, defined, 37, 47, 65
Footnotes to statements, 440
Franchises, 261, 277, 278
Freight costs, 130
Full disclosure, 7
Funds, 455. *See also* Statement of changes in financial position

Garner v. Murray rule, 351
General Accountants Association (GAA), 8
General accounting system, 493-504, 515
General journal, 208, 209, 211
adjusting entries, 90, 97, 99, 107, 108, 144, 175, 176, 211, 504
closing entries, 73, 74, 175, 176
compound entries, 44
in conjunction with special journals, 175-177
correcting entries, 175, 176
expansion of, 159-175
and expense accounts, 55
and payroll, 220
posting from, 39-44
split entries, 111
General ledger, 68, 70, 75, 110, 245
with adjusting and closing entries posted, 91, 107, 108, 109, 131, 140, 211
posting to, 158, 162
and subsidiary ledgers, 156-159, 160-175, 179-181
and work sheet, 100
Gifts
of assets, 10, 298
of treasury stock, 325
Going-concern concept, 6-7
Goodwill, 15, 201, 277, 278-279, 348-349
Gross
margin inventory method. *See* Inventory
margin on sales, 128, 134, 233, 236, 239, 248, 249

Gross (Cont.)
price method, 128-129, 141
Group depreciation rates, 268-269

Historical cost. *See* Cost, historical
Horizontal analysis, 436

Imprest fund, 202
Income
bonds, 364
and disclosure, 440-442
and extraordinary items, 460
marginal, 575, 578, 580, 582
net, 16, 57, 68-69, 70, 72, 74, 99, 134, 136, 233, 239, 248, 249, 264
accounting method and, 88-89, 554-556
and comparative statements, 431-435
on work sheet, 100, 105
statement, 53, 68-69, 70, 156, 209, 455
and adjusting entries, 92, 93, 94, 95, 97, 98, 99, 100
all-inclusive concept, 440-442
approach, 2, 12
common-size, 436-437
comparative, 431, 433, 434, 579
current operating performance concept, 440-442
departmental, 583
dividends on, 319
interrelationship with other statements, 71, 74
manufacturing business, 502-504
merchandising, 127, 129, 133, 136, 138
in proprietorship, 338
work sheet section, 105, 110, 502
summary account, 71-73, 96, 131, 339
taxes, 69, 362
adjustment, 99-100
and abandonment, 585
bonds and, 364-365
and capital budgeting, 606-607
and comparative financial statements, 434
corporations, 99, 288
depletion allowance, 276
depreciation of fixed assets, 265
dividend tax credit, 288
investment income exemption, 288
partnerships and, 288, 343
proprietorships and, 388
use of LIFO costing, 237
Incorporated, 291
Incorporation, laws of, 287
Indirect labor. *See* Labor, indirect
Inflation, 274-275
Information flow chart, 156
Insurance, prepaid, 14, 63, 91
adjustment, 89, 91-92
Intangible assets. *See* Assets, intangible
Interest, 98-99, 563
compound, 617, 619-627
discount, 620
tables, 623-627
coupons, 563
defined, 617
earned, 98-99
effective, 385-386, 408, 409
ordinary annuity, 619, 621-623, 625 626
partnership profit distribution, 345-347, 349-350
present value, 619, 620-621, 623-625
rate on bonds, 361, 366, 368-375
simple, 617-619
short-cut calculations, 618-619
single sum, 619-620, 624
value of rent, 626-627
Interest payable accrued, 111, 361
bonds, 363, 366, 368, 370-371, 373-376
notes, 97, 382
paying, 111-112
Interest receivable accrued, 112
marketable securities, 399-401
notes, 91, 98, 112
receiving, 112
Interim statements, 140
Internal control, 219
accounts receivable, 219
cash, 199-201
defined, 199
and inventory, 249-250
special journals and, 161
voucher system and, 182
Inventory, 233-250
account for, 84
on balance sheet, 233, 235, 239, 243, 248, 497
beginning, 131-133, 139, 245, 249-250, 424
consistency, 244-245, 246
control, 5, 249-250, 519
cost accounting, 515, 519
cost, defined, 234
costing
changing methods, 244-245
specific identification, 234-235
economical buying quantities, 250

Inventory (Cont.)
ending, 131-133, 139, 233, 237, 239, 242, 248, 249, 424, 499-502
estimating
gross margin method, 235, 246-247, 248
retail method, 248
finished goods, 493, 499, 500, 504, 516, 517, 519, 523-524, 528, 555
levels, 250
materials, 494, 497-500, 504, 516, 523, 549
merchandise, 14, 15, 131-133, 136, 233, 245, 275, 421, 422
periodic, 131, 133, 234, 235-237, 241-243
FIFO costing, 231, 234, 235, 238, 239, 240-241, 243
and general accounting systems, 494, 504, 515
LIFO costing, 234, 235-236, 237-239, 241-242, 243
and perpetual compared, 238-239, 245-246
weighted average, 237, 238, 239, 243
perpetual, 131, 234, 239-243
FIFO costing, 238, 239, 240-241
and general accounting systems, 504
LIFO costing, 238, 239, 241-242
moving average costing, 237, 239, 242-243
and periodic compared, 238-239, 245-246
retail method, 248
specific identification, 234-235
systems, 234-235
turnover, 420, 423-424
valuation, 236, 237, 431, 438
basis, 233-234
importance, 248-249
lower of cost and market, 243-244, 248
methods compared, 238-239, 556
work-in-process, 423, 425, 497-498, 499, 504, 516, 517, 518, 521, 524-530, 547, 549-553, 555
on work sheet, 499-502
Investment register, 405
Investments, 399-409. *See also* Marketable securities
annual cost, 608-609
long-term, 15, 210, 399, 404-408
on balance sheet, 15, 210, 399
bonds, 15, 406-407
notes, 408
stock, 15, 404-406
net cash, 602-604, 605, 606-607
opportunity, 600
payback, 610
in plant and equipment ratio, 424-425
rate of return, 429-430
temporary, 399-404
bonds, 399-400, 408
stock, 400, 402
valuation, 402, 404
in subsidiaries, 404, 407-408
Investors' ratio, 427-428

Jacket voucher, 182-183
Job order cost sheet. *See* Cost accounting
order cost system. *See* Cost accounting
Journal, defined, 43. *See also* specific journals
Journalizing, 40, 43, 53, 58-64, 110, 504. *See also* specific entries or journals
adjusting entries, 90, 92, 102

Labor, 493, 497, 518, 546-547
direct, 494, 495, 496, 498, 516-517, 520, 521, 522, 523, 549
indirect, 496-497, 516-517, 520, 523
Land, 10,11, 15, 18, 34-35, 60. *See also* Plant and equipment
Last-in, first-out. *See* Inventory
Leasehold, 261, 277, 278
Ledger, defined, 43. *See also* specific ledgers
Legal capital, 292, 313
Letters patent, 289
Leverage, 364, 365, 430
Liabilities. *See also* Bonds payable
accrued, 15, 98, 220
adjusting entries, 93-94, 97
contingent, 382-383, 384
current, 15, 65, 94, 97, 98, 100, 361-362, 374-375, 458
decreases of, 19, 33-36, 58-64
defined, 10
fixed. *See* Long-term
increases of, 19, 33-36, 58-64, 89-90
limited, 16
long-term, 361, 376
on balance sheet, 15, 16, 31, 367, 368, 370, 372, 375, 376, 379, 380, 404, 405, 407
defined, 16

Liabilities (Cont.)
ratio of plant and equipment to, 424-425
on work sheet, 105
Life, estimated useful, 264, 265-271, 277
LIFO. *See* Inventory
Limited, 291
Limited companies. *See* Corporations
Liquidating dividend, 314
Liquidation, liability, 15
partnership, 349-351
Liquidity, 13
Long-term cost apportionment, 91, 94-96
liabilities. *See* Liabilities; Bonds payable
Loss, net. *See* Net loss
Lower of cost and market
inventory, 243-244, 248
temporary investments, 402-403

Machine processing, 177-178
Make or buy decision, 582-583
Management by exception, 141-142
Manufacturing
general accounting for, 493-504, 515
overhead, 494, 495-497, 498, 500, 502, 516, 517, 518, 520-522
allocation, 500-502, 521-522
departmentalization, 502
ledger, 496-497, 516
overapplied, 520-522, 546, 551
and product pricing, 580
rate, 520-522, 546
special orders, 578-579
underapplied, 520-522, 546, 551
summary, 504
work sheet, 499-504
Margin
gross. *See* Inventory
on sales, 128
net operating, 134, 136
ratio, 428, 430-431
of safety, 576-578
Marginal
costs, 569, 579, 583
income, 554, 556, 575, 578, 580-582, 583, 585
direct costing, 554
planning, 577-578
pricing and, 580-582
statements, 575-576
Markdown, 248, 437
Market
rate on bonds, 366-375
value. *See* Value, market
Marketable securities, 10, 314, 399-404
bonds, 399-400
defined, 14
stock, 401-402
valuation, 402-404, 406
Markup, 248, 581
Matching revenue and expenses. *See* Expenses
Materiality, 7
Materials, 493-495, 496, 497, 543
job order system, 516, 518, 520, 521, 522, 523
in process cost system, 522, 523
on schedule of cost of goods manufactured, 494
in standard cost system, 546-549
on work sheet, 499-502
Merchandise accounts, 127-142, 245, 246
functions, 132-133
inventory. *See* Inventory
notes for, 380
Merchandising business, defined, 18, 127
Methods, accounting, 87-89
Mini practice case, special journals, 179-181
Mortgage payable, 16, 361, 376
Mortgages, investment in, 408
on bonds, 363, 364, 369-370, 371
Moving average costing. *See* Inventory

Natural resources, 261, 275-276
Net assets, defined, 11
Net cost of purchases, defined, 133
income, 16, 57, 263
accounting method and, 88-89
and bad debts, 210
on financial statements, 68-69, 70, 72, 74
and other revenue and expenses, 134, 136, 403
partnerships, 346, 347, 348
per share, 428-429
proprietorships, 99, 338
on work sheet, 100, 105
loss, 68-69, 72, 100, 105, 136
operating margin, 134, 136
price method, 130, 141
sales, ratio to plant and equipment, 425, 426
Nominal accounts, 71-73
rate, 366, 367
Noncurrent assets. *See* Plant and equipment

Noncumulative preferred stock, 315
Nonparticipating preferred stock, 315-316, 365
Nontrade accounts receivable, defined, 210
  notes receivable, defined, 210
No-par value. *See* Value, no-par
Notes
  defined, 10, 376
  long-term investments in, 408
  payable, 10, 60, 183, 361
    defined, 14, 15
    interest, 97, 111
    recording, 168, 170, 173
    to settle accounts payable, 381
    register, 175
  receivable, 381-384
    defined, 14, 209
    discounted, 380, 382-384
    dishonored, 382
    interest, 91, 98, 112, 399-401
    nontrade, 209, 210
    recording, 168, 169, 175
    to settle accounts receivable, 382
    trade, 210
    register, 175
  renewable, 376
  short-term, 376, 380
N.S.F. check, 203
Numbering accounts, 37, 64, 73

Objective evidence concept, 7
Office supplies, 14
  adjustments, 91
Ontario Business Corporations Act (1970), 323
Open charge accounts, 14, 15. *See also* Accounts payable; Accounts receivable
Operating
  capacity, 546, 574
  expenses, 127, 134, 136
  margin, net, 127, 134, 136
    ratio, 428, 430-431
Order of Chartered Accountants of Quebec, 8
Organization cost, 279
Original entry, book of, defined, 43
Other expenses, 134, 136
  revenue, 134, 136, 141, 271
Outstanding checks, 204, 207
Overage, cash, 202, 209
Overdraft, 203, 361
Overhead. *See also* Manufacturing overhead
  budgeted, 543, 553, 559
  and direct costing, 554
  fixed 546, 554, 556, 580, 582
  predetermined, 520-521, 551
  and standard costs, 543-546, 547, 549, 550-553
  variable, 554, 586
Owner's equity, 10, 11, 337, 347
  on balance sheet, 16, 17, 341, 343
  statement of, 340-341

Par value. *See* Value, par
Participating preferred stock, 315-316
Partners' equity, 11, 347
  statement of, 344-345
Partnership agreement, 342
Partnerships, 11, 16, 17, 99, 337, 342-351
  admission of new partner, 288, 348-349
  advantages, 17, 342-343
  balance sheet, 343, 348, 350-351
  capital accounts, 343-344
  defined, 17, 342
  disadvantages, 287, 343
  distribution of profits, 345-347, 349-351
  equity accounts, 343-345
  financial statements, 347-348, 349
  formation of, 342
  Garner v. Murray rule, 351
  income taxes and, 343
  liquidation, 349-351
  types, 342
Patents, 261, 277, 497
Payables. *See* Accounts payable; Notes payable
Payback, 610
Payroll, 219-220
  accrued, 15, 89-90, 111, 220
    paying, 220
  Canada Pension Plan, 219
  deductions, 219-220
  factory, 516-517, 523
  income tax deductions, 219
  provincial pension plan, 219
  Unemployment Insurance, 219
Pension plans, 219, 361, 376
Percentage analysis, 434-438
  break-even, 574, 576
  contribution, 571, 576
  horizontal, 436
  of safety, 576
  vertical, 436-438
Periodic inventory. *See* Inventory
Periodicity, 7
Permanent accounts, 71

Perpetual inventory. *See* Inventory
card, 516
Petty cash, 170, 182, 201-202
Planning, 5
Plant assets. *See* Plant and equipment
Plant and equipment, 261-276
on balance sheet, 15, 266, 270
as capital expenditure, 263
carrying value, 270, 274
classification, 14-15
cost, 262
defined, 14
depreciation. *See* Depreciation
discard, 270
disposal, 270-274
effects of inflation on, 274-275
ratio to long-term liabilities, 424-425
of net sales to, 425
to shareholders' equity, 425
replacement, 275
as revenue expenditure, 263
sale, 270
trade-in, 270, 272-274
turnover, 426
Position statement. *See* Balance sheet; Statement of changes in financial position
Postclosing trial balance, 64, 74, 109-110, 504
Posting, 43, 44, 58, 110
to accounts payable ledger, 157-158
from cash payments journal, 172-174
from purchases journal, 163-165, 180, 181
to accounts receivable ledger, 157-158, 169
from cash receipts journal, 167-170
from sales journal, 162-163
of adjusting entries, 90, 107, 504
from business documents, 176-177
from cash payments journal, 172-174
from cash receipts journal, 167-170
closing entries, 71-74, 109-110
defined, 40
direct, 176-177
from general journal, 38, 39-44
to ledgers, 65, 66-68
from purchases journal, 163-165, 180, 181
from sales journal, 162-163
Posting flow
from cash payments journal, 171
from cash receipts journal, 106
from general journal, 38
from purchases journal. 164
from sales journal, 162
Posting machines, 177-178
Preferred dividends, times earned, 424, 428
stock. *See* Stock, capital
Premium
bonds, 367, 368-376, 400, 408-409
stock, 295-296, 297, 303
Prepaid
insurance, 14, 63
adjustment, 89, 91, 92
items, defined, 14
rent, 56, 91, 92
Present value
capital budgeting, 600-602, 607-608, 609
expenditures, 602-606
compound interest, 619, 620-621, 623, 625, 626
excess, 602, 604
index, 604, 608
ordinary annuity, 619, 621, 622-623
Price-earnings ratio, 428-429
Pricing
inventory. *See* Inventory
product, 580-582
special orders, 578-580
Primary claims, 10
Principles, accounting. *See* Accounting principles; Accounting concepts
Prior-period adjustments, 440-442
Process cost system. *See* Cost accounting
Producing departments, defined, 522
Product pricing, 580-582
abandonment, 583-585
Production-unit depreciation method, 266-267, 275
Profit, partnership distribution, 345-347, 349-351
Profitability index, 604
Promissory notes, 362, 380-381
Proprietorship, 10, 11, 16, 17, 99, 287, 288
accounting procedures, 337, 338-341
capital accounts, 337, 338, 340
defined, 16, 17
Protest fee, 383
Punched-card equipment, 155, 178
Purchases
account, 129-130, 233
discounts, 130-131, 141, 172, 184
lost, 130-131, 141-142, 184, 262
net cost of, 133
Purchases journal, 160, 163-165, 173
posting from, 163-165, 180, 181

Purchases journal (Cont.)
posting flow from, 164
returns and allowances, 130, 175
and voucher system, 183
Purchases returns and allowances journal, 175

Qualified endorsement, 380
Quantitive decision models, 6
Quick assets, 422

Rate of return. *See also* Capital budgeting; Capital expenditure
on investment, 600, 602, 605, 606, 608, 609
on shareholders' equity, 430
on total investments, 429-430, 582
Ratio analysis, 419, 420-431
acid-test ratio, 420, 422, 431
accounts receivable, 420
average collection period, 422-423
capital budgeting, 600, 605
credit sales to receivables, 422-423
creditors' equity, 426-427
current ratio, 420-422, 427
equity ratios, 424, 426-427
inventory turnover, 420
investors', 427-428
limitations, 431
market value, 600
net income per share, 428-429
net operating margin ratio, 428, 430-431
sales to plant and equipment, 425
operating ratio, 428, 430-431
plant and equipment to long-term liabilities, 424-425
to shareholders' equity, 425
turnover, 426
price earnings ratio, 428-429
receivables turnover, 422-423
shareholders' equity, 426-427, 428
table of ratios, 438-440
times bond interest earned, 424, 427-428
times preferred dividends earned, 424, 428
yield rates, 428
Raw materials, 493
job order costing, 516
on manufacturing work sheet, 499
on schedule of cost of goods manufactured, 494
Real accounts, 72
Realization, defined, 349
Receivables, 199. *See also* Accounts receivable; Notes receivable
classification, 209
ratio of credit sales to, 422-423
sources, 209-210
turnover, 422-423
Reconciliation, bank, 203-209
Record date, 313
Registered bonds, 363
Relevant volume range, 572, 575
Rent
expense, 56, 59, 172
prepaid, 56, 91, 92
unearned, 93-94
Rents, annuities, 626-627
Replenishing petty cash fund, 201-202
Research and development, 279
Residual
claims, 10
value. *See* Value, residual
Resources, natural, 261, 275-276
Responsibility accounting, 543, 557-559
Restricted retained earnings, 323, 376, 379-380
Retail inventory method, 248
Retained earnings, 20, 54, 71, 287, 298-300, 313, 314-315 317-320, 321, 361
defined, 16
and dividends, 313, 314-315
and expense accounts, 56
restricted, 323, 376, 379-380
statement of, 71, 105, 106, 110, 347, 455
all-inclusive concept, 440-442
comparative, 433, 434
current operating performance concept, 440-442
interrelationship with other statements, 71, 74
manufacturing business, 503
merchandising business, 138
Retirement. *See* Bonds
Returns and allowances
allowance for, 130
purchases, 130, 133
sales, 128, 133
Revaluations, 287, 298
Revenue, 53-54, 68
accounts, 53-54, 58, 60, 63, 71-72, 73, 127, 128
accrued, 88, 91, 92, 94, 98-99, 111
apportionments, short-term, 91, 93-94
from bonds, 370
and cash basis, 87, 88

Revenue (Cont.)
expenditures, 263
matching expenses and, 68-69, 89, 210-211, 263, 275, 430-431, 434-435, 437
rules for recording, 54-55
and work sheet, 105

Salaries to partners, 346-347
Salary, 61. *See* payroll
Sales
account, 127-128
credit, ratio to receivables, 422-423
discounts, 128-129, 141, 165, 169
allowance for, 130
gross price method, 128-129, 141
not taken, 129, 141
and fixed costs, 569-573
gross margin on, 128, 134, 436-437
net, ratio to plant and equipment, 425
ratio to sales, 430-431
returns and allowances, 128, 175
allowance for, 130
and variable costs, 569-573
Sales journal, 160, 161-163, 168, 169
posting from, 162, 163
posting flow from, 162
Sales returns and allowances journal, 175
Salvage value, estimated, 94, 95
Schedule
of cost of goods manufactured, 494, 495, 499, 502, 515
of changes in working capital, 462
of equivalent production, 525-526, 527, 529
quantity, 525, 526-527, 529
of unpaid vouchers, 184, 185
Secured bonds, 362, 363-364
rates, 376, 408
Securities, marketable. *See* Marketable securities
Securities and Exchange Commission, 275, 426
Sequence, accounting, 43-44, 64-74
Serial bonds, 364, 376
Service business, defined, 18
charge, bank, 203
Shareholders' equity, 12, 20, 22, 33, 34, 53, 54, 57, 58, 68, 70, 128, 287-304, 362
on balance sheet, 16, 18-21, 31, 33, 34
and dividends, 314-315, 318, 321, 323
and expense accounts, 56
and inventory, 233, 249
ratio, 426, 427, 428
ratio of plant and equipment to, 425
return on, 430
sources, 296-297
on work sheet, 105
Shortage, cash, 202, 209
Short-term cost apportionments, 89, 91-93, 94
financing devices, 361, 380-384
discounting customer notes, 382-383
notes receivable financing, 382
promissory notes, 362
revenue apportionments, 91, 93-94
Sinking fund, 362, 376, 377, 378-380
bonds, 364
Small tools used, 497
Social accounting, 6, 7
Society of Management Accountants (SMA), 8
Solvency
measurement of long-run, 420, 424-428
measurement of short-run, 420-424
Source and Application of Funds, statement of. *See* Statement of changes in financial position
Source documents, 155
posting from, 176-177
Source and uses of cash, statement of. *See* Statement of changes in financial position
Special journals, 160-177, 179-181
advantages, 160-161
allowances journal, 175
cash payments journal, 160
cash receipts journal, 160, 165-170
check register, 175
combined, 174-175
in conjunction with general journal, 175-177
internal control and, 161
mini practice case, 179-181
notes payable register, 175
notes receivable register, 175
purchases journal, 160, 163-165
purchases returns and allowances journal, 175
sales journal, 160, 161-163
sales returns and allowances journal, 175
voucher register, 175
Special order purchasing, 578-580
Specific identification costing, 234-235
Split entries, 111

Split-ups, stock, 313, 320-321, 405
Stable dollar concept, 7
Standard cost system, 543, 553-556
  and budgets, 543-544
  comprehensive illustration, 546-553
  costs and, 543, 546
  defined, 530, 543
  flow chart, 546-547
  variances, 549-553
Stated capital, 292
  value, 291-292
Statement analysis. *See* Financial statements analysis
Statement of changes in financial position, 455-475
  all-financial resources concept of funds, 472-474
  cash basis, 474-475
  evolution, 455-456
  purposes, 456
  working capital basis, 456-472, 556
    analysis, 421-422
    classification by operations, 458, 459-462
    differences, 472
    preparation, 460-462
    purpose, 457-458
    sources and uses, 456, 458, 472
    T-account method, 462-472
Statement of owner's equity, 340-341
  of partners' equities, 344-345
  of retained earnings. *See* Retained earnings, statement of
  of sources and uses of cash. *See* Statement of changes in financial position
  of sources and uses of working capital. *See* Statement of changes in financial position
Stock, capital, 6, 18, 289-296. *See also* Dividends
  authorized, 292, 295, 323
  on balance sheet, 18
  and bonds compared, 362-363, 364-366, 376
  book value, 95, 313, 321-322, 385, 403, 409, 429
  certificate, 290, 301, 302, 303
  classes, 287, 289
  common, 289-290, 303-304, 313, 315, 319, 322, 365-366
  conversion of bonds to, 377-378, 472
  and debits and credits, 34, 58, 167, 169
  defined, 16
  discount, 295-296, 297
  dividend yield rate, 428-429
  earnings yield rate, 428-429
  issuance, 292-296, 301, 302, 319, 324-325
  long-term investment in, 15, 404-406
  market value, 291, 313, 319, 321-322, 402, 429, 600
  no-par value, 291, 292-293, 294-302, 314, 316, 365, 401
  par value, 290-291, 294-296, 302, 317, 320, 367-368
  preferred, 289-290, 304, 313, 315-317, 321, 322, 401
  premium, 295-296, 297, 303
  recording transactions, 291-294
  split-ups, 313, 320-321, 405
  stated value, 291-292
  subscriptions, 287, 301-304
  temporary investment in, 399, 401-402
  transfer, 288, 290
  treasury, 296, 313, 322-326
    donated, 325
  value of, 290-291
  watered, 291
Stockholders. *See* Shareholders
Store equipment, 15
  supplies, 14
    adjustments, 91, 93
Stores ledger card, 516
Straight-line
  amortization
    bond investment, 406-407, 408-409
    bonds payable, 370-371, 373
  depreciation, 94, 96
Subscribers' ledger, 302
Subscriptions, stock, 287, 301-304
Subsidiary, investment in, 404, 407-408
Subsidiary ledgers, 211, 214, 246, 405, 515, 520
  and general journal, 159, 160-177
  and general ledger, 156-159
Supplies, 29
  adjustments, 91, 93
Supporting documents, 440, 557
  posting from, 176-177
Surplus, capital, 288
  contributed, 295, 297-298, 324, 325
  distributable, 294
  donated, 287
Systems analyst, 156
Systems design, 155-156
Systems flow chart, 156

T accounts, 31, 33, 34, 36, 41, 132
T-account method, working capital statement, 462-472

Tangible assets. *See* Plant and equipment
Taxes, income. *See* Income taxes
Taxes, payroll. *See* Payroll
Temporary accounts, closing, 64, 71-73, 109
  investments. *See* Marketable securities
Three-column account form, 41
Three-digit system, 75
Time cards, 516-517
Tools used, small, 497
Trade accounts receivable. *See* Accounts receivable
  discounts, 142
  notes payable. *See* Notes payable
  notes receivable. *See* Notes receivable
Trade-in, 270, 272-274
Trademark, 15
Trading assets, 422
  on the bondholder's equity, 430
Transfer agent, 290
Transit, deposits in, 204
Transportation in, 130, 133
Treasury stock, 296, 313, 322-326
  donated, 325
Trend percentages, 431, 434-436
Trial balance, 31, 37-39, 131, 169, 338
  adjusted, 90, 93, 94, 103, 105, 107, 138
  errors, locating, 38-39
  errors not revealed by, 38
  financial statements from, 70
  postclosing, 64, 74, 109-110, 504
  preparing, 37-39, 43, 64, 67-68, 110
  on work sheet, 100, 102, 103, 138, 500
Trial and error method, 605, 608
Turnover
  inventory, 420, 423-424
  merchandise inventory, 422, 423-424
  plant and equipment, 426
  receivables, 422-423

Uncollectible accounts. *See* Bad debts
Unearned rent, 93-94
  subscriptions, 361, 372
Unit
  contribution margin, 571
  cost, 515, 526, 527-528, 529, 546, 570-571, 574, 575, 579, 581, 582
  economic, defined, 9
Unpaid
  voucher file, 184-185
  vouchers, schedule of, 184, 185
Unsecured
  bonds, 364
  notes, 376, 408
Useful life. *See* Estimated useful life

Valuation
  accounts, 211, 274
  bases, 426
  of long-term investments, 404-406
  of temporary investments, 402-404, 406
Value
  book, 95, 313, 321-322, 385, 403, 409, 429
  carrying, 95, 265-266, 270-274, 377, 425, 426, 602, 603
  defined, 234
  face, 366-374, 377, 378, 385-386, 399
  fair market, 262, 272-274
  market, 291, 319, 321, 402, 429, 600
  no-par. *See* Stocks, capital
  par. *See* Stocks, capital
  present. *See* Present value
  residual, 94, 264
  salvage, 94, 95, 264, 265-270, 276, 601
Variable costs, 544-546
Variances, 543, 544, 549-553
  budget, 552
  efficiency, 550
  interpretation, 553
  rate, 550
Vertical analysis, 436-438
Voucher jacket, 182-183
  register, 175, 183-184
  system, 182-185
    advantages, 185
    controlling account, 182
    internal control and, 182
Vouchers
  payable, 183, 184, 185, 361
  petty cash, 182, 201
  unpaid, 182, 185

Wages. *See* Payroll
Wasting assets, 261, 275
Watered stock, 291
Weighted average costing. *See* Inventory
Work in process
  inventory, 497-498, 499, 504, 516, 517, 518, 521, 524-530, 547, 549, 553, 555
  job order costing, 516, 517, 518, 520, 522
  process costing, 522-529

Work in process (Cont.)
standard cost, 547-550
on work sheet, 499-500
Working capital, 298, 300, 319, 380.
See also Statement of changes in financial position
flow, 456, 457
inventory, 423, 425
investment of, 423
from operations, 459-462
transaction classifications, 458-459
Working-hours depreciation method, 267
Work sheet, 100-107
adjusted trial balance section, 103, 105
adjusting entries, 90, 107
adjustments section, 100-105, 107, 500-503, 504
balance sheet, 105, 110, 503
closing entries recorded from, 109, 110
defined, 100
error on, 105
finished goods on, 500
income statement section, 105, 110, 499, 502
interim statements, 140
inventory on, 499-502
manufacturing business, 499-504
materials on, 499-500
merchandising business, 136, 138
net income or loss on, 100, 105
preparation, 100-107
preparation of financial statements from, 105-107, 110
trial balance section, 102-103, 500
work in process on, 499-500

Yield rate, 428-429, 627
table, bond, 384

Zeros, use in cents columns, 40-41